Educatio

International

Development

Education and International Development

An Introduction

Second Edition

Edited by Tristan McCowan and Elaine Unterhalter

BLOOMSBURY ACADEMIC
LONDON • NEW YORK • OXFORD • NEW DELHI • SYDNEY

BLOOMSBURY ACADEMIC
Bloomsbury Publishing Plc
50 Bedford Square, London, WC1B 3DP, UK
1385 Broadway, New York, NY 10018, USA
29 Earlsfort Terrace, Dublin 2, Ireland

BLOOMSBURY, BLOOMSBURY ACADEMIC and the Diana logo are
trademarks of Bloomsbury Publishing Plc

First published in Great Britain 2022

Cover design by Toby Way
Cover Image: Students attend primary school in rural Dodoma Region,
Tanzania © Jake Lyell / Alamy Stock Photo

A catalogue record for this book is available from the British Library.

A catalog record for this book is available from the Library of Congress.

Library of Congress Cataloging-in-Publication Data
Names: McCowan, Tristan, 1974- editor. | Unterhalter, Elaine, editor.
Title: Education and international development : an introduction /
Edited by Tristan McCowan and Elaine Unterhalter.
Description: Second edition. | London ; New York :
Bloomsbury Academic, 2021. | Includes bibliographical references and index. |
Identifiers: LCCN 2021004234 (print) | LCCN 2021004235 (ebook) |
ISBN 9781350119055 (paperback) | ISBN 9781350119062
(hardback) | ISBN 9781350119079 (ebook) | ISBN 9781350119086 (epub)
Subjects: LCSH: Education–Social aspects–Developing countries. |
Poor children–Education–Developing countries. |
Economic development–Effect of education on.
Classification: LCC LC2605 .E296 2021 (print) |
LCC LC2605 (ebook) | DDC 306.4309172/4–dc23
LC record available at https://lccn.loc.gov/2021004234
LC ebook record available at https://lccn.loc.gov/2021004235

ISBN: PB: 978-1-3501-1905-5
          HB: 978-1-3501-1906-2
          ePDF: 978-1-3501-1907-9
          eBook: 978-1-3501-1908-6

Typeset by Integra Software Services Pvt. Ltd.
Printed and bound in Great Britain

To find out more about our authors and books visit www.bloomsbury.com
and sign up for our newsletters.

Table of Contents

Part 2 Key Themes

Notes on Contributors

Monazza Aslam is an education economist with over fifteen years of experience working in international development. Her research has focused on teacher effectiveness, girls' education and women's labour market outcomes, political economy of education systems and school choice and school provision. Monazza is Honorary Senior Researcher at the Institute of Education, University College London, UK, and Managing Partner at the Oxford Partnership for Education Research and Analysis.

Sheila Aikman is Senior Research Associate in the School of International Development at the University of East Anglia, UK. She has held both academic and practitioner positions in the field of education and international development with a focus on language policy, socio-cultural change and gender equality. She draws on forty years of research in the Peruvian Amazon on education, knowledge and indigenous rights.

Monisha Bajaj is Professor of International and Multicultural Education at the University of San Francisco, USA. She is also Visiting Professor at Nelson Mandela University, South Africa. Bajaj is the author and editor of seven books, as well as numerous articles. She has also developed curriculum – particularly related to peace education, human rights, anti-bullying efforts and sustainability – for non-profit organizations and inter-governmental organizations, such as UNICEF and UNESCO.

Aaron Benavot is Professor of Global Education Policy at the University at Albany-SUNY, USA and Former Director of UNESCO's Global Education Monitoring Report. His research interests include the comparative historical study of basic education and the school curriculum, the monitoring of lifelong learning and the links between education and global citizenship and sustainability, especially climate change education.

Elaine Chase is Associate Professor in Education, Health Promotion and International Development at the Institute of Education, University College London, UK. Her teaching, research and writing explore the sociological dimensions of health, well - being and rights of individuals and communities, particularly those most likely to experience marginalization and exclusion.

Pablo Del Monte is Lecturer in Education in Te Kura Toi Tangata School of Education at the University of Waikato, New Zealand. His research draws on post-structuralist, ethnographic and narrative approaches, and focuses on youth educational trajectories and education policy enactment in disadvantaged neighbourhoods.

Joanna Härmä focuses on non-state actors' involvement in education, especially low-fee private schooling in developing countries; she has researched private schooling in India and many countries in sub-Saharan Africa. She has lived in Nigeria, working with state governments to improve their education data on public and private schools, and she has also worked at UNESCO. She is currently writing and teaching in international education at Edinburgh University, UK.

Mieke Lopes Cardozo is Senior Lecturer in Education and Inclusive Development at the University of Amsterdam, the Netherlands. Her teaching, supervision and international research collaborations focus on the role of education in relation to social justice and peacebuilding, in contexts including Bolivia, Indonesia, Myanmar, the Netherlands and Sri Lanka.

Caroline Manion is Lecturer in the field of comparative, international and development education at the Ontario Institute for Studies in Education, University of Toronto, Canada. Her research interests include equity, gender and education, the politics of education, educational leadership and policy, and global governance and educational multilateralism.

Stephanie Matseleng Allais is Research Chair of Skills Development and Professor of Education at the Centre for Researching Education and Labour at University of the Witwatersrand, South Africa. Her research is located in the sociology and political economy of education, focused on relationships between education and work. Her books include *Selling Education Out*; *Knowledge, Curriculum, and Preparation for Work* (with Yael Shalem); and *Implementing National Qualifications Frameworks Across Five Continents* (with Michael Young).

Tristan McCowan is Professor of International Education at the Institute of Education, University College London, UK. His work focuses on higher education and international development, particularly in Latin America and sub-Saharan Africa. His latest book is *Higher Education for and beyond the Sustainable Development Goals*, and he is the editor of the journal *Compare*. He is currently leading a multi-country Global Challenges Research Fund project on universities and climate change.

Karen Mundy is Professor of International and Comparative Education at the Ontario Institute for Studies in Education, University of Toronto, Canada. Her research interests include the global politics of education for all, educational policy and reform in sub-Saharan Africa, the role of civil society organizations in educational change, and global citizenship education.

Charlotte Nussey is Research Associate at the Institute of Education, University College London, UK, working on higher education and climate change. Her doctoral research explored adult education, gender and violence in rural KwaZulu-Natal, South Africa. She has been working in the field of education, gender and international development since 2008.

Rosie Peppin Vaughan is Lecturer in Education and International Development at the Institute of Education, University College London, UK. Her research focuses on transnational advocacy on girls' and women's education, and also draws on the capability approach and the concept of human development to explore the measurement of educational equality and social justice. She has completed consultancies for several international organizations, including Plan International, UNESCO and the UN Girls' Education Initiative.

Lerato Posholi is a PhD candidate at the Centre for Researching Education and Labour (REAL), University of the Witwatersrand, South Africa, and is currently a PhD visiting fellow at the University of Basel, Switzerland. Her research interests are in curriculum studies, social epistemology and decolonial theory. Her PhD project broadly looks at the question of knowledge and power in curriculum.

Anita Rampal is Former Dean in the Faculty of Education at Delhi University, India. She is an EC member of the International Commission on Mathematics Instruction, was Chairperson of the NCERT Primary Textbook Committees and is part of national and grassroots initiatives. She is associated with the Right to Education campaign and the people's science movement. Her areas of work are policy analysis, curriculum studies, science-technology-society studies, education for sustainable development and teacher education.

Shenila Rawal is an experienced applied economist specializing in education, labour markets and issues of gender and poverty. Her research has involved applying quantitative evaluation methods to analyse large-scale data sets and designing and implementing the collection of primary data as well as RCTs in education. She has extensive experience in leading and conducting evaluations and has lectured and supervised dissertations on a variety of topics at master's level in the field of economics of education.

Susan Garnett Russell is Associate Professor of International and Comparative Education at Teachers College, Columbia University, USA, and Director of the George Clement Bond Center for African Education. Her research focuses on citizenship and human rights in conflict-affected and post-conflict contexts, including Rwanda, South Africa and Colombia. Recent publications appear in *Comparative Education Review*, *Comparative Education* and *Harvard Education Review*.

Eva Sajoo is Researcher with a focus on Muslim societies, religion and women's rights, and diaspora communities, based at Simon Fraser University in Vancouver, Canada. She has previously been Research Associate with the Centre for the Comparative Study of Muslim Societies and Cultures, and at the Institute for Diaspora Studies.

Rebecca Schendel is Assistant Professor of the Practice and Managing Director of the Center for International Higher Education (CIHE) at Boston College, USA. Her research focuses on the relationship between higher education and human development in sub-Saharan Africa, with particular emphasis on questions of pedagogy, student learning and processes of institutional change.

Ritesh Shah is Senior Lecturer of Comparative and International Education at the University of Auckland, New Zealand. His scholarship and teaching focuses on education's role and function in processes of social transformation, particularly in conflict-affected states.

William C. Smith is Senior Lecturer in Education and International Development and Academic Lead for the Data for Children Collaborative with UNICEF at the University of Edinburgh, UK. His research focuses on testing;

learning metrics; and issues of quality, education and social development; and teachers and accountability. He previously worked at UNESCO's Global Education Monitoring Report and as a TJA Fellow with the OECD.

Gita Steiner-Khamsi is Professor of Comparative and International Education at Teachers College, Columbia University, USA, and Director of NORRAG. She has been seconded (until 2022) by the Graduate Institute of International and Development Studies to serve as faculty member in its interdisciplinary programmes. She has authored, edited or co-edited twelve books on topics related to comparative policy studies, globalization, public–private partnerships, comparative methodology and development studies.

Meera Tiwari is Reader at University of East London, UK. She is investigating the role of dignity in improving menstrual health in India and localizing SDGs in Newham, London, UK. Her recent publications examine discrimination of women before being born in parts of India and why India should train informal health providers to curb Covid-19.

Elaine Unterhalter is Professor of Education and International Development at University College London, UK. She co-directs the Centre for Education and International Development (CEID). Her research looks at gender, class and race inequalities in education, and processes for change. Her recent books are *Education, Poverty and Global Goals for Gender Equality* (with Amy North), and two edited collections: *Measuring the Unmeasurable in Education* and *Critical Reflections on Public Private Partnerships* (with Jasmine Gideon).

Ian Warwick is Associate Professor and a member of CEID at the Institute of Education, University College London, UK, where he leads the MA Education, Health Promotion and International Development. Ian's research is on the interface of education, health and well - being and focused on issues related to HIV prevention and AIDS care, sexualities and sex education, young parents, mental health, alcohol use as well as professional development, in low-, middle- and high-income settings.

Acknowledgements

This book has built on our experience of working in education and international development at the Institute of Education (IoE), now part of University College London (UCL), over twenty years. This second edition revises and updates chapters from the first edition, and includes some new work. Many of the people we need to thank remain the same, but there are some key additions. Our warmest and most profound thanks go to our many friends, students and colleagues, both at IoE and in the wider international and comparative education community, from whom we have learned enormous amounts, discussed and debated themes that recur through this book and with whom we have tried to put some aspirations into practice. Our understanding of these issues has also been formed and shaped by the numerous inspiring and insightful educators, activists and students with whom we have come into contact in our work in many countries in Africa, Asia and Latin America. Specific thanks are due to a number of others. Firstly, we owe particular debts to all the authors who have contributed chapters to this collection. The genre of writing an introductory text has been new to all of us, and we have had many months of dialogue. The process of updating material in a fast-moving field is challenging. While the new chapter authors had a body of work to build on, they also had new fields to synthesize. We thank all the authors for their time and generous engagement with this project. Secondly, in order to orient this book to the needs of students of education and international development, a perceptive group of students volunteered to read chapters in a penultimate draft of the first edition and give comments to authors. Our thanks remain to those we acknowledged in the first edition for excellent work in helping to deepen arguments, spot gaps and alert us to student needs. Revisions in the second edition have been guided by the comments of our students on the MA programmes in the Centre for Education and International Development (CEID) at UCL, and we are grateful for the questions they have raised and the new issues they have alerted us to. We would like to thank Mark Richardson at Bloomsbury for commissioning the second edition of the book and supporting the project with understanding and kindness through a number of ups and downs, heightened by the pressures of the Covid-19 pandemic. Thanks also to Ewan McCowan for organization of the bibliography. Our families and friends have seen some of the stress associated with bringing a book to completion, and have learned, with us, that a second edition can be as challenging as a first. We thank them a second time round for their support, good humour and the ongoing welcome distractions they offer. We dedicate this book to our own children – on Elaine's side, Joe, Rosa, Oliver, Sophie and grandchild Elijah, and on Tristan's side, Leon and Ewan, with our continued hope for lifelong education for all in the world into which new generations of children will be born.

Introduction

Tristan McCowan and Elaine Unterhalter

The Sustainable Development Goals (SDGs) were adopted at the United Nations Assembly in 2015 articulating a global vision to stimulate activity over fifteen years for 'humanity and the planet'. The SDGs gave prominence to education, understood as a lifelong process of learning. Education is delineated in the SDG framework not only as a goal (SDG4) in its own right with a set of targets but as a component of the targets for many of the seventeen SDGs and a key means to address the overall SDG aim of bringing an 'end [to] poverty and hunger' and ensuring 'that all human beings can fulfil their potential in dignity and equality and in a healthy environment' (UN 2016). The SDG project expresses values of universalism, rights and 'leave no one behind', mapping directions for policy that attempt to mobilize high levels of political support and practical action, taking account of planetary boundaries and the enormous and difficult changes associated with the altering climate. This book reviews how well positioned the education sector in low- and middle-income countries (LMICs) is to take up this role, considering the history of earlier engagements with ambitious national and global policy frameworks, the complexities of linking education and international development, conceptually and practically, and the nuance of the challenges associated with different areas of education. It also considers some of the setbacks associated with Covid-19, the issues these illuminate, and assesses some future directions.

The SDG framework was ambitious in 2015. The policies and the approach mapped to global and local collaborations came under considerable stress from 2016, as the United States, under the presidency of Donald Trump, withdrew from many multilateral frameworks. The Covid-19 pandemic in

2020 has threatened to derail many elements of what had been achieved in support of the SDGs (UN 2020a). The expansion of education provision worldwide, which had heretofore focused on access and quality, trying to overcome deep-seated barriers to inclusion and equity, has been stopped in its tracks. In nearly all the countries of the world, a majority of schools and universities were closed for many months in 2020 to contain the pandemic. Over this period many children had virtually no access to learning materials, and in many countries, feeding schemes, which had been based in schools, were halted for long periods. These effects were harshest in the poorest countries. United Nations Development Programme (UNDP) estimates showed that, during the second quarter of 2020, 86 per cent of children in primary education were out of school in countries with low human development – compared with just 20 per cent in countries with very high human development (UN 2020a, 5, 2020b). Digital provision through computers reached only the affluent, and attempts to use mobile phones were often limited because of access to handsets and the costs of data. Governments sought to use radio and television to deliver education content, but in nearly half of the poorest countries, this was not feasible. Studies highlighted that the poorest children had some of the least developed digital skills and limited access to hardware and connectivity, which meant they effectively missed nearly a whole year of learning (UN 2020a, 8, 2020b).

Studies of the effects of the coronavirus crisis and timing of action and inaction calculated large estimates of damage to decades of work on addressing poverty and marginalization (Omtzigt and Pople 2020). The sharp contraction of GDP around the world was only one indication of a multi-layered Covid crisis (Anand et al 2020). A United Nations Educational, Scientific and Cultural Organization (UNESCO) team estimated that in 2021 at least $210 billion would be cut from education budgets in LMICs due to declines in GDP. The funding gap between what was available in governments' education budgets and what was needed to deliver on SDG 4 would more than double in size to 29 per cent, compared to a proportion of 11 per cent anticipated before the pandemic (UN 2020c, 2020a, 6). Commentators noted that one effect of the pandemic was pressure to allocate resources to health and social safety nets, with less money to support teachers and develop strategies for gender equality or inclusion in schools, just at the time when this was most needed, with slowing GDP growth meaning domestic resource mobilization would be limited (ActionAid 2020, UN 2020c). Contractions in gross national income (GNI) in aid-giving countries will result in a reduction in the amounts given to aid-supported education projects. In the UK there are estimates of cuts of up to a third in aid to education (Watts 2020). This has ignited discussion of how education aid is best allocated and what the decision-making process over this should be (World Bank 2020, Bond 2020). In revising our opening chapter for the second edition of *Education and International Development: An Introduction*, as the multiple effects of the pandemic have become apparent, we have had to reconsider many of the key themes of this field of scholarship, trying to assess how they speak to a changed landscape of the confident positioning of education in relation to the SDGs only five years ago.

Many of the themes of the first edition of this book have, if anything, gained in significance. Ensuring access, progression and quality of education is difficult at any time, but more testingly so as the world experiences and tries to recover from a global pandemic, with many political, economic, environmental, cultural and social dimensions. These education-specific challenges themselves raise wider issues relating to culture, language, governance, sustainability, equalities, health and locale. These challenges, in turn, present questions regarding the aims of education, bringing into play contestations over political, moral and religious values and theories of knowledge. They also illuminate contemporary and historical social divisions, geo-politics and struggles over different kinds of power. All of these issues are central to this book and the study of education and international development. We can think of the Covid-19 moment as looking at these trends through water, which both magnifies these elements and changes them (Unterhalter 2020).

Schooling for all, as envisaged in SDG 4, has long been an international goal. The idea that all people, wherever they live and however poor they might be, should have the opportunity to develop their capacities to improve their own lives and create better societies has been a key notion articulated by social reformers in many different kinds of society for centuries. Yet history has proved that it is extraordinarily difficult to realize this widely shared aspiration. Providing access to schooling or other kinds of education for groups who are politically, socially and, sometimes, physically distant from those in power presents significant challenges. There are many accounts in academic works, travel books, journalism and advocacy through film, song and the speeches of political activists of how certain social groups have been shut out from learning. Sometimes this is because schools, for populations that are considered hard to reach, often require considerable resources; sometimes it is because of an intention to deny or limit access. Work on education that addresses poverty, inequality and injustice, therefore, challenges existing assumptions about how learning and teaching are organized. The chapters in this book explore these issues. They draw out some of the complex problems associated with understanding these questions, describe work that has been undertaken to engage with them and analyse some of the achievements and difficulties that have ensued. They also look forward to where concerns of policymakers, practitioners and researchers are going over the next decade.

The importance of education, and the considerable strides that still need to be made to ensure quality lifelong learning for all, has led to education having a prominent place within the SDG framework and in discussions of building resilience after the pandemic (UN 2015, UN 2020a, 2020c). The targets for SDG 4 deal with all phases of education, and many other SDGs – such as those which deal with ending poverty (SDG1), improving health and well-being (SDG3), assuring gender equality and women's empowerment (SDG 5) and providing decent work (SDG8) – have targets which refer to education. But the issue of the content of formal schooling and the indicators to assess what is learned are highly controversial, as debates about SDG targets, indicators and the content of learning indicate (Unterhalter 2019a; Tikly 2019; see also Chapter 10 of this volume). Some key issues this discussion raises concern what education should be common to all groups and cultures and what should be context-specific. Do measures of learning outcomes provide appropriate metrics for evaluating education? Contestation on themes like this lies at the heart of debates around education and international development, and this book addresses a number of these, presenting the arguments and their research base for those who seek an introduction to this field.

A logical approach to this topic might be to provide at the start a clear definition of the key terms 'education' or 'international development', and thereby elucidate the issue under discussion. While we do set out some guiding delineations in this chapter, we want to signal that the field of education and international development to a large extent resists this kind of approach. The area of investigation is characterized by complexity of the basic concepts and the multifariousness of their practical manifestations. We therefore need to acknowledge at the outset that any kind of definition entails a normative assertion. Defining what education or development is entails a statement of one's own personal values and priorities, and we set these out below, explaining some of the concerns that have guided the development of this book.

Nevertheless, some initial conceptual mapping is of use. 'Education', as employed in this book, is understood to consist of all levels of formal education – from early years, through primary and secondary to university – as well as non-formal education with adults and in some cases broader forms of learning in society. In keeping with practice at the international level, many of the chapters in this book focus on formal education for children, while retaining this broader understanding of the educational sphere and the whole of the life course. Ideas about education entail assumptions about the ontologies of learners and teachers, and their social relationships. Discussions about what is viewed as useful, appropriate or valuable knowledge; how this links with discussions of pedagogy; and formations of an education system all bear on the definition of education, which we are conceiving as wide in scope and have loosely specified so it can be differently interpreted in different chapters. We note that education may be understood in terms of the distinctions Tikly (2019) and Kreienkamp and Pegram (2020) draw, noting that it is both a complicated system with many formal relationships that go in different directions and a complex system that is open-ended with many processes interacting, defying control and prediction with many emergent bottom-up properties and non-linear outcomes. It is often in the tensions between the complicated systems of regulation of curriculum, pedagogy, management, assessment and evaluation and the adaptability of the complex system in defiance of these processes that many of the focal points of education and international development emerge.

The term 'development' when applied to countries or societies refers to a process of change over time – usually a positive change. As such, it is a minimal concept, given character by the specific political and moral positionings brought to it by its users. However, there is a more particular use of the word 'development' in relation to the historical moment post–Second World War and the process of change of the less wealthy and often newly independent countries of Africa, Asia and Latin America in conjunction with an increasingly elaborate architecture of development agencies. As stated by Gilbert Rist (2008, 13):

> Development consists of a set of practices, sometimes appearing to conflict with one another, which require – for the reproduction of society – the general transformation and destruction of the natural environment and of social relations. Its aim is to increase the production of commodities (goods and services) geared, by way of exchange, to effective demand.

As seen in Chapter 4 and elsewhere in the book, this dominant view of development identified by Rist has been challenged from a range of viewpoints in the past half century. There have been strong critiques from

Marxist and poststructural viewpoints, as well as resistance from indigenous groups and local populations drawing on alternative worldviews such as *ubuntu* and *buen vivir* (as discussed in Chapters 1 and 4). A school of post-development thinkers, many drawing on the work of Arturo Escobar (2011) and collected in the *Development Dictionary* (Sachs 1992), highlighted how ideas about development were an invention of the West, growing out of and maintaining colonial relationships, silencing the voices, experiences and aspirations of those who were dispossessed. In critiquing frameworks of development, these writers formulated challenges to the universalist and teleological assumptions linked with ideas about development evident in formulations such as Rist's. They advocated for different ways of thinking about voice, representation and a pluriversality of perspectives, paying particular account to those situated outside Europe and suggesting alternative ways of doing development including through different strategies for research and education (Ziaia 2020, McGregor 2009).

These currents raise many ethical questions regarding who defines development, how this process unfolds, what emphases are given and why, what relationships are formulated between ends and means, what is considered good and what is considered just and how or whether ideas about the limits and conditions of possibility are in play. Development is not just one process, and we need to clarify normative positions in our thinking about education and international development. We have both written about normative ideas on development associated with rights, freedoms, capabilities and equity in relation to education (Unterhalter 2007a, 2009, McCowan 2013, McCowan and Unterhalter 2013). Scholarship on development ethics has also begun to look at aspects of education (Drydyk and Keleher 2018). Clearly there is not a single model or goal of development, but whose goal should this be? This is a perennial question touched on by a number of chapters in this book.

The contested notion of development has led to difficulties with the concept of a 'developing country'. In spite of its use by many development agencies, the limitations of this term are plain to see: does it mean that other countries have stopped developing or do not need to because they exemplify an end point to which less developed countries should aspire? Nevertheless, the broadly optimistic tone of 'developing country' has made it preferable to previously used expressions such as 'underdeveloped countries' or 'Third World'. The term 'developing country' is used in some parts of this book in full awareness of its problematic nature, along with 'Global South', which, despite its dubious geographical accuracy, has some significant advantages in avoiding value judgements. The more technical expression 'low- and middle-income countries' is also used, which in its more factual basis avoids some of the dangerous, smuggled-in judgements of worth, although also establishing a hierarchy based on income, just one way of assessing what is valuable in a country.

This book provides an introduction to the field of education and international development. As such, and like all books of its type, it must start by excusing itself for its inability to cover the issues in the depth that would be needed for a full understanding of their complexity: further reading is indicated at the end of each chapter for this purpose. In addition, some important issues or dimensions have not been allocated a chapter in their own right – for example, gender, health and nutrition, pedagogy, technology, disasters and epidemics, governance and disability – but instead are covered transversely through the book with a number of chapters dealing with these themes. Some entirely new chapters have been added for this second edition – those on decolonization, privatization, learning metrics and sustainability – so as to address some of the emerging issues that are taking on increasing importance in the field.

This book brings together twenty-six authors working in the field, located in diverse countries and with a range of specializations in terms of research and practice. For each topic, rather than presenting a specific research study or line of argument, a broad overview is provided, covering the major debates, prominent research and evidence, as well as case studies of policies, initiatives and thinkers. In each chapter, boxes are provided featuring examples and case studies of the broader ideas at play: these are organized into the categories of 'policies', 'measurement and indicators', 'pathways to practice', 'actors' and 'concepts'. Indications of relevant websites, further reading and questions for discussion are also provided at the end of each chapter.

The book is intended for those engaging in academic studies of international development and education, as well as those working for development agencies and educational institutions around the world. The book relates both to the practice of educational development (the policy and planning processes, the training and deployment of teachers and the chalk-face work of teaching and learning) and the development of knowledge and analysis in the field through research. We have come to this project through our experience of teaching in this area, working with colleagues in schools, universities, development projects, activist campaigns and research projects in many countries of Latin America, Africa, Europe and Asia. We have drawn on networks that reach across continents, but we are aware that there are gaps and that many themes may only have been introduced in a preliminary way.

We see this book as a contribution to discussions that are ongoing regarding the definition of this area of investigation.

There are two principal parts to the book. The first covers the background needed for understanding the field, involving an account of its historical development since the Second World War (Chapter 1), the principal theories (Chapters 2 and 4), the emergence of the Education for All initiative (Chapter 3) and an overview of issues relating to research (Chapter 5). The second part takes a thematic view, covering in depth a range of issues, sectors, approaches and levels. The themes we have selected deal with citizenship, economic growth, inequalities, privatization, conflict, sustainability, religious and linguistic affiliations, and forms of adult skill formation, professional and higher education. The conclusion weaves an autobiographical reflection by a key individual who has been active in this field for forty years into a commentary on the themes of the book, and through it provides a reflection on the implications of these chapters for the new development landscape post-2015 and in the wake of Covid-19 pandemic. There are no chapters specific to particular countries or regions – instead references to diverse geographical locations are spread through the book: for example, discussions of Rwanda in Chapters 6, 11 and 16; of India in Chapters 6, 17 and 19; Bolivia in Chapter 12; Kyrgyzstan and Mongolia in Chapter 9; and Turkey and Indonesia in Chapter 12. Inevitably, some contexts and regions receive more attention than others, depending on the personal experience of the authors in question, the focus of development agencies themselves and the availability of research.

There are two principal relationships that can be observed between education and international development: first, that development includes education and second, that education drives development. In the first, education is *a part of* development – it is one of the institutions of society that extends itself and improves in the course of a country's becoming more developed. The task of researchers and practitioners then is to understand and overcome the barriers to this process of expansion and enhancement of education. This aim has underpinned the Education for All (EFA) initiative, analysed by Karen Mundy and Caroline Manion in Chapter 3.

Other chapters – such as Rebecca Schendel's and Tristan McCowan's analysis of higher education in Chapter 16 and Charlotte Nussey's assessment of adult education in Chapter 15 – look at these questions of overcoming barriers and understanding quality in relation to other phases of the education system. Gita Steiner-Khamsi in Chapter 9 focuses on the task of training and recruiting high-quality teachers, while Aaron Benavot and Will

Smith in Chapter 10 assess the initiatives to measure learning globally as a means of enhancing quality. Joanna Härmä in Chapter 18 analyses the extent to which privatization of education, and low-cost private schools specifically, are assisting in the achievement Education for All (EFA), or alternatively undermining it and leading to more unequal education systems.

But the optimistic undertow associated with the notion of development of EFA is not the only story linked with this area of investigation. The specific challenge presented by conflict and emergencies, and how these may be oriented towards development and the provision of education, is explored by Mieke Lopes Cardozo and Ritesh Shah in Chapter 11. The complexities of societies divided by generation, race, ethnicity and location and what they might mean for development are considered by Pablo Del Monte and Lerato Posholi in Chapter 4 and Elaine Unterhalter in Chapter 8, while the question of language and the medium of instruction through which so many notions of development are formulated is considered by Sheila Aikman in Chapter 13.

The idea that development should involve expansion and improvement of formal education does not then command universal agreement. In this way, general critiques of the development process as economic exploitation or cultural Westernization have been applied to education. These debates have recently come to the fore in struggles around decolonization, explored in Chapter 4, highlighting that formal education systems can serve the role of subjugation during colonization and afterwards in more subtle forms, unless a radical transformation of the curriculum and education system can take place. Religion is also a key source of contestation in relation to development, and Eva Sajoo in Chapter 12 provides an overview of perspectives and practices in relation to the place of values and religious beliefs in educational provision. In the concluding chapter, Anita Rampal reflects on her experience over decades with governments and social activists in India as she has worked to value local engagements and support the right to education in opposition to dehumanizing forces.

In the second relationship, attention is turned to the ways in which broader processes of development are underpinned by, and dependent on, education. The levels of education of a population can be seen to determine economic growth, democratization and a range of other positive outcomes. Susan Garnett Russell and Monisha Bajaj in Chapter 6 focus on the ways education has been harnessed in the formation of citizenship and the nation state, while Monazza Aslam and Shenila Rawal in Chapter 7 assess thinking from within economics on the role that education plays in growth, focusing initially on human capital theory and some of the extensions in recent decades. One of the ways in which education is tasked with enhancing economies is through the formation of skills and the developments of livelihoods, assessed by Stephanie Matseleng Allais in Chapter 14, highlighting some of the myths as well as the opportunities presented in the contemporary context. Finally, Chapter 17 focuses on the role of education in sustainable development, as envisaged by SDG 4.7, through environmental education and in fostering sustainable livelihoods.

Again, there is contestation in relation to the second principle. Education can be seen to promote the wrong kind of development (e.g. wealth accumulation and environmental destruction, rather than wisdom – as explored in Chapter 4) or restrict the benefits of development to the few. Elaine Unterhalter's discussion of social divisions and inequalities (Chapter 8), for example, shows how particular groups in society have been systematically excluded from forms of quality education that confer privileges in the broader society. In practice, these two relationships are closely linked, as the perceived role of education in driving development becomes a strong political and economic justification for its provision, leading to a potential virtuous cycle, or if adequate investments cannot be made, a vicious cycle. However, discussions of alternative development paradigms and approaches to radically re-envision development by linking this with substantive relationships of trust, abolishing hierarchies associated with aid and building democratic participatory processes suggest the need to promote different forms of education and linkages between communities (Wallace 2020, Kothari 2020)

These approaches suggest another, third, way in which we can view the relationship between education and development. Here, education becomes constitutive of development, with the line between the two increasingly hard to draw. We can see this relationship in the participatory approaches to development emerging from the 1970s involving community empowerment, in Freire's radical ideas on pedagogy, and in the emphasis on agency in the human development and human rights paradigms, in which human beings' emancipation and participation in collective decision-making – and consequently learning and personal development – are central. Michael Apple (2005) writes about critical education in ways that echo a number of alternative visions of development entailing processes of bearing witness to injustice, opening counter-hegemonic epistemological and pedagogic spaces, engaging in dialogues, keeping alive histories of radical action and providing supportive critiques, while acting in concert with radical movements. Some of these ideas are explored further in Tristan McCowan's chapter on theories of development (Chapter 2) and in Elaine Unterhalter's chapter on addressing and transforming inequalities (Chapter 8), and they are picked up by Anita Rampal in the concluding chapter.

However we conceive the relationship, the presence of education in international development work is unmistakable and growing and, given the normative and pragmatic complexities of the endeavour, requires constant critical reflection. This book aims to provide such a space, bringing together a range of voices from diverse geographical, sectoral and political locations to open up the key facets of the field for those engaging with the practice and study of education and international development.

This is a fast-moving area with changing configurations of actors making policy and identifying priorities. We are completing the revisions to this volume in the midst of the reassessments being made in the wake of the coronavirus epidemic. A number of scenarios have been produced regarding what kind of crisis or opportunity the pandemic presents. A report for the High Level Political Forum on the SDGs in July 2020 outlined setbacks, uncertainties and opportunities for the SDG agenda linked with supporting universal healthcare, robust social protection, more forceful action on climate change, better protection of land, water and biodiversity and greater recognition of sustainable production and consumption (UN 2020a). None of these scenarios deal explicitly with education, although the conclusion of the report draws out the significance of better governance and partnerships to achieve the SDGs. A policy brief produced by the UN in August 2020 notes shocks and aftershocks associated with the pandemic affecting all levels of education from early years to tertiary, widening inequalities in learning outcomes, leading to increased risk of dropout for the most vulnerable, significant needs of teachers for training and high levels of violence against girls and women anticipated. The report recommends enhanced planning and dialogue with the health sector, responsiveness to local conditions, to support schools re-opening safely, preserving education spending as a proportion of government budgets, increasing domestic resource mobilization and supporting co-ordination of aid (UN 2020b).

Much of the analysis done by UN organizations focuses on what government should do to lead the education recovery from the pandemic. However, even before the pandemic, discussion about education and political action with regard to education had expanded considerably from the remit of governments, parents and teachers. Technologies, and particularly information and communications technology (ICT), where large investments have been made by a small number of tech companies, have been associated with expanding access for some, but also with shutting out half the world who have little or no access to the internet.

During the pandemic, widespread mobilization has taken place in many countries noting some of the inequalities laid bare by Covid-19. The *Black Lives Matter (BLM)* social movement saw hundreds of thousands take to the streets worldwide in July 2020 in protest against racism, highlighting colonial histories associated with some education institutions and prompting what are sometimes called 'statue wars',[1] which highlight very different interpretations of particular histories and the ways these are commemorated. *BLM* and a number of the education protests associated with social movements in the last ten years have articulated left or liberal demands, such as protests at inaction on climate change initiated by Greta Thunberg and schoolchildren around the world, mobilizations for education equality, the recognition of indigenous language rights, an end to violence against women (VaW) in educational institutions, initially associated with the figure of Malala Yousafezi, but emerging sporadically in many countries, or critiques of old established autocracies. But a feature of this decade has also been a popular mobilization of right-wing social movements promoting nationalist demands around education, or advocating for particular religious groups, protesting at affirmative action policies or demanding the expulsion of immigrants from schools. The politics of education thus has become a major issue, not just in securing expansion of higher education or school provision but in supporting wider political, economic or environmental causes.

These popular mobilizations within the education sector, which sometimes focus on issues of curriculum and teaching, highlight how accountability for education has expanded, so that it is not only part of a narrow remit of political parties or school governance committees, but is seen as a key issue of widespread economic, cultural and political concern.

A second range of new actors who have become increasingly involved with education over the last decade is the private sector. The significant presence of the private sector in the field of education and international development has been growing over the last twenty years. A number of large education businesses emerged with multinational interests and engagement in the field of international education policymaking and provision (Ball 2012, do Amaral et al 2019). One of the key mechanisms for this has been public private partnerships (PPPs), which have been assiduously promoted within education, despite very little evidence of their capacity to support provision for the poorest or enhance equality (Verger et al 2020, Gideon and Unterhalter 2020). The pandemic has given considerable impetus to PPP arrangements, with very uneven effects. One response to the emergence of education PPPs and the growth of large numbers of private schools, particularly in urban areas in developing countries, has been the establishment of a regulatory framework, described in Chapter 18, drawing on international human rights law, national constitutions, civic activism and research collaborations to assess and reframe the tide of privatization. *The Abidjan Principles on the human rights obligations of States to provide public education and to regulate private involvement in education*[2] are guiding principles on the right to education adopted by human rights and education experts in Abidjan, Côte d'Ivoire, in February 2019 (Right to Education 2019, Abidjan Principles 2019). The principles distil a legal framework informed by international human rights law on the obligations of states to provide public education and to regulate private provision of education, including PPPs. Under the shadow of the pandemic, important exploratory work needs to be conducted as to whether human rights frameworks, including those that deal with violence against women (VAW) and indigenous rights, can be used in ways to design and enable processes of building back to support equalities.

The increased presence of the private sector has been driven partly through its key role in the links between technology and education. The Covid-19 pandemic has accelerated many of the trends of humanity's relationship with digital technology, many with a direct bearing on education. Human interactions are increasingly taking place via digital linkups, whether video or text based, and universities and many schools around the world have been moving their teaching online, contributing to the expansion of large tech companies. While these technologies have been indispensable in allowing teaching and learning to continue during lockdown, they raise some complex issues for education and social justice – the moral dimensions of the question often being ignored by advocates. There remains a digital divide, and while access to technologies is spreading rapidly, availability of quality connections is far from universal. Home learning requires not only bandwidth but also high levels of either learner autonomy or family support, both of which can be constrained in contexts of poverty. There are also ongoing issues of privacy in relation to the large amounts of data collected via online platforms and broader concerns around datafication of education, and of our lives more broadly. On the other hand, there are some promising signs that technology can facilitate greater levels of cooperation and sharing – with Wikipedia being a prime example – decentring traditional forms of production and distribution on the basis of purchasing power. These debates are certain to continue as the so-called Fourth Industrial Revolution gains pace, with the continued growth of social media and use of artificial intelligence in education.

A third group of new actors in policy making and practice in education and international development comprises those concerned with the security agenda. This stream of work was noted during the war in Afghanistan, with the military building schools and securing an efficient education system as part of the strategy of European and North American armies in Afghanistan (Novelli 2013a). In the last ten years, with the huge challenges of large numbers of refugees leaving Syria, education has become part of refugee compacts involved with complex geopolitics (Dryden Petersen 2016, Trimikliniotis 2019). Migration due to poverty, as well as displacement (internal and over borders) on account of conflict and persecution, has led to new educational challenges. Large numbers of children are now being educated outside of their home countries, leading to complex decisions around curriculum, and its relationship with language, culture and employment. Education has also been mobilized in the attempt to halt migration and to address violent extremism, in ways that have been controversial and of dubious effectiveness. The significance for post-2015 education and international development is an important theme, discussed in Chapter 11.

The climate crisis along with broader environmental challenges of pollution and biodiversity loss pose threats to educational provision and resourcing in the decades to come. Yet education also holds the key to bringing the deep shift in understandings and actions, which, along with research and innovation, can enable the human community to address these critical issues (McCowan 2019). Further emerging issues concern the geo-politics associated with the significant economic role played by China and the mobilization of education resources in support of it, seen in many education initiatives in developing countries, the numbers of students from developing countries who study in China and the contribution of China to UN policy (Welch 2018, Wu 2018).

We thus see education and international development as a field marked by much expansion of provision yet shifting because of changing politics, policies, networks and a questioning of some core ideas. Covid-19 as a global pandemic accentuates these concerns. This book scrutinizes these themes, helping to contextualize the conditions for realizing the education aspirations of the SDGs. The chapters explore why the SDGs have acquired particular policy and practice significance, which partnerships are taking them forward and why. They highlight how defining education and development is a complex process in which intellectual inquiry has developed in critical reflection on policy and practice. Indeed, instead of being a starting point, defining education and development can be seen as the ultimate goal of a work of this sort and indeed of the entirety of the field. This is not merely a question of finding a technical solution but a normative task touching on our most fundamental moral and political values and necessarily involving the participation of all, from grassroots to government, in sustained and open deliberation.

Part I

Histories, Ideas and Actors in International Education

1

Histories of the Field of Education and International Development

Elaine Unterhalter

Introduction

International development is an area with contested beginnings, perspectives, pathways, alliances and positions of critique. Writers and practitioners concerned with education have engaged with international development invoking a range of ideas, policies and practices. Yet the kind of role education has taken or been given in this process has often been dictated by other more powerful disciplines or alliances. Its potential to offer a space for critical reflexivity with regard to development has sometimes been undervalued, although this has shifted somewhat in the last decade. This chapter aims to provide a short background history of education and international development as a field of study, highlighting some issues for the theoretical reviews and analyses of issues that follow.

Beginnings

Accounts of origins can provide significant markers of how disciplines or fields of study view themselves and demarcate their boundaries. Education and international development emerged, together with international education, as sub-fields of comparative education. Unlike comparative education, which traces a clear lineage identifying foundational works, methodological orthodoxies and precisely formulated areas of dispute (Philips and Schweisfurth 2008, Cowen and Kazamias 2009), neither sub field claims a distinctive origin, theoretical orthodoxy or easily distinguishable streams of work. McGrath and Gu (2016), in editing an overview volume in the field of international education and development, note how the terrain is not marked by interactions between perspectives. They comment on areas where there are disputes with regard to what constitutes development, quality education and the relationship of public and private, but they do not see any sharp divisions (McGrath and Gu 2016, 4). In a later synthesis volume McGrath (2018) draws out a range of different meanings and settings for education before and after 'the development era', loosely identifying a number of thematic areas. In my view, particular lines of division, regardless of thematic focus, have become more evident as scholars have come to demarcate the field of inquiry with more precision. Two accounts can be given of the history of the field. These different origin stories highlight some clear disputes with regard to how development is understood and what approaches to education policy, practice and research are entailed.

The first origin story is a mainstream account which links the emergence of education and international development with development economics (Fagerlind and Saha 1983, Jones 2007). From the 1950s, development economics emerged as a distinctive disciplinary area concerned with the uneven experiences of industrialization in low-income countries and the nature of trade and exchange between resource-rich countries, usually colonies or former colonies, and various metropolitan centres. In this work education is viewed as an aid to economic growth, which is itself initially linked with enhancing industrialization (Chenery et al. 1988). According to this version of a beginning, education and international development is a key area of engagement for global organizations linked together through the UN family.

In January 1961, the United Nations (UN) announced that the 1960s would be the decade for development. The concept of development it used was expressed in the call to member states and their peoples to work together 'to accelerate growth of the economy of the individual nations and their social advancement' (United Nations 1961, 17). Although this portrayal of development invoked state and non-state processes and referred to economic and social relations, the emphasis was very much on economic development. A key target for the decade was increasing the annual rate of growth of aggregate national income to 5 per cent, although in the 1960s various UN agencies, such as the United Nations International Children's Emergency Fund (UNICEF) and United Nations Educational, Scientific and Cultural Organization (UNESCO), worked to broaden this remit to include aspects of education.

In this origin story education and international development emerges as a field of inquiry shaped by disciplinary orthodoxies and methodologies linked to economics. Its concept of development is powerfully connected to economic development. The field of inquiry is associated with powerful organizations which connect member states to UN organizations. These formulations of political economic relationships, policies, practices and forms of research shape the field, and the issues it focuses on, and explains what is researched and what is overlooked.

A second version of the origin story draws out how ideas about education and development had been a strand in the expansion of colonial or imperial rule for many centuries. This perception is captured in an epigram attributed to a black South African: 'When the settlers came, we had the land and they had the Bible. They told us to close our eyes, and when we opened them, they had the land and we had the Bible.' In the many impositions of colonial rule and anti-colonial confrontation from the sixteenth century onwards, claims about forms of development were made. Education was a key location for political, cultural and social contestation. The terrain of education and international development was marked by complex struggles over knowledge, how humans were defined and distinguished, differing views of progress, language, national and cultural identity. These contestations with regard to ontology, epistemology and culture within education were closely linked with struggles over land ownership, franchise, the deployment of labour, formulations of policy and relationships of practice and many different kinds of organization. In this origin story education and international development emerges as a field of inquiry linked with many areas of subaltern and dominant knowledge, contested claims to authority, to land, struggles over rights. Some works rest on arguments against racism and gender inequality, and some rest on defences of these processes. In this account inequality, discrimination, violence and aspirations to overcome these are as much part of the field of inquiry as growth or trade. Considerations of connection outside institutions of state power, as well as strategies of how to work inside these organizations, are a major theme. Education policy and practice may advance the interests of the powerful or articulate the views of the powerless and assist towards transformation. The pathways to change are not linear and may have many facets. There is not a single genre of research, or approach to policy and practice.

These two different accounts of beginnings come to be associated with two clear streams of work in this field. In the first stream research and analysis document how education supports the needs of the economy through building human capital and enhancing market relations. Later this stream of work comes to associate education with enhancing relations of good governance, building institutions and sometimes with addressing poverty (Andrews 2008, World Bank 2018). A key thread is the ways in which education is associated with the policies and practices of international organizations, many located within the UN family (Jones 2007, Duedahl 2016). The agenda here is often linked with making education effective, or enhancing the alignment between education and key development outcomes, and this is sometimes referred to as the 'what works' agenda (Unterhalter 2018a) because many works in this stream focus on effective delivery or include the notion of 'what works' in their title (e.g. Sperling and Winthrop 2015, Masino and Niño-Zarazúa 2016)

In the second stream of work, education is a contested terrain in which different values are articulated, stories of pain, dispossession, inequality and the effects of violence are articulated (see, for example, Dei and Kempf 2016, Madeira and Correia 2019). The capacity of education to address existing forms of power and powerlessness is debated and assessed. Critical accounts are formulated of institutions not just for inefficiencies in that they might not work well but for being complicit with existing formations of power and exclusion, and not working well for transformation (Zinn 2016). I have referred to this as an agenda oriented to articulating 'what matters' (Unterhalter, 2018). Sometimes this work highlights that 'what matters' is linked with advancing anti-colonial struggles, defending human rights, protecting the rights of indigenous people of those with disabilities, understanding gender equality in education or supporting sustainability.

Actors 1
Colonial History, Education and International Development

Authors who were critical of divisions associated with colonial political economy used the education they received to articulate a different vision of society. They present an alternate beginning point for the history of education and international development. Some key figures are as follows:

Olaudah Equiano (*c.* 1750–97) was born in southern Nigeria. In his autobiography *The Interesting Narrative of the Life of Olaudah Equiano or Gustavus Vassa, the African*, published in 1789, he describes how he was kidnapped with his sister at around the age of eleven, sold by local slave traders and shipped across the Atlantic to Barbados and then Virginia. Bought by a Royal Navy captain, he spent twenty years travelling the world and was ultimately able to make enough money to buy his freedom. He learned to read and write, becoming a prominent member of the campaign to abolish slavery. In the dedication of his autobiography, he depicts the horrors of the slave trade and his confidence in the liberal human values of Britain, its arts and science, which will resonate with his aim as an 'unlettered African' to become 'an instrument toward the relief of his suffering countrymen' (Equiano 1814).

Kartini (1879–1904) was the daughter of a Javanese landowner and regent (a local political official) under Dutch colonial rule. Kartini and her sisters were sent to school and she read widely in Dutch. She engaged in correspondence with a number of Dutch women and in her letters formulated a critical commentary on the colonial political economy and aspects of the rights of women. Kartini died in childbirth. Her letters were published in 1911 initially in Dutch as *Door Duisternis tot Licht (Out of Dark Comes Light)*. She has been an influential symbolic figure in postcolonial Indonesia, associated with the establishment of schools for girls, ideas about domesticity and feminism. In a letter of 1900 to a former teacher, Mrs Zeehandlelaar, she wrote: 'We wish to equal the Europeans in education and enlightenment, and the rights which we demand for ourselves, we must also to give to others' (Kartini 1920, 20).

Sol Plaatje (1876–1932) was born on a mission station in South Africa, where his Tswana-speaking parents were employed. He attended a mission school. He worked as a teacher, a telegraph clerk and a journalist; he also wrote a novel, many political commentaries and translated Shakespeare into Tswana. In 1913, he was a founder member and first secretary general of the South African National Congress that engaged with the British colonial authorities for political rights for black South Africans. He began writing *Native Life in South Africa*, an account of the hardships and discrimination associated with colonial rule, while on a journey by sea to London in 1913 to petition the British government to repeal legislation on land and labour. He was also part of a delegation in 1919 to the peace conferences at the end of the First World War that tried to gain recognition for the political rights of black South Africans, many of whom had fought in the war. While none of these petitions were successful in Plaatje's lifetime, he is today recognized for his political, social and literary contribution to South African scholarship. A passage in *Native Life* gives a flavour of his clear observations:

Whenever by force of character or sheer doggedness one Native has tried to break through the South African shackles of colour prejudice, the Colour Bar, inserted in the South African Constitution in 1909, instantly hurled him back to the lowest rung of the ladder and held him there. Let me mention only one such case. About ten years ago Mr. J. M. Nyokong, of the farm Maseru, in the Thabanchu district, invested about 1,000 Pounds in agricultural machinery and got a white man to instruct his nephews in its use. I have seen his nephews go forth with a steam sheller, after garnering his crops every year, to reap and thresh the grain of the native peasants on the farms in his district. But giving evidence before the Lands Commission two years ago, this industrious black landowner stated that he had received orders from the Government not to use his machinery except under the supervision of a white engineer. This order, he says, completely stopped his work. The machinery is used only at harvesting time; no white man would come and work for him for two months only in the year, and as he cannot afford to pay one for doing nothing in the remaining ten months, his costly machinery is reduced to so much scrap iron. This is the kind of discouragement and attrition to which Natives who seek to better their position are subjected in their own country. (Plaatje 1916)

The writers in Actors 1 all connect to a colonial relationship and seek to use the education tools provided by colonial rulers to refashion the structures of colonialism, associated with racism, slavery, the subjugation of women, the dispossession of land and the denial of political representation. The depth of the inequalities established under colonial rule, and the difficulties of achieving transformation through education alone, is evident from their life stories and the history of subsequent centuries.

Different forms of modernization and education were articulated in countries like Japan and Ethiopia, which were not colonized. Here, cross-national attraction to education ideas from many locales took diverse forms, not always passing in a singular direction, and not always expressing the dichotomy I have sketched associated with colonial relations (Rappleye 2007, Barnett 2012, Marzagora 2016).

Education, not just in the form prescribed by colonial rulers, was to be invoked as a key process of decolonization by leaders of anti-colonial movements, like Ambedkar in India and Nyerere in Africa. In the articulation of anti-colonial visions different emphases are given to education in the aspiration of anti-colonial movements to support the development of new kinds of people, enriched by wider insights than those conferred through colonial formulations. For example, Rabindranath Tagore (1861–1941) worked on writing about education and research and established a nexus of education institutions in India. His work delineates a form of curriculum to enhance knowledge and interpretation of tradition in multiple areas, synthesizing knowledge streams from West and East, noting the need to draw on science to solve real-world problems and build a cosmopolitan outlook (Mukerjee 2020). Another example is Rokeya Sakhawat Hossain (1880–1932), an innovative writer and social activist, born into an orthodox Muslim family in British-ruled Bengal. She founded a school, led a women's organization and built networks with other reformers who challenged hierarchical family structures and religious dogma. In her writings, which use multiple genres, she formulates a vision for education linked to enlightenment and women's empowerment in the face of existing political and social mores of exclusion, which dehumanize women. She highlights the importance of women's friendships and emphasizes how change happens partly through the practical work of establishing institutions (Qaysum and Hasan 2017). The examples of Tagore and Begum Rokeya show the stream of work with regard to 'what matters', drawing out complex rather than linear ways to think about education. They draw attention to multiple settings for education change, not just the state. Both Tagore and Begum Rokeya, although very engaged with specific places, also connected to transnational networks.

Transnationalism or international networking was also a feature of the writings exemplified in Actors 1. Their education ideas were developed through connections between people in different countries organized outside state relationships through political, religious or ethnic networks. Thus, for example, Christian anti-slavery campaigners helped publicize the work of former slaves documenting education and the struggle to be heard by Africans, or those of African descent in Europe and America (Thomas 2000). The wide circulation of Sol Plaatje's *Native Life in South Africa* was partly achieved because it was promoted by African American campaigners like W.E.B. DuBois and Marcus Garvey. Women social reformers from England made connections with women in India, engaging with questions of education for women and girls to connect across differences (Ramusack 1990). We can multiply these instances beyond these actors. For example, concerns with promoting ideas about Confucianism led to the establishment of the Tiong Hoa Hwee Kwan (THHK), founded in Batavia, now Jakarta, in 1900 by Chinese living in the East Indies, drawing on experiences of Chinese schools initially established in Japan (Suryadinata 1972). These international relationships, travelling along networks of affiliation, rather than formations of a bureaucracy, associated with UN organizations of aid relationships seen in the 'what works' stream, have also at some points been seen in global movements supporting Education for All (EFA) with regard to education rights (Mundy 2007) or gender equality in education (Unterhalter and North 2017).

The two readings of the history of education and international development indicate how the field of inquiry is diffuse and complex, marked by political, economic, social and cultural processes in which education intertwines with many relationships of power and powerlessness. Some views of education in both streams are formal and highly structured directed to address political, economic, cultural or health goals. Others, also associated with both streams, involve informal educational associations articulating wide ideas concerning parenthood, authenticity, equality or social justice. Some approaches are organized to emphasize the technical and the rational, and others the affective, the aspirational and emotional. Some combine the two seeking to link or translate from one framework to another expanding ideas about formal schooling to encompass wider, more general views of education drawing on frameworks concerned with human rights, equalities, human development or sustainability. Documenting networks, policy shifts and how ideas move and change form has been a prominent theme in comparative education (Steiner Khamsi and Waldrow

2012, Cowen, 2018). In reviewing some features of the debate between 'what works' and 'what matters' in education and international development (Unterhalter 2009, Unterhalter 2018a, 2018b, 2019a, 2019b), I have argued for the importance of seeing these streams as connected, even if the form of articulation is complex. If something matters, one needs it to work. Furthermore, one would only want something to work, if it mattered. In looking at some pathways through education and international development one can see some formations of connection, often linked with trying to make abstract ideas about social justice, such as the right to education, human development or gender equality, work in real life settings marked by difficult histories, fragile polities and economies and complex intersecting inequalities. We can mark these pathways of working towards connection as a third stream of work in education and international development. Thus pathways associated with connecting 'what works' and 'what matters' are evident at certain periods in some UN organizations, some civil society networks and some multi-disciplinary dialogues. Sometimes connection is enhanced, but sometimes it is evaded or changed so that the association of ideas, people or places is not productive.

Pathways: Connections or Disconnections?

We can read some of the pathways through the history of the field of education and international development as attempts to connect or disconnect the orientations of 'what works' with 'what matters'. Making 'what matters' work through constructing a global architecture for delivering human rights and universal education was a key initiative after the Second World War. The UN Charter of 1945 sets out the importance of enhancing cooperation between countries on education and addressing a range of social, economic and cultural problems. The Universal Declaration of Human Rights of 1948 lists education as a key right. Education was seen both as a right and to underpin peace building and international understanding, and therefore the mission of the UN as a whole. The establishment of the UN and the growth of international organizations after the Second World War becomes an important context for education and international development. Human rights become a key framing idea. UNESCO, the agency charged with overseeing the scientific, cultural and educational work of the UN, has principles of educational equality and the importance of negotiating between member states built into its Constitution. Throughout the 1950s, UNESCO organized regional conferences promoting access to free basic education, adult literacy and gender equality. As such, it was a locus for a particular engagement of education and international development work, which took seriously the role of the state, education rights and equalities. It thus attempts to bridge some of the concerns of 'what works' framing this around 'what matters'.

UNESCO did not only privilege economics, and placed particular emphases on aspects of planning (Ross and Genevois 2006) and cultural diversity (Pigozzi 2006). The association of education with modernization was a key theme (Mundy 1999b, Peppin-Vaughan 2010). Before 1990, UNESCO convened international meetings and discussions, developing resources and capacity on education rights, adult, technical, vocational and higher education. It also participated in the drafting of the major global instruments concerning education including the International Covenant on Economic, Social and Cultural Rights (1966) and the Convention on the Rights of the Child (1989). Technical expertise in education planning was developed through the International Institute for Educational Planning (IIEP) and large databanks of statistics through the UNESCO Institute for Statistics (UIS). These organizational formations linked to making processes work assumed particular importance as the EFA movement grew from 1990 (see Chapter 3). UNESCO was the lead UN organization associated with work on the Decade of Education for Sustainable Development (2005–14) and directed the formulation of the vision document adopted in 2015 *Education 2030*. UNESCO has oversight of assembling the data to monitor progress on targets under the SDG framework (see Chapter 10). In 2020 it launched an initiative to look into Futures for Education encouraging global conversations on 'how knowledge and learning can shape the future of humanity and the planet' (UNESCO 2020b). In all these initiatives there is a perception that policy frameworks and global convenings are a site of work to take forward 'what matters' with respect to education rights, equality and sustainability. How this is linked to understandings of 'what works' has been much debated (Tikly 2019, Unterhalter 2019a).

UNESCO's governance structures linked it closely to the concerns on which member states agreed to collaborate. Some limits of co-operation were highlighted in 2018 when the USA and Israel left UNESCO. But this departure did not derail the organization's focus on rights or efforts to try to connect an orientation concerned with 'what works' to one linked with 'what matters'. Indeed, this focus on delivery and connection with the policies and practices of governments intensified. The Covid-19 crisis saw both threads of work prominent in the support provided by UNESCO with a focus both on government provision of education to children out of school, or returning under the shadow of the pandemic, and discussions of future visions (https://en.unesco.org/covid19). These initiatives saw UNESCO sharing platforms discussing the effects of the pandemic on education with other UN agencies, who interpreted rights and equality somewhat differently.

A somewhat different emphasis with regard to how 'what works' can help deliver 'what matters' is evident in UNICEF. From the 1960s UNICEF and the World Bank began to take an interest in education. Because of the way each was governed, these organizations had levels of autonomy from the agreed concerns of *all* UN member states and consequently were able to approach the issue of education somewhat differently, compared to UNESCO. Their engagement with this area identified particular signature approaches to 'what works' for each organization (Jones 2012, Jolly 2014). UNICEF, initially set up to provide emergency relief to countries devastated by the Second World War, relied on donations from governments, private organizations and individuals. Governed by a Board made up of government representatives, elected by the United Nations Economic and Social Council, and led by an Executive Director, in its first decade of work, UNICEF focused primarily on children's health but started to broaden this in the 1960s, stressing a commitment to humanitarian work and developing planning for children, which was a particularly novel idea at the time. This entailed attending to child and maternal health; providing access to food and nutrition, and formal and non-formal education; and meeting children's psychosocial needs (Jolly 2014). In 1966, UNICEF received the Nobel Peace Prize for this work. From the 1970s, UNICEF's priorities shifted from short-term disaster relief to long-term engagement with programmes to address 'the "silent emergencies" of malnutrition, deadly disease, the AIDS pandemic, gender inequality and child abuse including child trafficking, child labour and child soldiers' (UNICEF 2006). It focused on working to address these contexts of education. This led to a new interpretation of 'what matters'. In 1989, UNICEF led on the adoption of the Convention on the Rights of the Child, signing up virtually every country in the world to uphold it. Getting global institutional frameworks to work to deliver on 'what matters' is thus a key approach. From the 1990s UNICEF has given particular attention to girls' education, and the UN Girls' Education Initiative (UNGEI) has been located in UNICEF since 2000. Interventions to protect child rights, support health and well-being and later equity have been the path through which UNICEF has attempted to connect 'what works' and 'what matters' for education (Jones 2006, Schaub, Henck and Baker 2017).

For the World Bank the connection between 'what works' and 'what matters' has generally swung most towards the stream of 'what works', with 'what matters' largely read through ideas about the economy. The World Bank was established in 1944 at the Bretton Woods Conference, which looked at establishing a global system to regulate exchange rates and the financial rules between countries, When the International Bank of Reconstruction and Development, which now forms part of the World Bank Group, was established, countries with large amounts of capital to invest in the bank, like the USA, took a leading role in deciding policy. The governance structures of the Bank tend to give more prominence to the concerns of the major shareholders, and the organization is thus less representative of the one country, one vote approach which governs UNESCO. This has meant that the World Bank has taken a distinctive line on education since the 1960s, sometimes differing from other UN organizations. Today it is a major development partner and also a prominent sponsor of research and centre of knowledge education. Its financial and intellectual strength often means that its work overshadows that of other UN agencies. It has promoted ideas, some of which are controversial among scholars of education and international development, about the importance of the private sector and the significance of strengthening education systems (Verger et al. 2017, Zapp 2017, Klees et al. 2020).

The World Bank's original mandate had not included lending to education, which was at that stage associated with private rates of return. However, in the 1960s, the case was made, by the Director General of UNESCO, among others, that investment in education was crucial to economic growth (Jones 2006). This led to changes in perspective at the World Bank, inaugurating a long period of engagement with research and policy discussion regarding education and international development, generally with a concern regarding growth, rates of return and system efficiency. In 1995, a key policy paper (World Bank 1995) argued that rates of return were significantly higher in primary education, and policy guidance, loans and research for around a decade took this direction. However, the World Bank currently sees its education mission in terms of a dual focus: 'to help countries achieve universal primary education and to help countries build the higher-level and flexible skills needed to compete in today's global, knowledge-driven markets' (World Bank 2014). It has been a prominent supporter of ideas about the learning crisis, associated with children in school in developing countries, but, as documented by many cross national tests, learning little with regard to literacy or numeracy outcomes (UNESCO 2016). In the 2018 *World Development Report* a particular vision of aligning a range of actors to deliver learning outcomes through education systems was formulated (World Bank 2018). Here there is significant emphasis on 'what works' to enhance learning outcomes, and 'what matters' is more narrowly specified than in some of the wide-ranging policy frameworks that had been led by UNESCO.

It can be seen that the pathways connecting 'what works' and 'what matters' go in different directions for different UN organizations, partly because of their governance structures and interpretations of their mission. Even more diversity is evident in civil society organizations, which link 'what works' and 'what matters' through pathways where there is an inter-mixture of activism, research, policy promotion and forms of educational practice. Opposition to structural adjustment in the 1980s and the enormous growth of civil society organizations in the 1990s in the wake of the end of the Cold War and in response to the HIV epidemic, led to non-governmental organizations (NGOs) and civil society organizations (CSOs) emerging as particularly important actors in the field of education and international development. Some global organizations became influential in the EFA movement after 2000, because of the programmes they set up in the 1990s (Tikly 2019). These organizations formulated their missions through concerns with rights and equality. In 2019 some were engulfed with scandal because of failure by some members of staff to act in accordance with these principles, raising questions about how transformative they really were (Marsh et al. 2020).

In the 1990s, some NGOs and CSOs began to develop and circulate specialist education knowledge, engage in policy development and advocacy and later become partners with academic and activist researchers. This work brought to the field of education and international development a new range of issues, different interlocutors, partnerships, methodologies and a new terrain for investigation (Fransman, Newman and Cornish 2017). Holding governments to account for the delivery of EFA has become a major concern for some NGOs (Unterhalter and North 2018, Unterhalter,Ron Balsera and Dorsi 2020), as has providing a platform for the marginalized. Some have worked closely with private sector foundations promoting aspects of neoliberalism (Brehm and Silova 2019). Here too there are connections made between 'what works', sometimes in signature education interventions, and 'what matters'.

Pathways to Practice 1
Selected Education Projects of NGOs

Save the Children Fund (SCF) was first established to help feed children at the end of the First World War. It was an early campaigner for children's rights and child protection. SCF undertakes humanitarian work around the globe. From 2000, it became involved with EFA and has developed particular expertise in programming and advocacy regarding education and conflict. From 2010 it partnered with DFID for delivery of initiatives linked to the *Girls' Education Challenge.*

ActionAid initially developed programmes to distribute donations to children living in developing countries. From the 1990s a key focus has been building activist coalitions through the Global Campaign for Education (GCE). It campaigns for education rights and develops projects that combine research, programming and advocacy. It campaigns for tax justice to support resources for education

Plan is a global children's charity, initially founded in the 1930s. It works on a range of projects with the world's poorest children. It has run the *Because I Am a Girl* campaign since 2007 and works at international, national and local levels against violence against girls and women.

A further pathway through education and international development as a field of inquiry is associated with the waxing and waning of the influence of other disciplines, and trans-disciplinary engagements. Unlike comparative education, which has a close association with history, scholars in education and international development work across disciplinary areas, suturing together different theorizations to help investigate features of practice, talking with many partners in different institutional locations. This is a feature of the stream of scholarship linked to 'what works' as much as to that linked to 'what matters'. The history of work in this area is thus characterized by hybridity and combinations of perspective. Some commentators have noted how hardwired some of the assumptions and power relations of the Global North have become in the field, with little acknowledgement or interest in redress, past histories of racism or epistemic exclusion (Sriprakash, Tikly and Walker 2019, Walker 2020).

These are astute criticisms of some features of work. But the field, because of its diversity, is hard to characterize only in this way.

From the 1960s, pathways through the field have been nurtured by the emergence of Development Studies as a particular area of enquiry. In this field, Development Economics, itself a highly heterodox field, has meshed with anthropology, sociology, politics, history, gender and women's studies, critical theory, queer theory, cultural studies and studies in information and communication technologies, environment and health (Desai and Potter 2013, Schech 2018). We can look at some of the routes through these processes of transdisciplinarity are, focusing on gender. The work of scholars on gender relations in developing countries, such as Naila Kabeer, Ruth Pearson and Maxine Molyneux (Jackson and Pearson 2005), was applied to work in education and international development establishing a new field of enquiry and highlighting the significance of gender equality and women's rights as areas that mattered and needed support to work (Stromquist 1997, Heward and Bunwaree 1999, Leach 2003, Aikman and Unterhalter 2005, Fennell and Arnot 2008). These studies went beyond some of the 'what works' approaches, outlined initially by researchers working for the World Bank (King and Hill 1993), who associated girls' education primarily with economic development. Other later formulations of 'what works' in girls' education saw this contributing significantly to all forms of development, not just economic growth (Sperling and Winthrop 2015). In the expansion of this area of enquiry, deeper complexities of gender inequalities within and beyond education have emerged (Unterhalter 2016, Unterhalter, Robinson and Ron Balsera 2020). Connections with livelihoods threatened by climate crisis, violence against women, a range of health issues, some made prominent through the COVID pandemic and difficulties in realizing empowerment have become apparent. This has led to the emergence of a more diverse and nuanced literature, drawing on many disciplinary resources, and concerned with trying to make gender equality in and through education work, and to generate new insights for scholarship and theory building about what matters.

Perspectives on Connection

How and why what works connects with what matters in education and international development has begun to be addressed by scholarly works looking at questions of scale, locale and discourse (e.g. Robertson 2005, Vavrus and Bartlett 2009, Unterhalter and North 2017, Takayama, Sriprakash and Connell (2017). Contested views of the global, the national and the local highlight different ways to frame and thus theorize and investigate both connected and dichotomous positionings of 'what works' and 'what matters.

From one perspective, the global can be thought of as a group of organizations that stand above or outside nation states, as exemplified by the structure of the UN and the relationships of EFA promoting policy and practice associated with either 'what works' or 'what matters'. From this perspective, aid or policy formulations or research approaches are given as loans or projects for development cooperation by powerful global organizations which make demands of nation states or local institutions. This perspective on education and international development generally entails writing about institutions with contrasting values, aims, scale and scope, and what happens when policy or practice formulated in one institutional setting moves or is moved to another. In this there is considerable cross-over with the mobilities theme in comparative education (Steiner Khamsi and Waldrow 2012; Sobe 2015). However, there are problems with delineating the global as always outside and different to the national or the local: it sets too stark a dichotomy. It also implies that the local is always somewhat parochial, inward looking, responding to national priorities and politics, receiving global initiatives in education policy and initiating little globally. This perspective suggests static understanding at both the global and the national levels.

A contrasting view sees the global as a set of sociocultural attitudes and dispositions which characterize the work of employees of particular kinds of organizations and networks, located globally, nationally and locally, who advance a particular set of ideas about education policy and practice *inside* nation states. This is the argument made by the school of neo-institutionalism, drawing on the work of John Meyer and others at Stanford University who have argued for a distinctive diffusion of Western-style education associated with the emergence of global institutions, international organizations and an increasingly common world culture evident after the Second World War (Meyer et al. 1997). In their argument, the take-up, for example, of ideas about transparent governance and accountability regarding education within governments and NGOs reflects the views of a particular class of advocates of this approach, who may be nationally located, for example working for a Department of Education or a large NGO to introduce school-based management committees which oversee the disbursement of aid and/or government capitation fees. The ideas of these supporters of what has been depicted as world culture, and the content of their views may be oriented to 'what works' or 'what matters', may come into conflict with advocates of other approaches. Sometimes these associations are portrayed as different and can be seen as linked to corruption, tradition or parochialism. From this perspective of analysis, it is not that one group is global and the other national. The group that articulates 'world culture' is also national but has a different network regarding patronage, ideas, funding and esteem. The group that opposes 'world culture' may well draw on ideas and affiliations that are not simply local. However, what this framework of analysis sets out to explain is why there has been a predominance of the groups with connections to centres of world culture.

This notion that the global is inside the national and the local is also a perspective advanced by students of international migrations of people or ideas, who show how there is no simple version of the global or the local in education or any other area and that people merge and mix ideas from many sources (Bjorkland, Hogland et al. 2016, Castles 2018). Thus money for education flows along diaspora channels: sent home by migrant workers to support their children's school fees or endow a classroom in their village or support a school association. Ideas about education also travel because of enhanced connectivity. Media portrayals or international conversations suggest particular ways of building or organizing a school. These ideas may be considered 'global' but may just be the outcome of diverse discussions on this theme as people criss-cross the world literally, virtually and in their imagination. From this perspective, poverty or marginality is not one set of static relationships as defined only by income. A person may be classed poor, earning little in a high-income country but have many significant networks in the low-income country in which she was born and, because of the remittances she sends, have considerable status in her community.

A third view is that the global can be understood as a set of ethical ideas about rights, capabilities and obligations which enjoin particular ways of thinking about what we owe each other regardless of our nationality and our particular beliefs. This is the argument a number of authors have made concerning how we understand rights, cosmopolitanism and what approaches we might take to evaluating the work of global, national and local initiatives in education (Sen 1999, 2009, Nussbaum 2000, 2007). In this argument, 'what matters' is not an abstract set of principles but a lived set of relationships with regard to what ethical evaluations are made about the processes of disbursement; the inclusivity of the relationships formed; and whether aims entail transformation or merely reproduction of existing structures of power. Both the state and the private sector need to be rigorously scrutinized for how they deal with, protect and advance rights and opportunities. Here, poverty needs to be understood as multi-dimensional, and the intersection of class, race, gender, ethnicity and age is investigated to develop relationships that are participatory, that take account of the complexity of context and that challenge injustices Dreze and Sen 2015, Reynolds et al. 2019).

These different ways of understanding the global, the national, the local and the relationships of 'what works' and 'what matters' for education illustrate both the diverse conceptual resources education and international development draws on and also the ways in which different kinds of policy and practice are discussed within particular framings. Scholarship in this field is often critically concerned with reviewing the implications of different framings in relation to each other.

Conclusion

This chapter outlines a broad history of education and international development, as a field of study which does not have a single theoretical lexicon, a set of foundational thinkers or a simple institutional location. It is a polyvalent area, drawing on different disciplines, engaging with some of the complexities of application and attempting to dialogue with policymaking through posing questions and offering critical reflection. I have sketched two different origin stories for education and international development, and these suggest two different pathways for policy, practice and research. The pragmatic demands of planning, which was a key feature of some beginnings in UN organizations, gave education and international development a particular flavour that was concerned to 'get things done'. This link to practice has remained a characteristic of the field, distinguishing it, in early writings, from Comparative Education, which had a more scholarly stance, with a tendency to stress its distance from practice. However, other older currents in education and international development draw on contested ideas about equity, equality, rights and decolonization, and are concerned to dig deeper into the ways ideas are formulated, who talks and who is silenced, and how efficiency might compromise what matters. The pathways that have sought to establish connections between 'what works' and 'what matters' have been associated with some UN organizations, NGOs, some multi-disciplinary debates and some normative understandings of the global, the national and the local. In the chapters that follow, which look at theory, research and practice, different ways of engaging or ignoring these questions can be discerned. This is a field in flux, where many ideas are contested, the direction of travel and place of arrival are not pre-given and the outcomes of debates are still to be settled.

Questions for Discussion

1. Which aspects of economics have played a key part in the history of education and international development, and why do you think they have been so influential?
2. How have features of international political economy shaped the histories of different UN organizations and affected the work they do on education?
3. Are the two positions of 'what works' and 'what matters' too polarized? What might deepen the division between them? What might connect them? Why?

Further Reading

Tikly, L. 2020, *Education for Sustainable Development in the Postcolonial World*, London: Routledge.

Verger, A., Altinyelken, H. K., and Novelli, M. (Eds.). (2018). *Global Education Policy and International Development: New Agendas, Issues and Policies*, London: Bloomsbury Publishing.

2

Theories of Development

Tristan McCowan

Chapter Outline

Introduction

The Organisation for Economic Co-operation and Development's (OECD, 2020) reflection on the impact of Covid-19 on education states:

> Because learning loss will lead to skill loss, and the skills people have relate to their productivity, gross domestic product (GDP) could be 1.5 lower on average for the remainder of the century. The present value of the total cost would amount to 69% of current GDP for the typical country. These estimates assume that only the cohort currently in school are affected by the closures and that all subsequent cohorts resume normal schooling. If schools are slow to return to prior levels of performance, the growth losses will be proportionately higher.

What we can observe here is an underpinning rationale for education: namely, that it provides individuals with the skills they need to succeed in work and by extension that economic growth is brought about by the investments that countries and individuals make in their skills. This view corresponds to that of human capital theory, one of the key frameworks that have driven international education practice over the past fifty years. That the OECD did not cite human capital theory is beside the point. This and many other theories orient practice and policy, whether or not they are invoked explicitly or used consciously.

This chapter outlines some of the major theories of international development that have influenced the work of supranational agencies, national governments and local actors since the end of the Second World War. It is intended not as a comprehensive overview of development theory but instead as a treatment that focuses on the principal *types* of theory (by political and epistemological orientation) and those that have had most relevance for the field of education. In each case, the major characteristics of the theory are outlined, as well as some of its well-known proponents and its implications for education. (Some of the implications of these theories for research are drawn out in Chapter 5.)

Yet two questions need to be addressed before turning to the specific theories: first, what exactly is 'theory', and second, why – given the apparently practical nature of the task of development – should we be interested in theory at all? In relation to the first of these questions, we might distinguish between what might be called 'big T' theory and 'little T' theory. There are theories that present themselves as 'theory X', have a coherent body of literature – usually with theoretical components and empirical applications – have researchers who utilize them explicitly and are publicly recognizable. Examples of these forms of theories are the theory of relativity, game theory or, in relation to international development, dependency theory. Yet there is another use of the term 'theory' that is more elusive and at the same time more present in our everyday lives. In this sense, theory is every abstraction from the concrete. Use of language to describe the world around us involves abstraction and representation, in particular in grouping and categorizing phenomena (e.g. use of the term 'animal' to denote a wide range of beings with some common characteristics). As an extension, we use theory to understand the causes of the phenomena we perceive (its explanatory function) and thereby to predict how phenomena will change or occur in the future (its predictive function). Furthermore, theory has a normative function in asserting how things *should* be in the world, particularly as regards human behaviour and social organization. All statements about the world, in this sense, are theory, as they are attempting to abstract from the actual instances to which they are referring.

The distinction between explanatory and normative aspects of theory is important in relation to international development. A theory of the explanatory type is human capital theory (HCT), which attempts to explain why some economies grow more rapidly than others and from which we can adopt strategies for ensuring growth in the future. *Normative* theories on the other hand make claims about what is of value in the world. The capability approach, for example, asserts that we should evaluate the desirability of social arrangements not on the basis of maximization of GDP alone but on the full range of freedoms that are accorded to people. Martinussen (1997), in a similar vein, distinguishes between three types of theorizing around development: 'concept' (the overarching vision of development), 'theory' (understanding the process of change and the conditions underpinning it) and 'strategy' (actions and interventions adopted to achieve the aims). Of course, we cannot separate completely the explanatory and normative dimensions – normally, explanatory theories are underpinned by normative assumptions (so HCT rests on the value of wealth accumulation, both individually and nationally) and normative theories may also have explanations of the world built into them (Marx's advocacy for socialism is partly normative, but is also based on a reading of the inherent contradictions of capitalism in practice).

Theory – particularly of the 'big T' variety – is often perceived to be intimidating (and it is fair to say that some theorists do little to make their work more accessible). Theoretical thought is portrayed as hard to understand, and moreover to be divorced from reality, because it is either irrelevant in terms of the characteristics of the current situation or too idealistic in terms of the practically feasible. According to this perspective, on one side we have 'theory' – lofty, dry, utopian and irrelevant – and on the other we have 'practice' – everyday, engaging, realistic and useful. However, it is important that we do not view theory in this way. In the first place, theory is not something we can choose to use or not. Understood as the fundamental abstract principles underlying specific instances, theory is within every practice, whether evident and known or not. When a government designs a set of policies for the education system – involving funding priorities, a framework of aims, curricular content and so forth – it is drawing on a range of principles relating to social justice, the good life and the nature of knowledge, whether or not these are made explicit. Likewise, every time teachers stand up in class, their practice of teaching is similarly informed by theories of an epistemological, political and moral nature.

We can identify three main reasons, therefore, for engaging with theory in the field of education and international development. First, as readers and users of research, it is important that we understand the theories that are being utilized by the authors. Second, as researchers, we will utilize a range of theories in collecting, analysing and interpreting data – and indeed in deciding what is and is not worth researching. Last, drawing on the idea above that theory is present in all practice, awareness of theory is essential for understanding the underpinnings of policies and practices with which we come into contact, allowing us more effectively to engage, critique and recast them.

The following sections will outline five paradigms of development theory: liberal capitalist, Marxist, liberal egalitarian, postmodern and radical humanist. In each of these, specific theories as well as a range of theorists are grouped. As stated above, this grouping is intended not as an exhaustive categorization of development theories but as a generative selection to highlight the major approaches. Some of the key components of these theories are outlined in Table 2.1.

The Liberal Capitalist Paradigm

A range of theories emerged after the end of the Second World War associated with promoting and sustaining economic growth and focusing on how countries could most effectively rebuild and restructure their economies. These theories have as their primary assumption that capitalism is the ideal or perhaps the only form of economic organization. They are for the most part universalist and assume that all countries' economies can and should be organized along similar lines.

'Development economics' emerged in the post-war period as a branch of the discipline addressing the specific conditions of the 'Third World'. However, by the late 1950s, theorists began to recognize the importance of social and cultural factors in facilitating or hindering economic growth (Desai 2012), leading to the emergence of *modernization* theory. In essence, this theory asserts that the key to economic growth is the transformation of the 'traditional' into the 'modern'. The US economist Walt Rostow (1960) put forward a model of economic development that envisaged countries moving through five phases:

Table 2.1 Paradigms of Development Theory

Paradigm	Vision	Strategy	Link to education	Variants
Liberal capitalist	Economic growth for 'catch-up' with developed countries	Modernizing economic activity and institutions, changing attitudes and enhancing workers' skills and productivity	Schooling instrumental in forming productive workers	Modernization theory Human capital theory Neoliberalism
Marxist	Ending economic inequalities and exploitation	De-linking from dependent relations with former colonial or neo-colonial powers	Education systems dependent on former colonial powers and reproduce unequal relations	Dependency theory World systems theory Social reproduction
Postmodern	Decentring of grand narratives of Enlightenment and progress	Critique of representation. Troubling/questioning concepts	Education serves to disparage indigenous cultures but also to articulate critical vision	Postcolonialism Post-development Queer theory
Liberal egalitarian	Equality of opportunity and fundamental entitlements, with individual agency, well - being and liberty	Constitutional guarantees, global obligations and individuals holding state to account	Educational opportunities must be distributed fairly and must equip individuals for full participation in society	Basic needs Human rights Human development/ capability approach
Radical humanist	Transformation of consciousness for the emancipation of the people and creation of a just society	Individual and collective empowerment through learning and action	Education is intrinsic to development; social transformation starts with learning; dialectic of reflection and action	Freirean approaches Critical pedagogy Participatory learning and action

(1)   The traditional society;
(2)   The establishment of the pre-conditions for take-off;
(3)   The take-off stage (The Big Push – marked by
     (i)   an increase in investment rate,
     (ii)   development of growth sectors of aggregate demand, and
     (iii) establishment of social, political and institutional frameworks);
(4)   The drive to maturity; and
(5)   The époque of high mass consumption (self-sustaining).

Rostow (1960, 19) stated:

> Above all, the concept must be spread that man need not regard his physical environment as virtually a factor given by nature and providence, but as an ordered world which, if rationally understood, can be manipulated in ways which yield productive change.

The process of modernization is seen to relate to both the institutions of society (legal systems, the market, political organization) and individuals' attitudes (becoming ambitious and entrepreneurial rather than superstitious and averse to change). Modernization theory, therefore, had a strong disciplinary presence from outside economics, including sociology (e.g. Inkeles and Smith 1975) and psychology (e.g. McClelland 1961). McClelland's psychological variant focused on the achievement motive, assessing the varying extents to which peoples around the world were motivated to succeed and thereby allow their nations to develop.

The connections to education are plain to see. The formal education system is itself an instance of a modern institution but also serves the function of 'modernizing' through inculcating a set of norms and attitudes, and forming skills for diverse functions in society. Just as the establishment of mass schooling systems had underpinned the formation of the modern state in Western Europe and North America (Green 2013), so they would need to in the newly independent countries of Asia and Africa. As argued by Unterhalter (2008), modernization theory linked in closely with the nation-building agendas of many newly independent countries, served by the development of mass education for national citizenship through a common language.

Human capital theory (which will be discussed in further detail in Chapters 7 and 14) can be located within this paradigm – although the focus is more on skills and other attributes for economic productivity rather than the broader norms or attitudes underpinning the modern state. Economists in the United States from the 1960s (e.g. Gary Becker [1964], Theodore Schultz [1961]) drew on the work of the eighteenth-century Scottish economist Adam Smith to assert the fundamental role of education in economic growth. Drawing on empirical data, they showed that differences in economic growth between countries could be explained by the level of education of the population (e.g. Psacharopolous 1994). On an individual level, investment in one's own education (as well as associated factors such as health) would enhance one's productivity and thereby one's earnings, and on a collective level, the increase in human capital stock would drive economic growth. Despite a range of concerns and challenges to the theory within the field of economics (e.g. screening hypothesis), human capital theory has prospered and is undoubtedly the key driving force for national investment in education and the advocacy of supranational agencies in low- and middle-income countries to this day.

Liberal capitalist approaches have had a significant revival in recent years through the ascendancy of free-market ideas associated with neoliberalism. Here, assertions of the ends of development as economic growth have been accompanied by claims that the means are through market-based competition, minimal state intervention and individual entrepreneurship and initiative. Neoliberalism has fuelled, and in turn been given impetus by, the processes of globalization and the intensification of transnational economic activity. Within education, it has expressed itself through the privatization of educational systems: first, the creation of quasi-markets and introduction of cost-sharing within public systems, and second, the growth of private providers, even serving low-income communities at the primary level in countries such as India, Nigeria and Ghana (Härmä 2020), as discussed in Chapter 18. In this model, education not only serves to form productive workers but also is a source of profit making itself. In higher education particularly, but also at the basic education level, there has been progressive financialization (Christophers and Fine 2020), with trading of education companies on the stock market, and accountability increasingly directed towards shareholders.

The liberal capitalist development model is subject to a range of critiques. First, it assumes that level of economic activity is the only or the primary feature of development. While the constituent theories attend to a range of aspects of society – such as education and political institutions – these are portrayed as instrumental in enhancing economic growth rather than being valuable in themselves. Is a materially poor, but safe, unpolluted, democratic and culturally and spiritually rich society necessarily worse off? Second, the liberal capitalist development model is relatively unconcerned with inequality. Human capital theory's roots in utilitarianism do ensure an element of egalitarianism, underpinned as it is by the idea that all people's human capital can and should be invested in. However, the modernization paradigm as a whole accepts significant resulting inequalities in status, function and wealth in society and sees little reason to address them for their own sake. Finally, liberal capitalism assumes a single model for development and one primarily based on the 'Western' model: Rostow's five stages – derived initially from Britain's trajectory of industrialization – are seen to apply to all countries. 'Modern', in this sense, is just code for becoming more like the capitalist countries of Western Europe and North America (and indeed the theory was utilized in the Cold War – see, for example, Rostow's personal involvement in Vietnam as adviser to Lyndon Johnson and advocate for the escalation of the conflict [Desai 2012]). There is no sense in this theory that there might be a range of 'moderns' or that it might be better in some ways to be 'traditional'. There have even been assertions of the 'end of history', with capitalism emerging as the only possible or viable economic model for the whole of humanity (Fukuyama 2006, Milanovic 2019).

All of the subsequent theories to be assessed in this chapter can be understood as responses to one or the other of these problematic aspects of the liberal capitalist paradigm. The next focuses on the aspect of economic inequalities, asserting that the purported helpfulness of these theories in fuelling growth in the poorest countries is, in fact, a mask for ensuring the latter's continuing domination by the rich world.

The Marxist Paradigm

There is a body of development theory emerging primarily in the 1960s and 1970s that can be broadly described as Marxist in that it provides a critical counterpoint to the approaches based on accumulation of capital outlined earlier. According to these views, 'the persistence of poverty was not an oversight, but a key dimension of capitalism, which required a reserve army of labour, who were poorly educated and impoverished' (Unterhalter, 2008). The most prominent of these is dependency theory. The basic principle of dependency is well expressed by this passage from Theotonio dos Santos (1970, 1):

> By dependence we mean a situation in which the economy of certain countries is conditioned by the development and expansion of another economy to which the former is subjected ... This theoretical step transcends the theory

of development which seeks to explain the situation of the underdeveloped countries as a product of their slowness or failure to adopt the patterns of efficiency characteristic of developed countries (or to 'modernize' or 'develop' themselves).

From this perspective, modernization is a deficit theory, placing the blame for lack of development with the poor countries themselves; for dependency theory, on the other hand, poverty is caused by the wealthy countries and the relations of dependency they have created. The world then consists of 'core' and 'periphery' countries, the latter engaged primarily in agriculture and mineral extraction, while the former reap the benefits through controlling flows of capital and high value industrial production. Cores and peripheries are also seen to exist within countries.

The theory emerged first from the work of Raúl Prebisch and Hans Singer, who in 1950 independently observed that the terms of trade for exporters of primary goods tended to deteriorate over time in relation to exporters of manufactured goods. Dependency theory is, therefore, initially an explanatory, rather than a normative, one, in the sense that it is based on the empirical claim that a country's dependency has an adverse effect on its economic prospects. It advocated import-substitution and ultimately 'delinking' from the international system as the best solution for the so-called Third World countries. Nevertheless, there is clearly a normative element, opposing the existence of an unequal world order and questioning the dominance of the Western powers over the rest of the globe.

Like Prebisch and dos Santos, many of the initial theorists of dependency theory were from Latin America – for example, the sociologist Fernando Henrique Cardoso, who went on to be Brazilian president – with the US-based thinkers Andre Gunder Frank and Paul Baran (exiles from Nazi Germany) also being influential. Immanuel Wallerstein's 'world systems theory' also drew heavily on dependency theory in asserting the continuing dominance of capitalist centres through binding peripheries and semi-peripheries into an interdependent global economic system. These thinkers also drew on earlier Marxist analyses such as that of Rosa Luxemburg, in which imperialism is attributed to the need for capital to go beyond national borders and incorporate and thereby exploit non-capitalist regions of the world.

Dependency theory relates first and foremost to the economic system – and as such, it has relevance for education as regards the funds that are available for educational provision. However, there have been more direct applications of the theory to education. From the 1970s onwards, researchers and theorists such as Ali Mazrui (1975), Philip Altbach (1977), Gail Kelly

(1982) and Martin Carnoy (1974) analysed the ways in which education systems in the South after independence continued to be dependent on the systems of the former colonial powers. They retained colonial languages within education, maintained similar curricula (focusing on Western subject matter) and relied on Western publishing houses. The implication was, as in the economy as a whole, that countries should delink and pursue their own educational course. A significant reform along these lines was carried out in Tanzania, through Julius Nyerere's vision of *Education for Self-Reliance* (1967). These changes to the education system oriented the curriculum and institutional forms away from the colonial model and tied them more closely to the realities of rural life and cooperativism, although, like Nyerere's broader designs for African socialism, they were unable to fully take root.

Ideas of dependency also resonate with theorists of social reproduction such as Bowles and Gintis (1976), Bourdieu and Passeron (1977) and Willis (1978), who showed that, instead of providing an opportunity for social mobility, education systems in Europe and North America merely reproduced existing social class inequalities. Educational dependency had its critics, however, with McLean (1983) and Noah and Eckstein (1988), for example, questioning the validity of the theory's transfer from economics to education and its oversimplification of relations between centre and periphery.

Dependency theory more broadly was rejected by supporters of capitalism-driven development as part of the broader ideological and political hostilities of the Cold War. This strong divide – and the marked lack of dialogue between the two sides in the 1980s – has been described as an *impasse* in development theory (Booth 1985), with neither global capitalism nor state socialism providing a viable or effective solution for the world's poor. As the 1990s unfolded, however, there emerged from the impasse a range of other theories and approaches, as will be explored in the following sections.

Postmodernism

Postmodernism is a broad current emerging in the twentieth century that critiqued and challenged the foundations of modernity and the Enlightenment. The European Age of Enlightenment developing from the seventeenth century had been founded on the use of reason in the pursuit of truth and the possibility of human progress through knowledge. Postmodernism, in contrast, asserted that there was no universal or objective basis for these claims to the true, the right or the good. In the twentieth century, a number of thinkers in literary criticism, linguistics, history and philosophy began to critique the ideas in their fields, highlighting their assumptions about universal structures and binaries, and asserting instead *poststructural* accounts. Michel Foucault (1965), for example, through a detailed historical analysis, aimed to show how dominant knowledge paradigms, such as the logic of rationality, had emerged over the ages through a confluence of contingencies. Dominant groups ensured that their version of reality was maintained in the ascendancy, and this *discourse* worked through others in society, marking the bounds of what was possible and impossible to think or know. Feminist thought has also been influential in this regard, in uncovering and critiquing the fundamental patriarchal assumptions of Enlightenment thought that could be used to portray women as lacking rationality and therefore incapable of political or cultural participation, thus legitimating oppressive structuring of societies. Theorists like Butler (1990) have examined how gender is *performative*, produced through day-to-day speech and acts, rather than being a stable essence. Queer theory, in turn, turned the lens on sexuality and gender identity, highlighting their socially constructed nature and deconstructing oppressive norms (Mason 2018).

Postmodern and poststructural ideas manifested themselves in the field of international development primarily in the form of postcolonialism. In a postcolonial paradigm, these ideas were applied to the relationship between the colonizer and the colonized. It was not just that physical violence had been inflicted on colonized peoples, nor that their natural wealth had been extracted and their economies locked into a relationship of dependency: they had begun to see themselves through the eyes of the colonizer and speak with the colonizer's voice. The imposed language and frames of thought had cast them in the role of 'other' – deficient and degenerate in relation to the norm. Thinkers such as Franz Fanon in *The Wretched of the Earth* (1963), Edward Said in *Orientalism* (1980), Gayatri Spivak (1988, 1999), Archille Mbembe (2001), Anita Loomba (2005) and a number of others developed variations on this perspective.

As Spivak (1988, 280–1) states:

> The clearest available example of such epistemic violence is the remotely orchestrated, far-flung, and heterogeneous project to constitute the colonial

subject as Other .... It is well known that Foucault locates epistemic violence ... in the redefinition of sanity at the end of the European eighteenth century. But what if that particular redefinition was only a part of the narrative of history in Europe as well as in the colonies? What if the two projects of epistemic overhaul worked as dislocated and unacknowledged parts of a vast two-handed engine?

The postcolonial paradigm also influenced the emergence of *post-development* thinkers (such as Arturo Escobar and Majid Rahnema), applying this mode of critique to conventional approaches to development (Escobar 1995, Rahnema and Bawtree 1997). Through this perspective, poverty and the need for external aid are constructions, with the development industry simply remoulding the Third World in a bedraggled image of the West. These concerns have resonated both with indigenous movements campaigning against cultural onslaught and with environmentalists opposing the destructive effects of Western models of wealth accumulation and resource extraction. Revolutionary movements such as the Zapatistas in Mexico have drawn on these critiques, as well as on anarchist ideas about the creation of utopias in the here and now, in the development of autonomous communities.

Educational applications of postcolonialism and post-development are, to a large extent, ones of critique: of revealing the hidden assumptions and veiled disparagement of indigenous cultures (e.g. Adjei 2007). In terms of alternative constructions, the focus has been either on recuperation of indigenous knowledge forms or on a fusion of indigenous and Western perspectives. Decolonizing education, in Andreotti's (2011) terms, is a process of 'learning to read the world through other eyes', of acknowledging the multiple perspectives on reality and refraining from imposing a single reading. An example in practice of the type of autonomous development advocated by the post-development theorists can be seen in the Unitierra initiative in southern Mexico (see Pathways to Practice 2). Decolonization and the postcolonial are further explored in Chapter 4.

A critique of postmodernism and postcolonialism is the lack of a clear path of action in response to the institutions of domination (Unterhalter 2007a). Proponents of the approach advocate a process of emancipation, through deconstruction and critique, and increasing awareness and therefore liberation from the enslaving thought forms, along with performance of alternatives. However, for many this response is insufficiently concrete and practicable given the pressing challenges and sufferings.

Pathways to Practice 2
Universidad de la Tierra (Unitierra)

The University of the Land, or in its Spanish acronym Unitierra, is a rare example of a manifestation in practice of the post-development paradigm. Created in the Mexican state of Oaxaca in 2001 (with a sister 'branch' in Chiapas), it aims to challenge fundamental conceptions of the educational institution. Drawing on the ideas of 'deschooling' of Ivan Illich, as well as contemporary post-development thinker Gustavo Esteva, it provides an opportunity for higher study for those who have become disillusioned with or dropped out of the mainstream education system. In the words of Esteva, the university has 'no teachers, no classrooms, no curriculum and no campus' (Barrón-Pastor 2010). Students come to the university with their own research and action projects, whether in philosophy, urban agriculture or video production, and develop these over a period of years through working with facilitators and developing initiatives in the community. Another important feature is that the university provides no formal qualifications. The key challenge of Unitierra remains that of whether young people will be willing to give up the exchange value of a regular degree for a more meaningful learning experience.

Liberal Egalitarianism

The liberal egalitarian theories do not take as a starting point the eradication of capitalist modes of production and the free market, although they do require a significant tempering of their workings in practice in accordance with social justice. In opposition to some versions of socialism, they also assert the primacy of individual liberty – guarding against the subordination of the individual to the collective; while in contrast to postmodern thought, they retain faith in the possibility of a universal morality and that concrete steps towards improvements in practice can be made. Some of the contributors to this paradigm have been economists – for example, Thomas Piketty (2013, 2019), whose revaluations of capitalism and inequalities have had significant reverberations in recent years. Yet there are also major contributions from philosophy and law, and the theories as a whole are characterized by an acknowledgement of the intrinsic importance of non-economic dimensions of life.

One version of this approach – that of human rights – has a long lineage but came to the fore in the period following the Second World War and the formation of the UN. The proclamation of the Universal Declaration of Human Rights in 1948 and the range of subsequent legally binding covenants and conventions have created a framework intended to guarantee a dignified life for all human beings independently of where they may be living. Rights-based approaches, which became influential in development work from the 1990s, recast the inhabitants of impoverished parts of the globe as rights-holders entitled to justice rather than beneficiaries of the charity of the privileged. A variant – the basic needs approach (e.g. Stewart 1985) – had also been influential from the 1970s, asserting the primacy of the task of ensuring a minimum levels for all of the world's population, although lacking the clear relationship between rights-holder (individual and community) and duty-bearer (primarily the nation state) of rights-based approaches. Unterhalter (2008) locates the later EFA movement's approach to educational entitlements and obligations within the basic needs paradigm.

A more recent variant is the human development approach, drawing primarily on the work on capabilities by Amartya Sen (1992, 1999) and developed by others such as Martha Nussbaum (2000, 2011) and Mahbub Ul Haq (1995). These approaches hold that development should be understood as the freedom for all people to do and be what they have reason to value (see discussion in Chapter 8). As such, it represents a departure from reductive emphases on economic growth and acknowledges the heterogeneity of human beings in terms of their life goals. It also represents a more general movement towards people-centred conceptions of development, with participation of local communities seen as having intrinsic and instrumental value – or even to be constitutive of development (McCowan and Unterhalter 2013). Martha Nussbaum's proposal for a list of central capabilities is presented in Concepts 1. The approach has also been influential in the development of the Human Development Index (HDI), which gauges education and life expectancy in addition to per capita GNI.

A primary application of these approaches to education is that education systems must distribute their benefits in an egalitarian manner: whether upholding for all the right or the capability to education. Yet there is also a reorientation of the aims of the educational process: in this way, education underpins the full set of human rights, empowering individuals to understand, exercise and defend their rights, or being a multiplier of capabilities. Central to this function is the task of fostering individual autonomy, the ability to choose between different life courses and enhance agency. Recent years have seen a flowering of literature on both rights-based approaches to education (e.g. Tomaševski 2001, 2003, UNICEF/UNESCO 2007, McCowan 2013, Coysh, 2017) and capabilities in education (e.g. Unterhalter 2003, Robeyns 2006, Walker and Unterhalter 2007, Mkwananzi 2019, Mtawa 2019). Practical manifestations of rights-based approaches have also been seen in UNICEF's rights respecting and child-friendly schools, for example, which aim to uphold the broad range of children's rights within institutions (including gender equality, health, nutrition and safety) as well as enhance knowledge of the Convention on the Rights of the Child and children's participation in the management of the school.

Liberal egalitarian approaches are not immune to critique from either the left or the right of the political spectrum. For capitalist libertarians, the efforts at redistribution place intolerable restraints on the individual freedom that

Concepts 1
Nussbaum's List of Capabilities

Martha Nussbaum has put forward a list of ten central human functionings, proposed as basic entitlements for all human beings around the world and a basis for national constitutions:

(1) *Life*
(2) *Bodily health*
(3) *Bodily integrity*
(4) *Senses, imagination and thought*
(5) *Emotions*
(6) *Practical reason*
(7) *Affiliation*
(8) *Other species*
(9) *Play*
(10) *Political and material control over one's environment*

While the list has had widespread recognition, there are also detractors, due to its universal pretensions. Amartya Sen himself has resisted the creation of a list of capabilities, on account of the need for local determination of needs and goals.
Source: Nussbaum (2000)

is supposed to be at the heart of liberalism. For Marxists, the entitlements guaranteed to marginalized populations are but a palliative, to provide some amelioration of conditions but ultimately perpetuating the unjust economic system. For poststructuralists, while these egalitarian approaches are less crude than the bulldozer narratives of modernization and Marxism, they are still riven with unfounded, culturally specific and ultimately dangerous assumptions of an epistemological and ontological nature.

Radical Humanism

The final section relates not to a coherent body of theory as such but to the work of certain theorists and practitioners who share a set of principles that distinguish them from the above theories – and importantly for this book, place a particular emphasis on the role of education in development. In these approaches, education is not a fruit of development or even a driver of development but is development itself. The process of learning, understood as the fundamental experience of emancipation, and the necessary engagement in it of all members of society, is both the means and the end of development.

The best-known of these thinkers is the Brazilian Paulo Freire (also discussed in Chapter 16), who formulated his ideas most famously in the book *Pedagogy of the Oppressed* (1972). In contrast to dominant state socialist advocates, he asserted that revolution needed to start not with the seizing of state power but with the transformation of the self and the emergence of critical consciousness. The collective development of understanding in the oppressed, and the consequent liberation of the oppressors, would lead organically and sustainably to the transformation of societal structures. These ideas, therefore, share some principles with dependency theory and postcolonialism but went beyond critique of the relics of colonial education systems to put forward a practical solution in the form of a set of pedagogical principles. Central to this vision is *dialogue* – understood not just as conversation but as a radical revisioning of the pedagogical relationship through which teachers approach learners not as empty vessels to be filled with knowledge (the so-called 'banking education') but engage with them in a shared and horizontal process of critical reflection and learning (Freire 1972).

Freire's ideas were taken up by a range of other thinkers, such as Augusto Boal (2000), in relation to theatre. Parallels can also be seen in the earlier thought of Mahatma Gandhi (Kumar 1994) and Julius Nyerere (1967) (as well as many others such as Steve Biko and Rabindranath Tagore), who in their distinct contexts advocated for an emancipatory education as a conduit for and actualization of social transformation. The participatory nature of Freire's political ideas found echoes in the participatory turn in development as a whole (e.g. Chambers 1997, Hickey and Mohan 2005), leading to fusions such as Participatory Learning and Action. ActionAid also adopted Freire's ideas in their REFLECT adult learning programme (as described in Chapter 10). Freirean approaches have been widely used in social movements in Latin America, and in political mobilizations elsewhere, such as the Rhodes Must Fall campaign in South Africa (Kane 2001, Andrews 2020). Radical humanist approaches are distinct from mainstream learner-centred reforms in education in their explicit commitment to political emancipation and social transformation rather than just effective learning.

Freire laid himself open to forceful critiques from feminist thinkers, on account of his use of language and inattentiveness to difference and to overlapping forms of oppression (e.g. Weiler 1996). Some (e.g. hooks 1996), while acknowledging deficiencies of his thought, have rekindled the principles in a way that is more attuned to gender and racial injustices – and these ideas have spawned a larger movement on the academic left under the label of 'critical pedagogy' (e.g. Giroux and McLaren 1986, Shor 1992). Ultimately, the greatest barrier of these approaches is the quietness of their voice in relation to the blare of global capitalism and even mainstream development. In the contemporary context, the idealism underpinning radical humanist thought is very often dismissed as impractical and excessively optimistic about human nature.

Conclusion

When weighing up these theories, it is important to recall their explanatory and normative functions. We may accept human capital theory as a valid explanation for economic growth but still reject it as a normative orientation for development (material prosperity is only one aspect of development, and the economic is just one of a range of valid aims for education). These theoretical debates rest on claims to fact and value, and to the interactions between the two.

The contrasting theories outlined in this chapter jostle for space in the contemporary landscape of development work. Strategy papers, policies and initiatives will commonly invoke ideas of educational rights, human capital theory and empowerment alongside – and sometimes in contradiction with – one another. Awareness of the theoretical is therefore an indispensable part of development work – in acknowledging the fundamentally political and moral nature of education and development, their epistemological and ontological assumptions, and navigating our own positionings in relation to them.

Questions for Discussion

1. Which theories of development appear to be most influential in international education? How do the theories adopted differ depending on the organization in question (supranational agency, NGO, local community etc.)?
2. What problems might there be in applying theories derived from other disciplines (e.g. economics, literary studies) to education?
3. Which kinds of research (in terms of both focus and design) are likely to be associated with each of the five paradigms?

Further Reading

McGrath, S., and Gu, Q. (Eds.). (2016). *Routledge Handbook of International Education and Development*, New York: Routledge.

Rahnema, M. and Bawtree, V. (1997), *The Post-development Reader*, London: Zed.

Unterhalter, E. (2007), *Gender, Schooling and Global Social Justice*, London: Routledge.

3

The Education for All Initiative and the Sustainable Development Goals: History and Prospects

Karen Mundy and Caroline Manion

Chapter Outline

Introduction

For more than half a century, international actors and national governments have focused their efforts on the achievement of 'Education for All' (EFA) using the frames of national development, poverty reduction and human rights to raise education to the status of a key global development priority. This chapter traces the development of international EFA efforts in the period after the Second World War.

When speaking of EFA, we refer both to
1) the set of concrete education goals, targets and indicators contained in formal EFA policy documents, the Millennium Development Goals (MDGs) and the Sustainable Development Goals (SDGs), as well as
2) the network of state and non-state actors operating at multiple scales (i.e. local, national, regional, global) actively promoting basic education of good quality for all.

In what follows, we begin by describing the origins of the EFA movement in the period after the Second World War, reviewing the changing roles played by bilateral donors, UN agencies and non-state actors and highlighting how these roles have been shaped by changes in the global geopolitical order. We assess the period after 2000, when the EFA movement gained increased momentum and new proponents. We conclude with a discussion of the EFA landscape within the context of the new global development agenda, set out in the SDGs framework, 2015–30, and current challenges to global governance.

The Origins and Evolution of 'Education for All'

After the Second World War, newly established international organizations and agreements helped to define a set of universal norms about educational rights and educational development. Brought together under the umbrella of the UN, the international community promised to uphold a universal right to education, first through the creation of the United Nations Educational, Scientific and Cultural Organization (UNESCO) in 1946, whose charter commits it to the achievement of 'full and equal opportunities for education for all' (UNESCO 1946) and second through Article 26 of the 1948 Universal Declaration of Human Rights, which states:

Everyone has the right to education. Education shall be free, at least in the elementary and fundamental stages. Elementary education shall be compulsory. Technical and professional education shall be made generally available and higher education shall be equally accessible to all on the basis of merit. (General Assembly of the United Nations 1948)

Geopolitical and interstate relationships shaped this new, universal commitment to education. Formal schooling was among the most significant of the cultural exports of colonial powers during the nineteenth and early twentieth centuries, leading to the widespread institutionalization of educational systems as part of the common apparatus of emerging nation states (Anderson 1991). When formal colonial rule ended (in most countries after the middle of the twentieth century), education remained deeply implicated in the neo-colonial relationships between Western countries and postcolonial societies – educational cooperation was one way to enhance geopolitical and economic ties. Education was also increasingly viewed, within the Western world and in newly independent colonies, as a significant contributor to economic development and growth. Many newly independent countries committed to improving access to education for their citizens and demanded support from the industrialized world to this end. Thus, a wide network of actors and activities focused on education for development emerged after the Second World War, shaped both by demands from newly independent governments and by the geopolitical interests and normative approaches of the predominantly Western hegemons of the world system (Mundy 2006, 2010).

Initially, UNESCO took the lead in international efforts to spur forward 'education for all', sponsoring ambitious regional conferences where regional and national targets for educational development were set in the late 1960s and 1970s (Chabbott 2003). Despite initial hopes, however, Western governments failed to fund UNESCO at levels sufficient to allow it to play a major role in the implementation of educational programming within low-income countries – its funding never rising above that of a medium-sized university. UNESCO's General Assembly became increasingly embroiled in Cold War politics, and its perceived politicization caused the organization to gradually lose the confidence of OECD governments in the 1970s and 1980s (Jones 1988, Mundy 1998, 1999).

By far the largest source of international financing and initiatives to emerge out of the post-war commitment to 'education for all' came from the newly formed bilateral aid programmes in the wealthy states of the Western world (United States Agency for International Development,

Canadian International Development Agency, etc.). Historically, more than three-quarters of all flows of foreign assistance to education have gone through bilateral channels (Mundy 2010). By the mid-1970s, virtually every industrialized country (including Japan and the Soviet Union) supported educational development through a bilateral foreign aid programme, though at varying levels of between 3 and 30 per cent of their total official aid. Yet, in contrast to the initial UN commitment to universal access to basic education, most bilateral aid for education in the period from 1960 to the mid-1990s focused predominantly on programmes of post-primary training, foreign scholarships and tertiary-level institution-building and was heavily tied to technical assistance from the donor countries (King 1991, Mundy 2006).

The 'education for development' regime that emerged was dominated by many small- to medium-sized, short-term, bilateral transactions, often working at cross-purposes. Bilateral efforts tended to have a geographical focus on former colonies or regions of geopolitical significance for the donor nation. For four decades (1960s through the 1990s) attempts at global-level coordination of bilateral education for development activities failed, and usually failed quite quickly. Examples of failure include: UNESCO regional conferences of the 1960s, OECD Development Assistance Committee (DAC) efforts to coordinate education sector activities among OECD members in the 1970s, the World Bank's initiative in sub-Saharan Africa in the 1980s and the Jomtien World Conference on Education for All (1990). In each case, international targets were set but not met. More importantly, the donor community failed to provide resources promised to meet these targets.

UNESCO's weakness created space for other, more entrepreneurial UN organizations to become active in educational development after the 1970s. The United Nations Children's Fund, UNICEF, had developed its own distinctive approach to educational development during the 1960s, targeting marginalized children. In the 1980s, it emerged as a significant player in debates about the appropriate roles and responsibilities of governments in the development of programmes targeting the basic needs of poor and vulnerable populations. In the 1990s, UNICEF embraced a new focus on children's rights, spurred forward by a growing advocacy movement among international non-governmental organizations. It, in turn, developed innovative programmes in the areas of girls' education and basic education (as, for instance, in its 'child-friendly schools' programme), playing a major role in establishing the principle that schools are protective institutions for children if adequately resourced and appropriately oriented to protecting children's basic rights (Phillips 1987, Jolly 1991, Black 1996, Fuchs 2007; see also Menashy and Manion 2016).

During the late 1970s and early 1980s, the World Bank emerged as an important international player in the education for development regime, becoming the largest source of multilateral finance for education. The Bank also became an increasingly influential thought leader, responsible for maintaining a strong focus on the link between educational development and economic growth, through its research on investments in human capital. In the 1980s and 1990s, the Bank was influential in designing a reform agenda for countries facing debt crises due to the loss of cheap international credit and in this context promoted the use of market-like mechanisms to ensure educational efficiency. The Bank emerged at the 'center of a neo-classical resurgence' in development economics: more responsible than perhaps any other organization for elaborating what has come to be called the 'Washington Consensus' agenda for low- and middle-income countries (Miller-Adams 1999). Around the world, governments were advised to restructure their education sectors by lowering subsidies to tertiary-level education and introducing user fees at this level and by encouraging efficiency-driven reforms at primary and secondary levels through the use of contract teachers, lowering of repetition rates and parental 'participation' in school costs often through the imposition of user fees (Hinchcliffe 1993, World Bank 1986, 1988, 1995, Alexander 2001, IEG 2011). Paradoxically, the era of structural adjustment contributed to substantial increases in the World Bank's lending activity in education, especially for primary schooling (Jones 1992, Mundy 2002, Jones and Coleman 2005, Resnik 2006, Klees et al. 2012).

In summary, it is worth highlighting some of the major features of the regime of actors and activities that emerged around the universal commitment to education for all in the period between 1945 and the late 1980s. As noted above, this regime was constructed primarily around bilateral flows of aid, with international organizations emerging as policy entrepreneurs. Dominated by 'official actors' – a handful of multi-lateral organizations (UNESCO, UNICEF and the World Bank) and bilateral aid organizations – Southern governments were the targets (or recipients) of the regime but often not active shapers of it (Samoff 1999, 2001). Furthermore, few non-governmental actors were involved or recognized within the official regime. They remained outside its conferences and conventions, despite the existence of international teachers unions and international humanitarian and religious organizations with an interest in education that predated official educational aid activities (Mundy and Murphy 2001). Despite various calls for global action, activities were primarily organized around bilateral intergovernmental relationships, with both the geographic focus of aid and the levels at which aid was targeted shaped by the geopolitical interests of the donor governments.

The diffuse nature of the educational-aid regime also played out in its growth as an epistemic and professional community (Chabbott 2003). From high-level 'man-power' planning to vocational education, non-formal education, adult literacy, higher education and back again, a vague and expansive menu of what was 'needed' was reported or endorsed in a succession of international conferences and publications. A growing professional expert community on educational development, largely housed within international organizations and research institutions, could do little to harness donors behind a common agenda because their own assessment of priorities changed so rapidly or diverged quite widely (Chabbott 2003). A fractious epistemic community allowed for a very loose coupling between rhetorical commitments and practical activities – creating, in effect, a smorgasbord of priorities and approaches from which donor countries might choose according to their own geopolitical and economic interests.

Most importantly, although the notion of a universal right to education figured strongly in the international discourse, EFA was not what was supported by major flows of foreign funding or technical expertise. In the period between 1960 and the late 1990s, most aid flows to education were focused at levels beyond primary schooling. Aid rarely supported the core costs borne by governments trying to expand access to their educational systems.

These features of international aid for education persisted into the 1990s, despite the new and ambitious framework that emerged from the World Conference on Education for All, a conference organized by the World Bank, UNICEF, UNESCO and the UNDP and hosted in Jomtien, Thailand, in 1990. The collapse of the Soviet Union in 1989, and the fiscal difficulties faced by Western states as they adjusted to greater international economic integration over the next decade, led to a precipitous decline in overall flows of aid, and an even steeper decline in aid for education, as illustrated in Table 3.1.

Tensions between the market-led liberalization programmes advocated by World Bank and the 'human development' models promoted by the UN led to heated debate rather than concerted action (Jolly 1991, Therien and Lloyd 2000, 2002). Instead of the 'peace dividend' (expected by many at the end of the Cold War), issues of global poverty and inequality were sidelined. The gap between rhetoric and reality in the implementation of EFA became particularly acute in the 1990s.

Table 3.1 Trends in ODA to Education and Basic Education Sub-sector (1989–99)

Year	Total ODA To Education (constant prices, 2011 USD million)	Total; ODA to basic education (constant prices, 2011 USD millions)
1989	10674.79	–
1990	11785.67	–
1991	11383.42	–
1992	9096.88	–
1993	9197.69	94.56
1994	7681.38	456.98
1995	8580.2	1056.65
1996	7338.91	886.23
1997	7609.73	997.33
1998	7748.43	995.18
1999	8342.83	1233.12

Source: OECD-DAC

2000–15: A New 'Education for All' Consensus

While it is important not to overstate the case, the education for development regime experienced significant changes in the decade after 2000. These changes are particularly dramatic when placed alongside what has been widely assessed as the failure of the international community to achieve the goals established for education in the 1990s, at the World Conference on Education for All in Jomtien, Thailand (Torres 2000, Chabbott 2003).

Three significant changes in the Education for ALL movement which emerged after 2000 are explored below:

(1) embedding education in a new consensus on global development and the construction of clear global educational targets and monitoring efforts;

(2) new forms of donor coordination and rising levels of aid for basic education; and

(3) the emergence of new actors and partnerships within the international education for development regime.

Embedding Education Goals in a New Consensus on Global Development

In the period after 1995, some of the most dramatic shifts in the education for development regime came on the heels of renewed efforts to build international consensus on how to deal with global inequality and poverty. The Millennium Development Summit and Millennium Development Declaration (2000) aligned the UN (and its agencies), the Bretton Woods institutions and OECD governments behind a unifying substantive framework for global development efforts (OECD/DAC 1996, United Nations General Assembly 2000). The Declaration set out eight Millennium Development Goals (MDGs) with time-bound, measurable targets. The MDGs included halving world poverty by 2015, reducing infant mortality by two-thirds, halving the spread of HIV/AIDS, combating malaria, halving the number of people without safe drinking water and promoting gender equity and environmental sustainability. The achievement of universal primary education and gender equity in education were goals numbers 2 and 3 in the MDGs (see Table 3.2). For education, a second set of more expansive 'Education for All' targets emerged in parallel to the MDGs, coming out of the UNESCO sponsored World Education Forum in Dakar in 2000. The widely endorsed Dakar framework established a more expansive set of six global education goals (only two of which overlap with the MDGs) (see Unterhalter 2013 for a history of recent education goal and targets).

Several authors characterized this new 'consensus' on development as part of a broader rapprochement between the neoliberal and pro-economic approaches to globalization and development endorsed by the International Monetary Fund (IMF) and the World Bank in the 1980s and 1990s, and the more equity and globalization-sceptic approaches adopted by the UN and some OECD governments (Therien 2002, 2005, Ruggie 2003). They locate the origins of this rapprochement in the need to respond to rising international protests against globalization and the aftermath of the East Asian economic crisis of the late 1990s (Stiglitz 2003). The rising importance of the European Union, with its more expansive approach to welfare state capitalism, also played an important part (Noel 2005). Education, which straddles both equity and productivity conceptualizations of development, has arguably benefited from this consensus. As Simon Maxwell summarizes, the post-2000 consensus on development 'encourage[d] internal and external trade liberalization, and simultaneously invest[ment] in health, education and good governance, so that people are able to take advantage of new economic opportunities' (Maxwell 2005, 3).

Anchored by explicit goals and targets, the new global consensus on international development was also backed up in new ways by efforts to hold governments to account to their development commitments. The Millennium Development Goals (including the two goals for education) were monitored formally by the UNDP (see for example UNDP 2012, 2013) and the World Bank (World Bank and International Monetary Fund 2013) as well as by many civil society organizations operating at the international and national level (i.e. Dyer and Choksi 2004, Global Campaign for Education 2004).

Among the new monitoring and accountability tools developed by the global community to track the achievement of global education commitments, the annual UNESCO Education for All Global Monitoring Report[1] (established in 2002 and renamed the Global Education Monitoring (GEM) Report in 2016) monitors EFA progress with assistance from the UNESCO Institute of Statistics. It originally focused on the six EFA goals endorsed by the 164 countries attending the 2000 Dakar World Education Forum – but now provides oversight on the Sustainable Development Goal #4 for Education. The GEM Report also tracks foreign aid to education and the share of domestic spending allocated to different levels of education, and it reports on the global financing gap (recently estimated at $39 billion annually) that needs to be filled to achieve the global goals (Global Education Monitoring Report 2018). Other efforts to track the implementation of the education MDGs included the Millennium Development Project 2005a, b and work at the Brookings Foundation (Sperling and Balu 2005).

Millennium Development Goals	EFA goals
1. Eradicate extreme poverty and hunger	1. Expand early childhood care and education
2. Achieve universal primary education	2. Provide free and compulsory primary education for all
3. Promote gender equality and empower women	3. Promote learning and life skills for young people and adults
4. Reduce child mortality	4. Increase adult literacy by 50 per cent
5. Improve maternal health	5. Achieve gender parity by 2005, gender equality by 2015
6. Combat HIV/AIDS, malaria and other diseases	6. Improve the quality of education
7. Ensure environmental sustainability	
8. Develop a global partnership for development	

New Forms of Donor Coordination and Rising Levels of Aid for Basic Education

One measure of the consensus on education during the decade after 2000 is the rise of overall aid for education and in particular for basic education, as can be seen in Figure 3.1. Although these substantial gains in international financing did not come close to filling the financing gap estimated for achieving the MDGs and the EFA goals, they do reflect a significant change in overall behaviour among donor governments and multilateral organizations.

Additionally, significant changes in the way in which aid to education is delivered occurred after 2000. The 2004 Rome Declaration on Aid Harmonization and the establishment and endorsement by UN agencies and OECD governments of the Aid Effectiveness Principles (Paris and Accra) formalized a significant (if uneven) shift in donor behaviour towards pooling of aid, provision of direct budget support (where aid is channelled directly into a government's budget) and sector-wide funding (where aid is given to support a sector budget). In education, this meant more coherent system-focused aid programmes that for the first time addressed the largest barriers to expanding access, including such recurrent costs as teachers'

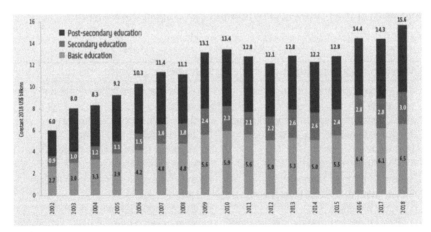

Figure 3.1 Total Aid to Education Disbursements, by Education Level, 2002–18. *Source: UNESCO and GEM Report 2020a, p. 3.*

salaries and teaching materials. What is sometimes not recognized is how frequently education has emerged as the key sector in which donors experiment with these historically novel efforts at donor coordination and pooling of resources (see Riddell 2000, Samoff 2004, World Bank 2018).

A further impetus to donor coordination in the education sector emerged from the Education For All Fast Track Initiative (renamed the Global Partnership for Education (GPE) in 2011), whose goal is to ensure that no developing countries with clear plans for achieving universal primary education (UPE) fail to make progress due to lack of resources (Unterhalter 2013). GPE acts by providing pooled funding, supporting coherent sector plans and assisting in the development of local coordination committees ('local education groups') comprised of donor agencies, Ministries of Education and civil society representatives (Global Campaign for Education and Oxfam International 2012, Global Partnership for Education 2012a, Global Partnership for Education 2012b, Mundy 2016).

Experimentation with pooled funding, direct budgetary support, the funding of recurrent costs of primary-level education and the creation of a new multilateral institution each suggest that EFA received significant recognition from the international community as a global public good in need of collective rather than unilateral action in the decade after 2000 (Figure 3.1).

New Actors

Another aspect of the new educational multilateralism that is unprecedented is the inclusion of new kinds of actors in both international and national EFA networks. It is not just that new partnerships with civil society and private sector organizations have come to be seen as essential by official political actors on the international stage (Ruggie 2003). There has also been a remarkable growth of effective transnational organizations and networks, representing coalitions of civil society and private sector actors (Menashy and Shields 2017).

As Mundy and Murphy (2001) have shown, in the early 2000s, transnational civil society advocacy networks on such issues as debt relief, ODA reform, children's rights and globalization increasingly took up the issue of the universal right to education as one part of their broader advocacy efforts. But the period after 2000 also saw the formation of robust transnational advocacy networks dedicated to EFA, such as the Global

Campaign for Education,[2] the International Network on Education in Emergencies[3] and the Consultative Group on Early Childhood Education.[4] Many of these networks have significant links to national civil society groups. By linking global advocacy to national accountability, these organizations can play a powerful accountability role vis-à-vis both donors and their home governments (Mundy and Murphy 2001, Mundy 2012, Verger and Novelli 2012). One early example often cited is of the civil society's efforts to end primary school user charges in Tanzania. In this case, research on the impact of user fees generated by Tanzanian groups was used by US NGOs to press the US government to halt funding to the World Bank if it imposed any form of user fees as part of its loan conditions. The World Bank subsequently removed this loan condition and the Government of Tanzania declared free primary education. The Tanzania experience in turn stimulated a number of other African governments to remove user fees in education and declare universal free primary education. Here, a new form of global accountability spurred significant advances in the achievement of 'education for all' (Alonso i Terme 2002, Sumra 2005, TEN/MET 2006, Mundy et al. 2007).

Several other types of new actors have emerged over the past fifteen years. Foundations – like the Open Society Foundations, the Mastercard Foundation and the Hewlett Foundation (among others) – suggest a novel appetite for supporting advocacy and accountability efforts in education as well as a new focus on social innovation. International think-tanks and consulting firms including, for example, the work of Pearson Foundation[5] and McKinsey and Company consulting on education and development are more recent entrants to the EFA field, signalling a new and expanding role for the private sector in the EFA movement (see, for example, studies by Blanchard and Moore 2010, Mourshed et al. 2010, Shuler 2010, Ball and Junemann 2012, Mourshed et al. 2013).

Bilateral donors from the BRICs and other emerging market economies have formed another set of new actors for EFA and educational development – including China, Russia, Brazil, Turkey, India and South Korea as well as some countries in the Middle East. In 2018, contributions by non-DAC bilateral donors accounted for 11 per cent of total aid to basic education (UNESCO and GEM Report 2020a, 5). Many of these emergent powers are also longstanding members of the major multilateral organizations engaged in education, where they have been active in calling for governance reforms to reflect the changing balance of power between Western and non-Western nations.

But caution is in order here. Characterized by sharply differing national approaches to economic and social development, these rising powers share a limited appetite for international regimes that constrain national sovereignty (including in such putatively domestic spheres as education). They are instead primarily focused on expanding their spheres of geopolitical influence on a bilateral basis and often use their foreign aid for this purpose, as, for example, China's use of foreign aid to leverage stronger relationships with resource rich African governments (Brautigam 2009).

At the same time, the growing voice of emergent economies in global decision-making is illustrated by the development of the Group of 20 (G-20), which has now replaced the G-8 as key global summit on world financial and economic matters. As Kumar explains, emergent economic powers have insisted that the G-20 officially adopt 'international development' as a specific area of attention, despite the preference among Western industrialized governments that the G-20 concentrate primarily on global financial and economic governance (Kumar 2010). To date, reference to education in G-20 communiqués relates to education for economic development and skills formation, reflecting a focus on working together to advance science, technology and skills to advance their own economic competitiveness (Gu et al. 2008, Woods 2008, Brautigam 2010, Nordveit 2011, Cammack 2012, Bracht 2013, Rodrik 2013).

From EFA to the Sustainable Development Goals

As documented above, much progress was made in the fifteen years from 2000 to 2015. Increases in national spending on education in developing countries, combined with better-targeted flows of aid to education, led to substantial improvements in universal access to primary education. Gender equity in education especially benefited: as reported in the UNESCO Global Monitoring Report, the incidence of severe gender disparity (fewer than nine girls for every ten boys in primary schooling) has become very rare and secondary-level gender disparities are declining in all but a few countries (GMR 2012, 106).

However, the gaps between EFA aspirations and EFA achievements remained significant. A variety of stocktaking efforts suggested that the record of the MDG era was mixed (UNESCO 2015, Education Commission

2016). International financing for education had stagnated as a proportion of overall aid flows, in contrast to the global health funding, where new funding was put in place for global health funds (i.e. GAVI and the Global Fund). Emphasis on pooled funding and sector-wide support was in decline. Equity issues persist – especially as related to stagnation in the number of out-of-school children world-wide, the effects of conflict and crisis on access to quality education. Persistent disparities in the educational life chances of children coming from lower-income families, those living in rural areas, those having disabilities and those who come from marginalized communities or ethnicities within countries were recognized in the work of the UNESCO EFA World Inequality Database on Education (http://www.education-inequalities.org/), demonstrating how interlocking sets of disadvantage (including income, ethnicity, location and gender) combine to ensure that the poorest children do not enter or persist in school.

Many governments and international observers also criticized the MDGs for their primary focus on universal access to basic education – citing inadequate attention to learning outcomes and to secondary and tertiary education in the MDG agenda. According to many analyses, the race to rapidly expand access to schooling had not led to better learning outcomes, particularly in foundational areas like literacy and numeracy (Hanushek and Woessmann 2007, World Bank 2011b, Pritchett 2013).

In 2013, the UN Secretary General launched a process that would lead to what was promised to be a new set of goals, applicable to all countries, rich and poor (UN Open Working Group 2013, United Nations 2013a, 2013b). Heated debate emerged among governments, development organizations and civil society on these goals for education – about the inclusion of specific learning targets (viewed by some as narrowing the scope of education); how to include equity targets and measure the gains made among the poorest and most marginalized populations; whether to expand the notion of basic education beyond junior secondary schooling and ensuring that an expanded set of goals brings more pressure to bear in areas neglected after 2000, like early childhood education and youth skills; and how to create goals that speak not only to poor countries but to the middle- and higher-income countries where educational disparities and deprivation persist. Indeed, much has been written about the complicated process of positioning and negotiation that lead to the final set of goals in 2015.[6]

Launched in 2015 at the United Nations Sustainable Development Summit, the seventeen SDGs of the 2030 Agenda for Sustainable Development officially came into force on 1 January 2016. SDG 4, focusing on quality education, aims to 'Ensure inclusive and equitable quality education and promote lifelong learning opportunities for all'.[7] Importantly, SDG 4 targets and indicators reflect considerations largely absent in the MDGs, as noted above, including education quality as well as early childhood education, adult education and learners with disabilities (among others). In this sense,

Table 3.2 SDG 4 Targets

4.1	By 2030, ensure that all girls and boys complete free, equitable and quality primary and secondary education leading to relevant and effective learning outcomes
4.2	By 2030, ensure that all girls and boys have access to quality early childhood development, care and pre-primary education so that they are ready for primary education
4.3	By 2030, ensure equal access for all women and men to affordable and quality technical, vocational and tertiary education, including university
4.4	By 2030, substantially increase the number of youth and adults who have relevant skills, including technical and vocational skills, for employment, decent jobs and entrepreneurship
4.5	By 2030, eliminate gender disparities in education and ensure equal access to all levels of education and vocational training for the vulnerable, including persons with disabilities, indigenous peoples and children in vulnerable situations
4.6	By 2030, ensure that all youth and a substantial proportion of adults, both men and women, achieve literacy and numeracy
4.7	By 2030, ensure that all learners acquire the knowledge and skills needed to promote sustainable development, including, among others, through education for sustainable development and sustainable lifestyles, human rights, gender equality, promotion of a culture of peace and non-violence, global citizenship and appreciation of cultural diversity and of culture's contribution to sustainable development
4.A	Build and upgrade education facilities that are child-, disability- and gender-sensitive and provide safe, non-violent, inclusive and effective learning environments for all
4.B	By 2020, substantially expand globally the number of scholarships available to developing countries, in particular least developed countries, small island developing states and African countries, for enrolment in higher education, including vocational training and information and communications technology, technical, engineering and scientific programmes, in developed countries and other developing countries
4.C	By 2030, substantially increase the supply of qualified teachers, including through international cooperation for teacher training in developing countries, especially least developed countries and small island developing States

the SDGs encompass an expanded set of areas for education, some that were first highlighted in two major world conferences on Education for All – in Jomtien, Thailand, in 1990, and a decade later at the 2000 World Education Forum in Dakar, Senegal.

The adoption of the global goals led to the launch of a range of new initiatives. In 2015, the former UK prime minister Gordon Brown established the International Commission for Financing Education, co-convened by the prime minister of Norway; the presidents of Malawi, Indonesia and Chile; and the director-general of UNESCO. Its 2016 report, 'The Learning Generation: Investing in Education for a Changing World', laid out a road map for revitalizing achievement of Education for All, calling for an emphasis on learning outcomes, innovative financing for education and enhanced focus on strengthening education systems' capacity for delivering quality education (Education Commission 2016). UNESCO, through regional meetings and convening the Education 2030 Steering Group, as well as through the monitoring work of the UNESCO Institute for Statistics and the GEM Report, continues to act as the global lead for SDG 4 (UNESCO Institute for Statistics and GEM Report 2019, 2020b, UNESCO and GEM Report 2019).

Looking to the Future: Trends and Debates

Where are we now with EFA? Five years into the SDG era, recent reporting from UNESCO suggests that the world will not see the achievement of the new SDG global goals for education, much as past global frameworks have failed (UNESCO 2016, xvii).

Four key areas of challenge remain. First, a stubborn number of children remain out of school – UNESCO projects approximately 220 million children, adolescent and youth will still be out of school in 2030 (see Figure 3.2).

Furthermore, primary completion rates in low-income countries still lag behind other countries, with an expected 79 per cent completion rate by 2030 on current trends, and disparities between the poorest and richest children continue to be widespread. Thus, in low-income countries, only 44 children in the poorest income quintile complete primary school for every 100 students in the richest quintile (UNESCO Institute for Statistics and GEM 2019). The UNESCO Institute for Statistics also reports vast gaps in learning outcomes for the poorest children and youth: while approximately half the children in

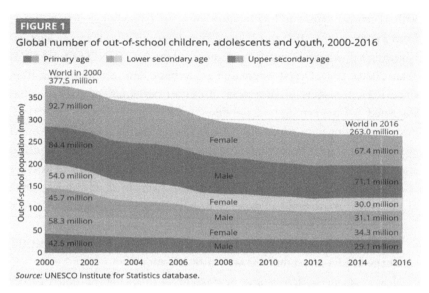

FIGURE 1

Global number of out-of-school children, adolescents and youth, 2000-2016

■ Primary age   ■ Lower secondary age   ■ Upper secondary age

Figure 3.2 Number of out-of-school children, adolescents and youth, 2000–16. *Source: UIS 2018, p. 2*

the world achieve minimum proficiency in reading and mathematics by the end of primary school, this number plummets to under 20 per cent in sub-Saharan Africa (UNESCO Institute for Statistics 2019). Basic infrastructure such as electricity and sanitation are unavailable in the poorest countries; the proportion of trained teachers is falling in Africa and South Asia.

Financing and donor coordination also remain as challenges (Burnett 2019). UNESCO estimates that for countries that meet targets for domestic financing established in the Education 2030 Framework for Action (UNESCO 2016), the education funding gap for low- and lower-middle-income countries is at least US$39 billion per year (UNESCO and GEM Report 2020a). International financing has not kept pace with this need, with the GEM Report Team indicating that 'a sixfold increase in the level of aid that goes to basic and secondary education' would be required, 'if low- and lower-middle-income countries were to achieve one year of pre-primary and universal primary and lower secondary education completion' (UNESCO and GEM Report 2020a, p. 1). Nonetheless, and after several years of stagnation beginning in 2010, over the past three years there have been some improvements in aid to education. In 2018, total aid to education reached US$15.6 billion, of which only US$6.5 billion is allocated to basic education, with 31 per cent going to low-income countries (showing an upward trend from 23 per cent in 2015) and 33 per cent to lower-middle-income countries (showing a downward trend from 46 per cent in 2015) (UNESCO and GEM Team 2020a, p. 4). Despite increased aid to basic and secondary education since 2017, the share of education in official development assistance has stagnated at 7 per cent of total aid flows, indicating a decline in education's priorities among donors (UNESCO Institute for Statistics and GEM Report 2019). Overall, aid is becoming more fragmented and low-income countries are still not receiving the highest share of education aid (Hares and Rossiter 2019). Moreover, the global Covid-19 crisis is likely to affect absolute flows of aid, as well as government expenditures, making the realization of SDG 4 targets less likely (UNESCO and GEM Report 2020a).

Against this backdrop, several trends and debates on how to meet the challenge of EFA going forward are worth attention.

New financing initiatives and new modes of financing: As noted earlier the MDG era saw new modes of financing for education, including better coordination and pooled financing of aid to education and the emergence of the Fast Track Initiative (now the Global Partnership for Education). In the SDG era, donor financing has moved away from pooled approaches, towards greater fragmentation and lower levels of coordination (Gehring, Michaelowa, Dreher and Spörri 2017, Burnett 2019). At the same time, innovations in financing for education abound.

Perhaps most notable are the new ventures that have resulted from the design work and advocacy led by the Education Commission. This includes the Education Cannot Wait (ECW) Initiative, which was formed in 2016 to respond to the need for increased education aid during humanitarian crises. ECW has mobilized over US$600 million since its inception (Education Cannot Wait 2020). The Education Commission has also been instrumental in the development of a new International Financing Facility for Education (IFFED), which aims to use financial guarantees from rich countries to amplify the education lending capacity of multilateral development banks in middle-income countries (Education Commission 2020, Barder and Rogerson 2018). Commission support has also helped launch the use of social impact bonds through the Education Outcomes Fund,[8] which will be piloted in Ghana alongside recent World Bank and GPE financing.

Alongside these new initiatives, there has been a substantial increase in philanthropic investments in education for development (OECD netFWD 2019) and a rising role for non-traditional donors, especially from Asia and the Middle East.

Renewed interest in results-based lending has grown alongside these new initiatives, with mixed implications for country ownership, holistic sector approaches and donor coordination.

The Learning Crisis: While many developing countries have concentrated their recent attention on universalization of secondary education, international development organizations have rediscovered learning as a central focus for development efforts (UNESCO Institute for Statistics 2017). Both the World Bank and UNICEF have announced new policy packages that link funding to improvements in learning outcomes, as measured by large-scale national and international assessments (UNICEF 2018, World Bank 2019a, 2019b). Yet there remain large-scale debates about how to define learning and related targets: civil society and many academic researchers have criticized international donor focus on foundational skills in reading and mathematics, calling instead for a more expansive vision of learning that includes noncognitive skills and '21st century' learning (Care, Kim, Anderson, Gustafsson-Wright 2017).

Privatization: Among the most heated areas of debate in the EFA landscape today is the use of private sector providers to meet national and global education goals (see Chapter 11). Low-cost private schooling has expanded around the world, significantly in low- and lower-middle-income countries. Influential global funders, such as the World Bank, as well as a network of philanthropic funders, have supported this expansion (Ball 2009, 2012, Nambissan and Ball 2012, Robertson et al. 2012, Verger 2012, Mundy and Menashy 2014, 2019, Srivastiva 2020). However, international civil society advocates have opposed it, including through a multi-year campaign that saw the launch of the Abidjan Principles[9] on the Right to Education and, more recently, policies from the GPE and the World Bank ceasing any support for private provision of schooling.

Conclusion

This chapter has explored the dynamic history of global 'education for all' efforts. Beginning with the highly aspirational commitments made under the umbrella of the UN in the wake of the Second World War, we have indicated how the realization of a global vision of a universal right to education has been shaped by global organizations and actors. The chapter identifies the period after 2000 as a very special one for global education commitments during which a geopolitical alignment of interests among Western states led to higher levels of consensus and collective action on global development goals and international education for all activities. The net results were significant, in terms of both increased access and equity in basic education and in terms of more effective aid modalities. Nonetheless, global EFA action focused on access and paid limited attention to equitable learning for all, and had other serious limitations.

In our final section, we discussed how EFA has been taken up within the Sustainable Development Goals. SDG 4, with its focus on quality and inclusive education, represents a return to the broader agenda of the original EFA goals adopted in Jomtien and Dakar, including attention to early childhood education and adult education.

We identify three significant trends that are shaping current global action around SDG 4: fragmentation of development aid, despite many innovations in financing; the tension between a developing country focus on expansion of secondary and tertiary education versus the more narrow agenda focused on foundational learning among international development organizations; and the expansion of privatized provision of education. Perhaps even more fundamentally, Education for All will be shaped by three wider threats – of environmental crises; geopolitical instability; and, as prominently demonstrated by Covid-19, the threat of global contagion. As recognized in SDG 4, education is also envisaged as making a fundamental contribution to these challenges. Such a vision will only be possible through coordinated efforts to support and reform education, both at national and international levels.

Questions for Discussion

1. How do international SDG targets and indicators constrain or enable global, national and local level action towards the achievement of quality education for all?
2. Do you think current global education goals and strategies sufficiently support broader global goals of poverty reduction and equity? Why or why not?
3. What challenges and opportunities for EFA might emerge from new donors to education (e.g. China, Brazil, India, Turkey, South Korea and Russia)?

4. How has the engagement of a growing number of non-state actors in EFA, including local, national and transnational civil societies, the private sector and philanthropic organizations, influenced EFA goals, strategies and outcomes?
5. In your view, what are the chances of success for recent international efforts to achieve EFA?

Further Reading

Bruns, B., Harbaugh Macdonald, I., and Schneider, B.R. (2019). 'The Politics of Quality Reforms and the Challenges for SDGs in Education,' *World Development, 118*: 27–38.

Mundy, K. and Read, R. (2017). 'Education for All: Comparative Sociology of Schooling in Africa and Beyond', in Bickmore, K., Hayhoe, R., Manion, C., Mundy, K., and R. Read (eds), *Comparative and International Education: Issues for Teachers, 2nd edition.* Toronto: Canadian Scholars' Press Inc, 303–34).

Verger, A., and Novelli, M. (2012). *Campaigning for 'Education for All': Histories, Strategies and Outcomes of Transnational Social Movements in Education*, Rotterdam, Spring.

4

Decolonial Perspectives on Education and International Development

Pablo Del Monte and Lerato Posholi

Introduction

Broadly, decolonization refers to a multi-faceted process at the end of colonial rule and can be used to describe the 'direct withdrawal of colonialism from the colonies' (Ndlovu-Gatsheni 2013b). There is a crucial distinction between 'decolonization' and 'decoloniality'. While these terms are often used interchangeably, and both refer to a concern with the effects of colonialism, decolonization, in the strict sense, is about reversing colonization and thus aims towards the removal of 'official' colonialism.

'Decoloniality' is a more encompassing term that involves decolonization but goes beyond the reversal of 'official' institutions of colonialism. Decoloniality is a framework for articulating and challenging the history and current configuration of the modern world, starting, crucially, with the placing of coloniality at the centre (Ndlovu-Gatsheni 2013b). Decoloniality is not a singular theoretical school of thought but a family of diverse positions that share a view of coloniality as the fundamental problem in the modern age (Ndlovu-Gatsheni 2013b, 13).

Aníbal Quijano coined the term 'coloniality of power' to refer to 'a global hegemonic model of power in place since the conquest of the Americas that articulates race and labour, space and peoples, according to the needs of capital and to the benefit of white European peoples' (Andreotti 2011b, 64). This articulation of power involves ensembles of relationships of labour as well as the creation of racial categories to separate the conqueror from the conquered (Quijano 2000). This matrix of power imposes the racial hierarchical dichotomy between the human and the non-human, and María Lugones (2014) adds that the 'coloniality of gender' imposes the distinction between 'man' and 'woman', as colonial categories. Coloniality is a 'global power structure that sustains asymmetrical power relations between the Euro-American world and the Global South' (Ndlovu-Gatsheni 2013b, 11). This notion surfaces the idea that despite the end of formal colonial administrations, colonial arrangements have not been dismantled but continue to govern contemporary societies, through articulations of labour, people and space that were generated in the emergence of modernity/coloniality (Maldonado-Torres 2007, 243).

Since the second half of the twentieth century, postcolonial, neo-colonial and decolonial studies have furthered the analysis and critique of the effects of colonialism in Africa, Asia and the Americas in all spheres of life – political, economic, cultural and epistemological. Different intellectuals, communities and bodies of knowledge have engaged with these kinds of pursuits since the very first Spanish colonies in the Americas. Recent and ongoing protests under the #BlackLivesMatter movement, the #RhodesMustFall student movements and various calls for the removal of colonial statues have all re-ignited the important issues of decolonization and decoloniality.

Decoloniality, then, is a political and epistemological movement that aims to critically expose the coloniality of the current global order (Ndlovu-Gatsheni 2015). The epistemological aims of decolonial perspectives, similar to postcolonialism, is to critique the colonial epistemic order and pursue forms of knowing and being otherwise (Bhambra 2014).

Concepts 2
Decolonial and Postcolonial Approaches

Both postcolonial and decolonial approaches emerge out of political developments contesting the colonial world order. However, there are some differences between these two traditions of scholarship.

The one difference is with regard to their genealogies. Decolonial thought draws more from the thought of intellectuals like Frantz Fanon and Aime Cesairé, whereas postcolonial thought draws from poststructuralist and neo-Marxist traditions of thought (Mignolo, 2011). Bhambra (2014) distinguishes between the two strands of scholarship in terms of their disciplinary origin and the geographical locations of scholars within the traditions. She describes postcolonialism as having emerged as an intellectual movement consolidating and developing the ideas of Edward Said, Homi K Bhabha and Gayatri C Spivak. On the other hand, decolonial scholarship, she maintains, emerged from the work of Anibal Quijano, Maria Lugones, Walter Mignolo and others. The geographical origin difference is that postcolonialism emerged from diasporic scholars from the Middle East and South Asia, and decolonial scholarship developed from the work of diasporic scholars from Latin America and Africa.

Another difference is that linguistically, decolonial theorists attempt to incorporate other languages, such as Spanish, into their thought. Postcolonial theory tends to stay with English as the main language of thought (Lim, 2019).

Lastly, postcolonial theory, it is argued, tends to work with the same dichotomy between subject and object fundamental to Western epistemology. Decolonial thought challenges this foundational distinction, and emphasizes the bio-politics and geo-politics of knowledge (Lim, 2019; Tlostanova & Mignolo, 2009).

This chapter provides an overview of decolonial frameworks and highlights their relevance for the field of education and international development. We specifically look at decolonization, and decolonial perspectives on education and international development from Africa and Latin America. We highlight two key insights from decolonial perspectives for thinking about education and international development. On a conceptual level, we discuss the decolonial critique of the prevailing and dominant interpretations of the concepts associated with education and international development. Specifically, we highlight the decolonial claim regarding the persistence of coloniality in education systems in Africa and Latin America through the dominance of Eurocentrism. On a practical level, we present some of the decolonial explorations developed in the broad field of education and international development,[1] for decolonizing education by challenging and displacing the unjust domination of Eurocentric models of education.

Latin American Thought, within and against Modernity/Coloniality

Critiques of colonization in Latin America, by Latin American intellectuals, can be traced back to indigenous chronicles of the Spanish colony. Throughout this history of ideas, various terms have been used to name the condition of the colonized, such as colonialism, neo-colonialism, dependency, internal colonialism, emancipation, coloniality and decoloniality.

Between the fifteenth and nineteenth centuries, the colonization of the Americas was told through a Eurocentric lens, whereby a 'new world' had been 'discovered'. In the presence of an unthinkable event, 'colonizers perceive something analogous to an unbridgeable gap between them and the colonized' (Maldonado-Torres 2016, 68). In Fanon's terms, they encounter what they see as a not-entirely human being (Fanon 2008, xii, quoted in Maldonado-Torres 2016). A new form of relationship is established within the European world: the relationship with the colonized. From a different locus of enunciation, and within the process of colonization, chronicles such as that of the Peruvian Indian Felipe Guamán Poma de Ayala *Nueva Crónica y Buen Gobierno* (New Chronicle and Good Government) show the perspectives of colonial subjects, who understood how their societies were being transformed, and posed critical views on the government of the colonies.

A relevant element to take into consideration when looking at the Latin American work on 'decoloniality' is that the processes of independence in the Americas during the nineteenth century took different forms from those in other continents. Maldonado-Torres (2016) presents three types of independence processes: the US Revolution, which was led by white men to the detriment of indigenous peoples; the Haitian Revolution, led by Black slaves, affirming racial equality and the end of slavery; and, broadly, Latin American revolutions, led by 'criollo' and 'mestizo' elites, as mixed-race inheritors of the two worlds, the indigenous and the European. Across the processes of independence in Latin America, different positions were taken in relation to a common assumption: that Europeanization was associated with modernization and development.

During the mid-twentieth century, at the same time that decolonization was taking place in Asia and Africa, Latin American independent nation states were seeking routes towards modernization and development, but they faced challenges that undermined such attempts. These were framed, through the work of a group of Latin American intellectuals, as 'dependency', as discussed in Chapter 2 of this book. Some of the renowned writers on dependency theory are Argentine economist Raúl Prebisch, Brazilian sociologist Fernando Henrique Cardoso and Peruvian political theorist Aníbal Quijano. Dependency theory postulated that there were structural conditions to capitalism that divided regions between metropoles and peripheries (see McLean 1983, for a critical account). Similar analysis and arguments were posed by intellectuals in Africa, such as Kwame Nkrumah (1966), who used the term 'neocolonialism' to name new forms of economic, political, cultural domination with Europe, after independence. This term was then used to understand forms of domination that operated across postcolonial countries (see Spivak and Young 1991).

While dependency theory was informed to a great extent by economic, sociologic and political analysis, the emergence of philosophies and theologies of liberation was seen in the Latin American intellectual landscape during the 1960s and 1970s, which influenced the work of Brazilian pedagogue Paulo Freire. While all these theories and approaches were heavily informed by Marxism, structuralism was being called into question by European continental philosophies, particularly those concerned with the importance of discourses and the relationship of knowledge and power. For example, during these decades, Enrique Dussel's[2] (2000) philosophy of liberation began to draw on French contemporary philosophy, such as Emmanuel Levinas.

During the 1990s, Latin American debates on decolonization and Latin American studies were expressed across a range of disciplines and were present in structural Marxist approaches and poststructural philosophies. Maldonado-Torres (2016) mentions two relevant groups at this time: Latin American subaltern studies, which looked at expressions of Latin American culture as subaltern knowledges – for example *testimonio*.[3] Prominent figures of this group are John Beverly, Ileana Rodríguez, Walter Mignolo (see Gugelberger 1998). The other influential group is the Modernity/Coloniality network, which has been in expansion since the 1990s both in its referents and in its interlocutors.

Modernity/Coloniality Dialogues

This network consists of a set of conversations between Arturo Escobar, Aníbal Quijano, Walter Mignolo, Enrique Dussel, Santiago Castro-Gómez, Ramón Grosfoguel, Nelson Maldonado-Torres, Catherine Walsh, Eduardo Mendieta, María Lugones and others (see Mignolo 2007). This group of scholars have developed critical perspectives on Eurocentric thought, producing 'alliances with the internal critique of modernity' as well as sustaining peripheric positions of 'border thinking' (Andreotti 2011b, 66). Regardless of the location of these thinkers in the current geopolitics of knowledge (some based in global universities, others in the Global South), they attempt to create a set of conditions for thinking at the peripheries of Eurocentric traditions of thought. They are inspired by efforts of Afro-Caribbean and Afro-Andean activists to create 'an-other world' (Maldonado-Torres 2016, 76), and look not only at the economic-political-cultural relations within specific territories but at the emergence of a new articulation of power that has become hegemonic across the globe, which Quijano called 'coloniality of power' (2000). The main propositions of this group are that the origins of modernity are not to be traced in European Enlightenment but in the colonization of America. This involves, on the one hand, understanding that colonialism is the 'darker side' (Mignolo 2011) of modernity. Although there is some discussion about how tight or loose the bond between modernity and colonialism is (see Rueda and Villavicencio 2018), this group argues that they should be thought of as interdependent. A further point that is involved in this approach is that modernity, therefore, is not solely a European process but a world phenomenon in which the colonies are a necessary and active feature. This is what they refer to as the 'planetary paradigm'. On these bases, they expose the errors of Eurocentric approaches, which have considered local European philosophies and epistemologies as universal – and thus continue to exclude, oppress and misrepresent the perspectives and cultures of postcolonial societies. Walter Mignolo (2002) refers to the subordination of non-European knowledges within the coloniality of power as a 'colonial difference' that sets the conditions for 'epistemic racism' (Andreotti 2011a). These effects may be evident or hidden, but they continue to operate as modernity/coloniality sets the conditions of possibility for education, teaching and learning.

Decolonization in and for Africa

Decolonization discourses in Africa emerged in the 1960s following the end of colonialism as part of debates about how Africa would move forward postcolonialism and post-independence. At the time, a key concern for decolonization was the political re-imagining of Africa and its development. Education was at the centre of efforts to re-imagine and reconstruct Africa for a better future. One key concern with education was how to disentangle it from colonial influences to make it fit for the postcolonial and independent aspirations of Africa. Decolonizing strategies of the time highlighted the need for education in Africa to break with the intellectual dependence on and servility to Europe and America that came with colonialism. Education was to be re-imagined and reconfigured to facilitate the liberation of Africans from intellectual and psychological effects of colonization, and to restore the dignity and centrality of African culture, experiences and modes of thinking. Calls and proposals were made by such scholars as Ngũgĩ wa Thiong'o to decolonize the minds of Africans and restore their humanity by centring and affirming their languages and cultural experiences as legitimate sources of knowledge (Wa Thiong'o 1992). The resurgence of decolonization in Africa has found its most prominent and forceful articulation in higher education institutions by students and academics. In particular, the 2015/16 South African student protests under the banner of #feesmustfall and #rhodesmustfall brought about a renewed interest in debates about decolonizing of universities across the globe.

Contemporary decolonial perspectives reveal and challenge the ways in which colonialism 'lives on' despite its formal ending. In particular, current decolonial arguments focus of upending and overcoming the epistemic effects of colonialism. In this way, decoloniality intersects with epistemic injustice concerns and critiques the underlying Eurocentric and colonial logic of education in Africa. Epistemic injustice centres on concerns about harms done to subjects in their capacity as producers and consumers of knowledge (Fricker 2007). Calls for decolonizing universities are driven by concerns that the Eurocentric and colonial structuring of higher education institutions in Africa perpetuate epistemic injustice – coloniality shapes and informs the norms and standards of what counts as knowledge and who contributes to knowledge (Posholi 2020). The Eurocentric and colonial structuring and orientation of higher education institutions is critiqued for positing Eurocentric forms of knowledge as the only valid knowledge. Earlier

Pathways to Practice 3
#FeesMustFall & #RhodesMustFall

A wave of student protests for decolonization erupted in South African universities around 2015/16, and followed across various universities in the world, most notably in the UK under #RhodesMustFall and campaigns such as 'why is my curriculum white?' Initially, the #FeesMustFall and #RhodesMustFall movements started in response to rising university fees at the University of the Witwatersrand and against the statue of Cecil Rhodes at the University of Cape Town respectively. These movements gradually culminated in the call for the decolonization of universities more broadly, and highlighted many issues including teaching and research practices, financial exclusion, outsourcing of workers, language policies, institutional racism as some of the key elements in need of decolonizing. At core, the calls for decolonization call for a more socially just higher education system. In 2020 #RhodesMustFall, re-ignited by the recent waves of anti-racism across the United States and Europe under #BlackLivesMatter movement, have called for the removal of the Cecil Rhodes statue in Oriel college, Oxford University.

For more information on #rhodesmustfall, see:

- https://rmfoxford.wordpress.com/
- https://www.theguardian.com/uk-news/2016/mar/16/the-real-meaning-of-rhodes-must-fall

attempts at decolonization by anti-colonial movements are often perceived as having been ineffective, to an extent, precisely because they neglected to realize and challenge the colonial epistemology that informs education in Africa (Ndlovu 2008, Ndlovu-Gatsheni 2013a, Nyamnjoh 2019).

As an epistemological project, decolonization places education as its central object. The core concern is to uncover and challenge the ways in which 'universities in Africa are sites for reproduction of coloniality' (Ndlovu-Gatsheni 2013b, 11). A starting point for many of the calls and efforts to decolonize education starts with the claim that education in Africa is colonial or Eurocentric, and to problematize this fact about education (Nyamnjoh 2012, 2019, Heleta 2016, Le Grange 2016, Mbembe 2016a, Ndlovu-Gatsheni 2013b). The central concern is that 'schools and universities in Africa are sites for the reproduction of coloniality working to produce alienated Africans who are socialized to hating the Africa that produced them, and liking the Europe and America that rejects them' (Ndlovu-Gatsheni 2013b, 11). To say of education that it is colonial or Eurocentric is, at core, to say that its content, structure and aims of education perpetuate coloniality, and the epistemic and social injustices that result from this.

There are various and diverse ways in which university education in Africa reflects and perpetuates coloniality. Nyamnjoh (2019) illustrates some of the ways in which curriculum and pedagogy, knowledge production practices, graduate choices for further study, language policies and institutional culture of universities in Africa continue to reproduce injustice along asymmetrical colonial power relations. Heleta (2016) argues that the same forms of discrimination brought about by colonialism continue to pervert our current educational institutions where you find curricula, for example, still marginalize knowledge that comes from or speaks to the marginalized Black people in South Africa. Knowledge itself is a core element identified as colonial in decolonial perspectives. Mbembe (2016b, 32), for example, argues that:

> What is wrong with our institutions of higher learning is that they are 'Westernized'. They are 'Westernized' in so far as they aspire to become local instantiations of a dominant academic model based on a Eurocentric epistemic canon – a canon that attributes truth only to the Western way of knowledge production.

The argument is that knowledge production and consumption in educational institutions in Africa is uncompromisingly Eurocentric/Western and foreign to the contexts and predicaments of Africa (Nyamnjoh 2019). As Ndlovu-Gatsheni (2013b, 11) puts it, 'Africa is today saddled with irrelevant

Actors 2

Prof Sabelo Ndlovu-Gatsheni is the founder of The Africa Decolonial Research Network (ADERN) based at UNISA in South Africa. The main goal of this network is to work with decolonial theory to produce Africa-centred scholarship to challenge the dominance of Eurocentric knowledge in Africa, and work towards developing a truly African university that is responsive to the needs of Africa.

https://din.today/sabelo-j-ndlovu-gatsheni-we-needed-to-shift-the-geography-of-knowledge-as-well-as-the-biography-of-knowledge/

knowledge that disempowers rather than empowers individuals and communities.' Hence we still have 'universities in Africa' instead of 'African universities' that are responsive to the needs and priorities of the African continent (Ndlovu-Gatsheni 2013b).

Decolonial Perspectives on Education and International Development

These sets of conversations, and tradition, have been taken up and used in the field of education, and more specifically international development and education, in the last years, expanding several fields of study.

One of the uses of the modernity/coloniality debate have been as tools for critique of hegemonic discourses on education development, looking at the circulation of policy discourses and the operation of policy technologies through supra-national actors (Aikman 2012, Shahjahan 2016, Nieto 2018). Shahjahan (2016), for example, has used a decolonial approach to study how international organizations such as the World Bank and the OECD 'reproduce a colonial geopolitics of knowledge production' (2016, 705) in global higher education policy. Understanding decoloniality as 'an ongoing logic of domination underlying imperial powers' (2016, 695), this work analyses how the OECD creates a discourse of colonial difference where national higher education systems and regions are classified 'according to their distance or difference from the optimum knowledge economy' (2016, 701). Also, how the World Bank is hired by governments to develop higher education policy, introducing Western neoliberal discourses of human capital and the knowledge economy into education systems that had not framed or represented their goals in such terms. Furthermore, epistemic racism continues to operate even in the case of high-performing Asian countries, like Japan, Taiwan, China and Singapore, which are framed as a 'negative reference' (Takayama 2017) or a threat (You 2020) by Western media and governments – unlike their European counterparts.

The decolonial tradition has clear links with studies that explore alternative frameworks to think development and education otherwise. Brown & McCowan (2018) draw on post-developmental approaches (Esteva 2009, Escobar 2011a) looking at *Sumak Kawsay* (or *Buen Vivir*, in its Spanish translation) as an indigenous cosmology that offers ways to think the relationship of humans with nature beyond the possibilities of Western traditions. More applied research draws on decolonial ideas to explore practices and institutions that are producing alternative forms of education, such as *Universidad de la Tierra* (UNITIERRA) in Mexico (Barrón-Pastor 2010), Intercultural University 'Amawtay Wasi' in Ecuador (Martín-Díaz 2017) or *Bachilleratos Populares* for Secondary Adult Education in Argentina (Said 2018). This lens has, therefore, foregrounded indigenous cosmologies and forms of education, as well as attempts to transform modern education from within and pursue alternative pathways to development.

Another relevant body of work is taking place in the field of pedagogy (Walsh et al. 2019, De Lissovoy 2019, Reyes 2019), and in sub-fields such as indigenous education (Nakata et al. 2012, Santana et al. 2018, Fleuri and Fleuri 2018), intercultural education (Aman 2017, Pineda et al. 2019), human rights education (Zembylas 2017) pursuing social change through education 'otherwise'.

Catherine Walsh (2015) sets a dialogue between Paulo Freire's pedagogy and the project of the coloniality/modernity group, in the search for pedagogic uses or interpretations of this group's work. In her essay she proposes a set of principles, arguing that the 'decolonial otherwise' continues to operate at the margins of the modern/colonial order, where 'pedagogies of resistance, insurgence, rebellion, disruption, transgression and re-existence' (2015, 16) are practiced. She presents an interesting example of a school in Chiapas, an *Escuelita Zapatista*, where the 'teachers' were members of the community that had been raised in the Zapatista struggle, where 'students' were not defined by their age or developmental stage, where each student was assigned a *votán* or guardian-translator-interpreter and where learning was experiential rather than prescribed by curriculum. Walsh emphasizes that as colonial difference continues to operate in the making of contemporary education, so does the impetus to the 'decolonial otherwise'. Similar efforts exist in South Africa, under the banner of 'ecologies of knowledge' to decentre Western knowledge in school and university, and promote African-centred epistemologies and knowledge (see Fataar and Subreenduth 2015).

Furthermore, decolonial approaches have provided lenses for a meta-critique on the very fields of study of education (i.e. comparative and international education) and their participation in the coloniality of knowledge production (Takayama et al. 2017; see also Vickers 2020, for a critique), both in its Eurocentric epistemic origins (Sobe 2017) and in the current geopolitics of knowledge production. Regarding the latter, Takayama (2016) exposes epistemic racisms across the European/non-European binary in the case of Asian academia, while Silova et al. (2017) explore strategies to 'delink' their studies in post-Soviet countries from Western hegemony. Acknowledging that coloniality is constitutive of the very forms of knowledge production of their (and this) discipline, Silova et al. (2017) explore 'juxta' forms of 'border thinking' where hegemonic and subaltern knowledges are deployed to create new imaginations and being otherwise as knowledge producers. These approaches show how coloniality, as a matrix of power, operates beyond the boundaries of postcolonial territories and administrations, in and through the colonization of knowledge.

Conclusion

The introduction of this volume describes two main ways in which we can characterize the relationship between education and development. One way is to think of education as part of development, in which case 'it is one of the institutions of society that extends itself and improves in the course of a country's becoming more developed'. The second way is to think of development as dependent on education, such that education is a condition for development. Decolonial perspectives consider education as both part of the institutions that need to change as society develops and as an important vehicle towards development. This is evidenced by narratives portraying the urgency of decolonization for a better African future (Ndlovu 2008, Nyamnjoh 2012, 2019, Ndlovu-Gatsheni 2013b, 2015). Implicit is a presupposition that education can serve as a vehicle for Africa's development.

However, the decolonial framework is critical of how we understand development as well as the form of education that might lead to development. Put simply, decolonial perspectives are critical of dominant Eurocentric notions of development and see the current form of education as unfit for serving the needs and future of non-Western regions because of its intricate entanglements with coloniality. Decolonial frameworks challenge the dominant narratives about development by exposing its roots in the colonial project of Eurocentrism where regions such as Africa and Latin America are deemed as undeveloped as long as they do not resemble Western countries. These perspectives challenge the popular notion that development is defined, and achieved through, adherence to Western standards and ideals (Ndlovu-Gatsheni 2013a). Decolonial critiques of education and development force us to ask critical questions regarding the role of education, particularly in postcolonial regions such as Africa and Latin America, in perpetuating the project of colonization and continuing its lingering forms of injustice.

Moreover, these critiques force us to critically question the relationship between education and development, and to pay careful attention to the Eurocentric character of this relationship. Importantly, decolonial perspectives remind us that education is intricately entangled with ideology. In this case, critical attention needs to be paid to the ways in which education perpetuates and enforces the Eurocentric notions of development and how development initiatives aimed at education then, in turn, apply those notions to promote colonial education. Decolonial perspectives foreground the epistemologies and voices silenced by modernity, towards new imaginations of what education and societies can be (Brown and McCowan 2018). This is observed in the creation of pedagogies 'otherwise' (Walsh 2015) as well as in the development of institutions that promote alternative forms of education, such as UNITIERRA.

Having illustrated that education in postcolonial contexts remains largely colonial, decolonizing approaches present a number of proposals and practical strategies about the different facets of education and how they need to be re-thought and transformed to challenge and reverse the coloniality that they conceal and promote. We do not have the space here for an exhaustive list of decolonial practical strategies in education. But the main decolonial strategy is to shift the places of enunciation of knowledge from the dominant West to the marginalized groups of regions such as Africa and Latin America. The key practical proposal from decolonization is that we reverse the dominance of Eurocentrism and its injustices by prioritizing and affirming knowledge from the experiences of marginalized groups (Mignolo 2007, Ndlovu-Gatsheni 2015, Le Grange 2016, Mbembe 2016a). This entails an important shift in the valuing system of knowledge, and works to create and affirm standards of value that are not Eurocentric. The 'trickle-down' effect of this shift will transform the many other facets of education.

The decolonial framework encourages us to be critical scholars and agents of development. It cautions against the common 'quickness' of so many well-intentioned development agencies, often situated in the Global North, to formulate and implement strategies for addressing what appears to be urgent problems in regions such as Africa and Latin America, while perpetually failing to diagnose and address the fundamental problem of coloniality that persists through systems of education in these contexts. The decolonial framework, at the very least, encourages us to be careful that we accurately diagnose the problems with education and development in these countries, and to ensure that we are critical of the development we intend for these regions.

Questions for Discussion

1. Why do we need decolonization in education?
2. Who has a say in what decolonizing means? Is this a global debate?
3. How does decolonization relate to other critical traditions of thought such as feminism and critical race theory?
4. What does decolonization mean for international development and international development institutions?

Further Reading

Andreotti, V. (2011), *Actionable Postcolonial Theory in Education*, New York: Palgrave Macmillan.

Kwoba, B., Chantiluke, R., and Nkopo, A. (Eds.). (2018), *Rhodes Must Fall: The Struggle to Decolonise the Racist Heart of Empire*, London: Zed Books Ltd.

Taverno-Haidarian, L. (2018). 'Why Efforts to Decolonise Can Deepen Coloniality and What Ubuntu Can Do to Help', *Critical Arts*, 32 (5–6)

5

Power, Participation and Partnerships in Research

Ian Warwick, Elaine Chase and Rosie Peppin-Vaughan

Introduction

In this chapter we introduce a number of issues to consider when reading, conducting and making use of research for education and development. We outline how the field has evolved within a competing set of ideas about the nature of education, of development and what constitutes meaningful impact in policy and practice. Such contestations inevitably raise issues of power and hierarchy with respect to who determines what research is important, how it is conducted, whose perspectives matter and the forms of evidence which are valued.

A core aim of this chapter is to assist readers to identify how they might position themselves in relation to others involved in research endeavours (Rowe 2014, Jafar 2018, Hope, Brugh, and Nance 2019). Reflecting on and understanding positionality in research is an essential ethical matter if, as we argue, the process of generating new knowledge is to meaningfully engage those affected by an issue in decisions that affect their lives.

The chapter begins with a brief overview of how research in education and international development has evolved. This is done by presenting two contrasting schools of thought as anchors for the debate (while hoping readers can see there are rather more currents at play than we can address in this short chapter). We then explore how the perceived nature and function(s) of education and of research in education and international development shape the conceptual framing and design of research and how it is conducted. We conclude with a discussion of ethical practices in research, noting the importance of collaboration when planning and conducting research and of making use of findings in epistemically just ways.

Research for Education and Development

In order to understand how research in education and development has evolved, we need to consider the relative prominence of the different policy, practice and research actors involved and the values, principles and theories which drive their approach. There have emerged two broad schools of thought, or ideal types (Tickly and Bond 2013), with respect to what research in the field is for and how it should and could be conducted. While in practice most research is more complex and nuanced, these ideal types nonetheless have some explanatory value in understanding what drives research for education and development and how the field has arrived at where it is.

On the one hand is an approach which has largely been promulgated by multilateral agencies such as the World Bank. Such organizations hold significant power in shaping global agendas in education and the nature and direction of related international cooperation through 'knowledge-based' aid and research (Mason et al. 2019, 2). These agencies have established an approach and ethic to research which, in its 'ideal form', seeks evidence which is 'neutral' and 'objective' and which advocates methods such as econometrics, cost-benefit analyses and randomized control trials. Typically underpinned by human capital theory on the role of education, this school of thought tends to adopt a top-down approach to the formulation of research problems and questions and often has a regulatory function. Such attempts to generate acontextual, value-free knowledge belies their underlying positivist and 'big science' assumptions (Mason et al. 2019). These often underpin the funding of research, which seeks to endorse ideas related to evidence-based policy and forms of 'best practice' that are believed to be generalizable across contexts.

On the other hand is a school of thought which is critical of the stance of development agencies and how they maintain power differentials within the field. Its authors take issue with the uncritical international transfer of research modalities in the area of international development cooperation (Mason et al. 2019). Typically driven by a theory of human rights and underpinned by ethics of respect, dignity and valuing difference, this school of thought seeks to unsettle assumptions of what constitutes best practice in the field and ideas that such practice can be transplanted across contexts (Mason et al. 2019). It has the explicit goal of centring knowledges and voices which have hitherto been silenced and marginalized (Santos 2012) and is as concerned with the research process and the particularities of the contexts within which it is conducted as it is with its objectives. Again, in its 'ideal' form, it is informed by more interpretivist and participatory methodologies and underpinned by an explicit code of ethics which seeks to decolonize the research process (Chilisa 2020) and promote epistemic justice (Walker 2020).

While some of the complexities of real-world research funding and practice are picked up later in the chapter, these idealized types help illuminate some of the tensions between objectivist and subjectivist approaches in social and educational research – particularly with regard to the nature of social and educational worlds, how one comes to understand these fields and what values drive research, especially with regard to notions of participation and partnerships. To help readers understand a little of the nature of the field of study and how knowledge might be generated about it, we next draw a distinction between the theoretical and conceptual framing of research (Crawford 2019).

Theoretical Positionality – Education and Development

In order to identify on what educational research might focus, how it might be conducted and to what ends findings might be used, it is useful first to step back and consider people's perspectives on how education and development 'work' to bring about particular outcomes – that is, identifying the theoretical framing or positioning of research.

Education, in its broadest sense, existed in all countries before the introduction of formalized education systems. However, such formality often came to be *the* taken-for-granted way that education was understood and delivered (Harber 2014). Understanding education in a relatively simple, somewhat formal and mechanistic way, where inputs and mediating variables lead to certain outcomes, rather reduces it to a deterministic set of technoscientific practices, often hiding its 'normative and political dimensions' (Sriprakash, Tikly, and Walker 2019), 686). Alternatively, considering how education 'works' in a more complex systemic way suggests that it is intimately related to its wider cultural environment and it involves people who are in a constant process of creating and interpreting meaning and who also bring their own agency to bear on educational processes (Biesta 2015), a point we return to below.

Moreover, the very purpose of education may be understood as somewhat normative, whether aiming to create a nation state, with compliant workers and family forms which service a state focused on economic growth (Harber, 2014) or inspired by, among other things, social justice and cultural diversity (UNESCO 2015). It may be important, here, to step back to consider how normative assumptions inform how education in a particular context is made use of with regard to three kinds of functions: to qualify people to work and live, to socialize them and to expect them to become a particular sort of subject in society (see Biesta 2015). Kadiwal and Jain (2020), for example, note the use of civics textbooks in India and Pakistan to reform the subjective character of citizens so that they would be transformed into dutiful, obedient, virtuous and subservient citizens of a paternalistic state. Development, too, is informed by its own set of underlying assumptions related, among other things, to whose values and visions inform policy and programming, the sorts of outcomes intended and the timescales by which change is expected (Sumner and Tribe (2008) (see introduction to this volume).

To return to ideas of positionality, the broad theoretical positions of the field that we and others hold about a field of study – here, education and development – are likely to influence how research itself is conceptualized and conducted (Crawford 2019).

Given the contested nature of educational research in international development, particular positions will inform policy drivers, funding calls for research, the preparation of proposals and the enactment of research itself (Mason, Crossley and Bond 2018).

Conceptual Positionality – Research Approaches and Designs

The disputed nature of education and of development outlined above, along with what type of research is seen to be of value, means that educational research has followed a range of trajectories over time. Studies in the field have been informed by and generated a number of approaches and designs (as well as methods), a few of which are discussed in this section.

Approaches

By research approaches, we refer to the underlying assumptions that inform research. For example, positivism, based on the possibility of constructing value-free objective knowledge alongside the development of universal causal laws, has been influential in research about education and international development (Mason et al. 2019). (We discuss this in relation to randomized controlled trial study designs below.)

Since the second half of the nineteenth century, the assumptions underpinning a positivist view of social research have been challenged, with new approaches, or paradigms, being developed, alongside innovations in research designs and methods. Positivism, with its somewhat mechanistic and reductionist view of nature, social life and of people themselves, became increasingly critiqued for its inattention to inner experience and individual moral choice (Mason et al. 2019). As we outline below, this led to more naturalistic approaches – assuming people were deliberative, intentional, creative and what they thought, felt and did was contextually situated. Enquiry, it was argued, should focus on people's natural states rather than as subjects within a manipulated research design (Cohen et al. 2018).

Since the 1970s, post-positivist approaches, where knowledge is understood as conjectural and challengeable, were accompanied by ideas associated with postmodernism and post-structuralism. Taken together (although Cohen et al. [2018] caution against conflating the two theories) these argued for 'multiple interpretations of a phenomenon', according to 'legitimacy to individual voices' and abandoning 'the search for deterministic, simple cause-and-effect laws of behaviour and action' (Cohen et al. 2011, 28). Complexity theory, which engages with ideas around networks and systems (and, as noted earlier, may be a useful way to understand education), suggests that educational research should pay attention to notions such as recursivity, connectedness and emergence (Cohen et al. 2018). For example, with regard to education, feedback to students has a regulatory function which affects learning. Connectedness views students as linked to one another, to their families, the environment, support agencies and technologies. Emergence might display itself when individual students join together to build a shared community of understanding and concurrently take action to advocate for change. An example, here, is young people's engagement with climate change in Brazil through participatory action research (Trajber et al. 2019).

Critical and transformative research approaches add to this complexity by interrogating, critiquing and seeking to unsettle taken-for-granted ways of knowing, being and doing (Cohen et al. 2011; Chilisa 2020) with the aim of empowering particular constituencies hitherto marginalized and/ or oppressed. Related to, but not the same as transformative approaches, Chilisa (2020) suggests a postcolonial indigenous research paradigm questions the extent to which certain constructions of the world have been deeply influenced by colonial and postcolonial eras and may legitimize the continuance of unequal global economic arrangements – including those related to education. She makes the case for a distinct postcolonial, indigenous research paradigm that is relational with regard to the nature of social life, how we generate knowledge about it and the values informing research. She argues that research should be responsible (so as to pursue social justice which resists dominant [colonial] ideologies) (see also Walker 2020), reverential (so as to engage with spirituality), respectful (in that the research process is guided and owned by a community) and reflexive (so that it seriously considers the use of power in research).

A postcolonial position seeks to reveal the assumptions and power relations which pervade research conducted on 'developing countries' by Western researchers (Mazrui and Mazrui 1996, Tikly 1999). Hence, research can be seen 'as a significant site of struggle between the interests and ways of knowing of the West and the interests and ways of resisting of the Other' (Tuhwai Smith 2012, 2). Smith discusses ways in which research has been openly challenged by communities and indigenous activists regarding ethnocentric assumptions, racist attitudes and practices, and exploitative research. She and others have suggested as a way forward the development of alternative methodological approaches located in the 'South' (e.g. Halai and William 2011, Park 2011, Robinson-Pant 2013, Chilisa, 2020).

Designs

Informed by the sorts of paradigmatic assumptions discussed above, research designs provide the methodological framework or plan for educational enquiry. Although some research designs have been limited in their engagement with the multifaceted nature of education, we note examples of how experimental designs, surveys as well as close-focused or in-depth studies have been developed to enquire into complexity and contextuality.

Experimental Designs and Randomised Controlled Trials

Often aligned with a positivist approach, randomized controlled trials (RCTs) or other experimental research designs are seen by many to offer definitive answers to educational problems. Such experimental approaches explore the effects of particular interventions on a population of interest by manipulating one or more independent variables and measuring the degree to which this manipulation accounts for variance in outcome. Imported from medical research, RCTs have been applied to social policy and gained some popularity amongst development agencies. They feature as part of an agenda to discover 'what works' (Mason et al. 2019) or really, what *has* worked (Biesta 2010). Proponents argue that they are important as a tool for rigorous testing of policy initiatives.

Despite their strengths, there are a number of disadvantages to experimental approaches, and RCTs in particular have not been introduced without controversy to the field of education. The assumptions underlying the research design and the interventions they investigate must be scrutinized. Such designs can be resource-heavy, require substantial financial investment and often generate evidence for a particular point in time rather than providing any longer-term or sustained analysis of what is happening. While some analyses may be able to demonstrate strong

Measurements and Indicators 1

A randomized controlled trial with theoretically informed follow-up by Loyalka and colleagues report on a large-scale, randomized evaluation of a national professional development (PD) programme in China (Loyalka et al. 2018). Six hundred teachers were randomized into four different groups: PD only, PD plus follow-up, PD plus evaluation of PD content knowledge and no PD. Their analysis of data from teachers and 33,492 students from 300 schools identified that involvement in the PD programme improved neither teacher nor student outcomes after one year.

Rather than settling on the simple conclusion, as many RCTs do (Gorur et al. 2018), that 'professional development has no impact', Loyalka and his team sought to find out why by enquiring into causal chain effects.

Informed by a literature review on professional development, the team enquired into issues of quality and tested key features of the professional development programme against a theory-based understanding of the ways that professional development might operate. Through interviews, teachers reported that they found the content of the PD programme too abstract and its teaching too rote and passive. Loyalka et al. concluded, among other points, that policymakers may wish to invest in PD programmes that are more closely aligned with educational theory and practice related to professional learning and its application.

associations between certain input and outcome variables, demonstrating causality is more problematic; strong correlation may be caused by latent or confounding variables that are not being measured. Critics argue that RCTs rarely provide useful evidence unless accompanied by theoretical work which can explain what determines the effects that have been observed (Morrison 2009, Deaton 2010; Gorur, Sellar, and Steiner-Khamsi 2018). While they may be able to answer 'whether' a particular intervention has brought about particular outcomes, they do so through a process of complexity reduction (of the contextual and recursive nature of education) often with a focus on single issues, and do little by way of meaningfully engaging with the intricacies of education and development (Biesta 2015; Mason et al. 2019).

Enquiring into what has led to particular sets of outcomes can be done by way of complementary designs through which qualitative information is gathered (see Measurement and Indicators 1).

Framing research theoretically is also of value when reviewing research. For example, Carr-Hill, Rolleston, Schendel and Waddington (2018) foreground their systematic review of effectiveness of school-based decision-making in improving educational outcomes with a wide-ranging theoretical framework. They used this to inform the literature search, analysis and synthesis. While recognizing that donors often promote the idea of local school decision-making as leading to improved educational outcomes, the authors proposed that outcomes are more likely the result of a complex range of causal pathways.

Large-scale Surveys

The complexities involved in finding out about people's lives through social and educational research can also be reflected through the use of large-scale surveys. These aim to capture information about educational circumstances from a wide constituency for comparison and analysis, possibly involving surveys of educational conditions in one location across a number of time periods. They may also have a cross-national element, allowing comparison between different countries. Examples include data compiled and published by UNESCO in the Global Education Monitoring Reports[1] and data from the OECD's Programme for International Student Assessment (PISA).[2] Such surveys can cover thousands or even millions of individual children, although some surveys are considerably smaller. They may involve the collection of basic educational data (such as enrolment, transition, achievement) or more specific questions tailored to particular research agendas, administered via questionnaires and interviews.

Surveys offer some unique and distinct benefits. The scale of data collection may provide an overall picture about a particular issue and may allow for greater generalizability as well as comparisons over location and/or time. However, surveys have their limitations, and because of the scale of data collection and the claims to generalizability, it is important to scrutinize the underlying assumptions, especially in terms of sampling (have any significant groups been omitted for example?), the validity of questions (what factors might influence how questions are understood and answered truthfully?) and reliability (will different groups understand and respond to the questions in the same way?).

Some time ago, Broadfoot (2004) cautioned against over reliance on statistical data in education, a concern more recently raised too by Gorur et al. (2018). Broadfoot claimed that too much emphasis on league tables and 'rankings', often only based on relatively small differences in scores and reflecting only certain criteria such as exam achievement, detracts from scrutinizing the actual quality of education. Moreover, statistical data must be analysed and interpreted correctly, and so those reading findings arising from such data should be wary of their manipulation for particular political agendas. It is also important to beware of the tendency to recourse to numerical data in the mistaken belief that it is more trustworthy or meaningful than other data. There are many instances where other forms of data may be more appropriate when answering particular research questions. Comparing such educational data across developing countries may be particularly problematic, such as significantly different political and economic trajectories and varied social and cultural contexts (Mason et al. 2019).

Nonetheless, when used for more than providing acontextual snapshots of education, surveys can have value. Although longitudinal study designs for international development in general and education in low- and middle-income countries in particular are not common, there is a growing recognition of the value of longitudinal research for sustainable development (see Measurement and Indicators 2). Banati and Oyugi (2019), for example, identified nineteen longitudinal survey studies focusing both on sustainable development and education.

Measurements and Indicators 2
Young Lives: A Longitudinal Cross-country Study

Young Lives has shed light on the drivers and impacts of child poverty, as well as the factors that influence successful transition into young adulthood, with particular emphasis on the labour market and education. One aim of the study has been to inform policymaking and programming.

Established in 2002, the project started to follow the lives of 12,000 children in Ethiopia, India (in the states of Andhra Pradesh and Telangana), Peru and Vietnam, and in two cohorts, those born in 1994–5 and 2001–2.

By conducting research in four countries, the project has been able to report on trends and explore commonalities as well as differences with regard to child development in each country. Through the use of two cohorts, it has been possible to compare the same young people at different ages to identify in what ways their lives and those of their communities have changed.

Young Lives is a rare example of a longitudinal project focusing on education (among other areas) in low- and middle-income countries and combines regular quantitative surveys of the children and their care-givers with in-depth qualitative research on a sub-sample. The main themes explored are the nature of and associations between poverty and inequality, health and nutrition, education, gender, child protection as well as work-related expertise.

(See: https://www.younglives.org.uk/)

In recent years, the availability of data, through surveys, social media or other means, has given rise to new digital methodologies which make use of large datasets – often referred to as the collection and analysis of 'big data' (Gorur et al. 2018). Analyses may produce new insights into, for example, formal and informal education among young people by tracking their pupil movement in and around educational settings, networks and associations through which learning takes place, words and phrases commonly used when searching electronically and patterns of commenting on issues via social media. As with other research, contextuality is important – not only with regard to whose big data methodologies inform research but also whether or how findings can be generalized from analyses of 'Western' datasets on, for example, young people's lives, to a plural Global South (Milan 2019). Analyses of large datasets are routinely conducted by non-academic organizations and raise questions about the distinctiveness and necessity of locating research in universities (Gorur et al. 2018). However, Dencik et al. (2019, 880) argue for the use of 'big data' to be accompanied by a concern with 'data justice' – 'to illuminate the contradictions, the challenges, along with the social, political, economic and cultural implications associated with the process of datafication'.

Close Focus and In-depth Research

Given the importance of understanding the contextuality of education outlined earlier, it is perhaps a disservice to include the range of qualitative approaches and designs which can address this complexity (such as, grounded theory, ethnographies, auto-ethnographies, qualitative/flexible case studies, critical discourse analysis, narrative research, participatory learning and action, to name just a few) by way of a few short paragraphs. However, the special issue of Forum for Development Studies – 'Qualitative Method/ologies in Development Studies' (Arntsen and Waldrop 2018) – provides a sense of the sorts of research designs that can provide in-depth understandings of people and the contexts in which they find themselves. The articles combine detailed accounts of ethnographic approaches with discussions about their underlying theoretical perspectives. The collection spans three continents and focuses on schools and classrooms in conflict-affected South Sudan, engages with hip-hop musicians in Uganda, examines vote-buying in a Mexican village, makes use of household histories to give substance to an impact evaluation in Ethiopia and explores women's everyday lives in Botswana and India.

An example of the complexities of young people's identities and their relation to the benefits and harms associated with education was identified in a study of young people's accounts of citizenship in Pakistan (Kadiwal and Durrani 2018) (Pathways to Practice 4).

While 'thick descriptions' and 'thick comparisons' (Gorur et al. 2018, 5) arising out of small-scale studies can provide information about micro-, meso- and macro-factors that affect people's lives, such findings (as with those from more fixed experimental and survey designs) need also to be accompanied by their own theoretical and conceptual framing. Theory is a way of identifying what might come to be the focus of a study while simultaneously absenting

Pathways to Practice 4
Using postcolonial theory to understand the role of education in identity construction in Pakistan

The study used postcolonial/decolonial theories as analytical tools to explore young students' negotiation of their citizenship identities at the intersection of their class, gender, religious and ethnic identifications in the conflict-affected setting of Pakistan. Findings, drawing on data from participatory focus group discussions, highlight that rather than asking for humanitarian help and charity, the young people demanded the transformation of conditions that produce poverty and conflict. In this sense, while they may have failed to identify themselves as global citizens, they exercised critical global citizenship. Participants expressed a sense of outrage and the desire to take action but had limited capacity for transforming the roots of inequities and conflict. They believed in the power of education to enable them to do this and strived for it, sometimes risking their lives. However, education itself was also discussed by participants as a major enabler of inequities and conflict in Pakistan. Students' positioning appeared to be influenced by the way conflict and education intersected with their social class, school type, neighbourhood, gender, migration, ethnolinguistic and religious backgrounds. Due to these complexities, it was difficult to ground their experiences in any single marker of their identity.

(Source: Kadiwal and Durrani, 2018)

factors, issues, variables not covered by that theory – such as whether and in what ways same-sex sexualities are discussed in postcolonial writing (Pallotta-Chiarolli 2020, Chilisa 2020). The concepts associated with research designs and methods operate similarly. They help people come to know about certain issues and, through informing policy and its enactment via programming and practice, may also create particular realities or truths about how things 'are' (Gorur et al. 2018). Whether small or large scale, whether making use of flexible or fixed designs, whether post-positivist or postcolonial, transparency is needed regarding the assumptions about a field of study and how knowledge about that field is being created through research.

These issues, we would argue, not only are related to technical understandings about how research might best be conducted but are also informed by cultural, social and political considerations – all of which require reflection on research ethics.

Ethics in Research: From Procedures to Reflective Practice

Ethical considerations are core to any research and particularly important to address in low- and middle-income countries where there are likely to be inherent inequalities among those involved (particularly with respect to the power dynamics between the researcher and the researched). Ethical research is scaffolded by notions of research *integrity*, defined as: honesty; rigour; transparency and open communication; care and respect (for humans, animals, the environment and cultural objects); and accountability (Universities UK 2019, 6). Research integrity seeks to ensure that studies are conducted according to appropriate ethical, legal and professional frameworks, obligations and standards, and that the research environment is underpinned by a culture of integrity.

While foregrounding ethics has gained global traction in recent decades, this has been uneven and the infrastructures for ethical research governance vary enormously across the globe. Much work in the Global North has focused on 'building capacity' for research ethics in low- and middle-income countries, particularly in relation to biomedical health research (Ndebele et al. 2014). However, there has been an increasingly robust critique of research governance infrastructures designed in the Global North and transplanted to contexts in the Global South (Walsh et al. 2016). Notions of ethical imperialism (Schrag 2010, Tikly and Bond 2013, Israel 2018) point to how such frameworks are predominantly based on universalist and individualized understandings of ethics which tend to exclude other belief and social systems, ignore colonial and neo-colonial experiences and which fail to engage with, and learn about, local knowledges and contexts (Santos 2007).

Tikly and Bond (2013) refer to a postcolonial research ethics which involves a process of decentring European thought and which is fundamentally emancipatory, situated and dialogical. Hence values and ethics form part of a dialogue between ideas of human dignity and its equivalents within, for example, African *Ubuntu*, Islamic *umma* or Hindu *dharma* as well as engaging with Western universalist ideas of human rights (Santos 2007, Tikly and Bond 2013, Seehawker 2018). Such a dialogue, it is argued, re-centres notions of humanness, relating positively towards others, trust, care and social justice. A postcolonial approach strives for cognitive justice with respect to giving appropriate value to Global South epistemologies and ways of knowing, particularly when they come into contestation with those from the Global North. It also seeks to bolster the importance of Global South research ecologies and promote leadership for research by universities in low- and middle-income countries (Cloete et al. 2015).

Practising ethics, therefore, involves being informed by local norms and protocols (rather than importing these from elsewhere) and valuing not only what is written down but what is spoken about too. Such considerations suggest a shift from a set of decontextualized ethical procedures towards an ethics and way of designing and conducting of research which assumes a reflective and critical stance, which is dynamic and adaptive to context and differing views, values, experiences and perspectives (Crossley and Watson 2003).

Towards Equitable Partnerships in Research: Decentring Values and Assumptions

An ethics of research along the lines discussed above not only transcends ideas of 'doing no harm' in and through research interactions but also more fundamentally informs all stages of the research process. Accordingly, this brings us to questions of equity and justice with respect to research partnerships (Walker 2020).

Whether producers or users of research, it is vital to consider the underlying purpose of generating new knowledge. The positivist tradition has tended to constitute the researcher as extractive or piratic (Tilly 2017) – that is, findings or data are used for the purposes of others outside of the context within which they are generated and often in ways which are opposed to the best interests of those being 'researched'. Whilst such research (as long as it adheres to the core elements of research integrity) may well receive ethical approval, it may still fall short of the type of ethical scrutiny outlined above.

Yet research can equally be driven by values which consider exploration of the world as a collaborative, shared endeavour underpinned by ideas

Pathways to Practice 5
LIDC-MLT: Towards a Migration
Research Strategic Agenda

One example of an attempt to decentre the process of research agenda setting is the ESRC/AHRC-funded London International Development Centre – Migration Leadership Team (LIDC_MLT). Between 2018 and 2020 the MLT was commissioned to develop a strategic agenda for global migration research and inform funding allocations from UK Research and Innovation (UKRI). A series of global conversations enabled migration scholars, practitioners, civil society organizations and artists from across the globe to set research priorities and shape the strategic research agenda from their own priorities. This was achieved whilst engaging with broader issues of how best to build and sustain equitable and sustainable partnerships for migration research as well as what constitutes meaningful impact across diverse cultural contexts (LIDC-MLT 2020).

of participation and the intention to unsettle existing power structures and epistemic injustices (Walker 2020). Such studies might, for example, build on the critical role of civil society and informal education in tackling inequalities through their understanding of national and local histories and contexts. Mohanty's analysis of community responses to Covid-19 illustrates how civil society actors' expertise in responding to one crisis, extreme communal violence in Delhi, enabled them to act with immediacy when faced with an evolving epidemic (Mohanty, 2020). Making known such expertise, social networking, community education and advocacy requires the research agenda, approach and process of analysis to be co-designed in ways which enable those affected by an issue to be closely involved in producing knowledge to inform solutions to it (see Pathways to Practice 5).

The Nature of 'Impact'

The impact of any research endeavour relates directly to its original objectives, its intended outcomes and audiences. In their 'ideal' forms, the schools of thought outlined in the introduction to this chapter suggest very different ideas about research impact and the sorts of uses findings will be put to. The regulatory approach implies that future funding for research or innovation might hinge on whether the research undertaken can demonstrate sufficient effectiveness and value for money. The rights-informed approach, on the other hand, might emphasize the value of more subjective accounts and multiperspective analyses of issues and may provide the basis of advocacy initiatives for certain marginalized groups or causes. In theory, while both scenarios might generate impactful research, whether they are evaluated as such will depend on the values and attitudes of those making such an assessment.

In their edited review of partnerships in international research to strengthen evidence-informed decision-making, Georgalakis and Rose (2019) highlight four dimensions of research impact: conceptual, capacity building, instrumental and building networks and connectivity. Importantly, and linked to the earlier discussion in this chapter, the review suggests how the possibility of generating impact hinges on sustained partnerships between researchers, intermediaries, evidence users and beneficiaries which are formed on notions of equity, fairness, bounded mutuality and sustained interactivity.

Generating impact is also contingent on communicating research findings in meaningful and useful ways to different audiences. Recent years have observed a fundamental shift in emphasis by research funding bodies beyond academic impact (traditionally garnered through peer-reviewed academic journal articles) towards encouraging researchers to make research more relatable to diverse policy and public audiences (Cairney and Oliver 2018, Ross-Hellauer et al. 2020). This has led to recognizing the value of dialogue and interactive engagement involving performance arts, theatre, animation, film and increasingly the use of digital mechanisms such as podcasts, video and webinars. It has also coincided with closer collaboration between different strands of research funding which bridge the natural, physical and social sciences, as well as arts and humanities (LIDC-MLT 2020).

Conclusion

Based on notions of decolonizing and decentring scholarship we have purposefully situated power, participation and partnerships at the heart of considerations of how educational research is envisioned and enacted in low- and middle-income countries. We have outlined how extant hierarchies of power and the nature of relationships between those involved in research inevitably shape decisions about what is researched, who researches it, how research is conducted, which findings are produced and how they come to be used.

We have suggested that positioning oneself in relation to such debates, as well as coming to understand the positionality of others, is an important ethical matter if inequitable power relationships are to be re-formed rather than reproduced. Still, the changing nature of education and international development, and the studies funded about it, makes alignment with a cognitively just approach to research a necessary ongoing commitment.

Questions for Discussion

1. In what ways do relations of power affect how research policy is framed, how research is planned and how it is conducted?
2. In what ways is understanding positionality an ethical as well as technical issue in research?
3. What sorts of partnerships are needed to help ensure research addresses issues of data and cognitive justice?
4. How might issues of power and partnerships affect the ways that research findings come to be used?

Further Reading

Chilisa, B. (2020). *Indigenous Research Methodology*, London: Sage.
Crossley, M, and Watson, K (2003) *Comparative and International Research in Education: Globalisation, Context and Difference*, London: Routledge.
Gorur, R., Sellar, S. and Steiner-Khamsi, G. eds. (2018). *World Yearbook of Education 2019: Comparative Methodology in the Era of Big Data and Global Networks*, Abingdon: Routledge.

Part 2

Key Themes

6

Schools, Citizens and the Nation State

S. Garnett Russell and Monisha Bajaj

Introduction

Scholars have long discussed the dual nature of schooling: on the one hand, education can be used to indoctrinate and socialize youth, while, on the other, it has the potential to foster critical thinking and enhanced civic capacity among children and their families. The purpose of this chapter is to examine the multiple roles and functions of education in the process of inculcating civic identity and nation-building. The chapter explores literature in the field of international and comparative education over the past five decades about schools, citizenship and political socialization, highlighting key studies that have advanced our understanding of the relationships among schools, citizens and the state. We highlight issues of global governance as they pertain to shifting perspectives on schooling, particularly in the contemporary era of Education for All (EFA) mandates and international goals, such as the Sustainable Development Goals (SDGs), related to increasing educational access and quality. We also engage current issues of globalization, human rights, migration and educational policy to explore how national school systems respond to global demands, trends and pressures.

Within diverse countries, curriculum and schooling are oriented to different notions of what it means to be an ideal citizen, and these may change in distinct historical moments. Utilizing cases studies from Rwanda, South Africa and India, we further discuss some of the ways education has resulted in conflict in some instances and in greater social cohesion in others. Even in nation states not affected by violent conflict or authoritarian political regimes, shifts in how the nation is positioned in the global economy can influence how education is envisioned. For example, India's changing educational landscape since its independence in 1947 has recast children and families – at least discursively – from being passive recipients of state services to becoming active agents in the education process, arguably, in line with its greater integration into the global economy in recent years (Bajaj 2014). Systematic reforms have created mechanisms for greater community participation and input in schooling, offering individuals and non-governmental groups increased involvement in educational processes as part of a more active form of citizenship (see Pathways to Practice 6). Periodic audits that compare indicators cross-nationally, such as PISA and TIMSS (Trends in International Mathematics and Science Study), have motivated policy action in the face of global pressures or trends; further, national and regional systems of accountability provide new venues of agency for local actors. Hence, in some cases, this has resulted in increased participation of local citizens in local governance over schools and education policy. However, there remain questions of government capacity for implementing change; in many nation states in the developing world, vast differences exist between government schools in regions with varied access to resources, across urban-rural divides and with distinct historical trajectories of educational development. Countries, such as India, have at times implemented innovative financing measures to reduce imbalances across states through grants from the federal government to equalize resources (see Mukherjee 2014).

As we highlight different country examples of schooling and society in different periods, it is important to remember that education is embedded within larger social processes. Social stratification linked to race/ethnicity, religion or income – and also complex historical processes – can result in unequal forms of citizenship that schooling can perpetuate (see Chapter 8). More affluent families can opt for private schools when government systems fail to provide high-quality or accountable educational services (or in the case of widespread pandemics). However, the majority of students in most low- and middle-income countries have no choice but to rely on government schooling or, as many do by the end of primary school, opt out of schooling altogether (UNESCO 2010). Given that schools are a key site for children to learn about their political system and their society broadly, high dropout rates pose a challenge to the development of a civic identity.

Schooling and Citizenship

With the shift from agrarian to industrialized societies, the state has played an increasingly important role in the education and socialization of citizens. Although the rise of mass schooling is associated with this more prominent role, the nature and the extent of the involvement of the state in schooling is also contested (Fuller 1991).

Education systems contribute to the construction of a 'civic culture' or the desired norms and attitudes of citizens with respect to government at different levels (Almond and Verba 1963). One aim of citizenship or civic education is to transmit knowledge and skills about political institutions and civil and political rights and duties within a democratic society (Abowitz and Harnish 2006). Traditional notions of civic education, originating in the European context during the eighteenth and nineteenth centuries, derived from the concept of the individual linked to the nation state and focused on promoting national values and patriotism. In contrast, some current forms of citizenship education aim to develop engaged and active forms of citizenship. Under this model, citizenship education is concerned not only with teaching about political institutions, rights and duties but also with instilling attitudes of 'civility' towards different groups of citizens across race, class and religion (Kymlicka 2001). Within a liberal democracy, a perspective on civic education is that it contributes to the 'conscious social reproduction' of political values, attitudes and behaviours of citizens (Gutmann 1999, 34).

The expansion of mass schooling served an important role in the consolidation of the nation state and in the creation of a unified national civic identity, particularly in Western European countries beginning in the late eighteenth and early nineteenth centuries. Public education systems replaced forms of religious schooling in favour of universal state-funded schooling (Green 2013). In the latter part of the nineteenth century and particularly after the Second World War, states expanded universal and compulsory education as part of a larger project of nation-building which aimed to incorporate citizens within a particular form of state and associated views of society (Ramirez and Boli 1987, Meyer et al. 1992). The rise of mass schooling was linked to the rationalization and 'scientization' of social organization, including the rise of a bureaucratic form of government and emphasis on the formation of the individual. Formal schooling played an important role in the process of state formation and political socialization. Schools were used to promote particular values linked to ideas of a shared national identity, presenting themes regarding a national history, language and culture (Resiner 1922, Bendix 1964, Tyack 1966, Weber 1976, Hobsbawm 1977) and invoking national myths and symbols (Smith 1986).

The expansion of mass education can be explained according to several different theoretical perspectives. Institutional theorists argue that schooling functions to organize societies, classify and assign values to individuals and transform social roles through rituals and myths (Meyer 1977). For example, commonly held assumptions about mass education serve to define notions of the nation, citizenship and ideas about rights and duties.

A functionalist perspective on schooling explains the expansion of mass education as a response to the needs of a modern, industrial society through providing training and socialization to students in preparation for a stratified labour force (Feinberg and Soltis 2009). Dreeben (1968) emphasizes the role of schooling in socializing students for an industrialized economy through teaching them norms such as independence and achievement, skills that are valued in such an economy's labour force.

While a functionalist perspective is that education is equally accessible to all students regardless of social attributes, a Marxist view considers education as perpetuating societal inequalities through the transmission of values and status cultures; thus, schools reproduce social relations both through structure and socialization in accordance with social class (Bowles and Gintis 1976, Kallaway 1984, Nkomo 1990, Chisholm 2004). Hence, while schooling, and citizenship or civic education in particular, can be used for the purposes of inculcating notions of civic identity and moral values, education can also perpetuate and reproduce existing inequalities within society through hidden curricula and political ideologies favouring a dominant class (Bowles and Gintis 1976, Anyon 1980, Giroux 1983). Bowles and Gintis (1976) argue that the main purpose of education within a capitalist society is to legitimate economic inequality and socialize citizens into behaviour traits along class lines. Other scholars have noted that the 'hidden curriculum' in schools implicitly contributes to the reproduction of unequal social relations through imparting divergent cognitive and behavioural skills necessary for working in a factory or in menial labour across different groups linked with their future positions in the labour force (Apple and King 1977, Anyon 1980) (see Table 6.1).

In addition to reproducing and exacerbating existing societal inequalities along class lines, education may also be manipulated to produce intolerant and hyper-nationalistic citizens, particularly in conflict-ridden or non-democratic societies. Under these circumstances, civic education may be used to divide society across different ethnic/racial or religious groups and to promote negative stereotypes, nationalist and divisive sentiments and inter-group violence (Bush and Saltarelli 2000, Smith 2005, Johnson and Stewart 2007). However, a number of authors argue that the education system can also be used to foster a unified notion of civic identity and to transmit liberal values in conflict-affected societies through implementing civics education that defines civic identity in global human rights terms and promotes a liberal notion of citizenship (Bush and Saltarelli 2000, Minow 2002, Smith and Vaux 2003, Weinstein et al. 2007). For example, in South Africa, citizenship education emphasizes human rights and multiculturalism (Kruss 2001) (Table 6.1).

Moreover, in the field of international and comparative education, understandings of the relationships between schooling, citizenship and civic identities have been enriched by postcolonial and poststructural insights and critiques (as discussed in Chapter 2 of this book). These approaches interrogate development as a 'regime of representation' (Escobar 1995), and further examine how dominant notions of civic identity are shaped and sometimes imposed on subordinated groups through 'epistemic' (Spivak 1988) and 'symbolic' (Bourdieu and Passeron 1977) violence. As a result, what it means, for example, to be 'Rwandan', 'Indian' or 'South African' must be understood and complicated by larger analyses of power and its asymmetries in each context.

Each of the theoretical perspectives highlighted above could be applied to understand – with differential interpretations – conditions and dynamics in educational development in a particular context. The rise of globalization and the global flow of educational trends and reforms have also influenced how nation states and schools cultivate citizenship.

Globalization and Global Governance

'Globalization' emerged as a term in the mid-1980s to explain the increasing economic, social and political interconnectedness or the 'compression of the world and the intensification of consciousness of the world as a whole' (Robertson 1992, p. 8). Globalization, at the economic, political and cultural levels, has significantly impacted the nation state, and education systems in particular. Nation states have increasingly shifted their orientation from a national and inward-oriented perspective to a more globalized post-national vision de-linked from a territorially bound nation state, although the degree of engagement with global processes varies by context. In an increasingly globalized world, nation states are influenced by global norms and policies such as EFA, although the level of influence on national policies varies across states. And certainly, more recently, the move towards increased nationalism in the face of greater integration and the retreat from global institutions (e.g., the US's withdrawal from UNESCO in 2019) complicates our understanding of how global convergence occurs in educational policymaking and other realms of governance.

Rather than being merely socialized by state education systems, citizens are now envisioned as rights-bearing, both within their nation state and in the global community, actively involved in holding the state accountable for the provision of quality education. Consequently, social citizenship has been increasingly globalized as transnational actors advocate for social rights related to education and accountability across levels. Mundy (2008) argues that civil society organizations play an important role in advocating for the engagement of citizens and social equality within the context of EFA activities at a local, national and international level. In the case of Brazil, a middle-income but highly unequal society, McCowan (2009) documents the role of civil society in promoting initiatives in the education sector

Table 6.1 Theoretical perspectives on the notion of citizenship and schooling

	Assumptions	Views of schooling	Role of citizen	Key authors
Institutionalist	Legitimating myths in place for the expansion of schooling (individual and national progress), socialization – Standardization – Models, scripts and identity. – Emphasis on common features of market, bureaucracy and individuals	Similar organization of schools throughout the world regardless of level of development, local culture. Expansion of mass education	Cohesive notions of citizenship passed down through rituals and symbols and participation in particular social formation shared in the nation state	See Meyer et al. (1992), Ramirez and Boli (1987)
Functionalist	Schools provide for equal opportunity (merit) – Schools serve societal interests. – Schools follow universal norms/standards	Schools for the development of a capitalist economy; modernization	A sense of solidarity among citizens and integration of different functions develops, although roles are differentiated through schooling	See Dreeben (1968)
Marxist	Education reproduces capitalist class relations – Schools serve the dominant class/powerful groups – Schools favour the perpetuation of the dominant class/status groups	Schools reproduce societal inequalities	Citizens emerge from schooling believing in the legitimacy of stratified social relationships through what Bourdieu and Passeron (1977) terms the 'symbolic violence' enacted by the curriculum on students. In addition, they are trapped by structures of class inequalities	See Bowles and Gintis (1976), Luykx (1999), Nkomo (1990)

Pathways to Practice 6: ASER Reports

The role of citizen and non-governmental actors in ensuring educational quality has increased. A non-governmental organization in India, the ASER Centre, which is part of the larger educational organization Pratham, developed a learning tool for language and mathematics to assess the quality of learning (as opposed to just rates of access). 'Aser' means 'impact' in Hindi and also stands for the Annual Status of Education Reports conducted by the organization. These annual reports have found that less than 50 per cent of fifth-standard (grade) students are able to read a simple Standard Two-level passage like the one below (translated into English). Since launching the first annual report in 2005, ASER's model has been replicated in other countries such as Pakistan, Kenya, Uganda, Mali and Senegal, offering communities greater information about how government schools fare. Citizen activists and policymakers can then use this information for interventions and reform. For instance, the Indian state of Rajasthan has incorporated a type of assessment developed by ASER into their state curriculum and the Government of India mentions ASER's findings in its five-year plan (2012–2017) (Figure 6.1).

Story

Seema is a little girl. Her mother gave her a book. It had lots of stories and nice pictures. Seema reads it every morning on her way to school. She learned many words. Her teacher was very happy. The teacher gave Seema another book. It had more stories. She showed it to all her friends.

Para

I go to school by bus.
The bus has four wheels.
It has many windows.
It is blue in colour.

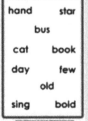

Figure 6.1 *Source: See: http://www.asercentre.org/*

to increase access to education, civic knowledge and active involvement in school management. For instance, the Plural School seeks to include marginalized students, the Voter of the Future programme aims to develop active citizenship among youth and the 'Landless Workers' Movement' (MST) provides education as part of a larger social movement (McCowan 2009, Tarlau 2019).

Global Citizenship Education

Within the context of a more globalized world, some notions of citizenship have shifted from a national territorially bound idea to a post-national global perspective emanating from a universal human rights framework (Soysal 1994). Consequently, education systems have been influenced by globalization, with new models of globalized national systems emerging in response to the increasing inter-connectedness across nation states. Hence, citizenship education in some contexts is conceived in terms of global human rights, enumerating both rights and responsibilities beyond the scope of the nation state (Smith and Vaux 2003, Suarez 2008). A globalized notion of citizenship education carries the dual purpose of developing understandings of obligations as national and global citizens with particular appreciation of ethnic, cultural and linguistic diversities (Banks 2004).

Global citizenship education is seen by its advocates to encompass important issues of human rights, democracy, social justice and social cohesion within a globally interconnected world (Davies 2006). Thus, the intention of global citizenship education is to foster a notion of citizenship not simply attached to a particular nation state but also engaged with the broader world and indeed humanity as a whole (Davies 2006). A number of notions of civic education have moved towards a post-national model, embracing a cosmopolitan notion of citizenship linked to a global community rather than one bound to the nation state (Buckner and Russell 2013).

In some nations, curricula and textbooks reflect both a regional and global notion of citizenship. Schissler and Soysal (2005) find that narratives in European textbooks increasingly emphasize the nation and citizen within a global framework. In an empirical cross-national study of 559 secondary textbooks from seventy-six countries across North America, Europe, Latin

America, Africa and Asia, Buckner and Russell (2013) find an increasing emphasis on discussions of globalization and global citizenship over the period of time from 1970 to 2008 in textbooks across both Western and non-Western countries. However, other studies of textbooks have also found that the focus on the nation and nationalism persists in textbooks during the period from 1955 to 2011, particularly in countries recently emerging from conflict (Lerch, Russell and Ramirez 2017). Moreover, in recent years, there has been a surge of populist nationalism and a backlash against liberal and global models, as evidenced by the ascent of Donald Trump in the United States, Brexit in the UK and the rise of authoritarian populism from Hungary to Brazil to India (Norris and Inglehart 2019).

Citizenship and Human Rights Education

The shift towards a more global notion of citizenship education emphasizes multiculturalism, human rights and diversity and draws attention to the emergence of an international human rights legal and normative framework. Civic education in many countries now incorporates discussions of these themes (Suarez 2008). Under this model of citizenship education, the learner is conceived of as an active citizen and a rights-bearer. In this way human rights education has become an important component of a globalized vision of citizenship education.

Human rights education (HRE) aims to provide learners with skills and knowledge regarding universal human rights utilizing learner-centred methods (Tibbitts 2008, Bajaj 2012). While there are many variants of HRE, there is broad agreement about certain core components. First, most scholars and practitioners agree that HRE must include both *content* and *pedagogical processes* related to human rights (Tibbitts 2002, Flowers 2003, Bajaj 2012). Second, most literature discusses the need for HRE to include goals related to cognitive (content), attitudinal or emotive (values/skills) and action-oriented components (Bajaj 2012). Consequently, the emphasis on citizenship as an individual rights-bearer has transformed the notion of education from passive to interactive, whereby citizens are situated as active and engaged stakeholders who can hold the government accountable for the provision of quality education.

Education in Post-conflict South Africa and Rwanda

In a post-conflict context, education can be used to fuel inter-group tension and intolerance; alternatively, education may play an important role in promoting reconciliation and inter-group tolerance (Bush and Salterelli 2000, Davies 2004). The cases of South Africa and Rwanda illustrate the role of education in promoting a unified identity in the aftermath of inter-group conflict, namely apartheid and the 1994 genocide, respectively.

For South Africa, 1994 marked the end to apartheid, an institutionalized system of racial discrimination, and the transition to a democratic society. Under apartheid, implemented under the victory of the National Party in 1948, the racially segregated education system was utilized for the process of socializing distinct racial identities, differentiating the white minority population from the black majority population, also divided on grounds of race and ethnicity. Education legislation sought to implement separate and inherently unequal education systems and curricula for different racial groups and to inculcate disparate values and social identities across groups (Jansen 1990, Soudien 2010).

Following the first democratic elections in 1994, the expansion of access to education across racial and ethnic groups has been paramount in the re-building of society. The education system plays an important role in the process of reconciliation and fostering a new civic identity in the post-apartheid era both through the integration of previously segregated schools and through the revision of the national curricula to eliminate nationalist and racist elements. With the end of apartheid and the transition to democracy, the newly elected government led by the African National Congress (ANC) sought to implement new education policies and reforms with an emphasis on rights, social justice and nation-building (Chisholm 2005). The right to education and instruction in the mother tongue is enshrined in the 1996 Constitution (Chapter 2, Section 29). Subsequent reforms, such as the 2005 Curriculum, have sought to emphasize outcomes-based, learner-centred pedagogy and human rights, although these reforms have been difficult to implement and their capacity to overcome persistent race and class divisions has been limited (Soudien 2010).

The government has drawn on a global human rights discourse in the curriculum and textbooks to address the violent past (Russell, Sirota and

Ahmed 2019). For example, in a ninth-grade social studies textbook, human rights are framed in both global and local terms: the Universal Declaration of Human Rights is directly compared to the Bill of Rights in the South African Constitution (Barnard et al. 2007). However, while national education policy and curricula express a global vision of citizenship linking the national notion of the 'rainbow nation', comprised of different racial and ethnic groups to global diversity, South African students' lived experience of citizenship is not so rosy, as disparities persist across racial, class and ethnic groups at the school level (Jansen 2002, Soudien 2004, Carter 2012). Hence, despite an attempt to eradicate deeply entrenched social and racial inequalities, unequal access to quality education and the persistence of dominant cultural norms perpetuate inequalities at the school level and make the task of citizenship education particularly pointed (Carter 2012, Russell and Carter 2019).

In Rwanda, education played a role in creating negative group stereotypes, contributing to the 1994 genocide. During the colonial era and after independence from the Belgians, unequal access to education and biased curricula and classroom practices created tensions between the Hutu and Tutsi (Rutayisire et al. 2004, Gasanabo 2006, King 2008, Mclean Hilker 2011). Unequal power relations and access to resources fuelled waves of inter-group conflict following independence in 1959 culminating in the 1994 genocide, where more than 800,000 Tutsi and moderate Hutu were killed in 100 days (Prunier 1995). Following the genocide, the government banned the teaching of Rwandan history in schools since there was no agreed-upon version of the past (Freedman et al. 2008); only in 2010 has the government developed new textbooks for teaching Rwandan history, which emphasize a singular and official version of the past (Russell 2020).

In the post-genocide era, the government draws on education as a tool for nation-building to foster reconciliation and a unified national Rwandan identity rather than one tied to ethnic groups. In this vein, educational policy documents and curricula emphasize global elements and rights-based terminology such as references to international human rights conventions, framing citizenship both in national and global terms; correspondingly, students identify as both national and global citizens (Russell 2020). However, in contrast to South Africa, where a multicultural nation is acknowledged through aspects of language policy and a multi-perspectival view of history, in Rwanda, post-conflict identity is de-ethnicized and linked to a broader national identity framed in terms of patriotism and unity. Thus, while civic education draws on global rights terms, a unified national identity is emphasized over multiculturalism (Russell 2020). Furthermore, while both countries draw on rights language within the civics curricula, in South Africa, citizenship education aims to foster dialogue between different groups, while in Rwanda the goal is to promote a unified civic identity as Rwandans – despite contested narratives of historical events – rather than to promote critical discussion. These cases demonstrate the difficulties inherent in using education for nation-building and creating a civic identity in post-conflict nations with a divided past.

The Right to Education in India

As nation states such as Rwanda and South Africa reconsider how schooling fits into larger political and economic goals, the role of the citizen is also renegotiated given shifting global, national and local mandates pertaining to education. India, a large and diverse nation state of more than 1.2 billion residents, implemented the 'Right to Education Act' in 2010 that seeks to recast how children, youth and families engage with the state around schooling. The shifting discursive positioning and initial steps towards enactment of the legislation offer insights into the complex relationship between state schools and the citizens they serve.

The right to education was identified in the original framing of the Indian Constitution (1950) as a 'directive principle', distinguished from the fundamental rights enshrined in that document. Access to schooling was made a priority but not a right for all Indians (Premi 2002). India liberalized trade and made formal decisions to integrate firmly into the global economy in the mid-1980s, and decisively in 1991. Concomitant with this sea change in Indian governance, educational policy moved into greater alignment with the notion of a right to education prominent in global educational discussions of the time given the UN's adoption of the Convention on the Rights of the Child in 1989 and the first global Education for All Summit in Jomtien (1990).

India's changing perspectives on the relationship between the state, schools and citizens are evidenced in policy frameworks when examined over time. For example, in 1978 the National Curricular Framework for Teacher Education posited the purpose of teacher education 'to develop Gandhian values of education such as non-violence, truthfulness, self-discipline, self-reliance, [and] dignity of labor [to achieve] the goals of

Pathways to Practice 7
Citizenship in Rwanda

In civics education in Rwanda, conceptions of citizenship are portrayed in both national and global terms. For example, in the textbook seen in Figure 6.2, students learn about citizenship rights deriving from the national constitution and about human rights linked to the UN system (Russell 2020).

Rights and responsibilities

Citizens' rights and human rights

The constitution gives the citizens of Rwanda rights. Many of these rights are based on the **human rights** listed by the United Nations. The government must respect and protect these rights.

Identify the responsibilities shown in the pictures below.

Human rights
- We have a right to life and security from attack.
- We have a right to shelter and food.
- We have a right to basic education and health care.
- We have a right to equality under the law.
- We have a right to think, write and move freely within our own country.
- We have a right to religious belief and conscience.
- We have a right to vote and take part in government activities.
- We have a right to trial if we have been suspected of committing a crime.

Responsibilities
As well as rights, we also have responsibilities.

Figure 6.2 Grade 6 social studies textbook *Source: Bamusananire et al. (2006)*

building up a democratic, secular, and socialist society' (as cited in Bajaj 2012, 44). An excerpt from the updated National Curricular Framework in 1998, soon after India's greater integration into the global economy, demonstrates increasing convergence towards global educational priorities at that moment: '[The objectives of teacher education are]... to sensitize teachers towards the promotion of social cohesion, international understanding and protection of human rights and child rights; [and] to sensitize teachers and teacher educators about emerging issues such as environment, ecology, population, gender equality, etc.' (as cited in Bajaj 2012, 44). In recent years, teacher education frameworks have included language related to learner-centred and critical pedagogies, peace, democracy and citizenship (Bajaj 2014).

In 2010, the Right to Education (RTE) Act came into force after several years of discussion and debate, shifting education from a non-binding principle to an enforceable right in Indian constitutional law and providing all children aged between six and fourteen years the right to free and compulsory education in a school within one to three kilometres of their home. There are several provisions in the RTE Act that deepen the legal claims individuals and families can make on the government, and a considerable onus is placed on state governments to increase spending in order to be compliant (Bajaj 2014). For example, the Act makes schooling for all children (including those with disabilities) compulsory; requires that state governments provide a primary school within one kilometre of every village/dwelling; sets aside

Policy 1
National Commission for the Protection of Child Rights, India

In 2005, the Indian Parliament issued an order for the creation of a National Commission for the Protection of Child Rights, which began operations in 2007. The vision of the Commission, as stated in its 'Citizen's Charter', is that 'All children enjoy their basic and inalienable rights i.e. survival, development, protection and participation in accordance with the Constitutional framework, law, policy and the United Nations Convention on the Rights of the Child, across the country'. Children, parents and community members can make complaints to the National Commission (or the State Commissions that have emerged throughout the country since 2007), followed by inquiries into the alleged offences. Local access to national- and state-level bodies with authority to intervene in situations of abuse has reformulated how individual citizens engage with the state, especially since corruption and a lack of transparency regularly characterize local bureaucracies (Gupta 2012).

25 per cent of all private school admissions for children from 'weaker sections' of society; mandates all schools have libraries with adequate materials; requires that women make up at least half of school management committees (also commonly known as parent–teacher associations); and bans teachers from offering private lessons, a common way that educators supplement their income and neglect their teaching duties during the school day (Bajaj 2014).

Positing access to schooling as a human right, as India has done in its RTE Act, provides citizens the ability, at least in theory, to hold governments accountable. Some critics, such as the non-governmental ASER Center, have argued that the inordinate focus on access and structures of education have actually resulted in *declining* educational quality. Nonetheless, rights frameworks may facilitate the agency of children and their families in demanding their right to schooling as opposed to being passive beneficiaries or targets of interventions (typically framed in larger efficiency terms rooted in arguments for economic development) (Robeyns 2006, McCowan 2013). Reframing citizens' role in education (and other public services) from passive to active is resultant from myriad influences ranging from global trends to local activism influencing how domestic policy gets adopted. India's educational policy shifts reflect the growing recognition of individual agency and human rights vis-à-vis social goods, such as state schooling. Perhaps further exercise of citizen accountability may ultimately lead to increased educational quality, though greater attention to shifts in the relationship between state schooling and citizenship is required to better examine outcomes and impact.

Citizenship, Education and Migration

In an era of globalization and global governance, the issue of global migration has important implications for ideas around citizenship and the provision of education. While national education systems were established by nation states in order to educate and socialize their citizens, such as in the cases of Rwanda, South Africa and India mentioned above, with increasing levels of global migration, the traditional view of schools to create an 'imagined political community' (Anderson 1991) and unified citizenry has been called into question (Waters and LeBlanc 2005).

With the highest number of forcibly displaced persons on record – more than 70.8 million – of which more than 25 million are refugees, meaning they have crossed international borders (UNHCR 2019), the responsibility of nation states has shifted from providing education only to their citizens to non-citizens as well. While refugee-hosting countries, particularly in the Global South, have started to include non-citizens within their national school systems with shifts in global policies (UNHCR 2019), questions remain as to what language these students should be taught, what curriculum they should follow and whose history they should learn. Moreover, with the average length of displacement now more than twenty years, non-citizen students, including refugees and asylum-seekers, face an 'unknowable future' (Dryden-Peterson 2017). The challenges of providing relevant education for displaced populations have resulted in what Banks (2017) terms as 'failed citizenship' or the denial of rights and privileges of citizenship due to their racial, ethnic or religious identity.

Conclusion

This chapter demonstrates the multiple relationships among schools, citizens and nation states across the globe in distinct historical periods and in particular country case studies. Education has the potential to offer students tools for critical social analysis and to build informed civic identities and social cohesion as the cases of South Africa and India demonstrate. However, as has too often been seen, education also carries the potential to fuel divisiveness, intolerance, inter-group conflict and violence, as illustrated in the case of Rwanda. In the contemporary period, global dialogue and discussion through the EFA Summits and the SDGs as well as coordinated donor aid – both multilateral and bilateral – have sought to influence greater uniformity in quality measures and accountability mechanisms, although these may take different shapes and forms in distinct contexts. Greater complementarity between local and global notions of citizenship has permeated most national education systems internationally.

The shift in the notion of national citizenship to a global, rights-based active citizenship – in discourse if not entirely in practice – has important implications for greater citizen involvement in accountability and local governance for the provision of higher quality education. Within the context of a globalized world, greater levels of inter-connectedness have led to a more global and cosmopolitan notion of citizenship education, at least discursively, as well as transnational mechanisms within the realm of international educational policy that seek to match 'policy talk' with 'policy action' (Tyack and Cuban 1997). In addition, recent increases in forced displacement and the rise of nationalism have implications for the role of schools in educating both citizens and non-citizens. The complex relationship between schools, citizens and nation states is constantly evolving and shifting, with reformers and activists consistently advocating for education to bring about greater equity and citizen participation across the globe.

Questions for Discussion

1. How do different theoretical perspectives explain how education systems inculcate values and ideas about citizenship through schooling?
2. How do conceptions of national and global citizenship differ?
3. In what ways do education systems seek to transmit values and ideas of citizenship through curriculum, pedagogy and school practices?
4. Consider the dual nature of education and provide some examples or cases where civic education may result in positive or negative outcomes. Why is education for nation-building and civic identity particularly contentious in a post-conflict context?
5. What are the challenges of globalization for education reforms and civic identity? In what ways does globalization positively or negatively impact education systems? How has global migration impacted education systems?

Further Reading

Bajaj, M. (Ed.) (2017). *Human Rights Education: Theory, Research, Praxis*, Philadelphia: University of Pennsylvania Press.

McCowan, T. (2009), *Rethinking Citizenship Education: A Curriculum for Participatory Democracy*, New York: Continuum.

Stromquist, N. and Monkman, K. (2014), *Globalization and Education: Integration and Contestation Across Cultures* (2nd ed.), Maryland: Rowman and Littlefield.

Useful Websites

International Association for the Evaluation of Educational Achievement
(IEA), Civic Education Study: http://www.iea.nl/cived.html
Human Rights Education Association (HREA): http://www.hrea.org/
United Nations 'Path to Dignity: The Power of Human Rights Education' film
https://www.ohchr.org/EN/NewsEvents/Pages/
ThePowerofHumanRightsEducation.aspx

7

The Education–Economic Growth Nexus

Monazza Aslam and Shenila Rawal

Introduction

Economic growth, the increase in goods and services produced within an economy over time, has been seen as a fundamental goal for countries the world over. It is not surprising, therefore, that examining the growth process and its relationship with education has been the subject of research over many decades. Economic growth has mainly been credited to increases in physical capital and the skills, knowledge and experience of individual workers in a country (embodied by their education), broadly termed 'human capital'. Increases in productivity arising from technological innovation and the development of new products and services are also seen to enhance economic growth. The last few decades have also seen influential supranational organizations, such as the World Bank and UNESCO, promoting the use of policies aimed at developing skills and training the workforce to stimulate economic growth and to foster social and socio-economic development in a bid to develop a 'knowledge economy'.

The role of human capital has been a universal component of both theoretical and empirical analyses of economic growth with 'skills of the population' entering theoretical debates within a number of the key growth models (discussed below). Although human capital includes education, health and aspects of social capital, the most commonly used measure of human capital is education (variously defined as schooling attainment, that is the highest level of schooling completed or more recently by cognitive skills). There are at least three reasons why one would expect to find a relationship between education and economic growth. Firstly, education increases the level of human capital within a country, which, in turn, would potentially increase labour productivity. Secondly, education has the potential to increase innovation in an economy, thereby promoting technological advancements in not only products but also processes, which all promote growth. Thirdly, the diffusion and transmission of knowledge is facilitated through education in that it increases the ability of these new technologies to be understood and implemented widely, further promoting economic growth (Hanushek and Woessmann 2020). However, these theoretical predictions have not been equivalently backed with such conclusive empirical evidence on quantifying the exact relationship between education and economic growth. This is particularly true given that other aspects such as family environment, health, nutrition and so on also play an important role in contributing not only to education but also to economic growth. Furthermore, early research that focuses only on the quantity of schooling may not provide an accurate estimate of this relationship given that research has shown that the quality of education also matters (ibid.).

It is apparent from observing the more successful economies such as South Korea and Taiwan that living standards have increased as the education levels have gone up. In South Korea, for example, primary and secondary enrolment rates have been near universal since 1990, and it was estimated that in 2019, 70 per cent of twenty-four to thirty-five-year-olds in the country had completed some form of tertiary education, the highest percentage worldwide (OECD data).[1] Coupled with this is the fact that since the 1960s, South Korea has set unprecedented growth records with GDP tripling in just the past twenty years.[2]

Evidence from a diverse set of developing countries such as India, Pakistan, Kenya, Ghana and Tanzania also indicates that individual earnings are linked to education levels, suggesting that more educated workers are more productive (Hanushek and Woessmann 2008). Logically, one would therefore expect this linkage between individual education and earnings (and higher productivity) to translate into a link between education and incomes at the macro country or regional level: if individuals with more education can command higher earnings, surely countries with a higher number of educated workers should be able to do so as well. The argument runs that, if education is viewed as an 'investment' at the individual level, that is, if spending on education is viewed as yielding some future return or benefit, so too can it be seen as such at the country level with countries investing in human capital as they would in physical capital (Stevens and Weale 2004). This chapter provides an overview of the education and economic growth relationship. It aims to address the question of *why* one would expect there be a relationship between education and economic growth in the first place.

Education is known to have both intrinsic and instrumental value. The former is based on the notion that education is valuable 'in itself', while the latter derives from the financial and non-financial benefits it confers. Education, for instance, is known to improve earnings, improve labour market outcomes, reduce mortality and improve health. A summary of the literature indicating a strong relationship between education and health is provided in Cutler and Lleras-Muney (2006). For example, research has shown that those with more education are more likely to live longer in a range of developed and developing countries such as the United States, Bangladesh, Korea and China, to name a few. A recent study shows that the most highly educated white men in the United States live on average fourteen years longer than the least educated Black men.[3] Because education is believed to be so valuable, it has also consistently ranked at the forefront of agendas at both the national and international levels.[4]

Education and Economic Growth: Theory

What causes economic growth? This question has been puzzling economists for centuries. The discipline of economics offers numerous explanations for why one would expect a relationship to exist between education and economic growth at both the micro and macro levels. There are both direct and indirect influences of education which may impact growth at these levels. At the micro level, these include, for instance, increased individual earnings (direct), improved health and increased parental involvement in children's education (indirect) and so on. At the macro level, some of the benefits include lower population growth, better health of the population and the labour force, as well as a general increase in the size of the labour force. Within this nexus, the role of externalities is also crucial. These are the spill-over benefits to other people in society as a result of another person's increased education. For example, crime rates are lower in societies where people are better educated or there is increased civic participation and so on.

Neoclassical growth theories have emphasized investment in capital as key to economic growth. However, the inability of these 'older' theories to explain the divergent growth paths of various economies led to the development of newer theories (discussed below).

Human Capital Theory

One of the most important ideas is the notion that marketable skills of workers are a form of 'capital' in which workers make a variety of investments. Broadly speaking, 'human capital' pertains to any stock of knowledge or skills workers have (innate or acquired) that contributes to 'productivity'. The much renowned human capital theory (HCT henceforth) proposed by Becker in the 1960s claims that better educated workers, on average, earn higher wages because they are presumed to have become more productive as a result of their education. A key advantage of this definition is that it allows incorporating not only years of schooling but also other broad characteristics such as school quality (variously defined as discussed below) and training which have a bearing on productivity and can thus be seen to constitute human capital investments. Measurement and Indicators 3 summarizes the 'micro' underpinnings of HCT.

Measurement and Indicators 3: Rates of Return to Education

This view of education as an investment measures the impact of education on earnings and other outcomes using 'returns' to various levels and types of education. This is done by comparing the private and social benefits of education with the costs, that is, by the 'return to education'. Returns to education may be both economic (increased earnings) and non-economic (lower infant mortality, enhanced civic participation, reduced crime rates, etc.). Similarly, returns to education may be private – that is, accruing to the educated individual only – or they may be social in that they confer benefits to others (e.g. in the form of externalities). A case in point is evidence from rural Ethiopia which has shown the externality effects of education in agriculture when educated farmers raised the productivity of their uneducated neighbours in pursuit of their own economic interests (Weir and Knight 2007).

There is a plethora of estimates of 'earnings functions' estimating the relationship between education and earnings to different levels of education (primary, secondary, higher), different types of education (general versus vocational) and to different subjects (medicine, law, agriculture, humanities, etc.), and these estimates are variously used for policy and evaluation purposes. For instance, while individual rates of return estimates may inform individuals on which types of education and training to get, social rates of return can help policymakers decide the return on various investments that have been or are going to be made.

The focus of most of the economics literature has been on the estimation of economic returns to education. There is a very large body of research that has examined this presumed association between individuals' education and their productivity. Productivity is measured either by a farmer's physical output (such as tonnes of maize) or, in urban settings, by the individual's wages/earnings. The rates of return to education are computed by either the cost–benefit method, where the benefits of an investment such as education are compared to the costs, or by the Mincerian regression method (owing much to the work of Jacob Mincer 1974).The latter method has proved most popular in recent years in being more flexible than the former in controlling for worker characteristics. It is based on using cross-sectional data on a sample of workers of various ages and education levels in a given place and time; for example, in its most simplified form, it involves conducting regression analysis linking individual earnings with schooling and experience. Mincer (1974) showed that the 'return' to schooling is the extra earnings an individual will earn as a result of one extra year of schooling.

Regressions have been fitted on numerous countries, and on average, the return to schooling varies between 0.08 and 0.15. In other words, education substantially increases earnings (an additional year of schooling increases lifetime earnings by between 8 and 15 per cent). If earnings reflect productivity, one can conclude that education improves productivity. This is the human capital interpretation of education. And this is what provides the economic efficiency rationale for investments in education. Psacharopolous (1994) and Psacharopolous and Patrinos (2004), applying Mincer's approach, summarize evidence on the pattern of returns to schooling at various levels of education across the developing world. These estimates have since been updated and the patterns largely remain the same (see Psacharopolous and Patrinos, 2018).

The HCT interpretation of education is not without its critics. There are many challenges to this view: on is the potentially damning critique of 'ability bias', which argues that the 'return' to education is biased due to the fact that more able individuals may earn more as well as be more educated. Therefore, much of their increased earnings are wrongly attributed to education when they should be attributed to their ability which cannot be easily measured and accounted for in these calculations.

Another challenge to HCT has also been posed by the screening or credentialist hypotheses (Spence 1974) that challenge the interpretation that education enhances workers' productivity, arguing that employers may be using education as a way of identifying the most able workers. In this model, employees signal their skills to employers by acquiring certain educational certifications and employers pay higher wages to them because they presume that the proportion of employees with high abilities is higher among the most educated. However, quality empirical evidence, on the balance, has largely overcome most of these criticisms and the broad consensus still holds: education confers large benefits to individuals in the form of increased earnings and these can be seen to be arising due to productivity increases rather than due to any other reason (see, for instance, Boissiere et al. 1985, Card 2001, Hanushek 2003, 2005, Hanushek and Woessmann 2008, 2009, among others).

Scaling the notion of individuals with higher education levels commanding higher earnings (due to greater productivity) to the macro level, one would expect that increasing the average level of education among the workforce would raise the average level of productivity, which will then raise average and total incomes of the country thereby leading to economic growth.

Neoclassical Growth Theories

The neoclassical approaches to economic growth associated with the work of several economists (see below) emphasized the accumulation of capital through investment (financed by saving) as key to growth. The basic tenet of this was that the accumulation of capital promotes more capital-intensive production and a higher level of output per worker. The neoclassical view of growth indicated that as capital is accumulated, each additional unit of capital contributes less than the previous one (notion of diminishing returns). As a result, one would expect developing countries to grow faster compared to more developed countries as they have smaller endowments of capital. Low levels of saving in poor countries were therefore considered a key reason for low growth in these countries. Moreover, while technological progress was not explicitly modelled in earlier theories, it was seen as a key determinant of growth in that it would be through (exogenously determined) technological progress that productivity of all factors that are inputs in production is improved so that greater levels of output may be achieved for a given level of inputs.

Neoclassical growth theories owe much to Denison (1962), who used the 'Solow growth accounting framework' to examine factors contributing to economic growth in the United States over 1910–60. Growth accounting exercises attempt to estimate the effects of contributory factors or 'sources of growth' on the rate of growth of national output (usually measured in terms of the rate of growth of Gross Domestic Product [GDP] or the total market value of a country's output). The role of human capital in determining growth in national income is explored in the literature using 'growth accounting' techniques to carve up growth rates into fractions of growth attributable to education and other inputs. Early growth models (Solow 1956) did not include education or human capital specifically and treated all labour as homogenous regardless of the education levels. The findings of these studies could not explain large proportions of growth, thereby suggesting that much of this unexplained growth was in part due to education, which had not been effectively accounted for.

New Growth Theories

In the new or endogenous growth models, education and training were kept as a central focus and situated within the production process itself rather than as external inputs. Propounded in the late 1980s, 'new growth theories' gave 'learning' a central place in their explanations for economic growth (Romer 1986, Lucas 1988, Barro and Sala-i-Martin 2004). In opposition to Mankiw, Romer and Weil's support for the Solow model (Augmented Solow Model), others have argued that growth should be modelled in an *endogenous* framework (hence often called endogenous growth theories), that is, that investment in human capital, innovation and knowledge are significant contributors to economic growth and not external forces. This theory also focuses on the positive externalities of an educated economy which leads to economic development. These positive externalities mean that if left to individuals (who are presumed to only consider private benefits to education), they would not acquire as much human capital as may be optimal when considering the additional social benefits to others from their education. This provides a basis for the prescription that governments should subsidize/ provide education in the interest of the greater good and economic growth.

Human capital rather than physical capital yields persistent and high per capita income growth primarily because humans, unlike machines, have the capacity to learn. As a result, investments that increase people's skills and productivity rather than yielding diminishing returns are capable of generating constant or even increasing returns. Unlike neoclassical theories where it is not clear why innovation occurs, new growth theories emphasize externalities and the role of spill-overs with the development of technological knowledge. In particular, investments in learning have positive externalities; that is, they improve the productive capacities not only of the person who acquired the education but also of those around him or her because of spill-overs in knowledge and learning.

Testing the Theory: Empirical Evidence on Education and Economic Growth

There is an extensive literature that attempts to determine the extent to which the rate of growth in an economy can be attributed to increases in human capital and specifically to education. Typically, testing the education–growth relationship at the macro level involves estimating Equation 7.1:

$$\Delta Y_j = a + bY_{j,t-1} + cS_{j,t-1} + dZ_{j,t-1} + e_j \ (7.1)$$

where ΔY_j is the economic growth of country j, Y_{t-1} is level of income of country j in the initial time period, S is average years of schooling in country j in initial time period and Z is a vector of variables such as capital and other variables deemed to determine growth in the initial time period, while e is the residual or the unexplained portion. In essence, this model attempts to establish and quantify the relationship between the change in GDP (growth) of a country with factors such as the levels of education of workers within that country and other potential explanatory variables such as the crime rate in a country, existence of democracy and so on.

Models such as in Equation 1 are usually estimated using data on a cross-section of countries spanning a period of time that can range from five to twenty years, depending on the availability of data. Some studies use average schooling levels, while others use different indicators of human capital such as literacy rates in the population and so on. There are other variants to this basic model, but broadly speaking, this is the underlying structure adopted by studies aimed at testing the relationship between education and economic growth. The evidence is mixed on this relationship premised on the endogenous growth theory notion of a positive significant effect of 'schooling' on economic growth. Studies on a range of developing countries by Barro and Sala-i-Martin (2004) and Benhabib and Spiegel (1994) find that schooling (however defined) has an *insignificant* effect on per capita growth, while those by Temple (2001), Gemmell (1996), Krueger and Lindahl (2001), to give just a few examples, find a positive association between education and growth.

One of the main reasons for the disagreement in the results of empirical studies arises from different measures of education and in how human capital is defined. Some studies, for instance, have looked at the impact of the level or stock of education (typically measured by the average years of schooling), while others have used a measure of the flow of investment in education (for instance measured using school enrolment rates). Considerable debate has been generated in empirical analyses. For example, there has been controversy about whether it is *level of years of schooling* (as predicted by several models of endogenous growth) or *change in years of schooling* (as predicted in basic neoclassical frameworks) which is the more important driver of economic growth. Early evidence, such as in Benhabib and Spiegel's (1994) cross-country study, found a positive effect of schooling levels on economic growth, but none of changes in schooling. However,

Temple (1999) shows that the findings of this study are debatable due to data problems. Considerable evidence has also emerged that there was substantial measurement error in the education data (Krueger and Lindahl 2001), and it is well known that measurement error biases results based on the change in schooling variable more. Different studies have used different variables to measure human capital at the primary, secondary or at the tertiary level of education with the result that the varied estimates relate to different levels of education and are hence not directly comparable. For example, junior secondary education may mean something different in India as compared to Ghana and may not contain the same grade groups. Varying dependent variables to measure growth and using different samples and sub-samples of countries also make comparisons arduous.

Rapid economic growth has often been accompanied by educational expansion as seen through the examples of the Asian Tiger economies (although it is worth noting that the causal direction may work the other way, in that more wealth may allow the education system to grow). There are, however, also examples of economic growth accompanied by poor educational expansion. Cases in point are provided by sub-Saharan Africa (e.g. South Africa). There have even been some studies that consistently find a negative association between education and growth (see for instance Patrinos 1994, Mingat and Tan 1996, Pritchett 2001). Arguably, there are several reasons for either a lack of a relationship between educational expansion and economic growth or indeed the finding of a negative relationship in some economies (e.g. failure to account for the costs of education and the failure to account for the quality of education). Another explanation is related to misguided policies that emphasize higher education (with large shares of educational budgets devoted to this sector as opposed to the building blocks at the primary and secondary levels) with a resultant elitist education system of poor quality education that is also inequitable (Bennell 1996a).

Quality of Education and Economic Growth

The most commonly used measure of human capital in empirical growth analyses has been the level of school attainment in a country. This measure of human capital, however, is based on the strong presumption that learning in one year of schooling is the same across all countries – an individual acquiring one year of schooling in Peru, for instance, learns the same as one in the United States. This is obviously too strong an assumption to hold in reality. Moreover, there is also an implicit assumption that human capital is only developed through formal schooling. However, this is contrary to the evidence (especially from the developing world) that strongly indicates that learning via families, peers and so on also contributes to the development of human capital. The former assumption has also been tested in micro-analyses of Mincerian Returns to Schooling (discussed in Measurement and Indicators 3), where it has been shown that the returns to 'quality' schooling (measured using cognitive test scores) are at least as high as the returns to the 'quantity' of schooling (typically measured using years of schooling completed by an individual), if not higher. Some of the most renowned studies indicating this relationship between human capital (using the newer definition based on quality) and individual earnings are summarized in Hanushek and Woessmann (2011), who argue that the available estimates of returns to cognitive skills indicate strong returns to schooling quality especially in developing countries and the large magnitude of the effects show that educational quality concerns are not only very real for developing countries but that they cannot and should not be ignored in empirical estimates.

Much in line with the micro literature, while early macro studies of growth empirics also focused on the 'quantity of schooling' as measures of human capital, more recent studies place a stronger emphasis on the 'quality of schooling' acquired. As a result, there has been a clear move in empirical literature from using enrolment rates and years of schooling to measure human capital to the use of international test scores to arrive at more convincing measures of learning. To measure human capital more accurately, Hanushek and Kimko (2000) introduced mathematics and science skills from international assessments into growth regressions. This pioneering study found that the 'quality' of schooling was significantly positively related to economic growth in the countries studied. More specifically, the authors find that adding schooling quality to the base specification (conditioning only on initial income and school quality) boosts the explained variation in GDP per capita among the thirty-one countries in their sample from 33 per cent to 73 per cent. Moreover, the effect of schooling 'quantity' is greatly reduced and largely insignificant.

This approach of controlling for schooling quality in growth regressions has been extended by a number of authors (discussed below), and the evidence indicates that economic growth is very closely related to the cognitive skills of the population. Broadly speaking, empirical literature based on this reinterpretation of human capital suggests that the view that schooling quality is a better measure of learning dramatically alters the role of education in the process of economic development. Hanushek and Kimko's (2000) findings are robust to numerous concerns, including the possibility that schooling might be the actual cause of growth, but may reflect attributes beneficial to growth or that the observed relationship between schooling and growth is indicative of reverse causality – better student performance is the result rather than the cause of growth. Appleton, Atherton and Bleany (2008) also corroborate this evidence showing the education quality–growth relationship to be robust to controls for reverse causality. It would appear that ignoring quality differences in schooling very significantly misses the real importance of education for economic growth. This issue of quality is even more crucial considering the rapid increase in private provision of education in some developing countries. In a number of countries children studying in private schools have increased access to education, at a low cost, and some studies report that private schools provide education more efficiently than government schools (see Kingdon 1996 for India and Aslam 2009 for Pakistan). For example, extensive work by Tooley and others (2007, 2011, etc.) in India and various African states has illustrated that large proportions of children in the developing world are being educated by low-cost private schools that seem to yield better results than their state counterparts despite much greater teacher salary expenditures in the latter. Given this, and the chronic frustration with the efforts to improve state-run schools, Tooley recommends policymakers to shift their focus to improving private schools and expanding access to them. However, it must also be highlighted that while research has shown the existence of a private school advantage, given the poor levels of achievement in both state and private school sectors, a marginal advantage in private schools will not address the equity issues related to the inadequate education received by many of the developing world's children.

Hanushek and Woessmann's (2008) study extends Hanushek and Kimko's (2000) analysis and provides new evidence using more recent data, over a longer time period (1960–2000) and extends the sample from thirty-one to fifty countries. Using the mean of maths and science scores to measure 'schooling quality' differences across countries, the authors find that cognitive skills largely acquired through formal schooling are the key drivers of economic growth. The authors also find that the effect of schooling quality is twice as large in low-income (below-median income) countries as compared to the high-income countries. The authors conclude that their evidence provides strong reasons to believe that the quality of education, linked to particular subject specialisms, is causally related to economic outcomes. Recent research has also shown that skills, as measured by ability and learning outcomes, do matter for earnings attainment. Overall, it has been estimated that a 1 standard deviation increase in school performance results in between 12 and 15 per cent increase in earnings (Patrinos and Psacharopoulos 2020, 62). The evidence would suggest that in high-income and middle-income countries, the highest returns exist at the upper ends of the wage distribution; however, in lower income countries, the returns appear to be higher at lower ends of the wage distribution (ibid.). A persistent concern in developing economies appears to be the relatively low rate of return to primary education particularly for females. The study by Patrinos and Psacharopoulos (2020) concludes that the global average rate of return to schooling is 9 per cent and whilst returns on investment in education provide useful indicators for the private returns to education, more research is still needed in estimating the social returns to education and this area remains a research priority. It must also be noted that quality learning may come from formal schooling, from parents, peers or neighbourhoods. Regardless of the source, a more skilled workforce is seen to result in stronger economic growth.

However, the contention that the quality of schooling determines a nation's rate of economic growth has been challenged by Breton (2011). The author claims to demonstrate that Hanushek and Woessmann's (2008) statistical results are 'invalid' due to misspecification of the growth model and because the test score data used is not representative of the workforce during the growth period. When the author statistically corrects for these flaws, the evidence appears to contradict Hanushek and Woessmann's findings:

> [The] paper shows that when the effect of either international test scores or years of schooling attainment is estimated with appropriate data in a properly specified model, either measure can explain cross-country differences in national income … average schooling attainment explains a larger share of income variation across countries and has greater statistical significance than average test scores.
>
> (p. 766)

Moreover, criticism is extended to the assumption that school quality can be appropriately proxied by test scores. The key problem according to Breton is that the presumption that average scores proxy for human capital confuses the precision of a standardized test with its accuracy as a measure of a nation's human capital. Average test scores at ages nine to fifteen (as used by Hanushek and Woessmann 2008) are not appropriate proxies for human capital in high- or low-income countries. In high-income countries, a large share of education arguably occurs at university level, where it creates human capital not measured in tests aimed at nine to fifteen-year-olds. In low-income countries, on the other hand, many students leave school before age fifteen. The author also cites evidence that strongly indicates that the home environment seems to matter more than school quality in determining student achievement and the existence of large private tutoring expenditures in some countries and so on, all of which arguably imply that test scores do not really measure school quality.

The empirical evidence, therefore, is somewhat mixed. Moreover, in recent years, some authors have called for placing a stronger emphasis on estimating the 'total macro return to education' by accounting for the non-market externalities and indirect effects of schooling in determining the education–growth relationship. In this regard, the study by McMahon (2010) contributes to the literature by attempting to provide a comprehensive estimate of the total macro return to education, taking into account non-market externalities and indirect effects of schooling. His findings suggest that conventional methods underestimate the true economic return to schooling and the evidence strengthens the prescription for more investment in schooling.

Conclusion

Human capital is increasingly seen as the main engine of economic growth. While human capital encapsulates health, education and other forms of social capital, the role of education has been viewed as one of the strongest in determining both individual and national outcomes. The relationship between education and economic growth has therefore been well debated and studied in both the theoretical as well as the empirical literature. In particular, new growth theories bring education firmly back into the driving seat of growth by reducing the limitations of neoclassical growth theories specifically by allowing increasing returns to scale via endogenous technological change essentially linked to human capital accumulation. The empirical evidence has been more difficult to interpret. One of the key reasons for this has been the fact that empirical testing of the relationship between schooling and economic development has faced numerous methodological challenges. These range from which measures to use for growth, what sample sizes of countries are analysed and most critically how to measure human capital and specifically education. Broadly speaking, very stringent and carefully conducted studies find powerful direct effects of education on economic growth. Krueger and Lindahl (2001) and Temple (2001) find the relationship to be stronger when externalities are specifically accounted for and largely indicate that the relationship is clearer and stronger when schooling quality rather than schooling quantity alone is considered. As a result, the last decade or so specifically has seen strong emphasis on the importance of human capital on economic growth and the recognition that the key determinant of differences in living standards among countries is human rather than physical capital.

Questions for Discussion

1. Why does education not always bring about economic growth?
2. Does human capital theory provide a strong basis for the education–growth relationship? Why?
3. Why has it proved so difficult to empirically estimate the education–growth relationship?
4. Can you think of the potential challenges to estimating rates of returns to education in micro analyses?
5. What are the specific 'external' benefits of education which may cause the social benefit/return to exceed the private benefit/return?
6. Which of the education externalities would you expect to be most significant in terms of producing economic growth?
7. Which, in your view, is the best measure of school quality? Why?

Further Reading

Psacharopolous, G. and Patrinos, H. (2004), 'Returns to Investment in Education: A Further Update', *Education Economics*, 12(2): 111–34.
Hanushek, E. A. and Woessmann, L. (2011), 'The Economics of International Differences in Educational Achievement', in Hanushek, E. A. Machin, S. and L. Woessmann (eds), *Handbook of the Economics of Education*, Vol. 3, Amsterdam: North Holland

Useful Websites

The World Bank (includes Edstats): http://www.worldbank.org
OECD: http://www.oecd.org/
UNESCO (includes UIS data): http://www.unesco.org/education
Centre for Economics of Education ((LSE/IOE/IFS): http://cee.lse.ac.uk
National Bureau for Economic Research: http://www.nber.org
Gapminder: http://www.gapminder.org/

8

Addressing Intersecting Inequalities in Education

Elaine Unterhalter

Introduction

Participation at all levels of education has increased enormously over the past twenty years, but this trend has not been uniform or equitable.

The Global Education Monitoring (GEM) Report noted 258 million children out of school in 2020, with 773 million youth and adults not able to read. Exclusion was most pronounced for the poor and children with disabilities (UNESCO 2020a). Assessments of some economic effects of Covid-19 at the end of 2020 indicated 24 million students from pre-primary to tertiary education in 180 countries were at risk of not returning to education (UNESCO 2020b). Although since 2000 there has been a dramatic expansion in education provision around the world, with growing proportions completing primary school, making a transition to secondary school and increasing numbers entering tertiary education, this expansion has not been equitable. Some social groups and regions have benefited, while others have been excluded or received very inadequate provision. Inequality has been as much a thread in the development of EFA, as government commitment or aid. Inequalities in education connect with other forms of social injustice. Understanding how and why these processes come about is an important aspect of working towards change.

Inequality, Social Division and Intersectionality

Forms of social division can generate inequalities. Often inequalities can amplify each other, and this process is one feature of what is termed intersectionality, associated with the work of Kimberlé Crenshaw (1989, 1991). Crenshaw argued, in the context of the United States, that African American women needed to take account politically and analytically of the ways in which they were subordinated as women, as Black women, and as Black women workers. Intersectionality investigates 'the complex, cumulative way in which the effects of multiple forms of discrimination… combine, overlap, or intersect especially in the experiences of marginalized individuals or groups' (Crenshaw 1989). This insight has had enormous influence on how inequalities are understood, highlighting the complex processes needed to bring change.

Inequality in educational, political, economic and social relationships presents complex definitional challenges. Every individual in the world is similar and different to others. But some similarities and differences, and the ways they interconnect, are given significance at particular times and places, influencing educational experiences and outcomes. When my children were in primary school in London in the 1990s, their classmates were all shapes and sizes: Some very tall, some short. Some were third generation living in the neighbourhood; some just arrived as immigrant families. Some, like my children, had one parent from the UK and one not. In their classrooms, as they learned to read, physical size was not a significant social division. Whether or not a family could use English was, and whether or not they had spare income to spend on additional activities outside school to enhance knowledge of English. These connected forms of social division affected how much additional support the teacher needed to provide when she organized reading practice. The way in which the local authority funded the school to provide language support was also significant. Ten years later at university, my children's fellow undergraduates were once again of different sizes, but there was less socio-economic mix. Few self-defined as from BAME (Black, Asian and Minority Ethnicity) backgrounds. At that time this was not a major issue in universities' thinking about policy and practice. These experiences are typical of the demographic of participation in different phases of education in the UK in the early twenty-first century, where size is not a marker of social division, but language, socio-economic status, race and ethnicity can be, eliciting particular forms of education response.

By contrast in Rwanda, at the time of the 1994 genocide, size was often taken to be a marker of being Tutsi, a member of a stigmatized group. Regardless of community stature, level of education and socio-economic position, size could lead to ostracism, attack and murder, even for children at school. International and local political processes meant limited and inadequate actions were taken to protect people. Thus social divisions may have their origins in biology, how one looks, or in social relations, in the language one speaks, which faith one practices or whose political views one supports. Sometimes intersecting social divisions, or social and biological differences intensify injustices, and sometimes one marker of social division is sufficient to result in exclusion. Whether or not these markers result in inequality, and what the educational consequences of these inequalities are, depends on historical conditions, the balance between structures and institutions that reproduce or try to change inequalities, and how intersectionality and agency work.

Five Forms of Inequality

There are various ways of grouping inequalities to distinguish how they operate in particular contexts. Here are five ways for thinking about inequality, each with different dynamics within education.

Firstly, we can think about inequalities in relation to distributional arrangements, which are sometimes described as vertical inequalities. These determine how much of a particular resource – wealth, income, food or years in schooling – a person has. The social relationships in a country associated with laws, policies, practices and everyday interactions may allow distributional inequalities to persist or may work to ameliorate some features. Forms of redistributive taxation, social protection like basic income grants or free education are common areas of policy engagement to address vertical inequalities. Vertical inequalities are generally analysed as existing between politically, economically and socially defined groups, and their implication in the forms of distribution of wealth or education has long histories (Piketty 2019). The formation of these groups is associated with the ownership, distribution and consumption of resources, but the groups are often delineated as if the difference between groups was natural, for example based on biology for men and women, or on geography, for those living in rural or urban areas, or on employment in different kinds of occupation for households delineated by socio-economic status (SES). Charting vertical inequalities allows us to note the unequal distribution of opportunities for access to and completion of particular levels of formal education for different groups delineated in this way. The World Inequality Database in Education (WIDE) allows us to see this by country for different groups of children differentiated by gender, socio-economic status (SES) and rural or urban location (https://www.education-inequalities.org/).

Vertical inequalities can be associated with an individual's assets, income, control over natural resources like land, or forms of political, social and economic power. We can term this an inequality of what amount. The World Inequality Report (Alvaredo et al. 2018) drew on national income and wealth accounts, estimates of offshore wealth, household income and wealth surveys, fiscal and inheritance data. It showed income inequality varied across regions, with the share of total national income accounted for by the top 10 per cent of earners lowest in Europe (37%) and highest in Africa, India, Brazil and the Middle East (55–61%). The growth of inequalities within countries, they argue, is linked with education distribution, taxation regimes and approaches to addressing poverty. There are a number of ways of ranking how unequal this distribution within countries is, with the Gini coefficient and the Palma index (see Measurement and Indicators 4) being the most well known.

Secondly, we can think of inequalities as associated not so much with how much is distributed but the social and cultural construction of relationships between groups, which may entail inclusion and tolerance or exclusion, discrimination, criminalization and, in extreme cases, genocide. Frances Stewart has termed this horizontal inequality, noting the deep-seated hatreds and

Measurement and Indicators 4: Measures of Income Inequality and Their Adaptation for Education

The Gini coefficient measures inequality in distribution, and is used in measuring levels of income. A Gini coefficient of zero expresses perfect equality, where all values are the same, for example, where everyone has the same income. A Gini coefficient of one (or 100%) expresses maximal inequality among values (e.g. for a large number of people where only one person has all the income or consumption and all others have none, the Gini coefficient will be nearly one). World Bank estimates put South Africa, Namibia and Haiti as the countries with the highest Gini index. Thomas, Wang and Fan (2001 used data on education attainment in eighty-five countries between 1960 and 1990 to develop an education Gini looking at relative distribution. A wider range of data and countries drawing on five-yearly data of Gini coefficients of education for 146 countries for the years 1950–2010 is provided by Ziesemer (2016).

The Palma index is the ratio of the richest 10 per cent of the population's share of gross national income divided by the poorest 40 per cent's share. Using the Palma index allows us to see better some of the effects in changes in the share of national income of the poorest or richest and develop an understanding of some of diversity in terms of distributional outcomes (Palma and Stiglitz 2016). Palma (2019) looks at what causes growth in the shares of distributional inequality for the rich. This includes the kinds of education received.

relationships infused with fear which shape treatment of groups, constructed on ideas about race, ethnicity, religion or gender (Stewart 2002, 2008, 2009). This form of inequality can draw on deeply held animosities by dominant groups with regard to the religious beliefs, cultural or political values, and aspirations of a stigmatized group. Views about bodies, feelings and emotions are often invoked in expressions and activities linked to this form of inequality. We can think of this form of inequality as primarily concerned with personal features, and thus it is an inequality of whom. Horizontal inequalities may account for some of the ways particular groups of children are treated in school by peers or teachers. Often these inequalities are so deeply woven into the norms of an institution that that they need very concerted attention to unpick how ideas about deficit or worth operate. For example, what times meetings take place, how many lavatories are available, who can travel safely – all have considerable bearing on the management of work in a school, but exclusions associated with these processes may be so normalized that horizontal inequalities linked with them are not noted. Meetings that are held very early or very late may exclude those who have to take care of young children. Limited sanitation or safe access to an educational site limits participation of some. Addressing inequality of whom might require attention to both the organization of education institutions and the attitudes of those within.

Thirdly, we can think of inequalities as associated with unequal processes. Amartya Sen (1999), in formulating the capability approach, highlights how inequality is a feature not only what is distributed but whether the social conditions are arranged to produce good levels of quality of life, and whether the processes of distribution are considered fair by those who are involved. Fair processes might entail open scrutiny and public deliberation about distribution, working out how to take account of a plurality of views, and understand intrinsic and instrumental values of education. For example there is a difference between two teenage girls who do badly in their school-leaving examination. One attended a well-resourced school but chose to spend time going out to enjoy music and time with friends. One attended a very well-resourced school, had heavy duties of work looking after younger siblings at home and, although she wished to study, had little time to do so. If we evaluate these as the same outcome (or functioning), we fail to understand the different and unequal processes involved. Many commentators on Sen's work build on his insight that equality demands not just equal amounts of income or education but equal distribution of capabilities, that is opportunity and potential, what one has reason to value. These capabilities need to be taken into account when evaluating functionings, that is achieved states, such as completing a level of education. The capability of a person 'reflects the alternative combinations of functionings the person can achieve and from which he or she can choose' (Sen 1992, 39) The capability approach entails evaluating individual levels of achieved well - being, freedoms to achieve well - being, the social arrangements, institutions and procedures for change which may or may not support these processes (Sen 1999, Nussbaum 2011, Robeyns 2017). Process inequalities can affect the selection of relevant capabilities for distribution (Robeyns 2017), the reasoning and discussion processes entailed in choice formation (Watene 2016, Meeks 2018), and the epistemic forms given legitimacy in evaluating social arrangements (Walker 2019). Process inequalities are also evident with regard to which people are able to exercise agency in relation to choice (Crocker 2008, Drydyk and Keleher 2018, Clark, Biggeri and Frediani 2019). We can think about this form of process inequality as comprising an inequality of *how*. This has bearing on how education policy is made, how practice is conducted. Unequal processes may be evident in how academic or vocational tracks through school are valued, how particular subjects or knowledge forms confer prestige and wealth on those who study, teach and excel in examination, while other subjects attract the opposite. We can remark on process inequalities in how decisions are taken regarding funding for schools and the pay of teachers. Process inequalities would be evident if a high growth sector of the economy gets inordinately more investment for teaching and research, linked to the lobbying by an inner circle of political advisors, compared to softer areas, concerned with education for children with disabilities, or mental health, whose advocates are not so influential. Education research and the evaluation of evidence are a key element in either the perpetuation of process inequalities or attempts to change these.

Fourthly, we can think of inequalities as intersectional. Intersectionality is widely used as an analytic tool for institutions and organizations to address inclusion, to consider fairness and to think about equity (Collins and Bilge 2016: 2–3), highlighting that social inequality entails an exercise of power drawing on axes of social division, for example race, class, gender, sexuality, disability and age. These operate not as discrete entities, but work together. These regimes of inequality, their overlaps and the ideas that make them appear justified, require continued processes of critical reflection to understand how they work and how best to address change. Intersectionality thus operates as a problem-solving tool, helping us to understand how different forms of inequality connect, for example inequality of what amount, working with inequality of whom and inequality of how. It thus considers how power operates interpersonally, and between institutional and discursive forms. McCall (2005) outlines three approaches to intersectionality: A first approach is intra-categorical, which considers, for example, how race and gender inequalities may augment each other. This is most evident in work on distribution and considers inequality of what amount. A second approach is inter-categorical which looks at the way power is structured to develop inequalities. This combines looking at vertical, horizontal and process inequalities. A third approach is anti-categorical, highlighting how sometimes the very discourses used to describe inequalities inscribe particular assumptions of deficit or exclusion. Naming is a particular form of inequality of how.

Concepts 3: Intersectionality, Gender and Education

Unterhalter, Robinson and Ron Balsera (2020) adapt McCall's three categories of intersectionality:

a) **A description of overlapping differences within groups defined by gender**: This requires analysis of differences and similarities in education within broad formations of social division. For example, noting that education experiences and relationships are different for girls and boys from racialized, classed or ethnicized groups in particular countries, depending on history, policy and practice. This entails refinements in looking at inequality of what amount.

b) **An analysis of interlocking institutions and formations of gendered power and powerlessness**: This requires analysis of reasons why structures which produce vertical, horizontal and process inequalities in education associated with gender exist and persist and are maintained by laws, economic, political and social relationships in spite of laws on education for all, because everyday political/economic and sociocultural relationships undermine this policy in practice. This entails understanding inequality of what, whom and how.

c) **A critique of existing descriptions of gender, race, ethnicity or disability**. This form of intersectionality questions the ways in which social categories such as gender, ethnicity, disability and class are used in education research, policy and practice. Who uses these categories for which audiences, and what do they signal? This is a form of inequality of how.

Fifthly, we can think about inequalities as simple or complex. The authors of the UNDP Human Development Report UNDP (2019, 30–51) distinguish between basic capabilities needed for protecting against extreme deprivation and enhanced capabilities associated with agency, and the capacity to make choices about work, affiliation or mobility. This distinction between forms of capabilities is made in slightly different terms in work by

Sen (1992) and Nussbaum (2001) in formulating key ideas in the capability approach. In reviews of inequalities in human development made before the Covid pandemic, UNDP (2019) noted there had been a reduction in inequality of distribution of basic capabilities, such as access to primary education, minimal health services and simple technologies. But there has been a widening of inequalities in relation to enhanced capabilities, such as quality education, enhanced health care provision and high-speed internet. Over a lifetime the lack of complex capabilities could establish enhanced inequality. This analysis suggests that inequality in one domain may co-exist with forms of equality in another, and that much refinement and nuance is needed for thinking about equality and equity.

Inequalities in Education

These different ways of thinking about inequality are evident in research on education and international development. More attention has been given to vertical inequalities, that is, how much schooling people receive. How particular groups do not access progress of complete schooling is a regular theme in UNESCO's annual Global Education Monitor, where groups are identified by gender, location and SES. Most SDG4 indicators assess vertical inequalities when considering whether targets have been reached (Wulff 2020b, Unterhalter 2019a) In high-income countries discussions of class construction and the reproduction of class inequalities through education look at inequalities of *what amount*, of *whom* and of *how* (Skeggs 2004, Breen et al. 2010, Mullen 2010, Stevens and Dworkin 2019) associated with how race, class and gender intersect in these processes (Brah and Phoenix 2013). Analysis of the intersection of multi-dimensional inequalities in education has been done for some developing countries (e.g., Choudhary Muthukkumaran and Singh 2019, Hunter 2019, Mpofu and Ndlovu-Gatsheni 2020) but has only recently been included in mainstream discussion of EFA, such as the 2020 GEM Report.

Inequalities in education can be described and assessed in several ways. One focuses on inequalities of opportunities, that is, whether certain groups or individuals are subject to discrimination and subordination in access to or participation in education. Inequalities in opportunity may be the result of vertical, horizontal, process or intersectional inequalities, and may be the outcome of a denial of basic or complex capabilities. A second approach focuses on inequalities in experiences associated with the process of education, such as pedagogic interactions and features of quality. This kind of analysis tends to be associated with accounts of horizontal or process inequalities. A third concerns inequalities of outcomes, that is, whether with the same experience of schooling, some groups or individuals attain less well, than others, or experience exclusion, prejudice and degradation in the work they undertake or in their social, cultural or political engagement. Analysis of this links to all the five ways of thinking of inequality detailed above. The capability approach, as outlined by Sen (1992, 1999) and Nussbaum (2001, 2011), prompts investigation into the connection between opportunities, outcomes, processes and agency in education (Robeyns (2017).

A further facet of inequalities in education concerns the inequalities between different countries or regions with regard to the levels of education of the population, the efficiency and equity of the education system in providing schooling and the ways in which political economy forms unequal education relationships associated with uneven investments in research, innovation and forms of epistemic injustice and exclusion (UNESCO 2020a, UNDP 2019). Forms of global inequality may undermine educational equality. Thus a country may expand EFA and address national educational inequalities, but still find itself tied into global systems associated with exploitative labour, high levels of interest charged on the finances needed for social protection of the poor and environmental fragility. These systemic inequalities between regions or locales might also be found within a country.

It is useful to think about inequalities in education and the forms these take drawing on three metaphors I have used in work examining aspects of gender and poverty (Unterhalter 2012b). Inequality may be judged in terms of crossing a particular line: for example, completing a primary cycle of schooling, reading up to a certain level or earning a certain wage. Inequality in educational opportunities might describe those groups based, for example, on race, gender or ethnicity who do or do not cross this line of opportunities, experiences or outcomes.

Generally, in this analysis these groups are delineated descriptively, drawing on a form of analysis that I have termed gender as a noun (Unterhalter 2007a). This form of descriptive categorization can be extended to delineate groups noted in terms of differences of race, ethnicity or SES. From this perspective the site of the inequality is assumed to be given by some feature of biology – for example female sexual organs, or skin colour – or a descriptive feature of ethnic belonging – for example being born Jewish or Kurdish. It may also be associated with the locale in which one lives, for example a suburb or a slum.

Countries or regions can be grouped descriptively in this form, for example as low, middle or high income, which is then taken to be explanatory of all features of why they may not meet particular education or health targets. They can then be compared in terms of the proportion of their population that do or do not have certain levels of education, and this can be read together with interpretations of economic growth or political integration or assessments of health. The EFA Global Monitoring Report reviews demographic information to show which groups fall below a line of completing primary or junior secondary school. This information can be read together with certain health or economic outcomes to delineate countries in terms of human development. The implication from this meaning of education opportunity is that taking all groups over a particular line of educational sufficiency, for example completing a primary or secondary cycle, having knowledge and skill in particular areas of learning outcomes, will help secure more equality and wellbeing with regard to economic distribution or levels of health. But the critique in UNDP (2019) points out that looking at these processes as averages masks some of the forms of inequalities.

This view of equality as crossing a line can be read as applying to groups who experience vertical inequalities associated with socio-economic status. It tends to treat horizontal inequalities, of race, ethnicity or gender, as though they were vertical inequalities. The challenge for groups who might define themselves in terms of gender, ethnicity or race is to cross over the line of educational sufficiency associated for example with years in school or attaining a particular learning outcome. This approach does not suggest any other remedy, for example, with regard to how the stigmatized group is regarded or understood, whether they are protected by anti-discrimination laws, whether tolerance and inclusion is practised or how the actions of individuals from that group are supported or undermined.

A second metaphor to think about inequalities is as a net of inter-meshing structures of exclusion. With regard to gender, I have associated this approach with what I term gender as an adjective (Unterhalter 2007a). This looks at process and intersectional inequalities and the ways they are formed by particular institutional arrangements. An ensemble of institutions and practices bears on shaping the distinction between basic and enhanced capabilities. Features of gendered power and the discursive and structural inscribing of inequalities may be associated with how ideas about race, class, ethnicity, nationality or disability operate. This perspective entails documenting the unequal allocation of resources between men and women, or different racialized groups, the ways in which institutions, such as laws, regulations and education systems, may inscribe and sustain inequalities. It considers how these processes diffuse though culture and language, into the private sphere and the sexual division of labour pervading household decisions over resources, time and esteem. Within education, gendered or racialized power shapes how aims of education are formulated, curricula developed, textbooks written, teachers trained, schools organized and evaluated.

In this analysis school might mirror and reproduce forms of discrimination found in the wider society. The net of educational inequalities stretches into many experiences of provision. In some societies curriculum may confirm a racist reading of history and textbooks convey sexist portrayals of women. In some contexts the languages some children speak at home are denigrated at school, and children who do not have mainstream language backgrounds are not well supported to learn a majority language. No one celebrates or teaches their minority language. Studies of these processes may highlight how teachers articulate assumptions that poor children are stupid, not motivated to learn, justifying why they ignore particular learning needs. Another feature of this net of educational inequalities concerns the arrangements for distributing money and expertise to schools with the result that by accident or design more money and other resource goes to children with higher status, rather than greatest need. Children whose families do not conform to social norms, through choice, or because of disasters, such as war, famine or lack of work, fall outside this system and have minimal provision or highly restricted access. Children whose families are nomads, refugees or stateless experience not only the difficulties of multiple migrations but also the discrimination of education systems that do not understand, which fail to address the inequalities they suffer (Dyer 2006, 2014, Fiddian-Qasmiyeh 2015, Gerrard and Sriprakash 2019). Children from many different backgrounds live as street children, some having come to towns looking for schooling or money, some having been abandoned or run away from difficult family experiences (van Blerk 2012, Anangisye 2020). The formal institutions of the school which assume an established family and its rhythms of interaction do not always address the needs of these children. Thus assumptions and institutional conditions all weave together, and trap the educational aspirations of children who come from groups which suffer exclusion and discrimination. The net of deeply ingrained practices do not make it easy for them to make progress in their learning, even when they have opportunities to enter school. Moreover the net of discrimination associated with educational opportunities is often replicated with regard to education outcomes. Children who are most discriminated against at school often attain at the lowest level. This becomes a vicious cycle of low school achievement linked with exclusions from adequately paying work and centres of decision making, in turn cementing a culture of denigration of the views of the less educated. This can be accompanied by a denial to these groups of adequate health care, nutrition or economic resources. Vertical inequalities associated with distribution, horizontal inequalities associated with esteem and process inequalities can intertwine to make the net a trap, from which it is difficult to escape.

A third metaphor to think about inequalities in education is as a fuel. When looking at gender, I have linked this with what I have termed gender as a verb, that is the way people 'do' gender in enacting changing forms of identity and belonging, which may differ, say between the public and the private realm, or in formal and informal educational spaces or in different regional contexts, associated or disassociated from a politics of sexuality (Unterhalter 2007a). Performing gender can be similar to enacting class, race or ethnicity. For all of these aspects of social division some forms of enactment might be dangerous and invite vicious retributions, while others might enable the boundaries to be pushed and injustices to be challenged. Fuel powers movement and change. Some social activists, keenly aware of the inequalities in education in developing countries, have analysed them and worked for transformation. Social activists in India in the 1970s drew on Freirean ideas about adult education, and linked campaigns demanding expansion of education with social activism to transform the interconnected inequalities of the society. 'Empowerment' was the term they used for this action which linked feminist and other activists to confront not just patriarchy but also inequalities of class, race, ethnicity, caste and religion. This built an integrated and connected social activism which challenged the ideologies that justified social inequality, and the material patterns of distribution and control. The notion of empowerment was a form of educational fuel to change unequal opportunities and outcomes and urged a transformation of institutions, structures and organizations, such as the family, the state, markets, education and the media (Batliwala 2007, 558–60). The meaning of the word 'empowerment' in education has changed over the decades and can be associated with mere token changes, although it has also been documented linked to expanding opportunities and agency (Unterhalter 2019b, Murphy-Graham and Lloyd 2016, Williamson and Boughton 2020).

Sometimes fuel, if used in excess or in some kind of combination, can be poisonous. Actions by social activists confronting education inequalities sometimes had unintended harmful consequences for those advocating them, while failing to change some of the existing structures of power. Thus, for example, social activists who campaigned for indigenous language rights, to use schools to protect cultures and social relations threatened by changes in political economy, found that fluency in indigenous languages could not secure protection against forces that expropriated land or advocated a different political vision (Aikman 2012). Feminist education activists who raised issues about gender inequalities sometimes found themselves marginalized in organizations and the issues they put on the table ridiculed (Morley 2011). It has often been difficult for the regions or countries who have suffered the most from education and other inequalities to gain access to centres of power concerning education policymaking; decisions regarding the distribution of resources; and evaluations of curriculum, pedagogy and management that bear on education opportunities and outcomes. For example, there is an under-representation of southern scholarship or communities of research and practice in global education policy and planning, and the approaches many governments take (Connell 2013, Walker and Martinez-Vargas 2020).

From the perspective of seeing inequalities as a fuel, sometimes connections are made between social activism to challenge the links between horizontal and vertical inequalities, but sometimes the injustices associated with horizontal inequalities might trump those linked with vertical inequalities. Thus action for change might be taken by those who are members of a stigmatized group, regardless of whether they come from higher or lower classes in that group and do or do not have other options. A positive example of this social activism drawing on identities formed through horizontal inequalities might be a faith-based group, with some highly educated members engaged in teaching street children and campaigning against poverty. A negative example of this social activism would be terrorist crime that draws on the experiences of injustice of particular groups to organize schools and incite violence and hatred against others (Davies 2014).

It can be seen that inequalities in education are multi-dimensional. They are to be understood and addressed through evaluating social contexts inside and outside school, opportunities, agency and outcome. Data from different approaches to assessing children's learning in South Africa show that children who continue to attend the schools that were discriminated against under the apartheid era, and come from the poorest socio-economic groups, continue, twenty years later, not to learn well, while children from higher socio-economic quintiles, who attend schools that were functional under apartheid, learn well (Spaull 2013). Schools, because of location, the fragility of parents' livelihoods, forms of poverty and the unevenness of inputs, reflect the inequalities in the society (Allais, Cooper and Shalem 2019). The more socially distant a particular group is from centres of power, the harder it is for children from that group to do well in relation to formal assessments of learning. This does not mean that children from that group do not value attending school.

Children living with HIV, some of whom find it very hard to concentrate at school, and who may face ostracism and bullying, told researchers that attending school was an important aspiration (Campbell et al. 2010). Data collected from children out of school during Covid-19 in Uganda documented how eager they were to return to studies, to take examinations and to reconnect with friends, as the isolation had been felt most profoundly by girls kept at home (Parkes, Datzberger et al. 2020). While nets of inequalities in the wider society can reproduce in schools, thinking about inequality as fuel can help us understand some of the commitment of children to participate in education, even when this is not always easy or comfortable.

Research has recently begun to document how violence is a feature of inequalities associated with schooling, particularly school-related gender-based violence (SRGBV) which has started to attract scholarly attention (Parkes 2015) and policy and practitioner engagement (Postmus and Davis 2014, UNGEI 2014, Parkes et al. 2020). This violence takes the form of corporal punishment, bullying, sexual harassment and assault. High stakes testing and pressures associated with enhancing the quality of education can exacerbate this (Vanner 2018). While much more work is needed to understand which structural and symbolic dimensions of inequality drive this process, and how the inequalities associated with gender might connect with other vertical and horizontal inequalities to legitimate the perpetration of this violence, these features of inequality have been noted across countries (Parkes and Unterhalter 2015) and detailed work to build coalitions to address this has been initiated in partnerships between UN organizations, governments, teacher unions and other education actors (UN Women 2016, Parkes et al. 2020).

Equality, Equity and Quality in Education: Strategies to Address Inequality

Strategies to address inequalities in education have been developed by governments, multi-lateral organizations, the non-state sector, informal local groups, families and households. Some of these focus on vertical inequality and getting particular groups across a line signified by years in school, literacy or numeracy attainment, or passing a particular examination. A few consider the complex interrelationships that make inequality a net or a fuel. There has been some debate as to whether what is to be aimed for in thinking about educational inequalities is equality or equity. A focus on equality raises the issue outlined in Amartya Sen's famous question (Sen 1993) – equality of what? Does equality mean equality of inputs – such as school income per pupil, time on task in school, levels of teachers' training or access to school? Equal amount of inputs fails to take account of the diversity of people and the historical contexts in which they receive schooling. Equality of outputs is also inappropriate for assessing education, as not all children will reach the same level of learning at the same time. This has led many commentators to formulate an approach to addressing inequalities in terms of equity, which carries concerns with addressing fairness, different needs and forms of redress (Unterhalter 2009, McCowan 2016, Carney and Schweisfurth 2018). The idea of equity attends to some of the complexities of different forms of inequality. Policy documents from UNESCO also stress inclusion, and SDG 4 places emphasis on *No child left behind.*

Free primary education (FPE) has been a major strategy in virtually every country in the world to expand access and support children to stay at school. Legislation on free primary education has been accompanied everywhere with a huge surge in demand for schooling. When resources are stretched so that quality does not accompany universal access, highly stratified systems can emerge. Under these conditions schools may impose local charges or parents seek additional private support for children to learn. While free primary education has been a firm commitment of many governments, revenues for free secondary school have not been as easy to assemble, and in many poor countries secondary schools differ depending on the income of families. Conditional and unconditional cash transfers, which give money directly to poor families to incentivize their children staying in school, have been widely used in Latin America and Africa and have generally been positively evaluated with regard to access to school, and supporting learning (Fiszbein et al. 2009), although Levy and Schady (2013) draw attention to the need to look not just at participation but also at the quality of service. Other equality-enhancing processes to reduce vertical inequality in education include a just tax regime or approaches to address uneven quality through more teacher training and support and more learning resources for schools. The provision of a free meal at school has also been used to support poor parents sending their children to school and to improve children's health and nutrition to enhance learning. Sometimes these schemes are linked with community development supporting local farmers who grow the food, and community members who cook. Other strategies to expand access include establishing primary schools close to where children live and providing mobile schools, which travel with nomadic pastoralist families. Building community relations to support children in schools in very poor neighbourhoods has also been documented (Bonal and Tarabini 2016).

Education Sector Plans (ESPs) can be a key part of this process, directing resources to schools or regions with the greatest need, and strategies have been developed to enhance knowledge of gender in work on ESPS through UNGEI's Gender responsive Education Sector Plan (GRESP) project identified planning as a key lever where change could be effected towards gender equality at education system level, noting the importance of deepening knowledge of gender and capacity among a key cohort involved in education planning (GRESP 2019). In 2020 UNESCO supported the development of Profiles Enhancing Education Reviews (PEER) assessments to evaluate how countries' laws and policies approached inclusion, taking note of local definitions, school organization, governance, learning environments, teachers, monitoring and evaluation. In both GRESP and PEER there is a concern to ground equitable and inclusive policies in local education systems and processes. However, both are focused at the level of a state's institutions and much work is still needed to engage with many local organizations associated with education.

These strategies for inclusion generally focus on understanding inequality in education as a line, and there is still only a patchwork of initiatives towards equity and inclusion that deal with aspects of the net of unequal relationships that establish and reproduce inequalities, and that provide some of the fuel to transform these. Some examples of equality-enhancing processes are associated with affirmative action in employment together with clear leadership to address racism and sexism in education workplace and pedagogic cultures. Teacher education and continuing professional development are key components of supporting work on multi-dimensional equality and equity. So too is in-depth work with schools, communities, government and employers looking at the causes of poverty, exclusion, intersectional inequalities and how change can be formulated and sustained. There is a need to build equalities, equity and inclusion from the bottom, the middle and the top and connect these processes, not leave a medley of disconnected initiatives.

Conclusion

This chapter has distinguished between different ways of understanding inequalities in education and shown how these frameworks affect the approach taken to change. To date most attention has been given to work on forms of inequality that entail crossing a line, and least to unravelling the netlike forms of structural inequality and drawing on the fuel or agency of those who experience inequalities. There has been a tendency to think about schooling and equality in terms of giving an equal amount to all people. This equates schooling with medicine and makes EFA or the expansion of higher education something like giving a vaccination that will eradicate poverty or ignorance. But inequalities in education, like those in health, are complex. Some are socially determined, some rest on individual experiences and some are an interplay of human agency with technologies, geographies and historical patterns. Addressing inequalities in education is not like giving a single dose to vaccinate against polio. It is much more like working on cancer, identifying that the illness takes many forms; that social and individual circumstances affect its incidence and treatment; and that the interplay between inputs, systems, relationships, care, and individual engagement and emotion are all significant parts of this undertaking. Connecting opportunities, outcomes and processes in thinking about equality in education is complex and requires policies, practices and research agendas that can work multi-dimensionally. There is still a long way to go to develop the understanding and experience to take this forward.

Questions for Discussion

1. Why is it easier to treat horizontal inequalities in education as vertical inequalities?
2. Why do inequalities in educational opportunities appear to be mirrored in inequalities in educational outcomes? What could change this process?
3. Consider how an education planner and a classroom teacher would approach addressing access and quality to reflect the three frameworks for thinking about addressing inequalities outlined? What would be similar and different in their approach to practice?

Further Reading

Collins, P. H. and Bilge, S. (2016), *Intersectionality*, John Wiley & Sons.

Piketty, T. (2019), *Capital and Ideology*, Cambridge, MA, Harvard University Press.

Parkes, J. (ed.) (2015), *Gender Violence in Poverty Contexts: The Educational Challenge*, London: Routledge.

9

Teachers and Teacher Education Policies

Gita Steiner-Khamsi

Introduction

The education of teachers and their effectiveness have become objects of academic investigation as well as applied policy learning. In fact, the area of teacher-related policies has taken on such a monumental significance in educational research that it has tended to eclipse alternative explanations for why some educational systems do better than others in terms of student achievement. Nowadays, policymakers are outward oriented and proclaim that they are keen to learn what has worked in other countries. Formulated differently, cross-national policy borrowing is nowadays the rule and not the exception. This chapter draws on the example of teacher policy to warn against the 'cargo-cult' (Cowen 2000) that has elevated the comparative preoccupation with isolating features of the educational system to undeserved notoriety.

In this chapter, I will identify three fundamental systemic differences that are relevant in the area of teacher policy.[1] Educational systems educate, manage and regulate teachers differently depending on whether the system

1. is decentralized or centralized,
2. hires and pays teachers based on the overall workload or based on the actual teaching hour and
3. conceives the teacher education degree as a pedagogical or a generalist degree.

Other differentiations apply but are not elaborated on in this chapter. For example, there are vast differences in what promotion criteria educational systems tend to use (performance versus experience) and what teacher accountability system they have in place (intrinsic versus extrinsic control). In an era of globalization, it has become common to use the method of comparison to emphasize commonality over difference. In this chapter, I draw on the full scope of the method of comparison and use it for the inverse purpose: I will stress difference over commonality in order to understand the particular logic or idiosyncrasies of educational systems. This chapter differentiates between universal challenges that all educational systems face and system-specific challenges that only similar systems share. Arguably, an international comparative perspective helps us to identify similarities and differences and, in this case, to develop a typology of system features that matter for teacher-related policies.

Global Trends in Teacher Policy

There are several reasons why teacher education and effectiveness have attracted so much attention. First, the shortage of qualified teachers is a global phenomenon. UNESCO Institute of Statistics (UIS) estimates that

69.8 million teachers are needed worldwide to achieve the Sustainable Development Goal (SDG) 2030 of universal primary and secondary education. At primary level, there is a shortage of 24.4 million and at secondary level 44.4 million teachers. These estimates take into account the international benchmarks for class size (40 for primary and 25 for secondary school) but do not address the large number of teachers that are hired despite their insufficient professional qualification (UIS 2016). Arguably, the non-availability of qualified teachers constitutes one of the greatest barriers to offering free and compulsory primary education in some countries and expanding schooling from ten to eleven or twelve years in others. The shortage in secondary schools is especially acute in specific subjects (Maths, Science, English). The 2006 PISA study mentions the shortage of qualified teachers in science subjects explicitly and attributes low student outcomes in science to the lack of qualified science teachers: in Kyrgyzstan, for example, 62 per cent of all schools report vacancies in science. Almost all of these schools (59 per cent countrywide) cope with this shortage by filling their vacancies with teachers who take on additional lessons in science or by assigning non-qualified teachers (i.e. teachers qualified in other subjects but with no training in science) (CEATM 2008). The latter practice – redistribution of vacant hours to substitute teachers or non-qualified teachers – is the most common strategy used at the school level to cope with teacher shortage.

Second, beginning with the EFA Fast Track Initiative (2002) and continuing with the SDGs, international donors and aid-recipient governments alike have subscribed to performance-based criteria of aid effectiveness. Nowadays, the benefits to the 'end users' are at the core of aid effectiveness evaluations. Therefore, for educational reforms the question has become: how have students benefited from the intervention or, more narrowly, have learning outcomes increased as a result of the reform or the project?

Naturally, IEA- and OECD-type international student achievement tests are increasingly used as policy instruments for learning lessons, adopting 'best practices', or for selective policy borrowing. More than once, the educational systems of Finland, Hong Kong, Japan, Singapore and South Korea have been identified not only as the best performing educational systems in terms of reading, science and maths but also as the models for 'best practices' in recruitment into teaching and teacher education. The strong correlation assumed between teaching and student outcomes has led to a global race over how to maximize teacher effectiveness. Within a short period of time, teaching has become one of the most studied and most regulated professions with high expectations and yet a host of unsolved issues.

The third reason why teacher policy studies have raised such high expectations is related to finance: salaries constitute by far the largest item on any national education budget. In more than half of all developing countries, personnel remuneration absorbs 75 per cent and more of the national education budget (UIS 2013), leaving too little room for other important items such as teaching/learning supplies, maintenance of facilities, targeted support for poor students and for students with special needs and professional development of staff. The situation is even more precarious in fragile states where, besides reliance on donor-financed teacher salaries, there exist a host of other issues such as, for example, lack of a banking registration and distribution system (Dolan et al. 2012). Thus, it is also for financial reasons why teacher education and teacher effectiveness have been treated with priority in policy studies.

In sum, teachers have a significant impact on student learning, yet their number is neither sufficient nor are they, in many developing countries, adequately paid. There is agreement on what needs to be done: a wide range of authors and institutions, ranging from OECD (2005) to McKinsey (2010), emphasize the importance of attracting, developing and retaining effective teachers. What the studies do not sufficiently identify, however, are the vast differences in educational systems that account for system-specific challenges and therefore call for system-specific rather than universal solutions for the effective recruitment, development and retention of teachers.

Universal Key Challenges of Teacher Supply

Comparative methodology requires that we first identify commonalities between cases, contexts or systems before we subject them to a comparison. There exist, in fact, at least three key challenges of teacher supply that lend themselves as *tertium comparationis*. It is proposed here that all educational systems have to tackle the following three key challenges of teacher supply that are related to three factors: characteristics of the student body, teaching workforce and the school. From a comparative policy perspective, the questions become:

Characteristics of the student body
What provisions do educational systems put in place to ensure that all students, regardless of their social, cultural and economic backgrounds,

and with different abilities, needs and interests, are taught by teachers with relevant qualifications?

Characteristics of the teaching workforce
How do educational systems ensure that the teaching workforce reflects the composition of the student body in terms of gender, ethnicity, religious affiliation, political affiliation, sexual orientation and so on?

Characteristics of the school
How do educational systems manage to equip schools in remote rural areas, in post-conflict areas and in other hardship posts with qualified teachers? There is a strong correlation between location of school and size of school: schools in remote rural areas are typically small and they cannot afford to hire one teacher per grade or one teacher per subject area. Therefore, for educational systems that operate with per capita financing, that is, where the school budget is affected by the size of the student body, the challenge of attracting and retaining qualified teachers to such areas can be nearly insurmountable. Small schools not only have a smaller budget available but often represent schools where teachers are required to teach under more difficult pedagogical circumstances, notably teach in a multi-grade setting (primary school) or teach several subjects for which they were not initially trained (secondary school).

Needless to state, some educational systems are more successful than others in coping with these three key challenges of teacher supply. This chapter does not attempt to evaluate educational systems in terms of how they deal with these challenges. I also do not try to explain the reasons for the success or failure of equitably supplying all students and all types of schools in a country with a teaching force that is not only qualified but also diverse, reflecting the composition of the student body. This chapter rather explores the vastly different approaches to dealing with these three key challenges.

Towards a Typology of Teacher Policy Systems

The argument made here is that several features of an educational system determine how it addresses the three key challenges of teacher supply. For reasons of illustration, I will confine myself to three fundamental system

Table 9.1 System determinants of teacher supply

Key feature	At one end of the spectrum	At the other end of the spectrum
Employment	Highly decentralized	Highly centralized
Salary structure	Set according to weekly workload	Set according to weekly teaching hours
Teacher education	Pedagogical degree	Generalist degree

differences mentioned above that account for why there are different challenges, calling for different policy solutions, in varied educational systems. Table 9.1 presents them in an overview.

Employment of Teachers: Decentralized versus Centralized

It appears at first sight that highly centralized educational systems experience fewer problems with teacher shortages in remote rural areas: they assign newly qualified teachers to a post and have policies in place that make a transfer from that post to another, more attractive location, nearly impossible. Rural–urban differences in living standards, notably access to electricity, safe water, transportation, are substantial in developing countries. It is therefore not surprising that many developing countries used to have highly centralized systems in which teachers, at times in combination with a service-rule regulation (e.g. mandatory service in a remote location for two years), were despatched to teach at a school with low-living standards. This used to be, in principle, an equitable solution that ensured not only that schools in rural areas had a constant supply of teachers but also that all schools, regardless of their location, could rely on the same type of qualified teachers.

There is a risk, however, that such systems produce unmotivated teachers and 'ghost teachers', that is, teachers who, rather than taking up the assigned post, trade it internally with someone from the location or sub-contract the job to someone who is not qualified. Sub-contracting is such a common practice in South Asia, including in the teaching profession, that a specific term (Urdu: *theka system*) is assigned to characterize this particular feature

Policy 2
Teacher Deployment in the Soviet Union

The Soviet education system (1922–91) had a centralist governance structure of this sort in place which subscribed to equal access to education. The Ministry of Education assigned graduates of teacher education studies to vacant positions. Some were in remote rural areas at great distance from the region of origin of the teacher education graduates. All kinds of control and reward mechanisms were in place to ensure the 'new specialists' assumed their position and remained in post for the first few years after graduation. After the move from a planned to a market regulated economy, arrangements eroded for enforcing service regulation in remote areas. Higher education in former Soviet countries expanded exponentially throughout the 1990s partly because colleges and universities were permitted to charge for tuition. Two groups of students emerged: those that received a scholarship from the government budget ('budget students') and those that paid tuition ('contract students'). Up until the first years of the millennium, governments in the countries of the former Soviet Union tried to enforce the service requirement at least for 'budget students'. The scholarship was contingent on working for the first two to five years after graduation at a teaching post that was selected by the Ministry of Education, sometimes in an unattractive location. However, the outcome was mixed. A World Bank study on higher education reported a low university-to-work transition rate (Brunner and Tillett 2007, 119). In 1999, three-quarters of graduates did not show up at the assigned post. Only 24 per cent of the 'budget students' assumed the position the Ministry of Education had assigned to them. The ratio improved over the next few years as additional policies were put in place to compensate for the lack of control mechanisms available in a free market economy where graduates may choose the profession and apply for a position at a location of their choice. The struggle continues to find an alternative to the coercive deployment centralist governments tend to use. Policy responses range from depositing a sizeable amount in a savings account the new teacher may only access after the completion of the mandatory service requirement[2] to hiring underqualified teachers who undergo professional development while working in an unattractive school location.

of the system. These and other practices are captured in the term 'ghost teachers' that has unfortunately experienced inflationary usage because of the erroneous assumption that all ghost teachers cash their salaries without carrying out the job. The phenomenon is offered as an explanation for interpreting the incongruent information on staff records at school, district and central level.

In the UNICEF ESARO Study on Teachers in Swaziland, which I worked on, we compared teacher information at the school level ($N = 96$) in two districts and at the central level (UNICEF ESARO and UNICEF Swaziland 2010). We found incongruent information between the various databases. The conflicting information related to very basic facts, including the quota size (number of entitled positions) and the actual size of the teaching staff. The inaccuracy of information led to hiring freezes, delays with approving updated quota and other problems that could feasibly be avoided with a more effective management and deployment system. Very often, centralized systems are slow and entrenched in bureaucratic processes to the extent that schools, parents and communities – at their own expense – find ways to hire additional teachers, most commonly as contract teachers. These coercive measures damage the public image of teaching. In Malawi, the teaching workforce is predominantly male, except in the cities where most teachers are female. Female teachers successfully made the argument to the Teaching Commission that they should stay with their families, following their husbands to work in the city (UNICEF ESARO and UNICEF Malawi 2011). Transfer for 'compassionate reasons' is also discernible in Pakistan, where transfer requests are more easily granted to female teachers who follow husbands to urban areas.

Centralized hiring practice, in which the district, rather than the school, hires teachers, implies that schools have no control over hiring, firing or managing teachers. This has negative impact on schools in rural districts. Thus, rural districts may end up paying for teachers who are then transferred to urban school districts and no longer work for rural district schools. There is a shortage of teachers in the rural areas even though official records at school, district and province level indicate the positions as filled.

Tremendous international pressure is currently being exerted on centralized teacher management and deployment systems to shift decision-making authority over hiring, transfer and promotion of teachers from the central to the school level. School-based management is a 'travelling reform' that has generated pressure on educational systems. Devolution of decision-making is considered to be more efficient because school principals, schools boards or school management committees are able to hire teachers directly, fill vacancies quickly and with fewer bureaucratic hurdles. However, rather than assuming that one governance structure (e.g. centralized or decentralized) is more effective than another, I recommend we understand the idiosyncrasies of each type of system for addressing key challenges of teacher supply.

While school-based management allows schools to act more efficiently on issues related to human management, they also have to deal with other challenges: of inequity and corruption, which they may be less well equipped to respond to. Since schools are in competition with each other over attracting the most qualified teachers by providing material and immaterial incentives (salary supplement, staff development options, work conditions, etc.), school-based management tends to work better in an affluent environment and in contexts where there is no sharp rural–urban divide. Unlike centralized systems, decentralized systems cannot issue an order to teachers to take on a post in an unattractive location. Rather, they resort to incentives and support structures to lure and retain teachers in schools considered difficult (Mulkeen and Chen 2008). Inequality becomes a major concern for decentralized, market-driven educational systems. Since rural schools cannot possibly keep up with their competitors in urban settings, decentralized systems have developed – often with the support of development partners – a series of pilot projects and policies to offset their comparative disadvantage. Several countries have set up branch campuses in rural districts. Others have actively promoted pre-service teacher education using blended learning, correspondence studies or distance learning so that pre-service teacher education students do not have to abandon their communities but rather complete their degrees while working as 'student teachers' in rural schools. Attempt to bring pre-service teacher education closer to a rural population – and overcome geographical, cultural and linguistic distance – should be interpreted as a positive sign of a policy that is pro-poor.

Salary Structure: Weekly Workload versus Weekly Teaching Load

A fixed, regular and predicable monthly salary for a teacher in a developing country often does not materialize; this is frequently the root cause of teaching being considered an unattractive profession. In 2006, the World Bank commissioned a study on teacher salaries in Mongolia as part of the

Public Expenditure Tracking Survey (World Bank 2006). Working on this, we were surprised to find the salary structure fragmented, that is, composed of a low base-salary and supplemented with all kinds of items such as stipends for additional teaching hours, serving as a class teacher, grading student notebooks, managing a lab at school and so on. Since these supplements were not always paid in full but rather depended on the arbitrary assessment of the education manager of whether the teacher properly graded student notebooks (the use of red ink was at the time mandatory to make supervision easier), effectively managed the class (supplement deductions were made for students that cut class) and took care of the lab (salary supplement deductions were made for broken equipment), teachers were not able to predict their monthly take-home salary.

Follow-up studies in Tajikistan, Kyrgyzstan, Mongolia and a six-country study in Central and Eastern Europe and the Commonwealth of Independent States region (UNICEF CEECIS 2011) confirmed the post-Soviet legacy in the region: all educational systems used to have a teaching load system (Russian: *stavka*) in place through which additional teaching hours helped boost the low base salary of teachers. In school year 2007/8, the salaries of teachers in the post-Soviet region (EU accession countries excluded) ranged (in US dollars) from $47 to $215 per month. The relative salary was not only low but also below the national wage average, ranging from 53 per cent to 92 per cent of what others with a similar level of education earned (Steiner-Khamsi and Harris-van Keuren 2008). As a result, teachers fight over who gets assigned additional teaching hours, regardless of whether these additional hours are in the subjects for which they trained or whether they substitute for teachers of other subjects on study, maternity or sick leave.

Figure 9.1 illustrates the complex salary structure in the post-socialist region, using Tajikistan as a case. Since the publication of the study, the salary structure in Tajikistan has undergone reform integrating the various supplements (over ten) into two (class teacher and notebook checking) (see Steiner-Khamsi 2007).

The fragmented picture in Tajikistan is indicative of the teacher salary structure in the Central and Eastern Europe and Commonwealth of Independent States (CEECIS) region, where the base salary is low, the benefits of appointment as a civil servant attractive and dependence on additional income great. This can take the form of teaching additional hours through private tutoring, providing special classes or requiring unofficial contributions by parents. The fragmented salary structure is a legacy of the communist past where all workers were supposed to be paid equally and,

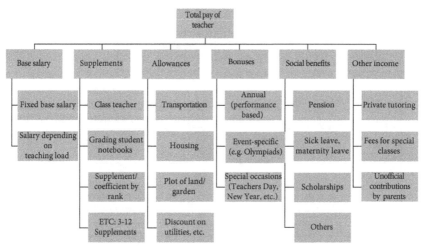

Figure 9.1 Total pay of teachers in Tajikistan. *Source:* UNICEF CEECIS (2011).

depending on the actual work, would receive professional supplements. At that time all workers were considered public servants and received, from today's perspective, generous 'social benefits', including free housing and a plot of land.

Each approach to teachers' pay faces its own kind of challenges and calls for its own kind of solutions. The teaching load system, to which most post-socialist countries and many developing countries adhere, is flexible and allows teachers to work part-time at a school and part-time as a farmer or a merchant. Put positively, the teaching load system allows schools in rural areas to recruit qualified teachers part-time who would, otherwise due to better compensation, work outside the profession. The teaching load system also makes it possible to recruit teachers who only wish to work part-time because of family or household commitments or responsibilities for a second job. Put negatively, the teaching load system enables governments in developing countries to pay low salaries, enlist teachers for part-time positions, rely on teachers making money off additional teaching hours and seeking additional income from jobs outside school, collecting (official and unofficial) fees paid by parents and engaging in private tutoring. Such work conditions generate periodic or seasonal teacher absenteeism (especially during harvesting) and put great pressure on teachers to secure income from multiple sources. Figure 9.2 summarizes key features of the two different salary structures.

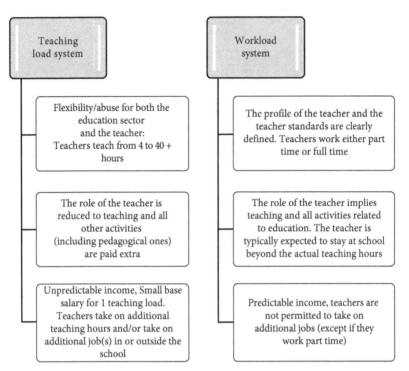

Figure 9.2 The divide between salary systems. *Source:* UNICEF CEECIS (2011: 77).

It can be seen that in the Teaching Hours System (18–24 hours of teaching per week), carried over from the Soviet past, all additional activity is compensated separately; the workload system (35–40 hours of work per week, including all activities at school) is currently in place in countries of the Global North and West. Twenty years after the move to a demand/supply driven market-economy, several post-Soviet countries dropped the previous system and adopted the weekly workload system.

Teacher Education: Pedagogical Degree versus Generalist Degree

An international comparative perspective brings to light fundamentally different curricula of pre-service teacher education: at one end of the spectrum are educational systems that place great weight on pedagogical knowledge, and at the other end, systems that conceive teacher education as a generalist degree. It is also important to differentiate *within* a system: the curriculum of secondary pre-service teacher education tends to be more subject-specific and less pedagogical than the one that prepares students to teach at primary level. Unsurprisingly, recruitment into teaching is particularly difficult for secondary school because the curriculum is subject-specific and the teacher education students identify more with the subject-specific knowledge (e.g. maths) than with the methodological-didactical elements of their studies (e.g. maths education). Recruitment into teaching at primary level faces challenges of a different kind: so many primary school teachers are needed that colleges in developing countries tend to attract school graduates with low academic achievement who enrol because they lack more attractive study alternatives.

In many countries, regardless of whether they are low-income or high-income, more than half of the graduates from pre-service teacher education never enter the teaching profession. Furthermore, those who assume a teaching position are at risk of leaving the profession within the first few years. This also applies to OECD countries, where the teacher salaries tend to be attractive. In the Canton of Berne in Switzerland, for example, 80 per cent of those who quit the profession do so in the first ten years of their service (Herzog et al. 2007). What is a cause for concern in Switzerland is not only the great attrition rate but also the negative selection of those teachers that stay: the motivation for those who remain in the profession is not so much related to pedagogical aspects of the work but rather the flexible work schedule. The option to work part-time appears to be especially attractive for women: 68 per cent of all female teachers in Switzerland work part-time as compared to 34 per cent of the male teachers. The teaching profession in many countries has become increasingly 'feminized' for all the wrong reasons, such as, for example, flexibility of the work schedule or low pay.

The low transition rate of graduates from pre-service teacher education entering the teaching profession is especially pronounced in education systems where teacher education studies are considered a generalist degree. In these countries, recruitment into teaching is low. Figure 9.3 shows recruitment into teaching deals with the key stages of professionalization and covers a cycle from the moment school graduates apply to pre-service teacher education through acceptance of a teaching position and the decision to stay in the profession.

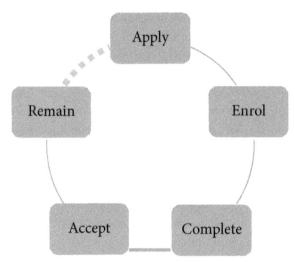

Figure 9.3 Key Stages of recruitment into teaching. *Source:* UNICEF CEECIS
(2011).

Several research questions arise when the full cycle is examined:

Who applies to pre-service teacher education, who chooses to accept a
    position as a teacher and who stays in the profession?
How difficult/easy is it to be admitted to pre-service teacher education as
    compared to other degree programmes in higher education?
How selective is admission into pre-service teacher education?
How many admitted teacher education students have 'survived' by the end
    of their studies?
Of those who complete their degree, how many accept a teaching position
    and, of these, how many indeed show up at the assigned school?
Two to five years later: how many of the newly qualified teachers are still
    working in the profession?

From an international comparative perspective that is interested in
understanding the logic of an educational system, it is important to note that
the five indicators constitute a cycle (Figure 9.3). In this case it is a vicious
cycle: governments tend to lower the admission criteria if the retention of
qualified teachers at the workplace is low and if there is a great demand for
teachers. This, in turn, negatively affects the public image of the teaching
profession and contributes to the unpopularity of the profession.

Although recruitment into teaching has been researched academically for
many years, it has only in recent years drawn the attention of government
officials and the general public. The two high-performing educational

Measurement and Indicators 5
Five Measures of Teacher Recruitment

In teacher education research, recruitment into teaching is a key variable used to investigate the effectiveness of teacher education and to shape effective teacher development strategies. Five measures are certain:

(1) *Admission rate*: Number of applicants admitted to a teacher training diploma or degree programme.
(2) *Enrolment rate*: Number of admitted applicants that actually enrol in a pre-service teacher training diploma or degree programme.
(3) *Completion rate*: Number of teacher training students completing their three- or four-year training programme.
(4) *Transition rate*: Number of graduates accepting a teaching position upon graduation from teacher training.
(5) *Retention rate of newly qualified teachers (NQT)*: Number of NQTs that remain in teaching posts two years (or five years) after graduation.

systems of Finland and Singapore are closely associated with effective recruitment into teaching: the admission criteria for teacher education are rigorous, the survival rate of those who actually graduate from teacher education is high and most graduates go on to become teachers. The educational systems of Singapore and Finland (league leaders in IEA and OECD studies) have received so many accolades for their teacher education systems that policymakers from other countries project features into these two systems that at times are only loosely related to reality. Naturally, not all nations have as rigorous a selection scheme for teacher education applicants as Singapore and Finland. Even fewer countries succeed in convincing their teacher education graduates to work as teachers. Figures 9.4 and 9.5 draw on the indicators (all except transition rate), presented above, and illustrate recruitment into teaching in Singapore and Kyrgyzstan.

Singapore was ranked at the top in science and maths in TIMSS 2003, and the Kyrgyz Republic scored at the bottom in PISA 2006 (ranked 57 out of 57 countries) and PISA 2009 (ranked 65 out of 65 countries). As Figure 9.3 illustrates, teacher education institutions are extremely selective in Singapore, and universities only accept 20 per cent of those that apply. Almost all those who enrol complete their course of study and then, upon graduation, start working as teachers.

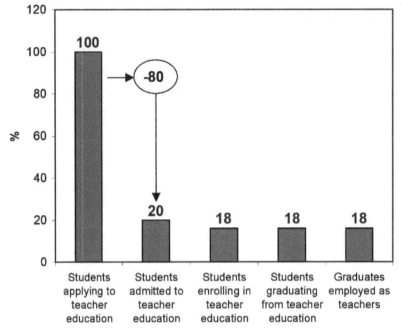

Figure 9.4 Effective recruitment into teaching (Singapore). *Source:* McKinsey (2010).

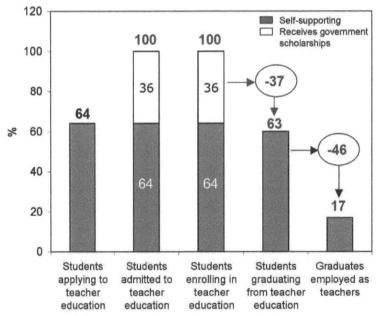

Figure 9.5 Ineffective recruitment into teaching (Kyrgyzstan). *Source:* Steiner-Khamsi and Teleshaliyev (2019)

The situation is entirely different in the Kyrgyz Republic. Figure 9.4 illustrates the high attrition rate during teacher education, pointing to a huge waste of resources. In an attempt to combat teacher shortage, the Government of the Kyrgyz Republic treats the teaching profession as a priority and allocates a disproportionately large number of scholarships to university students in pedagogical specializations: 36 per cent of all teacher education students who are admitted receive government scholarships (i.e. are 'budget' students). During the five-year teacher education diploma programme, 37 per cent of those enrolled either abandon their studies or switch to another programme over the course of their studies. Only 63 per cent of those who start teacher training actually obtain a higher education diploma with a teaching specialization. Of those that complete their studies with a teacher education specialization, very few (17 per cent) end up working as teachers.

It goes without saying that the contexts vary considerably. Teaching is an attractive profession in Singapore and, for a variety of reasons (low and fragmented teacher salaries, difficult working environment), an unattractive one in the Kyrgyz Republic. Teacher education institutions in Singapore closely collaborate with the Ministry of Education, and admitted students already have a workplace guaranteed upon graduation. The curriculum is geared towards teaching and is therefore pedagogical in orientation. They can afford to be highly selective, whereas the same institutions in Kyrgyzstan only remain in operation because they use two negative selection criteria. First, they absorb students who were turned away in other degree programmes because they achieved low scores in university entrance examinations. Second, they attract those who depend on government scholarships. The pre-service teacher education curriculum is a generalist degree and focuses on general knowledge and subject-specific knowledge rather than pedagogical skills and competencies. Colleges and universities either do not require teaching practice, readily exempt students from completing a teaching practicum and reduce it to a few short visits in the affiliated lab school or have organized the practicum experience (up to ten teacher education students per class) so poorly that there is little to gain in terms of teaching competencies. Given the low transition rate of graduates, the focus of externally funded initiatives tends to be on in-service rather than pre-service teacher education. Understandably, international donors and NGOs prefer to strengthen in-service programmes for practising teachers rather than investing in a generalist pre-service teacher education degree.

There exist, of course, a great number of educational systems that range between the two extremes: a pedagogical degree (Singapore) versus a generalist degree (Kyrgyzstan). In Pakistan, for example, the majority of teachers first complete a generalist undergraduate degree (2 year BA or BSc) and only afterwards, if they do not secure a job, enrol in a professional teacher education degree (BEd) to work as teachers (USAID 2013). This practice of 'life-long learning of teachers' or life-long accumulation of higher education degrees is manifested in the salary scheme, referred to as 'service rule regulation' in Pakistan. With every new degree, teachers are promoted to the next salary level.

In many countries, state-run teacher education has ceased to be the dominant form of professional development for teachers. At one end of the spectrum are standardized sophisticated teacher certification programmes (e.g. International Baccalaureate) and at the other end, a boom in modularized short certificate programmes (e.g. Teach for Chile, Teach for India and Teach for the Philippines).

Every educational system is a bounded system with a specific set of cause–effect relationships, its own logic and regulatory mechanisms that ensure the system logic is perpetuated. This logic may be undermined or subverted: in Pakistan, for example, the great value attached to qualification has led to an explosion of private colleges and universities that sell certificates and degrees or issue them with minimal attendance or performance requirements.

Conclusion

By demonstrating some fundamental differences that exist between teacher policy systems, this chapter makes a case against uncritical transfer of reform packages from one context to another.

It extends an invitation to reverse the current homogenization trend and acknowledge fundamental differences rather than similarities between educational systems. I have done so in light of the busy global trade of educational reform packages that are catapulted and more and more (literally) sold from one corner of the world to another without any regard for already existing, more participatory and possibly more effective 'home-grown' reform initiatives. The field of international educational development is fuelled with ignorance, misconceptions and prejudices about the capacity of 'locals' to bring their own educational systems in line with (vaguely or broadly) defined 'international standards'. Rather than understanding the logic of each educational system, international donors use standards developed in the Global North as a yardstick to evaluate reforms in the Global South. Examples are the export of school-based management, teacher reforms and a host of other reform packages that were blindly transferred regardless of context and despite already existing provisions in the local context (Verger et al. 2013). Not only were such imported reforms simply added on top of already existing local reform initiatives but worse they disempower local policy actors at the expense of global ones.

Questions for Discussion

1. Do differences in the types of institutions in which teachers are given initial training affect how they are viewed with regard to discussions of pedagogy and work conditions?
2. What are some of the effects of the transfer of policies regarding teachers between countries and organizations?
3. Explore some of the cultural, political and economic factors that explain differences in teacher management and salary systems.

Further Reading

Landman, T. (2014), *Issues and Methods in Comparative Politics: An Introduction* (4th Edition), London and Oxford: Routledge.

Verger, A. Altinyelken, H. K. and De Koning, M. (2013), *Global Managerial Education Reforms and Teachers*, Brussels: Education International Research Institute.

Quality Education and Global Learning Metrics

William C. Smith and Aaron Benavot

Introduction

In significant ways 2015 marked the 'quality' turn in international education policy. The adoption of the 2030 Agenda for Sustainable Development,[1] including a separate goal on education (SDG 4), institutionalized the notion of quality education in international development discourse (Wulff 2020a). In contrast to the Millennium Development Goal, which focused exclusively on universal primary completion (Schwandt 2012, Smith 2018), SDG 4 captured widespread consensus about the value and importance of quality education and learning. This chapter raises questions about this global shift towards quality education and learning: 'How is quality being understood?', 'Whose quality is being recognized and acted upon?' and 'What metrics have evolved to measure quality and learning?'

Quality education is not a new concept in academia. Educators like Dewey, Bloom, Montessori and Freire explored the nature and purposes of education (Schwandt 2012, Napier 2014) and theorized about quality. And yet, quality embodies an equivocal term – universally accepted, highly visible, but lacking a clear and rigorous definition. Synonyms for quality education include excellence, meeting standards and fitness for purpose (Cheng and Tam 1997). Even though 'quality' has been central to education research, it remains a contested notion. As Ball (1985) asked over thirty years ago, we are often left to wonder 'What the hell is quality?'

Usage of the term 'quality' in education research has increased in recent decades (Pons 2012). In part, this can be traced to cross-country comparisons of educational achievement, which raised questions about the quality of learning generated by different education systems. The highly influential US report *A Nation at Risk* (US National Commission on Excellence in Education 1983) presented evidence of poor performance of the United States on cross-national learning assessments, creating intense media attention which instigated major shifts in education discourse, policy and practice for years afterwards. Much of the discussion made reference to the 'dilemma of *quantity versus quality*' (Napier 2014, 6, emphasis original). While the global expansion of primary and secondary education brought unprecedented numbers of children into schools, in many contexts it also resulted in larger class sizes, fewer prepared teachers and inadequate instructional materials, generating concerns about the provision of quality education. By the late twentieth century many national policies focused explicitly on improving quality education, setting aside 'earlier attention given to such priorities as educational expansion and school access' (Adams 1993, 3).

Conceptualizing Quality Education

To better understand the multifarious definitions of quality, we briefly explore three questions. (1) Does the definition purport a single, universal understanding of quality education or does it recognize differences based on local context? (2) Does the definition capture a broad, holistic view of education, or does it only focus on specific aspects within the larger system? and (3) Does the definition only refer to formal schooling or are non-formal and informal educational frameworks included as well?

Universal versus Locally Defined

Is quality the same to everyone, everywhere? Epistemological assumptions of a single, uniform reality underlie views that definitions and standards of quality can be universally applied to education around the world. This approach is often accompanied by absolute thresholds or benchmarks that all education stakeholders must reach, regardless of context (Harvey and Green 1993). Global goals and targets in education generally rely on claims of universality, assuming that 'it is both desirable and feasible for all students, regardless of resources and support, to perform at the same levels' (Spreen and Knapczyk 2017, 3). Beyond comparing countries or systems, it has been argued that a single, global understanding of quality can generate support for education among donor partners and policymakers (Sayed and Moriarty 2020).

Universal definitions and applications of quality have been critiqued by national governments and educators. Even amongst countries that agree on a goal of quality education, there is little consensus as to whether definitions of quality should be constructed at the global or national level (Wulff 2020a). Recognizing how contexts, including culture and tradition, are intertwined with the purposes and aims of education, it is not surprising that respondents from different countries and local communities provide a range of illustrations when describing quality education (Adams 1993). Indeed, education is complex and highly contextualized, which makes quality 'open to many interpretations and operationalisations' (Napier 2014, 1).

Holistic versus Partial Understanding

Should quality reference specific aspects of an education system or reflect a more holistic understanding of the system? Although sometimes criticized as overly linear (see Napier 2014), quality of education has often been framed as consisting of input, process, outputs and outcomes (Adams 1993). Partial definitions of quality typically focus on outputs and outcomes, recognizing that measurable improvements in quality can be viewed as a 'real anticipated increase in effectiveness' (Adams 1993, 7). The glaring omission of process-oriented measures is one way that conceptions of quality education have been narrowed (Unterhalter 2019a).

A holistic approach to quality recognizes the interdependence inherent in education. Outputs and outcomes would not be singled out since they rely on both inputs (e.g. adequate infrastructure, well-prepared teachers, and relevant and sufficient instructional materials) and processes (e.g. classroom practice and teacher–parent communication) (Spreen and Knapczyk 2017). A widely used comprehensive conceptualization of quality education was advanced in the 2004/5 Education for All (EFA) Global Monitoring Report (UNESCO 2005). Core dimensions of this framework of quality education include context, enabling inputs, learner characteristics, teaching and learning, and outcomes. UNICEF (2007), based on a children's rights perspective, and the World Bank (Heneveld and Craig 1995), focusing on school effectiveness, have also advanced comprehensive frameworks of quality (Tawil et al. 2012).

Formal Schooling versus All Forms of Education

Is quality limited to school-based education? The vast majority of conceptualizations of quality education can be better characterized as quality schooling, as they mainly capture experiences of students in formal education. Such approaches prioritize some types of knowledge over others and fail to capture quality in diverse forms of lifelong learning in non-formal and informal settings. Non-formal education (NFE), which caters to people of all ages, is typically provided in courses, workshops or seminars of shorter duration in settings outside of school (e.g. community centres, faith-based organizations, museums, workplaces). While NFE is institutionalized, intentional and planned by an education provider, it does not lead to certification. Informal education refers to intentional or deliberate forms of learning that are less organized and structured, such as those that occur in daily life at home, work or in the local community. They are typically self-, family- or socially directed (UIL 2009). Most conceptions of quality education pay scant attention to non-formal and informal learning opportunities despite their pervasiveness in peoples' lives (Livingston et al. 2008).

Additional Considerations

At least three additional points can be considered in reference to conceptions of quality. First, understandings of quality education differ by level and type, from early childhood to higher education, from vocational training to adult education. Comparing quality across levels is problematic, since the purposes and objectives at each level vary significantly (Adams 1993; see

Hunkin 2018 for example of early child education). Second, how does time, and its relationship with the desired aim of education, shape the definition of quality education? Specifically, is education an end in and of itself or a means to other ends? If the latter, are short-term or longer-term effects the focus of improving quality education?

Finally, as we explore, how does the measurement of quality change the definition of quality? If more holistic principles of quality are operationalized using narrowly defined measures, the original meaning of quality education gets lost (Smith 2018). This often occurs when quality become quantified in concrete indicators and measures. Numbers are constructed to ease communication (Lingard et al. 2012) of complex notions; the resulting 'evidence' is then perceived by experts and the public alike as legitimate (Robertson 1999, Napier 2014). Overly complex notions of quality, which are not easily measured, become drastically reshaped or discarded in the operationalization process (Sayed and Moriarty 2020). This raises questions of whether quality indicators measure what we value or whether we disproportionately value what we measure (Sayed and Ahmed 2015).

Whose Quality?

Given the contested nature and multiple understandings of quality, it is critical to ask: Who defines quality and who benefits from a given definition of quality? Conceptions and discussions of quality are neither apolitical nor objective. Instead, they reflect ideas advanced by actors who are shaped by history and ideology, in positions of asymmetrical power relations and established hierarchies (Napier 2014). Lacking a widely held consensus definition, notions of quality are embedded in different ideological perspectives, including human capital, human capability, social justice and cultural recognition, as explored in Chapter 2 of this volume (Tikly and Barrett 2011, Luong and Nieke 2014). Below we briefly review two dominant perspectives influencing education policy and respective definitions of quality: education as human capital and education as a human right.

The human capital approach is utilitarian in nature, focusing on education as an instrument towards economic ends (Sayed and Moriarty 2020). This approach views quality in partial terms, since the emphasis is primarily on outputs and outcomes. Managerialism and performativity are avenues to improve quality, understood as improvements in learning as measured by assessment results or test scores (Benavot and Smith 2020). The main justifications for using test scores to operationalize quality are: (1) their ability to provide quick and simply communicated information for policymakers (Smith 2018), (2) the public belief in test scores as an objective measure that provides appropriate input for evidence-based decisions (Schwandt 2012) and (3) literature highlighting the connection between test scores and economic growth (e.g. Hanushek and Woessmann 2015; for a critique, see Komatsu and Rappleye 2017). Quality, from a human capital perspective, is often also associated with notions of 'value for money' or 'value added' (Adams 1993) and is strongly linked to accountability (Spreen and Knapczyk 2017).

A rights-based or humanistic approach to quality posits that education is a legally binding and universal human right (Aubry and Dorsi 2016) and a good in itself (Spreen and Knapcyzk 2017). Such an approach embodies a broader conception of quality, incorporating inputs and processes, in addition to outputs and outcomes (Benavot and Smith 2020), together with an emphasis on structural impediments to rights fulfilment (Wulff 2020a). Teachers are accorded a higher priority as are the availability of equitable learning opportunities, both inside and outside of school (Benavot and Smith 2020).

Debates over education as human capital and education as a human right have been ongoing for decades. In the formulation of the SDGs the tension between the two perspectives came into sharp relief (see Unterhalter 2019a, Sayed and Moriarty 2020, Wulff 2020a). Some suggest that, given the role of powerful actors and funding priorities generally supportive of human capital approaches, alternative perspectives of quality and society are being undermined (Fisher 2009, Slee 2013), which narrows the societal changes envisioned in the SDGs. Others viewed the enhancement of quality education in non-instrumental terms as a crucial condition for a more holistic social, political, economic and environmental transformation (Wulff 2020b).

Global Metrics of Quality Education and Learning: Historical Roots

Data-driven approaches to education have grown in scope and visibility in recent decades. The emphasis on evidence-based policymaking, and results-oriented funding assumes that education constructs like 'quality education' and 'learning' can be modelled and measured. Valid and reliable data can be produced, permitting comparisons across countries and education systems.

International organizations have prioritized quality education and learning in policy declarations, and this has had implications for data collection and indicator construction. Experts and organizations have adopted various strategies to measure and monitor quality dimensions in education, especially in terms of learning outcomes. Most models have viewed learning as a production process: inputs → processes → outputs → outcomes. Below we briefly review international policy discussions on quality education and learning, and select measurement strategies undertaken.

In 1990, participants to the World Conference on Education for All (WCEFA) in Jomtien, Thailand, committed themselves to an 'expanded vision of basic education', which would meet the basic learning needs of all children, youth and adults by the year 2000. Until this meeting international policy priorities in education had mainly focused on ensuring universal access to education and the provision of free and compulsory primary education (all specified in Article 26 in the Universal Declaration of Human Rights). The WCEFA reflected a shift in discourse from universal access to *access plus learning*. Meeting the learning needs of all children and youth meant improving the provision of quality education and ensuring its relevance to students:

> The focus of basic education must... be on actual learning acquisition and outcomes, rather than exclusively upon enrolment... participation... and completion... Active and participatory approaches are particularly valuable in assuring learning acquisition and maintenance, allowing learners to reach their fullest potential.
>
> (The Inter-Agency Commission for the WCEFA 1990a, 35)

And yet, although the WCEFA strengthened international consensus on quality education and learning, there was no such consensus on what quality education entailed or which indicators or metrics should be used to measure improvement in inputs or outcomes of schooling:

> The quality of learning activities has traditionally been defined in terms of the inputs to a programme, institution, or system. Preferably, measures of output... should be used as substitutes for or, at least, complements to the input measures. Measures of the learning process ... are least commonly used to indicate learning quality because of methodological problems .... Therefore, the definition and analysis of learning quality has relied excessively on input and output measures without a clear understanding of how available inputs are transformed into desired outputs.
>
> (The Inter-Agency Commission for the WCEFA 1990a, 41–2)

The Inter-Agency Commission for the WCEFA (1990b) confirmed the contested debates regarding quality education and learning metrics during the conference. Delegations discussed, for example, whether the emphasis should be on foundational skills, like literacy or numeracy, or a broader spectrum of relevant learning outcomes. They wondered whether quality should be defined as a minimum common level of learning to be achieved by all learners. Some were concerned about the devaluation of learning that is neither tested nor assessed – learning that contributes to the 'development of the creative potential of the individual, of imagination, of spiritual and aesthetic values, of community spirit' (The Inter-Agency Commission for the WCEFA 1990b, 14). Similarly, some cautioned against an overly 'utilitarian approach to learning' and argued that learning 'is a process of growth, and not a product to be acquired: learning is a journey, not a destination' (The Inter-Agency Commission for the WCEFA 1990b, 14).

While Jomtien attested to the ongoing debates over quality education and learning, little progress was made. The World Bank, the dominant source of external funds for basic education in low- and middle-income countries, lamented the decline in quality education with some caveats. A major World Bank report (Lockheed and Verspoor 1991), circulated during the WCEFA and published afterwards, stated:

> We frequently hear that 'the quality of education in developing countries is eroding.' The truth of this statement depends on the indicator of quality used. If … one considers inputs as the sole indicator, quality appears to have declined, since the inputs available per child have declined. If … one considers the output of education – children's learning – as the indicator of quality, we are hard pressed to say anything since so little research has been done comparing children's learning over time …. Improving the quality of primary education therefore means ensuring that more of a nation's children complete the primary cycle having mastered what was taught.

By the 2000 World Education Forum (WEF) in Dakar, Senegal, few internationally comparable indicators of quality education and learning were available. The synthesis review of EFA achievements (UNESCO 2000a) reported evidence on expenditures per pupil (as a % of GDP), enrolments in pre-primary, primary and secondary education, and textbook availability, but nothing on learning outcomes. These 'proxy variables'

> are used in assessing learning achievement … On these indicators, there are big problems in many countries. In South Asia and in Sub-Saharan Africa, less than three out of four enrollees reach grade 5 …. In the least developed

countries taken together, only half reach this level and many drop out after the first or second grade. Student-staff ratios and levels of teacher education are poor in many countries.

(UNESCO 2000a, 43–4)

Despite the paucity of valid or comparable measures of learning, broad consensus as to the value of quality education continued unabated:

Quality is at the heart of education, and what takes place in classrooms and other learning environments is fundamentally important to the future well-being of children, young people and adults. A quality education is one that satisfies basic learning needs and enriches the lives of learners and their overall experience of living.

(para 42)

Indeed, of the six EFA goals established at the WEF, one was devoted entirely to quality education (EFA Goal 6): 'Improving all aspects of the quality of education and ensuring excellence of all so that recognized and measurable learning outcomes are achieved by all, especially in literacy, numeracy and essential life skills.' Another goal (EFA Goal 2) makes reference to the value of quality education: 'Ensuring that by 2015 all children, particularly girls, children in difficult circumstances and those belonging to ethnic minorities have access to complete free and compulsory primary education of good quality.'

In the ensuing years the EFA Global Monitoring Report – mandated to monitor progress of the six EFA goals – developed a comprehensive multi-dimensional model of quality education, while continuing to utilize 'proxy variables' to monitor progress (UNESCO 2005). It not only reported newly published data on learning outcomes from international and regional learning assessments but also examined data on spending per pupil, completion or retention rates in primary education, student–teacher ratios, annual hours of instruction, access to and use of learning materials (textbooks) and access to qualified and well-trained teachers. Many of these proxy variables were limited in global coverage and of indeterminate reliability. Data gaps were common – for example, beyond inconsistent and unreliable data collection, evidences of inequalities by sub-region, district or school were lacking. In general, the EFA Global Monitoring Report noted that countries facing challenges in providing quality education experienced similar challenges in achieving other EFA Goals (UNESCO 2005).

During the 2000–15 period, national and international efforts to measure student learning levels intensified. Following the first Programme for International Student Assessment (PISA) in 1999, there was an unprecedented growth in the number and frequency of learning assessments – international, regional and national assessments – based on the assumption that learning is the crux of quality education and needs to be measured (Kamens and Benavot 2011). The World Bank further emphasized learning outcomes in most of its education projects, and in 2011 published a new strategy document entitled *Learning for All* (World Bank 2011b). During this period the first formal efforts to establish a global learning metric began. Advancing a broad model of learning domains and quality education, the Brookings Institution and UNESCO's Institute for Statistics convened the Learning Metrics Task Force (LMTF),[2] which highlighted Learning Champions[3] in different world regions and the scalability of select learning projects in developing countries.[4]

In sum, by 2015, there were significant advances in the availability, coverage and comparability of data on quality education, particularly data on student learning levels. Media coverage of quality issues, most prominently the rankings of countries in international learning assessments, grew as did narratives aimed at reforming the provision of quality education. Governments and policymakers became committed stakeholders in measuring quality education and learning. These efforts, as we discuss below, culminated in the reporting of internationally validated data on country learning levels along a single global metric.

Global Learning Metrics (GLMs) in the Sustainable Development Goals

A global learning metric (GLM) constitutes a platform allowing scores from different countries and assessments to be mapped onto a single, standardized metric with identified benchmarks and evaluated over time (Benavot and Smith 2020). The rise of standardized testing in the latter half of the twentieth century (Smith 2014, Kamens and Benavot 2011) was a central condition for the spread of GLMs. These efforts were supported, in part, by a belief that 'the quality of educational practices can be unambiguously quantitatively measured and that such measures are sufficiently precise and robust to be aggregated into policy-relevant rankings' (Meyer 2017, 17). Assessment outcomes are seen as comparable, objective and a rapid accountability tool that can be used to evaluate nationally funded reforms and interventions (Smith 2018). As the preeminent measure of quality (Murgatroyd and

Sahlberg 2016, Smith 2016), results in international assessments not only help legitimize country reform agendas but become a goal in themselves, as initiatives are established to improve country performance on GLMs (Fischman et al. 2019).

With the adoption of SDG 4 in 2015, metrics around quality education and learning expanded significantly. As Wulff (2020a) demonstrated, the creation of the SDG for education 'coincided with a broader push for learning metrics and large-scale assessments' (p. 21). SDG 4, originally negotiated as a broad global goal for education to reflect quality, became more narrowly defined by a small group of technical experts (King 2017). Political questions, including who sets the agenda and whose interpretation should be valued, were largely avoided (Sayed and Moriarty 2020).

Education targets and indicators in SDG 4 accelerated the construction of GLMs. Specifically, a disproportionate amount of attention and resources focused on the global indicator for SDG 4.1 (Smith 2019). It reads: 'Proportion of children and young people (a) in grades 2/3; (b) at the end of primary; and (c) at the end of lower secondary achieving at least a minimum proficiency level in (i) reading and (ii) mathematics, by sex' (UN 2017).[5] Not only is this global indicator weakly aligned with the broad aims of the associated target (Smith 2019), it also fails to reflect the lengthy debates that preceded its formulation. The global indicator emphasizes a narrow, human capital understanding of quality education (Unterhalter 2019a) and effectively undermines a rights-based perception of quality (Sayed and Ahmed 2015).

Turning SDG 4.1.1 into a GLM: Key Actors

The development of a valid and robust GLM is a challenging conceptual and technical task. The UNESCO Institute of Statistics (UIS) has a mandate to lead development of the underlying methodology (Benavot and Smith 2020). As 2015 neared, UIS was fully motivated to pursue a GLM suggesting that 'learning goals and targets in the post-2015 agenda will only be meaningful if they are underpinned by empirically derived common numerical scales that accommodate results from a range of different assessments of learning outcomes' (UIS et al. 2014, 1). In the early stages, UIS pointed to data illustrating the challenge ahead. For instance, in 2017 they estimated only one-third of countries participated in a high-quality cross-national assessment that would allow for reporting (UIS 2017a).

The Global Alliance to Monitor Learning (GAML) was one of several expert groups created by UIS to aid the development of SDG 4 indicators. Created as an 'umbrella initiative to monitor and track progress towards all learning-related Education 2030 targets' (UIS 2016), GAML has been the most active and better resourced of the expert groups (Smith 2019). Although membership is open to anyone willing to contribute, composition of GAML has a historical legacy dating back to the Learning Metrics Task Force (LMTF) (Fontdevila 2020).

Created in 2012, the LMTF was a multi-stakeholder partnership focused on driving global education towards an 'access plus learning' agenda (LMTF 2013). The emphasis on the technical measurement of learning (Fontdevila 2020) led some to suggest that the LMTF was conflating quality with benchmarking (Soudien 2013). At the end of the LMTF multiple questions remained, including whether measures of learning should be limited to those in school and whether a broad or narrow scope of learning should be adopted (Fontdevila 2020).

The Learning Metrics Partnership (LMP) acted as a bridge between the LMTF and GAML (Fontdevila 2020). Led by UIS and the Australian Council for Educational Research (ACER), the goal of the LMP was to 'develop a set of nationally and internationally-comparable learning metrics in mathematics and reading, and to facilitate and support their use for monitoring purposes in partnership with interested parties' (UIS and ACER 2014, 1). ACER has historically administered and consulted in the development of assessments, such as PISA and TIMSS (Fontdevila 2020). More recently they championed a 'universal learning progression', where student achievement across assessments would be converted into universal learning progression units (ACER 2019).

As GAML is self-funded, donors often dominate the conversation (Benavot and Smith 2020). Amongst the largest supporters of GAML are the UK Department of International Development (DFID), Australia's Department of Foreign Affairs and Trade (DFAT) and the Hewlett Foundation (UIS 2017b). After initially supporting UIS's production of the GLM as part of the £6.4-million 'Best Education Statistics for Improved Learning' programme (Benavot and Smith 2020), in 2018 DFID dedicated another £4.6 million to further develop SDG 4.1.1 and other learning-related indicators (Smith and Benavot 2019). UIS donors now commonly earmark contributions for measuring learning outcomes (Wulff 2020a) and donor support has increased in areas where there is a perception measurable impact is possible (Fontdevila 2020).

SDG 4.1.1 as a GLM: Current Conceptualization

Following considerable efforts SDG 4.1.1 was formalized as a GLM. In October 2019, the Inter-Agency Expert Group indicators upgraded SDG 4.1.1 to a tier 1 indicator (Montoya and Senapaty 2019) with data available in 146 out of 193 countries (IAEG-SDGs 2019). Tier 1 classification indicates the indicator is conceptually clear with an 'internationally established methodology and standards are available, and data are regularly produced by countries for at least 50 per cent of countries and of the population in every region where the indicator is relevant' (IAEG-SDGs 2020, 2). Originally a tier 3 indicator with no established methodology, significant efforts were made in prioritizing SDG 4.1.1 amongst other global education indicators.

The general framework for the present GLM was agreed upon at the May 2017 meeting of GAML, which concluded that a global reporting scale would be created. At its centre would be a common metric, on which international, regional and national assessment scores could be mapped (UIS 2017a). Developed over a three-month period in 2019, this common metric is now known as the Global Proficiency Framework. Focusing on mathematics and reading for grades two to six, the Framework 'articulates the minimum knowledge and skills that learners should be able to attain along their learning progressions at each of the targeted [grades 2/3 and end of primary] grade levels in the two subject areas' (GAML 2019, 3). Four proficiency levels or Global Proficiency Descriptors – does not meet, partially meets, meets and exceeds – are identified for each grade and subject. Donors continued to play a substantial role, with GAML pointing out that work on the Framework 'reflects close matches with the education goals, objectives, and indicators of donor agencies including UNESCO, USAID, DFID, the World Bank, the Global Partnership for Education, and DFAT' (GAML 2019, 4). The twenty-eight contributors to the framework included overall contributors and expert groups for reading and mathematics. Amongst the seven overall contributors, over half represented USAID. UIS was solely represented by its director (GAML 2019).

With the Framework completed, decisions were made prioritizing which assessment would be used for mapping purposes. The first selection criterion is grade of the assessment, with those best matching the target grade chosen. Within the aligned grade, international assessments would be the desired choice, followed by regional and national assessments with population-based assessments identified as a final resort (Montoya 2019). As UIS has previously indicated they will not push for new tests (UIS 2017a), it is unclear to what extent national assessments will be reshaped to meet the robust requirements for participation or when mapping (if at all) will proceed to population-based assessment – which are the only assessments that capture out-of-school children but may need significant modification to map onto the Framework.

Three processes (see Table 10.1) would be used to map assessments onto the Framework (see Gustafsson 2018, for the costs and benefits of each process): statistical recalibration, policy linking (at times called social moderation) and statistical linking. Statistical recalibration is more established and was explained in detail by the World Bank in their work on harmonized test scores (Altinok et al. 2018). Policy linking provides a lost-cost option that

Table 10.1 Processes used to map assessments onto the global proficiency framework

	Assessment taken	Mapping process	Link to GLM
Statistical recalibration	International or regional assessment	Statistically matching scores to a single scale (such as TIMMS) which overlaps with Framework	Converted equivalency score placed onto single global scale
Policy linking	National assessment	Local experts review each question of national assessment and evaluate whether correct answers match global definition of minimum proficiency	Equivalent cut-off score for minimum proficiency allows the national assessment to be mapped onto single global scale
Statistical linking	National assessment	Common test items that are mapped to the Framework and global proficiency levels are implanted into national assessments	Equivalency score, based on results of common items, are used to place countries onto single global scale

strengthens national assessments by ensuring benchmarks are in place, while providing local ownership (USAID 2019). Statistical linking is a more challenging process (Lazendic et al. 2019) that 'requires testing the same students using multiple assessments or testing the same item across multiple assessments' (USAID 2019, 4). The aim of this approach is to create a Rosetta Stone booklet, which would enable the translation of all tests that draws from it onto the Framework. It is currently being piloted in Chile, Colombia and Guatemala with results expected in 2021 (Cayuman Cofre 2019).

With the GLM conceptualization and mapping process formalized multiple challenges remain. Low capacity in low-income countries may limit the policy and statistical linking ability of some, and with the prioritization of international assessments, we may see additional participation in international assessments, to the detriment of strengthening national systems. Additionally, GAML discussions on how to factor in out-of-school children to the GLM for SDG 4.1.1 are ongoing, with present thinking focusing on statistical adjustments to country proficiency level, based on their level of out-of-school children (UIS 2019).

Alternative GLMs: Fragmentation of the Field?

The construction of a new universal GLM challenges the relative advantage of other international organizations doing comparative work that evaluates 'quality' cross-nationally (Fontdevila 2020). The desires and creations of alternative measures to SDG 4.1.1 and other education indicators threaten to fragment global attention and undermine the substantial efforts of UIS and GAML (GEM Report 2018). Amongst the potential competing agendas is that of the OECD. Their PISA assessment is the largest, and often considered the most influential, international assessment. The OECD has made clear its aspiration to have all countries participate in PISA by 2030 (Ward 2016), with national assessments better aligned with PISA. Addey (2017) found that this was already the case in countries such as China, Canada, Norway, Paraguay and Ecuador, with country national assessments adopting PISA proficiency levels. While the World Bank has been an active partner in proposing and developing the statistical recalibration process for the GLM for SDG 4.1.1, it has recently challenged the current metric. Using its dataset of harmonized test scores (Altinok et al. 2018) as a basis, the World Bank has recently developed and pushed out two new global measures of learning: the Human Capital Index and the Learning Poverty Indicator (see Measurements and Indicators 3).

Measurements and Indicators 3
World Bank's Human Capital Index and Learning Poverty Indicator

The World Bank revealed two complementary measures in 2018 and 2019: the Human Capital Index (HCI) and the Poverty Learning Indicator (PLI). The HCI uses five components to calculate future expected human capital with an aim to provide 'policy guidance for more and better investments in human capital' (World Bank 2018, 64). Scores on the HCI range from 0 to 1. A value of 0.50 indicate that a child born today in that country would receive only 50 per cent of the human capital by their eighteenth birthday, relative to a child born in a country expecting full education and health (Kraay 2019).

The five components of the HCI include survival (probability of survival to age five), two indicators capturing health (adult survival rate and under-five stunting rate), education (expected years in school) and harmonized learning outcomes (Kraay 2019). Deriving harmonized learning outcomes is done in a similar manner to statistical recalibration (see Table 10.1). Harmonized scores are mapped onto the TIMSS scoring scale with the TIMSS advanced international benchmark used to signify full quality education (Kraay 2019). Compared to the UIS GLM, the World Bank's harmonized learning outcomes do not include national and population-based assessments (Patrinos and Angrist 2018).

Three key assumptions of the HCI have been challenged. First, Stromquist (2019) questions whether the TIMSS benchmark is appropriate for measuring top performance. A very small percentage of students hit the benchmark score of 625, and in the 2015 TIMMS, no country met the benchmark (Mullis et al. 2016). In addition, Liu and Steiner-Khamsi (2020) identify a score penalty in the synchronization process, undermining the HCI assumption that, once harmonized, countries would be on an equal playing field. Finally, the HCI assumes quality is captured through a test score and that that measure of quality will not change over the education lifespan of the child (Kraay 2019).

The World Bank used the global average HCI score of 0.56 to justify the need for its new LPI (World Bank 2019a). The LPI claims to capture the percentage of the world's ten-year-olds unable to read and understand a simple story. Achievement data from early grades, primary and other assessments of ten-year-old children are combined with out-of-school numbers (100% of which are considered non-proficient) to create this minimum proficiency measure (World Bank 2019b).

Conclusion

Drawing on previous commitments, the international community in 2015 adopted the most extensive education agenda ever conceived. SDG 4 prioritizes equitable and inclusive quality education and lifelong learning. Its targets and indicators include learning-related benchmarks for pre-primary, primary and secondary education, as well as adult literacy and numeracy. Other aspects of lifelong learning – technical, vocational skills and ICT skills, as well as knowledge, values and skills related to sustainable development and global citizenship – are also included.

Yet, a narrow set of learning outcomes, mainly in reading and mathematics, have been prioritized. International organizations and aid agencies have focused resources on the creation of GLMs in these areas, while other, more complex subject domains, such as global citizenship, remain 'under development'. Propping up GLMs in reading and mathematics at the expense of other learning priorities will diminish and devalue learning in non-assessed domains. Moreover, current assessments convey a deficit model in which knowledge and skills of learners from poor, marginalized or indigenous backgrounds are undervalued, partly since their acquisition occurs outside of school in non-formal or informal settings.

The measurement of school-based learning in GLMs is not simply a technical activity but also a political activity. Powerful actors (e.g. World Bank, GPE, European donors, Education Commission, OECD) are supporting – financially and otherwise – the construction of a 'leading' GLM to promote SDG 4 advocacy. The longevity of this GLM is, presently, dependent on this external funding. Unless learning assessments come to be viewed as a public good, appropriate for the local context, with sustainable national funding, their impact on evidence-based policymaking will be limited.

Questions for Discussion

1. How has quality education and learning come to be conceived and operationalized in your country?
2. To what extent are GLMs fit for purpose? Whose political and economic interests do they serve?

3. How are countries likely to react upon seeing their students' proficiencies ranked on a global metric?
4. How would you describe the relationship between GLMs and the provision of quality education at the school level (e.g. teacher preparation, curriculum development, classroom practices)?

Further Reading

William C. Smith (ed.) (2016). *The Global Testing Culture: Shaping Education Policy, Perceptions, and Practice*, Oxford: Symposium Books.

UNESCO. (2005). *EFA Global Monitoring Report 2004/2005: Education for All: The Quality Imperative*, Paris: UNESCO.

Wagner, D. A., Wolf, S. and Boruch, R. F. (eds.) (2018). *Learning at the Bottom of the Pyramid: Science, Measurement, and Policy in Low-income Countries*, Paris: UNESCO-IIEP.

Antonia Wulff (ed.) (2020) *Grading Goal Four: Tensions, Threats, and Opportunities in the Sustainable Development Goal on Quality Education*, Leiden: Brill Publishing

Useful Websites

The Global Education Monitoring Report (GEM Report): https://en.unesco.org/gem-report/

World Bank's Human Capital Project (Human Capital): https://www.worldbank.org/en/publication/human-capital

GAML (Global Alliance to Monitor Learning): http://gaml.uis.unesco.org/

UNESCO Institute for Statistics (UIS): http://uis.unesco.org/

11

De Facto and By-design Privatization of Education in Developing Countries

Joanna Härmä

Chapter Outline

Introduction

The issue of fee-charging schools and their impacts on national and international development has over the last two decades ignited rigorous debate focusing largely on questions about whether these schools are making a contribution and what type of public and civil society response is appropriate. Do we abandon hope regarding government provision in places where this is failing, following a path of 'by-design' privatization by throwing our weight behind specific government policies that support the flourishing of non-state schools? Or do we focus on expansion and improvement of government provision because only schools operating entirely outside of the market will serve the poor and bring the difficult-to-reach into school? What do we do about the hundreds of thousands of private schools that already exist as part of a growing wave of *de facto* privatization, where schools have developed entirely outside of their country's regulatory mechanisms? The most divisive issue has been this *de facto* 'mushrooming' of low-fee private (LFP) schools targeting the relatively poor in urban slums and rural villages where they can attract sufficient numbers of children. The question of privatization in education does not just pertain to the rapid growth of fully private schools in a variety of locations across the world; encouraged by bilateral and multilateral donor agencies, many governments are trying various types of public–private partnerships despite considerable lack of success with these approaches in rich country contexts.

It is as a result of insufficiently planned and under-funded primary school universalization campaigns in the 1990s and 2000s that enrolments burgeoned virtually overnight, with negative implications for the quality of education following swiftly. In contexts where a sufficient share of parents had some disposable income, individuals began to open small private schools within their communities, and many of those who had been paying to access government schools with other like-minded families fled these same schools when their enrolment registers were filled with poor and marginalized students, whose peer effects better-off families shunned. This first wave of mass privatization in some countries and parts of countries of the Global South would set the scene for other forms of privatization to be purposefully introduced through partnership arrangements.

This chapter provides an introduction to the issue of privatization in education in economically less-developed contexts, beginning by defining the types of privatization that are becoming increasingly commonplace. The first part of the discussion introduces market theory, how choice and competition are purported to hold significant promise for educational improvement and how education 'markets' behave in today's messy reality. A second part discusses LFP schools as the single most significant type of private player in education, while the followed by a consideration of questions of accessiblity, quality and equity at low-fee private schools' considers questions to do with these schools related to accessibility and affordability, evidence regarding quality, and lastly the equity implications of these schools. A third part looks at public-private partnerships and discusses the rise of the concepr of branded school chains. A forth pat cooks at regualtion of not state provision.

Defining the Types of Privatisation in Education

Privatization in or of education would seem to imply the implementation of a policy to turn a hitherto government service private. Both government- or privately run services may or may not attract the payment of user fees, but where government provision is privatized or children are pushed towards the private sector, this is usually accompanied by government funding. Private actors in education can take a range of different forms: they can be individuals, small, medium and large companies, non-governmental organizations, community groups or faith-based groups which establish and run one or more schools. These might be structured as charitable or other non-profit entities, or as for-profit businesses. These might be funded entirely from user-fees, entirely from government funds, entirely from charitable or religious mission funds, or some combination of these sources. Schools both public and private are meant to operate within the rules and regulations of the country. Some countries allow for-profit providers, while others do not. In practice even those claiming to operate not-for-profit often find ways to hide or otherwise obscure their accruing of profit, while, counter-intuitively, those openly established to seek profit may make no profit at all. Most governments expect school operators to come forward for registration with the relevant ministry (Baum, Cooper, and Lusk-Stover 2018), which usually entails meeting some minimum standards (usually focused on facilities and teachers' qualifications). Those who apply for and gain registration are considered legal, 'registered', 'recognized' or 'approved' schools, while those that do not apply or fail to meet the minimum standards are essentially illegal and must 'fly under the radar'.

The most-discussed form of private involvement in education in developing countries in the last two decades has been the LFP school, variously referred to as 'low-cost', 'affordable' or 'budget' schools. These schools are generally relatively small (or at least they tend to start out small), having been established by an individual or a partnership of individuals or family members as a fee-paying alternative to government schools within the local community. In some rural areas and in many urban slums that grow up in and around major cities in the Global South, these schools do not simply provide an alternative but sometimes comprise the only schooling option within a reasonable distance from people's homes. These schools make up the vast majority of *de facto* privatization taking place today and are run entirely on parental user fees, while in some contexts community schools play a significant role at both primary and secondary levels, depending on the context. It is often the case that communities build and establish schools, intending that one day these schools will be adopted by and funded through the government system. While these types of non-state schools are flourishing in a number of locations in the Global South, more expensive private schools pre-date these schools and exist where low-fee schools have taken off, as well as where they are yet to do so. Such private options for middle and wealthier classes, having existed for decades and more, often started through early missionary activities under colonial rule. In most countries a range of private schools exist, ranging from those serving the lower middle classes up to the elites.

Other forms of privatization tend to be planned and even funded by government authorities or international donors or philanthropic bodies. Increasingly we see public–private partnerships (PPPs) being tried as a way to inject broadly one or more of three things: greater access, quality or efficiency where these have been seen to be lacking. These ends can be achieved, at least partly, through paying for students to attend private schools through vouchers or direct subsidies; contracting out the management of government schools to private organizations; or contracting with private organizations to provide training, curriculum materials, technology-enabled 'solutions' (EdTech) to support teachers or other support services.

The Theory of Choice and Market Competition

Milton Friedman is considered the father of vouchers and a pioneer of education market thinking, writing that governments should ideally have no role in the provision of education, to allow parents free rein to choose a school for their children (1962). His theoretical writings suggest that schools competing against each other in a context of full parental choice would diversify their offerings and compete against one another, leading to upward pressure on educational standards. In adapting his ideas to developing country contexts, proponents suggest that private schools are more efficient and cost effective, achieving greater learning outcomes. They suggest that teachers in LFP schools put in greater effort and are less frequently absent due to the conditions of much greater accountability under which they work. This is because proprietors of LFP schools have a market incentive to please their clients (parents) by keeping standards high, meaning that they are willing and are able to let teachers go who fail to live up to the necessary standard (Tooley and Dixon 2006, Tooley, Dixon and Stanfield 2008, Dixon, Humbleand Tooley 2017). This direct accountability to the fee-paying client who can withdraw their child at any time is said to be the key factor in the greater care and activity exhibited at LFP schools, contrasted against government schools, whose teachers do not face any direct accountability to parents.

Returning to Friedman, he acknowledged the 'neighbourhood effects' of education through which society would suffer if some parents did not educate their children, for example due to inability to pay user fees or because of lack of interest or motivation to send children to school. The suggested solution to this is to provide families with vouchers that they could spend at the private school of their choice. Friedman envisaged another role for government in addition to funding: government would stipulate a minimum level of education that all individuals should attain for the good of society and would also regulate schools. Friedman recognized that in rural areas with insufficient local populations to support a range of different schools in constant competition with one another, his market competition theory would not work, suggesting only that transportation was improving and that fewer and fewer people were living in rural areas.

There are many reasons why market theory does not work out in practice in the education sector. Firstly, for competition to work as theorized, there must be a range of options accessible to parents (i.e. several options that

POLICY 3
Chile and the World's Longest-running Education Privatisation Experiment

Perhaps the most famous and one of the longest-term neoliberal experiments with education privatization has taken place in Chile. The country was a democratic welfare state from 1925–73, and had a successful education system, with 80 per cent of primary and secondary school pupils attending the government school system (Castro-Hidalgo and Gomez-Alvarez 2016, 23).

The key education reform introduced in 1973 under Augusto Pinochet was the introduction of a voucher system, with funding attached to pupils' school attendance, rather than simply enrolment, while state subsidies were given to private individuals willing to start new private schools. Many parents who were not poor used the vouchers to move their children to private schools, and with the system allowing schools to be selective in their admissions policies and to charge 'top-up' fees, already somewhat privileged families could use the voucher to access even more expensive schools, and schools could choose to exclude less able pupils that would be more challenging to teach. At the same time teacher training was downgraded and salaries reduced. The voucher programme resulted in the poorest being left behind in the government schools, while becoming poorer due to rampant inflation (Castro-Hidalgo and Gomez-Alvarez 2016, 25). The fact that voucher funding depended on the actual attendance of children had a negative impact on schools in poor neighbourhoods, because the children of increasingly poor families often had to miss school to work for their families or to care for siblings.

In 1989 the voucher experiment was deepened, with a law allowing voucher schools to introduce a compulsory charge to families, which further spurred growth in voucher school numbers. By 2012, half of all school enrolments were in the private subsidized sector; 45 per cent were in government schools, while the remaining 5 per cent were attending private, independent schools. With the loss of all better-off peers to the private-subsidized sector, test results were almost certain to be worse in government schools. This led to a distorted perception that government school teachers were providing worse-quality education when it turns out that the reverse is actually the case: government schools have proven more effective over a longer term at improving student learning than private independent or private subsidized schools (Castro-Hidalgo and Gomez-Alvarez 2016).

The results of this more than four-decade experiment in school choice are very low scores on international assessments such as PISA and staggering socioeconomic stratification which is mirrored in school enrolments (OECD 2012). 'This is radical stratification, a sort of apartheid in education', as Waissbluth states, 'decreasing social mobility throughout children's entire life cycles. This apartheid education system is 'not working for anyone' (Castro-Hidalgo and Gomez-Alvarez 2016, 40), as evidenced by Chile's PISA scores which have not improved, while the system is characterized by intense stratification (OECD 2012c). The effects of this type of stratification can be felt throughout the system, not just by the poor, as made clear by Carnoy (2016):

> systems in places like ... Chile in the 1990s and early 2000s experienced growing income inequality along with growing disparity in the quality of schools available to more and less affluent children. One of the great ironies of this concentration of low social class students into low-performing schools is that it contributes to students suffering academically even in high social class schools. The mass of low achieving students/schools sets a (low) standard for the entire system. Parents of high social class children in their private or selective public enclaves believe that their students' relatively high achievement is proof that they are doing exceptionally well academically. This is not true.

In recent times certain reforms have taken place to mitigate some of the damage done by the voucher system in Chile, including the end of selective admissions practices in voucher schools. However, the country's education system remains highly unequal and with lower quality than that seen in the government-dominated system of Cuba (Carnoy 2016).

parents could realistically access, and have the required transport and adequate finances available to meet the associated costs); there must not be any monopoly provider; lastly, there must be objective, reliable information regarding school quality for families to use to make informed decisions. In practice in most contexts these conditions are not satisfied. In addition, government schools that, for the most part, do not rely on user fees, user satisfaction or minimum enrolment numbers, distort the market, in that they exist entirely outside of market logics and imperatives. Positively, this allows them to target the poorest and hardest to reach; negatively, where there is no support, monitoring or accountability for staff, this can mean that there is little pressure to maintain standards.

With regard to competition between private schools, the expected positive outcomes are often not forthcoming because parental preferences are often not what is expected or predictable, meaning that their key focus is typically not on teachers, their knowledge and pedagogical preparation and ability to do the job, and any ostensibly 'rational' insights into the quality of teaching at the school. Rather, in a range of contexts where schools compete to attract families, they tend to focus on public appearances, first and foremost through the school's building, facilities and general appearance, and secondarily through the uniforms, advertising and even school buses where applicable. This is common in richer country contexts (Lubienski 2006) as well as in a range of sub-Saharan African and South Asian contexts. In developing countries, access to reliable information regarding school quality is all but nonexistent (Härmä 2020), while in richer countries parents often judge based on published examination results or 'league tables'.

Low-fee Private Schools in Developing Countries

Since the 1990s, the small, independently and individually owned private schools referred to here as LFP schools have become the most common form of non-state schools, particularly in sub-Saharan Africa and South Asia, but increasingly in Latin America and parts of East Asia. The typical LFP school starts small with pre-primary classes and possibly some children in the lower one, two or three primary grades. Where the numbers are very small, multigrade teaching is the norm, until sufficient numbers of children enrol to allow for the hiring of additional teachers. These schools then add a grade level each year and seek to attract additional enrolments at all grade levels (Härmä 2011a, 2011b, Härmä and Moscoviz 2019). Fees are kept as low as possible to attract additional families, and this means that teacher salaries are invariably extremely low, but tend to be somewhat higher when schools grow sufficiently in size and reputation to charge somewhat higher fees (Rose 2002, Tooley and Dixon 2005b, Srivastava 2006, Andrabi, Das and Khwaja 2008, Härmä 2015, Kamat, Spreen and Jonnalagadda 2016, Kingdon 2017). Whether teachers are likely to be qualified, trained teachers or not depends on the teacher training system within the country, and the proportions of LFP school teachers who are properly qualified varies enormously between countries.

The typical LFP school tends to be smaller than a government school or more middle-class private school, and a large share of their attraction is that they are many (hence their small size) and so can be found closer to many people's homes. A key perception amongst parents is that they take better care of their students, stopping them from leaving school at any point in the day to roam around (Härmä 2013, Rolleston and Adefeso-Olateju 2014, Dixon, Humble, and Tooley 2017). A key aspect of the LFP school model is the direct accountability of the school to the fee-paying parent. This accountability rests on parents' abilities to remove their children should they become dissatisfied; proprietors are keenly aware of this and so try harder to satisfy parents (Tooley and Dixon 2005b). While private schools must maintain some level of standards to justify the fee paid, this ability of parents to change schools is often overblown, as education does not lend itself to the type of switching that is applicable to other more basic commodities in a market (Härmä and Siddhu 2017). In addition, parents tend to have a much hazier idea regarding school quality, and tend to base their school choice decisions more on proximity to home and their relationship with the proprietor and the faith they have in the school's ability to care for the child (Härmä 2011a, 2013b). The fee level also necessarily plays an important part in school choice, and while parents do favour better buildings, many LFP schools exist in sub-standard and even temporary structures, lacking sufficient space, toilets and other important infrastructure, as well as often employing unqualified teachers (Rose 2002, Srivastava 2007, Akaguri 2011).

Data on LFP schools are scarce, with new schools opening continually, and no data existing regarding 'churn' in the market, i.e. the schools that fail and close down. Markets are changing all the time; eighteen months after documenting schools in rural villages in Uttar Pradesh in 2006 (Härmä 2008), 25 per cent of the study schools had closed down. However, in 2020, many more schools at higher-fee levels have opened, with few of the very low-fee schools remaining. Illustrative of the wider pattern in Lagos, a 2016 sample study found that only 17 per cent of the 179 schools studied had been in existence in 2000, and fully 42 per cent had been established in the previous five years (Härmä and Siddhu 2017, 18). Likewise, in sample studies of Lusaka and Kampala it was found that 46 per cent and 32 per cent were established within the last five years, respectively (Härmä 2016c, 5, Härmä, Hinton and Pikholz 2017, 6). In addition, many do not come forward to seek registration with the government authorities because of the difficulties anticipated with meeting the regulatory requirements, and the fear of having to bribe officials (Härmä and Adefisayo 2016), and so are not counted in the school census.

What is known is that where the LFP sector has taken off in response to government failure to keep pace with demand and failure to provide education of sufficiently good quality, the numbers have been growing significantly. Development of these schools is not uniform across countries; they are less common in poorer parts of countries and in rural areas, and the continents of greatest development are sub-Saharan Africa and South Asia. In some of the poorest countries, however, private school 'markets' have not taken off to the same extent, even where government education is of very poor quality, as in Maputo and Dar es Salaam, where few private schools exist (Härmä 2016a, 2016b). In addition, the governments of Mozambique and Tanzania have been found to have higher capacity to enforce their own stringent regulatory regimes (Unterhalter and Robinson 2020). However, even in some ostensibly very poor contexts, some private schools may be found: in Juba and Monrovia many private schools were documented, likely due to the extreme dysfunctionality of government systems in South Sudan and Liberia (Tooley et al. 2013, Longfield and Tooley 2013).

What the Evidence Tells Us about Affordability and Access, Quality and Equity at Low-fee Private Schools

Affordability and Access

The second wave of the debate on LFP schools, once the initial phase of doubting their growing ubiquity ended, concerned their affordability and accessibility to the poor. Tooley and Dixon have been the strongest proponents of the view that LFP schools are affordable to the poor (Tooley and Dixon 2006). It is generally accepted that the poorest of the poor are unlikely ever to be able to afford to pay user fees; however, Tooley and Longfield (2016) show that the very cheapest LFP schools may well be within reach of the moderately poor. They point out that analysing affordability based on the costs associated with attending the *average* LFP school is likely to show that the poor are unable to access them, while the poor are likely to be able access the *cheapest* (and likely lowest-quality) LFP schools in their area.

There is now a strong body of evidence that shows that few families in the poorest two quintiles of wealth are attending private schools. The UK's Department for International Development (DFID) carried out a 'rigorous literature review' on the role and impact of private schooling in developing countries in 2014, which found that there was no positive evidence to support claims as to private schools' affordability to the poor (Day-Ashley et al. 2014). My research, starting in Uttar Pradesh, India, in 2006 through to research in Central Region, Ghana, in 2019 has found consistently that while a few truly poor families send their children to private schools, these tend to be exceptions who have a particularly favourable earner-to-dependent ratio within the household, for example. From rural Kwara State (Härmä 2016d) to rural and urban Central Region in Ghana, the relationships are clear. In the latter study, only 2.9 per cent and 12.8 per cent of the private schools' primary four pupils were drawn from the poorest and second-poorest quintiles (respectively). The corresponding figures were 25.9 and 22.4 per cent for government schools (Härmä and Moscoviz 2019, 26). Additional evidence findings similarly include Rolleston and Adefeso-Olateju (2014) for Ghana and Nigeria; Akaguri (2013) for Ghana; Alcott and Rose (2016) for Kenya, Tanzania and Uganda; Singh and Sarkar (2012) for Andhra Pradesh; and Härmä (2009) for Uttar Pradesh, India; but this list of evidence is far from exhaustive.

With regard to the geographical reach of these schools, they tend to cluster in low-income areas and slums that develop within and around major cities, which tend to absorb the large numbers of rural to urban migrants. As such, they prove generally accessible in terms of distance from home to the poor in the cities where they have developed; however, it must be noted that LFP schools are far from homogenous, and even within the same low-income area, they can vary greatly in cost and quality. Fee levels are a major determining factor in accessibility and school choice for most families; however, the other associated costs add considerably to the true cost, with the main tuition fee often amounting to only around half of the complete costs as reported by schools and families. Private school parents must also provide uniforms, textbooks, writing materials and must pay a host of other fees usually, including registration and examination fees. Depending on the context schools may also charge sports fees, building or development fees, information technology fees, parent–teacher association fees, to name the most common. Parents of government school children are also often expected to pay for some of the same costs, for example uniforms and writing materials, and they may be asked to pay a small sum towards registration and examinations, depending on the country and the local context. These costs are usually much less, however, as they are often not expected to supply textbooks and they often opt to under-supply their children with writing materials. Uniform policies tend to be stricter in government schools; private school proprietors are loath to turn away potential clients based on their ability to pay for uniforms.

Quality

Parents choose a private option over a government option (where both exist) largely due to perceptions of the former providing better quality education. However, there is no literature to date that finds LFP schools as a rule (in any context) using any better or more 'innovative' pedagogy than at government schools. Indeed, where many teachers are unqualified or have received very poor quality training, methods tend to consist of 'chalk-talk' (writing on the board and lecturing to the whole class), and rote-learning techniques with simple question–answer in class, often involving sing-song replies in unison to simple questions asked by teachers. There is little pedagogy that gets children to demonstrate true mastery of subject matter or to apply knowledge and mastered concepts to new or novel situations or examples (for a detailed discussion of pedagogical methods and teacher knowledge and skills, see Ngware et al. 2013). In addition, teachers often have to spend significant time writing material on the board for children to copy into exercise books, because many children come to school without the requisite textbooks (Akaguri 2011, Milligan et al. 2017, Härmä and Moscoviz 2019).

There is a growing body of research on whether a 'private school effect' exists, basing judgements on test scores and taking into account children's background characteristics. Essentially all of the research shows a raw test-score advantage over government school students, which tends to become greatly reduced once the socio-economic background of the students is taken into account or 'controlled for' in the analysis. However, test scores should be considered no more than a highly imperfect proxy for students' learning for a host of reasons, including schools' ability to engage in cream-skimming at the time of enrolment and during examinations.

Many studies find a private school advantage in India after controlling for background characteristics (Tooley and Dixon 2006, Muralidharan and Kremer 2006, Kingdon 2007, Goyal and Pandey 2009). Alcott and Rose find a private school advantage in India and Pakistan based on ASER data, but that additional private supplemental tuition played a considerable role in learning (Alcott and Rose 2015). Andrabi and colleagues find a significant private school advantage in Pakistan (Andrabi et al. 2010), while Amjad and Macleod (2014) found that private schools participating in a public–private partnership in Pakistan did not provide a test score advantage once the use of private supplemental tuition was factored in. Tooley and Dixon find a positive effect of private school attendance on learning outcomes in Ghana and Nigeria, as well as in India (Tooley and Dixon 2006, Tooley et al. 2010).

Not all of the research is unanimous, however. Chudgar and Quin (2012) did not find a private school advantage in their research on India and, most crucially for equity, found that higher-fee private schools were associated with higher test scores, meaning that the poor accessing the cheapest private schools were not found to be benefitting from their expenditure. Ngware and colleagues (2013) found similarly that the cheaper schools were associated with much less of an advantage over government schools than higher-fee schools. An evaluation of learning in private schools in four local government areas in Lagos found that there was quite a small but statistically significant 'private school effect' in relation to government schools. Yet only half of the private schoolchildren, tested in the first part of their primary three year on a test of primary two material, were found to be achieving at the level expected for their grade in English literacy, and in numeracy this was only 6 per cent (EDOREN 2015).

Even where private schools are found to be providing a slight advantage, it is usually the case that all schools are not performing at an objectively acceptable level of quality. Wadhwa notes that 'even [private schools] are not producing learning outcomes that are anywhere near grade level competency' (Wadhwa 2014, 21) – indeed, in absolute terms the results are abysmal, with only 62.5 per cent of private schoolchildren in grade five being able to read a grade two-level text. What is even more dismaying is the 42.2 per cent of government schoolchildren who could do the same. This evidence regarding India is similar to that found in Ghana (Härmä and Moscoviz 2019) and Nigeria (EDOREN 2015), where very few children are learning the desired minimum, with private schools essentially failing just somewhat less badly than government schools. Indeed, Alcott and Rose's various papers as well as their paper with Gruijters (Gruitjers, Alcott, Rose 2020) suggest that the key determinant of children's learning is the socio-economic background of the family.

Equity Implications

There are clear implications for equity where a slightly better option is available only to those who can pay, and where all those who can pay, choose to do so, leaving the poorest behind. Government schools in these contexts have become 'ghettoized', the preserve of nearly the poorest and most marginalized in society, while the very poorest are likely to be out of school entirely. Ghettoization means that a school has become locked into a downward spiral, where teachers become increasingly demotivated; there are fewer parents with 'voice' in society to care and to push for improvement; and there are often in some cases ever-fewer students (although this is not the case in densely populated urban areas where need is still great), and so the cycle of decline continues. Under these conditions, attendance at government schools becomes stigmatized (Härmä 2008, Joshi 2014). There is also stratification by fee-level within the LFP school sector, with several studies finding that fee levels are correlated with learning levels (Ngware et al. 2013, EDOREN 2015). Where LFP schools have mushroomed, inequity and stratification are undoubtedly exacerbated, with negative ramifications on society, as noted by Carnoy (2016).

The too-common underfunding of education services, particularly at the levels most often accessed by the poor (pre-primary and primary levels), inevitably has negative equity implications. However, there are many countries where the funds available are less an issue than the way they are spent, with much wider political economy factors at play that are not amenable to a simple funding solution. For example, in India, teachers' salaries are extremely high,[1] but accountability in the system is lacking (Kingdon and Muzammil 2008). In other countries, such as Liberia, funding is a key issue for the government overall; however, there are still serious political economy issues at the national parliament level that explain the level of funding that the education sector (and what levels within the sector) receives from the Ministry of Finance. For the foreseeable future, it is inevitable that parents with any disposable income will continue to pay for both insufficient tax revenue collection and poor spending decisions within government systems.

The Allure of Name-brand Schools and Public – Private Partnerships

With the LFP sector made up of constellations of hundreds and thousands of unconnected, atomized, individual efforts, often serving only between 30 and 200 children each, many minds have focused on the question of how to raise standards in LFP schools. Those who see more potential in improving and expanding private schools as compared with government schools have suggested two overlapping approaches. Firstly, the idea of chains of private schools under a single for-profit or not-for-profit owner or corporation is a way of getting around the 'information problem' in education 'markets'. Tooley draws parallels with the way in which fast-food restaurant chain customers come to expect a certain level of quality when they visit branches of any particular chain (Tooley 2007), so it is suggested that chains of schools could operate under a recognized 'brand name', just as other types of businesses do, which would serve to inform the client about what to expect at one of these branded schools. This is already being tried by corporations like Bridge International Academies (operating in Kenya, Uganda and Nigeria), Rising Academies (in Sierra Leone), Omega Schools (in Ghana, recently acquired by Rising Academies), SPARK Schools (in South Africa) and Schole (in East Africa); however, their progress is slow due to the difficulties inherent in the chain school business model. These more prominent chains are mostly foreign-owned or at least have significant foreign investment; there are some small national chains in several countries. However, none of these (national or international) tend to operate at truly low-fee levels, and none have managed to reach anything like the scale that government school systems or the collective total of individually owned schools have (Srivastava 2016).

Related with the chain schools idea is the recent trend towards public private partnerships (PPPs). These can take a variety of forms, from vouchers for parents to spend at private schools to other types of direct financial support; arrangements to supply training and materials (often ICT-enabled) to government systems; and lastly 'outsourcing' or private management PPPs which entail government schools being handed over to a non-state entity to manage. Outsourcing proves controversial because these arrangements affect civil service teachers who are often represented by strong unions, meaning that it would be extremely difficult for a government to grant the private operator the same type of control over staffing that fully private schools have. PPPs are becoming increasingly common in developing countries, such as Pakistan, Uganda, Liberia, Côte d'Ivoire and parts of Nigeria. The evidence is at best mixed, and at worst (for efficiency and equity) these schemes miss out the most marginalized children, at least partly negating the point of such schemes (Patrinos, Barrera-Osorio and Guaqueta 2009, Carr-Hill and Murtaza 2013, Aslam, Rawal and Saeed 2017, Afridi 2018, O'Donoghue et al. 2018). There are serious concerns regarding the growth of PPPs that involve foreign corporations providing chain schools, including that these corporations often use lawyers and court cases to evade national regulation; they could become 'too big to fail' and threaten national sovereignty; and they will lead to the extraction of profit from the 'bottom of the pyramid' to benefit rich northern company owners and shareholders.

Regulating Private Actors in Education

Regulation is a key issue with regard to the involvement of private actors in education and is directly linked with the subject of publicprivate partnerships. In an ideal world, all organizations that are involved with children would be well regulated first and foremost with child protection in mind (relating to school staff and premises), and secondly to ensure that private schools are providing education of an acceptable quality. At the current time there is no documented case of a developing country context with a significant LFP sector that is well-regulated for either one of these two key concerns.

DFID's rigorous review of the evidence on LFP schooling found that

> there is consistent evidence across a range of contexts that attempts by governments to intervene in the private education sector are constrained by a lack of government capacity, understanding and basic information on the size and nature of the private sector. Attempts … to apply regulatory frameworks suffer from poor implementation.
>
> (Day Ashley et al. 2014, 35)

This finding is reinforced by the work of Baum and colleagues at the World Bank (2018), who state that in their study of nineteen focus countries, the capacity to enforce regulations was found to be lacking. In addition, in Lagos, Nigeria, the place with the most stringent requirements of those studied, there was no impact on dampening private school growth, but that proprietors simply chose to evade regulation and fly under the radar. Heyneman and Stern (2014) note that in some countries regulations are only on paper, and are not enforced.

In addition, some papers have managed to document that schools' interactions with government authorities are often marred by rent-seeking. Inspectors for the most part focus their attention on physical inputs such as buildings, furniture and sanitation; they also tend to inspect schools' records, but very rarely do they undertake classroom observation or make any effort to ascertain the level of quality on offer at a school. Tooley and Dixon (2005) document reports of corruption in the system of school regulation and oversight from school proprietors and District Education Officers, while my own work documents that respondents in Abuja, Accra and Kampala

POLICY 4
The Abidjan Principles and Regulating the Non-state Sector

The Abidjan Principles on the human rights obligations of States to provide public education and to regulate private involvement in education' (www.abidjanprinciples.org) were formally adopted in February 2019, bringing together key education, human rights and community stakeholders and advocates. The Principles draw implications from established international human rights law principles and treaty provisions for education, rather than establishing any new legal provisions for states to ratify (or not). The key focus is the duty bearer of the right to education: the national government, and the document outlines the duties that governments have with regard to ensuring the right through their own educational provision at the system level, as well as through any non-state schools that operate within the national territory. Some private education stakeholders have viewed the principles as a potential threat, arguing that they go beyond the scope of existing international human rights law, that they impinge upon national sovereignty and that they will be difficult to enforce (Global Schools Forum 2019). In reality, the text was painstakingly drafted and then scrutinized repeatedly by legal experts and an extended commentary document provides the legal basis for all points contained in the document, derived from international law already accepted by large numbers of national governments. There is, therefore, no additional encroachment onto national sovereignty, while national sovereignty can be threatened by large-scale private involvement of, for example, chains of private schools. Rather, the document pulls together and interprets for the reader a large number of disparate provisions that pertain to the education domain. Crucially, the document places the greatest emphasis on the role of the government with regard to the right to education, highlighting the need to ensure this right rather than abdicating responsibility to the private sector.

While early drafts of the Principles placed an overly onerous obligation on governments with regard to regulation of private schools, as well as setting an unrealistically high bar for all private providers to reach (when taking into account the level of development of many countries to which the Principles pertain), the final draft had eliminated such impossible goals as insisting that all private schools pay teachers at the same level as civil service teachers. The document also embraces the principle of progressive movement towards full regulation and improved standards at private schools, recognizing particular contextual challenges. The final set of Principles has now been adopted or recognized by an expanding number of international organizations and education stakeholder groups, and is serving to raise the profile of this issue with many national governments and international organizations.

reported both corruption and general incapacity to regulate the private sector (Härmä 2019). Afridi's research shows corruption in the oversight of Pakistan's education PPP (Afridi 2018), which is highly significant because, freed of the responsibility to provide schooling under a PPP, two of the state's *main roles* under a PPP are meant to be regulation and quality assurance. Ultimately, the often overly stringent regulations that exist on paper are ineffectual and only have the effect of driving private schools underground.

Conclusion

Privatization in education in developing countries is a fraught issue which strongly divides opinions between two quite distinct 'camps'. On one side are those who believe that the provision of education should be the preserve of governments and that it is inequitable to allow fee-paying for an important service like education, particularly at the compulsory schooling levels. This side of the debate adheres to the view that encouraging school choice tends to fracture the education system and lead to greater stratification in education and in the wider society. On the other side are those who suggest that school choice is a key way to bring about better-quality education through schools having to compete in the market to attract clients. They even suggest that government schools might raise their standards for fear of losing all of their students. They suggest that partnership arrangements (which still require considerable government involvement) that mean children are supported financially by the government to access a non-state option will ensure social equity.

The evidence to date is overwhelming in suggesting that where private schools have 'mushroomed' governments have neither the capacity (of any sort) nor the political will to effectively regulate government or private schools. The suggestions of choice proponents beg the question, if governments were able to manage the non-state sector effectively and run a public–private partnership well, why would they not choose to turn these managerial abilities on their own schools instead? In addition, there is the danger that companies capitalizing on PPPs could become powerful enough within a given country context to threaten the host's sovereignty and authority over education while siphoning off wealth from poor families. By way of contrast, individually owned LFP schools keep the earnings of local people circulating in the local economy and represent a truly local and context-sensitive response to the needs of local people. These schools are getting on with what they are doing, providing a sort of long-term emergency response to the current learning crisis facing so many countries, while there continues to be a role for government provision in reaching the poor. The complexity of the major issues facing national education systems means that there are no simple or fast solutions available.

Questions for Discussion

1. What are the potential benefits for educational development of at least partial reliance on fee-paying private schools?
2. What are the equity implications of at least partial reliance on fee-paying private schools?
3. What is more important (and why): ensuring compliance with regulations and ensuring all teaching staff are qualified to national standard, or quickly scaling up access to education outside of constrained government budgets?
4. What are the pros and cons of individually/locally owned LFP schools and international corporate-owned chains of private schools?
5. How important is direct accountability at the school level in ensuring acceptable standards in schools?
6. What types of organizations are likely to make the greatest use of the Abidjan Principles and how will this tool be used? Can the Principles be used with regard to private actors or solely with regard to the state as duty bearer?

Further Reading

Härmä, J. (2020), *Low-fee Private Schooling and Poverty in Developing Countries*, London, Bloomsbury.

Day Ashley, L., Mcloughlin, C., Aslam, M., Engel, J., Wales, J., Rawal, S., Batley, R., Kingdon, G. Nicolai, S., Rose, P. (2014), *The Role and Impact of Private Schools in Developing Countries*, London: University of Birmingham, Institute of Education, Overseas Development Institute, UK Aid.

Srivastava, P. and Walford, G. (2007), *Private Schooling in Less Economically Developed Countries: Asian and African Perspectives*, Didcot: Symposium Books

12

(Re)examining the Politics of Education in Crisis and Conflict-affected Contexts

Mieke Lopes Cardozo and Ritesh Shah

This chapter reflects the equal input and scholarly contribution of each of the two co-authors irrespective of the order in which the names appear.

Introduction

From the age of eleven, Malala Yousafazi gained international fame for her active role in detailing her life under Taliban rule and for promoting the rights of children, particularly girls, who were being denied their right to education by ongoing conflict in Swat Valley, Pakistan. On 9 October 2012, Taliban militants shot Malala in the forehead while she rode a bus back from school, in a brazen attempt to silence her concerns. Malala survived the attack, and ten months later, she stood before a crowd at the United Nations in New York on her sixteenth birthday and proclaimed:

> I speak not for myself, but so those without a voice can be heard. Those who have fought for their rights. Their right to live in peace. Their right to be treated with dignity. Their right to equality of opportunity. Their right to be educated.[1]

Applauding Malala's vision and resilience, former British prime minister Gordon Brown, the UN's Special Envoy for Global Education, reflected that 'her dream that nothing, no political indifference, no government inaction, no intimidation, no threats, no assassin's bullets should ever deny the right of every single child … to be able to go to school'.[2]

Reality, however, paints a different picture. Approximately 75 million children each year have their schooling interrupted by a range of shocks and stressors – such as natural hazard impacts, outbreaks of disease or famine, climate change, gender – or school-based violence, violent conflict and economic shocks (UNESCO-IIEP 2011, Global Campaign for Education 2016). Worrying estimates from the UNESCO Institute of Statistics (2018) indicate that within contexts of conflict and crises, nearly 50 per cent of students may be out of school. The Inter-agency Network for Education in Emergencies (INEE) in their *Gender Guidance Note* adds to this picture that girls very often participate less than boys in education in conflict-affected settings, and they also tend to suffer disproportionally during disasters (INEE 2019b).

Research today is exploring the dynamic relationship between education, crisis and conflict, to understand how education is both affected by and effects a range of shocks and stressors, including insecurity, violence and natural disasters. In this chapter, we explore current dilemmas and complexities within the field of education in situations of crises and conflict, and new approaches to critically assessing how and if education can work towards transforming the underlying conditions of adversity and contribute to a more equitable and socially just society. Firstly, we sketch the context of rising concerns and international responses to the complex relation between education in conflict or crisis situations, highlighting emerging debates on resilience of education in emergencies. Secondly, we continue by outlining the merging of development, diplomacy and defence in international interventionism and how this impacts on education systems and actors in multiple ways. This leads us to discuss the multiple faces of education in conflict and consequently offer a social justice inspired framework for analysing education sector governance and praxis in conflict and crisis called 'the 4Rs'. We conclude by discussing how the debate on education and peacebuilding can move forward, moving beyond a problem-solving approach.

Rising Concern for the Impact of Crises and Conflict on Education

In recent times, it has become clear that climate change and weather variability, population growth, migration and displacement, local and global price shocks, illness and disease, political instability, violence and armed conflict are combining in complex and uncertain ways, threatening the lives and livelihoods of people and eroding hard-won development gains, including education (Shah 2019). The most recent global development compacts – namely the Sustainable Development Goals (SDGs), the Sendai Framework for Action and the Incheon Declaration – all recognize these mounting threats, and argue for a need to protect education from a mounting number of risk factors through increased attention and investment in conflict and disaster-prone regions of the world.

Alongside the immediate impact on the communities and nations where conflict and crisis are occurring are the flow-on effects to hosting communities and nations for displaced peoples. The numbers of peoples displaced by conflict and natural disasters are currently at an all-time high, with over 70 million refugees and internationally displaced peoples globally (UNHCR 2018, 2). Many end up 'flee[ing] to neighbouring developing countries, whose education systems are already weak and face limited capacity to support new populations' (UNESCO 2013, 2). The clearest example of this in recent times are Syrian refugees who fled the civil war in the country throughout the 2010s. The majority reside in the neighbouring countries of Jordan, Lebanon and Turkey, where public services, including education, were already struggling to function effectively before the Syrian refugee crisis. While all three of these countries have extended the right to education to the Syrian refugee population, there remain significant issues about the quality and reach of the provision which is provided to both Syrian refugees and other vulnerable populations in these countries. The result is that significant numbers of learners may enter into schooling but drop out in these education systems because their needs are not adequately considered in the education that is provided (Carlier 2018). Beyond access, then, are also questions about a system's capacity to provide quality, relevant education for all in a context of conflict and crisis. Failure to consider this, as we later explore, may in the long run undermine education's proven potential to build human and social capital, prepare communities for future risks and support stronger state–society relations.

Concerns about threats facing the education sector in times of conflict and crisis are long-standing. When the international community assembled in Dakar in 2000 to review global progress against the 1990 Education for All targets, it was agreed that greater focus and attention needed to be given by the international community to conflict affected contexts (CACs). While mention was made of this in the main text of the Dakar Framework for Action, there was no clear sense of what additional commitment should or would be needed to address the challenge of educational provision in CACs, and none of the six EFA goals made explicit the issue of conflict in the targets that were set (Smith and Vaux 2003). Ten years later, the 2011 UNESCO

	Estimated # of OOSC in emergency countries (In millions)	Total # of OOSC in the World (in millions)	Estimated share of OOSC in Emergency Countries
Preprimary (one year before primary only)	15.3	39.7	39%
Primary	32.9	63.3	52%
Lower Secondary	23.7	61.1	39%
Upper Secondary	32.3	138.5	23%
Total	104.2	302.7	34%

Figure 12.1 *Out-of-school children (OOSC) and youth from conflict- and disaster-affected settings* (see https://data.unicef.org/resources/a-future-stolen/), Table 3.

Global Monitoring Report (GMR) reiterated that with less than five years left to 2015, it was conflict-affected states that remained most off-track to achieving most of the Education for All goals set out in 2000, with nearly 50 per cent of the out of school population located in CACs (UNESCO 2011). As illustrated in Figure 12.1, more recent analysis by UNICEF indicates the situation has not changed, and children living in CACs continue to be those most likely to have their right to a quality education denied.

Several explanations are behind this situation. One is that inadequate attention has been given to thinking about educational system resilience in the contexts of crises and conflict which are increasingly recurrent. Driven instead by piecemeal solutions and responses to immediate threats, there has been an unwillingness, until recently, to consider the need for short-term humanitarian action to link up more coherently with long-term developmental and systems-focused responses prior to and in the midst of a crisis (Nicolai et al. 2019). When a resilience focus to response has been employed in CACs, it often falls short of ensuring structural and systemic-change (see Box 12.1). The result is that the medium- and long-term capacities of education systems to prepare for and protect against known and potential threats are lacking, and when a crisis hits, it is unable to maintain equitable access to quality education for all in the midst of adversity. This can lead to prolonged education disruption, permanent dropout of learners from schooling, weakened learning outcomes and long-term psychosocial concerns for learners (Nicolai and Hine 2015, Ireland 2016). In the long run this leads to a vicious cycle where reduced or limited access to schooling in the midst of a crisis can have profound impacts on countries and regions around the world seeking to recover and transform afterwards, particularly when entire generations of children may have never gone to school or had their schooling interrupted prematurely. This undermines opportunities for these future generations to be productive, active members of society and for the social contract between citizens and the state to be reinforced and strengthened (Smith and Ellison 2015).

Alongside this, relatively low levels of humanitarian funding continue to be allocated for education in emergency situations, despite the fact that conflicts today are more protracted and affect greater portions of the civilian population than in decades prior. According to UNESCO, 'while humanitarian aid to education reached a historic high in 2016, increasing by 55% from 2015 to 2016, it still receives only 2.7% of total aid available, amounting to 48% of the amount requested.'[3] This contrasts with an uncomfortable reality where humanitarian crises are on the rise in various parts of the world.

Funding for education in crisis contexts is suffering because education is not seen as a priority for humanitarian aid, and because development donors do not always see the clear link between development and crisis contexts. Despite the tripling of humanitarian financial assistance in recent years, the share of the total that goes to education has barely risen, standing at a mere 2.3 percent in 2018.

(INEE 2019a, 4)

Concepts 4
The Rise of Resilience as a Narrative for Action in CACs

In recognition of the increasingly complex and interconnected relationship between conflicts and disaster, as well as the need to bridge the short-term action typical of humanitarian response, with the longer-term view of developmental programming, resilience strengthening efforts have become much more common in the Education in Emergencies (EiE) community. A review of key EiE texts from 1990 to the present suggests that the term's use in recent years has proliferated, and regularly features centre-stage in key EiE policy texts and framing documents (Shah et al. 2019). Oftentimes, however, this concept has been used uncritically, and with the unintended impact of limiting possibilities for seeking transformative action which addresses the root causes of adversity.

Specifically, the concept's translation into EiE interventions has thus far focussed primarily on strengthening individual or community level resilience, and often for the purposes of coping with adversity. This is because much of the evidence standing behind this work is founded in human psychology or anthropology, which has sought to identify a range of individual and environmental assets which learners draw on in times of adversity to maintain positive learning outcomes. Such research identifies that traits such as having hope, purpose, social competence, problem-solving skills, emotional regulation and a sense of place and future were all critical to being resilient as an individual. This has then led to the rapid expansion of efforts to equip learners with these social emotional competencies through targeted programmes of support with the belief that in times of adversity, resilience becomes a resource to draw on (Shah et al. 2019). O'Malley (2010b, 489) critically observes that 'elements formerly identified as human "attributes", such as courage, will-power, fortitude and character, have been reconfigured as "coping strategies" or "skills" that can be learned by anyone'. This view has also had the (un)intentional impact of making young people, schools or communities accountable for their own circumstances in times of adversity. MacKinnon and Derickson (2013) link such narratives to the project of 'responsibilisation', where the power of the state or other external actors is replaced by offering the resources, initiative and capacities of individuals and communities to help themselves. It also tends to ignore underlying power structures which might purposely be acting to worsen the vulnerability of some to conditions of risk (Shah 2015).

In response, the past two decades have seen an increasing level of international advocacy and attention given to the urgency of supporting education in conflict-affected settings. For example, advocacy networks such as the INEE have arisen and produced guidelines for provision of education in situations of conflict and disaster; international NGOs such as Save the Children have made children affected by conflict a key concern of their action and advocacy work, and funding bodies, such as The Global Partnership for Education (GPE), have targeted support to conflict-affected states under the hope that education can 'promote peace-building and conflict mitigation, and foster economic growth' in such contexts. These campaigns also continue to highlight concerns over funding, as mentioned above, and to mobilize additional funding for education in times of conflict and crisis. For example, the 2015 Oslo Summit on Education for Development urged governments, non-governmental organizations and civil society, foundations and the private sector to mobilize funding for education in emergencies. This was followed by the launch of the Education Cannot Wait Fund during the World Humanitarian Summit in Istanbul in 2016, which aims to increase funding and provide this in more flexible ways, to support coordination between various stakeholders, support national ownership over funding and address both immediate and longer-term needs.[4] While on the one hand, this increasing international interventionism and action in contexts of crisis and conflict is long overdue, it also comes with new challenges.

Increasing International Interventions in Situations of Conflict: Impacts on Education

The last twenty years have seen a marked rise in Western interventionism in internal conflicts and reconstruction efforts – for example Kosovo (1999–2008), Timor-Leste (1999–2012), Solomon Islands (2003–13), Afghanistan (2002–present), and Iraq (2003–11), Syria (2013–present), Yemen (2015–present) – under the guise of nation and state-building by the United Nations or other regional stabilization initiatives (Novelli and Lopes Cardozo 2012). Driven by the desire to prevent a state failing or lapsing towards failure and threatening regional and international security, interventions have increasingly focused on a strategy of winning the hearts and minds of citizens (Novelli 2010). The restoration and reform of education service delivery is seen to be a key component of this strategy. It is based on the assumption that widespread, highly visible education policy changes can win public support for a new political order, but conversely poor educational provision is perceived as a symbol of state incompetence (Alubisia 2005).

The distribution of aid among severely conflict-affected countries reflects the impact of the melding of diplomatic, defence and development efforts in conflict-affected contexts. Figure 12.2 illustrates how aid to education has been increasingly targeted to a small group of conflict-affected countries such as Afghanistan, Iraq and Pakistan. Other conflict-affected countries, such as Cote D'Ivoire, Chad or the Democratic Republic of Congo, remain much more poorly resourced, despite the fact that financing gaps within the education sector are equally as large in these countries (UNESCO 2011, 174). Such data suggest that educational aid is unevenly distributed towards those where international diplomatic and defence efforts are most pronounced.

This evolution has also led to international actors supplementing or substituting the capacity of the state to deliver educational services during reconstruction. Such was the case in Timor-Leste, where for several years following the nation's referendum for independence from Indonesia in 1999, the UN caretaker government and other international actors involved in peacekeeping operations rebuilt schools, recruited new teachers and procured new instructional materials. Action in those initial years was driven by the pragmatic concern of getting children into school,

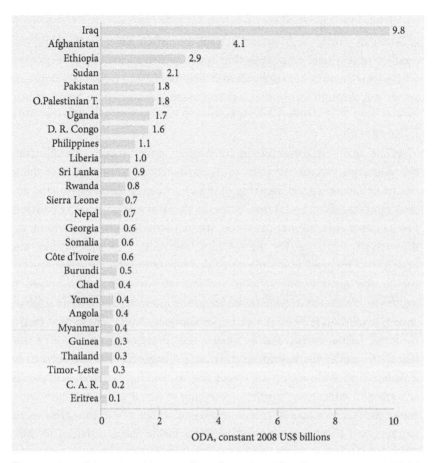

Country	ODA
Iraq	9.8
Afghanistan	4.1
Ethiopia	2.9
Sudan	2.1
Pakistan	1.8
O.Palestinian T.	1.8
Uganda	1.7
D. R. Congo	1.6
Philippines	1.1
Liberia	1.0
Sri Lanka	0.9
Rwanda	0.8
Sierra Leone	0.7
Nepal	0.7
Georgia	0.6
Somalia	0.6
Côte d'Ivoire	0.6
Burundi	0.5
Chad	0.4
Yemen	0.4
Angola	0.4
Myanmar	0.4
Guinea	0.3
Thailand	0.3
Timor-Leste	0.3
C. A. R.	0.2
Eritrea	0.1

ODA, constant 2008 US$ billions

Figure 12.2 *Education aid to conflict affected and fragile states* (see UNESCO GMR 2011, 173, Figure 3.14: Some conflict-affected countries receive far more aid than others, http://unesdoc.unesco.org/images/0019/001907/190743e.pdf).

rather than ensuring that the education that was provided was of quality or relevant to the lives of children. Actions included the mass recruitment of individuals to fill the void left by the mass exodus of teachers from other parts of Indonesia who fled after the 1999 referendum, the reconstruction and rehabilitation of school buildings, and the provision of learning resources and a new curriculum plan for primary schooling. The results were astonishing with regard to access, as children across the country flooded into schools. Today, however, the nation still deals with a legacy of this period of strong external involvement. In particular, the majority of teachers remain un/underqualified for the positions they have assumed, and children learn from internationally procured curricula and textbooks which have little local relevance (Shah 2011, 2012). The result is that many children in Timor-Leste attend school, but often learn very little. Post-conflict educational reconstruction must be driven by a long-term view where teacher training, curriculum development and policy development are driven through local processes and systems, rather than being driven, provisioned and delivered by external actors (Tawil and Harley 2004, INEE 2011).

While renewed commitment of Western governments to supporting the education sector as part of reconstruction is on the one hand positively welcomed, the blurring of lines between defence, diplomatic and development efforts by external actors is also a matter of growing concern. For example, educational provision (particularly for girls) became a key discursive justification for the military intervention in Afghanistan, and educational progress was a means of demonstrating the alleged success of the occupation. Building schools and strengthening education helped to legitimate continued outside influence in the internal affairs of the Afghani state (Novelli 2011, Novelli and Lopes Cardozo 2012). These new tactics have put humanitarian and reconstruction projects in the country, and elsewhere, under increasing scrutiny, as aid organizations are seen to be 'collaborating' with occupying forces and/or warring factions. Specifically, schools and educational projects receiving external assistance have come under increasing attack in recent years, jeopardizing both the safety of aid workers and those learning and working inside these activities (Novelli 2010, 2011, 2013b, Novelli and Lopes Cardozo 2012).

From the 'Two Faces' to the 'Many Faces' of Education's Relationship to Conflict

We had to leave behind all of our possessions. The only thing we could bring with us is what we have in our heads, what we have been taught – our education. Education is the only thing that cannot be taken from us.

(Women's Refugee Commission, in Perlman Robinson 2011, 1)

This statement of a Sudanese refugee woman who fled from Darfur to Chad in 2004 conveys the importance of education to those affected by emergencies.

It illustrates how communities often place high value on education in conflict-affected settings and perceive it as one of the few protective measures in situations of insecurity or instability (Smith and Vaux 2003, Smith 2005, Winthrop and Kirk 2008, Novelli and Smith 2011, UNESCO 2011b, Winthrop 2011, Save the Children 2013). Great importance has been, and continues to be, given to the restoration of education provision due to its visible and important role in restoring/reconstructing state legitimacy and the important function as a peace dividend that education can play (Rose and Greeley 2006). Education has been noted to have an important role in reconciliation or nation-building goals, through the messages and shared values it can promote – in essence promoting a form of social cohesion that can be often lost during conflict (Fukayama 2001, Tawil and Harley 2004). In post-conflict periods, education can provide for psychosocial recovery, normalcy, hope and the inculcation of values and skills for building and maintaining a peaceful future (Sommers 2002, 18). For example, children in crisis are particularly vulnerable to physical and emotional harm, and need new and different knowledge, skills and learning experiences to cope with these issues. Matters such as land mine education, health education (water, sanitation and hygiene (WASH) or HIV/AIDS education) and disaster preparedness (earthquake safety, for example) are critically relevant in such moments (Kirk 2006, 2).

Beginning with Bush and Sartarelli's (2000) landmark report, *The Two Faces of Education in Ethnic Conflict*, research started to suggest that restoring educational provision after conflict is insufficient if the goal is to promote what Johan Galtung (1975, in Smith et al. 2011, 12–13) calls positive peace – specifically, 'the absence of structural violence, the presence of social justice and the conditions to eliminate the causes of violence'. This goal identifies that peace is not just about the absence of violence but rather an ongoing process of active social repair and reform. What Bush and Saltarelli noted was that while education has the *potential* to serve such a role in post-conflict societies (what they call the *positive face* of education), it can equally do more harm than good. Specifically, this report suggested that the content, organization, governance and student experience of schooling can all be contributors to further conflict, if considerations are not given to how these domains might have fuelled conflict in the first place. In the long run ignoring these issues can lead at an individual and community level to increasing rates of non-participation in schooling through absenteeism and drop-out, and at a societal level to public dissatisfaction with education and the state as the main duty-bearer for providing this service.

What is increasingly noted in the literature is that particular educational aspects (such as equity, relevance, management considerations) and conflict dimensions (such as security, economic factors, political representation) operate in contingent and specific ways. Education, in itself, is rarely the panacea for conflict transformation that it is envisaged to be, and paradoxically, particular dimensions of the education system or its location within the post-conflict political economy in which it finds itself may render it to do more harm than good. Following on this, and drawing on the work of Salmi (2000 in Seitz 2004), we contend that education is related to matters of conflict and violence in two ways: (1) direct violence/conflict where schools become ideological battlegrounds for control in conflict-affected states and instances where physical harm is being done (e.g. attacks on teachers, physical punishment of students), or alternatively serve a protective function against such conditions; or (2) indirect violence, through which social injustices and inequalities are perpetuated and legitimized in discriminatory or (culturally, linguistically, politically, etc.) biased schooling practices, provoking social exclusion and the seeds of further conflict, or alternatively actively seek to redress such conditions through more inclusive schooling practices.

Researching Education for Peace and Reconciliation through a Social Justice Lens

In order to bridge the spectrum on causes of conflict and violence, on the one hand, and opportunities for peacebuilding and reconciliation, on the other hand, we now introduce a social justice-inspired framework for analysing education sector responses and action in CACs. The framework was developed with colleagues in the context of the Research Consortium on Education and Peacebuilding, a collaboration with UNICEF's Peacebuilding, Education and Advocacy (PBEA) programme. This '4Rs framework' (Novelli, Lopes Cardozo and Smith 2017) adapts Nancy Fraser's (1995, 2005) three-dimensional conceptualization of social justice (redistribution, recognition, representation) and combines this with insights on reconciliation. In the three subsequent sections, we link this to the first three Rs that together

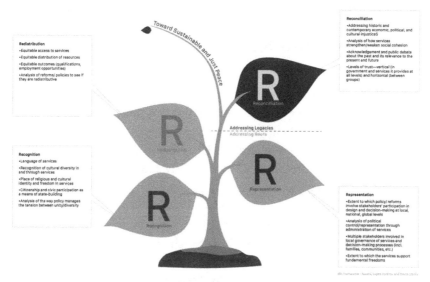

Figure 12.3 The 4Rs Framework. Source: Adapted from Novelli, Lopes Cardozo and Smith, 2017, redesigned by Adrian Serezo for the Early Childhood Peace Consortium Report (2018)

help to understand the underlying causes and drivers of inequalities and conflict: (1) redistribution of safe and equitable educational access and opportunity; (2) socio-cultural recognition and educational relevance; and (3) transparency, participation and representation. We identify how these domains might interface with the legacies of conflict, and both the challenges and potential for reconciliation. We would like to stress that while we separate these categories out for analytical purposes, they are in reality closely interlinked. The key underpinnings of the 4Rs framework are visualized in Figure 12.3, which is an updated version of the figure published in 2017 (Novelli et al.), redesigned by Adrian Serezo for the Early Childhood Peace Consortium Report (2018). The 'original' 3Rs as developed by Fraser are closely connected to the roots, while the 4th R of reconciliation is connected to addressing the legacies of conflict, and growing towards sustainable and just peace. Importantly, however, each context requires a specific and tailored approach to understanding and addressing the various dimension of injustices included in this framework, requiring adaptations to these Rs as needs be.

Redistribution of Safe and Equitable Access and Opportunities

In several contexts, such as Rwanda, Liberia, Kosovo and Sierra Leone, research has shown that a lack of equitable access[5] to schooling amongst the civilian population served as a grievance amongst fighting parties and fuelled further conflict (Dupuy 2008). In the case of Rwanda, schooling opportunities during the colonial period disadvantaged the Hutu majority, and favoured the Tutsi minority, who were deemed to be intellectually and culturally superior. Over time, it led to the Tutsis assuming a near monopoly on political, administrative, cultural and economic control of colonial society. After independence, the tide turned against the Tutsis, and strict quotas were put in place by the Hutu-majority to limit access of Tutsis to schooling. The result is that since independence, 'schools have had little influence in promoting national unity' (Weinstein, Freedman and Hughson 2007, 55). Rather, blatantly discriminatory practices, such as enforced racial quotas, led to growing alienation of the Tutsi minority, and youth in particular, who fled the country throughout the 1980s and banded together to form the Rwandan Patriotic Front army who would later become embroiled in the country's bloody civil war in the early 1990s. The Rwandan example is a prime case of the fact that 'those who control political and economic power tend to allocate priority of educational opportunities first and foremost to their own children and then to those who are next in line in maintaining the power holder's position of interest' (Degu 2005, 138).

It is possible, however, to consider how opportunity and access can more equitably be re-allocated in the post-conflict moment. Doing so requires careful consideration of the barriers that have traditionally disadvantaged particular groups from attending school. Actions towards the positive face of education might include a fairly distributed access to schooling facilities, with equal resources and opportunities for all groups of learners. When speaking about acute emergency situations, or even longer sustained situations in refugee camps, the instalment of school tents or similar ad hoc constructions can be crucial to offer a daily structure and safe space for children. But also in more protracted situations of conflict, or during a post-conflict phase, it is crucial to prioritize safe and secure access (including protecting children and teachers from attack, school premises free of gender-based violence and discrimination, and teaching pedagogies which encourage children's expression) and to redistribute educational resources to ensure that targeted resources are directed at marginalized students.

An example of where such efforts have been successful is Aceh, a province in Northwestern Indonesia, where after emerging from nearly thirty years of conflict in 2005, the provincial government made a serious and sustained commitment to addressing educational disadvantage suffered by the province and populations within it due to conflict. They eliminated school fees, increased targeted support to conflict-affected regions/populations and made a legal commitment to directing the province's resource revenues to education (Shah and Lopes Cardozo 2014). Compared to other parts of Indonesia, the province now enjoys higher-than-average participation rates across the early childhood, primary, pre-secondary and secondary schooling sectors. Examination results for the province are also close to national averages, suggesting improvements in quality. Data also suggest that the most conflict-affected districts of the province now have enrolment rates and examination results either at or above the provincial average, with educational inequality greatly reduced from the time of the conflict (BAPPENAS and UNICEF 2019).

Socio-cultural Recognition and Educational Relevance

When education is not perceived to be relevant by particular groups, it can be a significant conflict-trigger. A lack of recognition of the diversity of learners and their needs in terms of relevance can occur within the curriculum when the language(s) of instruction effectively exclude particular linguistic (and often minority) groups or leads to further segregation in societies. In Sri Lanka, this has led to a segregated education system that reflects a power imbalance between the Sinhalese majority and Tamil minority groups. From 1983 to 2009 Sri Lanka was embroiled in a violent conflict between the Sinhalese-dominated government and the Liberation Tigers of Tamil Eelam (LTTE), who were fighting for an independent state in the north-eastern regions of the island. The ethnically driven conflict led to a separation of the two groups in society and within the schooling system, where Sinhalese-speaking students attended Sinhalese medium schools (the majority language) and Tamil-speaking students attended Tamil medium schools. This helped to perpetuate the notion of a divided country and deepen entrenched hostilities (Lopes Cardozo 2008).

Exclusion can also occur when learning content presents biased or intolerant messages towards specific ethnic or cultural groups. Presenting certain negative stereotypes of 'the other' (ethnic, linguistic, religious) groups as being violent or untrustworthy can fuel distrust between students in a classroom, or in the broader community and society. In Sri Lanka, history textbooks and content, in particular, have been noted to be biased and exclusive of Tamil minority views (Davies 2011, Lopes Cardozo and Hoeks 2014). In Sri Lankan schools, history classes have had little attention for an understanding of how history is politically manipulated or an exploration of recent roots of conflicts and mistakes made by all involved parties, as 'Tamils are portrayed as "filthy" invaders, fought by heroic Sinhalese kings' (Orjuela 2003 in Lopes Cardozo 2008, 26). This has resulted in the case of Sri Lanka in government-driven attempts for reconciliation being perceived by parts of society as disingenuous. Rather, community-driven approaches for reconciliation, led, for instance, by minority Muslim communities in the north of the country, have shown greater promise for success (Duncan and Lopes Cardozo 2017).

The converse problem can also exist, wherein attempts to sanitize the content of the curriculum following conflict or ethnic tension by removing any references to difference, citizens feel that important questions of identity and struggle are artificially glossed over, leaving little space for a critical reflection of the past and the lessons that could potentially be drawn from it. Such is the case with the curriculum in Rwanda, which insists on the presentation of a one-nation narrative despite the very real sense of identity based on ethnic belonging/difference which exists in the country, and the desire of the education system to encourage critical thinking and engaged citizenship following conflict (Paulson 2011).

For this reason, some authors have argued for a critical intercultural pedagogy which respects minorities as indigenous rather than identifying them as infiltrators, and a pedagogy that stays away from uncritical and stereotyping forms of multiculturalism that do not take into account issues of religion, race, class or gender (Davies 2011, Keddie 2012, 9). An example of this is evident in Bolivia, where a national reform process began in 2006, under the presidency of Evo Morales (2006–19). The aim was to develop a new critical intercultural/intracultural curriculum that would begin to decolonize the minds of all (indigenous and non-indigenous, male and female) Bolivians. The curriculum aims to respond to the ongoing social conflict within the nation caused by centuries of colonialism, racism and deeply entrenched poverty and inequality that were the product of these conditions. It builds on the notion to *live well* (enough, and not better to the expense of some). Bolivia's education law developed under the Morales government was built on 'liberatory pedagogy', partly inspired by the philosophy of Paulo Freire (1970). It encourages personal development, a critical understanding of one's own and others' cultural identities and a critical awareness of reality 'in order to change it' (Article 3.14, ASEP law, in Lopes Cardozo 2011). The implementation of this set of reforms in practice, however, has been met with considerable challenges, including a lack of resources to train teachers accordingly, and resistance from politically opposing groups in society (Lopes Cardozo 2009, 2011, 2012a, 2012b). With changes in the political directions of new governing actors with the end of the presidency of Morales at the end of 2019, it remains to be seen in what ways, and how far, the underlying aims for an intercultural and decolonizing education system within the reform and curriculum will impact educational realities of teachers and students; as well as how long-standing a commitment to this bold new direction in education will be.

Transparency, Participation and Representation

The way in which management functions and processes within education systems are laid out, and how stakeholders' participation is facilitated within them, can foster constructive interactions and relationship building, or promote distrust and entrench intolerance. Political representation should ideally be promoted through fair ethnic, linguistic and gender-balanced representation at multiple scales of educational governance. For example, centrally controlled and managed educational provision can lead to a general lack of accountability and transparency between citizens and the state, particularly when educational resources and services are seen to be inequitably deployed. This has been the case in Liberia, where a culture of highly centralized government control of education continues, despite long-standing issues of political power being wielded in exclusionary ways, which serve self-interest rather than the national good. While the current government has made promises to reform the educational civil service and decentralize control, the system remains prone to high concentrations of power at the central level with rampant charges of corruption and growing public perception that the central government, and in particular current political leadership, has little political will or concern for improving education service delivery. According to one report, this remains 'the core of political, economic, social and environmental fragility [in the country], both in the past and in the present' (UNESCO-IIEP 2011, 44).

As a solution, mechanisms such as school-based management and decentralization of authority, control and provision to local levels have been promoted for their potential to promote citizenship, social inclusion and cooperation, and also can potentially increase levels of accountability, transparency and participation between educational service providers and communities (Dupuy 2008, Edwards and Higa 2018). In the case of Afghanistan, community-based and community-managed schools have proven to be an important and vital component of the national education system, as they have increased the value and relevance of education in communities where high distrust and concern for centrally provisioned educational services remain. The communities maintain strong oversight of these schools and are responsible for planning, monitoring and evaluating the nature of education that is provided to their children, including the ability to employ local teachers who may not have the appropriate qualification but are seen to have a keen sense of understanding the needs and wishes for education from the community itself. The government of Afghanistan has, over time, worked to incorporate these schools into its national system by providing their teachers with in-service support, resources and teaching materials as part of a recognition that these schools provide an important complement to centralized educational provision (Kirk and Winthrop 2008). Others have noted with concern, however, that decentralization of management functions onto the backs of community-based committees, who often assume such responsibilities without adequate training, resourcing or support, is often a ploy to substitute rather than complement state-based provisioning of education (Poppema 2012). Additionally, research findings from Indonesia and post-conflict Cambodia have indicated that these committees are prone to elite capture, and that despite being given authority, citizen-actors are afraid, unwilling or unaccustomed to challenging professional educational actors (Bjork 2006, INEE 2009). Such dynamics severely undermine the ability of such governance arrangements to constructively improve authentic representation and participation.

Moving the Debate Forward: Education and Peacebuilding beyond Problem-solving

As acknowledgement has grown of the complexities we note above, a new research agenda has begun to take shape – one that actively explores how education might contribute to goals of social justice and transformation, and longer-term peacebuilding. Novelli and Smith (2011, 7) contend how 'peacebuilding is essentially about supporting the transformative processes any post-conflict society needs to go through, and these changes unfold over generations. Developments through the education sector represent a very important part of this transformative process, with huge potential to impact positively or negatively'. They further stipulate how the emerging literature 'argues that education can contribute to peacebuilding more effectively if interventions and reforms are conducted at the sector level and by contributing to political, economic and social transformations in post-conflict societies' (ibid., 12). In addition, attention should continuously be paid to the longer-term sustainability of donor interventions during or immediately after conflict, so that impact extends beyond short-term 'problem-solving' approaches to longer-term structural improvements of the education sector. Hence, what this new research agenda seeks to respond to is *how*, *why* and, most critically, *under what conditions* education and peacebuilding processes can support each other.

This new research agenda responds to several shortcomings of prior work in the field. For one, research has been too focused in the past on approaching the issues of education and conflict from a problem-solving approach – namely identifying how to get the system back up and running – rather than paying close attention to education's location within a broader governance and social change agenda (Smith et al., McCandless, Paulson and Wheaton 2011). As we have suggested in prior sections, it is insufficient to restore educational provision without any consideration for the cultural, political, economic and social structures it feeds into and belongs to. It also limits education's potential to act as a transformative measure, by accepting the status quo and identifying all educational problems as the fault of the education system itself. The examples illustrated throughout this chapter show how many of the challenges facing education in conflict-affected settings are the product of historical (and colonial) legacies, long-standing social and economic structures, and political regimes and affiliations of power and privilege. These issues extend well beyond the borders of education itself.

Additionally, with the growing influence of international interventions in domestic conflicts, there needs to be acknowledgement that 'conflict and its resolution is shaped by a range of structures, institutions and agents that operate below, around, above and beyond the nation-state (local government, national state, neighbour states, regional agreements, supranational bodies, other nation-states)' (Novelli 2011, 7). This is especially true as regards the contemporary field of education and peacebuilding, which is located in a 'complex and highly unequal system of local, national, regional and global actors, institutions and practices', as we have suggested earlier (Novelli and Lopes Cardozo 2008, 483).

Finally, as Davies (2013, 3) notes, research that has tried to link particular actions and interventions in the education sector, to particular outcomes in conflict-affected societies, is severely flawed. She remarks, 'input-output models do not work in social terms, as too many messy contextual factors and power interests intervene. The "attribution gap" is too huge. Even if conflict were to decrease, it is almost impossible to trace this back to something in education.' For that reason she notes that positivist, reductionist and deterministic understandings based on mapping clear cause–effect relationships between education and conflict are wholly insufficient. Her observation is one that is duly noted in an INEE (2011, X) synthesis report, which concluded that 'the issue of discriminating the interlinking and cross-cutting dynamics between [various] domains' made it 'apparent that a full understanding of fragility dynamics was necessary before beginning to tease out how education interacts and interfaces with indicators of fragility'.

Where this perspective falls short is in its failing to undertake a more comprehensive analysis of the cultural, political and economic nature of the root causes of a conflict situation – which is vital to understand when thinking about education's role, function and purpose in post-conflict reconstruction. Additionally, the education and conflict literature has often been too *state-centric* in its modes of analysis, largely failing to acknowledge processes and actors operating in levels above, below and beyond the formal state.

For this reason, approaches drawing on cultural political economy analysis are helping researchers and policymakers to identify education's location within the broader society, historically and at present (Robertson and Dale 2015). Such frameworks for analysis provide a tool for understanding the ways in which: (1) education is both a reflection of and a contributor to past, present and future social relations, experiences and practices (the cultural); (2) the ways in which education fits into existing relations of production, distribution and exchange in society (the economic); and (3) how and by whom education's purpose, role and function in society have and are being determined and governed (the political) in such contexts. Rather than presenting an evolutionary or consensual process of change, educational policy production, reproduction, modification and adaptation become located within highly contested projects of state, nation and region-building. This more critical perspective helps us begin to understand the context, political will and motivations of various actors involved in education projects in conflict-affected states. It allows us to see the many faces education has in relation to conflict and fragility – faces we have attempted to demonstrate through some of the examples in this chapter. A cultural political economy perspective has also informed the development of the 4Rs Framework (Novelli et al. 2017) presented earlier. This framework brings together the economic dimension of *redistribution*, the socio-cultural dimension of *recognition*, the political dimension of *representation* and the interconnected dimension of *reconciliation*, and it allows for a more holistic understanding of the role of education in hindering or fostering transformations towards peacebuilding and social cohesion in societies.

While highlighting the complexities of the field, and suggesting that education is not necessarily the panacea for preventing conflict, we retain our optimism about the potential of education to serve a transformative role in society. In this regard, we side with Malala's Yousafzai's urgent call to choose books over bullets, and her continued optimism, despite the adversities she has faced. As she herself noted in her speech at the UN, 'The wise saying, "The pen is mightier than the sword," it is true. [...] let us pick up our books and our pens, they are the most powerful weapons. One child, one teacher, one book and one pen can change the world.'

Questions for Discussion

1. Education cannot create peace and equality on its own. What structural dimensions of conflict-affected societies would need to be examined and potentially changed for education to effectively achieve such goals?
2. How does conflict challenge the rights-based provision of education, and conversely how might a rights-based argument for educational provision fuel conflict?
3. How might increasing external interventionism in educational reconstruction threaten the ability of education systems to promote messages of economic redistribution, cultural recognition/ relevance, political representation and reconciliation that should be part of education's function as part of peacebuilding?
4. Teachers are often perceived as crucial actors in education (reform) processes. Can you reflect on specific challenges educators face in times of conflict or post-conflict reconstruction?

Further Readings

Bengtsson, S. and Dryden-Peterson, S. (eds) (2018), *Education, Conflict and Globalisation*, New York: Routledge.

Lopes Cardozo, M. T. A. and Maber, E. J. T. (eds) (2019), *Sustainable Peacebuilding and Social Justice in Times of Transition: Findings of Education in Myanmar*. Cham (Switzerland): Springer.

Mundy, K. and Dryden-Peterson, S. (eds) (2011). *Educating Children in Conflict Zones: Research, Policy, and Practice for Systemic Change – A Tribute to Jackie Kirk*, New York: Teachers College Press.

Useful Websites

The Inter-agency Network for Education in Emergencies – INEE website http://www.ineesite.org provides a plethora of information related to education in conflict and emergencies.

Education Cannot Wait Campaign (https://www.educationcannotwait.org) is the first global pooled fund dedicated to education in emergencies and protracted crises.

The Education, Conflict and Crisis Network (ECCN) (https://www.eccnetwork.net/resources) has an excellent, curated set of resources for guidance and research on education in crisis and conflict.

UNICEF's Peacebuilding, Education and Advocacy programme was a four-year, multi-country programme which sought to explore how education might make inroads to peacebuilding. A significant component of this work was research carried out by a range of international and local partners, the evidence which is available here: https://inee.org/collections/education-peacebuilding

13

Education, Religion and Values

Eva Sajoo

Chapter Outline

Introduction

Religion has often been seen as a barrier to development initiatives. Education is a particularly sensitive area because it inevitably involves the transmission of values – a contested terrain. Further issues arise in terms of access for vulnerable groups such as females and minorities and with respect to the religiously phrased attitudes affecting such groups that may be disseminated in educational settings. Instead of viewing religion and education as competing goals, can development initiatives incorporate religion or religious values to increase the participation of target communities and integrate new skills with existing identities? What are the dangers of adopting this approach, and what benefits might it offer?

This chapter will map the emerging arguments for incorporating religion in development strategies generally before turning to their application to education in particular. The focus will be on Muslim examples in education, since these have been some of the most high profile and controversial in recent years. However, the principles explored here are applicable across religious traditions. Whether religion- and values-based education models can provide sufficient academic competence and a balanced, pluralist context for learning will be examined through reference to contemporary models in Afghanistan, Indonesia and Pakistan. Reference will also be made to how these questions are being approached in industrialized countries, and some of the dangers of religious education. It is beyond the scope of this chapter to provide a thorough examination of the ways in which religious schools may be incorporated or regulated in national education systems. My purpose here is to examine the question of whether it may be useful to attempt to do so.

Is Religion a Barrier?

The antipathy towards religion and religious values embedded in education is relatively recent in Western countries but pervasive. The first schools and universities in Europe, which emerged in the early twelfth century, were instituted by the Church, and religious institutions had a dominant role in the design and provision of education for centuries thereafter. The impact of the Enlightenment – notably in the eighteenth century – with its emphasis on rationalism sometimes accompanied by rebellion against religious authority made it possible to begin to view knowledge and education as separable from religious values. This shift was encouraged by preceding centuries of European conflict in which religious identity was a divisive factor.

Subsequently, the doctrine of secularism which emerged in the nineteenth century, with its separation of religious and political institutions, has increasingly been interpreted both philosophically and practically to suggest that the only appropriate role for religion is in private life. State-funded institutions, like public schools, ought not to be associated with religious identity or values (Canadian Secular Alliance 2009, National Secular Society 2013). One of the most strident interpretations of secularism was the 1905 French law on the Separation of the Churches and State, which put religious institutions under formal state control – and gave birth to the doctrine of *laïcité* (Keddie 2003). More than mere institutional separation, this version of secularism demands the subordination of individual particularities to the unifying, rational ethos of the French Republic. The purpose of this model was to create a neutral public space; the privatization of religion would ensure freedom of belief. This concept has led to several high-profile controversies over religious symbols in schools and other public spaces, both in France and in countries which have adopted its model, such as Turkey and Tajikistan.[1]

In a development context, by the mid-twentieth century the decline of public religion was taken to be both a natural and desirable part of industrialization and rising standards of living. Theorists of secularization and modernization (Comte 1880, Weber 1904, Durkheim 1912, Freud 1927, Berger 1967) asserted that religion belonged to an earlier stage in human evolution and was fast becoming obsolete. Irrelevant at best, and often seen as obstructive, for modernist theorists of development, religion has been associated with irrational ideas, uneven educational priorities and entrenched inequalities. John Dewey, whose influence on educational philosophy was profound, asserted, in his 1934 book *A Common Faith*, that religion would be replaced by a focus on social improvement.

Despite confident predictions of its demise, religion continues to be a significant factor in the lives of people across the world. Indeed, as many commentators have noted (Thomas 2003, Micklethwait and Wooldridge 2009, Toft et al. 2011), its visibility and impact seem to be increasing. Ignoring this reality is increasingly untenable and puts development practitioners at risk of resembling the 'one-eyed giants' (Goulet 1980, 481) they have been described as by some critics. In failing to recognize the significance of faith in the lives of individuals and communities, development practitioners alienate some of their most important stakeholders and jeopardize the success of their projects (Figure 13.1).

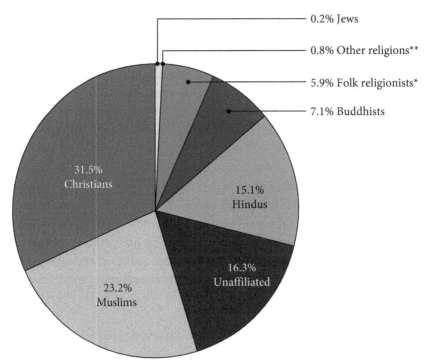

0.2% Jews

0.8% Other religions**

5.9% Folk religionists*

7.1% Buddhists

31.5%
Christians

15.1%
Hindus

16.3%
Unaffiliated

23.2%
Muslims

Figure 13.1 Size of major religious groups, 2010. *Source: Pew Research Center, 'The Global Religious Landscape,' © 2012, http://www.pewforum. org/global-religious-landscape-exec.aspx*

Why Involve Religion?

Amartya Sen (1999) and Martha Nussbaum (2003, 2011) challenged the conception of poverty and development with the 'capabilities approach'. This framework, most associated with Sen's landmark book Development as Freedom (1999), defined poverty not in quantitative economic terms but as deprivation of freedom, which has economic as well as social implications. Economic growth is a means of development not its ultimate goal. Rather, 'expansion of freedom is viewed as both (1) the primary end and (2) the principle means of development' (Sen 1999, 36).

Substantive freedom is measured by the 'capabilities' or 'functionings' available to individuals. 'Capabilities' may be thought of as abilities or potential to choose the kind of life that a person has reason to value. 'Functionings' are the actual things so valued and attained (Sen 1999,

74–6). To put it another way, capabilities are our range of choices and functionings are how we choose to exercise them – or those of our desired states that we actually achieve.

The first reason for engaging with religion in development is therefore conceptual. In applying Amartya Sen's definition of development as freedom, it must be acknowledged that religion is one of many possible goals or goods that individuals and communities may aspire to. It is not reasonable to view such aspirations as a type of 'false consciousness' from which societies may be expected to emerge after sufficient exposure to the technological goods of modernity. As Gerrie ter Haar puts it, 'the very idea of empowerment, a buzzword in the development industry, implies that people are acknowledged both as the means of development and as its ultimate end' (2011, 8). The rights-based concept of development that emerges alongside the capabilities approach requires balancing religious freedom alongside other basic human rights (Deneulin and Bano 2009). It is impossible to ignore the various conceptions of the good life that communities may hold – including those constructed around religion – without becoming guilty of paternalism.

The second reason is pragmatic. Religious leaders and organizations already play a significant role in many communities across the developing world. They often have both infrastructure and authority. As a result, development practitioners have begun exploring ways to make use of these enviable resources for goals ranging from conflict resolution to poverty alleviation and public health (Haynes 2007, Marshall 2010). A prime example of this partnership is Tostan, a Senegalese NGO committed to ending the practice of female general mutilation (FGM). Many Senegalese believe this traditional practice is religiously mandated; Tostan's response was to engage religious leaders in the process of changing community attitudes (Marshall 2010). As a UNICEF (1995) report put it:

> Religion plays a central, integrating role in social and cultural life in most developing countries ... there are many more religious leaders than health workers. They are in closer and regular contact with all age groups in society and their voice is highly respected. In traditional communities, religious leaders are often more influential than local government officials or secular community leaders.
>
> (Haynes 2007, 150)

If ignored, religious networks may be disengaged from – and in some cases, even hostile to – various development programmes. In societies where religion and religious identity are important for a range of reasons, any perception that a medical clinic, programme or school is a threat to religious identity or values can result in the mobilization of community resistance. Religion has often been invoked in opposition to various development projects, including education. One notable example of this is the militant Islamist group Boko Haram, which has been active in Nigeria. Its name roughly translates 'Western education is forbidden'. They have attacked more than 300 Nigerian schools between 2009 and 2013 (Mark 2013), and were behind the high-profile kidnapping of more than 200 girls from a school in Borno state in April 2014. In Afghanistan, which will be discussed in more detail later, an unprecedented school building programme which began in 2002, led by government and NGOs, has come under sustained attack by militants. The most commonly cited reason for their opposition to these schools is their perceived separation from 'Afghan' or 'Islamic' values and the suspicion that such schools are simply transmitting a foreign agenda (Human Rights Watch 2006, Yacoobi 2011). Failing to engage with religious values, concerns and identity facilitates the construction of religious identity versus secular development as oppositional projects. This does nothing to further development goals and may lead to project underperformance or failure.

Religion and Education

While there is an increasing willingness to find ways to cooperate with religious groups and mobilize support through religious values in some development organizations, including UNICEF (Haynes 2007) and the World Bank (Marshall 2010), the idea of doing this in educational contexts may raise particular objections. The prospect of religion in the classroom is a polarizing one, and has galvanized debates in developing and Western countries alike. The crux of the debate is really what we take the purpose of education to be and how best to accomplish those objectives.

Even in secular, post-industrialized countries, there are a range of perspectives on the role of religion and moral values in education. School prayers and overtly Christian teachings and moral frameworks have largely been removed from public schools in Europe and North America, as secularism is widely interpreted to mean that state institutions should not be formally or preferentially affiliated with any particular religion. Rather than identify the school with any particular practice, religion is either excised as something that belongs in the private sphere or is taught as a general

Religious Education course intended to provide impartial information about various religious traditions and faith communities (Department of Education, UK 2010).

This transition has not been without controversy, and there remains among some communities in Western Europe and North America a high demand for 'faith schools'. These are private institutions which teach state-recognized curriculum but may also offer further courses on religious subjects. In addition, religious principles permeate the identity and organization of the learning environment – the context as well as the content.

In the UK in 2017, for example, 6,177 faith schools received some state funding, representing just over 36 per cent of national primary schools. In some cases they are entirely state-funded, while others receive only partial funding (Department of Education, UK 2012, 1). The majority are Church of England schools, but this number includes Catholic schools and a few Jewish, Muslim and Hindu schools as well. This raises the question of whether the state ought to be involved in supporting educational institutions that promote a particular version of religious identity and values. Here is a brief summary of the main arguments against this arrangement.

Education should be about preparing students to be economically productive and democratically literate members of plural societies (Sen 2003, 2006). Curricula must offer basic skills (literacy, numeracy, technology) and a framework for understanding the democratic political process and students' future role in it. Religious education does not further either of these goals and should therefore occur in private settings (home, church) or schools funded entirely by private means.

The purpose of education is to create independent rational capacity in students in order to give them the ability to autonomously choose their own goals (Downey and Kelley 1978). Religious education, by its very nature, judges some goals and choices to be superior to others and encourages students to conform to a pre-constructed moral framework. It does not equip them to think for themselves. Religious education is not about developing rational capabilities but rather about reproducing a religious community through indoctrination (White 1982). This makes it incompatible with the objectives of public education.

Faith schools, by their very existence, keep children in an environment which reinforces a particular religious identity. This does not allow them to learn from encountering diverse views and does not prepare them well for living in a society where they must work with and respect people with radically different values (Short 2002, Burtonwood 2003).

The secular state must remain impartial – showing no preference for any particular religious community or creed (Macedo 1995, Habermas 2006). This means the state is neutral towards the choice of identity, of any faith affiliation or none. The provision of state funding for schools that promote a particular religious identity is seen, particularly by some atheist/humanist organizations and other faith communities, as a violation of neutrality.

The responses of faith communities to such criticisms are instructive, not only because they are similar across Europe and North America but also, as we shall see, because they have much in common with the perspective of faith communities in developing countries.

Faith communities make the following responses: viewing education as the mere acquisition of marketable skills is an inadequate account. Education is the cultivation of the person and includes their intellectual, emotional, physical, moral and spiritual capacities. This definition is also found in certain liberal perspectives on education (Arthur 2003). Religious

Policy 5
Religious Schools and the State

Religious schools have often been subject to tensions between their right to determine how their community values and beliefs are expressed in the educational context, and their need to conform to state legislation regarding such matters as non-discrimination, gender equality and curriculum content. 'Free schools' in the UK can be set up at the request of communities, in response to perceived educational needs and priorities. These schools receive state funding, and many free school applications are from religious groups (Department of Education 2013, 1). In 2009 in the UK, the Jewish Free School lost a case in which the school rejected a male applicant on the grounds that his mother's Jewish conversion was not recognized by the school's Orthodox chief rabbi. The Supreme Court ruled in favour of the student, viewing the school's rejection as an instance of racial discrimination (Shepherd and Butt 2009). Where religious schools receive state funding, similar issues have emerged over hiring policies that privilege teaching applicants with particular religious beliefs or only admitting students who profess the religion that guides the school (Pring 2005).

schools promise a more holistic approach to education, recognizing that parents are often unable to address all these areas. They point out that this educational model often produces academic scores that are ahead of those found in public schools.

The secular public school model is not neutral with regard to life choices and values despite the assumptions of its supporters. By excluding religion from the classroom, the implicit message is that non-religious worldviews are privileged and religious values are irrelevant (Callan 2000). Parents have a right to educate their children in a manner consistent with their religious identity, and public schools often present students with values that explicitly contradict those of various religious communities.

This issue is exacerbated with regard to ethnic/religious minorities. Some fear complete assimilation, such as the Amish in the United States, who withdraw their children from high school to preserve their religious values, or the increasing popularity of home-schooling among religious communities in North America. Others may regard the state as showing preference to other communities: Catholics in the UK have regarded state institutions as linked to the Church of England, which is Protestant. Members of the Alevi community in Turkey have alleged that the general religious education course administered in secular state schools actually privileges the Hanafi interpretation of Islam and denies their understanding of Islam and Alevi identity as Muslims (Zengin vs. Turkey 2007). In Ethiopia, where up to 34 per cent of the population is Muslim (World Population Review 2020), there are fewer state schools in Muslim communities than Christian ones. Further, state schools are often viewed as reflecting the values and identity of the Orthodox Christian population, making Muslims reluctant to enrol (Haynes 2007, 186).

Developing Country Contexts

While these debates surrounding religious schools remain animated in Europe and North America, they are heightened in developing countries, where additional factors come into play. One of the major challenges of educational provision is state capacity. The role played by faith schools can be very significant where the state is unable to provide basic education throughout the country, when it is unaffordable for families or when state schools are overcrowded or of poor quality.

The term 'faith schools' here encompasses a broad range of institutions, from schools that teach state curriculum, as well as additional courses or activities related to religion, to schools which teach only religious subjects. The significance of religion as part of the educational system depends very much on the particular format in which it is being delivered.

In the Democratic Republic of Congo, Christian schools 'have played a definite role in educational provision' (Haynes 2007, 182) since colonial times. They remain a major part of the educational system mainly because the state lacks the resources to provide and oversee nationwide schools. Togo and Tanzania are in the same position, as post-independence, state intentions to take over the administration of church schools were thwarted by lack of capacity (Haynes 2007, 182–3). To attempt to expand access to education in these countries while excluding religious organizations would be a failure to mobilize available resources effectively.

Turkey

In Turkey, the presence of religious schools is a direct response to the state's attempt to eradicate or control the presence and understanding of religion. Late Ottoman Turkey had a variety of schools, religious, mainstream and military, all of which had some religious elements in their curricula. Under Ataturk's Unification of Education law (1924) all religious schools were closed and religious teachings eliminated from surviving schools (Ozgur 2012, 32–3). *Imam-hatip* schools were then created to train religious functionaries with a state-approved version of Islam. Instead, after adding vocational training to their curriculum in 1973, and changes to university transfer regulations in 1983, these Islamic schools have provided a religiously grounded education to their students, the majority of whom have pursued secular careers (Ozgur 2012, 34, 45–6).

The attempt to create a secular education system in Turkey which was not religiously neutral but rather 'religion free' failed to take into account the ongoing demand for religiously informed education. As a result, *imam-hatip* schools have emerged as an official educational alternative, offering both religious and regular academic courses. Currently there are approximately 750,000 students enrolled in *imam-hatip* middle schools, and 650,000 enrolled in *imam-hatip* high schools, out of a total of 5.5 million and 5.7 million respective students nationwide (Genc 2018).

Religion has also been re-integrated into regular state schools, in part to ensure that any interest in religion is met with an officially approved version (Ozgur 2012, 48).This takes the form of a mandatory religion and ethics course, which begins in fourth grade and continues through high school, taking one to two hours of class time a week (Meral 2015). The purpose of the course has been to provide students with an 'essence' of the principles of Islam without getting into differences of interpretation or sectarian doctrines. The course also discusses other religions, with a view to comparing the similarities and differences among religious movements, but the focus is on Muslim traditions since these are most familiar to the majority of the population (Genc 2018). Under the AKP government since 2012, religious courses on Islamic subjects are offered as electives in state schools, in addition to the mandatory religion and ethics course already mentioned (Genc 2018). This has not been without controversy, as some Muslim minorities and other religious minorities within the country, as well as non-religious citizens, perceive that the government is providing a Hanafi version of Sunni Islam with state support through school curriculum.

Pakistan

In Pakistan, the role of traditional Muslim religious schools, known as madrasas, has been the focus of much scrutiny. More than 9,000 such schools are officially registered, with an unknown number operating unofficially. One Pakistan-based research report set the number at 35,000, and other research suggests that only 10 per cent of the total number of these schools are registered (Reynaud 2019). Estimates of the number of children enrolled in these schools stand at 2.26 million (Shafiq, Azad and Munir 2019), though subsequent studies indicate that these figures do not differentiate between students enrolled full time in madrasas and those who may attend supplementary classes there after regular school hours in a state school (Andrabi et al. 2005). Madrasas were actively encouraged under the administration of Zia ul-Haq (1977–88), who, in addition to overseeing a politicized new curriculum designed to produce 'Islamic guerrillas' (Mamdani 2004), also provided equivalence measures to integrate them into the national education system. In large part, the continued growth of madrasa education across the country is a response to an impoverished national education system which notoriously lacks basic infrastructure and committed teachers (Reynaud 2019). Only 68 per cent of primary school–aged children and 43 per cent of secondary aged–children are enrolled in a school of any kind (World Bank 2018), and madrasas offer free classes and often free room and board (ICG 2002). They are thus especially attractive to orphans and the poor who would otherwise be unable to access education in any form (Bashir and Ul-Haq 2019).

Madrasas serve communities that suffer from an educational gap, but it is unclear that they are able to fill it. Although the number of children who attend madrasas as their principle source of education may be small, the content of this education has failed to move beyond traditional emphasis on the Quran and religious scholarship, except in the incorporation of an increasingly politicized religious identity (Schmidle 2007). Madrasas are based on a particular interpretation of Islam (*madhab*) and usually include arguments for refuting and de-legitimizing other interpretations (ICG 2002), thus encouraging intolerant sectarian identities. A further concern is that the curriculum often encourages negative views of women and minorities (Marshall and Van Saanen 2007). Analyses of textbooks used in Pakistani madrasas indicate an acceptance of violence (Mamdani 2004, 137) and an exclusive representation of women in traditional roles. Rigid portrayals of religion, women and minorities are an issue in government schools as well (Bashir and Ul-Haq, 2019).

For the students who attend madrasas as their main source of education, the failure of these schools to supply adequate knowledge outside the religious sphere does not prepare them well for employment or participation in a democratic society. The content of education is of great concern, because radical views emerging from these institutions are dangerously wrapped in the mantle of religious legitimacy. Not only are these views conveyed to the much larger number of students who attend madrasas for supplementary classes, they may acquire legitimacy in larger social and civil circles. In response, a madrasa reform programme has been in operation since 2002 (ICG 2002, 24), attempting to show madrasa instructors how religious education can be reconciled with secular subjects, along with tolerance and respect for human rights (Marshall and Van Saanen 2007). This reform programme took on new urgency after a terrorist attack on an Army Public School in 2014. The Government of Pakistan responded with a National Action Plan (NAP) to counter religious extremism. One of its key objectives was to require all madrasas to be registered and to oversee some regulation of their teachers and content. However, this initiative has been met with significant resistance (Shafiq, Azad, and Munir, 2019). Critics of the education system in Pakistan point out that madrasas have tended to reinforce sectarianism, because although there are various *madhhabs*, or traditions of religious interpretation, within Islam, the instructors will emphasize that their particular version is the correct one. However, others have pointed the finger at the inadequate national education system in state schools, with their impoverished curriculum and poor learning outcomes as the root cause of susceptibility to extremism among young people (Shafiq, Azad and Munir, 2019). In any case, many students move between state-run schools and madrasas regularly, and religious studies are taught in both. It seems likely that a more effective national education system would greatly reduce the number of children who attend madrasas alone because poverty makes this their only viable option.

Pathways to Practice 8
The Afghan Institute of Learning

Afghanistan is a country that has been rebuilding its national education system from a point of almost complete destruction since 2001. Decades of conflict have created physical and social barriers to accessing education, particularly for girls. The Back to School Campaign of 2002 was an initiative led by the Afghan government, with extensive support from NATO partners and NGOs. It succeeded in increasing student enrolment from I million to 6 million between 2003 and 2008 (Wardak and Hirth 2009, 2). However, in 2005, a concerted series of threats and attacks from insurgent groups, particularly in southern provinces such as Kandahar, Helmand and Zabul began to shut down the new schools or prevent students and staff from attending them (Human Rights Watch 2006 IRIN 2009). As of 2018, the number of attacks had continued to increase dramatically, closing 1,000 schools by the end of the year. More than 3 million children, or about half of school aged children are currently out of school (UNICEF 2019).

Education has become politicized and in the eyes of militants is part of a 'Western' or 'foreign' attempt to destroy Afghan culture or values. 'Islam' has been used as an ideological line of demarcation, separating indigenous Afghans from suspicious foreigners and projects they sponsor. In part, this is because under the Soviets in the 1980s education was a government requirement, and boys and girls were forcibly enrolled in secular schools. The resentment this created in some parts of the country lends a heightened tension to the idea of education supported by foreign parties. This is yet another challenge to providing education in Afghanistan.

One successful response to this has been the Afghan Institute of Learning (AIL), founded by Sakena Yacoobi. It began as a female-run NGO in the refugee camps of Peshawar, Pakistan, providing training in response to a community request for more female teachers. From its small beginnings, the AIL has expanded into Afghanistan and supported more than 300 learning centres for students, teacher training and health education. They have also been successful despite insurgent attacks on other educational projects.

Yacoobi attributes her success to the principles of community engagement they have used. She explains: 'There are traditional concerns about the need and relevance of education for girls, concerns about the religious and cultural appropriateness of the curriculum, and suspicion about education from foreign agencies potentially embedded with foreign values and political agendas' (Yacoobi 2011, 312). The AIL responded by ensuring that both their programmes and staff were culturally sensitive: this meant incorporating religion in the classroom and in the deportment of its staff. When they offered workshops on human rights for women (including education), they grounded them in Quranic principles and Islamic precedents. As a result, not only did women enrol in larger numbers, they were then equipped to convince their male family members to support their ongoing education using arguments that had *internal*, local legitimacy. Similar principles have worked in the establishment of community-based education classes in remote areas far from government schools. The Steps Toward Afghan Girls Education Success (STAGES II) Project, operating since 2013 and funded by a coalition of foreign development partners, works with local religious leaders, parents and families to change attitudes towards female education. In many cases, they have been successful in setting up classes and accelerated learning programmes for girls who have never been to regular school (Banks 2017). By deliberately engaging with religious leaders, they have been able to soften resistance to girls' education, and some classes even take place in rooms located in local mosques.

While Turkey represents an unsuccessful attempt to make education entirely secular, Pakistan's madrasas are a vivid illustration of the dangers of permitting religious authorities to run the educational programme autonomously in some parts of the country. In both countries, religion remains an important factor in the lives of many citizens, as it does in many other parts of the world. The question is how that reality should be reflected in the provision of education.

Indonesia

One country which has responded creatively to the need to balance secular and religious education components is Indonesia. There are now multiple 'streams' in its education system which incorporate students from a range of backgrounds, providing various levels of religious teaching where desired but equipping all students with the basic skills required for employment and democratic citizenship.

The *pesantren* is the Indonesian version of a traditional religious school. They were the first organized communities of learning, present as early as the sixteenth century (Azra et al. 2007). Initially, they were groups of students gathered around a religious scholar, known as a *kyai*. The learning model was not merely a system of information transfer; *pesantren* education included a direct mentoring relationship with the *kyai*, devotional exercises, and often work on the property. This work could take the form of agricultural labour or some other activity which sustained the enterprise, in lieu of formal fees (Lukens-Bull 2000).

The curriculum usually included study of the Quran, the hadith, Islamic jurisprudence and *tasawwuf* (Islamic mysticism) as well as particular texts in which the *kyai* or local scholars were expert (Azra et al. 2007).

In 1912, an Islamic association known as Muhammadiya formed under the leadership of Kyai Hajji Ahmad Dachlan (Azra et al. 2007, 184). They pioneered a new educational model which incorporated more formal, structured practices such as fixed class hours, textbooks and examinations and added secular subjects to the curriculum (Azra et al. 2007). The combination of religious subjects with general education and marketable skills soon made the schools very popular. This hybrid model was called the madrasa. It is important to note here that while the madrasa has been an institutional form of education in many Muslim countries as early as the ninth century, in Indonesia the term refers only to this very recent educational model. Recognizing in the success of madrasas the demand for more broadly marketable skills, many *pesantren* began to explore various methods of incorporating general subjects into their curriculum (Azra et al. 2007).

Today, the Indonesian education system is dual. While in state schools religious education is an obligatory subject in every grade (Afrianty and Azra 2005), an equivalent madrasa category exists parallel to secular schools at every level (UNESCO 2008, 3). The 1975 'Agreement of Three Ministers' provided that madrasas following government curriculum and retaining a balance of 70 per cent general studies to 30 per cent religious studies would be recognized as equivalent to state schools (Afrianty and Azra 2005, 20). The National Education Law of 1989 completed the integration of madrasas into the national education system, making them in effect 'general schools with an Islamic identity' (Afrianty and Azra 2005, 20).

The recognition accorded to madrasas is both a response to an increasing demand for Islamic education and a way of ensuring control over the curriculum and instructional quality on offer. If Indonesia had left religious education outside the national system, the number of students enrolled in madrasas would certainly be lower due to concerns about eligibility for higher education and mainstream employment. However, by recognizing the widespread desire for both religious values and secular education, the Indonesian government has reduced the tension between religious identity and economic utility which afflicts some other Muslim societies. In fact, some scholars (Azra 2003) view religious schools as a prophylactic: thorough grounding in religious education prevents students from crediting literal interpretations of the Quran and religiously packaged radicalization efforts.

Though educational figures in Indonesia are approximate, current estimates are that registered madrasas serve 31 per cent of junior secondary and 36 per cent of senior secondary students, while unrecognized madrasas have recently expanded dramatically and now serve 17 per cent of students (Asadullah 2020). According to the World Bank in 2019, schools registered under the Ministry of Religious Affairs accounted for 15 per cent of the national total for formal education institutions (World Bank 2019b).

Madrasa student failure rates in national exams are 2.5 times higher than those of students from state schools, but the fact that madrasas tend to have a higher percentage of students from rural and poor families and receive less state funding must be taken into account in interpreting these figures (Azra et al. 2007, 182). However, in terms of gender equality, religious schools do very well. Figures from the 1990s show that in madrasas the gender ratio was equal; indeed, the girls' enrolment rate was actually 10 per cent higher than that of boys at the senior secondary level. *Pesantren* also boast little gender gap in the enrolment ratio (Hefner 2009). These figures are on par with those for the national education system as a whole, which achieved gender equality in the period 2000–3. Girls now outperform boys in national examinations and have a 3 per cent higher graduation rate at the senior secondary level (UNESCO 2007, xv–xvi). The literacy rate for adults is 91 per cent, and for youth, the figure is 98 per cent (UNESCO 2006a, 1). These statistics demonstrate a highly effective commitment to EFA – even more impressive given that Indonesia is the most populous Muslim-majority country and the fourth largest education system in the world.

However, as with Turkey, the government's support of Muslim schools has empowered certain versions of Islam over others. The Ministry of Religious Affairs has been instrumental in affirming a version of religious orthodoxy that is conservative and Hanafi Sunni in its expression, at the expense of more liberal or local forms of Islam. Religious minorities, including Shi'a Muslims and Christians have also found their positions weakened by the state's involvement with Muslim organizations and pressure from the National Council of Ulama (MUI) (Van Bruinessen 2018).

Analysis

There are two key considerations in understanding education in developing contexts. First, religious schools are often a response to internal demands from the community for values-based education which affirms communal identity or to external gaps in state capacity to provide quality education that is affordable and physically accessible. In many cases, both factors may be present.

Faith-based organizations (FBOs) (of which Muhammadiya in Indonesia and the Afghan Institute of Learning are examples) are potential assets in attempts to expand educational access. Indonesia represents a state attempt to partner with religious schools and provide avenues for their integration into the national education system in exchange for adherence to certain standards (such as the percentage of non-religious education in the curriculum). Insisting that secular education is the only acceptable model may backfire when the state is unable to provide such schools to all citizens. Religious schools, which often serve poorer, more isolated communities, are then left in limbo – their graduates unable to be assimilated into mainstream society because their education is not recognized. Even when the state has the capacity to provide secular schools in every community, there may be non-economic barriers to access. For minority communities, some aspects of state education may be seen as suspicious or even hostile. This can lead to low performance or enrolment rates.

Gender barriers may also be present. Religious education environments may be perceived as physically safer for female students. Some Muslim communities object to mixed-sex classrooms and will withdraw their girls. If there are no other recognized educational options, it is the female students who pay the price. Permitting a religious education option, integrated into the national education system and subject to scrutiny, allows such students to obtain the economic skills that will provide them with the best chance of autonomy as adults.

Development practitioners, working to expand education in low state capacity environments, may have much to learn from the successes and local knowledge of FBOs. This has been reflected in the emerging efforts to engage with religious development actors noted at the beginning of this chapter. However, there are hazards in seeking out such partnerships too. When international development organizations or the state engage with local FBOs, they will be exposed to the understanding of a religious tradition that motivates that particular organization (or at least, its leadership). While this can be useful, it would be dangerous to take that particular understanding to be the 'authentic' or uncontested version of any religion. A senior male authority figure may express views which he justifies in religious terms; these may be quite different from those one might hear from younger members of the religious community or from female ones. The first danger in engaging with religious organizations is therefore empowering a particular version of that religion as authoritative (Balchin 2011).

A second concern is the teaching offered in religious education settings. Does it have a negative impact on the students' capacity for pluralism, either by explicitly teaching that people with different beliefs are inferior or simply by minimizing exposure to others who do not adhere to the same religious understanding? The Muslim Brotherhood is an FBO which, among other social services, provides education in impoverished neighbourhoods – not just in Egypt but across the Middle East. The version of Islam that they espouse is very conservative and concerns Muslim feminists and democrats alike. Their mission is the 'awakening' of Muslim societies that they see as lapsed, and their version of Islam is the only one they recognize (Ahmed 2011b). Such teachings are of increasing concern in the wake of the series of political uprisings and revolutions that has been called the 'Arab Spring' and the increasing sectarianism evident in Syria and the Gulf States. As in Pakistan, when education includes the inculcation of an intolerant version of religious identity, the risk of heightening social conflict is all too real. Transitional societies are often those in which state capacity is lowest and the scope for FBOs to provide education is the largest. They are also societies in which the need for tolerant, unifying versions of identity is the most acute.

No less significant is the importance of female education. The economic and social impacts of female education and employment are one that developing countries can least afford to ignore (Schultz 2001). While incorporating religious schools into the national system may provide access to girls who would otherwise be excluded from school, the nature of what they are taught is critical. Religious education programmes may hinder the rights of women by teaching female subordination either as doctrine or as part of the 'hidden curriculum' (the attitudes, understandings and expectations that are communicated through the behaviour of teachers, staff and classmates in the educational context). In such an environment, the potential of the education girls receive is significantly curtailed, because while they learn new skills, they also learn how little they are expected to use them.

In view of these various risks, any incorporation of religious organizations in development projects or the national education system must include some system of regulation to ensure that the education on offer does not encourage parochialism or gender inequality. Some critics would say that such criteria would eliminate religiously based education as an option anywhere. This would be a mistake. In development settings, the inclusion of religious principles and conduct in education may increase participation and reduce the perception that the education provided is part of a 'foreign' agenda. The existence of such schools undermines radical narratives that would portray the state or development organizations as the enemy of religious communities.

Conclusion

This chapter has sought to examine the promise and peril of embedding religion within an educational context. While there are undeniable risks in encouraging faith-based schools and education programmes, there are risks attached to excluding religious actors from education and development efforts as well. Development must respect people as ends in themselves, with the aspirations and values that they cherish. For many people across the world, 'faith is no mere label attached to the surface of the self; it is a constituent of the self' (Callan 2000, 60). Religious authority is often a decisive influence which can be harnessed in support of education or against it.

Apart from the principle of recognizing the aspirations, identity and concepts of education that particular communities of faith may cherish, education in development contexts involves additional factors. Low state capacity for educational provision often necessitates the participation of civil society actors, both NGOs and FBOs. Further, the provision of education by non-state actors is particularly vulnerable to perceptions that the educational objectives are foreign – if not hostile – to the values of local communities. In view of these considerations, insisting on a strictly secular programme of education may not be the most effective way to pursue education for all.[2]

Questions for Discussion

1. Outline one example of the inclusion of religion in an education programme (e.g. curriculum subject, specialist schools), and compare and contrast how different perspectives (e.g. human capital theory, human rights, postcolonial theory) might lead you to evaluate the outcomes of this initiative.
2. What are the advantages and disadvantages of prohibiting the discussion of religion in state schools? How do different approaches to citizenship colour how these advantages and disadvantages are viewed?
3. How has the history of religions in particular contexts affected approaches to faith-based schools by governments? How do the approaches taken by governments differ from those of the leadership of faith communities?

Further Reading

Deneulin, S. with Bano, M. (2009), *Religion and Development: Rewriting the Secular Script*, London and New York: Zed Books.

Gardner, R. Cairns, J. and Lawton, D. (eds) (2005), *Faith Schools: Consensus or Conflict*, Abingdon, Oxon: Routledge.

Sivasubramaniam, M. and Hayhoe, R. (eds) (2018) Religion and Education: Comparative and International Perspectives, Oxford: Symposium Books.

14

Languages and Identities

Sheila Aikman

Chapter Outline

Introduction

This chapter investigates choices made in relation to the languages of schooling, language pedagogies in classrooms and ways learners use language. That the languages used in and around schools are the results of choices made by institutional power holders such as policymakers and curriculum writers might seem obvious, but the chapter asks how teachers and students mediate, or 'enact', official language and education policy and how they use language in classroom interactions. It also considers pupils' and parents' language expectations with regard to schools.

The language policies and language practices of schooling flow from particular ways of thinking about what language is and the positive and negative identities attributed to languages and their speakers. Three orientations towards language(s) inform different approaches to schooling: first, there are situations where one dominant language is associated with economic development, opportunity, prestige and inclusion. Schooling is expected to foster and nourish learners so this language becomes an investment for individual and national economic development. This orientation has led to investing a single language with authority and status and consequently monolingual schooling in the dominant language. A second, though not mutually exclusive, orientation which informs the selection of languages for use in school stems from a view of language and languages as resources for human and social development. Here, linguistic diversity, or multilingualism, is considered a cultural resource and a right. Multilingual education has been promoted in many countries as a stepping stone to monolingualism and proficiency in the dominant language. But multilingualism can be valued on its own terms. For Canagarajah and Liyange (2012), researching language and education in South Asia, a multilingual individual refers to someone with a repertoire of more than one language, where each language is viewed as separate and discrete as if that person had two or three monolingualisms. In terms of multilingual societies, they note how particular languages are linked to particular identities or geographical locations, and particular languages are seen as bounded and distinct from one another.

A third orientation towards languages in schooling, informed by research in sociolinguistics and linguistic anthropology, investigates how young people use languages, dialects and genres in fluid and incomplete ways drawing from personal 'linguistic repertoires'. With this approach speakers are viewed as plurilingual, each with their personal tool-kit of language skills. A plurilingual orientation does not view schooling as learning first one language and then another (additive multilingualism) or a situation where one language supplants another (subtractive bilingualism which means that as you learn one language, you lose proficiency in another). It recognizes that learners may have different degrees of proficiency or competence in several languages. Where there has been migration and social upheaval, for example in Mozambique over the long period of war (1977–94), speakers of different African languages became more mixed and less tightly geographically located. Rural classrooms could comprise a diversity of language speakers with different strengths and abilities in different languages. In urban classrooms, where there has been rapid migration to the cities or movements of internally displaced peoples or refugee populations (Davies 2004), it may not be possible to identify a common first or second language. Indeed, in such situations young people may have complex repertoires of multiple and incomplete languages and practices (Garcia and Flores 2012).

Ethnologue is an online and print publication which provides information about living languages across the globe. It is continually updated as languages grow, change, shrink or disappear as a consequence of the ways they are valued and used. Today of 7111 living languages, 537 (8.69 per cent) are used in institutions, such as schools, government and the mass media, while 2895 (40.71 per cent) are classed as endangered. The *Ethnologue* authors note that a language becomes endangered when its users begin to teach and speak a more dominant language to their children. Of the 51.23 per cent of languages classed as 'stable', children are still learning and using these languages but changing situations can propel them into decline and endangerment (Eberhard et al. 2019, www.ethnologue.com). Given these statistics, what can be said about the languages taught in schools, how they are valued and why they are chosen?

The two country case studies in this chapter, Nepal and Bolivia, offer insights into these questions and demonstrate the diversity and complexity of expectations and demands for languages in schooling. The Nepal case reveals the persistence of a one-language-one-nation practice over time in the face of multilingual national policies and linguistic diversity, while the Bolivia case highlights the importance of school language policy in shaping a new society based on recognition of linguistic and cultural plurality. These case studies offer insights into language regimes, which are 'political constructs, where ideologies function as linguistic and discursive practices' and are 'fluid and constantly changing across time and space' (Coronel-Molina 2017, 1).

The term 'language in schooling' is used throughout the chapter to stress the focus on schooling and educational institutions and systems rather than education and learning more generally. However, a distinction is made between a language or languages of instruction, which refers to the language(s) used for formal teaching and learning (sometimes referred to as the 'medium of instruction') and the learning of a language which may or may not take place through the school 'language of instruction'. Moreover, informal language practices abound in schools: used by teachers to help learner comprehension, used by learners together in the spaces beyond classrooms, used by staff in staffrooms. These are language practices which are not officially sanctioned by the education system but which are part of students' and teachers' communicative repertoires.

National Development and Monolingual Education Policies

In many countries, the languages of instruction and the languages learned have roots in a nineteenth-century European vision of one common language for all, where this language was intended as a unifying force and symbol of national identity. This vision was driven by the belief that the coherence and cohesion of a society and its governability benefit from the existence of just one language (Blommaert and Verschueren 1998, 191). And such (implicit or explicit) ideologies have been embedded in top-down and centrally controlled policies based on assumptions that languages can be effectively taught and developed through rational and linear processes of policy design and implementation (Rizvi and Lingard 2010). In the twentieth century, newly independent nations adopted monolingual policies to aid processes of economic development though not always the language of the former colonial power. Thus indigenous languages were adopted, such as Kiswahili in Tanzania (Brock-Utne 2012), Bahasa Indonesia in Indonesia and Nepali in Nepal (see Policy 6).

Such attitudes to language(s) in schooling emerge from ideologies about what a language can and cannot do and are 'largely tacit, taken-for-granted assumptions about language statuses, users and uses' (Tollefson 2006, 47), giving such beliefs a 'common sense' feel to them. Blommaert and Verschueren (1998) identify two persistent assumptions made about a one-language-one-nation ideology: an assumption that multilingualism is an obstacle for societal and national integration and an assumption that efficient government as well as economic growth, development and a society free from conflict is hampered by multilingualism. Schooling holds the promise of access to prestige or high-status languages – to the language of institutions, of further education, of the law and the media – reinforcing a ranking and hierarchy of languages (Woolard 1998).This ranking places oral languages on the lowest rung where, without a literate form of the language and without a written history and knowledge base, they are judged unfit for schooling purposes and practices (Skutnabb-Kangas 2000). In this way literate, international languages such as French, Spanish, Chinese and English have come to be highly valued and desired.

The English language achieved a status of world language through its spread and uses associated with imperialism, colonialism and 'linguistic pragmatism'. It has been employed by international industry and commerce as well as being the language of many global organizations since the end of the Second World War (Phillipson 1992, Bhatt 2001, 532, Pennycook 2006). With the English language at the centre of economic, financial and political globalization, there has been what Sonntag (2003) describes as a 'scramble for English', because the language is viewed as a carrier of modernity. Its supposed promises of social mobility lead many parents to turn away from home languages and seek access to English for their children through private English-language schooling. Since the 1990s in the United States there has been a strong English-only movement influencing a preference for English language schooling which serves to reinforce a particular concept of American national identity (Schmidt 2006).

The effects of monolingual language choices made by institutional decision makers based on ideological beliefs about certain languages as inherently beneficial for economic development and social cohesion make education difficult for speakers of other languages in many parts of the world. Alidou (2009), writing about the effects of French monolingual language-of-instruction education in West African countries, notes that in Niger more than 50 per cent of school-aged children do not go to school and of those who do attend school, 70 per cent experience serious academic problems and high drop-out before completing primary school. In situations where learners' home languages (sometimes called mother tongue) are excluded and ignored, children may not fully master the language of instruction. In Vietnam, learners who have little access to the national prestige language, Vietnamese, are taught by highly trained but monolingual Vietnamese-speaking teachers, with the assumption that this 'immersion' approach, which provides only access to Viet, will aid their acquisition of Viet and, through it, their efficient social and economic inclusion. However, for many young learners, being immersed in a language which they do not understand and rarely hear outside of school has the effect of alienating them from schooling, 'silencing' them leading to drop out (Aikman and Pridmore 2001, Lewin 2007).

In the global effort to achieve EFA and the SDGs through national planning and international funding mechanisms, new arguments are being made for the importance of multilingual education. UNESCO, an institutional proponent of multilingual education, has argued for the benefits of learners learning to read and write in their home language. A total of 221 million school-age children speak home languages that are not recognized in schools, demonstrating that education systems seldom reflect linguistic diversity, despite the strong association of low levels of educational achievement and speaking minority

Policy 6
A Case Study of Nepal[1]

Nepal, situated in the Himalayas, is highly diverse in terms of languages and ethnic identity with an estimated 122 languages, of which 121 are indigenous.[2]

From the 1950s onward, under the Panchayat system of 'partyless democracy' the country promoted monolingual nationalism, which viewed Nepali as the vehicle for national unification and development. This relegated all other languages to inferior status, with little recognition in the school system. These languages were silenced in the school, the playground and many other social spheres (Sonntag 1995, Pradhan 2002). The experience of monolingual nationalism powerfully shaped education policy in Nepal and its legacy is still felt today – particularly in terms of opportunities for employment. The establishment of multi-party democracy in the 1990s brought a new constitution that enshrined a commitment to linguistic pluralism and educational and cultural rights (Whelpton 1997, Weinberg 2013). But, in practice, monolingual schooling continued with a lack of policy support for mother tongue instruction and resistance to the use of local languages in administration and schools (Sonntag 2003). The Maoist 'People's War' (1996–2006) led to a new commitment to linguistic pluralism and promotion of the language and cultural rights of indigenous nationalities. However, since the end of the war these policies have been associated with a period of weak governance and ineffective language policy.

Given the political constraints and lack of educational choice, non-Nepali-speaking parents often find themselves in an ambivalent position – wanting their children to retain their home language (often associated with ethnic identity) while being influenced by a pragmatic desire for their children to acquire the elite languages of power and to access employment and higher education. Greater linguistic freedoms have become available, but people show little commitment to educating their children in local languages (Gellner 2001). Instead, schools take on the role as institutions for the promotion of dominant and foreign languages. This trend is illustrated with the growth of English language private schooling since the 1990s. The adoption of English medium instruction is not informed by nationalist concerns or by those of indigenous minorities (though in some cases it is adopted as an alternative to Nepali). But in the age of internet and global communication, English instruction offers parents and students access to a high-status langue useful regionally and globally.

languages (UNESCO 2016a). Evidence emerging from international monitoring and testing suggests that monolingual teaching is a significant factor in educational disadvantage and marginalization. The UNESCO GEM Report provides evidence of learners' disadvantage in tests when the language of the home and school are different. It demonstrates the extent of learning inequalities depending on whether the children speak the language of assessment at home or not (UNESCO 2016b). The 2007 TIMSS found that students who reported never speaking the test language at home scored 20 per cent lower than those who always spoke the language at home[3] and the Progress in International Reading Literacy Study (PIRLS)[4] conducted in thirty-five countries found lower average reading achievement when the language of schooling and testing was different from that at home (Pinnock 2009).

Research from the 1980s has been widely used to support bilingual or multilingual education. It demonstrates the cognitive advantage of learning to read and write in the familiar home language before embarking on a second language, as skills in language and literacy developed in the familiar home language aid the acquisition of literacy in the second language (Baker 1988). Thus organizations such as the World Bank (2012) support a 'transitional' additive and instrumental approach for bilingual or multilingual education, where home-language literacy learning is considered a 'bridge' to achieving literacy proficiency in the dominant language. In this way, the assumption that multilingualism is a problem and a barrier to development is maintained, perpetuating ideas about the benefits of monolingualism.

Language Rights and Multilingual Education

Hornberger (2002) discusses three ways of viewing language(s): as a problem, as a resource and as a right. Monolingualism views non-dominant languages as a problem; multilingualism views them as a resource. The view of language as a right differs from these. Skutnabb-Kangas (2000, Skutnabb-kangas and Phillipson 1994) has written and campaigned widely for the importance of language rights as human rights, concerned with ensuring meaningful participation for speakers of all languages in public institutions – such as schooling – and in democratic processes. Language rights have emerged from minority and indigenous peoples' movements which have demanded the right to use, maintain and develop their languages on equal footing with the majority population and their dominant languages.

For over a decade, indigenous peoples debated their rights at the UN drawing on the moral authority derived from their experience of cultural,

Policy 7
UN Declaration on the Rights of Indigenous Peoples 2008[5]

Article 14
  (1) Indigenous peoples have the right to establish and control their educational systems and institutions providing education in their own languages, in a manner appropriate to their cultural methods of teaching and learning.
  (2) Indigenous individuals, particularly children, have the right to all levels and forms of education of the State without discrimination.
  (3) States shall, in conjunction with indigenous peoples, take effective measures, in order for indigenous individuals, particularly children, including those living outside their communities, to have access, when possible, to an education in their own culture and provided in their own language.

Declaration on the Rights of Persons Belonging to National or Ethnic, Religious and Linguistic Minorities 1992[6]
Article 4: States should, where appropriate, take measures in the field of education, in order to encourage knowledge of the history, traditions, language and culture of the minorities existing within their territory. Persons belonging to minorities should have adequate opportunities to gain knowledge of the society as a whole.

social and linguistic persecution and discrimination. This process resulted in 2008 in the Declaration on the Rights of Indigenous Peoples. Today, some governments have ratified the UN Declarations on indigenous rights and minority rights and enacted national legislation to provide minority languages and their speakers with some of the protections and institutional support that majority languages enjoy. More recently the UN decreed 2019 as the International Year of Indigenous Languages. This has raised awareness of the consequences of the endangerment of indigenous languages across the world and their importance as 'strategic resources for good governance, peacebuilding, reconciliation and sustainable development' (UN 2019) (see Policy 7), and national legislation provides important starting points for the development of education programmes designed to maintain and in some cases revitalize minority languages. This revitalization has happened in all regions, including Europe, where Welsh and Catalan have achieved legal recognition. Such legal status, as Hornberger and Johnson (2011, 285) argue, can both open and close implementation and ideological spaces for different kinds of language interaction and new language in schooling practices. Intercultural bilingual schooling in Latin America offers some examples of this (Lopez 2020).

Multilingual Education for Inclusion and Equity

Drawing on language as a right, a human development approach proposes different aims, policies and practices for language in schooling. Researchers and programmes are concerned with ways in which multilingual education can increase inclusion by respecting learners' home language environment and the language abilities they bring (Hornberger 2002, Lopez 2009, May and Sleeter 2010). They raise questions about the value, quality and status of languages in relation to questions of inequality and injustice. Inequalities of access, participation and outcomes in schooling can lead to restricted access to written and spoken resources and restricted opportunities for employment and social mobility. Parents who do not speak the official language in which their children are being educated may have less opportunity to engage with teachers, education authorities and homework. But May and Sleeter (2010) argue that an emphasis on respect for cultural and linguistic difference fails to recognize the inequalities of power relations between groups. Investigating languages as sites of power and authority helps to identify the ways that particular notions about identity, aesthetics, morality and epistemology shape language use, school policy and values about the person or social group (Woolard 1998, 3).

Sociolinguistic research, looking at languages within their wider 'ecology', compares languages to living species which evolve, grow, change and die. From this perspective, languages are not autonomous and discrete, bounded and fixed through linguistic description but, rather, organisms which interact and change within a wider physical, social and political environment (these are discussed in terms of 'language evolution', 'language environment' and 'language endangerment' themes in Hornberger 2002). In contrast to national education policy-oriented research with a strong top-down and institutional focus and commitment to international assessments and testing, language ecology research has produced fine-grained and detailed qualitative insights into relational dynamics between languages, dialects and questions of status and language domains and power in schooling. Studies of the 'linguistic ecology' of classrooms and ethnographies of communication (Gumperz and Hymes 1972) are today being complemented by anthropological studies of speech communities and sociolinguistic ethnographies of schooling (Wyman 2012).

While high-income country researchers have led the way in sociolinguistics and studies of the linguistic anthropology of schools and classrooms, a number of studies shine a light on dynamics of language choice and practices in low-income countries, examining the ways that teachers and students shape language policies through their practices in different contexts (Hornberger and Johnson 2011). Researchers are investigating gendered language uses (Cameron 1998, Higgins 2010); language choice and school/community interactions (Hornberger 1988 in Peru); practices of vernacular medium education (Ramanathan 2005 in India); language and schooling for diaspora communities (Canagarajah 2008 in Sri Lanka); schooling and processes of language 'loss' and language 'shift' (McIvor and McCarty 2017 in the USA); and mixing and switching languages in the context of migration and mobility (Blackledge and Creese 2017). This research views languages as fluid, changing and used by young people for communicative needs in changing worlds (Wyman 2012).

Sociolinguistic research into the myriad varieties of English that have developed in their own right across the globe, such as Liberian English, African American English and Indian English, has undermined the idea of English as having one definitive identity and status. Comparisons between Singaporean English and Malaysian English indicate how these varieties have diverged in the postcolonial period and been shaped by their users and their contexts (Blommaert et al. 2005). While English may be a global

Figure 14.1 Types of multilingual pedagogies and their orientations. (Source: Garcia and Flores 2012.)

Type of Pedagogies// Assumptions	Bilingual Subtractive (transitional)	Bilingual/multilingual Additive	Multilingual pedagogies
Type of language education	Learning in two languages: the home language and the dominant prestige language. The two languages are compartmentalized in the classroom.	Learning in two languages: the home language and the dominant prestige language. The two languages are compartmentalized in the classroom.	Learning in many languages – to reflect the student composition, including the prestige dominant language. Languages intermixed in the classroom.
Bilingual orientation	Subtractive and linear (L1+L2-L1=L2)	Additive and linear (L1+L2=L1+L2)	Recursive or dynamic and complex (non-linear)
Languages viewed as:	Autonomous and discrete/ bounded.	Autonomous, discrete/bounded.	Fluid and dynamic, changing, partial and incomplete.
Expected outcome	First language gradually phased out and cease to be used with a shift to use of second (majority) language.	Second or third languages added and expectation that student will develop similar competences in both/all languages.	Teaching aims to foster students' competencies in multiple languages based on an individual's language resources.
Example	Transitional bilingual education programmes (e.g. World Bank 2020 Education Strategy)	Immersion programmes e.g. in Quebec, Canada, for English and French	Language revitalization programmes; linguistically heterogeneous classrooms

hegemonic force, it is also an important component of many people's plurilingual repertoires. From her research in India, Ramanathan (2012) calls for a move away from reified conceptions of English as 'cosmopolitan' and vernacular as 'parochial' and instead to open up spaces for examination of the meanings associated with language practices in constant flux, forever modified and constantly transformed.

From the ethnographic perspectives of such studies, what can be learned about multilingual classroom practices? Garcia and Flores ask about the kind of teaching and learning which supports social justice and the political participation of students. They argue that unless all students are taught in ways that support and develop diverse language practices, there cannot be any meaningful participation in schooling, education and society (2012, 232). They conclude that pedagogies of multilingual schooling should be adapted to the different sociopolitical conditions of school systems, and the shifting socio-educational spaces within schools, which are the products of specific communities' and educators' beliefs and values, varying students' experiences and multiple socio-educational goals (see Figure 14.1).

Costs are often raised as a barrier to multilingual pedagogies because of the production costs of texts and materials in languages other than the dominant literary language. Non-dominant languages may require the development of orthographies, grammars as well as learning and reading materials. But these financial costs need to be assessed in relation to the social, political and economic costs of continuing with monolingual policies and high levels of school drop-out (Pinnock 2009). There is also the question of what is at stake in the standardization and 'modernization' of oral languages. In the Amazon Basin, speakers of indigenous languages are rejecting alphabets and orthographies developed by missionary-linguists of the 1970s according to their particular ideological and academic agendas (de Souza 2005). Instead, they have instigated self-directed and collective processes of discussion and debate about how to represent their languages and their knowledges in written forms (Simon 2010).

Education Reform and the Challenges of Plurilingual Schooling

In a society that values plurilingualism, schooling will value the heterogeneity of learners' linguistic repertoires and work to support them to use and expand their resources. In her work on language and education in Corsica,

Jaffe (2012) discusses the way in which the idealized concept of monolingual national citizen is being replaced by that of pluricultural European/global citizen, where citizens have multiple identities and ever-widening linguistic repertoires. Where plurilingualism is valued, the linguistic capital of a minority speaker will be validated and this will promote participation in democratic practices (Jaffe 2012). However, the 'progressive ideal of the plurilingual citizen in European contexts coexists in an often unresolved tension with "older" discourses and their ideologies' such as monolingualism or multilingualism (Jaffe 2012, 83).

In Bolivia, struggles for recognition and rights by indigenous peoples and 'subaltern' groups led to the emergence of a new political project for a plurilingual intra- and intercultural society (Walsh 2009). As the Bolivian case study shows (Policy 8), education and language has been and remains at the centre of the struggle and the political project.

Policy 8
A Case Study of Bolivia

In Bolivia, a country of high Andes and wide Amazon basin and plains, with forty-two ethno-linguistic groups, the Aymara, Quechua and Guarani peoples are numerically the largest. Of the forty-two indigenous languages, two are extinct, two are institutionalized, eight are developing, four are vigorous, twelve are in trouble and sixteen are dying.[7]

The 1994 Constitution recognized Bolivia as multi-ethnic, pluricultural and linguistically diverse. An education reform in 1994 was designed to improve educational quality and inclusion through intercultural bilingual education. However, Bolivia's indigenous peoples rejected what they saw as the liberal foundations of the reform and its bilingual intercultural approach aimed at only the indigenous population. They found it to be perpetuating a linguistically, racially and culturally stratified society. Opposition to the reform brought social unrest, indigenous mobilization and political instability (Howard 2009, Lopes 2012).

The reform was accompanied by administrative changes which were critiqued for running roughshod over indigenous structures of authority and territoriality. Indigenous parents saw bilingual education as hampering their children's ability to learn Spanish and fulfil expectations of social mobility and economic productivity. Teachers were required to adopt a new and challenging pedagogy as well as teach in indigenous languages for which there was a lack of materials, despite a massive rollout of the programme (Gustafson 2009, Howard 2009)

In 2005 Evo Morales was elected to power with strong backing from the indigenous movement and coca producers. His government had a vision for democratic cultural and political 'decolonization' of the country through, among other things, the transformation of the education system. The Constitution of 2009, under the Morales government, articulated the concept of a plurinational state, new not only for Bolivia but within the Andean region (Howard 2010). The intercultural bilingual education of 1994 was reconceptualized as not only intercultural (in terms of relationships between cultural groups including the dominant Spanish-speaking group) but intra-cultural, strengthening indigenous people's diverse and plural cultural and linguistic identities across and within the nation. Schooling was to benefit the 'indigenous originary nations' on their own terms and through their autonomy over their own historical processes, epistemes and identities (Gustafson 2009). While the 1994 reform had organized the curriculum and language pedagogy around a 'common core' curriculum allowing for locally relevant adaptations, this reform for plurilingual, intra and intercultural schooling purported to give the collective users of language decision-making power over the development of their individual and societal linguistic repertoires. A decade later, Gustafson (2017, 52–3) suggests that, while gaps still persist between policies, practices and experiences, there has been a growth of linguistic networks comprised of indigenous teachers, intellectuals and experts who have negotiated relationships with the government. And, while there are still disjunctures between what the state says in support of indigenous language policy and the wider political and economic policies, discourses and actions, there is an ongoing transformation of indigenous languages.

The plurilingual and plurinational Bolivian state emerged within a context of tensions between global and national political and capitalist economic forces and resistance to these from different sectors. At the time of writing, Morales has had to flee Bolivia, facing charges of electoral corruption. In the fast-changing social, economic and political contexts, young Bolivians, like young people around the world, look to schooling and education to help them navigate the dynamics and contradictions of their societies. They face expectations of their language abilities from parental generations as well as new opportunities and challenges which 'ripple through societies to create a tidal wave of sociolinguistic change' (Harrison 2007 cited in Wyman 2012, 1).

Traditional bilingual pedagogies that compartmentalize languages – whether additive or subtractive models (see Figure 14.1) – are not designed to work with the linguistic complexity and heterogeneity of students' and teachers' linguistic repertoires or fit them for the pluricultural societies across Africa, Asia and America in which they live. A plurilingual schooling orientation recognizes that linguistically heterogeneous classrooms require flexible models of teaching and learning that focus on the processes of learning and interacting (Jaffe 2012). It is concerned with what students do with their multiple languages and forms of language in plurilingual classrooms and spaces. Pedagogies are necessarily subject to considerable variation, according to different sociocultural contexts (de Mejia 2012). They need to challenge theories of language learning based on the repetition of fixed grammatical structures and designed to support communication which takes place through a multiplicity of different ways of speaking (Hill and May 2011, Cooke and Simpson 2012, Garcia and Lin 2017).

Conclusion

This chapter has considered different explanations for the disparity between the diversity of languages around the globe and the focus of language in schooling on a few high-status languages, such as English. It has considered the choices people make about language(s) in schooling in terms of ideological orientation and how ideologies influence how languages are valued, the kinds of identities associated with them and what they are expected to be able to do for those who use them. A critical approach to languages in schooling warns against making simplistic linkages between languages and identities and raises the question not of what languages can do for people and society but what people and societies can do with language and languages.

Through the chapter we have also looked at language practices in schooling, asking about the kind of pedagogies that flow from different orientations. Recent qualitative research being carried out in different locations around the world is providing insights and understandings of the complex linguistic dynamics of twenty-first-century classrooms where plurilingual students manipulate language in creative and innovative ways. There is also increasing qualitative research into the complex linguistic societies in which young and adult learners live. The emerging picture is of sophisticated uses of languages and language forms by young people with their own ideas about what they want to do with language, expectations of what they can do with language and how they expect schooling to help them achieve it.

Questions for Discussion

1. What are 'languages' and what does it mean to think about individuals as having linguistic repertoires?
2. How do social, cultural and economic values become attributed to particular languages or forms of language (written, spoken, genres, dialects, etc.)?
3. Who decides which languages are used in the classroom and in what ways, for what purposes and with what outcomes?

Further Reading

García O., Lin A., May S. (eds.) (2017) *Bilingual and Multilingual Education. Encyclopedia of Language and Education* (3rd ed.). Springer: Cham.
Hornberger, N. and McKay, S. (eds.) (2010) *Sociolinguistics and Language Education*, Multilingual Matters: Clevedon.
Johnson, D. C. (2013) *Language Policy*, London: Palgrave Macmillan.

15

Livelihoods and Skills

Stephanie Matseleng Allais

Introduction

This chapter explores debates and research into the role of skills in development, specifically in relation to individual livelihoods and the conditions for their sustainability. Raising levels of skills in order to assist the prosperity of both individuals and nations is a common theme in educational research, in the popular media and in national policy in many countries around the world. A focus on skills is included in the work of international development and donor organizations. But which skills are needed by whom, and what role do they play in assisting individuals to improve their livelihoods and lives? A consideration of policies, projects, debates and research internationally suggests three main narratives about how skills contribute to individuals' ability to earn an income:

The first is the idea that giving poor, marginalized people basic technical, literacy and numeracy skills will improve their ability to gain a livelihood or improve the livelihood they already have.

The second is that countries need more people with vocational and technical skills as well as various 'generic' skills that are required by employers, sometimes described in terms such as 'core work skills', in order to improve general productivity and competitiveness, thereby contributing to raising employment levels as well as assisting individuals to earn better incomes.

The third is that economic and technological changes mean that countries need 'high skills' – in other words, more people with higher levels of qualifications, in order to ensure economic development and individual prosperity and fulfilment.

This chapter starts by examining each of these narratives. It then explores some complexities and debates about how skills relate to livelihoods.

Three Narratives of Skills and Livelihoods

Basic Skills to Support Basic Livelihoods

In the first narrative, 'skills' is used to refer to basic literacy and numeracy, as well as basic technical skills and 'know-how'. It sometimes also includes what are labelled 'generic' skills such as 'life skills', 'employability skills' or 'entrepreneurial skills'. These skills are believed to be essential for individual livelihoods and social progress in poor communities in developing countries. The idea of providing basic skills to support basic livelihoods is most likely to be found in the documents of aid agencies, non-governmental organizations, international organizations and corporate social responsibility programmes. Some examples include the Non-Formal Education and Livelihood Skills Training Programme,[1] aimed at providing livelihoods skills and placements to marginalized street children and slum-dwelling youth in Uganda, and the Caribbean Youth Empowerment Program,[2] which aims to equip 'vulnerable youth with the technical, vocational, entrepreneurship and life skills needed to develop sustainable livelihoods', to provide them with placement services and support them in serving as 'positive agents of change in their communities'. In India there is, among many other examples, the Market

Aligned Skills Training programme.[3] An example from Bangladesh is the Tools of Trade and Skills Training for Sustainable Livelihoods Options programme for the people of Faridpur district.[4]

The main idea is that people who have little chance of securing a job in the formal sector and are looking for options to generate income in order to sustain themselves and their families will be better off if they have more skills. Many programmes try to integrate 'life skills' training (sometimes seen as literacy and numeracy, sometimes as communication and interpersonal skills as well as things like budgeting and family planning), which is believed to support marginalized individuals to voice their interests and to find appropriate ways to represent them in social processes (Adam 2012). 'Life skills' are also seen as part of helping people to participate in social processes in their communities. Oxenham et al. (2002) suggest, for example, combinations of livelihood skills training and adult literacy education help improve poor people's livelihood. Firstly, there is a widely noted 'empowerment effect' – that learners acquire enhanced confidence and social re-sources which help them take initiatives to improve their livelihoods. Second, literacy and numeracy skills are a clear advantage in market transactions in the informal economy, and thus especially important for entrepreneurship. Thirdly, more productive agricultural or livestock practices result from learning new vocational skills.

The kinds of education which are envisaged in this narrative include formal literacy and numeracy classes as well as short formal training sessions to provide technical, entrepreneurial and life skills.

Non-formal training is also foregrounded as it is seen as a way of providing skills to people from poor socio-economic backgrounds who may not enter formal training because of fees and lost income during training or because they dropped out of school before completing primary school or people who want to upgrade or learn new skills (Adam 2012). In many countries, formal technical and vocational education and training is an option for a small minority of young people. Informal apprenticeships (forms of on-the-job training in the informal economy) are believed to offer many more young people an opportunity to learn a trade and enter the world of work (ILO 2012).

Combining vocational training with literacy education is believed to 'enable a very poor, illiterate labor force, especially rural women, to develop more productive livelihoods and take on increasingly active roles in transforming their families and communities' (Oxenham 2002). For example, it is hoped that formal provision of literacy skills can assist people who manage small businesses to keep better records, so a project in Senegal

Pathways to Practice 9
Basic Skills for Basic Livelihoods:
Support for *Jua Kali* Workers in Kenya

Jua kali is a name given to workers in the informal sector in Kenya, including traders and artisans such as car workers and metal workers. *Jua kali* means 'fierce sun' in Kiswahili, referring to the fact that most workers are outdoors under the hot sun, or shaded by plastic bags or maybe a sheet of tin roofing, because of lack of official premises (King 1996). Nearly 90 per cent of all businesses in Kenya operate in the informal sector. Skills are a key issue for *jua kali* workers: it is believed that improving both the level and quality of skills is necessary if the informal sector is to contribute to real economic growth by creating reasonable returns on the labour invested and improving productivity and competitiveness (Baiya 2003).

SITE (Strengthening Informal Training and Enterprise) was set up in Kenya as a non-profit organization with the mandate of supporting informal sector development through skills training. In the late 1990s, the organization implemented a skills upgrading project (Haan 2006, Adam 2012) with three major objectives:

- to upgrade the technical and managerial skills of master craftspeople, with a view to enabling them to diversify production,
- to strengthen the capacity of master craftspeople and improve the quality of training provided to their apprentices,
- to strengthen the capacity of selected vocational training institutes to support master craftspeople.

During the two and a half years project, forty-three courses were designed, and training material comprising worksheets, books and videos developed. Courses were conducted in technical and business skills with a few courses in pedagogy. A total of 419 masters and 284 apprentices were trained. It was hoped that an additional 1,400 received improved training from the participating master craftspeople (Adam 2012). An evaluation found the training of apprentices improved both in content and quality, with more focus on technical skills for production. The number of apprentices increased. *Jua kali* workers were able to raise their incomes by 14–20 per cent, and enterprises that participated employed 22 per cent more workers. Seventy-three per cent of the master craftspeople started to make new or improved products, and 58 per cent reached new markets. Apprentices stated that they had increased confidence in starting a business and in awareness of the financial aspects of running a business (Haan 2006, Adam 2012).

focused on providing cotton farmers with both improved agricultural skills and literacy. The project evaluation found that farmers who succeeded in the combination of a livelihoods and literacy programme were 6 per cent more productive than those who remained illiterate. They were also found to be more energetic in forming organizations to sell their crops, manage credit and serve the public interest (Oxenham 2002, Oxenham et al. 2002). Many interventions at the level of supporting survivalist enterprises try to supply other forms of assistance as well as skills, such as helping small businesses to access markets, access to credit and other services needed to establish and grow businesses (Oxenham 2002).

The notion of 'livelihood' in this narrative usually invokes survivalist activities in the informal sector, self-employment or home-based enterprise as the target groups are seen as unlikely to obtain work in the formal sector and as most developing countries have very small formal sectors (see Pathways to Practice 9). There is often a strong component of entrepreneurship. Some projects also try to provide individuals with skills that would assist them to enter formal labour markets, which is seen as offering better long-term prospects of a reliable income. This usually leads into the second narrative.

Technical Skills for Mid-level Occupations

When the focus is on enabling people to make a smooth transition to work in formal labour markets, policies are largely concerned with what are referred to as vocational skills, occupational skills or technical skills. Here 'skills' usually mean the technical knowledge required for mid-level occupations. Economic competitiveness is increasingly widely believed to rest on the skills of the labour force (Brown et al. 2001). This view is often presented in reverse: that a general lack of skills in the population is hampering economic development, thereby preventing the country in question from developing decent jobs. It is also argued that individuals are unable to find jobs because they do not have the right skills. For example, the ILO (Brewer 2013) cites a report by McKinsey which drew on survey data from nine countries and demonstrated that only 43 per cent of employers indicated they could find the skills they needed in their entry-level workers. This leads to what is described as a skills shortage, a skills gap or an 'education/labour market mismatch', which is argued to exist concurrent with rising unemployment rates, particularly for young people, in most countries around the world (Brewer 2013). The key idea is that education systems, particularly vocational education systems, are not producing the required skills. Jobs go unfilled because too few workers have the required skills. This hampers employers from expansion. It also prevents new international investments, particularly in developing countries. The kinds of educational programmes that this approach usually calls for are improved technical and vocational education and training.

Thus, over the past thirty years or so, many countries have put considerable focus on reforming their vocational education and training systems (McGrath 2012, Marope, Chakroun and Holmes 2015). Policy focus on technical and vocational education and training internationally has grown in recent years, as the World Bank, which mainly did not support this area in the 1970s, 1980s and 1990s, has increasingly given assistance to reforming vocational education systems. Many international organizations today provide aid money and technical assistance to developing countries in order to reform vocational education as well as to improve relationships between education systems and labour markets (McGrath 2012). At the same time, policy focus has shifted from building technical skills to providing skills as the basis for entrepreneurship (Allais 2012). Often, training is aimed at teaching people not only technical skills but also how to run a business. Other types of skills are also sometimes included, which are sometimes described as 'employability skills':

> the skills, knowledge and competencies that enhance a worker's ability to secure and retain a job, progress at work and cope with change, secure another job if he/she so wishes or has been laid off and enter more easily into the labour market at different periods of the life cycle. Individuals are most employable when they have broad-based education and training, basic and portable high-level kills, including teamwork, problem solving, information and communications technology (ICT) and communication and language skills. This combination of skills enables them to adapt to changes in the world of work.
>
> (Brewer 2013, 6)

Many countries have policies to encourage apprenticeships and other types of on-the-job learning. There is also a policy focus on encouraging employers to train, which could include giving employers subsidies for training, tax breaks and skills levies (OECD 2010). Another policy concern that has received increasing attention in the last twenty years is trying to find ways of formally recognizing various skills and abilities that people may have acquired outside of formal education, in the hope that such recognition

Policy 9
National Qualifications Frameworks as a Tool to Solve the Skills Gap

Over 150 countries are now implementing, developing or considering establishing national qualifications frameworks which aim to change the way qualifications and credentials are used hoping this will improve economies (UIL, Cedefop, and ETF 2017). Many involve employers, trade unions and other stakeholders in specifying the learning outcomes they require of education systems. Competence-based training has been introduced in many countries where policymakers believe that vocational education is too *supply-driven* by educational institutions, which are seen as inappropriately dominating decisions about what is taught with insufficient cognizance of employers' need. The idea is that learning outcomes and competences can be specified by employers to create more *demand-driven* education and training.

Two studies commissioned by the ILO (Allais 2010, 2017) compared qualifications frameworks in sixteen countries and six countries respectively, and found little evidence that they improved communication between education and training systems and labour markets. All countries in the study found it difficult to involve employers in designing qualifications, and it was even more difficult to involve trade unions. In nearly all of the countries with older qualifications frameworks, many qualifications had been developed but never used. However, Pevec-Grm and Bjørnåvold (2017) argue that in many European countries qualifications frameworks have been adopted with more modest goals, and have achieved some successes in supporting the restructuring, strengthening and/or regulation of national qualifications systems.

will help them in labour markets (Anderson and Harris 2006, OECD 2007). The rise of national qualifications frameworks, which are intended to improve relationships between education systems and labour markets as well as provide benchmarks for giving certificates to people who have gained skills and knowledge outside of education systems, is a contemporary policy initiative in part aimed at addressing this concern (Allais 2014).

Some analysts argue that the world of work has changed, but education systems have not kept abreast of these changes (e.g. Jutting and de Lauglesia 2009, Murgatroyd 2010). In developed countries, what is sometimes referred to as a 'labourist model' of capitalist work was established in the mid-twentieth century – stable jobs with long-term security benefits, fixed hours, established routes of advancement, subject to unionization and collective bargaining agreements (Standing 2011). Since the 1980s secure, well-paying industrial jobs were steadily disappearing in developed countries and these countries pursued 'labour market flexibility': they attempted to lower the cost of labour by being able to move employees around inside companies, to change job structures easily and to lower employment levels (Standing 2011, Kalleberg 2013).

These conditions are the same as those which have dominated labour markets for most people in developing countries (Jutting and de Lauglesia 2009). In recently industrialized countries, in general, the pattern of insecure work has continued rather than imitating the earlier industrializers with the 'labourist' model. For example, in China the urban workforce has grown from 95.1 million to 293.5 million from the 1990s to 2010, with dramatic changes in terms of sectors (e.g. agriculture decreased from 69.5 per cent to 40.8 per cent of the workforce between 1978 and 2010), but many of these new urban jobs are insecure and informal. There is a similar pattern in many fast-developing Asian countries, such as Singapore, Malaysia, the Philippines and India (Gallagher et al. 2011).

According to many researchers, this means that individuals need the skills to be able to cope with changing demands, the flexibility to quickly adapt to new work contexts and to innovate (Sahlberg 2006, Sahlberg and Oldroyd 2010). The OECD (2009, 1) argues:

> Developments in society and economy require education to equip young people with new skills and competencies, which allow them to benefit from the emerging new forms of socialisation and to contribute actively to economic development under a system where the main asset is knowledge.

This leads into the third narrative.

High Skills for Knowledge Economies

Since the 1970s, analysts such as Daniel Bell (1973), Peter Drucker (1969) and Alvin Toffler (1980) have argued that societies previously based on industrial manufacturing were being transformed into 'information societies' in which knowledge would become the dominant factor of production. New types of work were emerging, they suggested, particularly in information management, finance, marketing and sales (Carlaw et al. 2012). Supporting this view is the World Bank (2003, xvii), which notes that 'the global knowledge economy is transforming the demands of the labour market throughout the world. It is also placing new demands on citizens, who need more skills and knowledge to be able to function in their day-to-day lives' (World Bank 2003, xvii). D. W. Livingstone and David Guile (2012, iii) suggest that the existence of a 'knowledge-based economy' is 'widely taken for granted by governments, mass media, public opinion, and most scholars today'. What this implies for economic development is that an ever-increasing speed of innovation is required for economies to survive in globally competitive markets. Some have suggested that this will require or enable more input from workers, in turn giving them more autonomy and requiring more skills from them (Thompson and Mchugh 2002). This in turn implies that the current and prospective labour force must have higher levels of qualifications and engage in greater learning efforts throughout their lives (Livingstone and Guile 2012, xiii). More recently, the dominant discourse has shifted from the idea of a 'knowledge economy' to the notion of the fourth Industrial Revolution, and a focus on a range of skills believed to be needed to succeed in the new conditions that are or will be created by this putative revolution (Avis 2018).

In this narrative, the term 'skills' refers to high levels of professional and technical education, as well as a range of 'generic' skills; in other words, the word 'skills' means knowledge, which in turn leads to a focus on higher education (see Chapter 16). The kind of education that is implied to build these 'skills', higher education, has expanded dramatically in recent years. In 1900, a fraction of a per cent of the age cohort worldwide was enrolled in higher education; by 2000 approximately 20 per cent of the cohort was enrolled, and by 2007 the estimate was 26 per cent (Schofer and Meyer 2005, Altbach et al. 2009). Many countries have now moved beyond 50 per cent, and some beyond 80 per cent (UIS 2020), although comparative statistics in this regard can be misleading as the figures are for gross rather than net enrolments, and some countries include two-year degrees and other forms of post-secondary education that are excluded in other countries.

Unpacking the Relationships between Skills, Education and Livelihoods

Taken together, these widely held views all suggest that different kinds of skills are crucial to ensuring individual livelihoods: raising levels of general education and of technical skills needed in the world of work at various different levels will help individuals to earn more and will improve general economic and social development, which will in turn improve individual livelihoods. In other words, nations should focus on enhancing everyone's skills at all levels: at the survivalist level, at the mid-level of occupations and at the level of complex professional work, in order to assist the individuals concerned as well as the societies and economies in which they live. The OECD (2016, 4) puts it like this: 'a stronger emphasis has to be placed in promoting strong levels of foundation skills, digital literacies, higher order thinking competencies as well as social and emotional skills.' This is a straightforward but unhelpful policy conclusion as it does not help policymakers to make decisions about where to focus limited resources, particularly in poor countries. Further, a policy preoccupation with raising education levels does not always seem to have had the desired effects. Sociologists of work suggest that one reason for this is that in some jobs, there seems to be an increase in levels of knowledge used, and in many others, there have been decreases; 'deskilling and temporary low-skill employment contracts remain a core feature of "knowledge work"' (Kennedy 2012, 169). In many contemporary paid work settings, formal qualifications increasingly exceed job requirements (Livingstone 2009). This is especially true for the youngest and most well-educated, who are last in the queue for jobs. One common response to this phenomenon is to suggest that education institutions are producing the wrong skills. Another is to suggest that the 'skills gap' is actually a 'jobs gap'.

Skills Gap or Jobs Gap?

Mark Levine (2013) cites the Nobel laureate economist Paul Krugman, who shows that during the Great Depression, when aggregate demand and the country's job creation machinery had collapsed, workers were described as unadaptable and untrained, unable to respond to the opportunities which industry had to offer. A few years later, when preparations for the Second

World War gave the economy a massive boost, the 'skills gap' vanished, and those same workers who had been described as 'unadaptable and untrained' before were easily employed. Similarly, in Latin America, Claudio de Moura Castro (2000) discusses the strong national training institutions that were established in these countries as successful and prestigious, in some instances far more so than the schooling system in their countries. They trained several generations of highly skilled workers. However, the skilled workers worked in industries nurtured by import substitution policies. These industries later collapsed when economic and political problems led to import substitution being abandoned (Palma 2003). The weakness of the industrial sector was *not* caused by a lack of skills. The education institutions had met the needs of industry while industry flourished and while there were stable jobs within industry. But when skilled workers suddenly had no industry to work in, because of broader economic conditions as well as the responses of their governments to these conditions, education and training came under the spotlight.

Thirty years ago, Randall Collins (1979) demonstrated that technological change was not the driving force in rising credential requirements. More recently D. W. Livingstone (2012, 108) points out, education levels have risen dramatically faster than knowledge requirements in most jobs:

> The image of contemporary society inherent in post-industrial/knowledge economy and human capital theories proves illusory. While an aggregate upgrading of the technical skills needed for job performance is gradually occurring, our collective acquisition of work-related knowledge and credentials is far outpacing this incremental shift.

Further, there is not much evidence that 'knowledge workers' such as computer engineers and software designers have really gained greater power over such policy matters as making decisions about the types of products or services delivered, employee hiring and firing, budgeting or workload (Livingstone and Guile 2012). Hugh Lauder and Phillip Brown (2008) demonstrate that the majority of 'knowledge workers' operate in a global labour market for work that is high-skilled but low-waged. With David Ashton (Brown et al. 2008, 4), they also point out that while much contemporary policy literature in relation to the knowledge economy focuses on knowledge, innovation and creative enterprise, it has ignored the shift towards global standardization of work, along with efforts to 'capture' and digitalize knowledge that had 'previously remained locked in the heads of high-skilled workers'. They refer to this as 'Digital Taylorism'. Much 'knowledge work', they argue, is being standardized in much the same way that the knowledge of craft workers was captured and translated into the moving assembly line in the early twentieth century. Digital Taylorism involves a power struggle within the middle classes, for it depends on reducing the autonomy and discretion of the majority of well-educated technical, managerial and professional employees. Collins (2013) similarly argues that middle-class and white-collar jobs are being eradicated in the same way that earlier automation eradicated many working-class manufacturing jobs.

As pointed out above, one response to the phenomenon of rising levels of people with qualifications far higher than what is required for their jobs is to suggest that education institutions are producing the wrong skills or indeed that education systems should not be the focus of policy, because the skills required can be best learned in work.

What Are Skills?

But what kinds of skills do people need, and what is the best way of ensuring that they can acquire them? One common response to this question is to try to get employers to stipulate the competences that they require and then get educational providers to produce them. This is an apparently appealing and very widespread idea that has profoundly influenced vocational education and has recently also started to influence thinking about professional education (here referring to higher education which prepares people for a recognized profession). However, many problems arise when governments try to implement systems based on this idea (Wolf 2002, Allais 2010, Wheelahan 2010). In most instances, employers are not able to predict what skills and knowledge will be required in the future. There is no one employer view of qualifications because employers in any industrial or service sector also vary widely, in terms of size, in the way in which their service or production is organized and in their demands for knowledge and skills. Further, most employer organizations represent older, well-established industries, but new dynamic ones are seldom organized. Also, employers frequently have unrealistic expectations about what education institutions can achieve, and, when asked for their requirements, provide long wish-lists, in many instances, of skills which would be better learned in the workplace.[5]

In practice, getting statements of required competences from employers has tended to lead to narrow skills training for fragmented work processes in the immediate job at hand (Winch 2011). It also seems to lead to endless cycles of reform, trying in vain to get closer to an elusive idea of what employers *really* want in the workplace along with the constant reorganization of government agencies and quasi-governmental agencies (Keep 2007, Allais 2010, 2017, Brockmann et al. 2011). What immediately becomes apparent is that the notion of 'skill' is not a simple one. Sociologists who study the labour market argue that the notion of skill is socially and politically constructed. Skills are not objective phenomena that can be measured and accounted for, which individuals either do or do not possess. They are social constructs variable through time and space, and perceptions of skills are mediated by racial/ethnic and gender identity (Dunk et al. 1996). Francis Green (2011, 12) points out that 'certain jobs predominantly held by women are conceived as low skilled, which self-justifies the consent to low pay, which then reinforces their perception as low skilled, and not suitable for men, and of lower value than men's work'.

Christopher Winch (2011, 94) argues that in *informal* labour markets, skills are usually not formally recognized, 'even when the know-how required to carry out the work requires a high degree of manipulative and coordinative ability that is difficult to acquire, and the task concerned necessitates a low degree of tolerance for error'. In other words, he suggests that it is the nature of the structure of the labour market, and not anything inherent in the work, which leads workers to be classified as belonging to a recognized category of skilled labour. Charles Tilly (1988, 452–3) classically argued, as a historical concept, skill is a thundercloud: solid and clearly bounded when seen from a distance, vaporous and full of shocks close up. The commonsense notion – that 'skill' denotes a hierarchy of objective individual traits – will not stand up to historical scrutiny; skill is a social product, a negotiated identity. Although knowledge, experience and cleverness all contribute to skill, ultimately skill lies not in characteristics of individual workers but in relations between workers and employers; a skilled worker is one who is hard to replace or do without, and an unskilled worker one who is easily substitutable or dispensable.

The relationships between knowledge, skill and work are complex. Mastery of different forms of craft knowledge used to give workers some power in the labour market through systems like guilds. Bodies of theoretical knowledge create the possibility of professional work where abstract knowledge is acquired and then applied, and they create the possibility for research and innovation that create new possibilities for society. But work also affects knowledge and skills. For example, a casualized and fragmented labour market leads to narrow short-term training. It is very difficult for education institutions to develop programmes which both prepare learners for the workplace and also provide them with a broad education; it may also not be rational for learners to invest in such programmes. Where labour markets are dominated by casualized or constantly changing jobs, vocational education programmes tend to be either somewhat removed from the immediate needs of the labour market or comprised of ever-changing short courses in narrow skills (Allais 2012). Vocational education systems which have a better fit with the needs of industry tend to be located in contexts of a developed industry, stable employment and some degree of redistribution or social insurance (Iverson and Stephens 2008). All this suggests that the relationships between education and work are more complex than those suggested by human capital theory.

Different Theories about How Education Relates to Work

All three of the narratives are premised on a link between education and productivity: the idea that education pays off in labour markets because the knowledge and skills obtained through education improve productivity. This idea is most clearly stated in human capital theory (discussed in detail in Chapter 7), which has become naturalized in much thinking about education. However, many studies have pointed to serious conceptual deficiencies in the notion of human capital as well as severe difficulties in actually measuring the 'capital' obtained through education and the rates of return obtained or obtainable from it (e.g. Vaizey 1972, Blackman 1987, Ashton and Green 1996, Dunk et al. 1996, Brown and Lauder 2001, 2006, Fine 2001, Lapavitsas 2005). There are many alternative theories on how education relates to work and to labour markets, a few of which are discussed below. Many of them may be at play at the same time, with some dominating more in certain occupations or at certain times.

Some argue that education is a *positional good* (Spence 1973, Thurow 1976). From this perspective, employers are uncertain about the potential productivity of potential employees. They are unable to clearly ascertain what knowledge and skills they bring, let alone how these enhance or otherwise affect productivity. So they use educational qualifications as a screening device that gives broad information about individuals *relative to each other*. Others see education as a proxy for trainability: even though the knowledge obtained through education is not seen as useful, more educated people are viewed by employers as more trainable (Thurow 1976). So, for example, Stefan Collini (2012) argues that employers have traditionally sought arts and humanities graduates for top jobs in the UK not because they necessarily gain 'useful' skills through these courses but because these courses have historically attracted many of the brightest students. Education can also be seen as a legitimized means for social inclusion and exclusion: by demanding formal qualifications for access to jobs, employers (and sometimes unions) can control access to privileged positions (Murphy 1988, van de Werfhorst 2011).

All of these theories, like human capital theory, assume that employers will pay more for education or that it will pay off in self-employment through improved productivity; they differ in terms of the mechanism involved in this relationship. Other theories suggest that employers will not pay more for education. For example, the 'global auction' looks at how the liberalization of markets for highly skilled labour is driving down wages, as 'knowledge' workers in poorer countries are employed at the expense of their more expensive counterparts in richer countries (Brown et al. 2011). Still others suggest that education changes the nature of work, reconstituting the very foundations of society and the way work is organized, our understanding and expectations for peoples' capabilities, the nature of work and even what is useable knowledge for economic value (Baker 2009, 2011). Finally, Collins (1979, 2013) argues that the expansion of education has very little to do with the requirements of work but is rather driven by the inability of labour markets to absorb labour.

Rising unemployment has made conditions harder for workers; this was facilitated by government policies, particularly in the United States and the United Kingdom, which actively attempted to weaken unions, minimum-wage legislation and other protection for working people (Harvey 2005, Kalleberg 2013). The numbers of people in insecure work has dramatically increased since the 1970s, and is likely to increase again because of the Covid pandemic. Livingstone and Guile (2012) argue that struggling to obtain formal credentials, as well as other qualifications and experiences, in order to enhance job prospects has become a primary coping strategy for workers because of how work has become increasingly insecure, with shorter and shorter contracts. This aggravates qualification inflation: because qualifications are used as a significant screening device by employers, potential workers are obliged to strive for higher and higher levels of qualifications to improve their place in the job queue. The combination of qualification inflation and increasingly casualized work inevitably means that individuals undertake education programmes with little relationship to the workplaces that they find themselves in, which again leads to accusations that education systems are producing the wrong skills. It can also be seen reflected in the growing educational movement (usually pushed by companies offering services in the area) of 'micro-credentials', or offering certificates for little bits of learning of specific 'skills'.

The three narratives are also premised on the idea that education and training can have significant effects on society through changing individuals' attitudes towards jobs and work. This has been a major debate in educational research since Phillip Foster published his research on the 'vocational school fallacy'. The fallacy, according to Foster, was that changing the curriculum could change people's attitudes to the kinds of jobs they should aspire to. He argued that, instead, patterns of work and rewards that exist in both urban and rural areas surrounding educational institutions had a far greater impact on individuals' attitudes to work and on their career aspirations (Foster 1965). (See King and Martin (2002) and Lauglo (2010) for further and updated discussion of the vocational school fallacy.)

Ideologies and Illusions?

As Simon McGrath (2007) points out, while educationalists (and policymakers) place considerable emphasis on the role of education in development, much development literature places very little emphasis on education. Many researchers have argued not only that the relationships between skills and work are less plausible than they seem but also that the idea of a 'skills gap' is often a smokescreen for policymakers who feel powerless to intervene in their economies, or want an excuse for reforming their education systems. For example, policymakers may focus attention on the skills of peasant farmers (as per narrative one) at the same time as other policymakers from the same country are agreeing to trade deals that undermine farming in their country. Another example is provided by Levine (2013), who argues that in the United States the idea of a 'skills gap' is used by policymakers and business executives to justify unemployment and create the impression that it is caused by defects of workers as opposed to defects of the economic system.

It could also be argued that all three of the narratives overemphasize the role of individuals and self-help. For example, consider the idea of 'employability skills', which are seen as important at all levels of education and training and contained in some way in all three narratives discussed above.

Governments and policymakers used to talk about 'full employment'. After the Second World War, in many developed and developing countries, full employment was a major focus of much government policy. Governments used different combinations of welfare policies, state spending on infrastructure and state-driven industrialization to fight unemployment (Chang 2002, Crouch 2011). Secure jobs were the norm for most people in developed countries (Brewer 2013). By the late 1970s, however, in many Western countries unemployment and inflation were rising, the working classes were weakening and the system which had delivered strong economic growth and raised prosperity levels in the Western world was in crisis. Governments shifted from attempting to ensure employment to controlling inflation regardless of the effect on employment (Harvey 2005). Since then, collective welfare provision has been reduced in many countries where it previously existed, under the influence of neoliberal economic policy (Crouch 2011). Many argue that this is a key reason for the new prominence given to education in social policy: policymakers emphasize the role of education in creating individual prosperity in order to justify reducing collective welfare provision (Tomlinson 2009, 5). Thus, the neoliberal policy consensus has been that while governments cannot guarantee employment, they can and should assist individuals to become 'employable' or to develop 'marketable skills'.

In other words, instead of collective welfare systems, employment by the state in socially useful work and national development of industries which create jobs, citizens should enrol for education and training programmes that will make them employable. The emphasis on the skills of the workforce, and therefore on training, enabled governments to describe unemployment as a temporary phenomenon, resulting from economic change and individuals' (and educational providers') failure to meet the needs of the economy. The victim, rather than the system, is blamed for unemployment (Foley 1994). Many researchers argue that with the shift from full employment to employability, unemployment has been redefined as a learning problem that can and should be solved by individuals (Novoa 2002, Brown et al. 2011). The learner must be in a continual state of 'up-skilling and re-skilling' in order to respond to shifts in the world labour market (Spreen 2001, 62). This has led some to suggest that the notion of 'employability' implies that it is the moral duty of human beings to arrange their lives to maximize their advantage to the labour market, signifying a shift in the very meaning of life, whereby people are economically enslaved by 'opportunities' for employment (Brown 2006).

Thus, instead of an emphasis on collective responsibility for fellow citizens, policymakers have increasingly involved a discourse of duties, rights and responsibilities to ensure that individuals do not expect too much from the state. This has led to a policy preoccupation with skills as part of a 'self-help' agenda. This is one way of understanding why the notion of 'employability' has become so dominant. It also gives insight into the ubiquity of the concept of entrepreneurialism, which emerges strongly in policy documents related to all three narratives of skills and livelihoods.

Implications for Education Systems

All of this has had, and continues to have, considerable implications for education reform. It could be argued that rising levels of educational attainment are intrinsically good, as, even if the narratives discussed at the beginning of the chapter are over-simplistic, there is much that is valuable about education. There are many reasons, social, economic and from a human rights perspective, for the expansion of both general and vocational education in developing countries. But when education is positioned so centrally in public and policy discourse as the solution to economic problems, education is blamed when, inevitably, the economic problems do not go away (Grubb and Lazerson 2004). This leads to serial reform of education systems, which can be very demoralizing to educators and is often accompanied by constant criticism of education institutions and educators. Also, as discussed above, the emphasis on the putative roles of education in improving economic situations has led governments to seek reforms that 'vocationalize' education or to attempt to make it more 'relevant' to what are *perceived* or *claimed* to be the needs of employers. It has also been accompanied by a drive to privatize the provision of vocational education in many countries guided by a belief that more competition will lead to better and more relevant programmes (McGrath 2012). While rising education levels may have many positive aspects, there is a high cost for individuals who feel compelled to obtain higher levels of qualifications at considerable expense to families and taxpayers. Education does not create demand in the economy (Amsden 2010). Focus on creating demand-led vocational education may draw attention away from the need to create demand for skilled workers through industrial and economic policies.

In short, there are many reasons to believe that not only are the social and economic problems faced by most nations today bigger than a lack of skills but also that attempting to solve them through education may exacerbate the situation and may cause problems for education systems. This is a serious problem in many poor countries, which now experience rapidly rising mass but poor quality education, and have little capacity to improve quality or diversify offerings because of weak or non-existent economic growth and development (Allais 2020). One alternative is focusing on economic and social development first, with educational development following from it but not seen as the precondition for it (Amsden 2010). In other words, policies to develop skills need to follow industrial policy, social welfare systems and macro-economic policy focused on job creation and social development.

Questions for Discussion

1. Why is it commonly believed that young people today are less well equipped for work than their parents were? Could educational standards have declined? Do technological changes mean that work requires higher skills levels? If these perceptions are wrong, why are they so widely believed?

2. Is there a youth unemployment crisis or just an unemployment crisis? Are young people unemployed because they lack skills or because they are at the back of the queue for a diminishing number of jobs?

3. What are skills? How and where are they best acquired? How can we know what knowledge and skills will be of most value to individuals?

4. How different are the three narratives of skills and livelihoods? To what extent and in which ways do they support or contradict each other?

Further Reading

Lauder, H. Brown, P. Dillabough, J. Halsey, A. H. (2006), *Education, Globalization, and Social Change*, Oxford: Oxford University Press.

Livingstone, D. W. (2009), *Education and Jobs: Exploring the Gaps*, Toronto: University of Toronto Press.

Moore, R. (2004), *Education and Society: Issues and Explorations in the Sociology of Education*, Cambridge: Polity.

16

Adult Education: Movements, Policies and Processes

Charlotte Nussey

Chapter Outline

Introduction

At first glance, it seems easy to identify what is meant by adult education. When compared to children, adults have different educational needs, experiences and learning processes. But the word 'adult' itself has multiple interpretations: it can refer to a stage in the lifecycle, a status or a culturally determined set of ideals, qualities and rites of passage which are constructed around a particular identity. UNESCO (1976) keeps the definition open, stating that adults are simply 'those people whom their own society deems to be adult' – they hold a particular place in society in which they both recognize themselves and are recognized by others (Rogers 2002).

Since adults and adulthood are contested concepts, perhaps it is easier to start by defining the idea of adult education. But unpacking the notion of adult education also reveals great variation. There are different delivery systems – formal, non-formal, vocational, state, NGO or market-based provision. In parallel with these delivery systems, different conceptualizations of adult education emerge. For some, adult education is a form of filling the gaps, of teaching adults who, for a range of reasons, were unable to access education as children and who are viewed as lacking particular skills that are thought to be important to active citizenship and participation in the labour market. For others, adult education is part of a raft of lifelong learning strategies, embedded in our daily lives, which we begin as children and continue as we travel into our later years. As we start to explore the different conceptualizations of adult education, it becomes clear that, in some senses, 'defining adult education is an impossible task. It is such a multivalent and amorphous field, comprising different traditions, that definitions are bound to be exclusive, often deliberately so' (Mayo 2009, 269).

This chapter draws out some of the ways in which adult education has been conceptualized while recognizing the politics entailed in defining the field. Education is far from value-neutral but rather is infused with power and subject to prevailing discourses, which shape policies, processes and identities associated with being literate, illiterate, educated or uneducated.

Histories of adult education over the course of the last century tend to be shaped by three distinct but interlinked discourses (UNESCO 2006a, 153–9, Rogers and Horrocks 2010, 1–10). From the 1940s to the 1960s, ideals of modernization constructed a single 'right' form of education. During this period, when primary school was far from universal, adult education was seen as largely remedial, a way to make up the deficit of education not received in earlier years. Increasingly, adult education was also linked to notions of human capital and production, and the expansion of national economies (Levine 1982).

In the later 1960s, tensions around the Cold War played themselves out in socialist revolutions, particularly in Central and South America, and around decolonization in countries such as Mozambique and Tanzania, challenging the world order and questioning the dominance of capitalism. What Rogers and Horrocks (2010) call 'heterodox' ideologies proliferated, which saw education as one of many contributory factors that created rather than remedied inequality. Those excluded from education systems were seen as oppressed or disadvantaged, rather than in terms of deficit, and it was argued that new forms of adult education were needed that were different from formal schooling. Increased attention was paid to the variety of experiences of adult learners as gendered, raced and classed individuals who needed to be empowered and whose societies needed to be transformed.

Instead of trying to educate for conformity, or for liberation, adult educators by the late 1980s started to facilitate students creating learning in their own ways, for personal growth, rather than the occupational or economic concerns of the nation. Emphasis was placed on incidental, informal, 'lifelong' or 'continuing' learning (UIL 2009), but funding for adult education in developing contexts dropped as primary education became the focus of many governments and international organizations.

In the twenty-first century, lifelong learning has come to dominate the discourse. Lifelong learning places both age and learning on a continuum: education is seen as extending across the life cycle, while learning is seen to happen both in formal but also in non-formal settings, including the family or the workplace. At the same time, forms of adult education can be seen to be increasingly diverging. These expansions are captured in the shift in UNESCO's definition of adults, to now include 'all those who engage in adult education, even if they have not reached the legal age of maturity' (UIL 2019). In UNESCO's 2015 Recommendation on Adult Learning and Education (2015), this divergent field of lifelong learning is divided into three key domains, each associated with different 'skills': literacy and basic skills; continuing education and professional development (vocational skills); and liberal, popular and community education (active citizenship skills).

These different histories continue to impact understandings of adult education today. This chapter will begin by tracing them through the dominant discourses on adult education, in the work of UNESCO and the three international frameworks which have framed debates since

Policy 10
An Overview of Adult Education in South Africa

In South Africa, the 'Modernization' period from the 1940s was overlaid by Apartheid, during which time adult education for Black learners was primarily available in poorly resourced night schools, a parallel track to the segregated schooling system (Morrell et al. 2009). Adult education for workers was also provided by some mining and industrial companies (Prinsloo and Breier 1996). Basic literacy was thus associated with the skills needed for work and low-status participation in the labour market, which was also racially segregated.

In the 1970s, a number of NGOs ran literacy programmes inspired by the work of Paulo Freire. These semi-illegal projects were closely linked to the struggle against Apartheid, and broader work towards social transformation and liberation. With the transition to democracy in the 1990s, these NGOs broadly disappeared, as the country embraced a Constitution in which basic education for all was constructed as a right, including for adults, and the transformative agenda was absorbed into state machinery (Aitchison 2010).

Under this state provision of adult education, however, the emancipatory ethic was not well translated, despite intense consultation and debate. By the late 1990s, government emphasis on economic growth and employment was edging out the more socially transformative policies around reconstruction and development, with a corresponding shift in conceptualizations of adult education towards skills for work. Adult education spaces and initiatives were poorly funded, with high levels of drop-out rates, and short-term forms of delivery (Baatjes and Mathe 2004).

With the focus on EFA and the MDGs, South Africa initiated a number of campaigns to reduce illiteracy. *Kha Ri Gude*, or 'Let us Learn', was launched in 2008 and designed to reach 4.7 million learners by 2015 (McKay 2018). Drawing on Freirean themes, it aimed to empower marginalized groups and individuals, providing adult learners with 'practical' skills, including using ATMs and basic budgeting. Focused on communities, the campaign further offered significant opportunities for building supportive social networks to mediate multiple forms of inequality.

2000 – Education for All, the Millennium Development Goals and the Sustainable Development Goals. It will then turn to the measurement agenda which has arisen in parallel to these goals, and finally to consider three framings of adult education in more detail: adult literacies as plural situated practices, adult pedagogy through the work of Paulo Freire and finally a more detailed look at lifelong learning.

Adult Education on the Global Stage: International Frameworks and the Work of UNESCO

In international frameworks, adult education is often interpreted as adult literacy. This partly reflects the focus in wider education and development discourses on outcomes and measurements rather than the processes of learning (Barrett 2011), but also reflects a prevalent instrumental view of literacy as the key or tool by which other forms of adult education such as health or the broader range of skills for work might be accessed (UIL 2010, Hanemann 2019).

A commitment to literacy as a right has been at the top of UNESCO's agenda from its formation in 1946, and reiterated throughout the organization's history (UNESCO 2006b, Wagner 2011). By 1997, and the fifth International Conference on Adult Education (CONFINTEA V) held in Hamburg, it was argued that adult education is 'more than a right; it is key to the twenty-first century' (Resolution 2). The Hamburg Declaration held that 'Literacy, broadly conceived as the basic knowledge and skills needed by all in a rapidly changing world, is a fundamental human right', a world of knowledge-based societies in which literacy is a 'catalyst for participation in social, cultural, political and economic activities, and for learning throughout life' (Resolution 11). In this expanded definition, knowledge, skills and literacy are conceptually elided, positioning illiterate men and women as 'locked out' of 'knowledge-based societies', defining them as neither participating nor knowing. Expanding the right in this way problematically constructs illiterate identities through new frames of deficit, despite the clear intentions to provide a basis for increasing the promotion of adult education and learning at this conference.

UNESCO and others play a role in mobilizing for the expansion of adult education and learning programmes, holding examples of best practice, arguing for funding and developing testing mechanisms for internationally comparable data. In the case of CONFINTEA V, support for the right to adult education was mobilized through international partnerships, although there were still insufficient calls for renewed commitments to funding (Bhola 1998). This appeal for support and best practice from international, national and civil society bodies was reiterated in the CONFINTEA VI in Brazil (2009), and stressed in the Belém Framework for Action adopted at this conference, which was grounded in a conceptualization of adult education as 'lifelong learning' (UIL 2009, Torres 2011).

The focus from UNESCO and other organizations on literacy, and to a lesser extent on 'skills', was solidified in the EFA movement and the MDGs. Two EFA goals addressed literacy and skills: EFA Goal 3, which aimed to 'promote learning and life skills for young people and adults', and EFA Goal 4, which aimed to 'increase adult literacy'. The indicators used for these goals were enrolment and completion in technical and vocational education and training (EFA 3), and spending, enrolment and completion in adult literacy and basic education programmes (EFA 4). The indicator for EFA 4 also included numbers and percentages of adults who pass a basic literacy test, with a target to increase this level by 50 per cent by 2015. Reporting on progress towards these goals in global overviews such as UNESCO's annual Global Monitoring Reports (GMR), however, tended to remain focused on literacy rates (UNESCO 2013/2014, 384–91).

There was no mention of adult education or literacy in its own right in the MDGs. The only deployment of literacy in this framework was in terms of youth literacy rates, which were used as indicators to report progress towards universal primary education (MDG 2) and gender equality in education (MDG 3). While some have highlighted that this left adult education notably and problematically absent from the framework (Unterhalter 2013), others argued that particular skills or forms of knowledge which are associated with adult literacy thread their way throughout the achievement of the other MDGs (Robinson 2005). This reading of adult literacy, which highlights the correlations between increased maternal literacy and a range of health benefits (MDGs 4–6), between maternal education and enrolment of children in school (MDG 2) and between reducing poverty (MDG 1) and promoting gender equality (MDG 3), has been repeatedly underlined in the analysis of internationally focused reports and donor organizations but predominantly to mobilize support for girls' rather than women's education (King and Hill 1993, UNESCO 2006b, UNESCO 2013/2014, UNFPA 2014).

The emphasis on these surface correlations, however, obscures the complex processes behind social change. The association of women's literacy with a range of instrumental benefits also poses a kind of conundrum for feminist commentators. While many feminists want to recognize the traction of this kind of inter-generational argument for the promotion of women's education, others have critiqued it for serving to subordinate women's intrinsic rights to their role as mothers and have questioned the dominance of donor values which are often universalized and depoliticized (Robinson-Pant 2004a, Unterhalter 2005, Robinson-Pant 2008, North 2010).

In the 2030 Agenda for Sustainable Development, and the accompanying Education 2030 Incheon Declaration, there has been a renewed understanding of education as one of the main drivers of development (UIL 2019). Adults have a clear place within these declarations and the goals, targets and indicators which accompany them. Links are made in the target 4.3 of the educational goal between lifelong education and gender equality, with a call for 'equal access for all women and men' to affordable and quality technical, vocational and tertiary education, including university. Adults and youth are the focus of targets 4.4 and 4.6, which call for a 'substantial increase' in the proportion of youth and adults who have 'relevant skills' or who 'achieve literacy and numeracy'. At the same time, however, there is a lack of specificity regarding what would constitute an 'increase' in adult literacy rates or skills, as well as no current consensus on how to measure 'participation' in adult learning (UNESCO 2020, Elfert 2019). More generally, concerns have also been raised that the substantive aims of SDG 4 are translated into narrow metrics of 'functional' forms of literacy, and narrow notions of life skills (King 2017, Unterhalter 2019a). Measurement continues to shape how these goals enact force on policies and processes associated with adult education, as well as how to understand the 'problem' of how many of the world's population are seen to lack the requisite skills and knowledge. The following part of this chapter considers questions of measurement in more detail.

Global Measurements: Adult Literacy

Global measures and compilations of adult literacy rates remain a contested terrain. National censuses, for example, tend to capture self-reported literacy, and have been viewed as unreliable and context-specific snapshots, which are not conducted regularly enough to properly report on trends and progress (Maddox and Esposito 2011). Three particular globally focused measures of literacy aim to address the reliability and comparability concerns levelled at such self-reported figures, by including a combination of self-reporting and testing: the Demographic and Health Surveys (DHS) funded by USAID, UNESCO's Literacy Assessment and Monitoring Programme (LAMP) and the OECD's Programme for the International Assessment of Adult Competencies (PIAAC).

A critique of all three of these measures is that while they capture a particular notion of literacy, participation in adult literacy classes can be valued for a range of other reasons by adult learners, in addition to, or even entirely independent of skill acquisition. These benefits have been characterized as 'soft', as opposed to the 'hard' skills of reading and writing, and include benefits such as self-esteem, confidence or the building of networks and solidarity (Tett and Maclachlan 2007). Research exploring women's engagement with adult education, for example, further highlights that there is often a disjuncture between top-down policy and the way in which literacy programmes are received and at times resisted by those who participate in them (Robinson-Pant 2008, Chopra 2011, Nussey 2019).

A related critique is that the measures position adult learners' needs as equivalent to those of children. This conceptualization of adult basic education as a 'second road', which runs parallel to early childhood and primary education (Wagner 2011), constructs skills and knowledge as the ultimate destination for both adults and children, and literacy as the technical measurement of education, regardless of age. But there is no sense in either these measures or this second road narrative of how adult needs might be different to those of children or how they might use their literacy skills differently. The road metaphor instead holds illiterate adults as somehow transgressive, on the wrong track and without knowledge.

One response to both of these critiques, which recognizes the specificities of adult lives and reaffirms their power to define the range of literacies that they might value, is offered by a measure which draws on the capability approach (Maddox and Esposito 2011). This proposed measure puts to work capability notions of human well-being and plurality to reframe functional literacy, and define new thresholds for the ways in which we might make international comparisons by suggesting that a composite list of literacies, defined through public participatory processes, could provide the basis for fuller and more representative measures.

Measurement and Indicators 7: Definitions and Models for Measuring Adult Literacy

In the DHS, researchers ask members of a household to read a card with four 'simple' sentences written on it, which should 'be appropriate' to the country. Sentences such as 'parents love their children' and 'farming is hard work' are prepared for 'every language in which respondents are likely to be literate', although one option on the survey is that no card with the required language was available. Questions are then asked about engagements with newspapers, the radio and television. Respondents are finally categorized by the survey into those who 'cannot read at all', are 'able to read only part' and are 'able to read the whole sentence'. These categories of literacy status can in turn be held against aspects of learning and empowerment, such as knowledge about HIV and sustainable development, or attitudes to gender-based violence (Unterhalter 2013). Such literacy categories speak to the UNESCO 1958 definition, which defines literacy as being able to read a simple sentence (cited in Ahmed 2011b). These categories have been critiqued for the ways in which they define learners against fixed binaries of being either literate or illiterate, which map onto discourses shaping illiterate identities as 'primitive' or 'backward' (Gee 1986), and do not allow for the range of competencies and literacy practices that exist in most social contexts (Maddox and Esposito 2011).

LAMP was launched in 2003, designed to measure the 'continuum' of literacy skills and to more properly capture the notion of 'functional' literacy (UNESCO 2013/2014). Functional literacy, a concept which gained currency from the Second World War onwards (Levine 1982), aims to go beyond what UNESCO names 'actual' literacy, and into measures of literacy in use. LAMP tests in three domains of literacy – prose, documents and numeracy – and tries to ascertain whether literacy skills are sustained in everyday practices. The design of LAMP both follows and builds on other surveys, such as the OECD's International Adult Literacy Survey (IALS), which is only conducted in 'industrialized' countries using European languages and Roman alphabets, by introducing a wider range of languages and scripts. Implementation and capacity development issues meant that LAMP took five years to be piloted (Ercikan et al. 2008), however, and it was only piloted or fully conducted in ten low- and middle-income countries, meaning that it does not yet offer broad international comparisons.

PIAAC also aims to capture the UNESCO (2005) definition of learning as operating on a 'continuum' (cited in Ahmed 2011). The first results were released in 2013, conducted by the OECD in thirty three countries. As with UNESCO's LAMP, the measure combines self-reporting and direct-assessment, but with a focus on the development of 'higher order skills', particularly those associated with literacies in ICT and the world of work. The survey contains a module on skills use, which includes skills such as 'planning' and 'communication', to assess both 'skills necessary in the workplace' but also 'cognitive functioning'.

The 'Problem' of 'Illiteracy': 'What Gets Measured, Counts'

The concerns discussed above about the narrowing of focus of SDG4 to metrics of 'functional' literacy have led to extensive work to extend global comparative measurements beyond simple binaries of literate / illiterate. This work is shaped by broader critiques in the field of development that only 'what gets measured, counts'. This single story of literacy is quite striking. Over the last twenty years, very little has changed. The raw number of 'illiterate' adults has remained 'stubbornly high' at over 750 million, a fall of 12 per cent since 1990 but just 1 per cent since 2000' (UNESCO 2013/4, UNESCO 2020). Global youth and adult illiteracy thus becomes the 'problem' which adult education must solve, and the more nuanced reflections on lifelong learning or social transformations get lost. The logic of literacy measurement both shapes our understanding of what 'the problem' is and defines it as one that is intransigent; literacy is a right but one which continues to be denied to approximately one fifth of the world's adult population (UNESCO 2006b).

A number of dimensions of literacy and adult education have been focused on as the reasons for this intransigence. The first set is around funding, quality and retention rates – adult education receives less than 1 per cent of education budgets in many countries (UIL 2019), with the result that provision can be patchy and poorly coordinated, small-scale or short-term.

Reflecting this funding, adult education teachers or facilitators are often poorly paid or even voluntary, which can lead to low status for their work (Gizaw, Rogers and Warkineh 2019). They are, in addition, generally less well-trained than their primary and secondary teacher counterparts. This in turn can lead to poor attendance and retention rates among learners, when the complexities of adults' lives with competing priorities and needs interact with poor delivery of classes or material which is felt to be insufficiently relevant. In fifty country reports analysed by UNESCO, the quality of adult educators was cited as a key challenge. Some countries, such as Haiti, employed educators who were only educated themselves to the level that they teach, while in Chad educators held a minimum of secondary education but were only offered two weeks training. Opportunities for professionalization of the field, offered in Indonesia and Thailand for example, were directly linked to the availability of government resources (UIL 2009).

The problem of illiteracy is also spatialized in quite specific ways that speaks not only to countries that are less 'developed' but further to complex questions of language. The five countries with the lowest adult literacy rates, all in sub-Saharan Africa, all have high linguistic diversity; Chad, with a national adult literacy rate of 22 per cent, has a population which speaks 133 languages. The Central African Republic, Mali and South Sudan all have 70 to 80 different languages spoken. Women's literacy rates are also particularly low in these countries (UNESCO 2020, 268–70).

While there are similarities between some countries with low adult literacy rates, analysis since the mid-1980s highlights that the ten countries which account for 72 per cent of the global population of illiterate adults have followed very different trajectories in whether or not they have been able to reduce their illiterate populations over time. China has made enormous progress in reducing its total of illiterates, as has India, but in India, population growth has worked to cancel the gains made. In Nigeria, on the other hand, the number of illiterate adults increased by 71 per cent from 1991 to 2008 (Figure 16.1).

In addition to population increase, the problem of illiteracy is also often attributed to very high numbers of out-of-school children and youth, whether due to a failure of governments to expand school provision, poor educational quality or as the result of broader social issues such as conflict. Spending less than four years in school is particularly identified as a 'route' to youth illiteracy, highlighting that in many countries children may be inside school buildings but not necessarily learning (UNESCO 2020).

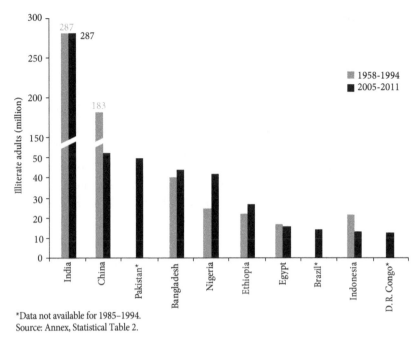

*Data not available for 1985–1994.
Source: Annex, Statistical Table 2.

Figure 16.1 Number of illiterate adults, 10 countries with highest populations of illiterate adults, 1985–94 and 2005–11. *Source*: Annex, Statistical Table 2.

The picture of national figures and trends is thus further complicated by inequalities at regional and local levels, in both developed and developing nations. In this final sense, therefore, illiteracy is constructed as a problem which is attributed to particular groups. The most obvious of these in the development discourse is women, who make up approximately two-thirds of the global illiterate population, a share which has remained more or less constant since 1990 (UNESCO 2020, 267). This gendered category can be further broken down by wealth inequalities, which mean that poor, often rural, women are likely to be illiterate, and a specifically named 'target' of illiteracy programmes in countries as diverse as Afghanistan, Pakistan, Zambia or Uganda. Family literacy programmes, increasingly popular in a range of countries, in part try to address such inter-generational issues of marginalization, while other projects address a range of issues that such communities face, such as a World Vision literacy project in Ghana that links to water and sanitation, or literacy programmes in Mozambique which cover environmental and health issues, including HIV (UIL 2009). High levels of illiteracy thus often map onto other forms of social inequality and deprivation, but in complex and non-linear ways.

Researching Adult Literacy: New Literacy Studies and the Ethnographic Model

The new literacy studies approach is particularly concerned with diversity of learners, as well as diversity of literacies in use. This body of work problematizes the idea of literacy as a straightforward acquisition of skills, and asks instead what it means to think of literacy as a social practice (Street 2001, Bartlett 2008). The approach argues that this practice should be conceptualized as multiple, and that literacies vary according to time and space and are contested in terms of power (Street 2003). In what Brian Street has termed the 'autonomous' model of literacy, which underpins much of the international development thinking and measurements discussed above, claims are made that literacy is a universal notion, which is 'natural' and objectively definable. Street argues that this is a deeply ideological position, an ethnocentric assumption which holds that literacy in and of itself is independent of cultural context and meaning, and will have autonomous effects, thus creating inequality for those who 'lack' it and advantages for those who gain it (Street 2011). He argues that the power to define and name what counts as literacy and illiteracy can sanction the imposition of dominant culture literacies onto minority groups, whether these literacies are Western in conception or belong to the dominant group(s) within a country. When definitions of literacy are restricted to a single, normative perspective, so too is the power to determine policy, design and fund international adult education programmes, and to assess their 'success'.

These critiques have been both grounded and further operationalized through a range of ethnographic research studies (Prinsloo and Breier 1996, Street 2001, Robinson-Pant 2004a, Rogers and Street 2012), which are characterized by long-term researcher engagement with adult education and understandings of literacies at individual and community levels. Such studies often deploy a variety of observational and participatory methods, including sketches or photography which document the ways in which texts such as maps, signs or shop arrangements mediate social interactions in a variety of different ways (Hamilton 2006). Engagements with signs painted onto walls, for example around voting processes in Ethiopia and Namibia, or warnings about noise levels in India, are often decoded through words and pictures in more than one language, highlighting the multiple ways in which meanings are made through different forms of literacy, which are time and context bound (Rogers and Street 2012, 65–82).

These studies pose challenges to orthodox pedagogies, in that they give accounts of the range of literacy practices which take place outside the context of school and schooled communities (Hamilton 2006). Often research notes, however, the continued resonance in these forms of adult education of the 'idea of a school' and the symbolic attraction to formal schooling expressed by adult learners (Robinson-Pant 2008). More work is needed, therefore, to unpack the ways in which power is located within multiple literacies with the result that some forms of literacy practices are invested with more social and economic capital than others (Papen 2005).

Contested Pedagogical Approaches: Freire, Social Movements and Empowerment

The problem of 'schooled' literacy in relation to adult education is also one that engaged the radical Brazilian thinker Paulo Freire. Freire's engagement with adult education throughout his works was one that was unapologetically political. Indeed, the methodology which he developed was considered such a threat to the old order in Brazil that he was jailed and later exiled, just after the military coup in 1964. For Freire, any claim that education is value neutral is in itself a political practice, designed to limit the potential of the oppressed to recognize the injustice which they experience. For Freire, the question therefore becomes not whether education is political but what a liberating model, as opposed to 'domesticating' model, might look like (McCowan 2006).

Perhaps the most illustrative metaphor which Freire employs to critique the 'domesticating model' is that of traditional educational processes as 'banking' (Freire 1970). Freire argued that education was suffering from 'narration sickness', in which students are constructed as empty vessels which the teacher 'fills' with pre-defined knowledge. This passive transferal of information is set against acts of cognition, in which students are actively engaged. For Freire, the banking model thus needed to be turned on its head, through the process of conscientization, by which students gain critical awareness. Conscientization takes place through two key pedagogical processes of dialogue and problem-solving, in which student–teacher dichotomies are destabilized since all are understood to be learning, and students themselves can start to value and evaluate their own experiences as well as to act on this new understanding.

When Freire published his seminal text, *Pedagogy of the Oppressed*, in 1968, he conceptualized this process of conscientization, or critical consciousness, as one operating within a context of class-based oppression. Throughout the text, his real-life examples are of students such as a 'peasant' who 'feels inferior to the boss because the boss seems to be the only one who knows things and is able to run things' (Freire 1970, 63). Knowledge, self-recognition, power and class struggle are thus intimately bound together, in 'reading the world' as well as 'the word'. The influence of Freire's thinking can be traced in many socialist movements for popular political education, and in a range of countries in both Latin America and sub-Saharan Africa, including Chile, Angola and Tanzania (Arnove and Graff 1987).

Pathways to Practice 10
Freirean Methods in the Nicaraguan Sandinista Literacy Campaign

Adult education formed a key intervention of the Sandinista rule (1979–90) in Nicaragua (Arnove and Graff 1987, Hanemann 2006). The campaign was concentrated over March–August in 1980, but began with a national census of all Nicaraguans over ten years old to determine literacy levels and locations of illiterate populations. The census itself became a miniature campaign, as it was conducted voluntarily and helped inform people about the upcoming literacy classes. It was established that approximately 75 per cent of the illiterate population were in remote areas, and so a cohort of voluntary *brigadistas* in the 'Popular Literacy Army' of secondary and university students went to live for five months in these mountain and rural areas with the families whom they taught. A scheme of training through supervision and radio programmes for these *brigadistas* was established, who were provided with teaching materials and encouraged to foster Freirean dialogue.

Over five months in 1980, official illiteracy rates were reduced from 50.3 per cent to 12.9 per cent. Literacy was held to be key for democratic participation and national reconstruction after the overthrow of the dictatorship, but also to increase political awareness and engagement through organizing around literacy classes, and to encourage cohesion across urban–rural and class divides. Despite some contestations over the reliability of these rates (Arnove and Graff 1987), and concerns that the effects of the campaign were short-lived, the campaign was notable for its highly successful mass mobilization of both volunteer teachers and learners. Altogether, more than one-fifth of the population participated directly in the campaign, approximately half of whom were female. The biggest reductions in illiteracy rates were in the least developed and most remote areas, politically engaging disempowered communities and providing local development projects alongside the literacy classes. Freire was often quoted in explaining the success of the campaign in these terms: 'this type of National Literacy Crusade is not a pedagogical program with political implications, but rather, it is a political project with pedagogical implications' (Hanemann 2006, p. 9).

In his later work, Freire acknowledged the critiques which had been made that his work inadequately addresses issues pertaining to race and gender as well as overlapping forms of oppression. These debates and engagements have also been taken on by different forms of critical pedagogy, which draw on his ideas around power, inequality and democratic values (Au 2011). ActionAid's *Reflect* (Regenerated Freirean Literacy through Empowering Community Techniques) movement also draws on Freire's methods, overlaid with participatory action research, to work on women's empowerment. Materials are generated by learners themselves, progressing from graphics to symbol cards and words which are elicited from knowledge of the community and learners' environments. Each graphic is designed to facilitate a starting point for Freirean critical dialogue, with increasing emphasis in the movement upon creating democratic spaces and analysing power (Fiedrich and Jellema 2003).

Lifelong Learning: Learning Embedded in Daily Lives

Both the Freirean and the new literacy studies approaches to adult education pay particular attention to the ways in which it is intricately bound in questions of experience. A third approach which also addresses experience focuses not on new forms of pedagogy, or new forms of researching and conceptualizing literacies, but rather the idea of learning itself. This is lifelong learning, which has already been discussed above as the dominant paradigm which has been translated into the language of SDG 4. As that discussion made clear, adult learning and education is central to lifelong learning, but the scope of lifelong learning is much broader than a focus on literacy, and encompasses the full range of technical, vocational and tertiary education, as well as formal education systems.

As a paradigm, lifelong learning draws on multiple discourses and approaches to (adult) learning and education. In one set of ideas, the paradigm has been associated with citizenship and democracy, most clearly expressed by the 'four pillars' of the Delors (1996) report on education: 'learning to know, learning to live together, learning to do and learning to be'. But as Delors himself reflected fifteen years after the launch of this famous report (Delors 2013), this understanding of lifelong learning has been overshadowed by more neoliberal interpretations of the paradigm. These have been particularly adopted by the European Union and the OECD, and associations with human capital and the 'knowledge economy' (Jarvis 2014), but are also evident in the language of some developing country policies, such as South Africa (Aitchison 2004, Walters 2006).

The breadth of the lifelong learning paradigm can thus be seen to be both its strength and its weakness. For some, the inclusion of lifelong learning offers space for connection between different components of learning systems, and gives renewed backing for calls for reforms of qualifications and the ways that indigenous, incidental or informal learning is recognized (Hanemann 2019). In countries such as Lao and Vietnam, work by government and NGOs respectively aims to do just that, building lifelong learning into comprehensive policies and approaches (Yorozu 2017). But for others, the different dimensions of the paradigm open rather than close space for increased inequalities, both within and between nations (Torres 2004, Elfert 2019), as well as across different lines of dis/advantage such as gender or class (Brine 2006, Leathwood and Francis 2006). In countries where basic education is of low quality, particularly for citizens who are poor, a 'compensatory' model of adult education continues to predominate, primarily focused on adult literacy (Preece 2009). In countries in Europe and the OECD, on the other hand, adults with 'high' skills are three times as likely to participate in training as those with low skills: 58 per cent versus 20 per cent. Lifelong learning opportunities are not equally available to all. In both developed and developing contexts, reaching disadvantaged groups remains a key challenge for meaningful enactment of the transformative agenda of the SDGs (UNESCO 2020).

Conclusions: Looking Forward

As this chapter has shown, there is the risk that adults continue to be rendered invisible in discussions of educational systems, targets and goals, except as the target for testing, and their needs are frequently undifferentiated from those of children. Lifelong learning, Freirean and new literacy studies approaches all start to question the ways in which adult learner identities are constructed and to critique the deficit models of adult education which underlie much of the international architecture. They also address questions of the process of adult education and learning rather than solely focusing on outcomes. But more work needs to be done to challenge divergences in approaches to adult education which exacerbate inequalities between and within countries, and continue to shape 'illiterate' identities which adhere to particular raced, classed or gendered positions, such as poor or female, without questioning the structural constraints that have led to deprivation.

Questions for Discussion

1. How would you define adult education? How would you best design measurements for the success of provision of this type of adult education?
2. Do you think that adult learners' needs should be thought of differently from those of children? Should they be further differentiated by gender, class or race? Why/why not?
3. How might you argue for adult education and learning, if you were trying to convince policymakers of its importance?

Further Reading

Elfert, M. (2018). *UNESCO's Utopia of Lifelong Learning: An Intellectual History*, Abingdon: Routledge.

Robinson-Pant, A. (2008), '"Why Literacy Matters": Exploring a Policy Perspective on Literacies, Identities and Social Change', *The Journal of Development Studies*, 44(6): 779–96.

Rogers, A. and B. Street (2012), *Adult Literacy and Development: Stories from the Field*, Leicester: National Institute of Adult Continuing Education (NIACE).

Useful Website

UNESCO Institute for Lifelong Learning: https://uil.unesco.org/

17

Higher Education and Development: Critical Issues and Debates

Rebecca Schendel and Tristan McCowan

Chapter Outline

Introduction

In the context of a low-income country struggling to provide even basic resources for all of its citizens, the provision of higher education (HE) might seem like something of a luxury. It is this perspective that has long dominated the international development discourse, particularly in light of empirical evidence presented in the 1980s that seemed to suggest that public investment in HE provided lower social return than investment in primary and secondary levels. The economic success of countries like South Korea, which focused on developing HE *after* achieving universal primary and secondary education, has reinforced the idea that HE is a sector of lower priority for developing nations (Pillay and CHET 2010).

In recent years, however, there has been a growing realization that development, even for the poorest countries, depends on a flourishing HE system. Universities are central to crucial societal tasks, including the formation of professionals in areas such as education, health and public administration; the creation, absorption and adaptation of new technologies; the strengthening of democracy and enabling of spaces for critique and scrutiny of government and policy; and the preservation, study and development of local and national culture and heritage. In particular, the emergence of the knowledge economy has placed new requirements on workers and intensified the need for HE. Knowledge-driven industries and the service sector have overtaken other industries as the greatest drivers of wealth throughout the world, and HE institutions are increasingly viewed as vital 'engines of development' (Castells 1994) within this context, as they support the adaptation of technology (Lucas 1988) and the development and management of enabling institutions (Glaeser et al. 2004, Persson and Tabellini 2006). As a result of these changes, HE has returned as an important component of the international development agenda, spurring reform and revitalization efforts within the HE systems of many low- and middle-income countries (LMICs).

This trend has been further supported by the renewed recognition of higher education in the Sustainable Development Goals (SDGs). In contrast to the Millennium Development Goals (MDGs), which focused almost exclusively on primary education, the SDGs include a goal for equitable access to tertiary education, and emphasize the crucial role of universities in achieving the full set of seventeen goals (McCowan 2019). The research, innovation and public engagement activities of universities, in addition to the education they provide, are a vital part of ensuring sustainable development and addressing the complex challenges of global pandemics and climate change.

This chapter explores the central debates on HE provision in LMICs. These include questions about funding for HE, particularly in view of its public and private benefits, and debates on how HE should be organized in order to reconcile often-conflicting demands for equity and quality. These are challenges for wealthy – as well as so-called 'developing' – countries, as all systems struggle to maintain high standards of teaching and research and equitably expand access in a context of constrained public funding (Unterhalter and Carpentier 2010).

Models of Higher Education in Low- and Middle-income Countries

It is difficult to delineate a clear definition of the term 'higher education', as it encompasses a variety of institutional types and models. Institutions such as Nalanda in fifth-century India and Al-Azhar Mosque in tenth-century Egypt functioned as centres of secular, as well as religious, scholarship and higher learning and could, in many ways, be considered the predecessors of modern HE. However, few contemporary institutions resemble these early culturally specific models. Instead, Western models of HE have largely been adopted across the globe (Altbach 2004, McCowan 2019), particularly in lower-income contexts, given their colonial legacies.

In the Spanish-American colonies, the first universities were established as early as the sixteenth century. However, in other parts of the world, HE hardly featured in the colonial period, with education largely restricted to primary and secondary levels (Lulat 2005). Most colonial governments believed that the number of qualified local people was insufficient to justify the establishment of universities, preferring to send bright young men to Europe to further their education (Ajayi et al. 1996).

This situation began to change in the British colonies in the 1920s and 1930s, as nationalist movements began to emerge, many of which were spearheaded by graduates of Western universities. In this context, the British authorities agreed to the establishment of colleges in many of their colonies. However, although most British universities followed a liberal, character-building model of university education, along the lines of Cardinal Newman's (1947 [1852]) recommendations, early colonial institutions could best be described as training colleges, emphasizing rote learning of the specific skills and knowledge necessary for working within the colonial bureaucracy (Ajayi et al. 1996, Lulat 2005, Tilak 2013).

Universities were not established in the French colonies until after 1945. These institutions were considered an extension of the French HE system and were placed under control of the French government's education department (Lulat 2005). In both the French and British empires, the new HE institutions aimed to enforce the values of the colonizing society and train individuals for service to the state (Nyerere 1968). The institutions were elitist and established in urban centres, and they required students to study in the language of their colonizers (Altbach 1998). Universities were therefore separated – physically, linguistically and intellectually – from the majority of the local population.

In the final years of the colonial era, the demand for HE became linked with national independence movements (Ajayi et al. 1996). As a result, upon gaining independence, many new governments solicited funding for the establishment of a national public university. These new institutions often imitated universities in the colonizing countries, as nationalist leaders felt that anything different would imply that former colonial subjects were intellectually inferior (Lulat 2005). In former British colonies, many universities such as the University of East Africa started as associate colleges of the University of London, and followed its curricular model, while in former French colonies, the Napoleonic model of centralized 'superior' institutes – focused on the 'learned' professions of law, medicine and engineering – was replicated through the establishment of institutions such as the *Ecoles Superieurs de Brazzaville* in Congo-Brazzaville (now the Republic of Congo). The Napoleonic model had already taken hold in most Latin American countries in the 1800s, following their independence from Portugal and Spain (Levy 1986). The central focus of universities in many former colonies, therefore, remained that of training a small percentage of the population for leadership positions, even after independence. This task was viewed as a public good, and, as a result, governments funded full scholarships for students who gained admission. However, a majority came from wealthy families, and many critiqued public money being spent disproportionately on the elite (Coleman 1986).

Arguments against this elitist model gradually took hold. In sub-Saharan Africa, the Association of African Universities (AAU), formed in 1967, claimed that Africa needed its own model of HE (Yesufu and AAU 1973). Casting aside both the Humboldtian and the Napoleonic model, the AAU argued that Africa needed 'developmental universities' that would focus explicitly on assisting government to reduce poverty in the region by training qualified 'manpower', discovering solutions to developmental problems through research and providing direct services to the surrounding community (IAU 1979). This model echoed the Latin American movement towards increasing the engagement of public universities with society, propelled by reforms at the University of Cordoba (Argentina) in 1918, and was largely inspired by the US land-grant university (Holland 2010). The 'developmental university' model was presented as having the potential to increase the impact of African HE by linking HE activities with wider developmental objectives. However, in reality, this ideal was never fully realized, largely because the emergence of the new model coincided with political changes across the region (Court 1980, Coleman 1986). As nationalist leaders were replaced by military dictatorships in many African countries in the 1970s, political support for HE began to wane, with many of the new leaders fearing that academics might publicly disagree with their policies. In some countries, this suspicion fuelled the violent persecution of academics (Ajayi et al. 1996). One extreme example is the 1972 kidnapping and disappearance of the vice-chancellor of Makerere University in Uganda, following his refusal to grant an honorary doctorate to one of Idi Amin's political appointees (Ajayi et al. 1996). Under such conditions, academic freedom was eroded, and many academics elected to leave the continent for positions in Europe and the United States (Lulat 2005, Mkandawire 2005). The decline of the 'developmental university' ideal was further exacerbated by severe financial constraints on the HE sector in the 1980s and 1990s, caused by a simultaneous decline in international aid to HE (due to the redirection of aid to primary education) and domestic support for HE (due to pressures on public education budgets under the policy of structural adjustment).

These historical influences, combined with international pressure to conform to institutional norms enshrined in global ranking systems (Altbach et al. 2009), have resulted in the replication of broadly similar models of HE across the globe. Significant heterogeneity continues to exist, however, *within* HE systems. 'Higher education' includes universities (typically multidisciplinary institutions), polytechnics and technology colleges as well as institutes that specialize in specific areas such as business, law and medicine. Teacher education colleges are classified as institutes of HE in some contexts and as secondary-level institutions in others. To further complicate the picture, HE is sometimes distinguished from *tertiary* education, which is a broader term encompassing the above but also including institutions of post-secondary learning, which provide shorter and more vocationally oriented courses. HE systems also include a mix of public and private (both non- and for-profit) institutions.

Key Debates and Issues

Funding

There has long been discussion around the legitimacy of public funding for HE in lower-income contexts. This debate rests largely on questions around the private and public benefits of HE, the former referring to the advantages that individual students gain through HE and the latter to those accruing to everybody in society. Marginson (2011) has also explored the notion of *global* public goods, reaching beyond national borders. The private benefit of HE is most often associated with the teaching function of universities, as individual graduates are seen to benefit personally through enhanced employment opportunities and higher earnings. Private benefits of research are also possible, as in the case of research and consultancy commissioned by corporations for commercial purposes. However, the research function of the university is generally seen to offer public benefit, as the new knowledge generated within universities can benefit all of society. Although most often associated with the private benefits of HE, the teaching pillar can also be viewed as a public good, as, in addition to the private benefits that accrue to professionals – such as doctors, teachers and social workers – as a result of their studies, there is an obvious public benefit to the constituencies with which they work. Research by Walker and McLean (2013) on pro-poor professionals, for example, explores the extent to which engineers and other professionals use their work for poverty reduction in South Africa.

Debates on the private and public benefits of HE have directly affected the funding of HE institutions across much of the Global South. In the early 1980s, attempts by education economists to model the public and private benefits of education resulted in the reduction of both international and domestic funding for HE in many low-income contexts. One of the most influential World Bank studies from this period (Psacharopoulos et al. 1986) indicated that, in developing contexts, the private return on investment in HE was substantially higher than the social return and public investment in primary education yielded double the social return to investment in HE. The Psacharopoulos report was subsequently criticized for its methodology and its lack of acknowledgement of the differential distribution of earnings across sectors of the economy (Bennell 1996a). However, the findings clearly motivated a move away from public subsidization of (and international support for) HE in many LMICs.

In recent years, the 'private good' argument has gained prominence in education policy throughout the world – including in high-income countries – as constraints on public funding have motivated governments to minimize public support for HE and move towards 'cost-sharing' arrangements, such as the charging of tuition fees (Altbach et al. 2009). Advocates of the 'public good' argument (e.g. Nixon 2011, Singh 2012, Locatelli 2017) maintain that there is a clear justification for taxpayer funding of HE, but this argument has lost momentum due to contemporary economic circumstances. However, it is possible that this balance may shift once again, particularly in the context of global challenges, such as climate change and pandemics, that can only be addressed through collective action. A number of countries have seen student protests in defence of free higher education or reduction in fees, in particular the Chilean mobilization in 2011 (Hernandez 2019) and the #feesmustfall protest in South Africa in 2015/2016 (see Chapter 4).

Empirical support for the role of HE in economic development has increased in recent years, as economists have developed new methods for incorporating 'externalities' into rate of return equations (such as increases in taxes, savings and consumption that tend to accompany higher wages) (Bloom et al. 2006). There have also been advances in methods for quantifying the non-market benefits of HE, such as improved health, reduced infant mortality, increased democratization, lower crime rates, improved environmental protection and increased levels of community volunteering (McMahon 2009).

Access

A second reason for the withdrawal of international aid for HE in the 1980s was the clearly elitist nature of many early HE systems across the Global South. HE systems – in all countries – have until recently been restricted to a very small proportion of the population. However, this is now being challenged in high-, middle- and low-income contexts alike. Expansion of primary and secondary systems and an increasing need for HE diplomas on the job market have led to intense demand for HE. Families throughout the world view HE as critical for social mobility, even in contexts in which graduate employment remains quite low (Altbach and Umakoshi 2004, Herrera 2006, Lebeau 2008, Tilak 2013, Marginson 2016). At the same time, states are aiming to increase the proportion of higher-level-educated individuals in the population in light of the apparent link between enrolment rates and economic competitiveness in the global knowledge economy (OECD 2008, Salmi 2017). While few LMICs can realistically aim for universalization in HE, a number of middle-income countries are moving rapidly towards massification (see regional statistics in Table 17.1).[1] Although welcomed by many, increased access to HE has created additional challenges for HE systems. The entry of new student populations with more limited academic preparation has challenged academic standards in many contexts. This trend has been compounded by the fact that expansion of the HE system has generally not been accompanied by corresponding funding, nor sufficient throughput of doctoral students (DAAD/British Council 2018, Yudkevich et al. 2020). Institutions have consequently been prevented from hiring sufficient staff to respond to the growing student numbers, leading to increasing student–teacher ratios and inevitable pressures on quality.

Tensions over massification are fundamentally linked to broader philosophical debates about the purpose of higher education in society: Is HE a training ground for future leaders and high-level professionals or an experience that can and should be available to all (McCowan 2012)? It could be argued that university expansion should not continue indefinitely in the context of graduate unemployment and that there should only be as many places as there are subsequent jobs for graduates. On the other hand, there is an argument that HE should be accessible to a broad proportion of the population, given that supply-led expansion might boost national productivity in the context of the global knowledge economy. Many systems have reconciled this tension through stratification: by maintaining a small elite core of high-quality universities but supplementing it with a demand-absorbing lower quality sector. Such a model carries inevitable implications for equity.

Table 17.1 Gross Enrolment Rate in Tertiary Education, 2000, 2010 and 2019

Region	2000	2010	2019
North America and Western Europe	60%	77%	80%
Latin America and the Caribbean	23%	41%	53%
Arab States	18%	23%	34%
South and West Asia	9%	17%	26%
Sub-Saharan Africa[2]	4%	7%	9%
World	**19%**	**30%**	**39%**

Source: UNESCO Institute of Statistics (2020) (figures to the nearest percentage point)

In fact, equity concerns are prevalent across LMICs. In many contexts, HE is only accessible to those who can afford to pay tuition fees. This issue has become more pronounced in recent years as institutions are increasingly charging fees in order to address their substantial financial shortfalls. Some, for example in East Africa, have also elected to introduce 'parallel streams', in which large numbers of fee-paying students enrol alongside those assuming free-of-charge places. Some countries, such as Brazil (see Policy 11), have chosen to expand access by maintaining free public universities but allowing the rapid expansion of a private sector to absorb the majority of the demand. Course fees vary dramatically at such institutions, largely in proportion to the quality or prestige of the course (McCowan and Bertolin 2020). Fee-paying structures are likely to disadvantage students from low-income backgrounds (Oketch 2003, Agarwal 2009). Although many governments are attempting to create student loan schemes to help with access, the fact remains that cost-sharing arrangements are likely to result in many young people either losing the opportunity to attend HE or graduating encumbered with substantial debts.

In some contexts, access is also limited to certain demographic groups. Although the international gender balance in HE has now tipped towards female students, males continue to dominate HE in parts of Africa and Asia. There is also evidence that minority populations and students from rural areas have trouble accessing HE in many contexts (see Naidoo 1998, Tilak 2013). In some cases, governments have responded to these inequities by introducing affirmative action policies: in Brazil, for example, quotas for African Brazilian students have been introduced, and there is now a federal law stipulating that 50 per cent of places in the elite federal universities should be reserved for underrepresented groups (Lee 2020).

Refugees are particularly vulnerable to barriers to access, due to their complicated legal and bureaucratic status in many contexts (UNHCR 2018). Qualified refugee students are not able to access higher education in many LMICs because of linguistic barriers, lack of requisite paperwork, unrecognized credentials from secondary school and cultural barriers, among others. As it appears likely that many LMICs will struggle with even higher numbers of refugees in the future, due to escalating conflict and other displacing circumstances linked to climate change, this is a particularly poignant challenge that must be jointly addressed by governments and HEIs.

Equality of experience and opportunity within the university is also an area of substantial concern in many LMICs. There is evidence that female and minority students often have more negative experiences within HE than their peers. In Ghana and Tanzania, for example, Morley (2011) found that female students face a number of obstacles during their university education, ranging from overt sexual harassment (and even the exchange of grades for sex) to more subtle cultural expectations related to marriage, child bearing and participation in certain academic disciplines.

Academic Quality, Relevance and Employability

There are also important issues related to the quality of HE available to students in LMIC contexts. As discussed in the previous section, limited funding has restricted institutional ability to hire additional lecturers to cope with rising student numbers, which has resulted in unacceptably large class sizes at many institutions. Limited funding has also led to a rapid decline in the wages of academics. As a result, many faculty members elect to find supplementary jobs, which limits their time for teaching, mentoring and research. Others opt to leave the sector altogether in search of more highly paid positions (Holm 2012). The lack of postgraduate programmes in many contexts, as well as a decline in the prestige of the profession, has also left very few new faculty members in the 'pipeline' (Tettey and PHEA 2009, Tilak 2013). As a result, the majority of university teaching staff worldwide now have only a bachelor's level degree (Altbach et al. 2009). In addition to these human resource implications, declining funding has curtailed the ability of institutions to invest in their infrastructure or maintain their libraries.

In recent years, there have been attempts to improve the quality of HE institutions in many LMIC contexts (see, for example, Inter-University Council for East Africa 2010, Brewis and McCowan, 2016). However, continuing funding pressures have fuelled a tendency to equate quality with efficiency. As a result, the emphasis has been on measures that allow the maximum number of students to complete their studies in the minimum time required. Critics argue that this focus on efficiency has actually further reduced academic quality as institutions have felt pressured to restrict their course offerings to subjects that are considered either useful for development or popular with fee-paying students (ADEA Working Group on Higher Education and AAU 2004, Assié-Lumumba and CODESRIA 2006, Mamdani 2007, Lebeau 2008, McCowan 2019).

The focus on particular academic subjects relates to wider discussions on the 'employability' of HE graduates (as discussed in Chapter 15). In many LMIC contexts, a mismatch can be identified between the number of employees needed for growth industries and the number of graduates in related disciplines (Agarwal 2009). STEM subjects (Science, Technology, Engineering and Mathematics) are particularly under-represented (Bloom et al. 2006). Some governments have reacted to this apparent 'skills mismatch' by setting enrolment quotas and/or providing scholarships for particular disciplines, in an attempt to incentivize the study of such subjects (Altbach et al. 2009). Critics of such policies have argued that universities should continue to support a wide diversity of academic subjects in order to cultivate all of the competencies necessary for a well-functioning society (see Smith 2014).

Measurement and Indicators 8
Fostering Critical Thinking in African Universities

The *Pedagogies for Critical Thinking: Innovations and Outcomes in African higher education* project (funded by the UK's Economic and Social Research Council and Department for International Development, 2015–19) assessed the impact of different forms of teaching on critical thinking skills. Eight departments or faculties at universities in Ghana, Kenya and Botswana with innovations to enhance teaching quality were selected to participate in the study, and matched with other similar institutions that had not implemented reforms. Assessments of undergraduate students in their first and third years showed that only some students were making significant gains over the course of their studies. The main factor influencing these gains was teaching orientation, i.e. the extent to which lecturers adhered to a facilitation rather than a transmission approach to knowledge (Kember and Gow 1994). These findings are significant as they show that adopting learner-centred methods in the classroom will only be successful if it is accompanied by deeper shifts in the teaching staff. These changes can best be brought about through carving out spaces for reflection and development in lecturers' busy schedules, and fostering a collaborative and supportive institutional culture.

Source: Schendel et al. 2020

Furthermore, a handful of recent studies have suggested that many graduates in LMIC contexts cannot demonstrate the skills necessary for employment – both in terms of technical ability in their chosen fields (Agarwal 2009) and in terms of more 'general' skills, such as critical thinking (Schendel 2015). Despite the crucial development implications of such findings, there remains only limited empirical analysis of how the quality of teaching and learning within HE institutions affects the employability of graduates or the sector's ability to contribute to development (Waghid 2009, Howell et al. 2020).

Research Capacity

Decades of underinvestment in HE in LIMCs has also limited the ability of universities to fully participate in the global research community. Research output from LMIC contexts is generally low (see De Ferranti et al. 2003, Di Gropello et al. 2012). African universities, for example, contribute only 1 per cent of international research output (Duermeijer, Amir and Schoombee 2018). These statistics are partially explained by financial realities, as many universities have been unable to equip their libraries and laboratories with the resources required for research and innovation. However, research output has also been negatively impacted by limited academic freedom in a number of contexts. The rise of a 'consultancy culture' has also redirected faculty energies away from basic academic research and towards funded consultancy opportunities (Mamdani 2007, Mohamedbhai 2008, Holland 2010). Limited interaction between HE and industry also appears to have had a negative impact on research productivity in many lower-income contexts (Didriksson 2008, Kruss et al. 2015), although this is a priority area for many countries, particularly those with strong technical institutions and some success in producing applied research (e.g. India) (Agarwal 2009).

Research output is also affected by norms within the global publishing industry. The hegemony of English as the primary language of academic discourse substantially limits the potential for non-Anglophone academics to distribute their work beyond their local context (Altbach 2016), as does the hierarchy of knowledge in global academic publishing, which tends to treat topics, research methods and forms of knowledge related to LMICs as largely peripheral and therefore privileges the work of academics from the Global North (Collyer 2018). In recent years, efforts have been made to address this imbalance (e.g. the establishment of the African Education Research Database),[2] but academics in LMICs continue to struggle to gain visibility for their work.

Internationalization

HE has become an increasingly transnational industry, with students frequently moving across borders. In addition to South-to-North student migration, which has been occurring since the colonial era, there is now a substantial amount of South-to-South student mobility. In South Africa, for example, over 90 per cent of international students come from other African countries (Lee and Sehoole 2015)). Although internationalization is a positive development for many HE systems, student mobility can lead to 'brain drain' as many departing students never return to their home countries. Of international doctoral students in the United States, for example, it is estimated that 80 per cent do not return to their home countries after graduation.[3] Although such outward migration has obvious implications for the technical capacity of the local workforce, some have argued that outward migration actually has a net positive effect on LMICs as remittances now account for a substantial proportion of many developing economies (Özden and Schiff 2006).

Internationalization has also changed the HE landscape in many countries (Unterhalter and Carpentier 2010). In response to increasing pressure on universities in high-income countries to expand their international programming, many institutions have established international branch campuses (e.g. the University of Paris's campus in Abu Dhabi, Carnegie Mellon University's in Rwanda and the University of Nottingham's campuses in China and Malaysia). While some herald the arrival of branch campuses as a boon for academic quality, others object to the neo-colonialist overtones of establishing a foreign institution, often exempt from domestic regulations, in a developing context. There are also concerns about equity, given that high tuition fees render most branch campuses unavailable to all but the wealthy, and internal 'brain drain', as branch campuses often recruit qualified faculty members from existing public institutions. Another change brought about by globalization is the increase in investment by international companies in HE franchises (e.g. investments by Apollo, Laureate and Pearson in Brazilian universities). HE institutions are also under increasing pressure to rise in the international rankings. As a result, there is a growing expectation that research will have a global dimension and will be strengthened by international collaboration. In Latin America, for instance, universities are encouraging staff to internationalize their research agendas and publish in internationally recognized academic journals (de Wit et al. 2005), presenting highly problematic implications in terms of epistemic justice and linguistic diversity (Walker and Martinez-Vargas 2020).

Recent Reforms

The challenges outlined above have been addressed through a range of reform initiatives, acting at both the system and institutional levels.

System-level Reforms

System-level reforms are often intended to address issues of access by expanding the capacity of systems to absorb increasing student demand for HE. Typically supported by multilateral and bilateral organizations (particularly the World Bank) and implemented through centralized Ministries of Education, system-wide reforms tend to include both efficiency measures, intended to bolster the capacity of existing institutions to absorb greater numbers of students, and expansion measures, intended to increase the number of HE institutions.

One of the most frequent efficiency measures within public HE systems is the introduction of 'niche' institutions, such as schools of business or institutes of technology. Niche institutions are seen to improve efficiency by concentrating resources and reducing 'overlap' (ADEA Working Group on Higher Education and AAU 2004). Diversification is advocated as a solution to the problems of both access and quality, as the assumption is that diversified HE systems can expand access to TE to a large proportion of the population while also ensuring quality by grouping students with similar interests – and, in some cases, levels of preparation – within the same institutions. In practice, it has proved difficult to truly diversify many HE systems. The reliance on student fees in many contexts has incentivized the convergence, rather than the diversification, of available models, as many institutions have started to introduce new academic programmes, often outside of their intended 'niche', in order to attract more fee-paying students (Ng'ethe et al. 2008). Nevertheless, a tendency that is evident is one of *stratification*, through which institutions become differentiated in terms of their quality or prestige, and as a corollary, in terms of the socio-economic backgrounds of their students (McCowan and Bertolin 2020).

Policy 11
Growth of the Private Sector in Brazil

While enrolments in private institutions are growing across the world, there are still significant differences across countries in terms of the size of the private sector. With 75 per cent of all enrolments in private institutions, Brazil is a critical case in this regard (INEP 2019). The country traditionally had a small number of mainly Catholic private institutions, but from the 1990s, a new breed of private institution started to emerge – teaching-focused, commercialized, highly attuned to the market and able to expand in a short time span. In terms of Geiger's (1986) typology, these institutions are best classified as being 'more', rather than 'better' or 'different', as their main function has been to absorb the excess student demand from the public sector.

This rapid expansion – facilitated by the neoliberal policies of the Cardoso administration in the 1990s – has enabled a rapid increase in access to HE, with some 6,373,000 of Brazil's 8,451,000 students now enrolled in private institutions (INEP 2019). Yet opinions are divided as to the desirability of this form of expansion (McCowan 2004, 2007). First, many of these institutions are little more than high schools, with poor facilities, uneven quality of teaching and mainly part-time hourly paid staff. Regulation has proved a challenge for the Brazilian authorities, particularly on account of the political influence of the owners of private universities. Second, the growth of the private sector has led to a stratification of opportunity, with the lower-cost institutions generally providing a lower-quality experience or at least lower prestige of qualifications on the job market. Third, there are concerns over transfer of public funds (in the form of loans and tax breaks) to the private sector, particularly in light of the fact that the majority of these institutions are for-profit. Given the apparent dependence of society on the private institutions for absorbing demand, and the limited ability of the public sector to expand, these tensions are unlikely to be resolved in the short term.

In light of constraints on public funding, there is also pressure to expand private HE provision (World Bank 2010), resulting in a dramatic increase in the number of private institutions in LMIC contexts (Fehnel 2003, McCowan 2004, Ng'ethe et al. 2008, Teferra and Knight 2008, Agarwal 2009, Levy 2011, 2018). While religious institutions have a long history, much of the recent private growth has been in commercially oriented and for-profit institutions. Private institutions are often supported for their ability to react more flexibly to 'market demand' (World Bank 2010). Some advocates also argue that they can provide a higher quality education, given their proximity to industry and employers, their access to alternative (i.e. non-governmental) sources of funding and the market-based competition that can be fostered between providers (World Bank and Salmi 1994, Task Force on Higher Education and Society 2000, UNESCO 2009a, World Bank 2009). However, this is often not the case in reality, as, in many contexts, there has been a proliferation of private providers of a very low academic standard (see Policy 11 and Materu 2007, Agarwal 2009, McCowan and Bertolin 2020). The expansion of private provision can also exacerbate problems of quality within the public sector. New private institutions often recruit faculty from existing public universities (Schendel et al. 2013). In many cases, lecturers assume these new positions in addition to their prior employment contracts, a phenomenon which negatively affects standards across the sector, as faculty members become less able to devote their full attention to teaching or research at any one institution (Teferra and Altbach 2004).

Institutional Reforms

Institutional reforms have also attempted to respond to challenges of both access and quality.

Many such reforms have focused on the financial health of public institutions. Some have aimed to reduce budgets, through the elimination of academic programmes, the reduction of 'excess' non-academic staff and/or the sub-contracting of services. Others have emphasized ways in which institutions can generate their own income, in order to supplement government funding. In general, these reforms have mirrored an international shift towards 'managerialism' in HE, in which HE institutions are increasingly pressured to adopt more traditionally corporate management structures in order to boost accountability and financial efficiency (Johnson and Hirt 2011).

Other reforms aim to build the academic capacity of institutions. Many of these reforms are implemented through 'partnership' models (Fraser 2009), in which HE institutions work collaboratively to address particular issues. Some prominent examples are the Higher Education Links Scheme, initiatives funded by the Partnership for Higher Education in Africa and the more recent Strategic Partnerships for Higher Education Innovation and Reform (SPHEIR) programme funded by the UK's Department for International Development (DFID) from 2016. Many of these interventions focus on building faculty capacity by providing short-term training courses, creating scholarships for postgraduate study and contributing to improvements in research infrastructure. Others aim to improve institutional governance and management, through the exchange of 'best practices', or to support technological infrastructure. Institutional partnerships have also helped to develop regional research consortia in many parts of the world. Although many partnerships rely on historical links between Northern and Southern institutions, South–South partnerships are also starting to have an impact on HE systems. China, for example, has cultivated a number of partnerships with universities in Africa, establishing Confucius Institutes on many campuses and investing in short- and long-term training programmes across the continent (King 2009).

New Modes of Delivery

Distance learning has long been advocated as a potential solution to the global access problem facing HE (Fehnel 2003, Task Force on Higher Education and Society 2000, Teferra and Knight 2008, World Bank 2009). Indeed, the world's largest universities – Indira Gandhi National Open University in India and the Allama Iqbal Open University in Pakistan, each of which enrols more than 3 million students – are distance learning institutions. Support for distance learning is not a new concept. The World Bank's African Virtual University (AVU), for example, has been in existence since 1997 (Teferra and Knight 2008). However, the emergence of high-enrolment models, such as MOOCs (Massive Open Online Courses), reignited debates around how online courses can support under-resourced

HE systems across the Global South and what dangers this form of provision might pose. The Covid-19 pandemic of 2020, which forced the curtailing of face-to-face provision in most of the world's universities, has also provided a significant boost to distance learning, with institutions rapidly creating online versions of their undergraduate and graduate courses.

Many argue that distance education has a fundamental role to play in LMICs, given that traditional brick-and-mortar universities are simply unable to respond to the immense demand for HE. Online programmes are seen by many to offer a low-cost, high-quality solution to this critical access problem. However, critics emphasize that distance education brings its own set of challenges. In order for students to benefit from online coursework, they must be familiar with both the use of a computer and the norms of self-guided instruction (Kapur and Crowley 2008). Neither can be assumed in many LMIC contexts. Furthermore, access to electricity and broadband connectivity remain significant challenges, particularly for those from less advantaged backgrounds (Klees 2002, Amutabi and Oketch 2003, Altbach et al. 2009). There are also neo-colonial implications to a reliance on courses designed for and within a Western university paradigm, and there is a lack of consensus on how best to regulate the quality of online educational provision, particularly in lower-income contexts without strong regulatory agencies (Materu 2007). Blended learning (i.e. a combination of face-to-face and online provision) has emerged as an innovative model that might offer opportunities for leveraging new technologies while also grounding HE provision in local circumstances. Hybrid institutions, such as the African Leadership University, keep their costs low by relying almost exclusively on online courses for their core curriculum, while also addressing some of the most common concerns about online instruction by providing students with in-person tutorial support. Such models do go some way towards addressing some of the most prevalent concerns about distance education, although neo-colonial critiques regarding who controls the core curriculum tend to remain a concern.

Digital technology also plays an increasingly important role in HE beyond distance education. In many institutions, technology is now implicated in all educational provision, including face-to-face courses, as it provides new tools for classroom interaction, assessment and feedback. Academic scholarship is also increasingly stored and accessed online rather than through physical libraries. The online platforms through which students access course materials and conduct assessments have allowed for the rise of learning analytics, through which student behaviours and performance can be analysed with a fine granularity (Williamson 2018). While these technologies may assist in providing early interventions for students, the entry of 'big data' into higher education has proved controversial, however, with concerns that it is being used for surveillance rather than student support, and commercial exploitation rather than enhancement of quality (Prinsloo and Slade 2017, Selwyn 2020). These processes are linked to the broader trend of 'unbundling' through which the package of higher education is increasingly separated out into its constituent parts, allowing for expansion of the market and enhanced profit-making activities (McCowan 2017, Ivancheva et al. 2020).

Conclusion

While universities in the poorest countries in the world provide a range of positive benefits to individuals and society – in terms of both economic growth and broader capabilities – in many cases these benefits are limited in magnitude (Oketch et al. 2014, Howell, Unterhalter and Oketch 2020). The potential impact of HE is clearly being constrained by a range of limiting factors: some relating to inputs (such as sufficient access to and quality of primary and secondary education, and sufficient funding for the sector); some to factors within the university (e.g. quality of teaching and learning and a relevant curriculum); and some to the characteristics of the external environment political conditions for academic freedom, the employment market, etc.).

Whether HE will ultimately deliver on the varied societal demands laid at its door depends on the commitments that states and their populations make to the HE sector – whether they ensure the sustainability of funding that allows for equitable access for all social groups, protect the academic freedom that enables high-quality basic research and allow for the free circulation of the benefits of HE across society. If these conditions are in place, HE is uniquely positioned to make a positive contribution to society and to merit a place at the forefront of the 2030 Agenda for Sustainable Development.

Questions for Discussion

1. To what extent is there a justification for public funding of higher education in low-income contexts?
2. How can public higher education systems balance the pressures of rising student numbers and the need to maintain quality standards?
3. What are the implications of the growth of private universities for equity and quality?
4. What contribution can distance education play in expanding opportunities for tertiary-level study?

Further Reading

Boni, A. and Walker, M. (2013), *Human Development and Capabilities: Re-imagining the University in the 21st Century*, London: Routledge.

McCowan, T. (2019), *Higher Education for and beyond the Sustainable Development Goals*, London: Palgrave Macmillan.

Salmi, J. (2017), *The Tertiary Education Imperative: Knowledge, Skills and Values for Development*, Leiden, Netherlands: Brill-Sense.

Useful Websites

Association of Commonwealth Universities: https://www.acu.ac.uk/

Centre for Higher Education Transformation, South Africa: http://chet.org.za/ Council for the Development of Social Science Research in Africa (CODESRIA): http://www.codesria.org/

International Higher Education: https://www.bc.edu/research/cihe/ihe.html

Partnership for Higher Education in Africa: http://www.foundation-partnership.org/

UNESCO International Institute for Higher Education in Latin America and the Caribbean: http://www.unesco.org.ve/index.php/en/home

18

Education, Environmental Crises and Sustainability

Meera Tiwari

Introduction

This chapter offers insights into the relationship between education, environmental crises and sustainability. Two decades into the twenty-first century, humankind is at the cusp of a seismic change that threatens the survival of up to 20–30 per cent of species currently sharing our planet (IPCC 2014). These changes will result in loss of habitat for humans and animals and lead to highly depleted stocks of natural resources for the future generations (IPCC 2018). Scientists further predict air pollution to become the biggest cause of premature death, killing an estimated 3.6 million people per year by 2050. This demands reimagining the intricate connections between how we live, what we value in life and how we want to achieve our aspirations. Education is a key part of this process.

The implications for low- and middle-income countries where most of the world's poor live are particularly severe in terms of loss of livelihood and habitat through flooding, water scarcity, food insecurity and human displacement. Regions in this category include sub-Saharan Africa and South and Southeast Asia. Many developing nations are situated in low-latitude countries and it is estimated that 80 per cent of the damage from climate change may be concentrated in these areas (IPCC 2014). According to the World Bank (2020), sub-Saharan Africa will experience frequent droughts and shifts in rainfall, resulting in food insecurity. Densely populated cities such as Kolkata and Mumbai will become more vulnerable to flooding, warming temperatures and intense cyclones. Depleted water sources from the Himalayas will reduce the flow of water into the Indus, Ganges and Brahmaputra basins with far-reaching adverse impact on the fertile agricultural belts that produce food for the subcontinent. In Southeast Asia, Vietnam's Mekong Delta, which produces most of the rice consumed by the population, is vulnerable to rising sea levels.

There is considerable injustice with regard to where carbon emissions are highest and where the most severe effects on climate change are felt. The global population has increased from just 2.5 billion people in 1950, to over 7 billion in 2020, and is expected to rise to 9 billion by 2050 (UN Population 2020).[1] When we look at levels of per capita consumption in terms of fossil fuel–based electricity, oil, transportation and household goods, we see different patterns in different countries. The populous middle-income countries such as China, India, Indonesia and Pakistan account for over 40 per cent of the contribution to global warming, but their per capita figures of carbon emissions are much lower than many high-income countries.[2] Thus, while India's carbon footprint, or contribution to global warming is 3rd in world, with 2654 metric tonnes of CO_2 emissions, its per person emissions are 2 metric tonnes placing it 82nd in the global ranking. In comparison, the United States ranks 2nd in its overall contribution to carbon emission with 5416 metric tonnes, and is also ranked very high with regard to emission per person of 17 metric tonnes, just below a few small island states or oil-producing nations, such as Saudi Arabia and Kuwait. Climate justice calls for support and policy based on per capita carbon emission and potential impact of climate change using a people-centred approach to improving human well-being. Education systems have a particular role in engaging all stakeholders in this process.

The following sections review climate change, environmental crisis and the role of education; they draw out how education has been linked with sustainability and how a sustainable development agenda charts how we can live respecting planetary boundaries. The discussion identifies some key areas where educational processes will enable the achievement of a sustainable development agenda, contributing to creating informed individuals who practice ecological responsibility.

Ecological Shifts, Environmental Crises and Education

The environmental crises associated with severe ecological shifts pose many challenges to education systems. Kwauk (2020) draws attention to the dilemmas and ambiguities exhibited by the education leadership at both the micro and macro levels in response to the climate activism of school children in 2019. The 'School Strikes for Climate' campaign led to millions of children and adults out on streets around the world. Teachers were divided as to whether to join or penalize students for missing school. Kwauk (2020) notes how this indicates a deeper problem with regard to how climate change has been viewed within the education sector. Alongside an active conceptual engagement, there has been uneven support for action, sometimes out of fear of violating academic process and rules. The biggest challenge for education systems is the reconfiguration required for all stakeholders to confidently place ecological precarity above all other priorities.

Ecology is the study of changes in an ecosystem. An ecosystem is a group of living organisms that live in and interact with each other in a specific environment. The earth's ecosystem comprises the life bubble created through an interaction between biotic factors – plants, animals and other living organisms – and the abiotic factors, such as weather, climate and landscape. Greenhouse gases are critical to life on earth, creating an insulating layer to maintain the optimum temperature conducive for plant and animal survival and propagation. But excess greenhouse gases cause the planet to heat up. In 2018, a report by scientists of the Intergovernmental Panel on Climate Change (IPCC 2018) warned of multiple crises resulting from rising global temperatures, including food insecurity, water scarcity, mass displacement of people through loss of livelihood and habitat. This confirmed the finding of a large community of scientists, who had noted rising planetary temperatures were caused by human activity (IPCC 2018). Evidence shows a steep increase in global warming since the Industrial Revolution, estimated to have resulted in a 1.0°C average rise above pre-industrial-level temperatures. Human activities that produce greenhouse gases have caused global temperatures to rise, resulting in long-term changes to the climate. Scientific models predict global warming will reach 1.5°C average rise above this level between 2030 and 2052 if anthropogenic emissions continue to increase at the current rates. Changes in the earth's ecosystem, triggered by global warning, have produced highly concerning ecological shifts posing challenges to resource availability for future generations and survival of several species. A wide range of activities shown to be responsible for causing global warming and damaging the planet include burning fossil fuels to secure energy requirements in construction, industry and transport; waste production and its disposal; urbanization and deforestation and glacial melting. Measurement and Indictors 9 gives a detailed explanation of these causes.

Measurement and Indictors 9: Causes of Global Warming

- Burning of fossil fuels (oil, coal and gas) to power factories, buildings and transportation. This releases gases that trap heat from the sun and warm up the earth leading to global warming. In 2018, global emissions from fossil fuels and cement production stood at 36.7 billion tonnes compared with 6.4 billion tonnes in 1950. Scientists believe that even to stay at the current levels of greenhouse gas concentrations in the atmosphere, the world needs to reach net-zero emissions by 2050 (Ritchie and Roser 2020). The net-zero emission or the climate neutrality concept is to reduce human activity caused greenhouse gas emissions close to zero and mop up the remaining by carbon removal from the atmosphere by forestation and/or by direct capture and storage technology.
- Waste production and its disposal often add to these harmful emissions and also threaten marine life. Decomposition of food waste creates large amounts of greenhouse gases. Estimates indicate around 88 million tonnes of food wasted annually in the EU (European

Commission 2016) result in over 3 billion tonnes of greenhouse gas emissions (Bravi et. al. 2020). In the UK approximately £9.7 billion are lost per year by throwing away unused food (Read 2019). Further, use of non-biodegradable materials in the world, such as plastic has risen steeply from just 2 million tonnes produced in 1950 to over 7.5 billion tonnes in 2015 (Geyer et. al. 2017). Prior to 1980, almost all plastic was discarded without recycling or any incineration. In 2015, 20 per cent was recycled and 25 per cent was incinerated. It is estimated that each year up to 13 million metric tons of plastic is left in the oceans and at least 800 species worldwide are threatened by this waste (Reddy 2020). The damage to marine ecosystems through non-biodegradable plastic waste is considered to be at the highest levels observed so far. There is growing evidence of fish, seabirds, sea turtles and marine mammals becoming entangled in and ingesting plastic debris, leading to drowning and suffocation. Some plastics that decompose more quickly into fine particles find their way into the sea food consumed by humans (Reddy 2020).

- Urbanization and deforestation: In 2018, more people lived in urban areas than in rural areas, with 55 per cent of the world's population residing in towns and cities. In 1950, 30 per cent of the world's population was urban, and by 2050, 68 per cent of the world's population is projected to be urban (UNDESA 2019). Meeting the infrastructure and food needs of the expanding urban population requires additional land, leading to deforestation. Thus, in addition to the greenhouse gases generated through transportation, building, heating and other urban activities, loss of forests depletes the ecosystem of trees that absorb greenhouse gases and release oxygen in the atmosphere. Tropical deforestation to meet expanding food and consumer needs is estimated to add 3 billion tonnes of greenhouse gases each year (Gourmelon 2016).
- Scientists note glacial melting and irreversible shrinking of the polar ice sheets that will cause sea level rises of over two metres around the world (Garbe et. al. 2020). This in turn will submerge several low-lying coastal regions with up to 650 million people currently living there.

While many of these adverse impacts have been worsening since the start of the Industrial Revolution, the last twenty years have seen the steepest increase in greenhouse emissions (IPCC 2018). This suggests rapid and some irreversible shifts in the planet's ecological system that have the potential to threaten the survival of several species and result in the loss of habitat for humans and animals. Advancement in technology since the Industrial Revolution has given people immense ability to use the environment and its resources for their own needs. This resource exploitation has been propelled by the emergence of free market economies, in which economic factors shape production, consumption, use of resources and treatment of waste.

There is a divergence in attitudes with regard to conceptions of environment evident in many Western societies, where the Industrial Revolution and free market economies emerged, and in several Latin American, African and Asian cultures. (Selin 2003).The perspective associated with many economic and environmental ideas developed in much of Europe and the United States views the environment as a free resource available for people, companies and countries to use in whichever way they like to achieve short-term profit maximization with little or no regard for long-term sustainable use. In contrast a number of non-Western cultures view nature as a larger earth system, where human beings are one among many actors. They emphasize co-existence and respect for nature, environment and other living beings (Selin 2003). Ideas of a free market are now being promoted in many regions where ideas about sustainability have had a long history. This has resulted in deforestation (Brazil, Indonesia, India) and expansion of extractive industries (e.g. DRC, Angola, South Africa and India).

Climate change has thus transformed into an environment crisis with serious implications for the current and future generations making urgent demands on education systems. The OECD's *Environmental Outlook to 2050: The Consequences of Inaction* (OECD 2001) alerted us in 2001 to global processes precipitating major damages to livelihoods:

- Pressures on the planet's ecosystem are now so great that future generations could face falling living standards.
- The population is expected to increase from roughly 7 billion people today to more than 9 billion in 2050. The global economy is expected to recover from the financial crisis and ultimately quadruple in size. However, the financial cost of failing to address climate change could

result in an up to 14 per cent loss in per capita consumption worldwide by 2050, according to some estimates.

- Pollution will become the biggest cause of premature death, killing an estimated 3.6 million people per year by 2050.
- Air pollution alone will be a major killer, overtaking both poor sanitation and a lack of clean drinking water as a global health threat.
- Due to dependence on fossil fuels, carbon dioxide emissions from energy use will grow by 70 per cent. This will help drive up the global average temperature by 3° to 6° Celsius by 2100. This far exceeds the internationally agreed-upon global warming limit of two degrees, but 3° may be the 'tipping point', where climate change could run out of control.
- Because the population will grow so dramatically, there will be a 55 per cent increase in demand for water, and 40 per cent of the world's population will be living under severe water stress. Groundwater depletion will be the biggest threat to agriculture and to urban water supplies, while pollution from sewage and waste water – including chemicals used in cleaning – will put further strain on global water supplies.
- Biodiversity will decline by 10 per cent on land, with the worst impacts felt in Asia, Europe and southern Africa.

These warnings alerted us to the planetary boundaries which would be ruptured if no action is taken to mitigate climate change. Since the publication of this OECD report, almost twenty years back, things have not got any better, with indications of further decline noted by the IPCC (2014, 2018). The notion of planetary boundaries (Rockström et al. 2009), proposed by internationally renowned scientists, identifies nine processes that regulate the stability and resilience of the Earth system. These boundaries comprise limits to the levels of ozone depletion, biodiversity loss and extinctions, chemical pollution, climate change, ocean acidification, freshwater consumption, land system, nitrogen and phosphorus flows, and aerosol use. Raworth (2017) illustrates the relationship between planetary boundaries and social foundations of human well-being in the twenty-first century (see Concepts 5). Failing to secure the social foundation of well-being within planetary boundaries will result in food insecurity, lack of educational opportunities and lack of housing, to name a few. Respecting or living within planetary boundaries will allow humanity to develop and thrive for generations to come. Crossing these boundaries increases the risk of generating large-scale abrupt or irreversible environmental changes with immediate and long-lasting damage to humanity's social foundation.

Whilst the problems of the climate crisis are largely physical (environmental), the causes and solutions lie more in people's attitudes, values and expectations, which are shaped by social and educational relationships. This leads one to reflect whether there have been missed opportunities in the domain of education policy and practice to engage with all people – young and old beyond the realms of universities and scientists. We have been alerted to a looming environmental crisis since

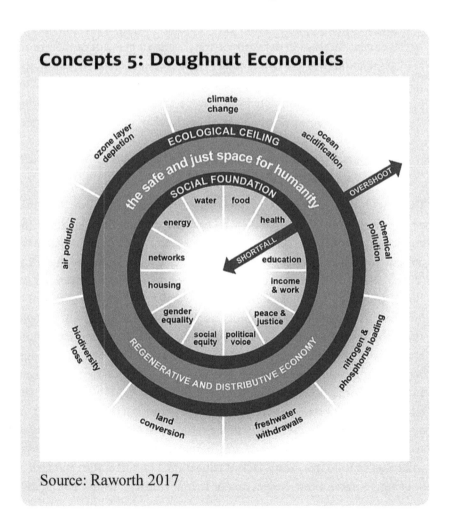

Concepts 5: Doughnut Economics

Source: Raworth 2017

1972 by the Club of Rome (Meadows et. al 1972), the Brundtland Report of 1987, the Earth Summit in 1992 and the focus of MDG 7 and its targets in 2000 to ensure environmental sustainability. The four targets included integrating the principles of sustainable development into national policies to reverse the depletion of environmental resources, reduce biodiversity loss, support sustainable access to clean and safe drinking water and basic sanitation, and secure substantial improvement in the lives of slum dwellers. In 2015, the targets had only partially been met, with much work remaining to reduce depletion of environmental resources and loss of biodiversity. Education systems had not been used sufficiently to expand knowledge of these issues. Kwauk (2020) notes much of the macro-level activity at global and national levels has been confined to glossy logo-filled websites with calls for lofty actions, high-level working groups, agenda-setting declarations and commitments. UNESCO's leadership has been critiqued (Jickling 2017) for lack of meaningful transformation at the grassroots, and little clarity on the role of key actors.

Against the backdrop of limited work within education systems in the last few years, grassroots actors have shown encouraging and inspirational leadership. Schoolchildren have highlighted the environmental crisis in real time using the tactic of the school strike and building an environmental movement, in a way that has communicated to all generations. The leadership shown by an inspiring seventeen-year-old environmental activist, Greta Thunberg, and many others like her, gained international recognition promoting the view that humanity is facing an existential crisis arising from climate change.

This activism builds on many decades of courageous leadership and social action in developing countries using many forms of educational engagement. Environmentalists such as Wangari Maathai, who led the Green Belt Movement in Kenya, and Rene Ngongo, a Congolese biologist, who dedicated his life to saving the Congo rainforest from deforestation and environmental degradation, both used education as key elements in their campaigns. Some activists have been killed for their work. Ken Saro-Wiwa, a Nigerian human rights activist and environmentalist, who pioneered the Movement for the Survival of the Ogoni People (MOSOP), was hanged. The Brazilian conservationist Chico Mendes was assassinated in 1988 and US-born environmentalist Sister Dorothy Stang was killed in Anapu, in the Amazon Basin, Brazil, in 2005. Both had promoted the cause of protecting the Amazon Rainforest. India has a multitude of environmentalists whose work continues to inspire grassroots action and engagement of youth. These include Sundarlal Bahuguna's 'Chipko Movement' in the 1970s, which mobilized the locals to protect trees; Vandana Shiva's work, which has publicized food sovereignty, rights of the Earth and women; and Chandi Prasad Bhatt, an Indian Gandhian environmentalist and social activist. The dedication of these activists has wide appeal for youth and community organizations in their home country and globally. In the Global North, the work of Sir David Attenborough has documented the environmental crisis for TV audiences of all ages, different educational levels and varied socio-economic backgrounds. The work of these activists indicates how education can help shape values, exchange information and guide action.

There is an emerging body of literature that draws attention to the educational implications of climate change. Reimers (2021) highlights the human competency and knowledge-enhancing attribute of education as being critical for humankind to adapt and mitigate the impacts of climate change. The knowledge expansion domain is vast, including individual and collective responsibility to the planet and sustainable lifestyle practices. Additionally, expansion of human competencies underpins innovation and inventions of technologies that can mitigate green house gas emissions, as evidenced in the electric car technology. However, translating the wider awareness of climate change into behaviour and societal change has been disappointing as noted by the Transforming Education for Sustainable Futures Study (TESF 2020). This study suggests a targeted approach to address the challenge of transforming climate literacy into behaviour change at the individual and collective levels. Thus, further adding a critical role that education needs to play in adaptation and mitigation of climate change by active engagement of the citizens in complementarity with technological solutions.

Sustainability and Education

The significance of education to address the environmental crisis has been somewhat underplayed, because the focus of the works that formulated ideas about sustainability did not consider the significance of this field of work. The origins of the discourse on sustainable development can be traced to the concerns regarding the exploitation of the global commons. Two pioneering bodies of research emerged in the 1970s and 1980s: *Limits to Growth* (Medows et al. 1972) and the Brundtland Report of 1987.

Medows et al. in 1972, alerted the world to three possibilities. First, they noted if present growth trends in world population, industrialization, pollution, food production and resource depletion were to continue unchanged, the limits to growth on this planet would be reached within 100 years, probably resulting in a rather sudden and uncontrollable decline in population and industrial capacity. A second trajectory, they argued, would make it possible to alter these growth trends and establish a condition of ecological and economic stability, which would be sustainable far into the future. The state of global equilibrium could be designed so that the basic material needs of each person on earth would be satisfied and each person would have an equal opportunity to realize individual human potential. Third, they concluded if the world's people decide to strive for the second outcome rather than the first, the sooner they were to begin working to attain it, the greater chances of success would be (Medows et al. 1972, 23–4). The study did not examine how education could be harnessed to enable the wider population to engage with these issues.

The Brundtland Report in 1987 articulated a critical relationship between current and the future human needs, thus defining sustainable development. The report – 'Our Common Future' – emphasized 'the possibility for a new era of economic growth, one that must be based on policies that sustain and expand the environmental resources base' (Brundtland 1987, 18). It highlighted interlocking crises between the needs of a global economy and a global ecology, emphasizing the environmental damage being caused by rapid economic growth and the dangerous levels of consumption of finite resources. Unfortunately, there was only scattered awareness in the society at that time of the adverse impacts of ecological degradation on economic growth. The report pointed to the pitfalls that lay ahead for human development in ignoring this relationship. It highlighted that the environmental crisis, the energy crisis and the development crisis were all entwined and parts of a single bigger crisis. The report warned of depleting local resources for the developing world, home to the majority of the world's poor. Around 90 per cent of the projected growth and population increase was expected to take place in already-burgeoning cities in developing countries. At the time of writing the report (1987) the majority of the developing countries had lower per capita income than at the beginning of the decade. The report drew attention to the increasing demand on the environmental resources, as a result of rising poverty and unemployment. Grounded within these concerns, the Brundtland Commission introduced the concept of sustainable development as one where the needs of the present generation are met without compromising the ability of future generations to meet their own needs. Sustainable development requires 'meeting the basic needs of all and extending to all the opportunity to fulfil their aspirations for a better life' (Brundtland 1987, 25).

The report's comprehensive call for actions, comprising several hundreds of action points in each domain, largely focused on policy and institutional infrastructure change and rebuilding policy processes to tackle sustainable development at national levels setting benchmarks to maintain human progress within guidelines linked to human needs and natural laws (Brundtland 1987, 281). But there was little detailed delineation of work to be done in education.

The idea of sustainable development has gained much impetus and attracted both intense attention and critique from a wide range of stakeholders (Shiva 1992, 2005, Bigg 2003, Stern 2006, Sachs 2008). The work of Elinor Ostrom (1990, 1993, 2006) has been particularly notable. Commentators acknowledge and endorse citizens and communities as key stakeholders in engaging with sustainable development, but a clear articulation of what kind of educational opportunities can enhance this engagement was not well developed.

Links are evident between people living in poverty and lack of education to support sustainable development. Using the Brundtland definition of sustainable development where the 'needs of the present generation are met without compromising the ability of the future generations to meet their own needs', people who are unable to satisfy even the most basic of their needs remain marginalized. Poverty reduces people's capacity to use resources in a sustainable manner and it intensifies pressure on the environment. Lack of information, and lack of access to education, limits people's ability to acquire the knowledge and skills required to change behaviour. Such communities face the immediate and urgent task of making their day-to-day ends meet and may not think about the future or the environment. This is illustrated by the common practice of using plastic and cardboard mix as cooking fuel in the densely populated urban slums in Mumbai.[3] Despite the harmful toxic fumes, the communities continue to use this cooking fuel because of their inability to purchase more expensive cleaner fuels. Fieldwork carried out in 2016 showed users were only partially aware of the damaging impact of the fumes, although they spoke of smoke triggering a cough while cooking. The wider impact of toxic fumes on the environment and on the health of all of the 600,000 slum dwellers was not mentioned. Absence of any educational input to raise awareness of the harms associated with the fuel used and the lack of any offer of alternative cooking fuel further excluded these slum-dwelling communities from engaging with knowledge and action to change practice and behaviour.

Environmental Education, the Decade of Education for Sustainable Development and SDG 4

There have been a range of initiatives to engage educationally with issues of the environmental crisis and sustainability. Environmental education (EE) emerged in the 1960s with a focus on education about environmental issues, such as air and water pollution, depletion and degradation of natural resources and concerns with rapid growth in worldwide population. The approach, as practised mostly in the United States, thus had a limited engagement with 'greening' the environment and producing knowledgeable citizens motivated to work towards solving wider environmental problems. Some viewed EE as limited to a curriculum intervention, which in turn made it difficult to be adopted in schools because of its mismatch with the regular disciplines delivered by an education system (Gough and Gough 2010). Global attention to this issue focused on policy change. Two key UNESCO-UNEP[4] international conferences held in Belgrade (1975) and Tbilisi (1977) provided insights that critiqued EE but also laid the foundations for education to play a key role in facing the challenges of environmental change. The critiques drew attention to the difficulties in the construction of the appropriate curriculum for environmental education, tensions in the conceptualization of the environment in relation to social understandings of the needs of humankind and problems in the implementation of EE in a mainstream curriculum. There were also concerns raised regarding the under-representation of views from developing countries (1977).

The Tbilisi conference was forthright in emphasizing the role of the education sector to engage students in teaching and learning about environmental problems. A critical approach was advocated that would encourage awareness of the complex factors associated with environmental problems. This was to be grounded in a broad range of teaching methods and set in many locales so that students could participate in planning their learning experiences. Opportunities were to be promoted to actively involve the education sector in working towards resolving environmental problems.[5] These insights continued to be part of the policy framework promoted during UNESCO's decade of education for sustainable development forty years later. However, while the Tbilisi outcomes and the UNESCO publications that followed recognized the leadership role of the education sector in shaping and driving an environmental education agenda and also acknowledged the importance of student engagement at the planning stage, there were several shortcomings. Weak implementation pathways to translate these ideas into practice and embed them in the national curricula have been noted (Gough and Gough 2010). Environmental education was located within the realm of specific communities associated with sections of the education system, with little or no attention given to raising wider societal awareness and promoting actions for lifestyle change.

Several workshops and conferences organized by UNESCO and other UN bodies between 1980 and 2000 were instrumental in the launch of the Millennium Development Goals (MDGs) in September 2000. Despite dedicated goals on education (MDG 2, MDG 3, Target 3A) and environmental sustainability (MDG 7), there was little connection between them suggested in this policy framework. It was the launch of the UN Decade of Education for Sustainable Development (DESD) for the period 2005–14 that offered a more focused agenda for education for sustainable development. Under UNESCO's leadership, a resolution was passed in 2002 to implement the DESD framework and define Education for Sustainable Development (ESD). This identified a sustainability–education partnership required to adopt principles of sustainable development in national educational curricula worldwide (Michelsen and Wells 2017). ESD identified drivers of knowledge, skills, perspectives, values that shaped four areas of emphasis: improving access and retention in quality education, reorienting existing educational programmes to address sustainability, increasing public understanding and awareness of sustainability, and providing training to workforce in all sectors (Michelsen and Wells 2017).

ESD drew on both the critiques of EE and also on some concerns regarding the leadership position the education sector could take in driving the agenda to resolve environmental challenges. ESD engaged with both formal and non-formal education expanding the remit of policy and practice to include knowledge, learning and teaching in problematizing environmental challenges and formulation of solutions beyond the boundaries of higher education and scientific institutions. Further, ESD engaged with charting out in detail a multitude of specific actions to raise public awareness and provide training programmes in different contexts (Michelsen and Wells 2017). ESD was intended to create a central space for sustainability knowledge exchange. It focused on the content change required to promote education for sustainable development, thus calling for improved public awareness, and new training in sustainability practices that would enable the embedding of the principles of sustainability to reshape education in creating a more sustainable future.

ESD did progress efforts to advance the sustainable development agenda in many societies, but there were many shortfalls between what was hoped for and what was achieved. DESD has been critiqued for offering a top-down framework that was unidirectional with hierarchical relationships with children in particular, ignoring collective input and co-production of knowledge (Cutter-Mackenzie and Rousell 2018, Kwauk 2020). This approach, commentators argue, deters grassroots engagement and activism of children and youth in spreading awareness and questioning our current lifestyles. ESD gave limited attention to embracing gender-driven actions to address the underlying problems of climate change, and gender inequality (Kwauk 2020). The ESD framework widened the stakeholder base involved with learning and teaching about sustainable development, yet pathways to enhance action to implement these ideas remained sparse at the end of the decade. For example, a survey of seventy-eight countries found that nearly three-quarters of national curriculum frameworks mentioned sustainable development (73 per cent), while just over a third referenced climate change (36 per cent) (Kwauk 2020).

Much more concerted effort in relation to education and sustainability was needed at global, national and local levels. The Sustainable Development Goals (SDGs), adopted by the heads of states of 193 nations on the seventieth anniversary of the United Nations on 25–27 September 2015, represent an urgent call for action by all countries, developed and developing linked in a global partnership. There is a clear acknowledgement that ending poverty and other deprivations must go together with strategies that improve health and education, reduce inequality and spur economic growth – all while tackling climate change and working to preserve our oceans and forests.[6] The word 'sustainable' occurs in the headline description of eleven of the seventeen SDGs (SDGs 2, 6, 7, 8, 9, 11, 12, 14, 15, 17 and 17), with SDG 13 being the climate action goal: take urgent action to combat climate change and its impacts. This reflects a concern to place the sustainability discourse as the centrality of the post-2015 development agenda.

The SDG education goal includes target SDG 4.7:

> ensure that all learners acquire the knowledge and skills needed to promote sustainable development, including, among others, through education for sustainable development and sustainable lifestyles, human rights, gender equality, promotion of a culture of peace and non-violence, global citizenship and appreciation of cultural diversity and of culture's contribution to sustainable development.

This is a positive step, but the indicators to assess progress on these initiatives offer a broad framework with little clarity on how to monitor and evaluate it. The only indicator of SDG Target 4.7 so far agreed does not guide particularly compelling actions:

> Extent to which (i) global citizenship education and (ii) education for sustainable development, including gender equality and human rights, are mainstreamed at all levels in: (a) national education policies, (b) curricula, (c) teacher education and (d) student assessment.[7]

In a comprehensive and insightful critique of SDG 4, contributions in the edited volume by Wulff (2020) draw attention to several pitfalls in the framing of the over all SDG 4 but also specifically with reference to Target 4.7. For example, despite the call for a new discourse to move away from our unsustainable ecological, social, economical, ethical and cultural models towards a sustainable paradigm (Wals 2007), the policy terrain remains largely unchanged. This has led to the continuation of the economic growth and social equity-led priorities over ecology and climate change (Wulff 2020).[8] McCowan (2020) focuses on how universities as home to knowledge creation and research can further influence the society and the environment, but a wide range of actions need to be planned and enacted. In a conceptual model that includes public engagement, the clearly articulated impact pathways to address current climate crisis, he suggests ways that offer potential to contribute to both framing of measurable indicators and also shape a new discourse identifying a sustainable paradigm. Another body of literature on environment and sustainability education (ESE) engages with connecting the discourse with government policy evident in the work of Lotz-Sisitka et al. (2020) in the context of South Africa. This study adds to the knowledge needed to develop an ESE research-policy interface, which can also contribute to more effective translation of the SDG Target 4.7 into practice.

Pathways to Practice 11
Two School Communities

KVS

KVS located in Nepal's Western district of Surkhet is run by the charity BlinkNow. This region is highly vulnerable to natural disasters, has erratic power supplies, with very high prevalence of extreme poverty and health inequalities. The adoption of 'rammed earth technology' has allowed the buildings to withstand extreme weather conditions. The school uses local knowledge to decide what and where to plant focusing on self-sufficiency. This includes growing nutritious food to be served as the school lunch, which may be the only meal for that day for many of the students. The school campus is carefully planted with edible and medicinal plants such as ginger, turmeric, fruit trees, sugar cane, sweet potato and asparagus. The seasonal vegetables and grains mimic local farming rotations. At KVS, the focus is not just on what the children are taught but about what they learn from the teaching environment. One learning environment is the on-site farm, where students learn about agriculture, animal welfare and husbandry (cows, turkeys, ducks, chickens and rabbits), beekeeping, mushroom propagation and more. Teachers of every subject have committed to teach classes on the farm or in the forest at least once a month. Each class has their own allotment to plant and nurture and the children enjoy the satisfaction of contributing their harvest to the school kitchen. As well as providing a valuable teaching tool, the farm plays an integrated role in the BlinkNow ecosystem. The cows, for example, provide milk for the charity's children's home, compost for the beds and biogas, and they consume the agricultural and food waste. In Nepal, cows represent prosperity, so their ownership also gives the school children semblance of Nepali traditions.

Source: Adams 2020

SECMOL

SECMOL is located in Leh, the capital of Ladakh in India. The region is a cold desert at high altitudes in the northeast border with China. The founder of SECMOL, Sonam Wangchuk, is a trained mechanical engineer who observed in the 1980s that the education system for the Ladakhi children was broken and irrelevant. Around 95 per cent of Ladakhi students used to fail in all important board exams. The few who managed to pass found no jobs in the region. This triggered

Mr Wangchuk and a few friends to launch SECMOL in 1988. SECMOL's campus utilizes solar energy for all its power, food and water needs. The SECMOL building is made up of rammed earth walls filled in with small wood pieces for insulation. The maximum usage of the solar power has greatly reduced the costs of running SECMOL, meaning the school does not require any funding. The SECMOL students manage the campus on their own tending the garden, milking the cows, maintaining solar panels, helping with construction work and kitchen duties. Students who failed their board exams multiple times and who joined SECMOL are now successful human beings. Mr Wangchuk helped build Ice Stupas, a discovery that has the potential to reduce the problem of water shortage significantly in regions like Ladakh. His work has brought in many awards including the *INR 100 million* from the Rolex Award for Enterprise, which he has used to set up the Himalayan Institute of Alternatives grounded in the philosophy of learning by doing, collaborating and reflecting on the past. The tenets are as follows:

(1) *Learn by doing: Move away from classroom learning as students imbibe the local culture and traditional knowledge while they work and learn alongside the local people in Ladakh. We believe in education that enriches both the body and mind.*

(2) *Collaborative Teaching: Students learn not only from academicians and industry experts but also from the local practitioners who are actually facing the challenges we want to tackle for the Himalayan region.*

(3) *Integrating traditional wisdom with technology: We develop sustainable models such as natural earth building passive solar houses and other such unique models that are efficient eco-friendly have low carbon footprint and draw from traditional practices.*

Source: https://www.hial.edu.in/about-us-ladakh/hial/

SDG Target 4.7 points to the need for education on sustainability, but more needs to be done to signpost how this can be achieved at multiple levels. Building on the idea of ecoschools, put forward by Arjen Wals (Peters and Wals 2016), one way is to support education projects that enable understanding from a young age of the ecological shifts that lead to climate change and environmental crisis and sustainable living. These shifts are captured by informed individuals (scientists) and draw on insights informed by the principles of sustainable development. This knowledge shapes ideas and pedagogy to create new knowledge, inform individuals and communities and thus support innovations to meet sustainability challenges. This interactivity allows for educational content to be relevant to the concerns of ecology, climate change and sustainable living to generate methods created by informed communities to support specific actions.

This three-way partnership between education, ecology and sustainability to educate and create sustainability-informed youth can be seen in two schools: The Kopila Valley School (KVS) in west Nepal and Students' Educational & Cultural Movement of Ladakh (SECMOL) in India (see Pathways to Practice 11).

The KVS uses 'rammed earth technology', which is a climate-sensitive technology to address the food requirements of school children, strengthening resilience to natural disasters, and insulation from extreme temperatures. The children in turn are key stakeholders in all aspects of the school activities by engaging directly, thus living, understanding and practising the principles of sustainability from a young age (Adams 2020). SECMOL, on the other hand, was founded on the principles of 'Bright Head, Skilled Hands and Kind Heart' (Ranjan 2019). Students become key stakeholders in running the school and are involved in building work using eco-friendly mud technologies, cooking food and managing expenses.

Conclusion

The environmental crisis largely propelled by human activity means humankind faces one of its biggest challenges that threatens the survival of our planet. Regions where most of the world's poor live are likely to have severe impacts in terms of loss of livelihood and habitat, water scarcity, food insecurity and human displacement. The role of education is ever more important now in reshaping our values and how we live in ways that conserve and respect environmental resources. Challenges in embedding this into curricula and pedagogy in formal and informal contexts are significant. One way to meet and overcome these difficulties is to educate children using environmental pedagogy from an early age as illustrated in the examples of the KVS and SECMOL schools.

Questions for Discussion

1. What are the key challenges confronting education systems in changing curriculum, pedagogy and assessment and helping to mitigate the environmental crisis?
2. Identify the main gaps in SDG Target 4.7, and critically discuss the proposed indicators with regard to achieving sustainable development.
3. This chapter has provided two examples of 'eco-schools'. Find similar schools in other parts of the world, and critically examine how they are creating sustainability informed citizens.

Further Reading

Shiva, V. (2020), *Reclaiming the Commons: Biodiversity, Indigenous Knowledge and the Rights of Mother Earth*, London: Synergetic Press.
Nagendra, H. (2018). 'The Global South Is Rich in Sustainability Lessons that Students Deserve to Hear.' *Nature*. Available at https://www.nature.com/articles/d41586-018-05210–0.

Conclusion: An Interview with Anita Rampal

Anita Rampal, Elaine Unterhalter and Tristan McCowan

Overview

The processes of education and international development addressed in this book are multifaceted. As with work on a gemstone, trying to bring out its brilliance, luminosity or vividness, these processes can be cut analytically in different ways. For example, we can understand the dynamics historically, examining different periods before and after the watershed of the Second World War and the formation of the UN or the emergence of the EFA movement from 1990. We can look at these delineating discrete historical periods or view them as a process of change over time, as seen in Chapters 1 and 3. Another perspective on these practices of education and international development is to divide up the analysis by country or region and to use a national or locational frame. Indeed, it can be argued, that none of the processes examined in the chapters of this book can be understood properly unless grounded in a deep, historically informed knowledge of the complexity of local and national contexts and of the interactions which reach beyond established locational framings, for example engagements with globalization or formulations of local identifications. While none of the chapters are restricted to a specific geographical location, in many instances the chapters provide elements of this contextual grounding – for example the discussion of citizenship and education in Rwanda (Chapter 6), educational reform in Bolivia (Chapter 12) and language and education in Nepal (Chapter 13). A third approach to examining this area draws on existing academic disciplines, showing the contribution, for example, of debates within economics (Chapters 7 and 15), anthropology (Chapter 13), politics and sociology (Chapters 6, 8 and 12) and comparative education (Chapters 1, 9 and 10).

In understanding the field of education, the gemstone is faceted in even more complex ways. One scheme for understanding its different dimensions is the Bray and Thomas (1995) 'cube' which divides education research by particular levels of administrative organization, population group and social sector. The problem with this kind of analysis is that the framework provided, which defines a region, a country or a school, prevents one seeing how there are different sites of engagement with education and international development. These inter-link, shift and change through complex processes in historically constructed moments. Particular ways of theorizing the problem, as set out in Chapters 1 and 2, might privilege particular sites, possibly the market, or the state, or the question of cultural authenticity. But, as considered in Chapter 14 on language, Chapter 13 on religion and Chapter 4 on decolonization, these framings are highly contested and shift in relation to a range of processes.

A different approach to understanding the field of education looks at the modalities of curriculum, pedagogy, assessment of learning and management. These themes run through nearly all the chapters, and one of the concerns of the book has been to examine how different processes of education and international development reveal these facets in different ways, for different kinds of learners, taking on board not only the years of childhood schooling but also the issues raised by higher education (Chapter 17) and adult education (Chapter 16). We have also been interested to document the processes that touch on practitioners, for example teachers or teaching assistants, or local government administrators.

While theoretical work in education and international development does not claim that the modalities of education in developing countries are special cases analytically, it does highlight how the complexities of history and locale mean that issues in education look different in these contexts, compared to those in 'developed' or high-income countries. This phenomenon is due in part to the historical conditions associated with colonialism, post-coloniality and global inequalities, as seen in the work on this history of this field of enquiry (Chapter 1), inequalities discussed in Chapter 8, conflict and emergencies (Chapter 12), the question of language (Chapter 14), livelihoods and skills (Chapter 15) and religion (Chapter 13).

One common feature of much of the work in this area is the concern to reach across particular kinds of boundaries. Sometimes this process connects a global terrain of policymaking like EFA with national policy frameworks and meso and micro levels of implementation. In other guises, this approach takes a normative theory like HCT or the capability approach and tries to examine how it works in guiding practice at global, national, sub-national and local levels.

The function of this book, then, may be different depending on the reader: for those engaged with international development work generally, it provides an introduction to the specific area of education, while for those involved at the chalk face in schools and educational projects, it provides the broader backdrop of international development theories and policies. For the reader well versed in social science it illustrates the messy realities at the local level, while for those engaged in a policy or practical task of development it highlights the overarching normative and analytical basis of that work.

A key challenge for us in editing the book has been to try to bring out how the theories, policies and debates covered in the chapters have emerged from and are acted out by real people in real places. Our own personal autobiographies combine experiences in Africa, Latin America and Asia of school teaching and adult education; work in politically oriented education campaigns; and academic research and teaching. We consider this thread of experience an important dimension of the analytical work in this area. Understandings and practices of education and international development – the abstract and concrete manifestations – are developed through a constant interaction, with each challenged and shaped by the other.

To illustrate this point, we are ending the book with an interview with Anita Rampal that draws out the connection between personal history, social location, practice and research. Anita Rampal is an Indian educationist and social activist. Through the interview, she sets out her life history, starting from her initial studies in physics to engagement with adult education in outreach projects for school curriculum reform, teacher education and academic leadership. In this interview, she portrays a life's work involving both critique of dominant approaches to policy and the active construction of alternatives. Having carried out the initial interview in 2014 for the first edition of the book, we returned to speak to Anita in

2020 for the second edition, so she could reflect on the significant global changes in the intervening period.

Interview with Anita Rampal

Anita Rampal and Elaine Unterhalter discussed the main themes of the book in April 2014 and September 2020. This is a shortened version of the discussion.

From the 2014 interview:

> *EU: You have been working in education and international development for many years and you've seen the area change. Could you tell us how you became involved in this work, some of your experiences and what you see as some of the major shifts over the period?*

> AR: From the mid-70s to late 80s, I was involved in a science education programme for rural schools in Madhya Pradesh. Many of us involved were scientists, and at the time I was doing my PhD in Physics at the University of Delhi. The programme's purpose was to try to make science a more interesting and accessible subject in schools, where it may have been very poorly resourced, as well as making it meaningful and relevant at a local level. The programme was then supported by two village-based voluntary groups. In general, the 70s was a period that saw a surge in voluntarism. People with professional degrees and training were looking to see how they could contribute to the issue of development. It was a big movement which encompassed people from numerous educational backgrounds, particularly from the sciences and engineering, who were ready to devote themselves to rural development. Most of us, especially in the sciences, had been educated in a format that conceived of the country almost entirely through its urban areas, so for us it was a very different exposure, of understanding diverse social realities.

> After 1975, I was doing my PhD as well as engaging with this programme, which also involved some of my teachers. We often found that we were conducting more exciting physics in this rural context because the network, and the group of scientists within it, was organized in a personal and democratic manner, unlike universities where supervisors can be intimidating. When we engaged with development work there, we found even the physics more engaging.

> A senior colleague of mine from the physics department who encouraged us to join this rural programme became my husband many years later – Vinod Raina. During the 70s, he was involved in the student politics and viewed education and development within a broader political context.

In the 80s, I joined the Faculty of Education at Jamia Millia Islamia in Delhi. The vice-chancellor of the university knew of my work in rural areas and requested that I engage directly with issues of restructuring of education at Jamia, where a large proportion of students was from very disadvantaged Muslim backgrounds. Later I was awarded a Nehru Fellowship at Teen Murti House to work on education and national development, where I chose to review what we had been doing in the extremely innovative Hoshangabad Science Teaching Programme (HSTP) for rural schools.[1] It was the first time in our country that voluntary groups and professional scientists had collaborated in a participatory curriculum development exercise. The state government had given us space in the development of the curriculum – including textbooks, low-cost experiments with a kit for every classroom, an open book examination, intensive teacher education programmes, annually and also in weekly block-level meetings. This had never happened before in India. The ramifications of that have been tremendous and much education reform in our country took inspiration from earlier efforts in the 70s and 80s. The National Curriculum Framework 2005, and before that efforts at decentralized planning and implementation at the block and cluster level, built on our experiences gained from this school project in Madhya Pradesh.

Around 1990, I began to engage more actively with the international community of development and education practitioners. I had been reviewing our work in science education and was beginning to get involved in the National Literacy Campaign. I had been associated with the People's Science Movement (PSM), which had collaborated with the central government in conducting a participatory literacy campaign, inspired by the Freirean approach of Latin American literacy campaigns. An NGO called the Bharat Gyan Vigyan Samiti (BGVS) was proposed. The Rajiv Gandhi government initially proposed the literacy mission linked to its vision of 'technology missions'. Our network, of which the Kerala Shastra Sahitya Parishad (KSSP) was a leading member and had worked in science popularization and environment policies resisting the Silent Valley Dam, instead negotiated a people-centred approach. In a state like Kerala, where education was to a large extent universalized, there were still questions about quality and relevance. In Ernakulam district a voluntary campaign showed that literacy could be linked to local development. The PSM network managed to convince the government and its Ministry of the campaign model, as some leading officials were keen to understand literacy from an empowering perspective.

The campaign sought to question the notion of education being a top-down model of knowledge transmission. The literacy campaign addressed how to bring in different kinds of knowledge how to make education participatory and how to relate people's disadvantages with their collective agency working for development. It sought to engage the whole community to address those who had been deprived of literacy and other social provision to work for transformative action.

EU: *How do these experiences speak to the chapters in this book?*

AR: As the chapter on skills indicates, there have been different views about the definition of 'skill' and vocational education in different contexts. The legacy of the Gandhian model of Basic Education, developed as part of India's anti-colonial freedom struggle, had called for 'education for life, through life' using a productive craft – weaving, carpentry, agriculture or pottery, etc. – as the medium of interdisciplinary hands-on learning. It also attempted to interrogate the traditional caste system that stigmatized the low castes and their vocations.

Much later, the issue of locally based curriculum development at the primary level was taken up by the District Primary Education Programme (DPEP). However, the model of education as a people's campaign, as the name Sarva Shiksha Abhiyan (SSA) implied ('abhiyan' means campaign), did not incorporate the campaign spirit. It was more a bureaucratic, top-driven, government programme for elementary schooling, as part of India's response to EFA, which tried to emulate the literacy campaign. In fact that campaign had been thwarted and bureaucratized through focus on imposed targets, individual testing and tardy processes of approval and funding. The chapter on EFA looks at how this process happened in other countries.

My engagement with our HSTP science programme led me to look at the literate traditions of science within oral cultures and to escape from dominant discourses surrounding knowledge, language and literacy. This led me to write a paper called 'A Possible Orality for Science?'[2] I had often found the discourse of international science education journals extremely constraining. They didn't understand where I was coming from or the cultural context in which we talked about a teacher, a learner or even science. The article got a very good response with people from different disciplines and from countries where science education reform through an STS (science-technology-society) approach[3] was being tried keeping in mind indigenous communities.

Jomtien was a very exciting juncture for EFA with a call for an expanded vision for education, not in the narrow terms of learning and competencies that had been dominant until that time. But what happened was that our government decided that EFA only applied to primary education, so the commitment to look at education for all was abandoned. Some of the chapters point out how this happened in other countries as well.

In the last decade we, meaning a large network of people working from a progressive and humanistic perspective towards a transformative approach to education, have seen that we could make a major contribution to the National Curriculum Framework (NCF) of 2005 and to the new textbooks that followed. (I was the chairperson of the National Council of Educational Research and Training (NCERT) Textbook Development Teams at the Primary Stage.) NCF 2005 followed a social constructivist approach supported by the ministry, locating the learner's knowledge in culture, while also critically empathizing with others in diverse cultural contexts. It demonstrated how learners bring with them various dispositions, world views and knowledge which is often dismissed by schools. Grassroots organizations exerted pressure because even though the government had amended the Constitution in 2002, it had not enacted the law and was telling individual states that they could introduce their own State Education Acts. Many movements worked concertedly, and due to the strength of the mobilization, the government relented and eventually brought in the RTE Act. Still there were a lot of struggles even after the Act; the private school lobbies contested it in court, which took up millions of rupees, claiming that the Act interfered with their freedom to run their schools. Luckily, the Supreme Court took a very strong stand and supported the Act, stating that this clause[4] was really to strengthen the social fabric of democracy, that it would help to bring children from different backgrounds together and that this is a shared responsibility for anyone who works in education because, in this country, education cannot legally be run for profit.

EU: *There was this huge promise associated with Indian independence, but in reality there's been a struggle to get the state to deliver. Nevertheless, the stories you tell of having access to the state and social-activists having access to the state are very compelling.*

AR: Yes, constantly there is this engagement. That's why the groups I have worked with, the networks, BGVS and the network of the People's Science Movement, consciously engage with the state. We did not set up our own schools; we engaged and pushed for policy to improve public provisioning. One of the basic criteria of the groups in our movement was that we remain a secular organization and that we do not accept foreign funds.

The chapter on religion raises a number of issues which I do not necessarily agree with. In the context of multicultural developing countries where religion has played a contested role in the shaping of dominant 'national' or sectarian identities and continues to be used for polarization, secular education is closely tied to a democratic vision for a just and humane society. For instance, in India, various religious denominations run schools that are recognized and affiliated to Boards of Secondary Education, where they may conduct optional sessions on religious education or value education. There has been a prolonged national debate on compulsory 'value education' which invariably gets linked to religious education, calling for the infusion of values in education to counter the perceived 'decline of traditional values in society'. Progressive educationists have resisted the introduction of separate subjects (even on issues of human rights, etc.), and instead have integrated across the curriculum critical understandings of democratic and secular values as enshrined in the Constitution, while also highlighting that education is never 'value free', dominated by the values of selection, segregation and individualistic competition, now even more aggressively promoted by the market. Moreover, unrecognized or private schools run by religious organizations which use their own curricular materials have raised concerns over the highly divisive content of education that promotes intolerance, reinforces stereotyping and leads to further segregation of children. Despite calls for a national Textbook Council, regulatory mechanisms at the state or central levels have not been found to be effective in dealing with such matters, which are not necessarily academic but dictated more by partisan political affiliations.

EU: *Thinking about education post-2015, do you have any sense about where you think this field of enquiry, of policy and practices, is going both in India and globally?*

AR: We are talking a lot at the moment about the issue of quality, which we feel has been compromised. I am wary about the way quality itself is conceived; we need to intervene to ensure that quality is tied with equity, and that our idea of quality should encompass a number of things, such as critical understandings and diverse knowledges, creativity and cohesion, not just very basic reading and writing for the poor, hi-tech for the rich.

For us now the most important thing is to determine just what it would mean to have a good equitable public education system. We also need to determine how we will look at quality in a way which is different from standardized tests and damaging assessments, which leads to the kind of unhealthy competition between bureaucrats and states, which works to keep teachers out. India has a big computer industry which unfortunately treats education as one of its markets. Now we have an increasing number of agencies coming in to offer assessments of children and teachers, with fancy statistics, rankings of schools, which is often a very seductive prospect for bureaucrats. There are a lot of pressures that we face from these different factors.

We would like to focus on the professional development of the teacher with particular emphasis on teacher autonomy, which is a long-term task. To this end there is much to be done. We have a National Council on Teacher Education, which is currently dealing with how to restructure our teacher education programmes which are, at present, in a bad state.

This is to do with the pressures in trying to implement the RTE when we don't have enough teachers. An estimated 80 per cent of our teacher education institutes are in the private sector and many are not doing well, functioning as teaching shops. We also have pressures from foreign universities which approach our government to set up new distance learning programmes for teachers, ignoring the need for more personal engagement to deal with disparities.

The question now is how do we withstand these external and internal pressures and create our own capacities? We want to create such capacities in tandem with our outlook on education, trying to look at teaching and learning in a more democratic way through children's and teachers' agencies and not just through the transmission of information.[5] Because at the moment our school system is highly discriminatory, this is unacceptable.

How can India claim to be an emerging country if this is the way we run our education system? 2015 and beyond is about redefining the way the education system looks at learning and knowledge, quality and equity. Right now in our state schools, there is a very misguided notion of quality: they think that the best students leave them because they don't teach in English, so overnight they are beginning to switch to English medium rather than as an effective second language, further damaging the meaning-making process.

EU: What I take you to be saying is that the future of the field is to concentrate on people. Linking education with care is where you'd see the compass of policy of practice and research?

AR: Yes, with empathy,[6] and engaging with it to the end. Engaging the agency of the learner from a young child to adolescence, encouraging them to look at education as an ongoing process, one which empowers the individual with the capacity to change one's surroundings and contribute to it and to look beyond the self – these have been and are our policies. When we led the literacy campaign for one decade, though they were more active in the rural areas rather than the urban, we saw young people so committed that they defined their identities through their work within the programme.[7] This may be too idealistic but I do think that we have seen it happen – it can be achieved. Though it is a significant challenge, we need to look at our educational system and ensure that socio-economic backgrounds are not determinants in the kinds of education that people receive.

I think we've made headway in fighting for rights. We've fought for the Food Security Act, which provides a midday meal as well as food for young children and their care givers. The rights framework is something we really have to continue to make progress in, also education for younger children (3–6 years), alongside the struggle for a more equitable system, and we hope for our future targets to be defined in these terms.

From the 2020 interview:

EU: *Since we last spoke six very challenging years have passed, even before we come to the pandemic. If you think back over the period from 2014, how much of what you hoped for has unfolded? How much do you think the processes you hoped for have been frustrated?*

AR: When I look back at what we thought in 2014, especially from our own country context, and also in terms of looking towards what would happen, when new international goals were being set up, we thought we would be looking at education differently. We were arguing that equity would be much more embedded in our notion of quality. There was this hope. In 2010, in India we had just started implementing the RTE for children of age 6–14 years. It went beyond the language of universal access. It made it clear there was a fundamental right of a child to have good quality education in a neighbourhood school. What was to be ensured was not just admission but admission, attendance and completion. Any barriers towards the child's completion were going to be legally dealt with. The system, sixty years after the Constitution directed the state to provide free and compulsory education, was now squarely in a rights framework. There was a lot of hope that the way the system was looking at education would change and that we would now be able to work differently with teachers and curriculum developers and other providers. But, in the last few years, the vision of *Agenda 2030* and the hopes we had of equitable, quality and inclusive education seem far away. Recently [July 2020], during the pandemic and with no parliamentary debate, a new national education policy has been approved for India. We have been waiting for this for thirty-four years. It was promised when the current government took office six years ago. The new policy document starts out saying an entire restructuring of education would be done, to make it inclusive with equitable quality in line with SDG4. But unfortunately, there is nothing in the policy detail on those issues beyond those opening statements. The restructuring envisaged is very damaging, completely stratifying this system even further than it is at present. It leaves the disadvantaged to their own resources. Teaching in the early years is to be left to community volunteers, not even professional teachers. The policy says that it is not going to focus on education inputs; it is only going to focus on outcomes. The present international discourse on learning outcomes is a damaging discourse of denial, especially for the disadvantaged, who need the most essential inputs, of a good school, qualified teachers and materials. Unfortunately, the focus on leaning outcome has been used by corporate interests to manufacture a crisis[8] and this emphasis has also been put into *Agenda 2030*.

Our new policy actually says that the Right to Education was too restrictive in terms of the basic requirements for a school. The system proposed is going to invite almost anyone to come in to run a school, through 'alternative models' or 'multiple pathways'. This paves the way to bring in private players under what it calls a 'public–philanthropic partnership', piously avoiding the term 'private' (as in public–private partnerships) as, by law, education has to be not-for-profit, though crass commercialization has not been stopped. This will also legitimize the global industry of low-fee private schools, and tens of thousands of single-teacher schools run by a right-wing organization. Most of these have been running through the Open School system, by circumventing any affiliation to a school board and the conditions of the Right to Education. So, unfortunately, what is happening in our country is that with this policy, you can use the idea of an open school to allow anyone to go through education in any form. In grade three, grade five and grade eight children will sit an open school exam. Teachers can use their own curricula, their own textbooks, and can just prepare children to take that exam. The policy also speaks of child-tutors. So schools which don't have enough teachers and where children are dropping out, those children who seem to be good at studies will now be doing peer tutoring.

It worries me that a good public education system, which is equitable, and which, in fact, we were talking about achieving for 2030 through SDG 4 is now going to be impossible. We have systems now, even national policies, which say that we won't talk about inputs. You don't even bother about who's a teacher because community volunteers come in. But in the present environment, communities are frequently being mobilized on a divisive agenda of citizenship. The policy also outlines that teachers' appraisal will be done, not only by the principal, and by their peers, but also by the community. This is highly problematic, especially since the policy recommends school teachers to be on probation for three years and college teachers for five years. The new form of teacher appraisal will allow non-state actors to have a key role. This is in a climate where our university teachers, who are standing up for social justice, standing against hate, against persecution of religious minorities, are being charged with false cases of 'terrorist and unlawful activities' against them, and even being put in prison. In this kind of an atmosphere, this policy is now going to allow anyone to enter a school system.

Even before Covid the Delhi government has been using private apps on smartphones, not face-to-face teacher training, for in-service teachers. Delhi has adopted completely market-based solutions, advised by organizations like *Pratham, Central Square Foundation* and *Teach for India*, which use principles of managerialism and efficiency, and segregate students into different sections, even at grade three for being 'slow learners'. An argument is made that they need a different pedagogy and even different exams. So there's a dumbing down of the curriculum for the disadvantaged, with a focus on what is called foundational literacy and numeracy. They claim to be doing something which is just appropriate for them, for their learning needs. For those who can afford a different kind of education, an elite private school, those will continue. So what is equitable and inclusive about this? In the government system, even the *anganwadi* worker for the Integrated Child Development Scheme (ICDS), herself not having completed school, is now being said to be the person who's going to work on foundational literacy and numeracy with children from ages three to five. Within the public school system some children are doing one curriculum and some another. This separation was pushed, unfortunately, by the economists and Nobel laureates Abhijit Banerjee and Esther Duflo, whose randomized control trials are said to show that this segregation works. The Nobel laureates have told the Delhi state government how to run education on a segregated basis and our best teachers from Delhi University, who teach in these schools, tell us of horror stories of what's going on within this divided system.

EU: The picture you're painting is gloomy with aspirations for building a public education system that have not come to fruition. Equity has been interpreted to mean separate but equal, although forced separation means there's no equality. The story in Delhi as you tell it is an extremely depressing one. Are there any states in India where this has been resisted?

AR: Kerala is still one state where they have really tried to work with the government system. In the last two years almost 500,000 students, as I remember, shifted from the private to the government system. There is a lot of energy from teachers in trying to work with open source technologies. I've been closely associated with them, especially with their curriculum reform. I talked to them and suggested that schools, which they call high-tech schools, should set up models of 'democratic' schools, so that all students are running these schools as much as possible. Students could be building new rooms, maintaining databases of the area, of the city. Students' agency is involved in the actual running of the school and students, taking responsibility, are given respect and recognition. All kinds of work then become doable and are legitimate. Some district institutions were telling me they were teaching courses like how to climb trees and pluck coconuts because there is no one to do that. The wages are higher in Kerala, people have forgotten how to climb up those trees and the coconuts are just dying on the trees. But people were looking down on those courses, and parents were saying, 'Please do only high tech'. We need to break this hierarchy between skill and knowledge, which is getting very deeply embedded and promoted in our education system. Our new education policy is proposing vocational education internships in grade six, instead of after grade 10. But we know what these courses are. There is no education; they are designed by industry as very narrow skill-based courses. So, as a counter to that, I hope that Kerala would be able to run different kinds of courses, and show us models of schools where children are able to do all kinds of work – build their own furniture, maintain their data resources and do water resource management or environmental testing – as part of their running the school. So for me, a democratic school is that, where students take charge, their agency can be realized and all kinds of rights are in alliance.

You know, last time I spoke about the Nai Taleem school started by Gandhi as a democratic project? I'm still involved with that school in terms of its work on education for sustainable development. But I think when a government system can actually run such a school, that would be a very heartening model to go by. I've also worked closely with Sikkim government in terms of their new textbooks. That is a small state which has taken sustainable development very seriously. They have restructured their textbooks, giving a basic understanding of education for sustainable development. It has been heartening working with the teachers.

EU: *In both states are these reforms linked to the balance of forces in the government or the levels of popular mobilization in those states?*

AR: Kerala has a long history, a tradition of socialist left movements. So right now, that is the case and they do not have much space for a very divisive right-wing agenda. Sikkim has had a long continuity, which is broken now, of a government, which was close to people who also trusted it. It is a small state and the social networks have been very close. They took the need to talk about sustainable development as a unique aspect of their own geographical, socio-historical location.

EU: *In the second edition of the book, we added chapters on quality, private provision, decolonization, sustainability and the environment. Do you think there are any other important issues in relation to global education that the readers of the book need to think about?*

AR: I know there is a chapter on learning metrics and the history of how this has evolved. But I would have liked to see a chapter just on assessment, its relation to learning, including approaches of assessment called authentic or culturally responsive. Every country now has started using the phrase assessment *for* learning and not *of* learning. But what they do is still based on behaviouristic understanding or the international managerial discourse of the science of evidence-based large scale assessments. There's been a debate we have been having with some neuroscientists while looking at assessment in a study for UNESCO.[9] I find that there is a lack of understanding of the nature of assessment and what can be done differently. It would be good to know whether anywhere in the world this is happening differently, using more decentralized teacher-based, culturally responsive forms of assessment within a public education system. We need to build more international understanding and solidarities around this, because it's almost as if everyone finds that there's no alternative. The push by funding agencies for those kinds of standardized, centralized assessments is getting very difficult to resist.

EU: *You're highlighting that we've engaged a lot in critique of these standardized systems, but we haven't spent time on alternatives and formulating a more responsive vision.*

AR: I would have also liked a chapter on digital justice. This huge market of online education is worrying, as it allows the computer industry to control the public education system. This is not education, just some kind of coaching or supplementary, individualized teaching and assessment, which is damaging. Online education, in my country right now, especially since the pandemic is being pushed to the hilt. Not just staring at a screen, I am concerned at the whole damaging process of customized, individualized, biased algorithms. I have been part of some seminars where I've seen enthusiastic young technology entrepreneurs who come with startups and a rhetoric that they have democratized education because they can reach the poorest child through a tablet. But they don't know anything about social processes of learning or about the history of algorithms, which computer scientists have written about, showing how these are biased. Algorithms are associated with facial recognition, surveillance and threats to data privacy. In the government schools in Delhi, there is a court case going on, about the breach of privacy of children and teachers from closed-circuit TVs in every classroom. Parents are being offered live broadcasts on their phones of their children in class. Poor parents are being told how important it is that they can monitor and feel assured of the security of their child. Hundreds of millions of rupees have been kept for this. There's a court case going on challenging this, but the government sticks to these initiatives. Teachers have to download apps made by private companies, on their phones, and the GPS has to be kept on all the time. They are told they have to be able to get notifications anytime of the day or night. It's actually surveillance of teachers and whether they are at work. Training has also become virtual. Even before Covid they had been doing trainings through apps. Teachers just have to look at a short video, do some multiple-choice questions, and within twenty minutes, they get a certificate that they're trained. They then send this certificate to the State Council. So the way digital technologies are being used and misused is a key issue. So is data privacy – children's data, teachers' data. During Covid all schools required parents to download an app, which was meant to be for Covid security, but it was not data protected. There is now every way to keep children's data. Data collected by governments has been used for their political campaigning. For example they send messages and SMS on special days or for elections, even on birthdays. On a child's birthday a parent can get a customized message from the chief minister saying we hope your child grows up to do as good work as our government is doing. The World Economic Forum had declared in 2019 that the market for education technologies was US$19 billion and that in five years it was expected to go up to US$350 billion. But now with Covid, we hear everyone celebrating the silver lining to Covid and the way online education has taken off, but there is much that needs to be looked at.

I also think we need to think about what are good humanist models of vocational education? The OECD, through its PISA tests, is imposing curricular changes in all countries which look at education for employment from a limited perspective only of the North. But have different countries developed courses that creatively integrate education with work in those socio-economic cultural contexts? Are these considered to be of equivalent status as the so-called 'academic' courses?

EU: *What do you think some of the themes emerging from the Covid pandemic are for thinking about education and international development?*

AR: One is this question of digital apartheid and a larger question of digital surveillance, privacy and justice. Another major issue is how education can counter the infodemic – the excessive misinformation, fear and prejudice that can be as dangerous as a pandemic.[10] I have written an article about how education can act as a vaccination against an infodemic. Finland starts off very early in in its education cycle teaching about what misinformation is, what disinformation or malinformation is, building an understanding about how to recognize fake news. In Kerala, I discovered during Covid that there was a programme running in one district about these issues which had been set up after the last Nipah virus epidemic. This is something that we in education really need to think of, not just because of Covid but also because of the post-truth reality of manipulated social media and echo chambers we are living in.

The Covid pandemic has showed us how governments can completely clamp down on any form of dissent to silence people questioning government policies, for example, on privatization. Over 100 million workers were forced to return to their villages during the lockdown, travelling thousands of miles on foot, without food or money. The economy is in serious regression. Our new education policy came in during Covid. It was in the making for the six years this regime has been in power. But it came during Covid when parliament was shut. So there is no parliamentary debate. Many repressive labour and environmental laws have been hurriedly enacted. A pandemic emergency can be used in authoritarian ways to curtail debate, silence people or put them into prison. Our Constitution, which stands for secularism, and not discriminating on the grounds of religion, had been amended before the pandemic. Thousands of people, including women and university students, had been on the streets peacefully protesting against the Citizenship Amendment Act. Our university students have now had false and dangerous charges, of sedition and of acts of terrorism, raised against them. For months they've been in prison, with no trial or bail. False confessions have been taken, and these have been used to implicate some of our best teachers in public universities. Academics and activists have had thousands of pages of chargesheets filed against them. Education has to take cognisance of how governments use an unprecedented pandemic to intimidate and clamp down on people.

EU: Events in India are very distressing. What do you think we can look forward to in the next ten years?

AR: Something we need to deal with in the next ten years is the rise of populist governments, which endorse divisive dispositions, and post-truth politics. We need to consider how does education – contextualized critical education, which allows learning through and from life – help engage with this present reality? This is where I find international solidarity is important. We need to understand that academic autonomy for institutions or for individuals is going to be a major challenge. International development will have to take cognisance of this. When human rights are being totally stifled, what is this international development community doing? Aren't we going to even look at basic human rights for our teachers and our students and our communities and the minorities? So for me, this is a crucial agenda for solidarity. We need to be able to speak truth to power. If there's one positive thing that I would like to underline that has given us hope in the past few years, it's young people speaking up, whether it's for climate justice in the movement inspired by Greta Thunberg, where youth could question political leaders and speak truth to power without being intimidated in the way adults would have feared. Our youth has spoken up about citizenship, in support of our Constitution. They are speaking up today against privatization and commercialization of education. This is the energy that we can look forward to. And I think if education can nurture this a little more consciously, and support it, through dialogic reflections, through readings across the world, sharing where things have happened, how campaigns and mobilizations have been taken up, it gives hope. And it gives a pedagogy of empathy, hope and strength.

Notes

Introduction

1   This term was used in the description of a seminar at UCL in July 2020 *Submerged histories – statues, stories, salvage https://www.ucl.ac.uk/ institute-of-advanced-studies/publications/2020/jul/submerged-histories-statues-stories-salvage*

2   https://www.abidjanprinciples.org

Chapter 3

1   http://www.unesco.org/new/en/education/themes/leading-the-international-agenda/efareport/

2   http://www.campaignforeducation.org/en/

3   http://www.ineesite.org/en/

4   http://www.ecdgroup.com/

5   http://www.pearsonfoundation.org/

6   See, for example, the Special Issue of the *Compare* Forum – post-2015 education and development agenda (2013, 43:6), UNESCO 2013a and b, Sayed and Ahmed 2015.

7   https://sustainabledevelopment.un.org/sdg4

8   https://www.educationoutcomesfund.org/

9   https://static1.squarespace.com/static/5c2d081daf2096648cc801da/t/5cc83 1a29e3a8d00018891ed/1556623838412/abidjan-Final-v8.pdf

Chapter 4

1   Given that this chapter is aimed at providing an overview and references to an English-speaking audience, we have limited the scope mainly to studies published in English.

2   Contemporary Argentine-Mexican author, whose work runs through philosophy, theology, history, pedagogy. Recognized as one of the most

influential Latin American intellectuals, he is a main exponent of the Philosophy of Liberation movement and the coloniality/modernity dialogues.

3   *Testimonio* has been defined as a narrative literary genre, which is told in the first person by a protagonist or witness, often written by a professional writer, which tells a life experience with the purpose of contributing to social change (Beverley 2008).

Chapter 5

1   https://en.unesco.org/gem-report/
2   https://www.oecd.org/pisa/

Chapter 7

1   https://data.oecd.org/eduatt/population-with-tertiary-education.htm
2   http://www.mckinsey.com/insights/asia-pacific/beyond_korean_style
3   http://www.newsonair.com/More-education-socio-econ-mic-benefits-equals-longer-life.asp
4   See http://www.unesco.org/new/en/education/themes/leading-the-international-agenda/education-for-all/the-efa-movement.

Chapter 9

1   I greatly benefited from discussing the outline of this book chapter with Arushi Terway.
2   The World Bank actively promotes the 'Young Specialist Deposit Scheme' in former socialist countries that had ineffective, mandatory service requirements in place and therefore experienced massive teacher shortage in rural areas. The programme is expensive and therefore is seen more as an emergency measure that is not sustainable without external financial assistance.

Chapter 10

1   https://sustainabledevelopment.un.org/post2015/transformingourworld. SDG 4 states, 'Ensure inclusive and equitable quality education and promote lifelong opportunities for all'.

2   https://www.brookings.edu/product/learning-metrics-task-force/
3   https://www.brookings.edu/wp-content/uploads/2016/11/global_111516_lmtf.pdf
4   https://www.brookings.edu/research/millions-learning-scaling-up-quality-education-in-developing-countries/
5   https://unstats.un.org/sdgs/indicators/indicators-list/

Chapter 11

1   Salaries continue to rise with each successive Pay Commission, the 7th having taken place in 2019.

Chapter 12

1   *The Independent*, 15 July 2013. The full text: Malala Yousafzai delivers defiant riposte to Taliban militants with speech to the UN General Assembly. [Newspaper article] http://www.independent.co.uk/news/world/asia/the-full-text-malala-yousafzai-delivers-defiant-riposte-to-taliban-militants-with-speech-to-the-un-general-assembly-8706606.html, last accessed 27 July 2013.
2   Reuters, by Michelle Nicols, 12 July 2013, Pakistan's Malala, shot by Taliban, takes education plea to U.N. [Newspaper article], http://www.reuters.com/article/2013/07/12/us-malala-un-idUSBRE96B0IC20130712, last accessed 24 July 2013.
3   Webpage UNESCO Global Education Monitoring https://en.unesco.org/gem-report/node/2299, last accessed 15 January 2020.
4   Webpage ECW, https://www.educationcannotwait.org/about-ecw/, last accessed 15 January 2020.
5   This is understood as access to both schooling itself and the resources that accompany it (i.e. quality teachers, sufficient instructional resources, etc.).

Chapter 13

1   See further the 1989 *foulard* affair in France, the 2005 headscarf ban in secular schools in Tajikistan, and Peres, R. (2012), *The Day Turkey Stood Still: Merve Kavakchi's Walk into the Turkish Parliament*, Reading: Ithaca Press.

2   This type, of course, is common in state schools in the UK, Australia, Turkey and parts of Canada – such as the province of Quebec.

Chapter 14

1   Thanks to Dr Bryan Maddox, University of East Anglia for this case study.
2   Ethnologue: http://www.ethnologue.com/world
3   https://nces.ed.gov/timss/results07.asp
4   TIMSS is an international assessment of the mathematics and science knowledge for students of ages between 9/10 and 13/14. TIMSS and PIRLS have been developed by the International Association for the Evaluation of Educational Achievement (IEA) for the purpose of comparing students' educational achievement across countries.
5   http://www.un.org/esa/socdev/unpfii/documents/DRIPS_en.pdf
6   http://www.ohchr.org/Documents/Publications/ GuideMinoritiesDeclarationen.pdf
7   http://www.ethnologue.com/country/BO

Chapter 15

1   http://www.unesco.org/uil/litbase/?menu=4&programme=101; http:// unesdoc.unesco.org/images/0014/001495/149513e.pdf; both accessed 2 July 2013
2   http://www.iyfnet.org/CYEP accessed 5 January 2014
3   http://aif.org/investment-area/livelihoods accessed 2 July 2013
4   http://practicalaction.org/faridpur_livelihoods accessed 2 July 2013
5   For example: Employability skills, Generic skills, Core skills, Technical skills, Vocational skills, Occupational skills, Life skills, Essential skills, Information skills, Self-management skills, Work and study skills, Numeric skills, Communication skills, Decision-making skills, Foundation skills, Basic skills, Interpersonal skills, Personal skills.

Chapter 17

1   In Trow's (1974) influential analysis, universalization is defined as an enrolment rate of at least 50 per cent of the population and massification as at least a 30 per cent enrolment rate.

2   https://essa-africa.org/AERD
3   https://www.nsf.gov/statistics/2017/nsf17306/report/international-students-staying-overall-trends/destination-when-leaving-the-united-states.cfm

Chapter 18

1   https://www.un.org/en/sections/issues-depth/population/index.html
2   Global Carbon Atlas http://www.globalcarbonatlas.org/en/CO2-emissions
3   Author's fieldwork in Deonar Slum, Mumbai, 2016.
4   United Nations Environmental Programme, established in 1961.
5   https://unesdoc.unesco.org/ark:/48223/pf0000032763
6   https://sdgs.un.org/goals
7   https://sdgs.un.org/goals/goal4
8   Komatu et al. in Wulff (2020).

Conclusion

1   For further information, see Rampal, A. (1992a), School 'Science in search of a democratic order?', *Social Scientist*, 20(7/8): 50–74; Rampal, A. (2000), 'Education for Human Development in South Asia', *Economic and Political Weekly*, 2623–31.
2   Rampal, A. (2002), 'Texts in context: Development of curricula, textbooks and teaching and learning materials', in R. Govinda (ed.), *India Education Report*, Oxford University Press, 153–66.
3   Rampal, A. (1992b), 'A Possible "Orality" for Science?', *Interchange*, 23(3): 227–44.
4   Rampal, A. (1994), 'Innovative Science teaching in rural schools in India: Questioning social beliefs and superstitions', in Joan Solomon and Glen Aikenhead (eds), *STS Education: International Perspectives on Reform*, Teachers' College Press, 31–8.
5   The Act requires a reservation of 25 per cent of places in private schools for children from disadvantaged backgrounds.
6   Rampal, A. (2012), 'Students' views on equity and justice in India's schools', in Christopher Day (ed.), *The Routledge International Handbook of Teacher and School Development*, Routledge, 243–53.
7   Rampal, A. and Mander, H. (2013), 'Lessons on food and hunger: A pedagogy of empathy for democracy', *Economic & Political Weekly*, 48(28): 51–7.

8   Rampal, A. (2008), 'Scaffolded participation of children: Perspectives from India', *International Journal of Children's Rights*, 16: 313–25.

9   Rampal, A. (2018), 'Manufacturing Crisis: The Business of Learning'. *Seminar, The Crisis in Learning, vol 706, June, 2018*, 55–9.

10 Rampal, A. (2020), 'We Are Fighting an Infodemic in the Time of 'Coronoia' https://thewire.in/media/coronavirus-infodemic-misinformation

Bibliography

Abidjan Principles (2019), 'Guiding principles on the human rights obligations of States to provide public education and to regulate private involvement in education (The Abidjan Principles)', *International Human Rights Law Review*, 8: 117–48.

Abowitz, K. K. and Harnish, J. (2006), 'Contemporary discourses of citizenship', *Review of Educational Research*, 76(4): 653–90.

Acemoglu, D., Johnson, S. and Robinson, J. (2005), 'Institutions as the fundamental cause of long-run growth', in Aghion, P. and Durlauf, S. (eds), *Handbook of Economic Growth*, Amsterdam: Elsevier, 385–472.

ACER. (2019), 'Centre for global education monitoring', Canberra: Australian Council for Educational Research (ACER). Available at https://www.acer. org/au/gem/learning-progression-explorer#faq-2.

ActionAid (2012), *Transforming Education for Girls in Nigeria and Tanzania: CrossCountry Analysis of Endline Research Studies*, London: ActionAid.

Adam, S. (2012), *Skills Development for Secure Livelihoods*, presented at the Triennale on Education and Training in Africa, 12–17 February 2012, Ouagadoudou. Available at http://www.adeanet.org/triennale/ Triennalestudies/subtheme2/2_3_01_Adam_en.pdf [accessed 3 March 2014].

Adams, D. (1993), 'Defining educational quality'. IEQ Publication #1: Biennial Report. Improving Educational Quality Project. Arlington, VA: Institute for International Research.

Adams, G.-K. (2020), 'The greenest school in the world?', *Permaculture*, 104, Summer 2020. Available at https://www.permaculture.co.uk/issue/ summer-2020.

Addey, C. (2017), 'Golden relics and historical standards: How the OECD is expanding global education governance through PISA for Development', *Critical Studies in Education*, 58(3): 311–25.

Adjei, P. B. (2007), 'Decolonising knowledge production: The pedagogic relevance of Gandhian Satyagraha to schooling and education in Ghana', *Canadian Journal of Education/Revue canadienne de l'Education*, 30(4): 1046–67.

Afrianty, D. and Azra, A. (2005), 'Pesantren and Madrasa: Modernization of Indonesian Muslim Society', Conference paper, http://azyumardiazra.com/ index.php?option=com_docman&task=cat_view&gid=20&dir=DESC&ord er=date&limit=10&limitstart=10 [accessed 15 April 2009].

Afridi, M. (2018), 'Equity and quality in an education public-private partnership: A study of the World Bank-supported PPP in Punjab, Pakistan,' August: 1–64. www.oxfam.org.

Agarwal, P. (2009), *Indian Higher Education: Envisioning the Future*, New Delhi: Sage.

Ahmed, L. (2011), *A Quiet Revolution: The Veil's Resurgence, from the Middle East to America*, New Haven, CT and London: Yale University Press.

Ahmed, M. (2011), 'Defining and measuring literacy: Facing the reality', *International Review of Education*, 57(1–2): 179–95.

Aikman, S. (1999), *Intercultural Education and Literacy*, Amsterdam: John Benjamins.

Aikman, S. (2012), 'Interrogating discourses of intercultural education: From indigenous Amazon community to global policy forum', *Compare*, 42(2): 235–57.

Aikman, S. and Pridmore, P. (2001), 'Multigrade schooling in "remote" areas of Vietnam', *International Journal of Educational Development*, 21(6): 521–36.

Aikman, S. and Unterhalter, E. (2005), *Beyond Access: Developing Gender Equality in Education*, Oxford: Oxfam.

Aikman, S. and Unterhalter, E. (2013), 'Gender equality, capabilities and the Terrain of quality education', in Tikly, L. and Barrett, A. (eds), *Education Quality and Social Justice in the Global South*, Abingdon: Routledge, 25–39.

Aikman, S., Unterhalter, E. and Boler, T. (2008), *Gender Equality, HIV, and AIDS: A Challenge for the Education Sector*, Oxford: Oxfam.

Aitchison, J. (2004), 'Lifelong learning in South Africa: Dreams and delusions', *International Journal of Lifelong Education*, 23(6): 517–44.

Aitchison, J. (2010), *A Review of Youth and Adult Literacy Policies: South Africa, Background Paper for the Global Monitoring Report 2010*, British Association of Literacy in Development (BALID), http://www.balid.org.uk/GMR/South%20Africa%20GMR%202010.pdf [accessed 13 April 2014].

Ajayi, J., Goma, F. A. and Johnson, L. K. H., G. A. and Association of African Universities (1996), *The African Experience with Higher Education*, Accra: AAU.

Akaguri, L. (2011), 'Quality low-fee private schools for the rural poor: Perception or reality? Evidence from Southern Ghana,' Consortium for Research on Educational Access, Transitions and Equity.

Akaguri, L. (2013), 'Fee-free public or low-fee private basic education in rural Ghana: How does the cost influence the choice of the poor?' *Compare* 44(2): 140–61. https://doi.org/10.1080/03057925.2013.796816.

Alcott, B. and Rose, P. (2015), 'Schools and learning in rural India and Pakistan: Who goes where, and how much are they learning?' *Prospects*, 45(3): 345–63. https://doi.org/10.1007/s11125-015-9350-5.

Alcott, B. (2016), 'Does private schooling narrow wealth inequalities in learning outcomes? Evidence from East Africa', *Oxford Review of Education*, 42(5): 495–510. https://doi.org/10.1080/03054985.2016.1215611.

Alexander, N. C. (2001), 'Paying for education: How the World Bank and IMF influence education in developing countries', *Peabody Journal of Education*, 76(3/4): 285–338.

Alexander, R. (2010), *Education for All, the Quality Imperative and the Problem of Pedagogy. CREATE Pathways to Access. Research Monograph No. 20*, Falmer: University of Sussex.

Alexander, R. (2014), 'Paper delivered at conference organised by Norwegian National Commission for UNESCO', *Norad, the Norwegian Refugee Council and the University of Oslo*. Oslo, 3 February 2014.

Alidou, H. (2009), 'Promoting multilingual and multicultural education in Francophone Africa', in Brock-Utne, B. and Skattum, I. (eds), *Languages and Education in Africa*, Oxford: Symposium Books, 105–132.

Allais, S. (2010), *The Implementation and Impact of Qualifications Frameworks: Report of a Study in 16 Countries*, Geneva: International Labour Office.

Allais, S. (2012), 'Will skills save us? Rethinking the relationships between vocational education, skills development policies, and social policy in South Africa', *International Journal for Educational Development*, 32(5): 632–42.

Allais, S. (2014), *Selling Out Education: National Qualifications Frameworks and the Neglect of Knowledge*, Rotterdam: Sense.

Allais, S. (2017), 'Labour market outcomes of national qualifications frameworks in six countries', *Journal of Education and Work*, 30(5): 457–70. https://doi.org/10.1080/13639080.2016.1243232.

Allais, S. (2020, forthcoming), 'Skills for industrialization in sub-Saharan African countries: Why is systemic reform of technical and vocational systems so persistently unsuccessful?' *Journal of Vocational Education and Training*.

Allais, S., Cooper, A. and Shalem, Y. (2019), 'Rupturing or reinforcing inequality? The role of education in South Africa today', *Transformation: Critical Perspectives on Southern Africa*, 101(1): 105–26.

Almond, G. A. and Verba, S. (1963), *The Civic Culture; Political Attitudes and Democracy in Five Nations*, New Jersey: Princeton University Press.

Alonso, I. and Terme, R. (2002), *The Elimination of the Enrollment Fee for Primary Education in Tanzania: A Case Study on the Political Economy of Pro-Poor Policies*, Washington, DC: World Bank.

Altbach, P. G. (1977), 'Servitude of the mind? Education, dependency and neo-colonialism', *Teachers College Record*, 79(2): 187–204.

Altbach, P. G. (1998), *Comparative Higher Education: Knowledge, the University, and Development*, Connecticut: Ablex.

Altbach, P. G. (2004), 'Globalization and the university: Myths and realities in an unequal world', *Tertiary Education and Management*, 10(1): 3–25.

Altbach, P. G. (2016), 'The imperial tongue: English as the dominating academic language', in *Global Perspectives on Higher Education*, Baltimore: Johns Hopkins University Press, 140–8.

Altbach, P. G., Reisberg, L. and Rumbley, L. E. (2009), 'Trends in global higher education: Tracking an academic revolution', *A Report Prepared for the UNESCO 2009 World Conference on Higher Education*, Paris: UNESCO.

Altbach, P. G., Reisberg, L. and Rumbley, L. E. (2010), *Trends in Global Higher Education: Tracking an Academic Revolution*, Paris: UNESCO.

Altbach, P. G. and Umakoshi, T. (2004), *Asian Universities: Historical Perspectives and Contemporary Challenges*, Maryland: Johns Hopkins University Press.

Altinok, N., Angrist, N. and Patrinos, H. (2018), *Global Dataset on Education Quality (1965–2015)*, Policy Research Working Paper 8314. Washington, DC: World Bank.

Altschuler, D. and Corrales, J. (2013), *The Promise of Participation: Experiments in Participatory Governance in Honduras and Guatemala*, London: Palgrave MacMillan.

Alubisia, A. (2005), *UPE Myth or Reality. A Review of Experiences, Challenges and Lessons from East Africa*, Oxford: Oxfam Great Britain and African Network Campaign on Education for All.

Alvaredo, F., Chancel, L., Piketty, T., Saez, E. and Zucman, G. (eds) (2018), *World Inequality Report 2018*, London: Belknap Press.

Aman, R. (2017), 'Colonial differences in intercultural education: On interculturality in the Andes and the decolonization of intercultural dialogue', *Comparative Education Review*, 61: S103–20.

Amjad, R. and Macleod, G. (2014), 'International journal of educational development academic effectiveness of private, public and private–Public partnership schools in Pakistan', *International Journal of Educational Development*, 37: 22–31. https://doi.org/10.1016/j.ijedudev.2014.02.005.

Amsden, A. (2010), 'Say's law, poverty persistence, and employment neglect', *Journal of Human Development and Capabilities*, 11(1): 57–66.

Amutabi, M. N. and Oketch, M. O. (2003), 'Experimenting in distance education: The African Virtual University (AVU) and the paradox of the World Bank in Kenya', *International Journal of Educational Development*, 23(1): 57–73.

Anand, P., Ferrer, B., Gao, Q., Nogales, R. and Unterhalter, E. (2020). 'COVID-19 as a capability crisis: using the capability framework to understand policy challenges', *Journal of Human Development and Capabilities*, 21(3): 293–9.

Anangisye, W. A. (2020), 'Voices of school-age street-children denied basic education in Tanzania', *The African Review*, 47(1): 223–46.

Anderson, B. (1991), *Imagined Communities: Reflections on the Origin and Spread of Nationalism*, London: Verso.

Anderson, B. (2006), *Imagined Communities: Reflections on the Origin and Spread of Nationalism*, London: Verso.

Anderson, P. and Harris, J. (2006), *Re-Theorising the Recognition of Prior Learning*, Leicester: NIACE.

Andrabi, T., Bau, N., Das, J. and Khwaja, A. I. (2010), *Are Bad Public SchoolsPublic 'Bads'? Test Scores and Civic Values in Public and Private Schools* Boston: Harvard Kennedy School.

Andrabi, T., Das, J. and Khwaja, A. I. (2008), 'A Dime a day: The possibilities and limits of private schooling in Pakistan', *Comparative Education Review*, 52(3): 329–55. https://doi.org/10.1086/588796.

Andrabi, T., Das, J., Khwaja, A. I. and Zajone, T. (2005), *Religious School Enrolment in Pakistan: A Look at the Data, Paper Number WPS3521*, Washington, DC: World Bank.

Andreotti, V. (2011a), '(Towards) decoloniality and diversality in global citizenship education', *Globalisation, Societies and Education*, 9(3–4): 381–97.

Andreotti, V. (2011b), *Actionable Postcolonial Theory in Education*, New York: Palgrave Macmillan.

Andreotti, V. (2011c), *Actionable Postcolonial Theory in Education*, New York: Palgrave Macmillan.

Andrews, G. (2020), 'Teaching gender and sexuality in the wake of the must fall movements: Mutual disruption through the lens of critical pedagogy', *Education as Change*, 24(1): 1–20.

Andrews, M. (2008), 'The good governance agenda: Beyond indicators without theory', *Oxford Development Studies*, 36(4): 379–407.

Angrist, J., Bettinger, E., Bloom, E., King, E. and Kremer, M. (2001), 'Vouchers for private schooling in Colombia: Evidence from a randomised natural experiment', *NBER Working Paper 8343*.

Anyon, J. (1980), 'Social class and the hidden curriculum of work', *Journal of Education*, 162(1): 67–92.

Apple, M. W. (2012), *Knowledge, power, and Education: The Selected Works of Michael W. Apple*. New York: Routledge.

Apple, M. W. and King, N. R. (1977), 'What do schools teach?' *Curriculum Inquiry*, 6(4): 341–58.

Appleton, S., Atherton, P. and Bleaney, M. (2008), *International School Test Scores and Economic Growth* (No. 08/04). CREDIT Research Paper.

Archer, M. S. (1979), *Social Origins of Educational Systems*, London: Sage.

Arnove, R. F. (1980), 'Comparative education and world systems analysis', *Comparative Education Review*, 24(1): 48–62.

Arnove, R. F. and Graff, H. J. (1987), *National Literacy Campaigns*, New York: Plenum Press.

Arntsen, H. and Waldrop, A. (2018), 'Introduction to special issue: Qualitative method/ologies in development studies', *Forum for*

Development Studies, 45(2): 185–9. https://doi.org/10.1080/08039410.201
8.1468408.

Arthur, J. (2003), *Education with Character: The Moral Economy of Schooling*,
London and New York: RoutledgeFalmer.

Asadullah, M. Niaz. (2020), 'Poor Indonesian families are more likely to send
their daughters to cheap Islamic schools', The Conversation.com, March 6.

Ashton, D. and Green, F. (1996), *Education, Training and the Global Economy*,
Cheltenham: Edward Elgar.

Aslam, M. (2009), 'The relative effectiveness of government and private schools
in Pakistan: Are girls worse off?', *Education Economics*, 17(3): 329–54.

Aslam, M., Rawal, S. and Saeed, S. (2017), Public–private partnerships in
education in developing countries: A rigorous review of the evidence,
London: Ark.

Assié-Lumumba, N. D. T. and CODESRIA (2006), *Higher Education in Africa:
Crises, Reforms and Transformation*, Dakar: CODESRIA.

Association for the Development of Education in Africa Working Group on
Higher Education and Association of African Universities (2004), *Higher
Education in Sub-Saharan Africa, with Specific Reference to Universities*,
Accra: AAU.

Atherton, A., Appleton, S. and Bleaney, M. (2013), 'International school test
scores and economic growth', *Bulletin of Economic Research*, 65(1): 82–90.

Au, W. (2011), 'Fighting with the text: Contextualising and recontextualising
Freire's critical pedagogy', in Apple, M. W., Au, W. and Gandin, L. A. (eds),
The Routledge International Handbook of Critical Education, London:
Routledge, 221–31.

Aubry, S. and Dorsi, D. (2016), 'Towards a human rights framework to advance
the debate on the role of private actors in education', *Oxford Review of
Education*, 42(5): 612–28.

Auguste, B., Kihn, P. and Miller, M. (2010), *Closing the Talent Gap: Attracting
and Retaining Top Third Graduates to a Career in Teaching*, London:
McKinsey & Company.

Avis, J. (2018), 'Socio-technical imaginary of the fourth industrial revolution
and its implications for vocational education and training: A literature
review', *Journal of Vocational Education & Training*, August, 1–27. https://
doi.org/10.1080/13636820.2018.1498907.

Ayres, D. M. P. (2000), *Anatomy of a Crisis: Education, Development and the
State in Cambodia, 1953–1998*, Honolulu: University of Hawai'i Press.

Azra, A. (2003), 'Bali and Southeast Asian Islam: Debunking the myths', in
Ramakrishna, K. and Tang, S. S. (eds), *After Bali: The Threat of Terrorism in
Southeast Asia*, Singapore: Institute of Defense and Strategic Studies, 39–58.

Azra, A., Afrianty, D. and Hefner, R. (2007), 'Pesantren and Madrasa: Muslim
schools and national ideals in Indonesia', in Hefner, R. R. and Zaman, M.

(eds), *Schooling Islam: The Culture and Politics of Modern Muslim Education*, Princeton and Oxford: Princeton University Press, 172–98.

Baatjes, I. and Mathe, K. (2004), 'Adult basic education and social change in South Africa (1994–2003)', in Chisholm, L. (ed.), *Changing Class*, Pretoria: HSRC, 393–420.

Babul, F. (2007), *Child-to-Child: A Review of the Literature (1995–2007)*, London: The Child-to-Child Trust.

Baiya, H. (2003), 'The quality challenges of Jua Kali training', *Norrag News*, 32: 94–7.

Bajaj, M. (2012), *Schooling for Social Change: The Rise and Impact of Human Rights Education in India*, New York: Continuum International Publishing Group.

Bajaj, M. (2014), 'The productive plasticity of rights: Globalization, education, and human rights', in Stromquist, N. and Monkman, K. (eds), *Globalization and Education: Integration and Contestation across Cultures*, 2nd edn, Maryland: Rowman and Littlefield, 55–70.

Bajaj, M. (ed.) (2017), *Human Rights Education: Theory, Research, Praxis*, Philadelphia: University of Pennsylvania Press.

Baker, C. (1988), *Key Issues in Bilingualism and Bilingual Education*, Clevedon: Multilingual Matters.

Baker, D. P. (2009), 'The educational transformation of work: Towards a new synthesis', *Journal of Education and Work*, 22(3): 163–91.

Baker, D. P. (2011), 'Forward and backward, horizontal and vertical: Transformation of occupational credentialing in the schooled society', *Research in Social Stratification and Mobility. Special Edition on New Directions in Educational Credentialism*, 29(1): 5–29.

Balchin, C. (2011), 'Religion and development: A practitioner's perspective on instrumentalisation', *IDS Bulletin*, 42(1): 15–20.

Ball, C. J. E. (1985), 'What the hell is quality?' in Ball, C. J. E. (ed.), *Fitness for Purpose – Essays in Higher Education*, Guildford: Society for Research into Higher Education & NFER-Nelson, 96–102.

Ball, C. J. E. (2008), 'New philanthropy, new networks, and new governance in education', *Political Studies*, 56: 747–65.

Ball, C. J. E. (2009), 'Privatizing education, privatizing education policy, privatizing educational research: Network governance and the "competition state"', *Journal of Education Policy*, 24(1): 83–100.

Ball, C. J. E. (2012), *Global Education Inc. New Policy Networks and the Neo-Liberal Imaginary*, London: Routledge.

Ball, C. J. E. and Junemann, C. (2012), *Networks, New Governance and Education*, Bristol, UK: Policy Press University of Bristol.

Ball, S. J. (1983), 'Imperialism, social control and the colonial curriculum in Africa', *Journal of Curriculum Studies*, 15(3): 237–63.

Bamusananire, E., Byiringiro, J., Munyakazi, A. and Ntagaramba, J. (2006), *Primary Social Studies: Pupil's Book 6*, Kigali: Macmillan Rwanda.

Banati, P. and Oyugi, J. (2019), 'Longitudinal research for sustainable development', *Zeitschrift für Psychologie*, 227(2): 149–53. https://doi.org/10.1027/2151-2604/a000368.

Banerjee, A. and Duflo, E. (2010), *Poor Economics: Barefoot Hedge-Fund Managers, DIY Doctors, and the Surprising Truth about Life on Less than $1 a Day*, London: Penguin.

Banks, J. A. (2004), 'Teaching for social justice, diversity, and citizenship in a global world', *The Educational Forum*, 68(4): 296–305.

Banks, J. A. (2017), 'Failed citizenship and transformative civic education', *Educational Researcher*, 46(7): 366–77.

Barber, M., Moffit, A. and Kihn, P. (2010), *Deliverology 101: A Field Guide for Educational Leaders*, London: Sage.

Barder, O. and Rogerson, A. (2018), *The International Financing Facility for Education*, Washington DC: Center for Global Development. https://www.cgdev.org/blog/international-finance-facility-education-wrong-answer-right-question.

Bardhan, P. K. and Mookherjee, D. (2006), *Decentralization and Local Governance in Developing Countries: A Comparative Perspective*, Massachusetts: MIT Press.

Barnard, J., Frank, F. and Kneen, B. (2007), *Social Sciences for the New Nation: Grade 9 Learner's Book*, Cape Town: Nasou Via Afrika Ltd.

Barnett, M. (2012), *Rastafari in the New Millennium: A Rastafari Reader*, New York: Syracuse University Press.

Barrera-Osorio, F., Fasih, T., Patrinos, H. A. and Santibáñez, L. (2009), *Decentralized Decision-Making in Schools: The Theory and Evidence on School-Based Management*, Washington, DC: The World Bank.

Barrett, A. M. (2011), 'A millennium learning goal for education post-2015: A question of outcomes or processes', *Comparative Education*, 47(1): 119–33.

Barrett, A. M., Crossley, M. and Dachi, H. A. (2011), 'International collaboration and research capacity building: Learning from the EdQual experience', *Comparative Education*, 47(1): 25–43.

Barro, R. J. (1991), 'Economic growth in a cross section of countries', *The Quarterly Journal of Economics*, 106(2): 407–43.

Barro, R. J. and Sala-i-Martin, X. (2004), *Economic Growth*, Massachusetts: The MIT Press.

Barrón-Pastor, J. C. (2010), 'Globalisation perspectives and cultural exclusion in Mexican higher education', in Unterhalter, E. and Carpentier, V. (eds), *Global Inequalities and Higher Education: Whose Interests Are We Serving?*, Basingstoke & New York: Palgrave Macmillan, 197–218.

Bartlett, L. (2008), 'Literacy's verb: Exploring what literacy is and what literacy does', *International Journal of Educational Development*, 28(6): 737–53.

Basch, C. E. (1989), 'Preventing AIDS through education: Concepts, strategies, and research priorities', *Journal of School Health*, 59(7): 296–300.

Bashir, Mohsin and Ul-Haq, Shoaib (2019), 'Why madrassah education reforms don't work in Pakistan', *Third World Quarterly, Taylor & Francis Journals*, 40(3): 595–611, March.

Batliwala, S. (2007), 'Taking the power out of empowerment–an experiential account', *Development in Practice*, 17(4–5): 557–65.

Bauch, J. P., Vietze, P. M. and Morris, V. D. (1973), 'What makes the difference in parental participation?', *Childhood Education*, 50(1): 47–53.

Baum, D. R., Cooper, R. and Lusk-Stover, O. (2018), 'Regulating market entry of low-cost private schools in sub-Saharan Africa: Towards a theory of private education regulation', *International Journal of Educational Development*, 60 (February 2017): 100–12. https://doi.org/10.1016/j.ijedudev.2017.10.020.

Becker, G. S. (1964, 1993), *Human Capital: A Theoretical and Empirical Analysis, with Special Reference to Education*, 3rd edn, Illinois: University of Chicago Press.

Bell, D. (1973), *The Coming of Post Industrial Society*, New York: Basic Books.

Benavot, A. and Smith, W. C. (2020), 'Reshaping quality and equity: Global learning metrics as a ready-made solution to a manufactured crisis', in Wulff, A. (ed.), *Grading Goal Four: Tensions, Threats, and Opportunities in the Sustainable Development Goal on Quality Education*, Leiden: Brill Publishing, 238–61.

Benavot, A. and Tanner, E. (2007), 'The growth of national learning assessments in the world: 1995–2006', Background paper for the Education for All Global Monitoring Report 2008: Education for All by 2015: will we make it.

Bendix, R. (1964), *Nation-Building and Citizenship; Studies of Our Changing Social Order*, New York: Wiley.

Benhabib, J. and Spiegel, M. (1994), 'The role of human capital in economic development evidence from aggregate cross-country data', *Journal of Monetary Economics*, 34(2): 143–73.

Bennell, P. (1996a), 'Rates of return to education: Does the conventional pattern prevail in sub-Saharan Africa?', *World Development*, 24(1): 183–99.

Bennell, P. (1996b), 'Using and abusing rates of return: A critique of the World Bank's 1995 education sector review', *International Journal of Educational Development*, 16(3): 235–48.

Berger, P. L. (1967), *The Sacred Canopy*, New York: Doubleday.

Berger, P. L. (1999), *The Desecularization of the World: Resurgent Religion and World Politics*, Michigan: Wm. B. Erdmans Publishing.

Berman, G., Hart, J., O'Mathúna, D., Mattellone, E., Potts, A., O'Kane, C., Shusterman, J. and Tanner, T. (2016), 'What we know about ethical research involving children in humanitarian settings: An overview of principles, the literature and case studies', Innocenti Working Paper No. 2016–18, UNICEF Office of Research, Florence.

Beverley, J. (2008), 'Testimonio, subalternity, and narrative authority', in Castro-Klaren, S. (eds), *A Companion to Latin American Literature and Culture*, Malden & Oxford: Blackwell, 571–83.

Bhambra, G. (2014), 'Postcolonial and decolonial dialogues', *Postcolonial Studies*, 17(2): 115–21.

Bhatt, R. (2001), 'World Englishes', *Annual Review of Anthropology*, 30: 527–50.

Bhola, H. (1998), 'World trends and issues in adult education on the eve of the twenty-first century', *International Review of Education*, 44(5–6): 485–506.

Bienen, H. (1974), *Kenya: The Politics of Participation and Control*, New Jersey: Princeton University Press.

Biesta, G. (2015), 'Education, measurement and the professions: Reclaiming a space for democratic professionality in education', *Educational Philosophy and Theory*, 1–16. https://doi.org/10.1080/00131857.2015.1048665.

Biesta, G. J. J. (2010), 'Why "what works" sill won't work: From evidence-based education to value-based education', *Studies in Philosophy and Education*, 29(5): 491–503. https://doi.org/10.1007/s11217-010-9191-x.

Bigg, T. (ed.) (2003), *Survival for a Small Planet*, London: Earthscan.

Bjork, C. (2006), 'Transferring authority to local school communities in Indonesia: Ambitious plans, mixed results', in Bjork, C. (ed.), *Educational Decentralization: Asian Experiences and Conceptual Contributions*, Dordrecht: Springer, 129–47.

Björkdahl, A., Höglund, K., Millar, G., van der Lijn, J. and Verkoren, W. (eds) (2016), *Peacebuilding and Friction: Global and Local Encounters in Post Conflict-Societies*, Abingdon: Routledge.

Black, M. (1996), *Children First: The Story of UNICEF Past and Present*, New York: Oxford University Press.

Blackledge, A. and Creese, A. (2017), 'Translanguaging in mobility', in Canagarajah, S. (ed.), *The Routledge Handbook of Migration and Language*, London: Taylor & Francis, 31–46.

Blackman, S. (1987), 'The labour market in school: New vocationalism and issues of socially ascribed discrimination', in Brown, P. and Ashton, D. (eds), *Education, Unemployment and Labour Markets*, Lewes: Falmer, 27–56.

Blanchard, J. and Moore, T. (2010), 'The digital world of young children: Impact on emergent literacy', *Research Presented by the Pearson Foundation*, London: Pearson Foundation.

Blommaert, J. and Verschueren, J. (1998), 'The role of language in European nationalist ideologies', in Schieffelin, B., Woolard, K. and Kroskrity, P. (eds), *Language Ideologies, Practice and Theory*, Oxford: Oxford University Press, 189–210.

Blommaert, J., Collins, J. and Slembrouck, S. (2005), 'Spaces of bilingualism', *Language and Communication*, 5: 197–216.

Bloom, D., Canning, D. and Chan, K. (2006), *Higher Education and Economic Development in Africa*, Massachusetts: Harvard University.

Boal, A. (2000), *Theatre of the Oppressed*, London: Pluto Press.

Bogenschneider, K., Little, O. M., Ooms, T., Benning, S., Cadigan, K. and Corbett, T. (2012), 'The family impact lens: A family-focused, evidence-informed approach to policy and practice', *Family Relations*, 61(3): 514–31.

Boissiere, M., Knight, J. B. and Sabot, R. H. (1985), 'Earnings, schooling, ability, and cognitive skills', *The American Economic Review*, 75(5): 1016–30.

Bonal, X. and Tarabini, A. (2016), 'Being poor at school: Exploring conditions of educability in the favela', *British Journal of Sociology of Education*, 37(2): 212–29.

BOND, (2020), ' How UK aid can stay on track, despite cuts and concerns at transparency' BOND News and views, 28 October 2020, online at https://www.bond.org.uk/news/2020/10/how-uk-aid-can-stay-on-track-despite-cuts-and-concerns-on-transparency.

Boni, A. and Walker, M. (2013), *Human Development and Capabilities: Re-imagining the University in the 21st Century*, London: Routledge.

Booth, D. (1985), 'Marxism and development sociology: Interpreting the impasse', *World Development*, 13(7): 761–87.

Bourdieu, P. and Passeron, J. C. (1977, reprinted 1990), *Reproduction in Education Society and Culture*, London: Sage.

Bowles, S. and Gintis, H. (1975), 'The problem with human capital theory – A Marxian critique', *American Economic Review*, 65(2): 74–82.

Bowles, S. and Gintis, H. (1976), *Schooling in Capitalist America: Educational Reform and the Contradictions of Economic Life*, New York: Basic Books.

Boyars. (Consulted in Spanish Illich, I. (2006) *Obras reunidas I y II*, Mexico: FCE.

Bracht, C. 'Will the BRICS deliver a more just world order?', *Guardian Weekly*, 8 May 2013. Available at http://www.guardian.co.uk/global-development-professionals-network/2013/may/08/brics-development-bank [accessed 14 December 2013].

Brah, A. and Phoenix, A. (2013), 'Ain't I a woman? Revisiting intersectionality', *Journal of International Women's Studies*, 5(3): 75–86.

Brautigam, D. (2009), *The Dragon's Gift: The Real Story of China in Africa*, Oxford: Oxford University Press.

Brautigam, D. (2010), 'China, Africa and the international aid architecture', *Working Paper No. 107*, Abidjan, Cote d'Ivoire: African Development Bank Group.

Bravi, L., Francioni, B., Murmura, F. and Savelli, E. (2020), Factors affecting household food waste among young consumers and actions to prevent it. A comparison among UK, Spain and Italy, Resources, Conservation and Recycling, Volume 153, February 2020, Article No. 104586

Bray, M. (1996), *Decentralization of Education: Community Financing*, Washington, DC: World Bank.

Bray, M. (1997), 'Community financing of education: Rationales, mechanisms, and policy implications in less developed countries', in Colclough, C. (ed.), *Marketizing Education and Health in Developing Countries: Miracle or Mirage?*, Oxford: Clarendon Press, 185–204.

Bray, M. (2000), *Community Partnerships in Education: Dimensions, Variations and Implications*, Paris: UNESCO.

Bray, M. (2003), 'Control of education: Issues and tensions in centralization and decentralization', in Arnove, R. F. and Torres, C. A. (eds), *Comparative Education: The Dialectic of the Global and the Local*, 2nd edn, Lanham, MD: Rowman & Littlefield, 204–28.

Bray, M. and Murray Thomas, R. (1995), 'Levels of comparison in educational studies: Different insights from different literatures and the value of multilevel analyses', *Harvard Educational Review*, 65(3): 472–91.

Breen, R., Luijkx, R., Müller, W. and Pollak, R. (2010), 'Long-term trends in educational inequality in Europe: Class inequalities and gender differences', *European Sociological Review*, 26(1): 31–48.

Brehm, W. and Silova, I. (2019), 'Five generations of NGOs in education', *Routledge Handbook of NGOs and International Relations*, Abingdon: Routledge.

Breton, T. (2011), 'The quality vs. the quantity of schooling: What drives economic growth?', *Economics of Education Review*, 30(4): 765–73.

Brewer, J. D. (2000), *Ethnography*, Buckingham: Open University Press.

Brewer, L. (2013), *Enhancing the Employability of Disadvantaged Youth: What? Why? And How? Guide to Core Work Skills*, Geneva: International Labour Organization, http://www.ilo.org/wcmsp5/groups/public/—ed_emp/—ifp_skills/documents/publication/wcms_213452.pdfaccessed[19 January 2014].

Brewis, E. and McCowan, T. (2016), *Enhancing Teaching in African Higher Education: Perspectives of Quality Assurance and Academic Development Practitioners in Ghana, Nigeria, Kenya and South Africa*, Manchester: British Council.

Brine, J. (2006), 'Lifelong learning and the knowledge economy: Those that know and those that do not – The discourse of the European Union', *British Educational Research Journal*, 32(5): 649–65.

Broadfoot, P. (2004), '"Lies, damned lies and statistics!": Three fallacies of comparative methodology', *Comparative Education*, 40(1): 3–6.

Brockmann, M., Clarke, L. and Winch, C. (2011), *Knowledge, Skills and Competence in the European Labour Market. What's in a Vocational Qualification?*, London: Routledge.

Brock-Utne, B. (2012), 'Language and inequality: Global challenges to education', *Compare*, 42(5): 773–94.

Brown, E. and McCowan, T. (2018), 'Buen vivir: reimagining education and shifting paradigms', *Compare*, 48: 317–23.

Brown, P. and Lauder, H. (2001), *Capitalism and Social Progress. The Future of Society in a Global Economy*, Basingstoke: Palgrave Macmillan.

Brown, P. and Lauder, H. (2006), 'Globalization, knowledge and the myth of the magnet economy', in Lauder, H., Brown, P., Dillabough, J. and Halsey, A. H. (eds), *Education, Globalization, and Social Change*, Oxford: Oxford University Press, 317–40.

Brown, P., Green, A. and Lauder, H. (2001), *High Skills*, Oxford: Oxford University Press.

Brown, P., Lauder, H. and Ashton, D. (2008), *Education, Globalisation and the Knowledge Economy*, London: Teaching and Learning Research Programme.

Brown, P., Lauder, H. and Ashton, D. (2011), *The Global Auction. The Broken Promises of Education, Jobs, and Incomes*, Oxford and New York: Oxford University Press.

Brundtland, G. (ed.) (1987), *Our Common Future: The World Commission on Environment and Development*, Oxford University Press, Oxford, http://www.worldinbalance.net/intagreements/1987-brundtland.php.

Brunner, J. J. and Tillett, A. (2007), *Higher Education in Central Asia. The Challenges of Modernization. Case Studies from Kazakhstan, Tajikistan, the Kyrgyz Republic and Uzbekistan*, Washington, DC: World Bank.

Bruns, B., Harbaugh Macdonald, I. and Schneider, B. R. (2019), 'The politics of quality reforms and the challenges for SDGs in education', *World Development*, 118: 27–38.

Buckner, E. and Russell, S. G. (2013), 'Portraying the global: Cross-national trends in textbooks' portrayal of globalization and global citizenship', *International Studies Quarterly*, 57: 738–50.

Burki, S. J., Perry, G. and Dillinger, W. R. (1999), *Beyond the Center: Decentralizing the State*, Washington, DC: World Bank.

Burnett, N. (2019), 'Invited essay: It's past time to fix the broken international architecture for education', *International Journal of Educational Development*, 68(1): 15–19.

Burtonwood, N. (2003), 'Social cohesion, autonomy, and the liberal defense of faith schools', *Journal of Philosophy of Education*, 37(3): 415–25.

Bush, K. and Saltarelli, D. (2000), *The Two Faces of Education in Ethnic Conflict*, Paris: UNICEF Innocenti Research Centre.

Butler, J. (1988), 'Performative acts and gender constitution: An essay in phenomenology and feminist theory', *Theatre Journal*, 40(4): 519–31.

Butler, J. (1990), *Gender Trouble*, New York: Routledge.

Cairney, P. and Oliver, K. (2018), 'How should academics engage in policymaking to achieve impact', *Political Studies Review*, 18(2): 228–44.

Caldwell, B. J. (2005), *School-based Management: International Institute for Educational Planning (IIEP), Paris, and International Academy of Education (IAE), Brussels*, Paris: UNESCO.

Callan, E. (2000), 'Discrimination in religious schooling', in Kymlicka, W. and Norman, W. (eds), *Citizenship in Diverse Societies*, Oxford: Oxford University Press, 45–67.

Cameron, D. (1998), 'Gender, language and discourse: A review essay', *Signs, Journal of Women and Culture in Society*, 23(4): 945–73.

Cammack, P. (2012), 'The G20, the crisis, and the rise of global developmental liberalism', *Third World Quarterly*, 33(1): 1–16.

Campbell, C., Skovdal, M., Mupambireyi, Z. and Gregson, S. (2010), 'Exploring children's stigmatisation of AIDS-affected children in Zimbabwe through drawings and stories', *Social Science & Medicine*, 71(5): 975–85.

Canadian Secular Alliance (2009), 'Public financing of religious schools'. Available at http://secularalliance.ca/wp-content/uploads/2009/10/csa-policy-on-public-financing-of-religious-schools.pdf [accessed on 5 October 2013].

Canagarajah, A. S. (2008), 'Language shift and the family: Questions from the Sri Lankan Tamil diaspora', *Journal of Sociolinguistics*, 12: 1–34.

Canagarajah, A. S. and Liyange, I. (2012), 'Lessons from pre-colonial multilingualism', in Martin-Jones, M., Blackledge, A. and Creese, A. (eds), *The Routledge Handbook of Multilingualism*, London: Routledge, 49–65.

Candappa, M., Arnot, M. and Pinson, H. (2010), *Education, Asylum and the 'Non-citizen' Child: The Politics of Compassion and Belonging*, Basingstoke: Palgrave Macmillan.

Card, D. (2001), 'Estimating the returns to schooling: Progress in some persistent econometric problems', *Econometrica*, 69(5): 1127–60.

Care, E., Kim, H., Anderson, K. and Gustafsson-Wright, E. (2017), *Skills for a Changing World: National Perspectives and the Global Movement*, Washington, DC: Center for Universal Education at Brookings. https://www.brookings.edu/wp-content/uploads/2017/03/global-20170324-skills-for-a-changing-world.pdf.

Carlaw, K., Oxley, L., Walker, P., Thorns, D. and Nuth, M. (2012), 'Beyond the Hype. Intellectual Property and the Knowledge Society/Knowledge

Economy', in: Livingstone, D. W. and Guile, D. (eds), *The Knowledge Economy and Lifelong Learning: A Critical Reader*, Rotterdam: Sense, 7–42.

Carlier, W. (2018), *The Widening Educational Gap for Syrian Refugee Children*, Amsterdam: KidsRights.

Carney, S. and Schweisfurth, M. (2018), *Equity in Education*, Oxford: Symposium Press.

Carnoy, M. (1974), *Education as Cultural Imperialism*, London: Longman.

Carnoy, M. (2016), 'Four keys to Cuba's provision of high quality public education', in Adamson, F., Astrand, B. and Darling-Hammond, L. (eds), *Global Education Reform: How Privatization and Public Investment Influence Education Outcomes*, London: Routledge, 50–72.

Carnoy, M. and Samoff, J. (1990), *Education and Social Transition in the Third World*, New Jersey: Princeton University Press.

Carpentier, V. (2010), 'Public-private substitution in higher education funding and Kondratiev cycles: The impacts on home and international students', in Unterhalter, E. and Carpentier, V. (eds), *Global Inequalities and Higher Education: Whose Interests Are You Serving?*, Basingstoke: Palgrave Macmillan, 142–71.

Carr-Hill, R. A., Katabaro, K. J., Katahoire, A. R. and Oulai, D. (2002), *The Impact of HIV/AIDS on Education and Institutionalizing Preventive Education*, Paris: International Institute for Educational Planning, UNESCO.

Carr-Hill, R. and Murtaza, A. (2013), 'Assessing possibilities of corruption: The example of the Punjab Education Foundation', in *UKFIET International Conference on Education and Development – Education and Development Post-2015: Reflecting, Reviewing, Revisioning*. Oxford.

Carr-Hill, R., Rolleston, C., Schendel, R. and Waddington, H. (2018), 'The effectiveness of school-based decision making in improving educational outcomes: A systematic review', *Journal of Development Effectiveness*, 10(1): 61–94. https://doi.org/10.1080/19439342.2018.1440250.

Carter, P. L. (2012), *Stubborn Roots: Race, Culture, and Inequality in US and South African Schools*, Oxford: Oxford University Press.

Castells, M. (1994), 'The university system: Engine of development in the new world economy', in Salmi, J. and Verspoor, A. M. (eds), *Revitalizing Higher Education*, Tarrytown, NY: Elsevier Science, 14–40.

Castles, S. (2018), 'Social transformation and human mobility: Reflections on the past, present and future of migration', *Journal of Intercultural Studies*, 39(2): 238–51.

Castro-Hidalgo, A. and Gomez-Alvarez, A. (2016), 'Chile: A long-term neoliberal experiment and its impact on the quality and equity of education', in Adamson, F., Åstrand, B. and Darling-Hammond, L. (eds), *Global Education Reform: How Privatization and Public Investment Influence Education Outcomes*, London: Routledge, 16–49.

Castro-Klaren, S. (ed.) (2008), *A Companion to Latin American Literature and Culture*, Malden & Oxford: Blackwell.

Cayumán Cofré, C. (2019), 'LLECE-ERCE: UNESCO´s large scale student assessment program in LAC', Presentation at 6th GAML Meeting on 27-28 of August 2019 in Yerevan, Armenia. Available at http://gaml.uis.unesco.org/sixth-meeting-of-the-global-alliance-to-monitor-learning/.

CEATM (Centre for Educational Assessment and Teaching Methods). (2008), *We Study for Life: The Results of the International Comparative Study of Functional Literacy of 15-Year-Old Pupils, PISA 2006*, Bishkek, Kyrgyzstan: CEATM.

Cervone, B. T. and O'Leary, K. (1982), 'A conceptual framework for parent involvement', *Educational Leadership*, 40(2): 48–9.

Chabbott, C. (2003), *Constructing Education for Development: International Organizations and Education for All*, New York: RoutledgeFalmer.

Chambers, R. (1997), *Whose Reality Counts?*, London: Intermediate Technology.

Chandler, D. P. (1998), *A History of Cambodia*, 2nd updated edn, Chiang Mai: Silkworm Books.

Chang, H. J. (2002), 'Breaking the mould: An institutionalist political economy alternative to the neo-liberal theory of the market and the state', *Cambridge Journal of Economics*, 26: 539–59.

Chattopadhyay, S. (2012), *Education and Economics: Disciplinary Evolution and Policy Discourse*, Oxford: Oxford University Press.

Chavkin, N. F. (1998), 'Making the case for school, family, and community partnerships: Recommendations for research', *School Community Journal*, 8(1): 9–21.

Chavkin, N. F. and Williams, D. L. (1993), 'Minority parents and the elementary school: Attitudes and practices', in Chavkin, N. F. (ed.), *Families and Schools in a Pluralistic Society*, New York: SUNY Press, 73–83.

Chenery, H. B., Srinivasan, T. N., Schultz, T. P., Behrman, J. R., Strauss, J., Rodrik, D. and Rosenzweig, M. R. (eds) (1988), *Handbook of Development Economics*, Vol. 4, Amsterdam: Elsevier.

Cheng, V. C. and Tam, W. M. (1997), Multi-models of quality in education, *Quality Assurance in Education*, 5(1): 22–31.

Chikoko, V. (2008), 'The role of parent governors in school governance in Zimbabwe: Perceptions of school heads, teachers and parent governors', *International Review of Education*, 54(2): 243–63.

Chilisa, B. (2020), *Indigenous Research Methodology*, London: Sage.

Chisholm, L. (2004), *Changing Class: Education and Social Change in Post-apartheid South Africa*, London: Zed Books Ltd.

Chisholm, L. (2005), 'The politics of curriculum review and revision in South Africa in regional context', *Compare*, 35(1): 79–100.

Chopra, P. (2011), '(Un) veiling desire: Re-defining relationships between gendered adult education subjects and adult education programmes', *International Journal of Educational Development*, 31(6): 634–42.

Choudhary, A., Muthukkumaran, G. T. and Singh, A. (2019), 'Inequality of opportunity in Indian women', *Social Indicators Research*, 145(1): 389–413.

Christophers, B. and Fine, B. (2020), 'The value of financialization and the financialization of value', in Mertens, Daniel, Zwan, Natascha van der, Mader, Philip (eds), *International Handbook of Financialization*, London: Routledge, 19–30.

Chudgar, A. and Quin, E. (2012), 'Relationship between private schooling and achievement: Results from rural and urban India', *Economics of Education Review*, 31(4): 376–90. https://doi.org/10.1016/j.econedurev.2011.12.003.

Chung, F. (1999), 'Education: A key to power and a tool for change – A Practitioner's Perspective', *Current Issues in Comparative Education*, 2(1): 1–6.

Clark, D. A., Biggeri, M. and Frediani, A. A. (eds) (2019), *The Capability Approach, Empowerment and Participation: Concepts, Methods and Applications*, New York: Springer.

Cloete, N. and Maassen, P. (2015), "Roles of universities and the African context," in N. Cloete, P. Maassen and T. Bailey (eds), *Knowledge Production and Contradictory Functions in African Higher Education*, Cape Town: African Minds.

CNTE (2013), http://cntrabajadoresdelaeducacion.blogspot.mx/ [accessed 15 December 2013].

Cohen, L., Manion, L. and Morrison, K. (2011), *Research Methods in Education*, London: Routledge.

Colclough, C. and Lewin, K. (1993), *Educating all the Children: Strategies for Primary Schooling in the South*, Oxford: Clarendon Press.

Coleman, J. S. (1986), 'The idea of the developmental university', *Minerva: A Review of Science, Learning and Policy*, 24(4): 476–94.

Collin, M. and Weil, D. N. (2020), 'The effect of increasing human capital on economic growth and poverty: A simulation exercise', *Journal of Human Capital*, 14(1): 43–83.

Collini, S. (2012), *What Are Universities for?*, London: Penguin.

Collins, R. (1979), *The Credential Society*, New York: Academic Press.

Collins, R. (2013), 'The end of middle-class work: No more escapes', in Wallerstein, I., Collins, R., Mann, M., Derluguian, G. and Calhoun, C. (eds), *Does Capitalism Have a Future?*, New York: Oxford University Press, 37–70.

Collyer, F. M. (2018), 'Global patterns in the publishing of academic knowledge: Global North, Global South', *Current Sociology*, 66(1): 56–73.

Comte, A. (1880), *The Positive Philosophy of Auguste Comte*, Trans. Harriet Martineau, C., New York: Belford, Clarke & Co.

Concern (2014), *Safe Learning Model*, London: Concern.

Connell, R. (2007), *Southern Theory: The Global Dynamics of Knowledge in Social Science*, Sydney: Allen & Unwin.

Connell, R. (2013), 'Using southern theory: Decolonizing social thought in theory, research and application', *Planning Theory*, 13(2): 210–23.

Cooke, B. and Kothari, U. (2001), *Participation: The New Tyranny?*, London: Zed Books.

Cooke, M. and Simpson, J. (2012), 'Discourses about linguistic diversity', in Martin-Jones, M., Blackledge, A. and Creese, A. (eds), *The Routledge Handbook of Multilingualism*, London: Routledge, 116–30.

Coombe, C. and Kelly, M. (2001), 'Education as a vehicle for combating HIV/AIDS', *Prospects*, 31(3): 435–45.

Coronel-Molina, S. (2017), 'Introduction: Indigenous language regimes in the Americas', *International Journal of the Sociology of Language*, (246): 1–6.

Court, D. (1980), 'The development ideal in higher education: The experience of Kenya and Tanzania', *Higher Education*, 9: 657–680.

Cowen, R. (2000), 'Comparing futures or comparing pasts?', *Comparative Education*, 36(3): 333–42.

Cowen, R. (2010), 'Then and now: Unit ideas and comparative education', in Cowen, R. and Kazamias, A. (eds), *International Handbook of Comparative Education*, Dordrecht: Springer, 1277–94.

Cowen, R. (2017), '2 The warp and weft of comparative education', *World Yearbook of Education 2018: Uneven Space-Times of Education: Historical Sociologies of Concepts, Methods and Practices*, 26: 26–40.

Cowen, R. (2018), 'Embodied comparative education', *Comparative Education*, 54(1): 10–25.

Cowen, R. and Kazamias, A. (eds) (2009), *International Handbook of Comparative Education*, Dordrecht: Springer.

Coysh, J. (2017), *Human Rights Education and the Politics of Knowledge*, Abingdon: Routledge.

Crawford, L. M. (2019), 'Conceptual and theoretical frameworks in research', in Burkholder, G. J., Cox, K. A., Crawford, L. M. and Hitchcock, J. H. (eds), *Research Design and Methods: An Applied Guide for the Scholar-practitioner*, 35–48, London: Sage.

Crenshaw, K. (1989), 'Demarginalizing the intersection of race and sex: A black feminist critique of antidiscrimination doctrine, feminist theory and antiracist politics', *University of Chicago Legal Forum*, 140: 139–67.

Crenshaw, K. (1991), 'Mapping the margins: Intersectionality, identity politics and violence against women of color', *Stanford Law Review*, 43(6): 1241–99.

Crocker, D. A. (2008), *Ethics of Global Development: Agency, Capability, and Deliberative Democracy*, Cambridge: Cambridge University Press.

Crossley, M. and Watson, K. (2003), *Comparative and International Research in Education: Globalisation, Context and Difference*, London: Routledge.

Crossley, M. and Tikly, L. (2004), 'Postcolonial perspectives and comparative and international research in education: A critical introduction', *Comparative Education*, 40(2): 147–56.

Crouch, C. (2011), *The Strange Non-Death of Neoliberalism*, Cambridge: Polity.

Cunningham, A. J. C. (2012), 'Understanding local realities of quality education in Kenya: Pupil, parent and teacher perspectives', *Research in Comparative and International Education*, 7(3): 296–341.

Cutler, D. and Lleras-Muney, A. (2006), 'Education and health: Evaluating theories and evidence', *National Bureau of Economic Research Working Paper Series*, Paper No: 12352.

Cutter-Mackenzie, A. and Rousell, D. (2018), 'Education for what? Shaping the field of climate change education with children and young people as co-researchers', *Children's Geographies,* 17(1): 90–104.

DAAD/British Council. (2018), *Building PhD Capacity in Sub-Saharan Africa.* https://www.britishcouncil.org/education/ihe/knowledge-centre/developing-talent-employability/phd-capacities-sub-saharan-africa.

Dale, R. (2000), 'Globalization and education: Demonstrating a "common world educational culture" or locating a "globally structured educational agenda"?', *Educational Theory*, 50(4): 427–48.

Davies, L. (2004), *Education and Conflict: Complexity and Chaos*, London: RougledgeFalmer.

Davies, L. (2006), 'Global citizenship: Abstraction or framework for action?', *Educational Review*, 58(1): 5–25.

Davies, L. (2011, unpublished paper) 'Promoting education in countries affected by fragility and/or conflict: Sri Lanka case study', Centre for International Education and Research, University of Birmingham.

Davies, L. (2013), 'Education, change and peacebuilding, Essay 1', *2013 FRIENT Working Group on Peace and Development.*

Davies, L. (2014), *Unsafe Gods: Security, Secularism*, London: Trentham.

Day Ashley, L., Mcloughlin, C., Aslam, M., Engel, J., Wales, J., Rawal, S., Batley, R., Nicolai, K. G. and Rose, S. P. (2014), *The Role and Impact of Private Schools in Developing Countries*, London: University of Birmingham, Institute of Education, Overseas Development Institute, UK Aid.

Dawson, W. P. (2009), '"Tricks of the teacher": Teacher corruption and shadow education in Cambodia', in Heyneman, S. P. (ed.), *Buying Your Way into Heaven: Education and Corruption*, Rotterdam: Sense, 51–74.

De Ferranti, D., Perry, G. E., Gill, I., Guasch, J. L., Maloney, W. F., Sanchez-Paramo, C. and Schady, N. (2003), *Closing the Gap in Education and Technology*, Washington, DC: World Bank.

De Lissovoy, N. (2019), 'Decoloniality as inversion: Decentring the west in emancipatory theory and pedagogy', *Globalisation, Societies and Education*, 17(4): 419–31.

De Mejia, A. M. (2012), 'Immersion education: En route to multilingualism', in Martin-Jones, M., Blackledge, A. and Creese, A. (eds), *The Routledge Handbook of Multilingualism*, London: Routledge, 199–213.

De Moura Castro, C. (2000), *Vocational Training at the Turn of the Century*, Frankfurt: Peter Lang.

Dencik, L., Hintz, A., Redden, J. and Treré, E. (2019), 'Exploring data justice: Conceptions, applications and directions', *Information, Communication & Society*, 22(7): 873–81.

De Sousa Santos, B. (2007), 'Preface', in De Sousa Santos, B. (ed.), *Another Knowledge Is Possible: Beyond Northern Epistemologies*, London: Verso, vi–xvii.

De Souza, M. (2005), 'The ecology of writing among the Kashinawa: Indigenous multimodality in Brazil', in Canagarajah, S. (ed.), *Reclaiming the Local in Language and Practice*, New Jersey: Lawrence Erlbaum, 73–98.

De Wit, H., Agarwal, P., Said, M. E., Sehoole, M. and Sirozi, M. (2008), *The Dynamics of International Student Circulation in a Global Context*, Rotterdam: Sense.

De Wit, H., Jaramillo, I., Gagel-Avila, J. and Knight, J. (2005), *Higher Education in Latin America: The International Dimension*, Washington, DC: World Bank.

Deaton, A. (2010), 'Instruments, randomization, and learning about development', *Journal of Economic Literature*, 48: 424–55.

Degu, W. (2005), 'Reforming education', in Junne, G. and Verkoren, W. (eds), *Postconflict Development: Meeting in New Challenges*, London: Lynne Reiner, 129–46.

Dei, G. J. S. and Kempf, A. (eds) (2006), *Anti-colonialism and Education: The Politics of Resistance*, Rotterdam: Brill/Sense.

Delors, J. (1996), *Learning, The Treasure within: Report to UNESCO of the International Commission*, Paris: UNESCO.

Delors, Jacques (2013), 'The treasure within: Learning to know, learning to do, learning to live together and learning to be. What is the value of that treasure 15 years after its publication?', *International Review of Education*, 59: 319–30.

Deneulin, S. and Bano, M. (2009), *Religion and Development: Rewriting the Secular Script*, London and New York: Zed Books.

Denison, E. F. (1962), 'Measuring the contribution of education (and the residual) to economic growth', in Study Group in the Economics of Education (ed.), *The Residual Factor and Economic Growth*, Paris: OECD, 13–55.

Department of Education, UK (2010), 'Religious education in English schools: Non-statutory guidance 2010'. Available at https://www.gov.uk/government/uploads/system/uploads/attachment_data/file/190260/DCSF-00114-2010.pdf [accessed 5 October 2013].

Department of Education, UK (2012), 'Voluntary and faith schools'. Available at http://www.education.gov.uk/schools/leadership/typesofschools/maintained/b00198369/volntary-and-faith-schools [accessed 5 October 2013].

Department of Education, UK (2013), 'More than 100 free school applications approved', https://www.gov.uk/government/news/more-than-100-free-schools-applications-approved [accessed 5 October 2013].

Desai, R. (2012), 'Theories of development', in Haslam, P., Schafer, J. and Beaudet, P. (eds), *Introduction to International Development: Approaches, Actors, and Issues*, 2nd edn, Oxford: Oxford University Press, 45–67.

Desai, V. and Potter, R. B. (2013), *The Companion to Development Studies*, London: Routledge 45–65.

Dewey, J. (1934), *A Common Faith*, New Haven, CT: Yale University Press.

Di Cesare, M., Sabates, R. and Lewin, K. M. (2013), 'A double prevention: How maternal education can affect maternal mental health, child health and child cognitive development', *Longitudinal and Life Course Studies*, 4(3): 166–79.

Di Gropello, E., Tandon, P. and Yusuf, S. (2012), *Putting higher education to work: Skills and research for growth in East Asia*, Washington, D.C.: World Bank.

Didriksson, A. (2008), 'Global and regional contexts of higher education in Latin America and the Caribbean', in Gazzola, A. L. and Didriksson, A. (eds), *Trends in Higher Education in Latin America and the Caribbean*, Caracas: IESALC, 19–50.

Dixon, P. and Tooley, J. (2012), 'A case study of private schools in Kibera: An update', *Educational Management Administration & Leadership*, 40(6): 690–706.

Dixon, P., Humble, S. and Tooley, J. (2017), 'How school choice is framed by parental preferences and family characteristics: A study in poor areas of Lagos State, Nigeria,' *Economic Affairs* 37(1): 53–65. https://doi.org/10.1111/ecaf.12214.

Do Amaral, M. P., Steiner-Khamsi, G. and Thompson, C. (eds) (2019), *Researching the Global Education Industry: Commodification, the Market and Business Involvement*, Berlin: Springer.

Dolan, J., Golden, A., Ndaruhutse, S. and Winthrop, R. (2012), *Building Effective Teacher Salary Systems in Fragile and Conflict-Affected States*, Washington, DC: Center for Universal Education at Brookings and CfBT Education Trust.

Downey, M. and Kelly, A. V. (1978), *Moral Education: Theory and Practice*, London: Harper & Row, Ltd.

Dreeben, R. (1968), *On What Is Learned in School*, Massachusetts: Addison-Wesley Pub. Co.

Dreze, J. and Sen, A. (2015), *An Uncertain Glory: India and Its Contradictions*, Princeton: Princeton University Press.

Drucker, P. (1969), *The Age of Discontinuity: Guidelines to Our Changing Society*, London: Heinemann.

Dryden-Peterson, S. (2016), 'Refugee education: The crossroads of globalization', *Educational Researcher*, 45(9): 473–82.

Dryden-Peterson, S. (2017), 'Refugee education: Education for an unknowable future', *Curriculum Inquiry*, 47(1): 14–24.

Drydyk, J. and Keleher, L. (eds) (2018), *Routledge Handbook of Development Ethics*, Abingdon: Routledge.

Duedahl, P. (ed.) (2016), *A History of UNESCO: Global Actions and Impacts*, Berlin: Springer.

Duermeijer, C., Amir, M. and Schoombee, L. (2018), 'Africa Generates Less than 1% of the World's Research; Data Analytics Can Change that', *Elsevier Web site*. https://www.elsevier.com/connect/africa-generates-less-than-1-of-the-worlds-research-data-analytics-canchange-that.

Duncan, R. and Lopes Cardozo, M.T.A. (2017), 'Reclaiming reconciliation through community education for the muslims and tamils of post-war Jaffna, Sri Lanka', *Research in Comparative and International Education*, 12(1): 76–94.

Dunk, T., McBride, S. and Nelsen, R. (1996), *The Training Trap: Ideology, Training, and the Labour Market*, Winnipeg/Halifax: Fernwoon Publishing.

Dunn-Kenney, M. (2013), 'Disciplining the teacher: The disembodied professional and the decline of vernacular wisdom in teacher education', *The International Journal of Illich Studies*, 3(1): 44–56.

Dupuy, K. (2008), *Education for Peace: Building Peace and Transforming Armed Conflict through Education Systems*, Oslo: Save the Children Norway.

Durkheim, E. (1912 [1965]), *The Elementary Forms of the Religious Life*, New York: Free Press.

Dussel, E. (2000), *Thinking from the Underside of History*, Lanham: Rowman & Littlefield.

Dyer, C. (ed.) (2006), *The Education of Nomadic Peoples: Current Issues, Future Perspectives*, New York: Berghahn Books.

Dyer, C. (2013), 'Does mobility have to mean being hard to reach? Mobile pastoralists and education's 'terms of inclusion', *Compare: A Journal of Comparative and International Education*, 43(5): 601–21.

Dyer, C. (2014), *Livelihoods and Learning: Education for all and the Marginalisation of Mobile Pastoralists*, Abingdon: Routledge.

Dyer, C. and Choksi, A. (2004), *District Institutes of Education and Training: A Comparative Study in Three Indian States*, London: DFID.

Early Childhood Peace Consortium (ECPC) (2018), *Contributions of Early Childhood Development Programming to Sustainable Peace and Development*, New York: Early Childhood Peace Consortium.

Eberhard, D., Simons, G. and Fennig, C. (eds) (2019), Ethnologue 22nd edn, Dallas, Texas: SIL International. Available at www.ethnologue.com.

EDOREN (2015), 'What are children in private schools learning?' Education Cannot Wait, *Results Dashboard*, April 7, 2020. Available at https://s30755.pcdn.co/wp-content/uploads/2020/04/ECW_Dashboard-Map-7-April-2020.pdf.

Education Commission (2016), *The Learning Generation: Investing in Education for a Changing World, a Report by the International Commission on Financing Global Education Opportunity*. Education Commission. Available at https://report.educationcommission.org/report/.

Education Commission (2020), *2020 Update: The International Finance Facility for Education (IFFEd)*. Education Commission. https://educationcommission.org/updates/2020-update-the-international-finance-facility-for-education-iffed/.

Education Reform Mexico (2013), http://www.presidencia.gob.mx/iniciativas/reforma-educativa/ [accessed 15 December 2013].

Edwards, D. B. and Higa, S. (2018), 'The global education policy of school-based management in conflict-affected contexts: Current reach, prominent rationales, and future research', *Policy Futures in Education*, 16(3): 306–20. https://doi.org/10.1177/1478210317742213.

EHEA (2012), 'Beyond the Bologna Process: Creating and connecting national, regional and global higher education areas: Statement of the Third Bologna Policy Forum', Bucharest, April 27th, Available at http://www.ehea.info/Uploads/Documents/BPF%20Statement_27042012_with%20additional%20event.pdf [accessed 11 February 2014].

Elfert, Maren (2019), 'Lifelong learning in Sustainable Development Goal 4: What does it mean for UNESCO's rights-based approach to adult learning and education?', *International Review of Education*, 65: 537–56.

Emanuela, D. G. and Marshall, J. H. (2011), 'Decentralization and educational performance: Evidence from the PROHECO Community School Programin Rural Honduras', *Education Economics*, 19(2): 161–80.

Emanuela, D. G., Tandon, P. and Yusuf, S. (2012), *Putting Higher Education to Work: Skills and Research for Growth in East Asia*, Washington, DC: World Bank.

Epstein, J. L. (1988), 'How do we improve programs for parent involvement?', *Educational Horizons*, 66(2): 58–9.

Epstein, J. L. (2011), *School, Family, and Community Partnerships: Preparing Educators and Improving Schools*, 2nd edn, Colorado: Westview Press.

Equiano, O. (1814, republished 1996), *The Interesting Narrative of the Life of Olaudah Equiano (Written by Himself)*, Oxford: Heinemann.

Ercikan, K., Arim, R., Oliveri, M. and Sandilands, D. (2008), *Evaluation of the Literacy Assessment and Monitoring Programme (LAMP)/UNESCO Institute for Statistics (UIS). Document IOS/EVS/PI/91*, Montreal: UIS.

Escobar, A. (1988), 'Power and visibility, development and the invention and management of the third world', *Cultural Anthropology*, 3(4): 428–43.

Escobar, A. (1995), *Encountering Development: The Making and Unmaking of the Third World*, New Jersey: Princeton University Press.

Escobar, A. (2000), 'Beyond the search for a paradigm: Post-Development and beyond', *Development (SID)*, 43(4): 11–14.

Escobar, A. (2007), 'Post-development as concept and social practice', in Ziai, A. (ed.), *Exploring Post-Development: Theory and Practice, Problems and Perspectives*, London: Routledge, 18–32.

Escobar, A. (2011), *Encountering Development: The Making and Unmaking of the Third World*, New Jersey: Princeton University Press.

Eshiwani, G. (1993), *Education in Kenya since Independence*, Nairobi: East African Educational Publishers.

Esteva, G. (1985), 'Development: Metaphor, myth, threat', *Development: Seeds of Change*, 27(3): 78–9.

Esteva, G. (1987), 'Regenerating people's space', *Alternatives*, 12(1): 125–52.

Esteva, G. (2006), 'Universidad de la tierra (Unitierra): The freedom to learn', in Fasheh, M. and Pimparé, S. (eds), *Emerging and Re-Emerging Learning Communities: Old Wisdoms and New Initiatives from Around the World*, Paris: UNESCO, 12–16.

Esteva, G. (2009), 'Beyond development: The good life.' [Más allá del desarrollo: La buena vida], *América Latina en Movimiento*, 445: 1–5.

Etzioni, A. (1995), *New Communitarian Thinking: Persons, Virtues, Institutions and Communities*, Charlottesville, VA: University of Virginia Press.

European Commission (2016), 'Estimates of European food waste levels', EU-FUSIONS Project, Available at www.eu-fusions.org/phocadownload/ Publications/Estimates-of-European-food-waste-levels.pdf.

Eurotrends (2009), *Study on Governance Challenges for Education in Fragile Situations: Aceh, Indonesia Country Report*, Brussels: European Commission, http://capacity4dev.ec.europa.eu/system/files/upload/ article/2010-10-28/Education_and_Fragility_Synthesis_Report-1.pdf [accessed 22 February 2014].

Fagerlind, I. and Saha, L. (1983), *Education and National Development: A Comparative Perspective*, Oxford: Pergamon Press.

Fägerlind, I. and Saha, L. J. (1989), *Education and National Development: A Comparative Perspective*, Oxford: Pergamon Press.

Facer, K., Lotz-Sisitka, H., Ogbuigwe, A., Vogel, C., Barrineau, S. (2020), TESF Briefing Paper: Climate Change and Education. Bristol, TESF, https://doi.org/10.5281/zenodo.3796143.

Fanon, F. (1963), *The Wretched of the Earth*, London: Penguin.

Fanon, F. (2008), *Black Skin, White Masks*, New York: Grove Press.

Fataar, A. and Subreenduth, S. (2015), 'The search for ecologies of knowledge in the encounter with African epistemicide in South African education', *South African Journal of Higher Education*, 29(2): 106–21.

Fehnel, R. (2003), 'Massification and future trends in African higher education', in Teferra, D. and Altbach, P. G. (eds), *African Higher Education: An International Reference Handbook*, Indiana: Indiana University Press, 73–81.

Feinberg, W. and Soltis, J. F. (2009), *School and Society*, New York: Teachers College Press, Columbia University.

Fennell, S. and Arnot, M. (eds) (2008), *Gender Education and Equality in a Global Context: Conceptual Frameworks and Policy Perspectives*, Abingdon: Routledge.

Fiedrich, M. and Jellema, A. (2003), *Literacy, Gender and Social Agency: Adventures in Empowerment. A Research Report for ActionAid UK*, London: Department for International Development, United Kingdom.

Fiddian-Qasmiyeh, E. (2015), *South–South Educational Migration, Humanitarianism and Development: Views from the Caribbean, North Africa and the Middle East*, Abingdon: Routledge.

Fincham, K. (2012), 'Nationalist narratives, boundaries and social inclusion/exclusion in Palestinian camps in South Lebanon', *Compare*, 42(2): 303–24.

Fine, B. (2001), *Social Capital versus Social Theory: Political Economy and Social Science at the Turn of the Millennium*, London and New York: Routledge.

Fischman, G. E., Topper, A. M., Silova, I., Goebel, J. and Holloway, J. L. (2019), 'Examining the influence of international large-scale assessments on national education policies', *Journal of Education Policy*, 34(4): 470–99.

Fisher, M. (2009), *Capitalist Realism: Is There No Alternative?*, Poole, UK: Orca Book Services.

Fiszbein, A., Schady, N. and Ferreira, F. (2009), *Conditional Cash Transfers: Reducing Present and Future Poverty*, Washington, DC: World Bank Publications.

Fleuri, R. M. and Fleuri, L. J. (2018), 'Learning from Brazilian indigenous peoples: towards a decolonial education', *Australian Journal of Indigenous Education*, 47(1): 8–18.

Flowers, N. (2003), 'What is human rights education', in Flowers, N.(ed.) *A Survey of Human Rights Education*, Hamburg: Bertelsmann Verlag, 107–18.

Foley, G. (1994), 'Adult education and capitalist reorganisation', *Studies in the Education of Adults*, 26(2): 121–43.

Fontdevila, C. (2020), 'Learning assessments in the time of SDGs: New actors and evolving alliances in the construction of a global field', in Wulff, A. (ed.), *Grading Goal Four: Tensions, Threats, and Opportunities in the Sustainable Development Goal on Quality Education*, Leiden: Brill Publishing, 262–79.

Forum, G. S. (2019), 'The "Abidjan principles" on private involvement in education: A useful framework or a step too far?' UKFIET Website. Available at https://www.ukfiet.org/2019/the-abidjan-principles-on-privateinvolvement-in-education-a-useful-framework-or-a-step-too-far/%0D.

Foster, J., Addy, N. A. and Samoff, J. (2012), 'Crossing borders: Research in comparative and international education', *International Journal of Educational Development*, 32: 711–32.

Foster, P. J. (1965), 'The vocational school fallacy in development planning', in Karabel, J. and Halsey, A. H. (eds), *Power and Ideology in Education*, New York: Oxford University Press, 356–66.

Foucault, M. (1965), *Madness and Civilization: A History of Insanity in the Age of Reason*, New York: Random House.

Fox, C. (2008), 'Postcolonial dilemmas in narrative research', *Compare*, 38(3): 335–47.

Fransman, J., Newman, K. and Cornish, H. (2017), '*Rethinking research partnerships: Discussion guide and toolkit*', London: Christian Aid.

Fraser, A. (2009), 'Aid-recipient sovereignty in historical context', in Whitfield, L. (ed.), *The Politics of Aid: African Strategies for Dealing with Donors*, Oxford: Oxford University Press, 45–73.

Fraser, N. (1995), 'From redistribution to recognition? Dilemmas of justice in a "Post-Socialist" age', *New Left Review*, 212: 68–93.

Fraser, N. (2005), 'Reframing justice in a globalized world', *New Left Review*, 36: 79–88.

Freedman, S. W., Weinstein, H. M., Murphy, K. and Longman, T. (2008), 'Teaching history after identity-based conflicts: The Rwanda experience', *Comparative Education Review*, 52(4): 663–90.

Freire, P. (1970, reprinted 1972), *Pedagogy of the Oppressed*, London: Penguin Books.

Freud, S. (1927), *Future of an Illusion*, New York: Norton.

Fricker, M. (2007), *Epistemic Injustice: Power and the Ethics of Knowing*, Oxford: Oxford University Press.

Friedman, M. (1962), *Capitalism and Freedom*, Chicago: University of Chicago Press.

Fuchs, E. (2007), 'Children's rights and global civil society', *Comparative Education*, 43(3): 393–412.

Fukuda-Parr, S. and Yamin, A. (2013), 'The power of numbers: A critical review of MDG targets for human development and human rights', *Development*, 56(1): 58–65.

Fukuyama, F. (2001), 'Social capital, civil society and development', *Third World Quarterly*, 22(1): 7–20.

Fukuyama, F. (2006), *The End of History and the Last Man*, New York: Free Press.

Fuller, B. (1991), *Growing Up Modern: The Western State Builds Third World Schools*, New York: Routledge.

Gallagher, M. E., Lee, C. K. and Kuruvilla, S. (2011), *From Iron Rice Bowl to Informalization: Markets, Workers, and the State in a Changing China*, New York: Cornell University Press, 1–14.

Galtung, J. (1975), 'Three approaches to peace: Peacekeeping, peacemaking and peacebuilding', in Galtung, J.(ed.), *Peace, War and Defence – Essays in Peace Research*, Vol. 2, Copenhagen: Christian Ejlers, 282–304.

Garbe, J., Albrecht, T., Levermann, A., Donges, J. F. and Winklemann, R. (2020), 'The hysteresis of the Antarctic Ice Sheet', *Nature*, 585(7826): 538–44.

Garcia, O. and Flores, N. (2012), 'Multilingual pedagogies', in Martin-Jones, M., Blackledge, A. and Creese, A. (eds), *The Routledge Handbook of Multilingualism*, London: Routledge, 232–46.

García, O. and Lin, A. M. Y. (2017), 'Extending understandings of bilingual and multilingual education', in García, O., Lin, A. and May, S. (eds), *Bilingual and Multilingual Education*, Encyclopedia of Language and Education, 3rd edn, Cham: Springer, 1–20.

Garcia, O., Lin, S. and May, S. (2017), *Bilingual and Multilingual Education*, Encyclopedia of Language and Education, 3rd edn, London: Springer.

Garnett, R. S., Sirota, S. L. and Kayum Ahmed, A. (2019), 'Human rights education in South Africa: Ideological shifts and curricular reforms', *Comparative Education Review*, 63(1): 1–27.

Gasanabo, J. D. (2006), 'School history and mechanisms for the construction of exclusive identities: The case of Rwanda from 1962 to 1994', in Braslavsky, C. (ed.), *Textbooks and Quality Learning for All: Some Lessons Learned from International Experiences*, Geneva: UNESCO, International Bureau of Education, 365–404.

Gee, J. P. (1986), 'Orality and literacy: From the savage mind to ways with words', *Tesol Quarterly*, 20(4): 719–46.

Gehring, K., Michaelowa, K., Dreher, A. and Spörri, F. (2017), 'Aid fragmentation and effectiveness: What do we really know?', *World Development*, 99: 320–34.

Geiger, R. L. (1986), *Private Sectors in Higher Education: Structure, Function and Change in Eight Countries*, Michigan: University of Michigan.

Gellner, D. (2001), 'From group rights to individual rights and back: Nepalese struggles over Culture and Equality', in Cowan, J., Dembour, M. and Wilson, R. (eds), *Culture and Rights: Anthropological Perspectives*, Cambridge: Cambridge University Press, 177–200.

GEM Report (2018), Is global education data heading toward fragmentation? World Education Blog. Available at https://gemreportunesco. wordpress.com/2018/09/19/is-global-education-data-heading-toward-fragmentation/.

Gemmell, N. (1996), 'Evaluating the impacts of human capital stocks and accumulation on economic growth: Some new evidence', *Oxford Bulletin of Economics and Statistics*, 58: 9–28.

Gender-Responsive Education Sector Planning (GRESP). (2019), Regional Workshop Eastern and Southern Africa, 5–8 November 2018. Nairobi, Kenya.

General Assembly of the United Nations (1948), 'Article 26, universal declaration of human rights'. Available at http://www.un.org/Overview/ rights.html [accessed 20 June 2006].

General Assembly of the United Nations (2010), *The Right to Education in Emergency Situations*, New York: UN General Assembly.

Gerrard, J. and Sriprakash, A. (2019), *Migration, Borders and Education: International Sociological Inquiries*, Abingdon: Routledge.

Gertler, P., Patrinos, H. A. and Rubio-Codina, M. (2008), *Empowering Parents to Improve Education: Evidence from Rural Mexico*, Washington, DC: World Bank, https://openknowledge.worldbank.org/handle/10986/6686 [accessed 21 December 2013].

Geyer, R., Jambek, J. R. and Law, K. L. (2017), 'Production, use, and fate of all plastics ever made', *Science Advances*, 3(7). Available at https://advances. sciencemag.org/content/3/7/e1700782.

Gideon, J. and Unterhalter, E. (ed.) (Forthcoming, 2020), *Critical Reflections on Public Private Partnerships*, Abingdon: Routledge.

Gillard, D. (2011), 'Education in England: A brief history', educationengland.com; www.educationengland.org.uk/history [accessed 16 January 2014].

Giroux, H. A. (1983), 'Theories of reproduction and resistance in the new sociology of education: A critical analysis', *Harvard Educational Review*, 53(3): 257–93.

Giroux, H. A. and McLaren, P. (1986), 'Teacher education and the politics of engagement: The case for democratic schooling', *Harvard Educational Review*, 56(3): 213–40.

Gizaw, A. M., Rogers, A. and Warkineh, T. Z. (2019), 'Leaving the job half done? An analysis of mid-term withdrawals by facilitators in some adult literacy learning programmes', *International Journal of Educational Development*, 65: 194–206.

Glaeser, E. L., La Porta, R., Lopez-de-Silanes, F. and Shleifer, A. (2004), 'Do institutions cause growth?', *Journal of Economic Growth*, 9: 271–303.

Global Alliance to Monitory Learning (GAML). (n. d.), *Learning Poverty. Global Alliance to Monitory Learning*. Available at http://gaml.uis.unesco.org/learning-poverty/.

Global Alliance to Monitory Learning (GAML). (2019), 'Global proficiency framework for reading and mathematics: Grade 2 to 6', Global Alliance to Monitor Learning (GAML). Background paper GAML6/REF16.

Global Campaign for Education. (2004), 'Learning to survive: How education for all would save millions of young people from HIV/AIDS'. Available at http://wwwcampaignforeducation.org/docs/reports/arch/learn.pdf.

Global Campaign for Education (2016), *The Fierce Urgency of Now: Delivering Children's Right to Education during Crisis*, Johannesburg: Global Campaign for Education.

Global Campaign for Education and Oxfam International (2012), *A More Ambitious, Effective Global Partnership for Education Briefing Paper*, Johannesburg: Global Campaign for Education.

Global Education Monitoring Report. (2017), *Aid to Education Is Stagnating and Not Going to Countries Most in Need*, Policy Paper 31. Paris, France: UNESCO-GEM Report. Available at https://unesdoc.unesco.org/ark:/48223/pf0000249568.

Global Education Monitoring Report. (2018), 'Fulfilling our collective responsibility: Financing global public goods in education', Policy Paper 34. Paris, France: UNESCO. Available at https://unesdoc.unesco.org/ark:/48223/pf0000261530.

Global Monitoring Report. (2012), *Global Monitoring Report: Youth and Skills: Putting Education to Work*, Paris: UNESCO.

Global Partnership for Education (2012a), *Strategic Plan 2012–2015*, Washington, DC: Global Partnership for Education.

Global Partnership for Education (2012b), *Making Education Aid More Effective: Monitoring Exercise on Aid Effectiveness in the Education Sector*, Washington, DC: Global Partnership for Education.

Golin, J. V. and McCowan, T. (2012), *The University of Latin American Integration: A New Model of Higher Education against the Odds*, Paper Presented at the European Conference on Educational Research (ECER), Cadiz, 19 September.

Gonzalez-Casanova, P. (2004), *Las nuevas ciencias y las humanidades. De la academia a la política*, Mexico City: Anthropos UNAM-IIS.

Gordon, I. J. (1977), 'Parent education and parent involvement: Retrospect and prospect', *Childhood Education*, 54(2): 71–8.

Gordon, I. J. and Breivogel, W. F. (1976), *Building Effective Home-School Relationships*, Massachusetts: Allyn and Bacon.

Gordon, T., Holland, J. and Lahelma, E. (2001), 'Ethnographic research in educational settings', in Atkinson, P. (ed.), *Handbook of Ethnography*, London: Sage, 188–203.

Gorur, R., Sellar, S. and Steiner-Khamsi, G. (2018a), Big data and even bigger consequences, in R. Gorur, S. Sellar and G. Steiner-Khamsi (eds.), *World Yearbook of Education*, London: Routledge.

Gorur, R., Sellar, S. and Steiner-Khamsi, G. (eds) (2018b), *World Yearbook of Education 2019: Comparative Methodology in the Era of Big Data and Global Networks*, Abingdon: Routledge.

Gough, A. and Gough, N. (2010), 'Environmental education', in Kridel, Craig (ed.), *The SAGE Encyclopedia of Curriculum Studies*, New York: Sage Publications, 339–43.

Goulet, D. (1980), 'Development experts: The one-eyed giants', *World Development*, 8(7–8): 481–9.

Gourmelon, G. (2016), How urban consumption lies at the root of deforestation, *GreenBiz*. Available at https://www.greenbiz.com/article/how-urban-consumption-lies-root-deforestation.

Goyal, S. and Pandey, P. (2009), 'How do government and private schools differ? Findings from two large Indian states', Washington, DC: World Bank.

Greany, K. (2012), *Education as Freedom?: A Capability-Framed Exploration of Education Conversion among the Marginalised: The Case of Out-Migrant Karamojong Youth in Kampala*, Unpublished PhD, Institute of Education, University of London.

Green, A. (1997, reprinted 2013), *Education, Globalization, and the Nation State*, Basingstoke: Macmillan.

Green, A. (2013), *Education and State Formation: The Rise of Education Systems in England, France and the USA*, 2nd edn, London: Macmillan.

Green, F. (2011), *What Is Skill? An Inter-Disciplinary Synthesis: LLAKES Research Paper 20*, London: Centre for Learning and Life Chances in Knowledge Economies and Societies.

Grubb, N. and Lazerson, M. (2004), *The Education Gospel: The Economic Power of Schooling*, Cambridge, Massachusetts: Harvard University Press.

Gruijters, R., Alcott, B. and Rose, P. (2020), 'The effect of private schooling on learning outcomes in South Asia and East Africa: A within-family approach', Working Paper No. 20/7., REAL Centre, University of Cambridge. 10.5281/zenodo.3686733.

Gu, J., Humphrey, J. and Messner, D. (2008), 'Global governance and developing countries: The implications of the rise of China', *World Development*, 36(2): 274–92.

Gugelberger, G. M. (ed.) (1998), *The Real Thing: Testimonial Discourse and Latin America*, Durham & London: Duke University Press.

Gumperz, J. and Hymes, D. (1972), *Directions in Sociolinguistics, the Ethnography of Communication*, New York: Holt, Reinhart, Winston.

Gupta, A. (2012), *Red Tape: Bureaucracy, Structural Violence, and Poverty in India*, North Carolina: Duke University Press.

Gustafson, B. (2009), *New Languages of the State: Indigenous Resurgence and the Politics of Knowledge in Bolivia*, Durham: Duke University Press.

Gustafson, B. (2017), Oppressed no more? Indigenous language regimentation in Plurinational Bolivia, *International Journal of the Sociology of Language*, Special Issue, Indigenous Language Regimes in the Americas, 246: 31–58.

Gustafsson, M. (2018), *Costs and Benefits of Different Approaches to Measuring the Learning Proficiency of Students (SDG Indicator 4.1.1)*, Information Paper No. 53. Montreal: UNESCO Institute for Statistics (UIS).

Gutmann, A. (1999), *Democratic Education* (rev. ed.), New Jersey: Princeton University Press.

Haan, H. C. (2006), *Training for Work in the Informal Micro-Enterprise Sector: Fresh Evidence from Sub-Sahara Africa*, Dordrecht: Springer.

Habermas, J. (2006), 'Religion in the public sphere', *European Journal of Philosophy*, 14(1): 1–25.

Hadden, J. (1987), 'Toward desacralizing secularization theory', *Social Forces*, 65(3): 587–611.

Halai, A. and William, D. (2011), *Research Methodologies in the 'South'*, Karachi: Oxford University Press.

Hamilton, M. (2006), 'Just do it: Literacies, everyday learning and the irrelevance of pedagogy', *Studies in the Education of Adults*, 38: 2.

Hammad, W. (2013), 'The rhetoric and reality of decentralisation reforms: The case of school-based management in Egypt', *International Studies in Educational Administration (Commonwealth Council for Educational Administration & Management (CCEAM))*, 41(2): 33–47.

Hammett, D. and Wedgwood, R. (eds) (2006), *The Methodological Challenges of Researching Education and Skills Development in Africa*, Edinburgh: University of Edinburgh Centre for African Studies.

Hanafin, J. and Lynch, A. (2002), 'Peripheral voices: Parental involvement, social class, and educational disadvantage', *British Journal of Sociology of Education*, 23(1): 35–49.

Hanemann, U. (2006), 'Nicaragua's literacy campaign', *Background Paper Commissioned for the EFA Global Monitoring Report 2006, Literacy for Life*.

Hanemann, Ulrike (2019), 'Examining the application of the lifelong learning principle to the literacy target in the fourth Sustainable Development Goal (SDG4)', *International Review of Education*, 65: 251–75.

Hanushek, E. (2003), 'The failure of input-based schooling policies', *Economic Journal, Royal Economic Society*, 113(485): F64–F98.

Hanushek, E. (2005), *Economic Outcomes and School Quality*, International Academy of Education & International Institute for Educational Planning, UNESCO.

Hanushek, E. and Kimko, D. (2000), 'Schooling, labor force quality and the growth of nations', *American Economic Review*, 90(5): 1184–208.

Hanushek, E. and Woessmann, L. (2007), 'The role of education quality for economic growth', *World Bank Policy Research Working Paper No. 4122*, New York: World Bank.

Hanushek, E. and Woessmann, L. (2008), 'The role of cognitive skills in economic development', *Journal of Economic Literature*, 46(3 (September)): 607–68.

Hanushek, E. and Woessmann, L. (2009), 'Do better schools lead to more growth? Cognitive skills, economic outcomes, and causation', *National Bureau of Economic Research*, Working Paper: 14633.

Hanushek, E. and Woessmann, L. (2011), 'The economics of international differences in educational achievement', in Hanushek, E. A., Machin, S. and Woessmann, L. (eds), *Handbook of the Economics of Education, Vol. 3*, Amsterdam: North Holland, 89–200.

Hanushek, E. A. and Woessmann, L. (2015), *The Knowledge Capital of Nations: Education and the Economics of Growth*, Cambridge, MA: MIT Press.

Hanushek, E. A. and Woessmann, L. (2020), 'Education knowledge capital, and economic growth', in Bradley, S. and Green, C. (eds), *The Economics of Education*, 2nd edn, Amsterdam: Elsevier.

Haq, M. U. (1995), *Reflections on Human Development*, New York: Oxford University Press.

Harber, C. (2014), *Education and International Development. Theory, Practice and Issues*, London: Symposium.

Hares, S. and Rossiter, J. (2019), *The State of Global Education in Six Charts*, Washington, DC: Center for Global Development. Available at https://www.cgdev.org/blog/state-global-education-finance-six-charts.

Härmä, J. (2008), 'Are low-fee private primary schools in rural Uttar Pradesh, India, serving the needs of the poor?', University of Sussex, Unpublished DPhil thesis.

Härmä, J. (2009), 'Can choice promote education for all? Evidence from growth in private primary schooling in India', *Compare*, 39(2): 151–65. https://doi.org/10.1080/03057920902750400.

Härmä, J. (2011a), 'Study of private schools in Kwara State', Abuja: DFID Education Sector Support Programme in Nigeria.

Härmä, J. (2011b), 'Low cost private schooling in India: Is it pro poor and equitable?', *International Journal of Educational Development*, 31(4). https://doi.org/10.1016/j.ijedudev.2011.01.003.

Härmä, J. (2013a), 'Access or quality? Why do families living in slums choose low-cost private schools in Lagos, Nigeria?', *Oxford Review of Education*, 39(4): 548–66. https://doi.org/10.1080/03054985.2013.825984.

Härmä, J. (2015), 'Private schooling and development: An overview', in Dixon, Pauline, Humble, Steve, Counihan, Chris (eds), *Handbook of International Development and Education*, Cheltenham: Edward Elgar, 171–99.

Härmä, J. (2016a), 'Is there a private schooling market in poor neighbourhoods in Maputo, Mozambique? Exploring the role of the non-state education sector', *Oxford Review of Education*, 42(5): 511–27. https://doi.org/10.1080/0 3054985.2016.1215612.

Härmä, J. (2016b), 'School choice in rural Nigeria? The limits of low-fee private schooling in Kwara State.' *Comparative Education*, 52(2): 246–66. https://doi.org/10.1080/03050068.2016.1142737.

Härmä, J. (2016c), 'Study of low-fee private schools in the slums of Dar Es Salaam, Tanzania', Chicago: CapitalPlus Exchange.

Härmä, J. (2016d), 'Study of low-fee private schools in the slums of Lusaka, Zambia', Chicago: CapitalPlus Exchange.

Härmä, J. (2019), 'Ensuring quality education? Low-fee private schools and government regulation in three sub-Saharan African capitals', *International Journal of Educational Development*, 66 (September 2018): 139–46. Available at https://doi.org/10.1016/j.ijedudev.2018.10.007.

Härmä, J. (2020), *Low-Fee Private Schooling and Poverty in Developing Countries*, London: Bloomsbury Academic.

Härmä, J. (2021), *Low-Fee Private Schooling and Poverty in Developing Countries,* London: Bloomsbury Academic.

Härmä, J. and Adefisayo, F. (2016), 'Scaling up: Challenges facing low-fee private schools in the slums of Lagos, Nigeria', in Prachi Srivastava, (ed.), *Low-Fee Private Schooling: Aggravating Equity or Mitigating Disadvantage?*, Oxford: Symposium Books, 129–52.

Härmä, J. and Siddhu, G. (2017), *Why Do Parents Default? Parental School Choice and Affordability in a Time of Recession*, Lagos: DFID Developing Effective Private Education Nigeria.

Härmä, J. and Moscoviz, L. (2019), *Learning in Ghana: Exploring the Challenges Faced by Pupils and Teachers at Government and Private Schools in Central Region*, Chicago: IDP Foundation.

Härmä, J. and Siddhu, G. (2017), *Parental Fee Default: Extent, Determinants and Implications*, Lagos: DFID-DEEPEN.

Härmä, J., Hinton, P. and Pikholz, L. (2017), *Low Fee Private Schools In Low-Income Districts of Kampala, Uganda*, Chicago: CapitalPlus Exchange.

Harvey, D. (2005), *A Brief History of Neoliberalism*, Oxford and New York: Oxford University Press.

Harvey, L. and Green, D. (1993), 'Defining quality', *Assessment & Evaluation in Higher Education*, 18(1): 9–34.

Hawes, H. (1990), *Question of Quality: Primary Education and Development*, Essex: Longman.

Haynes, J. (2007), *Religion and Development: Conflict or Cooperation?*, Houndmills, Basingstoke, Hampshire: Palgrave Macmillan.

Hefner, R. (2009), 'Islamic schools, social movements, and democracy in Indonesia', in Hefner, R. (ed.), *Making Modern Muslims: The Politics of Islamic Education in Southeast Asia*, Honolulu: University of Hawaii Press, 55–105.

Heleta, S. (2016), 'Decolonising higher education: Dismantling epistemic violence and Eurocentrism in South Africa', *Transformation in Higher Education*, 1(1): 1–8.

Heneveld, W. and Craig, H. (1995), *Schools Count: World Bank Project Designs and the Quality of Primary Education in Sub-Saharan Africa*, Washington, DC: World Bank.

Herrera, L. (2006), 'Higher education in the Arab World', in Forest, J. J. F. and Altbach, P. G. (eds), *International Handbook of Higher Education Vol. One*, Dordrecht: Springer, 409–21.

Herzog, W., Herzog, S., Brunner, A. and Müller, H. P. (2007), *Einmal Lehrer, Immer Lehrer? Eine vergleichende Untersuchung der Berufskarrieren von (ehemaligen) Primarlehrpersonen*, [Once a Teacher, Always a Teacher? A Comparative Study of Professional Careers of (former) Primary School Teachers], Bern: Haupt.

Heward, C. and Bunwaree, S. S. (1999), *Gender, Education and Development: Beyond Access to Empowerment*, London: Zed.

Heyneman, S. P. and Jonathan, M. B. S. (2014), 'Low cost private schools for the poor: What public policy is appropriate?', *International Journal of Educational Development*, 35: 3–15. https://doi.org/10.1016/j. ijedudev.2013.01.002.

Hickey, S. and Mohan, G. (2005), 'Relocating participation within a radical politics of development', *Development and Change*, 36: 237–62.

Hickling-Hudson, A., Matthews, J. and Woods, A. (2004), *Disrupting Preconceptions: Postcolonialism and Education*, Queensland: Post Pressed.

Higgins, C. (2010), 'Gender identities in language education', in Hornberger, N. and McKay, S. (eds), *Sociolinguistics and Language Education*, Clevedon: Multilingual Matters, 370–97.

Hill, M. (1991), *The Harambee Movement in Kenya: Self-Help, Development and Education among the Kamba of Kitui District*, London: Athlone.

Hill, R. and May, S. (2011), 'Exploring biliteracy in Maori-medium education: An ethnographic perspective', in McCarty, T. (ed.), *Ethnography and Language Policy*, London: Routledge, 161–84.

Hill Collins, P. and Bilge, S. (2016), *Intersectionality*, Cambridge: Polity.

Hillman, A. L. and Jenkner, E. (2002), *User Payments for Basic Education in Low-Income Countries, International Monetary Fund Working Paper No. 02/182*, Washington, DC: International Monetary Fund.

Himalayan Institute of Alternatives (2020), Available at https://www.hial.edu.in/

Hinchcliff, K. (1993), 'Neo-liberal prescriptions for education finance: Unfortunately necessary or inherently desirable?', *International Journal of Educational Development*, 13(2): 183–7.

Hobsbawm, E. (1977), *Age of Capital 1848–1875*, London: Abacus.

Holland, D. (2010), 'Higher education institutionalization in Malawi, 1964–2004', *Comparative Education Review*, 54(2): 199–222.

Holm, J. D. (2012), 'The brain drain within Africa', *The Chronicle of Higher Education, chronicle.com*, 9 October, http://chronicle.com/blogs/worldwise/the-brain-drain-within-africa/30554 accessed [12 January 2014].

Hooks, B. (1996), *Teaching to Transgress: Education as the Practice of Freedom*, New York: Routledge.

Hope, E. C., Brugh, C. S. and Nance, A. (2019), In search of a critical stance: Applying qualitative practices for critical quantitative research in psychology, *Community Psychology in Global Perspective*, 5(2): 63–39.

Hornberger, N. (1988), *Bilingual Education and Language Maintenance*, Dordrecht: Foris Publications.

Hornberger, N. (2002), 'Multilingual language policies and the continua of biliteracy: An ecological approach', *Language Policy*, 1: 27–51.

Hornberger, N. and Johnson, D. C. (2011), 'The ethnography of language policy', in McCarty, T. (ed.), *Ethnography and Language Policy*, London: Routledge, 273–89.

Hornberger, N. and McKay, S. (eds) (2010), *Sociolinguistics and Language Education*, Clevedon: Multilingual Matters.

Howard, R. (2009), 'Education reform, indigenous politics and decolonisation in the Bolivia of Evo Morales', *International Journal of Educational Development*, 29(6): 583–93.

Howard, R. (2010), 'Language, signs and the performance of power: The discursive struggle over decolonisation in the Bolivia of Evo Morales', *Latin American Perspectives*, 37(3): 176–94.

Hulme, D. (2010), 'Lessons from the making of the MDGs: Human development meets results-based management in an unfair world', *IDS Bulletin*, 41(1): 15–25.

Human Rights Watch (2006), *Lessons in Terror: Attacks on Education in Afghanistan*, 186: July issue.

Hunkin, E. (2018), 'Whose quality? The (mis)uses of quality reform in early childhood and education policy', *Journal of Education Policy*, 33(4): 443–56.

Hunter, M. (2019), *Race for Education*, Cambridge: Cambridge University Press.

Hunter, M. and Hachimi, A. (2012), 'Talking class, talking race: Language, class, and race in the call center industry in South Africa', *Social & Cultural Geography*, 13(6): 551–66.

IAEG-SDGs. (2019), 'Tier reclassification: review or reclassification between Tier I and II based on data availability', Presented at Tenth Meeting of the Inter-Agency and Expert Group on Sustainable Development Goal Indicators (IAEG-SDGs) on 21-24 October 2019 in Addis Ababa, Ethiopia. Available at https://unstats.un.org/sdgs/meetings/iaeg-sdgs-meeting-10/.

IAEG-SDGs. (2020), Tier classification of global SDG indicators as of 17 April 2020. Inter-Agency and Expert Group on Sustainable Development Goal Indicators (IAEG-SDGs). Available at https://unstats.un.org/sdgs/iaeg-sdgs/tier-classification/.

IEG [Independent Evaluation Group] World Bank. (2011), *World Bank Support to Education since 2001: A Portfolio Note*, Washington, D.C.: IEG/World Bank.

Illich, I. (1971, reprinted 1976), *Deschooling Society*, New York: Marion.

ILO (2012), *Upgrading Informal Apprenticeships: A Resource Guide for Africa*, Geneva: International Labour Organization.

Indonesia Ministry of National Development Planning and the United Nations Children's Fund (2017), *SDG Baseline Report on Children in Indonesia*, Jakarta: Bappenas and UNICEF.

Indonesia Ministry of National Development Planning and the United Nations Children's Fund (2019), *Achieving the SDGs for Children in Indonesia: Emerging Findings on Trajectories for Reaching the Targets*, Jakarta: BAPPENAS and UNICEF.

INEE (2009), *Education and Fragility in Cambodia*, Paris: UNESCO International Institute for Educational Planning.

INEE (2011), *Understanding Education's Role in Fragility, A* Synthesis of Four Situational Analyses of Education and Fragility: Afghanistan, Bosnia-Herzegovina, Cambodia and Liberia, Paris: UNESCO International Institute for Educational Planning.

INEE (2019a), *Achieving SDG4 for Children and Youth Affected by Crisis*, New York, NY. www.inee.org.

INEE (2019b), *INEE Guidance Note on Gender*, New York, NY. Available at https://inee.org/system/files/resources/INEE_GN_Gender_2019.pdf.

INEP (2019), *Censo da educação superior 2018*, Brasília: INEP.

Inkeles, A. and Smith, D. (1975), *Becoming Modern: Individual Change in Six Developing Countries*, Massachusetts: Harvard University Press.

International Association of Universities (1979), *The Role of the University in Developing Countries: Its Responsibility Toward the Natural and Cultural Environment*, Paris: International Association of Universities.

International Crisis Group (2002), 'Pakistan: Madrassas, Extremism, and the Military', ICG Asia Report Number 36. Available at http://merln.ndu.edu/archive/icg/pakistanmadrasasextremismandthemilitary.pdf [accessed 8 July 2013].

Inter-University Council for East Africa (2010), *A Road Map to Quality: Handbook for Quality Assurance in Higher Education*, Kampala: The Inter-University Council for East Africa/DAAD.

IPCC (2014) 'AR5 climate change 2014: Mitigation of climate change'. Available at https://www.ipcc.ch/report/ar5/wg3/.

IPCC (2018) 'PCC, 2018: Summary for policymakers', in Global Warming of 1.5°C. Available at https://www.ipcc.ch/site/assets/uploads/sites/2/2019/05/SR15_SPM_version_report_LR.pdf.

Ireland, S. (2016), *Education Disrupted: Disaster Impacts on Education in the Asia Pacific Region in 2015*, Singapore: Save the Children.

IRIN (2009), 'Afghanistan: 5 million children not in school', *Irin News*, Available at http://www.irinnews.org/Report.aspx?ReportId=84336 [accessed 15 May 2009].

Israel, M. (2017), Ethical imperialism? Exporting research ethics to the global South, in R. Iphofen and M. Tolich (eds), *The SAGE Handbook of Qualitative Research Ethics*, London: SAGE.

Ivancheva, M. P., Swartz, R., Morris, N. P., Walji, S., Swinnerton, B. J., Coop, T. and Czerniewicz, L. (2020), 'Conflicting logics of online higher education', *British Journal of Sociology of Education*, 41(5): 608–25.

Iverson, T. and Stephens, J. D. (2008), 'Partisan politics, the welfare state, and three worlds of human capital formation', *Comparative Political Studies*, 45(4/5): 600–37.

Harrison, K. D. (2007), *When Languages Die: The Extinction of the World's Languages and the Erosion of Human Knowledge*, Oxford: Oxford University Press.

Hernandez, I. (2019), 'The geographies of collective identity in the Chilean student movement', *British Journal of Sociology of Education*, 40(4): 475–89.

Jackson, C. and Pearson, R. (2005), *Feminist Visions of Development: Gender Analysis and Policy*, London: Routledge.

Jafar, A. J. N. (2018), What is positionality and should it be expressed in quantitative studies?, *Emergency Medicine Journal*, 35(5): 323–24. doi: 10.1136/emermed-2017-207158.

Jaffe, A. (2012), 'Multilingual citizenship and minority languages', in Martin-Jones, M., Blackledge, A. and Creese, A. (eds), *The Routledge Handbook of Multilingualism*, London: Routledge, 83–99.

Jansen, J. D. (1990), 'Curriculum as a political Phenomenon: Historical reflections on black South African education', *The Journal of Negro Education*, 59(2): 195–206.

Jansen, J. D. (2002), 'Political symbolism as policy craft: Explaining non-reform in South African education after apartheid', *Journal of Education Policy*, 17(2): 199–215.

Jarvis, P. (2014), 'From adult education to lifelong learning and beyond', *Comparative Education*, 50(1): 45–57.

Jensen, B. (2013), *The Myth of Markets in School Education*, Melbourne: Grattan Institute.

Jickling, B. (2017), 'Education revisited: Creating educational experiences that are held, felt, and disruptive', in Jickling, B. and Sterling, S. (eds), *Post-sustainability and Environmental Education: Remaking Education for the Future*, Cham, Switzerland: Palgrave Macmillan, 15–30.

Johnson, A. T. and Hirt, J. B. (2011), 'Reshaping academic capitalism to meet development priorities: The case of public universities in Kenya', *Higher Education*, 61: 483–99.

Johnson, D. and Stewart, F. (2007), 'Education, ethnicity and conflict', *International Journal of Educational Development*, 27(3): 247–51.

Johnson, D. C. (2013), *Language Policy*, London: Palgrave Macmillan.

Jolly, R. (1991), 'Adjustment with a human face: A Unicef record and perspective on the 1980s', *World Development*, 19(12): 1807–21.

Jolly, R. (2014), *UNICEF (United Nations Children's Fund): Global Governance That Works*, London: Routledge.

Jones, P. (1988), *International Policies for Third World Education: UNESCO, Literacy and Development*, London and New York: Routledge.

Jones, P. (1992, reprinted 2012), *World Bank Financing of Education: Lending, Learning and Development*, London: Routledge.

Jones, P. (2006), *Education, Poverty and the World Bank*, Rotterdam: Sense.

Jones, P. W. (2006), 'Elusive mandate: UNICEF and educational development', *International Journal of Educational Development*, 26(6): 591–604.

Jones, P. W. (2007), *World Bank Financing of Education: Lending, Learning and Development*, Abingdon: Routledge.

Jones, P. W. and Coleman, D. (2005), *The United Nations and Education: Multilateralism and Globalisation*, New York: RoutledgeFalmer.

Jordan, C., Orozco, E. and Averett, A. (2001), *Emerging Issues in School, Family, & Community Connections*, Texas: National Center for Family and Community Connections with Schools.

Joshi, P. (2014), 'Parent decision-making when selecting schools: The case of Nepal', *Prospects* 44(3): 411–28. https://doi.org/10.1007/s11125-014-9319-9.

Jutting, J. P. and de Lauglesia, J. R. (2009), *Is Informal Normal? Towards More and Better Jobs in Developing Countries*, Paris: OECD.

Kadiwal, L. and Durrani, N. (2018), Youth negotiation of citizenship identities in Pakistan: Implications for global citizenship education in conflict-contexts, *British Journal of Educational Studies*, 66(4): 537–58.

Kadiwal, L. and Jain, M. (2020), Civics and citizenship education in India and Pakistan, *Handbook of Education Systems in South Asia*, 1–27.

Kahn, R. (2009), 'Critical pedagogy taking the Illich turn', *The International Journal of Illich Studies*, 1(1): 37–49.

Kaldor, M. (1999), *New and Old Wars: Organized Violence in a Global Era*, Stanford, California: Stanford University Press.

Kallaway, P. (1984), *Apartheid and Education: The Education of Black South Africans*, Johannesburg: Ravan Press.

Kalleberg, A. L. (2013), *Good Jobs, Bad Jobs: The Rise of Polarized and Precarious Employment Systems in the United States, 1970s to 2000s*, New York: Russell Sage Foundation.

Kamat, S., Spreen, C. and Jonnalagadda, I. (2016), 'Profiting from the poor: The emergence of multinational Edu-businesses in Hyderabad, India.' https://doi.org/10.1002/9781119082316.ch10.

Kamens, D. H. and Benavot, A. (2011), 'National, regional and international learning assessments: Trends among developing countries, 1960–2009', *Globalisation, Societies and Education*, 9(2): 285–300.

Kamens, D. H. and McNeely, C. L. (2010), 'Globalization and the growth of international educational testing and national assessment', *Comparative Education Review*, 54(1): 5–25.

Kane, L. (2001), *Popular Education and Social Change in Latin America*, London: Latin American Bureau.

Kapur, D. and Crowley, M. (2008), *Beyond the ABCs: Higher Education and Developing Countries*, Washington, DC: Center for Global Development.

Kartini, R. A. (1920), *Letters of a Javanese Princess*, New York: CPSIA.

Kattan, R. B. (2006), *Implementation of Free Basic Education Policy*, Washington, DC: World Bank.

Kattan, R. B. and Burnett, N. (2004), *User Fees in Primary Education*, Washington, DC: World Bank.

Keddie, A. (2012), 'Schooling and social justice through the lenses of Nancy Fraser', *Critical Studies in Education*, 53(3): 263–79.

Keddie, N. (2003), 'Secularism and its discontents', *Daedalus*, 132(3): 14–30.

Keep, E. (2007), 'The multiple paradoxes of state power in the English education and training system', in Clarke, L. and Winch, C. (eds), *Vocational Education: International Approaches, Developments and Systems*, London: Routledge, 161–75.

Kelly, G. (1982), 'Teachers and the transmission of state knowledge: A case study of Colonial Vietnam', in Altbach, P. et al. (eds), *Comparative Education*, New York: Macmillan, 176–94.

Kelly, G. (2000), *French Colonial Education: Essays on Vietnam and West Africa*, New York: AMS Press.

Kelly, M. J. (2000), *Planning for Education in the Context of HIV/AIDS*, Paris: UNESCO, International Institute for Educational Planning.

Kember, D. and Gow, L. (1994), 'Orientations to teaching and their effect on the quality of student learning', *The Journal of Higher Education*, 65(1): 58–74.

Kennedy, P. (2012), 'The knowledge economy. Education, work, and the struggle to (re-) regulate the distinction between "necessary" and "free" labour time', in Livingstone, D. W. and Guile, D. (eds), *The Knowledge Economy and Lifelong Learning: A Critical Reader*, Rotterdam: Sense, 161–81.

Khamis, A. (2009), 'Cultures of learning', in Sajoo, A. B. (ed.), *A Companion to the Muslim World*, London: I. B. Tauris, 237–62.

King, E. (2008), *The Role of Education in Violent Conflict and Peacebuilding in Rwanda*, Toronto: University of Toronto.

King, E. and Hill, A. (1993), *Women's Education in Developing Countries: Barriers, Benefits, and Policies*, Washington, DC: World Bank.

King, K. (1991), *Aid and Education in the Developing World: The Role of Donor Agencies in Educational Analysis*, Essex: Longman.

King, K. (2009), 'China's cooperation in education and training with Kenya: A comparative analysis', *UK Forum on International Education and Training Bi-annual Conference*, Oxford.

King, K. (2017), 'Lost in translation? The challenge of translating the global education goal and targets into global indicators', *Compare*, 47(6): 801–17.

King, K. and Martin, C. (2002), 'The vocational school fallacy revisited: Education, aspiration and work in Ghana 1959-2000', *International Journal of Educational Development*, 22: 5–26.

Kingdon, G. G. (1996), 'Private schooling in India: Size, nature and equity effects', *Economic and Political Weekly*, 31(5): 3306–14.

Kingdon, G. (2007), 'The Progress of School Education in India', *Oxford Review of Economic Policy*, 23(2): 168–95. https://doi.org/10.1093/icb/grm015.

Kingdon, G. (2017), *The Private Schooling Phenomenon in India: A Review*, Bonn: IZA Institute of Labor Economics.

Kingdon, G. and Muzammil, M. (2008), 'A political economy of education in India: The case of Uttar Pradesh', *Oxford Development Studies*, 37(2): 123–44. https://doi.org/10.1080/13600810902874626.

Kirby, D., Obasi, A. and Laris, B. A. (2006), 'The effectiveness of sex education and HIV education interventions in schools in developing countries', *WHO Technical Report Series*, 938: 103–50.

Kirk, J. and Winthrop, R. (2008), 'Home-based school teachers in Afghanistan: Teaching for Tarbia and student well-being', *Teaching and Teacher Education*, 24: 876–88.

Kirk, K. (2006), *Education in Emergencies: The Gender Implications*, Bangkok: UNESCO Advocacy Brief.

Klees, S. (2002), 'World Bank education policy: New rhetoric, old ideology', *International Journal of Educational Development*, 22: 451–74.

Klees, S. (2012), 'World Bank and education: Ideological premises and ideological conclusions', *International Perspectives on Education and Society*, 16: 151–71.

Klees, S. J., Samoff, J. and Stromquist, N. (2012), *The World Bank and Education: Critiques and Alternatives*, Rotterdam: Sense.

Klees, S. J., Ginsburg, M., Anwar, H., Robbins, M. B., Bloom, H., Busacca, C., Corwith, A. et al. (2020), 'The world bank's SABER: A critical analysis', *Comparative Education Review*, 64(1): 46–65.

Knight, J. and Weir, S. (2006), 'Production externalities of education: Evidence from Rural Ethiopia', *Journal of African Economies*, 16(1): 134–65.

Komatsu, H. and Rappleye, J. (2017), 'A new global policy regime founded on invalid statistics? Hanushek, Woessmann, PISA, and economic growth', *Comparative Education*, 53(2): 166–91.

Kothari, A. (2013), *That Common Ground? Education, Marriage and Family in Middle-Class, Urban India*, Institute of Education (University of London): Unpublished PhD thesis.

Kothari, A. (2020), 'Earth Vikalp Sangam: Proposal for a global tapestry of alternatives', *Globalizations*, 17(2): 245–49.

Kraay, A. (2019), 'The World Bank human capital index: A guide', *The World Bank Research Observer*, 34: 1–33.

Kreienkamp, J. and Pegram, T. (2020), 'Governing Complexity: Design Principles for the Governance of Complex Global Catastrophic Risks', *International Studies Review*.

Krueger, A. B. and Lindahl, M. (2001), 'Education for growth: Why and for whom?', *Journal of Economic Literature*, 39(4): 1101–36.

Kruss, G. (2001), 'Towards human rights in South African schools: An agenda for research and practice', *Race Ethnicity and Education*, 4(1): 45–62.

Kruss, G., McGrath, S., Petersen, I.-H. and Gastrow, M. (2015), 'Higher education and economic development: The importance of building technological capabilities', *International Journal of Educational Development*, 43: 22–31.

Kumar, K. (1994), 'Mohandas Karamchand Gandhi', in Morsy, Z. (ed.), *Thinkers on Education Volume 2*, Paris: UNESCO, 47–65.

Kumar, R. (2010), 'A development agenda for the G20', *Policy brief prepared for the European Think-Tank for Global Action (FRIDE)*. Available at http://www.fride.org/download/PB_G20_6_eng_A_development_agenda_for_the_G20.pdf.

Kwauk, C. (2020), *Roadblocks to Quality Education in a Time of Climate Change*, Brookings Brief, Available at https://www.brookings.edu/research/roadblocks-to-quality-education-in-a-time-of-climate-change/.

Kymlicka, W. (2001), *Politics in the Vernacular: Nationalism, Multiculturalism, and Citizenship*, Oxford: Oxford University Press.

Lansdown, R. (1995), *Child-to-Child: A Review of the Literature*, London: Child-to-Child Trust.

Lapavitsas, C. (2005), 'Mainstream economics in the neoliberal era', in Saad-Filho, A. and Johnston, D. (eds), *Neoliberalism: A Critical Reader*, London: Pluto Press, 30–40.

Lareau, A. (2011), *Unequal Childhoods: Class, Race, and Family Life*, California: University of California Press.

Lauder, H. and Brown, P. (2010), 'Economic globalization, skill formation and the consequences for higher education', in Apple, M. W., Ball, S. J. and Gandin, L. A. (eds), *The Routledge International Handbook of the Sociology of Education*, London: Routledge, 229–41.

Lauglo, J. (2010), 'Revisiting the vocational school fallacy: A tribute to Philip Foster', *Comparative Education*, 46(2): 223–35.

Lazendic, G., Walker, M. and Adams, R. (2019), 'Options for reporting against 4.1.1 when using national assessment programs', Presentation at 6th GAML Meeting on 27–28 of August 2019 in Yerevan, Armenia. Available at http://gaml.uis.unesco.org/sixth-meeting-of-the-global-alliance-to-monitor-learning/.

Le Grange, L. (2016), 'Decolonising the university curriculum', *South African Journal of Higher Education*, 30(2): 1–12.

Leach, F. (2003), *Practising Gender Analysis in Education*, Oxford: Oxfam.

Leathwood, C. and Francis, B. (2006), *Gender and Lifelong Learning: Critical Feminist Engagements*, London: Routledge.

Lebeau, Y. (2008), 'Universities and social transformation in sub-Saharan Africa: Global rhetoric and local contradictions', *Compare*, 38(2): 139–53.

Lee, J. H. (2020), 'Policy and ideology collide: an examination of affirmative action for students of Brazilian public higher education', *Race Ethnicity and Education*. https://doi.org/10.1080/13613324.2020.1753673.

Lee, J. and Sehoole, C. (2015), 'Regional, continental, and global mobility to an emerging economy: the case of South Africa', *Higher Education*, 70: 827–43.

Lerch, J. C., Garnett Russell, S. and Ramirez, F. O. (2017), 'Wither the nation-state? A comparative analysis of nationalism in textbooks', *Social Forces*, 96(1): 153–80.

Levine, K. (1982), 'Functional literacy: Fond illusions and false economies', *Harvard Educational Review*, 52(3): 249–66.

Levine, M. V. (2013), *The Skills Gap and Unemployment in Wisconsin. Separating Fact from Fiction*, Milwaukee: Centre for Economic Development, University of Wisconsin-Milwaukee.

Levy, D. C. (1986), *Higher Education and the State in Latin America: Private Challenges to Public Dominance*, Illinois: University of Chicago Press.

Levy, D. C. (2011), 'Public policy for private higher education: A global analysis', *Journal of Comparative Policy Analysis: Research and Practice*, 13(4): 383–96.

Levy, D. C. (2018), 'Global private higher education: An empirical profile of its size and geographical shape', *High Education*, 76: 701–15.

Levy, S. and Schady, N. (2013), 'Latin America's social policy challenge: Education, social insurance, redistribution', *The Journal of Economic Perspectives*, 27(2): 193–218.

Lewin, K. (2007), 'Diversity in convergence: Access to education for all', *Compare*, 37(5): 577–99.

Lim, C. M. S. (2019), 'Appendix 1: Postcolonial and decolonial: "Same same but different"', in Lim, C. M. S. (ed.), *Contextual Biblical Hermeneutics as Multicentric Dialogue*, Brill: Leiden, 193–94.

Lim, D. (1999), 'Quality assurance in higher education in developing countries', *Assessment & Evaluation in Higher Education*, 24(4): 379–90.

Lingard, B., Creagh, S. and Vass, G. (2012), Education policy as numbers: data categories and two Australian cases of misrecognition, *Journal of Education Policy*, 27(3): 315–33.

Little, A. and Leach, F. (1999), *Education, Cultures, and Economics: Dilemmas for Development*, London: Routledge.

Liu, J. and Steiner-Khamsi, G. (2020), 'Human capital index and the hidden penalty for non-participation in ILSAs', *International Journal of Educational Development*, 73. https://doi.org/10.1016/j.ijedudev.2019.102149.

Livingstone, D. W. (2009), *Education and Jobs: Exploring the Gaps*, Toronto: University of Toronto Press.

Livingstone, D. W. (2012), 'Debunking the "knowledge economy". The limits of human capital theory', in Livingstone, D. W. and Guile, D. (eds), *The Knowledge Economy and Lifelong Learning: A Critical Reader*, Rotterdam: Sense, 85–116.

Livingstone, D. W. and Guile, D. (2012), *The Knowledge Economy and Lifelong Learning: A Critical Reader*, Rotterdam: Sense.

Livingston, D. W., Mirchandani, K. and Sawchuk, P. H. (eds) (2008), *The Future of Lifelong Learning and Work: Critical Perspectives*, Rotterdam: SensePublishers.

Lloyd, C. B. (2005), *Growing Up Global: The Changing Transitions to Adulthood in Developing Countries*, Washington, DC: National Academy Press.

Lloyd, C. B., Mensch, B. S. and Mensch, B. (2008), 'Marriage and childbirth as factors in dropping out from school: An analysis of DHS data from Sub-Saharan Africa', *Population Studies*, 62(1): 1–13.

LMTF. (2013), *Toward Universal Learning: Recommendations from the Learning Metrics Task Force*, Washington, DC: UNESCO Institute for Statistics and Center for Universal Education at the Brookings Institution.

Locatelli, R. (2017), Education as a public and common good: Revisiting the role of the State in a context of growing marketization, Unpublished PhD thesis, University of Bergamo.

Lockheed, M. E. and Verspoor, A. M. (1991), *Improving Primary Education in Developing Countries*, Washington, DC: World Bank.

London, N. A. (2003), *Pathways to Educational Transformation and Development: Policies, Plans, Lessons*, Toronto: Canadian Scholars' Press.

Longfield, D. and Tooley, J. (2013) *A Survey of Schools in Juba, South Sudan*. Newcastle: E. G. West Centre. Available at http://egwestcentre.files

Loomba, A. (2005), *Colonialism-Postcolonialism*, London: Routledge.

Lopes Cardozo, M. T. A. (2008), 'Sri Lanka: In peace or in pieces? A critical approach to peace education in Sri Lanka', *Research in Comparative and International Education*, 3(1): 19–35.

Lopes Cardozo, M. T. A. (2009), 'Teachers in a Bolivian context of conflict: Potential actors for or against change?', *Globalisation, Societies & Education*, 7(4): 409–32.

Lopes Cardozo, M. T. A. (2011), *Future Teachers and Social Change in Bolivia – Between Decolonisation and Demonstration, Delft*, Netherlands: Eburon.

Lopes Cardozo, M. T. A. (2012), 'Transforming pre-service teacher education in Bolivia: Form indigenous denial to decolonisation?', *Compare*, 42(5): 751–72.

Lopes Cardozo, M. T. A. (2012), 'Decolonising Bolivian education: Ideology versus reality', in Griffiths, T. G. and Millei, Z. (eds), *Logics of Socialist Education: Engaging with Crisis, Insecurity and Uncertainty*, Dordrecht: Springer, 21–35.

Lopes Cardozo, M.T.A. and Hoeks, C.M.Q. (2014), 'Losing ground: A critical analysis of teachers' agency for peacebuilding education in Sri Lanka', *Journal of Peace Education*, 12(1): 56–73.

Lopes Cardozo, M. T. A. and Shah, R. (2013), '*The Right to Education in Situations of Conflict-Affected and Fragile States – A Post-2015 Priority?*', NORRAG blog online publication. Available at http://norrag.wordpress.com/2013/09/16/the-right-to-education-in-situations-of-conflict-affected-and-fragile-states-a-post-2015-priority/ [accessed 2 December 2013].

Lopez, L. E. (2020), 'What is *Educacion Intercultural Bilingue* in Latin America nowadays: Results and challenges', *Journal of Multilingual and Multicultural Development*, DOI: 10.1080/01434632.2020.1827646.

López, L. E. and Sichra, I. (2017), 'Indigenous bilingual education in Latin America', in García, O., Lin, A. and May, S. (eds), *Bilingual and Multilingual Education*, Encyclopedia of Language and Education 3rd edn, Cham: Springer.

Lotz-Sisitka, H., Rosenberg, E. and Ramsarup, P. (2020), 'Environment and sustainability education research as policy engagement: (Re-) invigorating "politics as potential" in South Africa', *Environmental Education Research*, 1–29, DOI: 10.1080/13504622.2020.1759511.

Loyalka, P., Popova, A., Li, G. and Shi, Z. (2019), Does teacher training actually work? Evidence from a large-scale randomized evaluation of a national teacher training program, *American Economic Journal: Applied Economics*, 11(3): 128–54.

Lubienski, C. (2006), 'School diversification in second-best education markets: International evidence and conflicting theories of change', *Education Policy*, 20(2): 323–44. https://doi.org/10.1177/0895904805284049.

Lucas, R. E. (1988), 'On the mechanics of development', *Journal of Monetary Economics*, 22(1): 3–42.

Lugones, M. (2010), 'Toward a decolonial feminism', *Hypatia*, 25(4): 742–59.

Lukens-Bull, R. (2000), 'Teaching morality: Javanese education in a globalizing era', *Journal of Arabic and Islamic Studies*, 3: 26–47.

Lulat, Y. G. M. (2005), *A History of African Higher Education from Antiquity to the Present: A Critical Synthesis*, Connecticut: Praeger Publishers.

Luong, M. P. and Nieke, W. (2014), 'Conceptualizing quality education from the paradigm of recognition', *Journal of Education and Practice*, 5(18).

Luykx, A. (1999), *The Citizen Factory: Schooling and Cultural Production in Bolivia*, Albany: SUNY Press.

Macedo, S. (1995), 'Liberal civic education and religious fundamentalism: The case of God vs. John Rawls?', *Ethics*, 105(3): 468–96.

Machel, G. (1996), *Promotion and Protection of the Rights of Children: Impact of Armed Conflict on Children: Report by the Expert of the Secretary-General, Ms. Graca Machel, Submitted Persuant to General Assembly Resolution 48/157*, New York: United Nations General Assembly.

MacIntyre, A. (1984), *After Virtue: A Study in Moral Theory*, Notre Dame, IN: University of Notre Dame Press.

MacKinnon, D. and Derickson, K. D. (2013), 'From resilience to resourcefulness: A critique of resilience policy and activism', *Progress in Human Geography*, 37(2): 253–70. https://doi.org/10.1177/0309132512454775.

MacMullen, I. (2007), *Faith in Schools? Autonomy, Citizenship, and Religious Education in the Liberal State*, Princeton, NJ: Princeton University Press.

Macpherson, I., Robertson, S. and Walford, G. (2014), *Education, Privatisation and Social Justice: Case Studies from Africa, South Asia and South East Asia*, Oxford: Symposium.

Maddox, B. and Esposito, L. (2011), 'Sufficiency re-examined: A capabilities perspective on the assessment of functional adult literacy', *Journal of Development Studies*, 47(9): 1315–31.

Madeira, A. I. and Correia, L. G. (2019), 'Colonial education and anticolonial struggles', in Rury, J. and Tamura, E. (eds), *Handbook of the History of Education*, Oxford: Oxford University Press, 413–26.

Maeda, M. (2009), 'Education and cultural hybridity: What cultural values should be imparted to students in Kenya?', *Compare*, 39(3): 335–48.

Maeda, M. (2012), 'Financing corruption? Aid money and teachers' practices in Cambodia', *Norrag News*, 47: 74–76.

Maldonado-Torres, N. (2007), 'On the coloniality of Being', *Cultural Studies*, 21(2–3): 240–70. https://doi.org/10.1080/09502380601162548.

Maldonado-Torres, N. (2016), 'Colonialism, Neocolonial, Internal Colonialism, the Postcolonial, Coloniality, and Decoloniality', in Martínez-San Miguel, Y., Sifuentes-Jáuregui, B. and Belausteguigoitia, M., (eds.), *Critical Terms in Caribbean and Latin American Thought*, 67–78. https://doi.org/10.1057/9781137547903_6.

Mamdani, M. (2004), *Good Muslim, Bad Muslim: America, the Cold War, and the Roots of Terror*, New York: Pantheon Books.

Mamdani, M. (2007), *Scholars in the Marketplace: The Dilemmas of Neo-Liberal Reform at Makerere University, 1989–2005*, Dakar: CODESRIA.

Mankiw, N. G., Romer, D. and Weil, D. N. (1992), 'A contribution to the empirics of economic growth', *Quarterly Journal of Economics*, 107(2): 407–37.

Manor, J. (1999), *The Political Economy of Democratic Decentralization*, Washington, DC: World Bank.

Mansuri, G. and Rao, V. (2004), 'Community-based and – driven development: A critical review', *The World Bank Research Observer*, 19(1): 1–39.

Marginson, S. (2011), 'Higher education and public good', *Higher Education Quarterly*, 65(4): 411–33.

Marginson, S. (2016), 'The worldwide trend to high participation higher education: Dynamics of social stratification in inclusive systems', *Higher Education*, 72: 413–34.

Mark, M. (2013), 'Boko Haram leaders call for more school attacks after dorm killings', *Guardian*, 14 July 2013. Available at http://www.guardian.co.uk/world/2013/jul/14/boko-haram-school-attacks-nigeria [accessed 18 July 2013].

Marope, P. T. M., Chakroun, B. and Holmes, K. P. (2015), *Unleashing the Potential: Transforming Technical and Vocational Education and Training*, Paris: United Nations Educational, Scientific and Cultural Organization.

Marsh, M., McCook, V. S. and Fulu, E. (Forthcoming, 2020), Altruism, Saving Face and Maintaining the Status Quo, *World Development*.

Marshall, K. (2010), 'Development, religion, and women's roles in contemporary societies', *Review of Faith and International Affairs*, 8(4): 35–42.

Marshall, K. and Van Saanan, M. (2007), *Development and Faith: Where Mind, Heart, and Soul Work Together*, Washington, DC: International Bank for Reconstruction and Development, World Bank.

Martin, M. J. and Henry, A. (2012), 'Building rural communities through school-based agriculture programs', *Journal of Agricultural Education*, 53(2): 110–23.

Martin, T. (2003), 'Divergent ontologies with converging conclusions: A case study comparison of comparative methodologies', *Comparative Education*, 39(1): 105–17.

Martín-Díaz, E. (2017), 'Are universities ready for interculturality? The case of the Intercultural University "Amawtay Wasi" (Ecuador)', *Journal of Latin American Cultural Studies*, 26: 73–90.

Martinussen, J. (1997), *Society, State and Market: A Guide to Competing Theories of Development*, London: Zed.

Marzagora, S. (2016), *Alterity, Coloniality and Modernity in Ethiopian Political Thought: The First Three Generations of 20th Century Amharic-language Intellectuals*, Doctoral dissertation, SOAS, University of London, Unpublished PhD.

Masino, S. and Niño-Zarazúa, M. (2016), 'What works to improve the quality of student learning in developing countries?', *International Journal of Educational Development*, 48: 53–65.

Mason, C. L. (ed.) (2018), *Routledge Handbook of Queer Development Studies*, Abingdon: Routledge.

Materu, P. (2007), *Higher Education Quality Assurance in Sub-Saharan Africa: Status, Challenges, Opportunities and Promising Practices*, Washington, DC: World Bank.

Maxwell, S. (2005), 'The Washington consensus is dead! Long live the meta-narrative', *Working Paper WP/243*. Available at http://www.odi.org.uk/publications/working_papers/wp243.pdf [accessed 22 June 2007].

May, S. (2001), *Language and Minority Rights: Ethnicity, Nationalism and the Politics of Language*, London: Longman.

May, S. and Sleeter, C. E. (2010), *Critical Multiculturalism: Theory and Praxis*, London: Routledge.

Mayo, P. (2009), 'Flying below the radar? Critical approaches to adult education', in Apple, M. W., Au, W. and Gandin, L. (eds), *The Routledge International Handbook of Critical Education*, New York: Routledge, 269–80.

Mazrui, A. A. (1975), 'The African university as a multinational corporation: Problems of penetration and dependency', *Harvard Educational Review*, 45(2): 191–210.

Mazrui, A. M. and Mazrui, A. A. (1996), 'A tale of two Englishes: The imperial language in post-colonial Kenya and Uganda', in Fishman, J. A., Conrad, A. W. and Rubal-Lopez, A. (eds), *Post-Imperial English: Status Change in Former British and American Colonies*, Berlin: Mouton de Gruyter, 271–302.

Mbembe, A. (2001), *On the Postcolony*, California: University of California Press.

Mbembe, A. (2016), 'Decolonizing the university: New directions', *Arts and Humanities in Higher Education*, 15(1): 29–45.

McCall, L. (2005), 'The complexity of intersectionality', *Signs*, 30(3): 1771–800.

McCarty, T. (2012), 'Critical ethnography and indigenous language survival, new directions in language policy research and praxis', in McCarty, T. (ed.), *Ethnography and Language Policy*, London: Routledge, 31–52.

McCarty Romero-Little, M. E. and Zepeda, O. (2006), 'Native American youth discourses on language shift and retention: Ideological cross-currents and their implications for language planning', *International Journal of Bilingual Education and Bilingualism*, 9(5): 659–77.

McClelland, D. C. (1961), *The Achieving Society*, New York: Van Nostrand.

McCowan, T. (2004), 'The growth of private higher education in Brazil: Implications for equity and quality', *Journal of Education Policy*, 19(4): 453–72.

McCowan, T. (2006), 'Approaching the political in citizenship education: The perspectives of Paulo Freire and Bernard Crick', *Educate*, 6(1): 57–70.

McCowan, T. (2007), 'Expansion without equity: An analysis of current policy on access to higher education in Brazil', *Higher Education*, 53(5): 579–98.

McCowan, T. (2009), *Rethinking Citizenship Education: A Curriculum for Participatory Democracy*, New York: Continuum.

McCowan, T. (2012), 'Is there a universal right to higher education?', *British Journal of Educational Studies*, 60(2): 111–28.

McCowan, T. (2013), *Education as a Human Right: Principles for a Universal Entitlement to Learning*, London: Bloomsbury.

McCowan, T. (2016), 'Three dimensions of equity of access to higher education', *Compare: A Journal of Comparative and International Education*, 46(4): 645–65.

McCowan, T. (2017), 'Higher education, unbundling and the end of the university as we know it', *Oxford Review of Education*, 43(6): 733–48.

McCowan, T. (2019), *Higher Education for and beyond the Sustainable Development Goals*, London: Palgrave Macmillan.

McCowan, T. (2020), *The Impact of Universities on Climate Change: A Theoretical Framework*, Transforming Universities for a Changing Climate, Working Paper Series No.1. Available at https://www.climate-uni.com/resources.

McCowan, T. and Bertolin, J. (2020), *Inequalities in Higher Education Access and Completion in Brazil*, United Nations Research Institute for Social Development (UNRISD) Working Paper. Available at https://www.unrisd.org/unrisd/website/document.nsf/(httpPublications)/7A5AAF82DFF3CCCC8025854C004436AE?OpenDocument.

McCowan, T. and Unterhalter, E. (2013), 'Education, citizenship and deliberative democracy: Sen's capability approach', in Hedke, R. and Zimenkova, T. (eds), *Education for Civic and Political Participation: A Critical Approach*, London: Routledge, 135–54.

McCowan, T. and Unterhalter, E. (eds) (2015), *Education and International Development: An Introduction*, London & New York: Bloomsbury Academic.

McGrath, S. (2001), 'Research in a cold climate: Towards a political economy of British international and comparative education', *International Journal of Educational Research*, 21: 391–400.

McGrath, S. (2007), 'The role of education in development: An educationalist's response to some recent work in development economics', *Comparative Education*, 46(2): 237–53.

McGrath, S. (2012), 'Vocational learning for development: A policy in need of a theory?', *International Journal for Educational Development*, 32(5): 623–32.

McGrath, S. (2018), *Education and Development*, London: Routledge.

McGrath, S. and Gu, Q. (2016), *Routledge Handbook of International Education and Development*, London: Routledge.

McGregor, A. (2009), 'New possibilities? Shifts in post-development theory and practice', *Geography Compass*, 3(5): 1688–702.

McIvor, O. and McCarty, T. L. (2017), 'Indigenous Bilingual and revitalization-immersion education in Canada and the USA', in García, O., Lin, A. and May, S. (eds), *Bilingual and Multilingual Education. Encyclopedia of Language and Education*, 3rd edn, Cham: Springer, 421–438, 1–17.

McKay, Veronica (2018), 'Literacy, lifelong learning and sustainable development', *Australian Journal of Adult Learning*, 58(3): November 2018.

McKinsey & Co. (2010), *Closing the Talent Gap: Attracting and Retaining Top Third Graduates to a Career in Teaching*, London: McKinsey & Company.

McLean Hilker, L. (2011), 'The role of education in driving conflict and building peace: The case of Rwanda', *Prospects*, 41(2): 267–82.

McLean, M. (1983), 'Educational dependency: A critique', *Compare*, 13(1): 25–42.

McMahon, W. (2009), *Higher Learning, Greater Good: The Private and Social Benefits of Higher Education*, Baltimore: The Johns Hopkins University Press.

McMahon, W. (2010), 'The external benefits of education', in Brewer, D. J. and McEwan, P. J. (eds), *Economics of Education*, Amsterdam: Elsevier, 68–79.

Meadows, D. H., Meadows, D. L., Randers, J. and Behrens, W. W. (1972), *The Limits to Growth*, New York: Universe Books.

Meeks, G. (2018), 'On Sen on the capability of capabilities', in Comim, F., Fennell, S. and Anand, P. (eds), *New Frontiers of the Capability Approach*, Cambridge: Cambridge University Press, 12–52.

Memon, M. (2013), *Education Conference on Teacher Recruitment, Preparation, and Policy, August 20 –21*, Karachi: USAID Teacher Education Project.

Menashy, F. (2019), *International Aid to Education: Power Dynamics in an Era of Partnership*, New York: Teachers College Press.

Menashy, F. and Manion, C. (2016), 'The historical evolution and current challenges of the United Nations and global education policy-making', in Mundy, K., Green, A., Lingard, B. and Verger, T. (eds), *Global Policy and Policy-Making in Education*, West Sussex: Wiley Blackwell, 319–34.

Menashy, F. and Shields, R. (2017), 'Unequal partners? Networks, centrality, and aid to international education', *Comparative Education*, 53(4): 495–517.

Menezes De Souza, L. M. (2009), 'The cultural logics of indigenous
perspectivism and predation', *Paper Presented in the Literacy Inequalities
Conference*, University of East Anglia.

Meral, Ziya (2015), *Compulsory Religious Education in Turkey: A Survey
and Assessment of Textbooks*, United States Commission on International
Religious Freedom. https://www.uscirf.gov/sites/default/files/
TurkeyTextbookReport.pdf.

Meyer, H. D. (2017), 'The limits of measurement: Misplaced precision,
phronesis, and other Aristotelian cautions for the makers of PISA, APPR,
etc.', *Comparative Education*, 53(1): 17–34.

Meyer, J. W. (1977), 'The effects of education as an institution', *The American
Journal of Sociology*, 83(1): 55–77.

Meyer, J. W., Boli, J., Thomas, G. M. and Ramirez, F. O. (1997), 'World society
and the nation-state', *American Journal of Sociology*, 103(1): 144–81.

Meyer, J. W., Ramirez, F. O. and Soysal, Y. N. (1992), 'World expansion of mass
education, 1870–1980', *Sociology of Education*, 65(2): 128–49.

Michelsen, G. and Wells, P. J. (2017), *A Decade of Progress for Education
in Sustainable Development*, UNESCO, https://unesdoc.unesco.org/
ark:/48223/pf0000252319?posInSet=1&queryId=c5014f6a-4b30-4694-aabe-
151abc2bb275.

Micklethwait, J. and Wooldridge, A. (2009), *God Is Back: How the Global
Revival of Faith Is Changing the World*, New York: The Penguin Press.

Mignolo, W. (2002), 'The geopolitics of knowledge and the colonial difference',
The South Atlantic Quarterly, 101(1): 57–96.

Mignolo, W. (2007), 'Delinking: The rhetoric of modernity, the logic of
coloniality and the grammar of de-coloniality', *Cultural Studies*, 21(2):
449–514.

Mignolo, W. (2011), *The Darker Side of Western Modernity: Global Futures,
Decolonial Options*, Durham: Duke University Press.

Milan, S. and Treré, E., 2019. Big data from the South (s): Beyond data
universalism. *Television & New Media*, 20(4): 319–35.

Milanovic, B. (2019), *Capitalism, Alone: The Future of the System That Rules the
World*, Cambridge, MA: Harvard University Press.

Miller-Adams, M. (1999), *The World Bank: New Agendas in a Changing World*,
London, New York: Routledge.

Milligan, L. O., Tikly, L., Williams, T., Vianney, J. M. and Uworwabayeho,
A. (2017), 'Textbook availability and use in Rwandan basic education: A
mixed-methods study', *International Journal of Educational Development*,
54: 1–7. https://doi.org/10.1016/j.ijedudev.2017.01.008.

Mincer, J. (1974), *Schooling, Experience, and Earnings*, New York: Columbia
University Press.

Mingat, A. and Tan, J. P. (1996), 'The full social returns to education: Estimates based on countries' economic growth performance', *Human Capital Development and Operations Policy Working Papers*, No. HCD 73.

Minow, M. (2002), 'Education for co-existence', *Arizona Law Review*, 44: 1.

Mkandawire, P. T. (2005), 'African intellectuals and nationalism', in Mkandawire, P. T. (ed.), *African Intellectuals: Rethinking Politics, Language, Gender and Development*, Dakar, Senegal and London: CODESRIA Books with Zed Books, 10–55.

Mkwananzi, F. (2019), *Higher Education, Youth and Migration in Contexts of Disadvantage: Understanding Aspirations and Capabilities*, London: Palgrave McMillan.

Mncube, V. (2009), 'The perceptions of parents of their role in the democratic governance of schools in South Africa: Are they on board?', *South African Journal of Education*, 29: 83–103.

Mobini-Kesheh, N. (1999), *The Hadrami Awakening: Community and Identity in the Netherlands East Indies, 1900–1942*, New York: SEAP.

Mohamedbhai, G. (2008), *The Effects of Massification on Higher Education in Africa*, Accra: Association of African Universities.

Mohanty, S. (2020), From communal violence to lockdown hunger – Emergency responses by civil society networks, Delhi, India, *Interface: A Journal for and about Social Movements*, 12(1): 47–52.

Molina, S. C. (2013), 'Family, school, community engagement, and partnerships: An area of continued inquiry and growth', *Teaching Education*, 24(2): 235–8.

Molyneux, M. (2006), 'Mothers at the service of the new poverty agenda: Progresa/oportunidades, Mexico's conditional transfer programme', *Social Policy & Administration*, 40(4): 425–49.

Montoya, S. (2019), Reporting indicator 4.1.1. Presentation at 6th GAML Meeting on 27-28 of August 2019 in Yerevan, Armenia. Available at http://gaml.uis.unesco.org/sixth-meeting-of-the-global-alliance-to-monitor-learning/.

Montoya, S. and Senapaty, H. (2019), 'Linking data to get results: India shows how countries can use their national assessments for global reporting', World Education Blog. Available at https://gemreportunesco.wordpress.com/2019/11/18/linking-data-to-get-results-india-shows-how-countries-can-use-their-national-assessments-for-global-reporting/.

Morley, L. (2011), 'Sex, grades and power in higher education in Ghana and Tanzania', *Cambridge Journal of Education*, 41(1): 101–15.

Morley, L. and Lugg, R. (2009), 'Mapping meritocracy: Intersecting gender, poverty and higher educational opportunity structures', *Higher Education Policy*, 22(1): 37–60.

Morrell, R., Epstein, D., Unterhalter, E., Bhana, D. and Moletsane, R. (2009), *Towards Gender Equality: South African Schools During the HIV and AIDS Epidemic*, Scottsville: University of KwaZulu-Natal Press.

Morrison, K. (2009), *Causation in Educational Research*, London: Routledge.

Mourshed, M., Chijioke, C. and Barber, M. (2010), *How the World's Most Improved Systems Keep Getting Better*, London: McKinsey & Company.

Mourshed, M., Farrell, D. and Barton, D. (2013), *Education to Employment: Designing a System That Works*, London: McKinsey Center for Government/ McKinsey & Company.

Mpofu, B. and Ndlovu-Gatsheni, S. (eds) (2020), *The Dynamics of Changing Higher Education in the Global South*, Cambridge: Cambridge Scholars Publishing.

Mtawa, N. (2019), *Human Development and Community Engagement through Service-Learning: The Capability Approach and Common Good in Higher Education*, London: Palgrave Macmillan.

Mukherjee, A. (2014), *Targeting Education Financing on the Marginalized: Lessons from Implementation of Sarva Shiksha Abhiyan and Right to Education in India. Background paper prepared for the Education for All Global Monitoring Report 2013/4*, Paris: UNESCO.

Mukherjee, H. B. (2020), *Education for Fullness: A Study of the Educational Thought and Experiment of Rabindranath Tagore*, New Delhi: Routledge India.

Mulkeen, A. and Chen, D. (2008), *Teachers for Rural Schools: Experiences in Lesotho, Malawi, Mozambique, Tanzania and Uganda*, Washington, DC: World Bank.

Mullen, A. (2010), *Degrees of Inequality: Culture, Class, and Gender in American Higher Education*, Maryland: Johns Hopkins University Press.

Müller, D. K., Ringer, F. K. and Simon, B. (1987), *The Rise of the Modern Educational System: Structural Change and Social Reproduction 1870–1920*, Cambridge: Cambridge University Press.

Mullis, I. V. S., Martin, M. O., Foy, P. and Hooper, M. (2016), *TIMSS 2015 International Results in Mathematics*, Lynch School of Education, Boston College: TIMMS & PIRLS International Study Center.

Mundy, K. (1998), 'Educational multilateralism and world (dis)order', *Comparative Education Review*, 42(4): 448–78.

Mundy, K. (1999), 'Educational multilateralism in a changing world order: UNESCO and the limits of the possible', *International Journal of Educational Development*, 19(1): 27–52.

Mundy, K. (1999), 'UNESCO and the limits of the possible', *International Journal of Educational Development*, 19(1): 27–52.

Mundy, K. (2002), 'Education in a reformed World Bank', *International Journal of Educational Development*, 22(5): 483–508.

Mundy, K. (2006), 'Education for all in the new development compact', *International Review of Education*, 52: 23–48.

Mundy, K. (2007), 'Education for all: Paradoxes and prospects of a global promise', *International Perspectives on Education and Society*, 8: 1–30.

Mundy, K. (2008), *Civil Society and Its Role in the Achievement and Governance of 'Education for All.' Background Paper Prepared for the Education for All Global Monitoring Report 2009*, Paris: UNESCO.

Mundy, K. (2010), 'Education for all and the global governors', in Avant, D., Finnemore, M. and Sell, S. (eds), *Who Governs the Globe?*, Cambridge: Cambridge University Press, 333–56.

Mundy, K. (2012), 'The global campaign for education and the realization of "education for all"', in Novelli, M. and Verger, A. (eds), *Campaigning for 'Education for All': Histories, Strategies and Outcomes of Transnational Social Movements in Education*, Rotterdam: Sense, 17–30.

Mundy, K. (2016), 'Leaning in' on Education for All. CIES Presidential Address, *Comparative Education Review*, 60(1): 1–26.

Mundy, K. and Menashy, F. (2014), 'Investing in private education for poverty alleviation: The case of the World Bank's International Finance Corporation', *The International Journal of Educational Development*, 35(1–2): 16–24.

Mundy, K. and Murphy, L. (2001), 'Transnational advocacy, global civil society? Emerging evidence from the field of education', *Comparative Education Review*, 45(1): 85–126.

Mundy, K., Haggerty, M., Cherry, S., Maclure, R. and Sivasubramaniam, M. (2007), 'Basic education, civil society participation and the new aid architecture: Lessons from Burkina Faso, Kenya, Mali and Tanzania', in Mundy, K. (ed.), *Haki Elimu Working Paper 07.3*, Dar es Salaam: Haki Elimu.

Mungazi, D. A. (1992), *Colonial Education for Africans: George Stark's Policy in Zimbabwe*, New York, London: Praeger.

Muralidharan, K. and Kremer, M. (2006), 'Public and private schools in rural India.' DOI: 10.7551/mitpress/9780262033763.003.0005.

Murgatroyd, S. (2010), '"Wicked Problems" and the work of the school', *European Journal of Education*, 45(2, Part 1): 259–79.

Murgatroyd, S. and Sahlberg, P. (2016), 'The two solitudes of educational policy and the challenge of development', *Journal of Learning for Development*, 3(3): 9–21.

Murphy, R. (1988), *Social Closure: The Theory of Monopolization and Exclusion*, Oxford: Clarendon Press.

Murphy-Graham, E. and Lloyd, C. (2016), 'Empowering adolescent girls in developing countries: The potential role of education', *Policy Futures in Education*, 14(5): 556–77.

Mwiria, K. (1990), 'Kenya's harambee secondary school movement: The contradictions of public policy', *Comparative Education Review*, 34(3): 350–68.

Mwiria, K. (1991), 'Education for subordination: African education in colonial Kenya', *History of Education*, 20(3): 261–73.

Naidoo, R. (1998), 'Levelling or playing the field? The politics of access to university education in South Africa', *Cambridge Journal of Education*, 28(3): 369–83.

Nakata, N. M., Nakata, V., Keech, S. and Bolt, R. (2012), 'Decolonial goals and pedagogies for Indigenous studies', in *Decolonization: Indigeneity, Education & Society*, Vol. 1: 334–49.

Nambissan, G. B. and Ball, S. J. (2010), 'Advocacy networks, choice and private schooling of the poor in India', *Global Networks*, 10(3): 324–43.

Napier, D. B. (2014), 'Qualities of education: A diversity of perspectives and cases, worldwide', in Napier, D. B. (ed.), *Qualities of Education in a Globalised World*, Rotterdam: Sense Publishers, 1–18.

National Institute for Educational Policy Research (2011), 'A survey of disaster-prevention facilities in school'. Available at http://www.nier.go.jp/shisetsu/pdf/bousaikinou2011.pdf [accessed 12 September 2013].

National Secular Society (2013), 'Religious education briefing paper'. Available at http://www.secularism.org.uk/uploads/religious-education-briefing-paper.pdf [accessed 30 September 2013].

Ndebele, P., Wassenaar, D., Benatar, S., Fleischer, T., Kruger, M., Adebamowo, C., Kass, N., Hyder, A. A. and Meslin, E. M. (2014). 'Research ethics capacity building in Sub-Saharan Africa: A review of NIH Fogarty-funded programs 2000–2012', *Journal of Empirical Research on Human Research Ethics*, 9(2): 24–40.

Ndlovu, M. (2008), 'Coloniality of knowledge and the challenge of creating African futures', *Ufahamu*, 40(2): 95–112.

Ndlovu-Gatsheni, S. (2013a), 'Coloniality of power in postcolonial Africa: Myths of decolonization', Dakar: CODESRIA.

Ndlovu-Gatsheni, S. (2013b), 'Why decoloniality in the 21st century?', *The Thinker*, 48: 10–15.

Ndlovu-Gatsheni, S. (2015), 'Decoloniality as the future of Africa', *History Compass*, 13(10): 485–96.

Newman, J. H. (1947 [1852]), *The Idea of the University: Defined and Illustrated*, London: Longmans, Green.

Ng'ethe, N., Subotzky, G. and Afeti, G. and World Bank (2008), *Differentiation and Articulation in Tertiary Education Systems: A Study of Twelve African Countries*, Washington, DC: World Bank.

Ngware, M., Abuya, B., Admassur, K., Mutisya, M., Musyoka, P. and
     Oketch, M. (2013), 'Quality and access to education in urban informal
     settlements in Kenya,' October. Available at http://aphrc.org/wp-content/
     uploads/2013/11/ERP-III-Report.pdf.

Nicolai, S., Hodgkin, M., Mowjee, T. and Wales, J. (2019), *White Paper:
     Education and Humanitarian-Development Coherence*, London: Overseas
     Development Institute (ODI).

Nicolai, S. and Hine, S. (2015), *Investment for Education in Emergencies: A
     Review of Evidence*, London: Overseas Development Institute (ODI).

Nieto, D. (2018), 'Citizenship education discourses in Latin America:
     Multilateral institutions and the decolonial challenge', *Compare*, 48(3):
     432–50.

Nissen, C. J. (2005), *Living Under the Rule of Corruption: An Analysis of
     Everyday Forms of Corrupt Practices in Cambodia*, Phnom Penh: Centre for
     Social Development.

Nixon, J. (2011), *Higher Education and the Public Good: Imagining the
     University*, London, New York: Continuum.

Nkomo, M. O. (1990), *Pedagogy of Domination: Toward a Democratic
     Education in South Africa*, New Jersey: Africa World Press.

Noah, H. J. and Eckstein, M. A. (1988), 'Dependency theory in comparative
     education: Twelve lessons from the literature', in Schriewer, J. and Holmes,
     B. (eds), *Theories and Methods in Comparative Education*, Frankfurt am
     Main: Peter Lang, 165–92.

Noel, A. (2005), 'The new politics of global poverty', *Paper Presented at the
     Social Justice in a Changing World: Conference Graduate School of Social
     Sciences*, 10–12 March, University of Bremen, Germany.

Nordveit, B. H. (2011), 'An emerging donor in education and development:
     A case study of China in Cameroon', *International Journal of Educational
     Development*, 31(2): 99–108.

Norris, P. and Inglehart, R. (2019), *Cultural Backlash and the Rise of Populism:
     Trump, Brexit, and Authoritarian Populism*, Cambridge, UK: Cambridge
     University Press.

North, A. (2010), 'MDG 3 and the negotiation of gender in international
     education organisations', *Compare*, 40(4): 425–40.

Norton-Taylor, R. (2012), 'Russia overtakes UK and France in global arms
     spending league table', *Guardian*, 17 April 2012. Available at http://www.
     guardian.co.uk/world/2012/apr/17/russia-vertakes-uk-france-arms
     [accessed 15 May 2014].

Novelli, M. (2010), 'The new geopolitics of educational aid: From cold wars to
     holy wars?', *International Journal of Educational Development*, 30: 453–59.

Novelli, M. (2011), 'Are we all soldiers now? The dangers of the securitization of education and conflict', in Mundy, K. and Dryden-Peterson, S. (eds), *Educating Children in Conflict Zones: Research, Policy, and Practice for Systemic Change: A Tribute to Jackie Kirk (International Perspectives on Education Reform Series)*, New York: Teachers College Press, 49–65.

Novelli, M. (2013), *The Merging of Security and Development in the Education Sector: Discourses and Effects*, Educacao e Sociedade: revista de ciencia da educacao, 34(123): 345–70. ISSN 0101-7330.

Novelli, M. (2013), 'The new geopolitics of educational aid', in Majhanovich, S. and Macleans, A. (eds), *Economics, Aid and Education Implications for Development*, Geo-JaJa: Sense, 29–46.

Novelli, M. and Lopes Cardozo, M. T. A. (2008), 'Conflict, education and the global south: New critical directions', *International Journal of Educational Development*, 28: 473–88.

Novelli, M. and Lopes Cardozo, M. T. A. (2012), 'Globalizing educational interventions in zones of conflict: The role of Dutch aid to education and conflict', in Verger, A., Novelli, M. and Kosar Altinyelken, H. (eds), *Global Education Policy and International Development: New Agendas, Issues and Policies*, London: Continuum, 224–43.

Novelli, M. and Smith, A. (2011), *The Role of Education in Peacebuilding: Methodological Framework for Three Country Case Studies*, New York: United Nations Children's Fund (UNICEF).

Novelli, M., Lopez Cardoso, M. T. A. and Smith, A. (2017) 'The 4Rs framework: Analyzing education's contribution to sustainable peacebuilding with social justice in conflict-affected contexts', *Journal on Education in Emergencies*, 3(1): 14–43. ISSN 2518-6833.

Novoa, A. (2002), 'Ways of thinking about education in Europe', in Novoa, A. and Lawn, M. (eds), *Fabricating Europe: The Formation of an Education Space*, Dordrecht: Kluwer Academic Publishers, 131–55.

Nungu, M. (2010), 'Universalizing access to primary education in Kenya: Myths and realities', *Canadian Journal for New Scholars in Education*, 3(2): 1–10.

Nussbaum, M. (2000), *Women and Human Development: The Capabilities Approach*, Cambridge: Cambridge University Press.

Nussbaum, M. C. (2001), *Women and Human Development: The Capabilities Approach*, Cambridge: Cambridge University Press.

Nussbaum, M. C. (2003), 'Capabilities as fundamental entitlements: Sen and social justice', *Feminist Economics*, 9(2–3): 33–59.

Nussbaum, M. C. (2007), *Frontiers of Justice: Disability, Nationality, Species Membership*, Massachusetts: The Belknap Press of Harvard University Press.

Nussbaum, M. C. (2011), *Creating Capabilities: The Human Development Approach*, London: Belknap.

Nussey, Charlotte (2019), *Adult education, gender and violence in rural KwaZulu-Natal*, Unpublished PhD Thesis, UCL Institute of Education, University College London.

Nyamnjoh, F. (2012), "'Potted plants in greenhouses': A critical reflection on the resilience of colonial education in Africa', *Journal of Asian and African Studies*, 47(2): 129–54.

Nyamnjoh, F. (2019), 'Decolonizing the University in Africa', in Cheeseman, N. (ed.), *Oxford Research Encyclopedia*, Oxford: Oxford University Press, 1–36.

Nyerere, J. (1967), *Education for Self-Reliance*, Arusha: United Republic of Tanzania.

Nyerere, J. (1968), *Freedom and Socialism= Uhuru na ujamaa: A Selection From Writings and Speeches, 1965–1967*, Dar es Salaam: Oxford University Press.

O'Malley, B. (2010), *Education Under Attack*, Paris: UNESCO. Available at http://unesdoc.unesco.org/images/0018/001868/186809e.pdf [accessed 24 November 2013].

O'Donoghue, J., Crawfurd, L., Makaaru, J., Otieno, P. and Perakis, R. (2018), *A Review of Uganda's Universal Secondary Education Public Private Partnership Programme*, London: Ark Education Partnerships Group.

OECD (1996), 'Shaping the 21st Century: The Contribution of Development Co-operation', Available at http://www.oecd.org/dac/2508761.pdf [accessed 15 May 2014].

OECD (1997), *Parents as Partners in Schooling*, Paris: OECD.

OECD (2001), *Environmental Outlook to 2050: The Consequences of Inaction*. Available at https://read.oecd-ilibrary.org/environment/oecd-environmental-outlook_9789264188563-en#.

OECD (2005), *Teachers Matter. Attracting, Developing, and Retaining Effective Teachers*, Paris: OECD.

OECD (2006), 'Determinants of human capital formation and economic growth of African countries', *Economics of Education Review*, 25(5): 554–64.

OECD (2007), *Qualifications Systems: Bridges to Lifelong Learning*, Paris: OECD.

OECD (2008), *Tertiary Education for the Knowledge Society*, Paris: OECD.

OECD (2009), *International Conference on the New Millennium Learners: Brussels*. Available at http://www.oecd.org/edu/ceri/43737014.pdf [accessed 13 March 2014].

OECD (2010), *OECD Reviews of Vocational Education and Training. Learning for Jobs*, Paris: Organization for Economic Co-operation and Development.

OECD (2012), *Equity and Quality in Education: Supporting Disadvantaged Students and Schools*, Paris: OECD.

OECD (2013), *Education at a Glance. Key Indicators*, Paris: OECD.

OECD (2016), 'Skills for digital world. Working party on measurement and analysis of the digital economy', Background paper for ministerial panel 4.2, Paris: Organization for Economic Co-operation and Development. Available at http://www.oecd.org/officialdocuments/publicdisplaydocument pdf/?cote=DSTI/ICCP/IIS(2015)10/FINAL&docLanguage=En.

OECD, McCowan, T. and Schendel, R. (2014), *The Impact of Tertiary Education on Development: A Rigorous Literature Review*, London: Department for International Development.

OECD netFWD (2019), *Philanthropy and Education: Quality Education for All: Lessons and Future Priorities*, Paris, France: OECD Development Centre. Available at http://www.oecd.org/site/netfwd/NetFWD_ PolicyNoteOnEducation.pdf.

Oketch, M. O. (2003), 'Affording the naffordable: Cost sharing in higher education in sub-saharan Africa', *Peabody Journal of Education*, 78(3): 88–106.

Oketch, M., McCowan, T. and Schendel, R. (2014), *The Impact of Tertiary Education on Development: A Rigorous Literature Review*, London: Department for International Development.

Olowu, D. (2001), *Decentralization Policies and Practices Under Structural Adjustment and Democratization in Africa*, Geneva: United Nations Research Institute for Social Development.

O'Malley, B. (2010), *Education under Attack*, Paris, UNESCO. Available at http://unesdoc.unesco.org/images/0018/001868/186809e.pdf.

O'Malley, P. (2010), 'Resilient subjects: Uncertainty, warfare and liberalism', *Economy and Society*, 39(4): 488–509. Available at https://doi.org/10.1080/0 3085147.2010.510681.

Omtzigt, D. and Pople, A. (2020), The cost of doing nothing. The price of inaction in response to the COVID 19 crisis. Paper prepared for UN Office for the Coordination of Humanitarian Affairs (UNOCHA), Geneva: UNOCHA. Available at https://www.unocha.org/sites/unocha/files/ Cost%20of%20inaction%2010.07.20.pdf.

Onsomu, E. N., Mungai, J. N., Oulai, D., Sankale, J. and Mujidi, J. (2004), *Community Schools in Kenya: Case Study on Community Participation in Funding and Managing Schools*, Paris: International Institute for Educational Planning, UNESCO.

Ostrom, E. (1990), *Governing the Commons*, Cambridge: Cambridge University Press.

Ostrom, E. (2006), *Understanding Knowledge as a Commons: From Theory to Practice*, Cambridge MA: The MIT Press.

Ostrom, E., Schroeder, L. and Wynne, S. (1993), *Institutional Incentives and Sustainable Development: Infrastructure Policies in Perspective*, Oxford: Westview Press.

Oxenham, J. (2002), *Skills and Literacy Training for Better Livelihoods: A Review of Approaches and Experiences*, Washington, DC: World Bank.

Oxenham, J., Diallo, A. H., Katahoire, A. R., Petkova-Mwangi, A. and Sall, O. (2002), *Skills and Literacy Training for Better Livelihoods: A Review of Approaches and Experiences* (Africa Region Human Development Working Paper Series), Washington, DC: The World Bank, Africa Region.

Özden, C. and Schiff, M. W. (2006), *International Migration, Remittances and the Brain Drain*, Washington, DC: World Bank.

Ozgur, I. (2012), *Islamic Schools in Modern Turkey: Faith, Politics, and Education*, Cambridge: Cambridge University Press.

Pallotta-Chiarolli, M. (2020), Pre-colonial actualities, post-colonial amnesia and neo-colonial assemblage, *Sage Handbook of Global Sexualities*, London: Sage, 57–81.

Palma, G. (2003), 'Latin America during the second half of the 20th century: From the age of "ISI" to the age of "The End of History"', in Chang, H. J. (ed.), *Rethinking Development Economics*, London and New York: Anthem Press, 125–52.

Palma, J. G. (2019), 'Behind the seven veils of inequality. What if it's all about the struggle within just one half of the population over just one half of the national income?', *Development and Change*, 50(5): 1133–213.

Palma, J. G. and Stiglitz, J. E. (2016), 'Do nations just get the inequality they deserve? The "Palma Ratio" re-examined', in Stiglitz, Joseph and Basu, Kaushik (eds), *Inequality and Growth: Patterns and Policy*, London: Palgrave Macmillan, 35–97.

Papen, U. (2005), 'Literacy and development: What works for whom? Or, how relevant is the social practices view of literacy for literacy education in developing countries?', *International Journal of Educational Development*, 25(1): 5–17.

Park, J. (2011), 'Metamorphosis of Confucian heritage culture and the possibility of an Asian education research methodology', *Comparative Education*, 47(3): 381–93.

Parkes, J. (ed.) (2015), *Gender Violence in Poverty Contexts: The Educational Challenge*, London: Routledge.

Parkes, J. and Unterhalter, E. (2015), 'Hope and history: Education engagements with poverty, inequality and gender violence', in Parkes, J. (ed.), *Gender Violence in Poverty Contexts: The Educational Challenge*, London: Routledge, 11–29.

Parkes, J., Datzberger, S., et al. (2020), 'Young people inequality and violence during the COVID 19 lockdown in Uganda COVACS working paper', Available at https://osf.io/preprints/socarxiv/2p6hx/.

Parkes, J., Ross, F. J. and Heslop, J. (2020), 'The ebbs and flows of policy enactments on school-related gender-based violence: Insights from

Ethiopia, Zambia, Côte d'Ivoire and Togo', *International Journal of Educational Development*, 72: 102133.

Patrinos, H. A. (1994), 'Notes on education and economic growth: Theory and evidence', *Human Resources Development and Operations Policy Working Papers*, HRO: 39.

Patrinos, H. A. and Angrist, N. (2018), *Global Dataset on Education Quality: A Review and Update (2000–2017)*, Policy Research Working Paper 8592. Washington, DC: World Bank.

Patrinos, H. and Psacharopolous, G. (2020), 'Returns to education in developing countries' in Bradley, S. and Green, C. (eds), *The Economics of Education*, 2nd edn, Elsevier, 218–23.

Patrinos, H., Barrera-Osorio, F. and Guaqueta, J. (2009), *The Role and Impact of Public-Private Partnerships in Education*, Washington, DC: World Bank.

Patton, M. Q. (2015), The sociological roots of utilization-focused evaluation, *The American Sociologist*, 46(4): 457–62.

Paulson, J. (2011), 'Conflict, education and curriculum: Past, present and future trends', *Conflict and Education*, 1(1): 1–5.

Pennycook, A. (2006), 'Postmodernism in language policy', in Ricento, T. (ed.), *An Introduction to Language Policy: Theory and Method*, Oxford: Blackwell Publishing, 60–76.

Peppin-Vaughan, R. (2010), 'Girls' and women's education within UNESCO and the World Bank, 1945–2000', *Compare*, 40(4): 405–23.

Perlman Robinson, J. (2011), *A Global Compact on Learning: Taking Action on Education in Developing Countries*, Washington, D.C. Centre for Universal Education, Brookings Institution, http://www.brookings.edu/~/media/ Events/2011/6/15%20education%20compact/0609_global_compact.PDF [accessed 24 November 2013].

Persson, T. and Tabellini, G. (2006), 'Democracy and development: The devil in the details', *The American Economic Review*, 96(2): 319–24.

Peters, M. A. and Wals, A. E. (2016), Transgressive learning in times of global systemic dysfunction: Interview with Arjen Wals, *Open Review of Educational Research*, 3(1): 179–89.

Pevec-Grm, S. and Jens, B. (2017), 'Measuring the impact of national qualifications frameworks: Lessons and challenges', in UIL, Cedefop and ETF (eds), *Global Inventory of Regional and National Qualifications Frameworks 2017, Volume 1*, Paris: UNESCO, 34–50.

Philips, D. and Schweisfurth, M. (2008), *Comparative and International Education: An Introduction to Theory, Method and Practice*, London: Continuum.

Phillips, H. M. (1987), *UNICEF and Education: A Historical Perspective*, New York: UNICEF.

Phillipson, R. (1992), *Linguistic Imperialism*, Oxford: Oxford University Press.

Pigozzi, M. J. (2006), 'A UNESCO view of global citizenship education', *Educational Review*, 58(1): 1–4.

Piketty, T. (2013), *Capital in the Twenty First Century*, Cambridge, MA: Harvard University Press.

Piketty, T. (2019), *Capital and Ideology*, Cambridge, MA: Harvard University Press.

Pillay, P. and Centre for Higher Education Transformation (South Africa) (2010), *Linking Higher Education and Economic Development: Implications for Africa from Three Successful Systems*, Wynberg: Centre for Higher Education Transformation.

Pineda, P., Celis, J. and Rangel, L. (2019), 'On interculturality and Decoloniality: Sabedores and government protection of indigenous knowledge in Bacatá schools', *Compare*, 50(8): 1–18.

Pinnock, H. (2009), *Language and Education: The Missing Link. How the Language Used in Schools Threatens the Achievement of Education for All*, London: Perspective CfBT Education Trust.

Pinnock, H. (2013), *The Potential of Low-Cost Community Private Schools to Boost Children's Education in Lagos*, London: Save the Children Fund.

Plaatje, S. (1916), *Native Life in South Africa: Before and since the European War and the Boer Rebellion*, London: P. S. King.

Poppema, M. (2012), 'School-based management in post-conflict Central America', in Verger, A., Novelli, M. and Kosar Altinyelken, H. (eds), *Global Education Policy and International Development: New Agendas, Issues and Policies*, London: Continuum, 161–80.

Pons, X. (2012), 'The turn and the paths', *Education Inquiry*, 3(2): 123–47.

Posholi, L. (2020), 'Epistemic decolonization as overcoming the hermeneutical injustice of eurocentrism', *Philosophical Papers*, https://doi.org/10.1080/0556 8641.2020.1779604.

Postmus, J. and Davis, R. (2014), *Passing the Test: The Real Cost of Being a Liberian Student*, London: Save the Children Fund.

Pradhan, R. (2002), 'Ethnicity, caste and a pluralistic society', in Dixit, K. and Ramachandaran, S. (eds), *State of Nepal*, Kathmandu: Himal Books, 1–21.

Prakash, M. S. and Esteva, G. (2008), *Escaping Education: Living as Learning in Grassroots Cultures*, 2nd edn, New York: Peter Lang Publishing.

Preece, J. (2009), *Lifelong Learning and Development: A Southern Perspective*, London: Continuum.

Premi, M. (2002), 'India's literacy panorama', *Seminar on Progress of Literacy in India*. Available at http://www.educationforallinindia.com/page172.html [accessed 20 April 2014].

Pridmore, P. and Carr-Hill, R. (2010), 'Tackling the drivers of child undernutrition in developing countries: What works and how should interventions be designed?', *Public Health Nutrition*, 14(4): 688–93.

Pridmore, P. and Stephens, D. (2000), *Children as Partners for Health: A Critical Review of the Child-to-Child Approach*, London, New York: Zed Books.

Pring, R. (2005), 'Faith schools: Can they be justified?', in Gardner, R., Cairns, J. and Lawton, F. (eds), *Faith Schools: Consensus or Conflict?*, London and New York: RoutledgeFalmer, 51–60.

Prinsloo, M. and Breier, M. (1996), *The Social Uses of Literacy: Theory and Practice in Contemporary South Africa*, Johannesburg: John Benjamins Publishing Company.

Prinsloo, P. and Slade, S. (2017), 'Big data, higher education and learning analytics: Beyond justice, toward an ethics of care', in Daniel, B. (ed.), *Big Data and Learning Analytics: Current Theory and Practice in Higher Education*, Switzerland: Springer International Publishing, 109–24.

Pritchett, L. (2001), 'Where has all the education gone?', *World Bank Economic Review*, 15(3): 367–91.

Pritchett, L. (2013), *The Rebirth of Education*, Washington, DC: Center for Global Development.

Prunier, G. (1995), *The Rwanda Crisis: History of a Genocide*, New York: Columbia University Press.

Psacharopolous, G. (1994), 'Returns to investment in education: A global update', *World Development*, 22: 1325–43.

Psacharopolous, G. and Patrinos, H. (2004), 'Returns to investment in education: A further update', *Education Economics*, 12(2): 111–34.

Psacharopolous, G. and Patrinos, H. (2018), 'Returns to investment in education: A decennial review of the global literature', *Education Economics*, 26(5): 445–58.

Psacharopolous, G., Tan, J. P. and Jimenez, E. and World Bank Education and Training Department (1986), *Financing Education in Developing Countries: An Exploration of Policy Options*, Washington, DC: World Bank.

Puri, J. (1999), *Woman, Body, Desire in Post Colonial India*, New York: Routledge.

Qaysum, M. and Hasan, M. (2017), *2017A Feminist Foremother. Critical Essays on Rokeya Sakhawat Hossain*, Hyderabad: Orient Black Swan.

Quijano, A. (2000), 'Coloniality of power and eurocentrism in Latin America', *International Sociology*, 15(2): 215–32.

Rahnema, M. and Bawtree, V. (1997), *The Post-Development Reader*, London: Zed.

Ramanathan, V. (2005), 'Rethinking language planning and policy from the ground up: Refashioning institutional realities and human lives', *Current Issues in Language Planning*, 6(2): 89–101.

Ramanathan, V. (2012), 'Rethinking discourses around the "English-cosmopolitan" correlation: Scenes from formal and informal multilingual educational contexts', in Martin-Jones, M., Blackledge, A. and Creese, A. (eds), *The Routledge Handbook of Multilingualism*, Routledge: London, 66–82.

Ramirez, F. O. and Boli, J. (1987), 'The political construction of mass schooling: European origins and worldwide institutionalization', *Sociology of Education*, 60(1): 2–17.

Ramusack, B. N. (1990), 'Cultural missionaries, maternal imperialists, feminist allies: British women activists in India, 1865–1945', *Women's Studies International Forum*, 13(4): 309–21.

Ranjan, P. (2019) 'Sonam Wangchuk Interview', https://hundred. org/en/articles/sonam-wangchuk-on-the-role-of-innovation-in-education#2468e7f6.

Rappleye, J. (2007), *Exploring Cross-National Attraction in Education: Some Historical Comparisons of American and Chinese Attraction to Japanese Education*, Oxford: Symposium Books.

Ravn, B. (2005), 'The cultural context of parental participation Scandinavian/ Western European issues', in Hiatt-Michael, D. B. (ed.), *Promising Practices for Family Involvement in Schooling across the Continents*, Connecticut: Information Age Publishing, 241–63.

Raworth, K. (2017), *Doughnut Economics*, London: Penguin Random House.

Read, J. (2019), 'Bin it Britain: Nation loses £9.7bn per year throwing away unused food', VouchersCode. Available at https://resource.co/article/study-reveals-uk-wastes-97-billion-food-each-year.

Reddy, S. (2020), 'Plastic pollution affects sea life throughout the ocean', PEW Trust, https://www.pewtrusts.org/en/research-and-analysis/ articles/2018/09/24/plastic-pollution-affects-sea-life-throughout-the-ocean.

Reimers, F. (1997), 'The role of the community in expanding educational opportunities: The Educo schools in El Salvador', in Lynch, J., Modgil, C. and Modgil, S. (eds), *Equity and Excellence in Education for Development*, London: Cassell, 141–53.

Reimers, F. M. (2021), *Education and Climate Change: The Role of Universities*, Cham: Springer.

Reisner, E. H. (1922), *Nationalism and Education since 1789; A Social and Political History of Modern Education*, New York: The Macmillan Company.

Resnik, J. (2006), 'Bringing international organizations back in: The "education-economic growth" black box and its contribution to the world education culture', *Comparative Education Review*, 50(2): 173–95.

Reyes, G. T. (2019), 'Pedagogy of and towards decoloniality', in Michael Adrian Peters (ed.), *Encyclopedia of Teacher Education*, Berlin: Springer, 1–7.

Reynolds, J., Fine, B. and van Niekerk, R. (eds) (2019), *Race, Class and the Post-Apartheid Democratic State*, Durban: University of Kwazulu Natal Press.

Riddell, A. (2000), *Implications for Agencies of Pursuing Sector Wide Approaches in Education*, Unpublished paper.

Riddell, A. (2007), *Does Foreign Aid Really Work?*, Oxford: Oxford University Press.

Right to Education (2019), 'New landmark Abidjan Principles adopted', Right to education 13 February 2019. Available at https://www.right-to-education.org/news/new-landmark-abidjan-principles-right-education-and-private-actors-adopted-experts.

Rist, G. (2008), *The History of Development: From Western Origins to Global Faith*, 3rd edn, London: Zed.

Ritchie, H. and Roser, M. (2020), 'CO$_2$ and greenhouse gas emissions', *OurWorldInData.org.* https://ourworldindata.org/co2-and-other-greenhouse-gas-emissions.

Rizvi, F. and Lingard, B. (2010), *Globalizing Education Policy*, London: Routledge.

Robertson, H. (1999), 'In Canada – Bogus points', *Phi Delta Kappan*, 80(9): 715–16.

Robertson, R. (1992), *Globalization: Social Theory and Global Culture*, California: Sage.

Robertson, S. (2005), 'Re-imagining and rescripting the future of education: Global knowledge economy discourses and the challenge to education systems', *Comparative Education*, 41(2): 151–70.

Robertson, S. and Dale, R. (2014), 'Towards a "critical cultural political economy" account of the globalising of education', Paper delivered at conference of Comparative and International Education Societies, Toronto, Marh.

Robertson, S., Mundy, K., Verger, A. and Menashy, F. (2012), *Public Private Partnerships in Education: New Actors and Modes of Governance in a Globalizing World*, Cheltenham: Edward Elgar Publishing.

Robeyns, I. (2006), 'Three models of education: Rights, capabilities and human capital', *Theory and Research in Education*, 4(1): 69–84.

Robeyns, I. (2017), *Wellbeing, Freedom and Social Justice: The Capability Approach Re-examined*, Cambridge: Open Book Publishers.

Robinson, C. (2005), 'Promoting literacy: What is the record of education for all?', *International Journal of Educational Development*, 25(4): 436–44.

Robinson-Pant, A. (2001), *Why Eat Green Cucumbers at a Time of Dying? Women's Literacy and Development in Nepal*, Hamburg: UNESCO.

Robinson-Pant, A. (2004), 'Education for women: Whose values count?', *Gender and Education*, 16(4): 473–89.

Robinson-Pant, A. (2004), *Women, Literacy and Development*, London: Routledge.

Robinson-Pant, A. (2008), '"Why literacy matters": Exploring a policy perspective on literacies, identities and social change', *The Journal of Development Studies*, 44(6): 779–96.

Robinson-Pant, A. (2013), 'Book review: Research methodologies in the "South"', *Compare*, 43(4): 563–66.

Robertson, S. L. and Dale, R. (2015), 'Towards a "critical cultural political economy" account of the globalising of education', *Globalisation, Societies and Education*, 13(1): 149–70.

Rockström, J., Steffen, W., Noone, K., Persson, A., Chapin, I. I. I., Lambin, A. F., Lenton, E., Scheffer, T. M., Folke, M., Schellnhuber, C., Nykvist, H. J., Wit, B., Hughes, C. A., Leeuw, T., Rodhe, S., Sörlin, S. H., Costanza, S. P. K., Svedin, R., Falkenmark, U., Karlberg, M., Corell, L., Victoria, R. W., J. Fabry, V. J., Hansen, J., Walker, B., Liverman, D., Richardson, K., Crutzen, P. and Foley, J., 'Planetary boundaries: Exploring the safe operating space for humanity', *Ecology and Society*, 14(2): 1–33.

Rodrik, D. (2013), 'Leaderless global governance', *Project Syndicate: A World of Ideas*. Available at http://www.project-syndicate.org/commentary/leaderless-global-governance [accessed 22 February 2014].

Rogers, A. (2002), *Teaching Adults*, 3rd edn, Buckingham, Pennsylvania: Open University Press.

Rogers, A. (2006), 'Lifelong learning and the absence of gender', *International Journal of Educational Development*, 26(2): 189–208.

Rogers, A. and Horrocks, N. (2010), *Teaching Adults*, Maidenhead: Open University Press.

Rogers, A. and Street, B. (2012), *Adult Literacy and Development: Stories from the Field*, Leicester: National Institute of Adult Continuing Education (NIACE).

Rogers, R. (2004), *An Introduction to Critical Discourse Analysis in Education*, New York: Routledge.

Rogers, R. (2008), 'Critical discourse analysis in education', in Martin-Jones, M., de Mejía, A. and Hornberger, N. H. (eds), *Encyclopaedia of Language and Education: Volume 3 Discourse and Education*, New York: Springer, 353–68.

Rolleston, C. and Adefeso-Olateju, M. (2014), 'De Facto privatisation of basic education in Africa: A market response to government failure? A comparative study of the cases of Ghana and Nigeria', in Macpherson, I., Robertson, S. and Walford, G. (eds), *Education, Privatisation and Social Justice: Case Studies from Africa, South Asia and South East Asia*, Oxford: Symposium Books, 25–44.

Romer, P. M. (1986), 'Increasing returns and long-run growth', *The Journal of Political Economy*, 94(5): 1002–37.

Romer, P. M. (1994), 'The origins of endogenous growth', *Journal of Economic Perspectives*, 8(1): 3–22.

Rose, P. M. (2002), *Is the Non-State Education Sector Serving the Needs of the Poor? Evidence from East and Southern Africa*, Brighton: University of Sussex.

Rose, P. and Greeley, M. (2006), *Education in Fragile States: Capturing Lessons and Identifying Good Practices*, Sussex: Centre for International Development and Institute for Development Studies, University of Sussex.

Ross, K. N. and Genevois, I. J. (eds) (2006), *Cross-national Studies of the Quality of Education: Planning Their Design and Managing Their Impact*, Paris: UNESCO, International Institute for Educational Planning.

Rostow, W. W. (1960), *The Stages of Economic Growth: A Non-Communist Manifesto*, Cambridge: Cambridge University Press.

Rowe, W. E. (2014) 'Positionality', in Coghlan, D. and Brydon-Miller, M. (eds), *The SAGE Encyclopedia of Action Research* (Vols. 1-2), London: SAGE.

Rueda, E. and Villavicencio, S. (2018), 'Introducción', in Rueda, E. and Villavicencio, S. (eds), *Modernidad, colonialismo y emancipación en América Latina*, Buenos Aires: CLACSO, 9–18.

Ruggie, J. G. (2003), 'The United Nations and globalization: Patterns and limits of institutional adaptation', *Global Governance*, 9(3): 301–22.

Russell, S. G. (2020), *Becoming Rwandan: Education, Reconciliation, and the Making of a Post-Genocide Citizen*, Rutgers, NJ: Rutgers University Press.

Rutayisire, J., Kabano, J. and Rubagiza, J. (2004), 'Redefining Rwanda's future: The role of curriculum in social reconstruction', in Tawil, S. and Harley, A. (eds), *Education, Conflict and Social Cohesion*, Paris: UNESCO, International Bureau of Education, 315–73.

Sachs, W. (1992), 'Introduction', in Sachs, W. (ed.), *The Development Dictionary: A Guide to Knowledge as Power*, London: Zed Books, 1–5.

Sachs, W. (2008), 'Climate change and human rights', *Development*, 51: 332–37.

Sahlberg, P. (2006), 'Education reform for raising economic competitiveness', *Journal of Educational Change*, 7: 259–87.

Sahlberg, P. and Oldroyd, D. (2010), 'Pedagogy for economic competitiveness and sustainable development', *European Journal of Education*, 45(2, Part 1): 280–99.

Said, E. (1980), *Orientalism*, London: Routledge.

Said, S. (2018), 'Pedagogies of the south and political subjectivation: People´s high schools in Argentina as part of "Latin American pedagogical movements"', *Education Policy Analysis Archives*, 26(0): 86.

Salmi, J. (1999), *Violence, Democracy and Education*, Unpublished paper presented at the OXCON Conference, Oxford, UK (September 1999).

Salmi, J. (2017), *The Tertiary Education Imperative: Knowledge, Skills and Values for Development*, Leiden, Netherlands: Brill-Sense.

Salmi, J. and Verspoor, A. M. and International Association of Universities (IAU) (1994), *Revitalizing Higher Education*, Oxford: Pergamon for IAU Press.

Samoff, J. (1999), 'No teacher guide, no textbooks, no chairs: Contending with crisis in African education', in Torres, C. A. (ed.), *Comparative Education: The Dialectic of the Global and the Local*, Lanham: Rowman & Littlefield, 409–45.

Samoff, J. (2001), 'The evolution of education aid to Africa: Changing terminology, persisting practice', *Paper presented at the Annual Meeting of the Comparative and International Education Society*, Washington, DC.

Samoff, J. (2004), 'From funding projects to supporting sectors? Observations on the aid relationship in Burkina Faso', *International Journal of Educational Development*, 24(4): 397–427.

Santana, C. R., Mackinlay, E. and Nakata, M. (2018), 'Editorial', *Australian Journal of Indigenous Education*, 47: iii–iv.

Santos, B. d. S. (2012), "The public sphere and epistemologies of the South," *African Development*, 37 (1): 43–68.

Santos, T. D. (1970), 'The structure of dependence', *American Economic Review*, 60(2): 231–6.

Save the Children (2013), *Attacks on Education – The Impact of Conflict and Grave Violations on Children's Futures*, London: Save the Children, http://www.savethechildren.org.uk/sites/default/files/docs/Attacks_on_Education_0.pdf[accessed] 12 November 2013.

Sayed, Y. and Ahmed, R. (2015), 'Education quality, and teaching and learning in the post-2015 education agenda', *International Journal of Educational Development*, 4: 330–8.

Sayed, Y. and Moriarty, K. (2020), 'SDG 4 and the "education quality turn": Prospects, possibilities, and problems', in Wulff, A. (ed.), *Grading Goal Four: Tensions, Threats, and Opportunities in the Sustainable Development Goal on Quality Education*, Leiden: Brill Publishing, 194–213.

Scanlon, D. G. (1964), *Traditions of African Education*, New York: Bureau of Publications, Teachers College, Columbia University.

Schafer, M. J. (2005), 'Family contributions to self help schooling in Malawi and Kenya', *Rural Sociology*, 70(1): 70–93.

Schaub, M., Henck, A. and Baker, D. P. (2017), 'The globalized "whole child": Cultural understandings of children and childhood in multilateral aid development policy, 1946–2010', *Comparative Education Review*, 61(2): 298–326.

Schech, S. (2018), 'Culture and development: Contemporary debates and practices', in Fagan, G. H. and Cheltenham, Ronaldo Munck (eds),

Handbook on Development and Social Change, Cheltenham: Edward Elgar Publishing, 291–310.

Schendel, R. (2013), *A Critical Missing Element: Critical Thinking at Rwanda's Public Universities and the Implications for Higher Education Reform*, Unpublished PhD thesis, London: Institute of Education.

Schendel, R. (2015), 'Critical thinking at Rwanda's public universities: Emerging evidence of a crucial development priority', *International Journal of Educational Development*, 42: 96–105.

Schendel, R., Mazimhaka, J. and Ezeanya, C. (2013), 'Higher education for development in Rwanda', *International Higher Education*, 70: 19–21.

Schendel, R., McCowan, T. Rolleston, C., Adu-Yeboah, C. Omingo, M. and Tabulawa, R. (2020) Pedagogies for critical thinking at universities in Kenya, Ghana and Botswana: the importance of a collective 'teaching culture'. *Teaching in Higher Education*, DOI: 10.1080/13562517.2020.1852204.

Schenker, I. (2001), 'New challenges for school AIDS education within an evolving HIV pandemic', *Prospects*, 31(3): 415–34.

Schenker, I. and Nyirenda, J. M. (2002), *Preventing HIV/AIDS in Schools: International Bureau of Education Geneva, International Academy of Education Brussels*, Bellegarde: SADAG.

Schissler, H. and Soysal, Y. N. (2005), *The Nation, Europe, and the World: Textbooks and Curricula in Transition*, New York: Berghahn Books.

Schleicher, A. (2020), 'The impact of COVID-19 on education: Insights from *Education at a Glance 2020*', OECD. Available at https://www.oecd.org/education/education-at-a-glance/.

Schmidle, N. (2007), 'Reforming Pakistan's "Dens of Terror"', *Truthdig. com*. Available at http://www.truthdig.com/report/page2/20070122_nicholas_schmidle_reforming_pakistans_dens_of_terror/ [accessed 13 July 2013].

Schmidt, R. (2006), 'Political theory and language policy', in Ricento, T. (ed.), *An Introduction to Language Policy: Theory and Method*, Oxford: Blackwell Publishing, 95–110.

Schneider, A. (2003), 'Decentralization: Conceptualization and measurement', *Studies in Comparative International Development*, 38(3): 32–56.

Schofer, E. and Meyer, J. W. (2005), 'The worldwide expansion of higher education in the twentieth century', *American Sociological Review*, 70: 898–920.

Schrag, Z. M. (2010), *Ethical Imperialism: Institutional Review Boards and the Social Sciences, 1965-2009*, Baltimore, MD: John Hopkins University Press.

Schriewer, J. (2009), *Discourse Formation in Comparative Education*, New York: Peter Lang.

Schultz, P. (2001), 'Why governments should invest more to educate girls', *World Development*, 30(2): 207–25.

Schultz, T. P. (2004), 'School subsidies for the poor: Evaluating the Mexican Progresa poverty program', *Journal of Development Economics*, 74(1): 199–250.

Schultz, T. W. (1961), 'Investment in human capital', *American Economic Review*, 51(1): 1–17.

Schwandt, T. A. (2012), 'Quality, standards, and accountability: An uneasy alliance', *Education Inquiry*, 3(2): 217–24.

Seeley, L. (1899), *History of Education*, New York: American Book Co.

Seehawker, M. K. (2018), 'Decolonising research in a Sub-Saharan African context: Exploring Ubuntu as a foundation for research methodology, ethics and agenda', *International Journal of Social Research Methodology*, 21(4): 453–66.

Seitz, K. (2004), *Education and Conflict: The Role of Education in the Creation, Prevention and Resolution of Societal Crises – Consequences for Development Cooperation*, Berlin: German Technical Cooperation (Deutsche Gessellschaft fur Technische Zusammenarbeit (GTZ)).

Selin, H. (ed.) (2003), *Nature across Cultures: Views of Nature and the Environment in Non-western Cultures*, Dordrecht/Boston/London: Kluwer Academic Publishers.

Selwyn, Neil (2020), 'Re-imagining "Learning Analytics" … a case for starting again?', *The Internet and Higher Education*, 46, https://doi.org/10.1016/j. iheduc.2020.100745.

Sen, A. (1980), 'Equality of what?', in McMurrin, S. (ed.), *Tanner Lectures on Human Values*, Cambridge: Cambridge University Press, 197–220.

Sen, A. (1992), *Inequality Re-examined*, Oxford: Clarendon Press.

Sen, A. (1993), *Equality of What?*, Cambridge: Cambridge University Press.

Sen, A. (1999), *Development as Freedom*, Oxford: Oxford University Press.

Sen, A. (2003), 'The importance of basic education', Speech to the Commonwealth Education Conference, Edinburgh, published in *Guardian*, 28 October 2003. Available at http://people.cis.ksu.edu/~ab/Miscellany/ basiced.html [accessed 18 April 2009].

Sen, A. (2006), 'The uses and abuses of multiculturalism: Chili and liberty', *The New Republic*, 27 February 2006. Available at http://www.pierretristam.com/ Bobst/library/wf-58.htm [accessed 20 April 2009].

Sen, A. (2009), *The Idea of Justice*, London: Penguin.

Severino, J. M. and Ray, O. (2010), *The End of ODA (II): The Birth of Hypercollective Action: Center for Global Development Working Paper 218*, Washington, DC: Center for Global Development.

Shaeffer, S. (1994), *Participation for Educational Change: A Synthesis of Experience*, Paris: UNESCO International Institute for Educational Planning.

Shafiq, Muhammad, Azad, Abdul Razzaq and Munir, Muhammad (2019), 'Madrassas Reforms in Pakistan: A Critical Appraisal of Present Strategies and Future Prospects', *Journal of Educational Research, Department of Education, IUB, Pakistan*, 22(2): 152–168.

Shah, R. (2011), 'It takes two to tango: Partnerships in the education sector in Timor-Leste', *International Education Journal: Comparative Perspectives*, 10(2): 71–85.

Shah, R. (2012), 'Goodbye conflict, hello development? Curriculum reform in Timor-Leste', *International Journal of Educational Development*, 32: 31–8.

Shah, R. (2015), 'Protecting children in a situation of ongoing conflict: Is resilience sufficient as the end product?', *International Journal of Disaster Risk Reduction*, 14: 179–85.

Shah, R. (2019), *Transforming Systems in Times of Adversity: Education and Resilience*, Washington DC: USAID.

Shah, R. and Lopes Cardozo, M. (2014), 'Education and social change in post-conflict and post-disaster Aceh, Indonesia', *International Journal of Educational Development*, 38: 2–12.

Shah, R., Paulson, J, and Couch, D. (2020) 'The Rise of Resilience in Education in Emergencies', *Journal of Intervention and Statebuilding*,1 4:3, 303–26. https://doi.org/10.1080/17502977.2019.1694390.

Shahjahan, R. A. (2016), 'International organizations (IOs), epistemic tools of influence, and the colonial geopolitics of knowledge production in higher education policy', *Journal of Education Policy*, 31(6): 694–710.

Shepherd, J. and Butt, R. (2009), 'Jewish school loses appeal', *Guardian*, 16 December. Available at http://www.guardian.co.uk/education/2009/dec/16/jewish-school-loses-appeal [accessed 12 June 2013.

Shields, R. (2013a), *Globalisation and International Education*, London and New York: Continuum International Publishing Group.

Shields, R. (2013b), 'Education in conflict and emergencies', in Shields, R. (ed.), *Globalisation and International Education*, London/New York: Continuum International Publishing Group, 48–59.

Shiva, V. (1992), *The Violence of the Green Revolution: Ecological Degradation and Political Conflict in Punjab*, New Delhi: Zed Press.

Shiva, V. (2005), *Earth Democracy; Justice, Sustainability, and Peace*, Cambridge, MA: South End Press.

Shor, I. (1992), *Empowering Education: Critical Teaching for Social Change*, Illinois: University Chicago Press.

Short, G. (2002), 'Faith-based schools: A threat to social cohesion?', *Journal of Philosophy of Education*, 36(4): 559–72.

Shuler, C. (2010), *Industry Brief: Pockets of Potential: Using Mobile Technologies to Promote Children's Learning: Research Presented by the Pearson Foundation*, New York: Pearson Foundation.

Sifuna, D. (2006), 'A review of major obstacles to women's participation in higher education in Kenya', *Research in Post-Compulsory Education*, 11(1): 85–105.

Silova, I., Millei, Z. and Piattoeva, N. (2017), 'Interrupting the coloniality of knowledge production in comparative education: Postsocialist and postcolonial dialogues after the cold war', *Comparative Education Review*, 61, S74–102.

Simon, J. de D. S. (2010), 'Informe Final, Programa Regional Andino de Educacion Intercultural Bilingüe EIBAMAZ (Bolivia, Ecuador, y Peru 2005–2009) UNICEF and Government of Finland'. Available at http://www.monografias.com/trabajos-pdf4/informe-final-del-programa-eibamaz/informe-final-del-programa-eibamaz.pdf.

Singh, R. and Sarkar, S. (2012), 'Teaching quality counts: How student outcomes relate to quality of teaching in private and public schools in India', Oxford: Young Lives, Department of International Development, University of Oxford.

Skeggs, B. (2004), *Class, Self, Culture*, London: Routledge.

Skidelsky, R. and Skidelsky, E. (2012), *How Much Is Enough?: The Love of Money, and the Case for the Good Life*, London: Allen Lane.

Skutnabb-Kangas, T. (2000), *Linguistic Genocide in Education – Or Worldwide Diversity and Human Rights?*, New Jersey: Lawrence Erlbaum.

Skutnabb-Kangas, T. and Phillipson, R. (1994), *Linguistic Human Rights: Overcoming Linguistic Discrimination*, Berlin: Mouton.

Slee, R. (2013), 'Meeting some challenges in inclusive education in the age of exclusion', *Asian Journal of Inclusive Education*, 1(2): 3–17.

Smith, A. (1986), *The Ethnic Origins of Nations*, Oxford: Blackwell.

Smith, A. (2005), 'Education in the twenty-first century: Conflict, reconstruction and reconciliation', *Compare*, 35(4): 373–91.

Smith, A. and Ellison, C. (2015), *The Integration of Education and Peacebuilding: A Review of the Literature*, New York: UNICEF.

Smith, A. and Vaux, T. (2003), *Education, Conflict and International Development*, London: UK Department of International Development (DFID).

Smith, A., McCandless, E., Paulson, J. and Wheaton, W. (2011), *The Role of Education in Peacebuilding: Literature Review*, New York: United Nations Children's Fund (UNICEF).

Smith, P. (19 March 2014), 'Move over, STEM: Why the world needs humanities graduates', *Guardian*.

Smith, W. C. (2014), 'The global transformation toward testing for accountability', *Education Policy Analysis Archives*, 22(116).

Smith, W. C. (ed.) (2016), *The Global Testing Culture: Shaping Education Policy, Perceptions, and Practice*, Oxford: Symposium Books.

Smith, W. C. (2018), 'Quality and inclusion in the SDGs: Tension in principle and practice', in Ydesen, C., Morin, A. and Hamre, B. (eds), *Testing and Inclusive Schooling*, Oxford: Routledge, 89–104.

Smith, W. C. (2019), 'One indicator to rule them all: How SDG 4.1.1 dominates the conversation and what it means for the most marginalized', in Wiseman, A. W. (ed.), *Annual Review of Comparative and International Education*, United Kingdom: Emerald Publishing, 27–34.

Smith, W. C. and Benavot, A. (2019), 'What is there not to like about a global learning metric? *NORRAG Highlights*', Network for International Policies and Cooperation in Education and Training. Available at https://www.norrag.org/what-is-there-not-to-like-about-a-global-learning-metric-by-william-c-smith-aaron-benavot/.

Smith, W., Salinas, D. and Baker, D. P. (2012), 'Multiple effects of education on disease: The intriguing case of HIV/AIDS in Sub-Saharan Africa', *International Perspectives on Education and Society*, 18: 79–104.

Sobe, N. W. (2015), 'All that is global is not world culture: Accountability systems and educational apparatuses', *Globalisation, Societies and Education*, 13(1): 135–48.

Sobe, N. W. (2017), 'Travelling researchers, colonial difference: comparative education in an age of exploration', *Compare*, 47(3): 332–43.

Solow, R. M. (1956), 'A contribution to the theory of economic growth', *Quarterly Journal of Economics*, 70(1): 65–94.

Sommers, M. (2002), *Children, Education and War: Reaching Education for All (EFA) Objectives in Countries Affected by Conflict*, Washington, DC: World Bank.

Sonntag, S. K. (1995), 'Ethnolinguistic identity and language policy in Nepal', *Nationalism and Ethnic Politics*, 1(14): 108–20.

Sonntag, S. K. (2003), *The Local Politics of English: Case Studies in Linguistic Globalisation*, Maryland: Lexington Books.

Sotz, J. and de, D. S. (2010), *Informe Final, Programa Regional Andino de Educacion Intercultural Bilingüe EIBAMAZ (Bolivia, Ecuador, y Peru 2005–2009)*, UNICEF and Government of Finland. Available at http://www.monografias.com/trabajos-pdf4/informe-final-del-programa-eibamaz/informe-final-del-programa-eibamaz.pdf [accessed 20 February 2014].

Soudien, C. (2004), '"Constituting the class": An analysis of the process of "integration" in South African schools', in Chisholm, L. (ed.), *Changing Class: Education and Social Change in Post-apartheid South Africa*, Cape Town: HSRC Press, 89–114.

Soudien, C. (2010), 'What to teach the natives: A historiography of the curriculum dilemma in South Africa', in Pinar, W. F. (ed.), *Curriculum Studies in South Africa: Intellectual Histories & Present Circumstances*, New York: Palgrave Macmillan, 19–50.

Soudien, C. (2013), 'What's being overlooked in the post-2015 agenda for education?', *Compare*, 43(6): 838–42.

Soysal, Y. N. (1994), *Limits of Citizenship: Migrants and Postnational Membership in Europe*, Chicago: University of Chicago Press.

Spaull, N. (2013), 'Poverty & privilege: Primary school inequality in South Africa', *International Journal of Educational Development*, 33(5): 436–47.

Spence, M. (1973), 'Job market signaling', *Quarterly Journal of Economics*, 87: 355–74.

Spence, M. (1974), 'Competitive and optimal responses to signals: An analysis of efficiency and distribution', *Journal of Economic Theory*, 7(3): 296–332.

Sperling, G. and Balu, R. (2005), 'Designing a global compact on education', *Finance and Development: A Quarterly Magazine by the IMF*, 42(2): 38–41.

Sperling, G. B. and Winthrop, R. (2015), *What Works in Girls' Education: Evidence for the World's Best Investment*, Washington DC: Brookings Institution Press.

Spivak, G. (1988), 'Can the Subaltern Speak?', in Nelson, C. and Grossberg, L. (eds), *Marxism and the Interpretation of Culture*, Illinois: University of Illinois Press, 271–316.

Spivak, G. (1999), *A Critique of Postcolonial Reason*, Massachusetts: Harvard University Press.

Spivak, G. and Young, R. (1991), 'Neocolonialism and the Secret Agent of Knowledge', *Oxford Literary Review*, 13(1/2): 220–51.

Spreen, C. A. (2001), *Globalization and Educational Policy Borrowing: Mapping Outcomes-Based Education in South Africa,* Doctoral thesis, Columbia University.

Spreen, C. and Knapczyk, J. J. (2017), 'Measuring quality beyond test scores: The impact of regional context on curriculum implementation (in Northern Uganda)', *FIRE: Forum for International Research in Education,* 4 (1). https://doi.org/10.18275/fire201704011110.

Sriprakash, A. (2012), *Pedagogies for Development: The Politics of Child-Centred Education in India*, New York: Springer.

Sriprakash, A., Tikly, L. and Walker, S. (2019), 'The erasures of racism in education and international development: Re-reading the "global learning crisis"', *Compare: A Journal of Comparative and International Education*, 50(5): 676–92, 1–17.

Srivastava, P. (2006), 'Private schooling and mental models about girls' schooling in India', *Compare*, 36(4): 497–514. https://doi.org/10.1080/03057920601024958.

Srivastava, P. (2007). *Neither voice nor loyalty: school Choice and the low-fee private Sector in India*. Research Publications Series, Occasional Paper No. 134. National Center for the Study of Privatization in Education, Columbia University, New York.

Srivastava, P. (2016), 'Questioning the global scaling up of low-fee private schooling: The nexus between business, philanthropy and PPPs', in

Verger, A., Lubienski, C., Steiner-Khamsi, G., (eds.), *The Global Education Industry - World Yearbook of Education 2016*, New York: Routledge, 248–63.

Srivastiva, P. (2020), *Framing Non-State Engagement in Education*. Think Piece prepared for the 2021 Global Education Monitoring Report, Paris, France: UNESCO. https://unesdoc.unesco.org/ark:/48223/pf0000372938?locale=en.

Ssekamwa, J. C. and Lugumba, S. M. E. (2001), *A History of Education in East Africa*, Kampala: Fountain Publishers Limited.

Stacey, J. (1993), 'Good riddance to "the Family": A response to David Popenoe', *Journal of Marriage and the Family*, 55(3): 545–7.

Standing, G. (2011), *The Precariat: The New Dangerous Class*, New York: Bloomsbury.

Stark, R. (1999), 'Secularisation RIP', *Sociology of Religion*, 60(3): 249–73.

Statista (2020), 'Development of the world population until 2050', Plecher. H (2020). Available at https://www.statista.com/statistics/262875/development-of-the-world-population/.

Steer, L. and Wathne, C. (2009), *Achieving Universal Basic Education: Constraints and Opportunities in Donor Financing (Draft for Consultation)*. http://www.odi.org.uk/sites/odi.org.uk/files/odi-assets/events-documents/3674.pdf [accessed]3 February 2013.

Steiner-Khamsi, G. (2004), *The Global Politics of Educational Borrowing and Lending*, New York: Teachers College Press.

Steiner-Khamsi, G. (2007), *The Stavka System in Tajikistan: Background, Challenges and Recommendations for Teacher Salary Reform*, Dushanbe: Education Modernization Project.

Steiner-Khamsi, G. and Teleshaliyev, N. (2019), 'Ten-Plus-One Ways of Coping with Teacher Shortage in Kyrgyzstan: Before and After 2011', in Silova, I. and Niyazov, S. (eds), *Globalization on the Margins. Education and Postsocialist Transformations in Central Asia*, 2nd edn, Charlotte, NC: Information Age Publishing.

Steiner-Khamsi, G. and Harris-Van Keuren, C. (2008), *Decentralization and Recentralization Reforms: Their Impact on Teacher Salaries in the Caucasus, Central Asia, and Mongolia. Background Paper for EFA GMR 2009*, Paris: UNESCO.

Steiner-Khamsi, G. and Waldow, F. (eds) (2012), *World Yearbook of Education 2012: Policy Borrowing and Lending in Education*, Abingdon: Routledge.

Stern, N. (2006), *Stern Review on the Economics of Climate Change*, London: HM Treasury.

Stevens, P. and Dworkin, A. (eds) (2019), *The Palgrave Handbook of Race and Ethnic Inequalities in Education*, Cham: Palgrave Macmillan.

Stevens, P. and Weale, M. (2004), 'Education and economic growth', in Johnes, G. and Johnes, J. (eds), *International Handbook on the Economics of Education*, Cheltenham: Edward Elgar, 164–88.

Stevick, E. D. and Levinson, B. A. U. (2007), *Reimagining Civic Education: How Diverse Societies Form Democratic Citizens*, Maryland: Rowman & Littlefield Publishers.

Stewart, F. (1985), *Planning to Meet Basic Needs*, London: Macmillan.

Stewart, F. (2002), *Horizontal Inequalities: A Neglected Dimension of Development, Working Paper No. 1, Centre for Research on Inequality, Human Security, and Ethnicity (CRISE)*, Oxford.

Stewart, F. (2008), *Horizontal Inequalities and Conflict: Understanding Group Violence in Multiethnic Societies*, Basingstoke: Palgrave Macmillan.

Stewart, F. (2009), *A Global View of Horizontal Inequalities: Inequalities Experienced by Muslims Worldwide: MICROCON Research Working Paper 13*, Brighton: MICROCON.

Stiglitz, J. (1999), 'Knowledge as a global public good', in Kaul, I., Grunberg, I. and Stern, M. (eds), *Global Public Goods: International Cooperation in the 21st Century*, New York: Oxford University Press, 308–26.

Stiglitz, J. (2003), *Globalization and Its Discontents*, New York: W.W. Norton.

Stiglitz, J. (2003), 'What's "new" in new literacy studies? Critical approaches to literacy in theory and practice', *Current Issues in Comparative Education*, 5(2): 77–91.

Stiglitz, J. (2011), 'Literacy inequalities in theory and practice: The power to name and define', *International Journal of Educational Development*, 31(6): 580–6.

Street, B. V. (2001), *Literacy and Development: Ethnographic Perspectives*, London: Routledge.

Street, B. V. (2003), 'What's "new" in New Literacy Studies? Critical approaches to literacy in theory and practice', *Current Issues in Comparative Education*, 5: 77–91.

Street, B. V. (2011), 'Literacy inequalities in theory and practice: The power to name and define', *International Journal of Educational Development*, 31: 580–86.

Stromquist, N. (1997), *Literacy for Citizenship: Gender and Grassroots Dynamics in Brazil*, Albany: SUNY Press.

Stromquist, N. P. (2019), 'World development report 2019: The changing nature of work', *International Review of Education*, 65: 321–9.

Suarez, D. F. (2008), 'Rewriting citizenship? Civic education in Costa Rica and Argentina', *Comparative Education*, 44(4): 485–503.

Subedi, B. (2010), *Critical Global Perspectives: Rethinking Knowledge about Global Societies*, North Carolina: Information Age Publishing.

Sumra, S. (2005), *Commonwealth Education Fund Global Midterm Review: Tanzania Programme Report*, London: Commonwealth Education Fund.

Suryadinata, L. (1972), 'Indonesian Chinese education: Past and present', *Indonesia*, 14: 49–71.

Takayama, K. (2016), 'Deploying the post-colonial predicaments of researching on/with "Asia" in education: A standpoint from a rich peripheral country', *Discourse*, 37(1): 70–88.

Takayama, K. (2018), 'The constitution of East Asia as a counter reference society through PISA: A postcolonial/de-colonial intervention', *Globalisation, Societies and Education*, 16(5): 609–23.

Takayama, K., Sriprakash, A. and Connell, R. (2017), 'Toward a postcolonial comparative and international education', *Comparative Education Review*, 61: S1–S24.

Tarlau, R. (2019), *Occupying Schools, Occupying Land: How the Landless Workers Movement Transformed Brazilian Education*, Oxford: Oxford University Press.

Task Force on Higher Education and Society, World Bank and UNESCO (2000), *Higher Education in Developing Countries: Peril and Promise*, Washington, DC: World Bank.

Tawil, S., Akkari, A. and Macedo, B. (2012), 'Beyond the conceptual maze: The notion of quality in education', Occasional Paper #2. UNESCO Education Research and Foresight. Paris: UNESCO.

Tawil, S. and Harley, A. (2004), *Education, Conflict and Social Cohesion*, Geneva: International Bureau of Education, UNESCO.

Tawil, S., Akkari, A. and Macedo, B. (2012), 'Beyond the conceptual maze: the notion of quality in education', Occasional Paper #2. UNESCO Education Research and Foresight. Paris: UNESCO.

Teferra, D. and Altbach, P. G. (2004), 'African higher education: Challenges for the 21st century', *Higher Education*, 47: 21–50.

Teferra, D. and Knight, J. (2008), *Higher Education in Africa: The International Dimension, Massachusetts:* Center for International Higher Education Lynch School of Education, Boston College, and Accra; Association of African Universities.

TEGINT (2011), *Report of Baseline Study for the TEGINT Project Tanzania*, Dar es Salaam: ActionAid.

Temple, J. (1999), 'The new growth evidence', *Journal of Economic Literature*, 37(1): 112–56.

Temple, J. (2001), 'Growth effects of education and social capital in the OECD countries', *OECD Economic Studies*, 33(2): 57–101.

TEN/MET (2006), *Strengthening Education in Tanzania: CSO Contributions to the Education Sector Review 2006*, Dar es Salaam: TEN/MET.

Ter Haar, G. (2011), *Religion and Development: Ways of Transforming the World*, London: Hurst and Company.

TESF (2020), *Mobilising Capacities for Transforming Education for Sustainable Futures: Opening Spaces for Collaborative Action and Learning.* https://tesf.

network/resource/mobilising-capacities-for-transforming-education-for-
sustainable-futures-opening-spaces-for-collaborative-action-and-learning/
Accessed 25 November 2020.

Tett, L. and Maclachlan, K. (2007), 'Adult literacy and numeracy, social capital,
learner identities and self-confidence', *Studies in the Education of Adults*,
39(2): 150–67.

Tettey, W. J. and Partnership for Higher Education in Africa (2009), *Deficits
in Academic Staff Capacity in Africa and Challenges of Developing and
Retaining the Next Generation of Academics*. Available at http://www.
foundation-partnership.org/pubs/pdf/Tettey_NGA_Indicators_Dec2009.
pdf [accessed on 13 November 2013].

The Inter-Agency Commission (UNDO, UNESCO, UNICEF, WORLD BANK)
for the World Conference on Education for All (1990a), *Meeting Basic
Learning Needs: A Vision for the 1990s*, Background Document World
Conference on Education for All Meeting Basic Learning Needs Jomtien,
Thailand 5-9 March 1990, New York: UNICEF.

The Inter-Agency Commission (UNDO, UNESCO, UNICEF, WORLD BANK)
for the World Conference on Education for All (1990b), Final Report of the
World Conference on Education for All, Jomtien, Thailand 5-9 March 1990,
New York: UNICEF.

Therien, J. P. (2002), 'Multilateral institutions and the poverty debate',
International Journal, 57(2): 233–52.

Therien, J. P. (2005), 'The politics of international development: Towards a
new grand compromise?', *Economic Policy and Law: Journal of Trade and
Environmental Studies*. Available at http://www.ecolomics-international.org/
epal_2004_5_therien_towards_new_grand_compromise_...._.pdf [accessed
2 February 2014].

Therien, J. P. and Lloyd, C. (2000), 'Development assistance on the brink', *Third
World Quarterly*, 21(1): 21–38.

Thomas, H. (2000), *Romanticism and Slave Narratives: Transatlantic
Testimonies*, Cambridge studies in Romanticism 38, Cambridge: Cambridge
University Press.

Thomas, S. M. (2003), 'Taking religious and cultural pluralism seriously', in
Hatzopoulos, P. and Petito, F. (eds), *Religion and International Relations: The
Return from Exile*, New York: Palgrave, 815–41.

Thomas, V., Wang, Y. and Fan, X. (1999), *Measuring Education Inequality: Gini
Coefficients of Education*, Policy Research Working Paper, Washington DC:
The World Bank.

Thomas, V., Wang, Y. and Fan, X. (2001), Measuring education inequality: Gini
coefficients of education, Washington: World Bank Publications.

Thompson, P. and Mchugh, D. (2002), *Work Organisations. A Critical
Introduction*, 3rd edn, Basingstoke and New York: Palgrave.

Thurow, L. (1976), *Generating Inequality*, New York: Basic Books.

Tibbitts, F. (2002), 'Understanding what we do: Emerging models for human rights education', *International Review of Education*, 48(3/4): 159–71.

Tibbitts, F. (2008), 'Human rights education', in Bajaj, M. (ed.), *Encyclopedia of Peace Education*, North Carolina: Information Age Publishing, 42–59.

Tikly, L. (1999), 'Postcolonialism and comparative education', *International Review of Education*, 45(5/6): 603–21.

Tikly, L. (2011), 'Towards a framework for researching the quality of education in low-income countries', *Comparative Education*, 47(1): 1–23.

Tikly, L. (2019), *Education for Sustainable Development in the Postcolonial World: Towards a Transformative Agenda for Africa*, Abingdon: Routledge.

Tikly, L. and Barrett, A. M. (2011), 'Social justice, capabilities, and the quality of education in developing countries', *International Journal of Educational Development*, 31: 3–14.

Tikly, L. and Barrett, A. M. (2013), *Education Quality and Social Justice in the Global South: Challenges for Policy, Practice and Research*, Abingdon: Routledge.

Tikly, L. and Bond, T. (2013), 'Towards a postcolonial research ethics in comparative and international education', *Compare*, 43(4): 422–42.

Tilak, J. B. G. (2013), *Higher Education in India: In Search of Equality, Quality and Quantity. Essays from Economic and Political Weekly*, Hyderabad: Orient Blackswan.

Tilley, L. (2017), "Resisting Piratic Method by Doing Research Otherwise." *Sociology*, 51(1): 27–42.

Tilly, C. (1988), 'Solidary logics: Conclusions', *Theory and Society*, 17(3): 451–58.

Tlostanova, M. and Mignolo, W. (2009), 'Global coloniality and the decolonial option', *Kult*, 6(Special Issue): 130–47.

Toffler, A. (1980), *The Third Wave*, London: Collins.

Toft, M. D., Philpott, D. and Shah, T. S. (2011), *God's Century: Resurgent Religion and Global Politics*, New York and London: W.W. Norton & Company.

Tollefson, J. (2006), 'Critical theory in language policy', in Ricento, T. (ed.), *An Introduction to Language Policy: Theory and Method*, Oxford: Blackwell Publishing, 42–59.

Tomaševski, K. (2001), *Human Rights Obligations: Making Education Available, Accessible, Acceptable and Adaptable, Right to Education Primers No. 3*, Gothenburg: Novum Grafiska.

Tomaševski, K. (2003), *Education Denied: Costs and Remedies*, London and New York: Zed Books.

Tomlinson, S. (2009), *Education in a Post-Welfare Society*, 2nd edn, Maidenhead: Open University Press.

Tooley, J. (2006), '"De Facto" privatisation of education and the poor: Implications of a study from sub-Saharan Africa and India', *Compare* 36(4): 443–62. https://doi.org/10.1080/03057920601024891.

Tooley, J. (2007), 'Educating Amartech: Private schools for the poor and the new frontier for investors', *Economic Affairs*, 27(2): 37–43.

Tooley, J. and Dixon, P. (2005a), 'An inspector calls: The regulation of "budget" private schools in Hyderabad, Andhra Pradesh, India', *International Journal of Educational Development*, 25(3): 269–85. https://doi.org/10.1016/j.ijedudev.2004.09.001.

Tooley, J. and Dixon, P. (2005b), *Private Education Is Good for the Poor*, Washington, DC: Cato Institute. https://doi.org/10.1017/CBO9781107415324.004.

Tooley, J. and Dixon, P. (2007), 'Private schooling for low-income families: A census and comparative survey in East Delhi, India', *International Journal of Educational Development*, 27(2): 205–19.

Tooley, J. and Longfield, D. (2016), 'Affordability of private schools: Exploration of a conundrum and towards a definition of "low-cost"', *Oxford Review of Education*, 42(4): 444–59. https://doi.org/10.1080/03054985.2016.1197830.

Tooley, J., Dixon, P. and Stanfield, J. (2008), 'Impact of free primary education in Kenya: A case study of private schools in Kibera', *Educational Management Administration and Leadership*, 36(4): 449–69. https://doi.org/10.1177/1741143208095788.

Tooley, J., Bao, Y., Dixon, P. and Merrifield, J. (2011), 'School choice and academic performance: Some evidence from developing countries', *Journal of School Choice: International Research and Reform*, 5(1): 1–39.

Tooley, J., Dixon, P., Shamsan, Y. and Schagen, I. (2010), 'The relative quality and cost-effectiveness of private and public schools for low-income families: A case study in a developing country', *School Effectiveness and School Improvement*, 21(2): 117–44. https://doi.org/10.1080/09243450903255482.

Tooley, J., Longfield, D., Dixon, P. and Schagen, I. (2013), 'Private education in low-income areas of Monrovia: School and household surveys', no. November. Available at https://egwestcentre.files.wordpress.com/2014/07/liberia-report-2013-11-26-v5.pdf.

Topel, R. (1999), 'Labor markets and economic growth', *Handbook of Labor Economics*, 3: 2943–84.

Torres, C. A. (2011), 'Dancing on the deck of the Titanic? Adult education, the nation-state and new social movements', *International Review of Education*, 57(1–2): 39–55.

Torres, R. M. (2000), *One Decade of Education for All: The Challenge Ahead*, Buenos Aires: International Institute of Educational Planning.

Torres, R. M. (2004), *Lifelong Learning in the South: Critical Issues and Opportunities for Adult Education, Sida Studies 11*, Stockholm: SIDA.

Trajber, R., Walker, C., Marchezini, V., Kraftl, P., Olivato, D., Hadfield-Hill, S., … Fernandes Monteiro, S. (2019), Promoting climate change transformation with young people in Brazil: Participatory action research through a looping approach, *Action Research*, 17(1): 87–107.

Transparency International (2013), *Corruption Perceptions Index 2013: Transparency International*. Available at http://cpi.transparency.org/cpi2013/results/ [accessed 24 February 2014].

Trimikliniotis, N. (2019), *Migration and the Refugee Dissensus in Europe: Borders, Security and Austerity,* London: Routledge.

Trow, M. (1974), 'Problems in the transition from elite to mass higher education', in Carnegie Commission on Higher Education (ed.), *Policies for Higher Education*, Paris: OECD, 86–142.

Tuhwai Smith, L. (2012), *Decolonizing Methodologies: Research and Indigenous Peoples*, London: Zed Books.

Tuwor, T. and Sossou, M. A. (2008), 'Gender discrimination and education in west Africa: Strategies for maintaining girls in school', *International Journal of Inclusive Education*, 12(4): 363–79.

Tyack, D. (1966), 'Forming the national character: Paradox in the educational thought of the revolutionary generation', *Harvard Educational Review*, 36(1): 29–41.

Tyack, D. and Cuban, L. (1997), *Tinkering toward Utopia: A Century of Public School Reform*, Massachusetts: Harvard University Press.

UIL (2009), *Global Report on Adult Learning and Education*, Hamburg: UNESCO Institute for Lifelong Learning.

UIL (2010), *Belem Framework for Action*, Hamburg: UNESCO Institute for Lifelong Learning.

UIL (2019), *4th Global Report on Adult Learning and Education. Leave No One behind: Participation, Equity and Inclusion,* Hamburg: UNESCO Institute for Lifelong Learning.

UIL, Cedefop, and ETF (2017), 'Global inventory of regional and national qualifications frameworks 2017, Volume 1', Report produced by UNESCO Institute for Life Long Learning, European Centre for the Development of Vocational Training, and the European Training Foundation. Paris: UNESCO.

UIS (2011), *Global Education Digest 2011*, Montreal: UNESCO.

UIS (2013), *UIS Data Centre*, Montreal: UIS. Available at http://www.uis.unesco.org/Education/Pages/data-release-november-2013.aspx [accessed 23 February 2014].

UIS (2016), *Sustainable Development Data Digest. Laying the Foundation to Measure Sustainable Development Goal 4*, Montreal: UNESCO Institute for Statistics (UIS).

UIS (2017a), *Expanding Coverage for Global Indicator 4.1*, Montreal: UNESCO Institute for Statistics (UIS).

UIS (2017b), *The Global Alliance to Monitor Learning: Governance and Organization*, Montreal: UNESCO Institute for Statistics (UIS).

UIS (2019), Benchmarking for learning: linking 4.1.1 with broader issues in education policy. Presentation at 6th GAML Meeting on 27-28 of August 2019 in Yerevan, Armenia. Available at http://gaml.uis.unesco.org/sixth-meeting-of-the-global-alliance-to-monitor-learning/.

UIS and ACER (2014), *Learning Metrics Partnership*. UNESCO Institute for Statistics (UIS) and Australian Council for Educational Research (ACER), Available at http://uis.unesco.org/sites/default/files/documents/learning-metrics-partnership-a-capacity-support-and-policy-strengthening-initiative-to-develop-and-use-common-learning-metrics-mathematics-reading-2014-en_1.pdf.

UIS, Australian Aid, Australian Government Department of Foreign Affairs and Trade & Australian Council for Educational Research. (2014), *Learning Metrics Partnership: A Capacity Support and Policy Strengthening Initiative to Develop and Use Common Learning Metrics for Mathematics and Reading*. Montreal: UNESCO Institutes for Statistics (UIS).

Umemura, M. (1999), *Community Participation in Education: What Do We Know*, Washington, DC: World Bank.

UN General Assembly (2010), *Resolution On the Right to Education in Emergency Situations: A/RES/64/290*. Available at http://www.un.org/ga/search/view_doc.asp?symbol=A/RES/64/290 [accessed]7 November 2013

UN Women (2016), *Global Guidance on Addressing School-Related Gender-based Violence*, Paris: UNESCO Publishing.

UNDESA (2019), World Population Prospects 2019. Available at https://population.un.org/wpp/Publications/Files/WPP2019_Highlights.pdf.

UNDP (2012), *The Millennium Development Goals Report 2012*. Available at http://wwwun.org/millenniumgoals/pdf/MDG%20Report%202012.pdf. [accessed 3December 2013].

UNDP (2012) (2013), *The Millennium Development Goals Report 2013*, http://www.undp.org/content/dam/undp/library/MDG/english/mdg-report-2013-english.pdf [accessed 2 November 2013].

UNDP (2019), *Human Development Report*, New York: United Nations Development Programme.

UNESCO (n.d.), *Education for all by 2015*. Available at http://portal.unesco.org/education/en/ev.php-URL_ID=42579&URL_DO=DO_TOPIC&URL_SECTION=201.html [accessed 7 November 2013].

UNESCO (n. d.), 'UN decade of ESD', [website]. Available at https://en.unesco.org/themes/education-sustainable-development/what-is esd/undecade-of-esd.

UNESCO (1946), *Constitution*. Available at http://portal.unesco.org/en/ev.php-URL_ID=15244&URL_DO=DO_TOPIC&URL_SECTION=201.html [accessed] 7 November 2013.

UNESCO (2000a), 'Education for all assessment: Global synthesis'. Report submitted by the International Consultative Forum on EFA to the World Education Forum, Dakar, Senegal, April 2000. https://unesdoc.unesco.org/ark:/48223/pf0000120058.

UNESCO (2000b), *World Education Forum, Dakar. Final Report*, Paris: UNESCO.

UNESCO (2003), *Education in a Multilingual World: A Position Paper*, Paris: UNESCO.

UNESCO (2005), *EFA Global Monitoring Report 2004/2005: Education for All: The Quality Imperative*, Paris: UNESCO.

UNESCO (2006a), *Education in Indonesia: UIS Statistics in Brief*. Available at http://stats.uis.unesco.org/unesco/TableViewer/document.aspx?ReportId=121&IF_Language=eng&BR_Country=3600 [accessed 19 April 2009].

UNESCO (2006b), *EFA Global Monitoring Report: Literacy for life*, Paris: UNESCO.

UNESCO (2007), *Indonesia: EFA Mid-Decade Assessment*. Available at http://planipolis.iiep.unesco.org/upload/Indonesia/Indonesia_EFA_MDA.pdf [accessed 20 April 2009].

UNESCO (2008), *Indonesia: National Report*, 48th Session of the International Conference on Education, ICE, 'Inclusive Education: The Way of the Future', Geneva, 25–28 November 2008. Available at http://planipolis.iiep.unesco.org/upload/Indonesia/Indonesia_NR08.pdf [accessed 20 April 2009].

UNESCO (2009a), *Final Report: World Conference on Higher Education*, Paris: UNESCO.

UNESCO (2009b), *High-Level Group on Education for All. Tenth Meeting. Paris: December 9 –11, 2009*, Paris: UNESCO.

UNESCO (2011), *The Hidden Crisis: Armed Conflict and Education (Education for All Global Monitoring Report)*, Paris: UNESCO-IIEP.

UNESCO (2013a), *Children Still Battling to Go School, Policy Paper No. 10, July 2013*, Paris: UNESCO. Available at http://unesdoc.unesco.org/images/0022/002216/221668E.pdf [accessed 20 October 2013].

UNESCO (2013b), 'Concept note on the Post-2015 education agenda', *Document Submitted by UNESCO to the 37th Session of the General Conference*, UNESCO, Paris.

UNESCO (2013c), 'Education beyond', *2015 Report to the UNESCO General Conference, 37th session*, Paris: UNESCO.

UNESCO (2013d), *Learning in the Post-2015 Education and Development Agenda*, Geneva: UNESCO International Bureau of Education.

UNESCO (2014a), *EFA Global Monitoring Report*, Paris: UNESCO.

UNESCO (2014b), *EFA Global Monitoring Report: Teaching and Learning: Achieving Quality for All (2013/14)*, Paris: UNESCO.

UNESCO (2014c), *DME WIDE Nigeria, World Inequalities Database*. Available
at http://www.education-inequalities.org/countries/nigeria#?dimension=sex
&group=all&year=latest [accessed 12 April 2014].

UNESCO (2014d), *World Inequality Data Base on Education*, Montreal:
UNESCO

UNESCO (2015), *EFA Global Monitoring Report: Education for All2000-2015:
Achievements and Challenges*, Paris, France: UNESCO. Available at https://
reliefweb.int/sites/reliefweb.int/files/resources/232205e.pdf

UNESCO (2016), *Global Education Monitoring Report 2016: Education
for People and the Planet: Creating Sustainable Futures for All*, Paris,
France: UNESCO. Available at https://unesdoc.unesco.org/ark:/48223/
pf0000245752

UNESCO (2020a), *Drop out Rate in Primary Education*, Available at http://
data.uis.unesco.org/Index.aspx?queryid=156 [accessed 31 August 2020]

UNESCO (2020b), *Futures of Education Initiative*, Paris: UNESCO. Available at
https://en.unesco.org/futuresofeducation/

UNESCO (2020c), *Global Education Monitor – Inclusion and Education*, Paris:
UNESCO

UNESCO (2020d), *COVID-19 Education Response: How Many Students are at
Risk of Not Returning to School?* Paris: UNESCO Advocacy paper.

UNESCO and GEM Report (2019), *Beyond Commitments. How Countries
Implement SDG 4*, Paris, France: UNESCO. Available at https://unesdoc.
unesco.org/ark:/48223/pf0000369008.

UNESCO and GEM Report. (2020a), 'COVID-19 is a serious threat to aid to
education recovery' *Policy Paper 41*, Paris, France: UNESCO. Available at
https://unesdoc.unesco.org/ark:/48223/pf0000373844.locale=en

UNESCO and GEM Report (2020b), *Global Education Monitoring Report 2020:
All Means All*, Paris, France: UNESCO.

UNESCO and UNESCO Institute for Statistics (2013), Education for all Global
Monitoring Report: Policy Paper 09: Schooling for millions of children
jeopardized by reductions in aid *Policy Paper 09*, Paris: UNESCO.

UNESCO Institute of Statistics, http://www.education-inequalities.org/
[accessed April 2014].

UNESCO Institute of Statistics (2010), *Global Education Digest 2010:
Comparing Education Statistics Across the World (Special Focus on Gender)*,
Montreal: Unesco Institute of Statistics.

UNESCO Institute of Statistics (2013), *Education for all Global Monitoring
Report: Policy Paper 09: Schooling for Millions of Children Jeopardized by
Reductions in Aid, Policy Paper 09*, Paris: UNESCO.

UNESCO Institute of Statistics (2013), 'Gross enrolment ratio (%) in tertiary
education', in *UNESCO Institute for Statistics*, Paris: UNESCO.

UNESCO Institute for Statistics. (2017), *More Than One-Half of Children and
Adolescents are Not Learning Worldwide*, Montreal, Quebec: UNESCO

Institute for Statistics, Available at http://uis.unesco.org/sites/default/files/documents/fs46-more-than-half-children-not-learning-en-2017.pdf

UNESCO Institute of Statistics (2018). One in Five Children, Adolescents and Youth is Out of School (Fact Sheet 48), Paris: UNESCO-UIS. Available at: http://uis.unesco.org/sites/default/files/documents/fs48-one-five-childrenadolescents-youth-out-school-2018-en.pdf.

UNESCO Institute for Statistics (2019), *Combining Data on Out-of School Children, Completion and Learning to Offer a More Comprehensive View on SDG 4*, Information Paper No. 61. Montreal, Quebec: UNESCO Institute for Statistics (UIS). Available at http://uis.unesco.org/sites/default/files/documents/ip61-combining-data-out-of-school-children-completion-learning-offer-more-comprehensive-view-sdg4.pdf

UNESCO Institute for Statistics (UIS) (2020), *Education: Enrolment by Level of Education*. Available at http://data.uis.unesco.org/.

UNESCO Institute for Statistics and GEM Report. (2019), *Meeting Commitments: Are Countries on Track to Achieve SDG4?* Paris, France: UNESCO. Available at https://unesdoc.unesco.org/ark:/48223/pf0000369009

UNESCO-IIEP (2011a), *Education and Fragility in Liberia*, Paris: International Institute for Educational Planning, UNESCO.

UNESCO-IIEP (2011b), *Guidance Notes for Educational Planners: Integrating Conflict and Disaster Risk Reduction into Education Sector Planning*, Paris: International Institute for Educational Planning (IIEP).

UNFPA (2012), *Marrying Too Young: End Child Marriage*, New York: UN Population Fund (UNFPA).

UNFPA (2014), 'Promoting gender equality: Empowering women trough education'. Available at http://www.unfpa.org/gender/empowerment2.htm [accessed 4 April 2014].

UNGEI (2014), *Report of Paris Network Meeting on School Related Gender-Based Violence*, Bangkok: UNESCO Bangkok office.

UNHCR (2018), *Global Trends. Forced Displacement in 2018*, UNHCR, Geneva, Available at https://www.unhcr.org/statistics/unhcrstats/5d08d7ee7/unhcr-global-trends-2018.html.

UNICEF (1995), *Religious Leaders as Health Communicators*, New York, NY: UNICEF, quoted in Haynes, J. (2007), *Religion and Development: Conflict or Cooperation?*, Houndmills, Basingstoke, Hampshire: Palgrave Macmillan.

UNICEF (2006), 'UNICEF milestones'. Available at http://www.cf-hst.net/UNICEF-TEMP/CF-hst%20redesign/milestones.htm [accessed 22 April 2014]

UNICEF (2007), *Quality of Education*, New York: UNICEF

UNICEF (2009a), *Child Friendly Schools Manual*, New York: UNICEF.

UNICEF (2009b), *Child Friendly Schools Programming Global Evaluation Report*, New York: UNICEF.

UNICEF (2012), *The Convention of the Right of the Child. The State of the Worlds Children 2012*. Available at http://www.unicef.org/sowc2012/pdfs/SOWC-2012-The-Convention-on-the-Rights-of-the-Child.pdf [accessed 7 November 2013]

UNICEF (2013), *Children of Syria*. Available at http://childrenofsyria.info [accessed 9 September 2013]

UNICEF (2018), *UNICEF Strategic Plan 2018–2021: Executive Summary*. New York, NY: UNICEF. https://www.unicef.org/media/48126/file/UNICEF_Strategic_Plan_2018-2021-ENG.pdf

CECCIS, U. N. I. C. E. F. (2011), *Teachers: A Regional Study on Recruitment, Development and Salaries of Teachers in the CEECIS Region*, Geneva: UNICEF CEECIS.

UNICEF ESARO and UNICEF Malawi (2011), *The UNICEF ESARO Study on Recruitment, Utilization, and Retention of Teachers*, Nairobi and Lilongwe: UNICEF.

UNICEF ESARO and UNICEF Swaziland (2010), *Teachers: Recruitment, Development and Retention in Swaziland*, Nairobi and Mbabane: UNICEF.

UNICEF/UNESCO (2007), *A Human Rights-Based Approach to Education for All*, New York: UNICEF/UNESCO. Available at http://unesdoc.unesco.org/images/0015/001548/154861e.pdf [accessed 7 January 2014]

United Nations (1961), *Resolutions Adopted on the Reports of the Second Committee, United Nations Development Decade*, New York: United Nations.

United Nations (2000), *United Nations Millennium Project*. Available at http://www.unmillenniumproject.org/goals/gti.html [accessed 7 November 2013]

United Nations (2013a), *A Life of Dignity for All: Accelerating Progress Towards the Millennium Development Goals and Advancing the United Nations Development Agenda Beyond 2015, Report of the Secretary General*, New York: United Nations.

United Nations (2013b), A new global partnership: Eradicate poverty and transform economies through sustainable development *Report of the High-Level Panel on Eminent Persons on the Post-2015 Development Agenda*, New York: United Nations.

United Nations (2019), *2019 International Year of Indigenous Languages*. Available at http://www.un.org/development/desa/dspd/2019/01/2019-international-year-of-indigenous-languages/

UN (2020a), *The Sustainable Development Goals Report 2020*, New York: United Nations. Available at https://unstats.un.org/sdgs/report/2020/The-Sustainable-Development-Goals-Report-2020.pdf

UN (2020b), *Policy Brief: Education during COVID 19 and beyond*, New York: United Nations. https://www.un.org/development/desa/dspd/wp-content/uploads/sites/22/2020/08/sg_policy_brief_covid-19_and_education_august_2020.pdf

UN (2020c), *Financing for Development in the Era of COVID 19*, New York: United Nations. https://www.un.org/sites/un2.un.org/files/part_i-_executive_ summary_menu_of_options_financing_for_development_covid19.pdf

United Nations Development Programme (1999), *Decentralization: A Sampling of Definitions*, Working paper prepared in connection with the Joint UNDP-Government of Germany evaluation of the UNDP role in decentralization and local governance.

United Nations General Assembly (2000), 'United Nations millennium declaration', Available at http://www.un.org/millennium/declaration/ ares552e.pdf [accessed 10 June 2014]

United Nations High Commissioner for Refugees (UNHCR) (2019), 'Refugee education', in Hamre, Bjorn, Morin, Anne and Ydesen, Christian (ed.), *Testing and Inclusive Schooling*, Copenhagen: United Nations, 152–169.

United Nations Open Working Group on Sustainable Development Goals (2013), *First Interim Report*, New York: United Nations.

United Nations Secretary General (2012), *Education First – An Initiative of the United Nations Secretary General*, September 2012, New York. Available at http://www.globaleducationfirst.org/ [accessed 9 January 2014]

Unterhalter, E. (2003), 'The capabilities approach and gendered education: An examination of South African complexities', *Theory and Research in Education*, 1(1): 7–22.

Unterhalter, E. (2005), 'Global inequality, capabilities, social justice: The millennium development goal for gender equality in education', *International Journal of Educational Development*, 25(2): 111–22.

Unterhalter, E. (2007a), *Gender, Schooling and Global Social Justice*, London: Routledge.

Unterhalter, E. (2007b), 'Global values and gender equality in education: Needs, rights and capabilities', in Fennell, S. and Arnot, M. (eds), *Gender Education and Equality in a Global Context*, London: Routledge, 19–34.

Unterhalter, E. (2008), 'Social justice development theory and the question of education', in Cowen, R. and Kazamias, A. (eds), *International Handbook of Comparative Education*, New York: Springer, 781–800.

Unterhalter, E. (2009), 'What is equity in education? Reflections from the capability approach', *Studies in Philosophy and Education*, 28: 415–24.

Unterhalter, E. (2012a), 'Poverty, education, gender and the millennium development goals: Reflections on boundaries and intersectionality', *Theory and Research in Education*, 10(3): 253–74.

Unterhalter, E. (2012b), 'Mutable meanings: Gender equality in education and international rights frameworks', *Equal Rights Review* 8, 67–84.

Unterhalter, E. (2013), *Education Targets, Indicators and a Post-2015 Development Agenda: Education for All, the MDGs and Human*

Development, Working Paper Series, FXB Center for Health and Human Rights, Massachusetts: Harvard School of Public Health.

Unterhalter, E. (2014), 'Measuring education for the millennium development goals: Reflections on targets, indicators, and a Post-2015 framework', *Journal of Human Development and Capabilities*, 15(1–2): 176–87.

Unterhalter, E. (2016), 'Gender and education in the global polity', in Mundy, K., Green, A., Lingaard, B. and Verger, A. (eds) *Handbook of Global Education Policy*, New York: Wiley, 111–27.

Unterhalter, E. (2018a), 'Equity against the odds: three stories of island prisons, education and hope', in Carney, S. and Schweisfurth, M. (eds.) *Equity in and through Education. Changing contexts, consequences and contestations*, Leiden: Brill/Sense, 13–28.

Unterhalter, E. (2018b), 'Negative Capability? Measuring the unmeasurable in education', in Unterhalter, E. (ed.) *Measuring the unmeasurable in education*, Abingdon: Routledge, 1–16.

Unterhalter, E. (2019a), 'The many meanings of quality education: Politics of targets and indicators in SDG4', *Global Policy*, 10 (Suppl. 1), 39–51.

Unterhalter, E. (2019b), 'Balancing pessimism of the intellect and optimism of the will: Some reflections on the capability approach, gender, empowerment, and education', in Biggeri, Mario, Clark, David (eds), *The Capability Approach, Empowerment and Participation*, London: Palgrave Macmillan, 75–99.

Unterhalter, E. (2020), Opening remarks for UNESCO's Global Education Meeting Session on inclusion, equity and gender equality 20 October 2020. Recording available at https://en.unesco.org/news/gem-2020-ensuringfocus-inclusion-equity-and-gender-equality.

Unterhalter, E. and Carpentier, V. (2010), *Global Inequalities and Higher Education: Whose Interests Are We Serving?*, Houndmills: Palgrave MacMillan.

Unterhalter, E., Howell, C. and Oketch, M. (2020), 'The role of tertiary education in development', Research Report, British Council.

Unterhalter, E. and North, A. (2017), *Education, Poverty and Global Goals for Gender Equality: How People Make Policy Happen*, Routledge.

Unterhalter, E. and Robinson, L. (2020), *Private Education and Compliance with the Abidjan Principles: A Study of Malawi, Mozambique, Tanzania and Nigeria*, London: ActionAid.

Unterhalter, E., Robinson, L. and Ron Balsera, M. (2020, forthcoming) 'The politics, policies and practices of intersectionality: Making gender equality inclusive in and through education', Background paper commissioned for the UNESCO GEM Report Gender Review, Paris: UNESCO (To be published October 8 2020).

Unterhalter, E., Yates, C., Makinda, H. and North, A. (2012), 'Blaming the poor: Constructions of marginality and poverty in the Kenyan education sector', *Compare*, 42(2): 213–33.

Unterhalter, E., North, A., Arnot, M., Lloyd, C., Moletsane, L., Murphy-Graham, E., Parkes, J. and Saito, M. (2014, forthcoming), *Girls' Education and Gender Equality: A Rigorous Review of Literature*, London: DFID. Available at https://www.gov.uk/government/uploads/system/uploads/attachment_data/file/326205/Girls_Education_Literature_Review_2014_Unterhalter.pdf, accessed August 2014.

US National Commission on Excellence in Education. (1983), *A Nation at Risk: The Imperative for Educational Reform: A Report to the Nation and the Secretary of Education*, Washington, DC: The Commission on Excellence in Education.

USAID (2013), *Teacher Education and Policies in Pakistan. A Compilation of Subsector Review*, Islamabad: Teacher Education Project.

USAID (2019), Policy linking and SDG 4.1. Presentation at 6th GAML Meeting on 27-28 of August 2019 in Yerevan, Armenia. Available at http://gaml.uis.unesco.org/sixth-meeting-of-the-global-alliance-to-monitor-learning/.

Vaizey, J. (1972), *The Political Economy of Education*, London: Duckworth.

Van Blerk, L. (2012), 'Berg-en-See street boys: Merging street and family relations in cape town, South Africa', *Children's Geographies*, 10(3): 321–36.

Van de Werfhorst, H. G. (2011), 'Skills, positional good or social closure? The role of education across structural–institutional labour market settings', *Journal of Education and Work*, 24(5): 521–48.

Van Dijk, T. (2003), 'Critical discourse analysis', in Schiffrin, D., Tannen, D. and Hamilton, H. E. (eds), *The Handbook of Discourse Analysis*, Oxford: Blackwell, 352–71.

Vandemoortele, J. and Delamonica, E. (2010), 'Taking the MDGs beyond 2015: Hasten slowly', *IDS Bulletin*, 41(1): 60–9.

Vanner, C. (2018), '"This is a competition": The relationship between examination pressure and gender violence in primary schools in Kenya', *International Journal of Educational Development*, 62: 35–46.

Vavrus, F. and Bartlett, L. (2009), *Critical Approaches to Comparative Education: Vertical Case Studies from Africa, Europe, the Middle East, and the Americas*, New York: Palgrave Macmillan.

Vavrus, F. and Seghers, M. (2010), 'Critical discourse analysis in comparative education: A discursive study of "partnership" in Tanzania's poverty reduction policies', *Comparative Education Review*, 54(1): 77–103.

Verger, A. and Novelli, M. (2012), *Campaigning for 'Education for All': Histories, Strategies and Outcomes of Transnational Social Movements in Education*, Rotterdam: Sense.

Verger, A., Altinyelken, H. and Novelli, M. (2011), *Global Education Policy and International Development: New Agendas, Issues and Policies*, London: Continuum.

Verger, A., Fontdevila, C. and Zancajo, A. (2017), 'Multiple paths towards education privatization in a globalizing world: A cultural political economy review', *Journal of Education Policy*, 32(6): 757–87.

Verger, A., Kosar, A. H. and de Koning, M. (2013), *Global Managerial Education Reforms and Teachers*, Brussels: Education International Research Institute.

Verger, A., Moschetti, M. C. and Fontdevila, C. (2020), 'How and why policy design matters: Understanding the diverging effects of public-private partnerships in education', *Comparative Education*, 56(2): 278–303.

Vickers, E. (2020), 'Critiquing coloniality, "epistemic violence" and western hegemony in comparative education–The dangers of ahistoricism and positionality', *Comparative Education*, 56(2): 165–89.

Wadhwa, W. (2014), 'Government vs private schools: Have things changed?', Aser Centre, 19–21.

Waghid, Y. (2009), 'On the unattentiveness of South African higher education research to teaching and learning', *South African Journal of Education*, 23(6): 1126–32.

Wagner, D. A. (2011), 'What happened to literacy? Historical and conceptual perspectives on literacy in UNESCO', *International Journal of Educational Development*, 31(3): 319–23.

Wagner, T. (2008), *The Global Achievement Gap: Why Even Our Best Schools Don't Teach the New Survival Skills Our Children Need – And What We Can Do about It*, New York: Basic Books.

Walker, M. (2019), 'Defending the need for a foundational epistemic capability in education', *Journal of Human Development and Capabilities*, 20(2): 218–32.

Walker, M. (2020), 'Failures and possibilities of epistemic justice, with some implications for higher education', *Critical Studies in Education*, 61(3): 263–78.

Walker, M. and Martinez-Vargas, C. (2020), 'Epistemic governance and the colonial epistemic structure: Towards epistemic humility and transformed South-North relations', *Critical Studies in Education*. DOI: 10.1080/17508487.2020.1778052.

Walker, M. and McLean, M. (2013), *Professional Education, Capabilities and the Public Good: The Role of Universities in Promoting Human Development*, London: Routledge.

Walker, M. and Unterhalter, E. (2007), *Amartya Sen's Capability Approach and Social Justice in Education*, Basingstoke: Palgrave Macmillan.

Wallace, T. (2020), 'Re-imagining development by (re) claiming feminist visions of development alternatives', *Gender & Development*, 28(1): 31–49.

Wallerstein, I. (1996), *The Age of Transition: Trajectory of the World-System, 1945–2025*, London: Zed Press.

Wals, A. E. (ed.) (2007), *Social Learning towards a Sustainable World: Principles, Perspectives, and Praxis*, Wageningen: Wageningen Academic Publishers.

Walsh, C. (2009), *Interculturalidad, Estado, Sociedad: Luchas (De)Coloniales De Nuestra Época*, Quito: Universidad Andina Simón Bolívar.

Walsh, C. E. (2015), 'Decolonial pedagogies walking and asking. Notes to Paulo Freire from AbyaYala', *International Journal of Lifelong Education*, 34(1): 9–21. https://doi.org/10.1080/02601370.2014.991522.

Walsh, C., de Oliveira, L. F. and Candau, V. M. (2018), 'Coloniality and decolonial pedagogy: To think of other education', *Education Policy Analysis Archives*, 26(0): 83.

Walters, S. (2006), 'Adult learning within lifelong learning: A different lens, a different light', *Journal of Education*, 39: 7–26.

Wangenge-Ouma, G. (2007), 'Higher education marketisation and its discontents: The case of quality in Kenya', *Higher Education*, 56(4): 457–71.

Ward, M. (2016), PISA for development (PowerPoint presentation), Paris: OECD. Available at http://www.unescobkk.org/fileadmin/user_upload/epr/Quality/NEQMAP/1-1.PISA_for_Development_Michael_Ward.pdf.

Wardak, S. and Hirth, M. (2009), 'Ministry of education, Islamic Republic of Afghanistan: "Defining the Gaps: The Case of Afghanistan"', *INEE Global Consultation – Bridging the Gaps: Risk Reduction, Relief, and Poverty*, 31 March–2 April.

Wa Thiong'o, N. (1992), *Decolonising the Mind: The Politics of Language in African Literature*, Nairobi: East African Publishers.

Watene, K. (2016), *Valuing Nature: Māori Philosophy and the Capability Approach*, Oxford Development Studies, 44(3): 287–96.

Waters, T. and Kim, L. (2005), 'Refugees and education: Mass public schooling without a nation-state', *Comparative Education Review*, 49(2): 129–47.

Watts, R., (2020), 'Global Britain? Why a £4 bn cut to UK aid leaves little room to advance investments in children', *Save the Children blogs*, 27 November 2020. Available at https://www.savethechildren.org.uk/blogs/2020/global-britain-uk-aid-budget-cut.

WCEFA (World Conference on Education for All) (1990), *World Conference on Education for All: Meeting Basic Learning Needs, Final Report*, New York: Inter-Agency Commission, WCEFA.

Weber, E. (1976), *Peasants into Frenchmen: The Modernization of Rural France, 1870–1914*, California: Stanford University Press.

Weber, M. (1904), *The Protestant Ethic and the Spirit of Capitalism*, New York: Scribner.

Weiler, K. (1996), 'Myths of Paulo Freire', *Educational Theory*, 46(3): 353–71.

Weinberg, M. (2013), 'Revisiting history in language policy: The case of medium of instruction in Nepal', *Working Papers on Educational Linguistics*, 28(1): 61–80.

Weinstein, H., Freedman, S. and Hughson, H. (2007), 'School voices: Challenges facing education systems after identity-based conflicts', *Education, Citizenship and Social Justice*, 2(1): 41–71.

Weir, S. and Knight, J. (2007), 'Production externalities of education: Evidence from rural Ethiopia', *Journal of African Economies*, 16(1): 134–65.

Welch, A. (2018), Global ambitions: Internationalization and China's rise as knowledge hub, *Frontiers of Education in China*, 13(4): 513–31.

West, E. G. (1994), *Education and the State: A Study in Political Economy*, 3rd edn rev. and expanded. edn, Indiana: Liberty Fund.

Wheelahan, L. (2010), *Why Knowledge Matters in Curriculum*, London and New York: Routledge.

Whelpton, J. (1997), 'Political identity in Nepal: State, nation and community', in Gellner, D., Pfaff-Czarnecka, J. and Whelpton, J. (eds), *Nationalism and Ethnicity in a Hindu Kingdom*, Amsterdam: Harwood, 39–78.

White, J. (1982), *The Aims of Education Restated*, London: Routledge & Kegan Paul.

Wilkinson, R. and Pickett, K. (2009), *The Spirit Level: Why More Equal Societies Almost Always Do Better*, London: Allen Lane.

Williamson, B. (2018), 'The hidden architecture of higher education: Building a big data infrastructure for the "smarter university"', *International Journal of Educational Technology in Higher Education*, 15(1): 1–26.

Williamson, F. and Boughton, B. (2020), '"I can speak on this here": Empowerment within an Aboriginal adult literacy campaign', *The Australian Journal of Indigenous Education*, 1–8.

Willis, P. (1978), *Learning to Labour: How Working Class Kids Get Working Class Jobs*, Aldershot Gower: Saxon House/Teakfield Ltd.

Winch, C. (2011), 'Skill – A concept manufactured in England?', in Brockmann, M., Clarke, L. and Winch, C. (eds), *Knowledge, Skills and Competence in the European Labour Market. What's in a Vocational Qualification?*, London and New York: Routledge, 85–101.

Winkler, D. R. (1989), *Decentralization in Education: An Economic Perspective*, Washington, DC: World Bank.

Winthrop, R. (2011), 'Understanding the diverse forms of learning valued by children in conflict contexts', in Mundy, K. and Dryden-Peterson, S. (eds), *Educating Children in Conflict Zones*, New York: Teachers College Press, 123–37.

Winthrop, R. and Kirk, J. (2008), 'Learning for a bright future: Schooling, armed conflict, and children's well being', *Comparative Education Review*, 52(4): 639–61.

Wolf, A. (2002), *Does Education Matter? Myths about Education and Economic Growth*, London: Penguin.

Wong, S. W. and Hughes, J. N. (2006) 'Ethnicity and language contributions to dimensions of parent involvement', *School Psychology Review*, 35(4): 645–62.

Woodhead, M., Frost, M. and James, Z. (2013), 'Does growth in private schooling contribute to Education for All? Evidence from a longitudinal two cohort study in Andhra Pradesh, India', *International Journal of Educational Development*, 33(1): 65–73.

Woods, N. (2008), 'Whose aid, whose influence? China, emerging donors and the silent revolution in development assistance', *International Affairs*, 84(6): 1–17.

Woolard, K. (1998), 'Introduction: Language ideology as a field of enquiry', in Schieffelin, B., Woolard, K. and Kroskrity, P. (eds), *Language Ideologies, Practice and Theory*, Oxford: Oxford University Press, 3–35.

World Bank (1978), *Review of Bank Operations in the Education Sector*, Washington, DC: World Bank.

World Bank (1986), *Financing Education in Developing Countries: An Exploration of Policy Options*, Washington, DC: World Bank.

World Bank (1988), *Education in sub-Saharan Africa: Policies for Adjustment, Revitalization and Expansion*, Washington, DC: World Bank.

World Bank (1995), *Priorities and Strategies for Education*, Washington, DC: World Bank.

World Bank (2002), *Education and HIV/AIDS a Window of Hope*, Washington, DC: World Bank.

World Bank (2003), *Life Long Learning for Developing Countries*, Washington, DC: World Bank.

World Bank (2004), *El Salvador – Community Education Strategy: Decentralized School Management*, Washington, DC: World Bank.

World Bank (2006), *Mongolia: Public Financing of Education. Equity and Efficiency Implications*, Washington, DC: World Bank.

World Bank (2007a), *Guiding Principles for Implementing School-Based Management Programs*, Washington, DC: World Bank.

World Bank (2007b), *What is School-Based Management?*, Washington, DC: World Bank.

World Bank (2009), *Accelerating Catch-up: Tertiary Education for Growth in Sub-Saharan Africa*, Washington, DC: World Bank.

World Bank (2010), *Financing Higher Education in Africa*, Washington, DC: World Bank.

World Bank (2011a), *Education Sector Strategy 2020*, Washington, DC: The World Bank.

World Bank (2011b), *Learning for All: Investing in People's Knowledge and Skills to Promote Development*, World Bank Group Education Strategy 2020. Washington, DC: World Bank.

World Bank (2012), *2020 Education Strategy: 'Learning for All: Investing in People's Knowledge and Skills to Promote Development*, Washington DC: World Bank.

World Bank (2013), *World Bank Education Projects Database*, Available at: http://datatopics.worldbank.org/EdStatsApps/WProject/aProRpt.aspx [accessed 12 September 2013].

World Bank (2014), 'Education and the World Bank'. Available at http://web.worldbank.org/ [accessed 22 April 2014].

World Bank (2018), *World Development Report 2018: Learning to Realize Education's Promise*, Washington, DC: World Bank.

World Bank (2019a), *Ending Learning Poverty: What Will It Take?* Washington, DC: World Bank. Available at https://openknowledge.worldbank.org/bitstream/handle/10986/32553/142659.pdf?sequence=7&isAllowed=y.

World Bank (2019b), *Learning Poverty*. Policy Brief, Washington, DC: World Bank. Available at https://www.worldbank.org/en/topic/education/brief/learning-poverty.

World Bank (2020), World Bank Group, Climate Change Knowledge Portal, https://climateknowledgeportal.worldbank.org/region/africa/climate-data-historical.

World Bank (2020), *Cost-Effective Approaches to Improve Global Learning: What Does Recent Evidence Tell Us Are 'Smart Buys' for Improving Learning in Low and Middle Income Countries? (English)*. Washington, D.C.: World Bank Group. Available at http://documents.worldbank.org/curated/en/719211603835247448/Cost-Effective-Approaches-to-Improve-Global-Learning-What-Does-Recent-Evidence-Tell-Us-Are-Smart-Buys-for-Improving-Learning-in-Low-and-Middle-Income-Countries.

World Bank and Salmi, J. (1994), *Higher Education: The Lessons of Experience*, Washington, DC: World Bank.

World Bank and International Monetary Fund (2013), *Global Monitoring Report 2013: Monitoring the MDGs, Rural-Urban Dynamics and the MDGs*. Available at http://siteresources.worldbank.org/INTPROSPECTS/Resources/334934-1327948020811/8401693-1355753354515/8980448-1366123749799/GMR_2013_Full_Report.pdf [accessed 20 November 2013].

World Education Forum (2015), *Education 2030: Incheon Declaration and Framework for Action for the Implementation of Sustainable Development Goal 4*, Paris: UNESCO.

Wright, K., Daniel, T. and Himelreich, K. S. (2000), *Preparation for Building Partnerships with Families: A Survey of Teachers, Teacher Educators, and School Administrators*, Massachusetts : Harvard Family Research Project.

Wu, H. (2018), 'China's international student recruitment as "outward-oriented" higher education internationalisation: An exploratory empirical inquiry', *Compare: A Journal of Comparative and International Education*, 619–34.

Wulff, A. (2020a), 'Introduction: Bringing out the tensions, challenges, and opportunities within Sustainable Development Goal 4', in Wulff, A. (ed.), *Grading Goal Four: Tensions, Threats, and Opportunities in the Sustainable Development Goal on Quality Education*, Leiden: Brill Publishing, 1–27.

Wulff, A. (ed.) (2020b), *Grading Goal Four: Tensions, Threats, and Opportunities in the Sustainable Development Goal on Quality Education*, Leiden: Brill Publishing.

Wyman, L. (2009), 'Youth, linguistic ecology, and language endangerment: A Uip'ik example', *Journal of Language, Identity and Education*, 8(5): 335–49.

Wyman, L. (2012), *Youth Culture, Language Endangerment and Linguistic Survivance*, Clevedon: Multilingual Matters.

Yacoobi, S. (2011), 'Empowering women through education: Recipes for success', in Heath, J. and Zahedi, A. (eds), *Land of the Unconquerable: The Lives of Contemporary Afghan Women*, Berkeley: University of California Press, 309–20.

Yesufu, T. M. and Association of African Universities (1973), *Creating the African University: Emerging Issues in the 1970's*, Ibadan: Published by Oxford University Press for the Association of African Universities.

Yorozu, Rita (2017), 'Lifelong Learning in Transformation: Promising Practices in SouthEast Asia', *UIL: UNESCO Institute for Lifelong Learning. Publications Series on Lifelong Learning Policies and Strategies: No. 4*, Hamburg.

You, Y. (2020), 'The "new Orientalism": Education policy borrowing and representations of East Asia', *Compare*, 50(5): 742–63.

Yudkevich, M., Altbach, P. G. and de Wit, J. (2020), *Trends and Issues in Doctoral Education: A Global Perspective*, New Delhi: SAGE.

Zajda, J. I. and Gamage, D. T. (2009), *Decentralisation, School-Based Management, and Quality*, Dordrecht: Springer.

Zapp, M. (2017), 'The World Bank and education: Governing (through) knowledge', *International Journal of Educational Development*, 53: 1–11.

Zembylas, M. (2017), 'Re-contextualising human rights education: Some decolonial strategies and pedagogical/curricular possibilities', *Pedagogy, Culture and Society*, 25(4): 487–99.

Zengin vs. Turkey (2007), 'Judgement in the European Court of Human Rights 9/1/2008'. Available at http://hudoc.echr.coe.int/sites/eng/pages/search.aspx?i=001-82580#.

Ziai, A. (2007), 'Post-development discourse and its critics: An introduction to post-development', in Ziai, A. (ed.), *Exploring Post-Development: Theory and Practice, Problems and Perspectives*, London: Routledge, 3–17.

Ziai, A. (ed.) (2020), *The Development Dictionary@ 25: Post-Development and Its Consequences*, Abingdon: Routledge.

Ziesemer, T. (2016), 'Gini coefficients of education for 146 countries, 1950–2010', *Bulletin of Applied Economics*, 3(2): 1–8.

Zinn, A. (ed.) (2016), *Non-Racialism in South Africa: The Life and Times of Neville Alexander*, Johannesburg: AFRICAN SUN MeDIA.

Index

Boldface locators indicate figures and tables; locators followed by "n." indicate endnotes